ROBERT FALCON SCOTT

THE WORST EXPLORER

IN THE WORLD

ROBERT FALCON SCOTT

THE WORST EXPLORER IN THE WORLD

Buriton Field

independently published by the author
available from Amazon

ISBN   978 1 0799 4971 1

ACKNOWLEDGEMENTS

It has never been easier to research historical figures. In the past, assistants were essential for finding information and unearthing old and out-of-print books. Usually these were only to be found in large metropolitan and academic libraries. It would then be necessary to spend long hours transcribing or photocopying sections of texts, which themselves might have taken hours to find. The alternative would have been to obtain copies of the original volumes, which would have been extremely difficult and very expensive.

All that has changed. In addition to the vast body of primary-source and biographical material in print concerning Scott, we can now obtain reprints of books long out of print, at a reasonable price and within days of ordering. This in itself has transformed what is possible for researchers to accomplish. The internet has made a vast archive of photos, newspaper articles, original documents sold at auction, and facsimiles of diaries, letters etc, easily available.

If all this was not enough, it is now possible to publish one's material oneself, without having to go through dispiriting and time-consuming rounds of rejections by agents. Now, authors themselves can test whether the public will buy their work, rather than getting the verdict from an agent – which has always been less than optimal, and decidedly unsatisfying for the writer.

I pay tribute also to those Scott biographers who have brought to light primary source material.

The cover photo shows a corner of the wardroom on RRS *Discovery*, taken July 2019 by the author. With acknowledgement to Dundee Heritage Trust.

Design and production-editorial by FilM.

I am lucky to have as my best friend a skilled copy-editor, who has brought a superlative standard of editing to the text, and has provided unstinting support and encouragement. Any errors that remain are my responsibility.

Buriton Field
February 2020

CONTENTS

Contents

PART 3

1910 TO 1912

THE *TERRA NOVA* TO THE DEATH-TENT AND BEYOND

APPENDIX   479

BIBLIOGRAPHY   485

INDEX   499

INTRODUCTION

There are not many instances in history where a man with no experience nor interest in exploration suddenly finds himself being offered the leadership of a uniquely challenging national expedition.

What could have been the qualities that trumped any kind of relevant track record? What was so special about Robert Falcon Scott that made him the chosen one, the one who didn't need to know about nor have experience of, not just anywhere, but Antarctica, the most daunting place on earth?

The story begins one sunny day in the Caribbean in 1887, when Robert Falcon Scott was a midshipman on HMS *Rover.* He had caught the eye of one Clements Robert Markham, erstwhile junior Naval officer, frequent guest thereafter on Her Majesty's ships, leading light of the Royal Geographical Society, hankerer after a bygone age, and connoisseur of young men and boys.

It is customary among historians to take an urbane view of Markham, and to close the questions with the standard 'not a shred of evidence' mantra. Francis Spufford and Roland Huntford are notable exceptions – the first baldly calling Markham a liar, the second stating that he was 'a homosexual'. He was both, although the word homosexual doesn't cover the abusive and paedophiliac nature of his sexuality.

Markham hid in plain sight, never making a secret of his love of boys and the way he constantly sought them out; but he was almost certainly an abuser who took advantage of his status in relation to his objects. The fact that there is no direct evidence proves nothing. Where there is an abundance of circumstantial evidence, as in this case, only wilful blindness can explain why Markham has, until now, not been shown up for what he was. History shows that in an older man, an enduring high level of involvement with boys is seldom innocent.

But why should Markham's sexuality concern the history of Scott? The reason is that it led to inappropriate criteria for the selection of a commander for the *Discovery* Expedition of 1901. There is no other plausible explanation as to why Scott should have been chosen. As far as Markham was concerned, far from counting against him, Scott's naivety was an advantage. It meant he was open to receiving all the instruction Markham chose to give him. Together with his Royal Navy background, violet-blue eyes, vulnerability, a trim waist and an ability to turn on the charm, his lack of experience made Scott the perfect candidate.

If it hadn't been for Markham and his homo-erotic ideals, there would never have been a 'heroic age of exploration'. A more responsible approach would have put hardened ice-masters into the treacherous icy waters, Alpine guides on the mountains, dog-mushers on the trail, and professional scientists in serious laboratories on shore. There would have been no glamour-boys in uniforms and a crew of obedient sailors to serve them. Who knows what might have been achieved.

By 1900, the Royal Navy was no longer a ceremonial entity in search of a meaningful occupation, as it had been in Markham's day. Now it was 'going to the dogs', in his view, by being turned into a modern fighting force, with no time for jaunts to the ends of the earth in quests for PR coups and showy achievements. Germany was building a navy to rival the British, and Europe was alive with political change – much of it far from friendly, and loaded with potential for war.

All the evidence suggests that Scott lacked sufficient nerve to be in charge of a battleship. This much may have been apparent to his superiors at the Admiralty. He would have denied it himself, as he denied so many other uncomfortable truths, but Polar exploration was one way he could make his mark without having to face the dread possibility of commanding a battleship in action. Hence, the Admiralty appeared to have no objection when, out of the blue, he requested leave of absence to go on a journey to the ends of the earth, with no possibility of a recall within months, or even years.

And so, on 6 August 1901, Commander Scott found himself on his way to Antarctica as Captain of the *Discovery*, a brand-new purpose-built ship, with a hand-picked Naval crew, and every kind of support he could have wished for. He just about got away with this, his first expedition – but it was a close thing, and he was lucky not to lose the ship.

In 1908 he married Edith Agnes Kathleen Bruce. It is strongly suggested by her constant flirtations and need for admiration from just about every man who crossed her path that she suffered from Narcissistic Personality Disorder. Her childhood contains an abundance of causative elements, including the loss at an early age of both her parents, and an itinerant and comparatively loveless childhood thereafter.

This was an age when knowledge about child development was still rudimentary; and in a way she was lucky in that she had older siblings to provide a family context for her. Nevertheless, it is clear she bore the scars of parental deprivation. She had no insight into her own pathology. Instead, she was cheerfully dismissive of anyone's opinion but her own. Her last letter to Scott, on the eve of his departure on the *Terra Nova* (his second and last expedition), telling him she would be better off without him if he chose to play it safe, is a classic of narcissistic heartlessness and egocentricity.

But even the brilliant cast of characters, the harshest, remotest location on earth, and the final dramatic race for the South Pole cannot account for the extraordinary number of biographies, histories, re-enactments and commentaries that have proliferated in the wake of the failure of the British to be first at the Pole. For this, we must look at the wardroom table and the hunched figure at the head of it, propelled by chance into a role he was unprepared for and unsuited to, but with a talent for lively descriptions of the dramas and horrors resulting mostly from his own incompetence. The public has been entertained for a hundred years, and counting.

Scott's death was a case of suicide with collateral damage. 'Taff' Evans and 'Titus' Oates were victims of Scott's poor judgement and denialism, but Wilson and Bowers somehow found themselves going along with Scott's suicidal decision to continue to drag an unnecessarily heavy sledge. It is perfectly obvious that if they had been serious about getting home, they would have depoted anything not strictly necessary, and made all possible speed. The most plausible reason why they did not do so is because the last phase of the homeward journey over the Barrier was deliberately sabotaged by Scott. It was bad enough to have lost priority at the Pole, but when Taff Evans died on the Beardmore Glacier, his mind appears to have turned to alternative ways of salvaging his reputation.

As his final 'Message to [the] Public' shows, his primary worry was that the world would condemn his organisation and leadership. This suggests that he would have been looking for ways of diverting attention away from those issues by turning his failure into an example of a heroic but doomed last stand against the odds. As we know, he succeeded brilliantly.

The story of Scott of the Antarctic was, and continues to be, treasured by the nation as an example of a set of British values which embraces a purist conception of Antarctic travel. Birdie Bowers consoled himself for the loss of priority at the Pole by stating that at least they had got there by good British man-haulage.

But even that wasn't true. Scott had marshalled every transport he could think of to get him to the Pole, and they had all failed. Both the ponies and the tractors were ill suited to the conditions, and he hadn't wanted to know about the potential of dogs. He had fallen back on extreme human effort of necessity, and because it was the only thing he really trusted. He got to the Pole somehow, but it was a whole month too late. Having man-hauled part of the way was surely scant consolation.

This book dismantles a heroic iconography constructed over a hundred years. It is done in the interests of putting the record straight, and giving credit where credit is due – which has, in some cases, been a long time coming.

As there is little point in going over old material, I have bypassed many of the more well-known aspects of Scott's story. Instead, I have endeavoured, through meticulous reading of the diaries and other source material, to find motivations and personal investments likely to throw a new light on hitherto overlooked aspects of events.

I have used the term Barrier throughout to describe the Ross Ice Shelf – not only because it is more succinct, but also because it is contemporary with the era, and more consistent with how it was conceptualised at that time.

PART 1

1830 TO 1901

MARKHAM TO THE

DEPARTURE OF THE *DISCOVERY*

1

THE POPE OF STILLINGFLEET

In March 1912, as Scott, Wilson and Bowers lay dying in their frozen tent, an infinitesimal speck in an ocean of icy solitude, the man who was responsible for setting in motion the chain of events that culminated in that scene was enjoying the balmy delights of Estoril, one of his favourite seaside haunts.

Born 20 July 1830, Clements Robert Markham had been a very fortunate child, born into a family of hereditary ecclesiastical status, comfortably off, well connected, and in happy possession of a benign and indulgent *pater familias*. The Rev. David F. Markham was the Vicar of Stillingfleet, near York. On account of his grandfather having been private tutor to both George IV and William IV, the Reverend was also appointed Canon of Windsor in 1827, entailing a residence there for two months every year.

For the first eight years of Clements' life, he lived with his parents, his older brother, and a younger sister, in what appears to have been idyllic circumstances in the large and comfortable rectory of Stillingfleet. In later life, he often liked to remind people that he was by birth a Yorkshireman. However, in 1838 the Reverend was offered, and accepted, the rectory of Great Horkesley in Essex, a larger and more important parish. The family left Stillingfleet reluctantly, having spent many happy years there. Catherine, Clements' mother, was pregnant again, and gave birth to another daughter in December 1838. She ended up having six children: three sons and three daughters, of whom one son died in infancy, and another at the age of 22. Clements, however, lived to be 85, and might have lived beyond that if he hadn't set light to his blankets, having dropped off while reading by candlelight. [1]

Clements' father was a great reader, interested in a wide variety of subjects. He appears to have been equally comfortable at the King's dinner table as at his lathe in his workshop at home. Described as an active and strong man, he was fond of outdoor sports, interested in the study of medicine and, unusually for a man of his status, adept at carpentry and turning. These are the first clues that suggests he was a follower of Rousseau in his principles and values.

Jean-Jacques Rousseau had introduced into European society a sense of the virtue of natural simplicity, the integrity of the simple artisan, and the value of nature over urban sophistication. [2] The romantic notion of honest craftsmanship beguiled even Louis XVI, who provided training for his son as a locksmith. The fact that the Reverend sent his sons to a school run on those principles confirms that he had Rousseauist convictions, as does his encouragement of Clements' writings – even though at an early age they took the form of very personal and unflattering little pen-pictures, especially of the female visitors who came to the house. Clements also wrote detailed descriptions of other people's interiors as well as potted biographies of their servants. 'Their names are all enumerated, more especially those who were kind to him, and the positions they filled; whilst in some cases even their family histories are recorded.' Clements retained this habit all his life. Those who knew about it cannot always have felt comfortable in the knowledge that they might have been critically observed and written about.

Nevertheless, Clements' writing was made much of. He learnt how to write abstracts and abridged biographies of historical figures and nations, culminating in a 'History of England' in eight chapters, written when he was ten years old. Much to his delight, his father, being in possession of a small printing press, printed 20 copies of this, had them bound in leather covers, and distributed them among the family. 'By this act, the boy's literary ardour was so much gratified that he decided unhesitatingly upon becoming an author!' Clements was given a lot of freedom to develop and learn at his own pace, which was fast.

Jean-Jacques Rousseau, in spite of the fact that he forced the mother of his children to give away all five of their offspring to a Foundling Hospital, wrote a lengthy treatise on the rearing and education of children. *Émile* was published in 1762, and very soon became the child-rearing bible for benign and well-meaning parents and teachers throughout Europe and beyond. Children were henceforth to be freed from the iron yoke of compulsory subjects, rote learning and forced attendance. Taking as his starting point the 'natural goodness of the child', education was to consist of guidance and encouragement, in an environment where he was free to make his own discoveries, and act on his natural impulses. None of this applied so much to children born into poor households, it need hardly be stated.

And not everybody was impressed. According to Restif de la Bretonne: [3]

> Their hair straggles in a hideous and disgusting way ... They are no longer checked, but clamber on to you with their muddy feet. When you visit their parents, they deafen you with their noise, and just when their father or mother is about to reply to you on some

important matter, you see them choose instead to answer some childish question of their darling son or daughter ... it is *Émile* which is responsible for this provoking, obstinate, insolent, impudent, arrogant generation ...

A hint that something like this might have been the case with Clements is suggested by an anecdote which concerns an incident in church, when he was four years old. Bored, he started to pinch his older brother, which resulted in a fight. Clearly not amenable to a gentle (or even a firm) reprimand, Clements had to be carried out of church, kicking and screaming. What the rest of the congregation thought about the Reverend's parenting methods probably had much in common with Restif's view. On the positive side, however, he grew up to possess an unshakeable self-confidence and a highly skilled and fluent social persona, equipping him with the basics for a successful future.

Clements' mother seems an incorporeal entity: invisible, unmentioned, quietly producing a baby every three years or so, concerned with domestic matters and fulfilling her role as a rector's wife. A snapshot of her is a letter she wrote to Albert Markham, Clements' cousin. Albert had gone to live with Catherine in London, where she had moved after the Rector died in 1853. Albert had left home at 14 in order to prepare for entering the Royal Navy. To begin with, however, he was not successful. Catherine wrote to him saying: [4]

> I need not tell you, my dear boy, how much I feel for your disappointment, as I know how great it will be, but you must try and feel that we do not direct any of the events of this life ourselves. God has not thought it good for you that you should succeed in what you wish, but you may rely upon His goodness ... and you may be sure it will not eventually turn out to your disadvantage, though at present you cannot help feeling grieved, having for so many months turned your mind to this profession.

Here is someone who views life through the prism of religious doctrine, and who knows what God wants and thinks. This vein of fatalistic piety was common in Victorian society – a mindset that simultaneously claimed submission to divine ordination, yet possessed of an iron conviction consequent on being privy to God's thoughts, and therefore entitled to pronounce on events as though divinely sanctioned. It included a passive acceptance of suffering, interpreted as the will of God and a test of faith. It was a belief which will be encountered again as this story unfolds, and could be held partially to account for the continued existence of four frozen corpses moving glacially towards the sea, somewhere beneath the Ross Ice Shelf in Antarctica. The fifth, also on its way beneath the ice, is there for a different reason, but more about that later.

Clements is not likely to have responded positively to this brand of mothering. His cousin Albert was a zealous Christian all his life, but Clements gives the impression of having outwardly conformed, while lacking inner conviction. Clements may not have got on with his mother particularly well. There are a number of circumstances that suggest this might have been the case. The first, rather speculatively, is that the firstborn, David, might have been his mother's favourite. When news came that David was seriously ill, Clements was home on a short period of leave before going to the Arctic on a potentially dangerous mission. His parents cut short their time with him in order to rush to his brother's side in Madeira. (David died shortly afterwards in his father's arms, aged 22, leaving Clements as the only living son.) Even if David had not been the favourite, sibling rivalry might have made him appear so to Clements' waspish eyes, even if he was not.

There is also the strong likelihood that Catherine shared her husband's philosophies and principles. As such, she would have integrated the Rousseauist cult of *sensibilité,* and may well have been given to bursting into tears at the slightest provocation and fussing over trifles. Similarly, in an age when many women hired wet-nurses for their babies if they could afford it, which the Markhams certainly could, Catherine would have breastfed her babies *au naturel.* Judging by Clements' adult Apollonian aestheticism and connoisseurship, especially of good-looking boys and young men, he might very well have found her pregnancies and nursing habits repellent, her emotionality irritating, and her religiosity naive and bourgeois. If his father was a Rousseauist, Clements was a Voltairean.

After having been educated at home until nearly nine years old, Clements was sent to a school at Cheam, which was run on the 'Pestalozzi Method'. Johann Henrich Pestalozzi (1746–1827) was an experimental educator, who had taken up the ideas of Rousseau, and explored how these might be developed and implemented. The boys were never kept at their lessons for more than one hour at a time, after which they were sent out to 'air their brains' for the next hour. According to Clements' biographer, cousin Albert, the selection of the school was largely due to the fact that many of the friends and relations were being educated there. Nevertheless, I would assume that it accorded with the Reverend's ideas about child-rearing, and that he was in harmony with many of his social peers.

In Clements' own words: [5]

> When I went to Cheam I was a good-looking, well-made little boy of eight years and ten months, in a round jacket, turn-down collar over it, and a Tam o' Shanter cap, black with red squares round the edge. I was always called Pope. In my first half I had no friends, only G– as a protector; and I especially hated D– R   . But we at once

made friends in the second half, became devoted to each other, and were inseparable *until dearer friends came*. [his italics]

Dearer friends came at Westminster, where Clements was sent after three years at Cheam, in around 1841. Westminster was the *alma mater* of many generations of the Markham family. In *High Minds*, Simon Heffer relates that in 1833 a boy called James Anthony Froude was sent to Westminster. He boarded in the dormitories, where [6]

> No master was in the dormitories to supervise them. Relentless bullying by the younger boys, and thrashings by the elder ones for whom he had to fag, soon became the staples of Froude's life. He recounted being woken by having a lighted cigar pressed to his face, and having his legs set fire to in order to make him dance. He was also force-fed brandy to make him drunk. ... He was also starved by having food kept from him by the older boys; his clothes were either torn or stolen, and so were his books ... It would get worse after Froude left and, despite reforms in the 1840s, would still shock the Clarendon Commission in 1862 ...

In another case, WS Meyrick [7] relates that in the early 1860s Westminster was

> ... a den of savagery, not just because of the frequent kickings, but also because of the habit of some boys to cut other boys' hands with a paper knife.

Nothing of the kind seems to have been suffered by Clements. On the contrary, he was much impressed by the cloisters, '... and the air of mystery and antiquity that surrounded them ...'. He loved the nearby river, and [8]

> ... was wont to assert that Westminster School with all its attributes was a more wonderful and delightful place than he had ever imagined could exist even in his wildest dreams.

Evidently, Clements did not suffer the ritual humiliations and abuse that Froude and Meyrick underwent. He was too confident, too clever and too precocious for that. Clements never was, and never would be, a victim.

In later life he constantly alluded to the happy two years he spent at Westminster, and spoke of the affection and reverence he had for the school and its traditions. He continued to take the greatest interest in the lives and careers of the Westminster boys, and in later life was honoured to be elected a member of the governing body, and appointed a Trustee of Dr Busby's charity. The Trust, among other charitable works, repaired or rebuilt decayed cottages and farm buildings. Richard Busby (1606–1695), headmaster of Westminster for more than 50 years, was as famous for administering corporal punishment as he was for his ability, and once boasted of having birched 16 of the bishops then on the bench.

He was also satirised for placing a 'jingling padlock on the mind' in proclaiming the virtues of rote learning. Although this was all in the past, it is safe to assume that the Pestalozzi method became but a distant memory for Clements. A more rigorous, but in some ways more libertarian regime, replaced it, in the time-honoured fashion of the English public boarding school.

Clements was domiciled upstairs in one of the master's houses, a Mr Benthall, who lived with his servants on the ground, the first, and the second floors in a house in Little Dean's Yard. Well out of the way, Clements shared the very comfortable garrets with eight other boys: [9]

> Privacy was insured by what was called "pokering the door"; this consisted in driving a red-hot poker through the floor against the door, and letting the end rest on the ceiling below.

Although the word 'homosexual' did not come into widespread use until the end of the nineteenth century, by any other name it was known to be rife at public schools of the period: [10]

> Encouraged by a classical curriculum, whose literature, 'impregnated with *paederastia*' as it was, provided within the closed communities of the schools the intellectual authority which temporarily over-rode the social prohibitions against homosexual contacts.

If this brings to mind scenes of cultured and more-or-less-civilised same-sex practices, John Addington Symonds attests to a culture somewhat less refined, recalling that at Harrow in the 1860s: [11]

> Every boy of good looks had a female name, and was recognized either as a public prostitute or as some bigger fellow's 'bitch.' Bitch was the word in common usage to indicate a boy who yielded his person to a lover. The talk in the dormitories and the studies was incredibly obscene. Here and there one could not avoid seeing acts of onanism, mutual masturbation, the sports of naked boys in bed together.

Whatever Clements' individual experience was, he emerged from the cloisters of Westminster with a lifelong love of boys. In later life he often visited his old school, Westminster, mingling with the boys, bringing home a few of them for the weekend, treating them to dinner and visits to the theatre, and generally giving them a good time. For an older man to bring boys home for the weekend and 'give them a good time' would not be considered appropriate these days. The presumption of innocence is characteristic for a society in which anything else was unthinkable. The fact that so many biographers make the same assumptions today means that they have failed to update their understanding in line with what we now know is, and was, the pervasiveness of sexual abuse perpetrated by adults in unequal power relationships with children.

References

1   The Rev. David Frederick Markham. *A History of the Markham Family*

2   Simon Schama. *Citizens*, p. 155

3   P.D. Jimack. Introduction to Jean-Jacques Rousseau, *Émile*, p. xl

4   Markham, M.E. and Markham, F.A. *The Life of Sir Albert Hastings Markham,* p. 3

5   Admiral Sir Albert Markham. *The Life of Sir Clements R. Markham,* p. 8

6   Simon Heffer. *High Minds*, p. 177

7   *op. cit.,* p. 454

8   Admiral Sir Albert Markham. *op. cit.*, p. 13

9   *op. cit.*, p. 14

10   Michael S. Foldy. *The Trials of Oscar Wilde*, p. 191, n. 96

11   Amber Regis (ed.). *The Memoirs of John Addington Symonds*, p. 147

2

THE ROYAL NAVY, PACIFIC STATION

Family and social connections have, since time immemorial, been the most important determining factor in the career prospects of a young man. Clements would not therefore have been expected to neglect his aunt, the Countess of Mansfield, at whose house he was a frequent visitor while he was at Westminster. Generally agreed to have been a 'beautiful boy', engaging and lively, his aunt evidently found him entertaining enough to frequently join her and her guests at the dinner table at her home, Langham House, on the site of the current Langham Hotel. One evening, about two years after he'd started at Westminster, there happened to be present at dinner Rear-Admiral Sir George Seymour. Seymour was about to embark on a four-year mission as Commander-in-Chief, Pacific Station. After dinner, when the ladies had retired, Clements found himself sitting next to Seymour. The Admiral, no doubt impressed and entertained by the boy's precocious erudition and ability to hold his own in august company, suggested that Clements should enrol as a cadet and accompany him on his flagship, the *Collingwood*, on his four-year mission to the Pacific.

Who would have declined a personal invitation from the C-in-C, and what boy would not have felt the lure of exotic lands and potential adventure? The prospect fired his imagination – and what Clements wanted, Clements got, by and large. Before long he had been kitted out by a Naval outfitter and, sitting in his new cadet's uniform, he posed for his portrait in watercolours by Thomas Richmond. The portrait shows a pert, fresh and active ephebe, trim-waisted and small for his age, with a Beatles hairdo. We will never know what was in Seymour's mind when he invited young Clements. Clements would have displayed qualities that would have justified his selection on purely pragmatic grounds, no doubt, and any suggestion that it was more than that would have been met with a suitable show of disbelief and opprobrium.

Nevertheless, boys, and especially a 'beautiful' boy, as Clements was repeatedly said to have been, were known to be a central focus of seaborne sexuality. Officers had sex with boys, not each other. [1] On voyages where no contact with women was possible for long periods, officers were known to have their special boys; and Clements was not only an exceedingly good-looking boy, but had also been appropriately schooled. He was a great favourite with all the officers, one of whom described him as '... the most beautiful as well as the most engaging boy on board the ship'. Reference was made to '... his gentle, sweet manners and his extreme beauty'. [2]

HMS *Collingwood* was an 80-gun two-deck second-rate wooden sailing ship of the line, already becoming obsolete in the twilight of the age of sail, but still guaranteed to impress, which is why she was considered suitable for the mission. She had a complement of one flag admiral, 57 officers and subordinate officers, 483 petty officers and seamen, 150 marines, and 60 boys. Total 751. [3]

She made her way out of Portsmouth Harbour on 20 July 1844, Clements' 14th birthday. The fact that it was his birthday must have added to his sense of occasion as she put out to sea – the summer breeze billowing her sails, with her officers in uniform manning the quarterdeck, and the men manning the yards. His heart leapt as he looked around the grand old sailing ship, in his opinion not to be surpassed for grace and beauty by anything afloat: [4]

> ... her very appearance gave an air of power and grandeur that it
> was impossible to describe.

For now, it was only as far as Spithead, however, where final stores were taken on board, and last embarkations made. She finally set off for the Pacific on 7 September, after lunch with the Admiral (at which Clements was present), and inspections by the Prince of Prussia, the Duke of Wellington, and Prince Albert among others. Gradually emerging from a flotilla of boats and yachts with friends and family fluttering handkerchiefs, she at last sailed into the open sea on a fair breeze, bound for the Pacific. In addition to the 751 personnel, on this occasion she also carried the Admiral's family, consisting of his wife, four daughters, one son, and a full complement of servants of both sexes and, last but not least, a cow, for fresh milk. It was customary for flag officers to take their families when going on lengthy assignments in peacetime. Seymour's family were to live in Valparaiso while he and the ship showed the flag and made contact with other British ships and allies in the Pacific. Britain and France were at odds about how exactly to carve up Pacific Island protectorates, and were engaged in making decisions over the heads of the islanders, convinced that they had brought the blessings of Jesus and civilisation where once there were only heathens.

Clearly already massively favoured by being Seymour's protégé, Clements nevertheless had to take his place a as a lowly cadet, although of the 'gentleman' class, and a junior member of the midshipman's (snotty's) mess, or gunroom. In many ways this was a similar environment to Westminster. Once again Clements found himself part of a community of male adolescents. Gunrooms were notoriously riotous places where alcohol flowed freely, as it did in the rest of the ship, and one entertainment or another was usually on offer, often accompanied by a fiddle and a flute. The older boys would send the younger ones to bed at 9 pm, after which licentiousness and debauchery could be given free rein. One suspects that this rule was not always strictly enforced, and Clements probably felt free to include himself if the evening looked promising enough. The gunroom was described as [5]

> ... [not] exactly a gentlemanly little prep school for innocent youth: yet it was surely over-straining the bounds even of contemporary propriety to allow such very immature lads to mingle so promiscuously with far older *men* who adorned the same mess. [his italics]

Fortunately for Clements, his early years as an indulged child, and his later experience at Westminster, had equipped him with the confidence and nous to handle the challenges of the gunroom. They slept below, however; and even the officers' protégés had to descend into the 'stygian gloom' at night, and sling their hammock over their sea-chests in the dark corners of the fetid and airless orlop-deck, deep in the bowels of the ship. These boys ate, slept, worked and played together in close confinement, often unsupervised. It doesn't take much imagination, considering the ever-present libidinous urges of teenage boys, to paint a picture of debauched anarchy at times.

Clements was soon scribbling and sketching in his journal. The ship and all her internal arrangements were carefully drawn, and the daily routine was described in the smallest detail. The officers, too, were observed and criticised, including Admiral Seymour and Captain Smart: 'Smart by name and Smart by nature'. Clements, in spite of the fact he'd only been in the Navy a couple of months, and had not, prior to that, ever set foot on a ship, passes judgement on Captain Smart thus: 'a good sailor, a strict officer, and a rigid disciplinarian'. He was right insofar as that in his later career, Smart, having risen to Rear-Admiral, became so unpopular with seamen that he was reported to have difficulty manning his ship.

The Commander, Captain Broadhead, on the other hand, was 'admitted to be the smartest and best commander in the Service: his mouth was that of a sybarite when at rest, but in anger it was compressed; but he had a very winning smile and he was a good fellow'. Describing another man's mouth as 'sybaritic' would suggest that young Clements was not as innocent, as ingenuous, and as straightforward as he was painted by chroniclers, both then and now. It is the first hint that in later life he was more than simply a nostalgic oldster with a romantic attachment to boys and young men, who viewed the past through rose-tinted spectacles and nothing more, as claimed by virtually all historians, including Scott's most recent biographer, the mellifluous and patrician David Crane.

Clements was often invited to dinner with the Admiral and his family, as were other officers. The family atmosphere and light conversation was welcomed by all as a change from the well-worn Naval yarns and reminiscences that usually held sway at the Admiral's table. As it got warmer going south, the evenings were often spent dancing on the quarterdeck to the music of the ship's band. They dropped anchor for ten days at Rio de Janeiro. Clements and his mess-mates were given enough leave to explore the city and the surrounding countryside.

After leaving Rio, and a rough month at sea rounding Cape Horn, they arrived in Valparaiso, where Admiral Seymour assumed command of the Pacific Station. The Admiral's family disembarked here, much to the regret of the officers, among whom was 36-year-old Lieutenant Philip Horatio Townsend Somerville. Somerville also wrote a journal throughout the mission, [6] and paints a very different picture of life in the Pacific. From him we hear about the hardships and the seamier side – in contrast to Clements who, not unusually for a teenager, seems preoccupied mainly with his own affairs. Although Somerville's account wasn't published until many years afterwards, writing narratives of voyages was popular with those officers who kept detailed diaries and who had an interest in literature. They formed a potential source of extra income as, among many others, William Parry and Sherard Osborn attest.

For the crews, shipboard life was anything but a bed of roses. Accidents and injuries, often fatal, were not uncommon: men fell from aloft or were drowned, ruptures and hernias were common, as were respiratory diseases from damp and mouldy conditions. Pain had to be endured and illnesses suffered, often in stifling heat, frequently ending in death. This voyage was no exception: by the time they reached Valparaiso, three men had accidentally fallen overboard and drowned. Alcohol was also a frequent issue and responsible for many accidents and bad behaviour, as it was in the Navy generally, where ordinary crew members were routinely flogged for being drunk. The purser on this voyage, being a warrant officer, escaped this fate, even though he must have been an alcoholic, judging by the reported delirium tremens he suffered: [7]

> Most wardroom officers were far from being drunkards, but most
> of them were accustomed to carrying a good deal, and most of them
> carried it decorously enough.

The commander-in-chief himself was often laid up and had to be hoisted around due to gout, an alcohol-related affliction.

It took over three months to sail from Spithead to Valparaiso: plenty of time for Clements to start getting an idea of the quotidian realities of shipboard life, and for the novelty to start wearing off. Fourteen-year-old boys are not known for writing letters home, nor for missing home very much, but it is striking how homesick Somerville is in comparison to Clements. Although Somerville is older than Clements, the longing for family and home suffuses his journal. He passionately looks forward to letters from home, and often mentions his correspondence with his family in his journal. Clements' attention, on the other hand, is on a newly formed friendship with Lieutenant William Peel, the glamorous and inspirational Naval hero. Clements adored him, and spent many long night watches in his company, imbibing noble sentiments along with practical knowledge. Or so we're told.

William Peel, later to become Captain Sir William Peel VC KCB, was the third son of Prime Minister Sir Robert Peel, and is immortalised by a larger-than-life sculpture at the National Maritime Museum at Greenwich. He made a deep impression on Clements, who was heartbroken when Peel broke the news shortly after they anchored in Callao that that he had been ordered back to England. Clements writes, '... my heart is like lead. I went down into one of the cabins, and shed bitter tears'. Later in life, he was to frequently assert that his interest in the Navy diminished considerably after Peel's departure. Peel died in India in 1858 at the age of 33, of smallpox contracted while recovering from wounds sustained in fighting the Indian Mutiny. He received the highest award for gallantry and was regarded as a hero. His constant companion and young *Aide-de-Camp*, Edward St John Daniel, went to pieces after Peel's death – disgracing himself through alcohol, and going AWOL after shadowy allegations surfaced concerning indecent liberties taken with four subordinate officers. He was eventually stripped of his VC, won for bravery by Peel's side, turning up eventually in Hokitika, a gold prospector's town in New Zealand. He died there in 1868 at the age of 31, the cause of death being stated as 'delirium tremens'.

Something of Markham's emotions can be imagined when, many years later, he looked up at Peel's statue at the National Maritime Museum, as he is likely to have done. The blatant homo-erotic quality of the work contradicts the prudery associated with the Victorian era. A case of the 'emperor's new clothes', perhaps – but the fact that these things were never brought into the open protected people like Markham, whose sexuality would have been nothing but his own business if it hadn't been exploitative, abusive and instrumental in his criminally irresponsible decision to appoint someone as unprepared and unsuited as Scott to command what was, nominally at least, a national Antarctic expedition.

From Somerville we start to hear about the summary punishments meted out to the lower deck: [8]

> Four men were punished at 11.30 a.m. for desertion; among them
> was Edward Cairn who roared like a bull, and after being cast off,
> still continued to cry.

Another man dashed headlong overboard, rather than submitting to being clapped in irons for being drunk. In addition to Peel's departure, the floggings and summary punishments were also taking their toll on Clements' emotional commitment to the Navy. The men to be flogged would be stripped to the waist and lashed to a grating or other convenient post, always with their arms up, to inflict maximum pain. The bosun's mate, who usually carried out the punishment, would make a new cat-o-nine-tails for each flogging.

The whole ship's company would be ordered to witness the entire disgusting spectacle – not only the pain, but also the ritual humiliation and submission to authority that were important parts of the proceedings. The men were often reduced to whimpering wrecks, praying for mercy, blood running down their legs.

Flogging was only for the lower deck, of course. The sheer inconceivability of a flogging for a 'gentleman' is a measure of the gross humiliation it entailed. The captain had the freedom to order punishments at his own discretion for all those offences that did not require a court martial. This meant that the frequency and severity of punishments in the Royal Navy was mostly decided on an arbitrary basis. If you were unlucky enough to find yourself on a ship with a sadistic captain you could, as an ordinary seaman, expect to get flogged savagely for often quite trivial offences. Without appeal to a higher authority, the crew were at the mercy of their captain; experienced Jacks knew whose ships to steer clear of. The *Collingwood* seems to have been unexceptional in this regard and punishments, although not unusual, seem to have been moderate for the time.

Having settled the Admiral's family comfortably in Valparaiso, the ship continued on her voyage, anchoring eventually at Callao, the seaport of Lima, where they spent an initial two months. For Somerville, Callao had little to recommend itself, with its constantly roaring surf, its dreary and barren coastline, adobe houses, louche hotels and stench of rotting offal. Small groups of officers were given leave in turn to make trips into Lima, and Clements obtained leave to go on a two-day visit the day after Peel's departure. Well timed to take his mind off his chagrin, the trip allowed him to explore Lima in the company of three mess-mates and the Naval Instructor, visiting the places he'd read and written about as a young boy. Peruvian history, especially the ancient Inca civilisation, held a special fascination for him.

Peru presented few threats or moral dilemmas for Clements, in contrast to Somerville, who struggles with his conscience. In Callao, for example, he is tempted to gamble in the 'low' hostelry where they wait for the boat to take them to the ship. Clements, on the other hand, frequently refers to the outings, picnics and bathing sessions with his mess-mates in the nearby river Rimac. He also spent a lot of time on board reading the books the Admiral and other officers placed at his disposal, to read in their cabins, if he so chose. He is reported not to have liked the discipline and routines of the quarterdeck, preferring to do as he pleased, without responsibility to anyone. It must have been clear early on that he was not cut out for a career in the Royal Navy.

Nevertheless, he was especially favoured by being invited to spend a week as a guest of the Admiral's family when the ship again called at Valparaiso. He made the acquaintance of prominent Chilean families and members of the operatic company then performing there. A grand ball was given on board at this time, of which Clements writes, 'Nothing to be compared with it had ever been seen on board a man-of-war at Valparaiso or anywhere else. It was a perfect scene of enchantment.'

Next on the agenda was a trip to Tahiti and Hawaii. Temptations in the form of the Polynesian women were a challenge for men like Somerville, who tried earnestly to live up to the ideals of Christian propriety and sexual continence. In Honolulu he was '... horrified at the conduct of a woman there and have reproached myself for the course I took'. His heart is far from being right with God and 'evil thoughts and sinful ideas' oppress him, following another visit to Honolulu. There were no such temptations for Clements. Comments regarding the women of the South Pacific are conspicuous by their absence in Clements' story.

The *Collingwood* was not a strongly religious ship. Somerville finds the sincerity of his religious sentiments and practices scoffed at. 'Divine service is performed for conscience sake and to keep up appearances.' [9] – indicative of a pragmatic and worldly moral climate among the officers, who lived more by their own rules and those of the Navy than by those of the Church. One of the cardinal rules was that nothing should damage the honour of the Royal Navy; officers were very concerned that the honour of the service should always be upheld. A precocious and savvy boy like Clements would have understood perfectly what that meant, and he was discreet – not only then, but all his life, above all in matters of a personal nature.

The social or class background of the 60 boys of the gunroom mess was mixed. Groupings would have self-selected on the basis of class primarily, but also age and inclination. Clements seems to have been part of a clique, of which James Goodenough, 'Gallows' Jones, and Vesey Hamilton were members. James Graham Goodenough (1830–1875), later Commodore, had been at Westminster at the same time as Clements (although not lodged upstairs at Mr Benthall's), and was a star pupil on board the *Collingwood*. Their friendship was cemented on the occasion when Goodenough insisted on getting back to the ship after a long and exhausting excursion inland, during which Clements had been quite prepared to go AWOL. William Henry Jones-Byrom (1829–1867), aka 'Gallows' Jones, later Commander, served in China in 1857 under Sherard Osborn, about whom much more later. Vesey Hamilton (1829–1912), later Admiral Sir Richard Vesey

Hamilton, was in the Arctic with Clements, in the *Assistance* in 1850, where they were known to be close.

There would have been a hierarchy of cliques in the gunroom; in-groups and out-groups. Clements' status as a favourite among the higher echelons is likely to have caused resentment in some quarters. Some may not, moreover, have made a secret of their dislike. He may well have been on the receiving end of snide remarks, and there may have been gossip behind his back. This experience, and no doubt much else throughout his life, combined to build his defences to the point where in 1904 he was described by Sir Evan MacGregor, the Secretary of the Admiralty as a 'pachydermous gentleman'; i.e. a gentleman with a thick skin.

As a general rule, the older boys would have dominated, but there would also have been boys who were especially favoured, due to 'interest', looks, confidence, *savoir-faire*, and an ability to give as good as they got and more in the ribald badinage of gunroom culture. Assuming that the Greek model, famously disseminated by the English public schools, still broadly informed ideas of male sexuality in the gunroom, then, as David Halperin claims, the primary sexual distinction, as it was for ancient Athenian men, would have been between active and passive roles. Therefore: [10]

> ... as long as a male maintained a masculine phallocentric protocol, and assumed the insertive role, no matter what his sexual object choice – woman, boy, slave, or foreigner – he was, within the contemporary context, 'politically correct' in terms of his sexuality.

In a more inclusive interpretation of this view, the top boys could have demanded a range of sexual favours without being considered, or considering themselves ontologically or epistemologically 'inverted'. This would suggest that it was the anxious, sensitive, and submissive boys who would tend to be the natural victims and thus expected to supply sexual favours if and when these were demanded, either from other boys or officers.

Being inclined to party, be it picnics, dances, dinners, 'skylarking' or theatricals, Clements instigated activities and to a large extent orchestrated them. He was a controller of events, and is likely to have been the one in control in his relationships. Nothing happened without his consent; the only times he was a victim is when it suited him.

Although homosexuality was not an offence under English law until 1885, sodomy on board the Royal Navy was punishable by death until 1829. Fresh in their memory will have been the flogging around the Fleet, in addition to a year's imprisonment and discharge with disgrace, in 1842, of two seamen convicted of buggery. Charges like these would always have required a court martial, for men as well as officers. An officer convicted of a similar offence could expect to be dishonourably dismissed from the Navy and suffer ignominy for the rest of his life.

Unsurprisingly, some preferred to take their own lives. Food for thought is that, if Clements had indeed been sexually involved with any officer, he would have had enormous power over them, whether or not he had been a consenting participant.

He would have made sure that the framing of the offence would have favoured him, while casting maximum blame on the other. Clements would have been well aware that an accusation of that nature could spell disaster for the accused. On the other hand, shared intimacies between equals could lead to lifelong bonds, and certainly Clements seems to have enjoyed such bonds, which in the case of Vesey Hamilton, for example, he used much to his advantage.

Clements had a fundamentally dominant nature. He tended to insubordination, rebelliousness, conceit and impertinence. One example of this was when, after a series of events that culminated in a fit of rage, he struck a superior officer. An idea of the extent of his privileged status – and the way in which he was able to take advantage of it – can be inferred from what happened in the aftermath. It was customary for boys like Clements to receive a certain amount of education on board large ships like the *Collingwood*. One day, during lessons, Clements, in front of the class, drew attention to an error in the work set by the Naval Instructor, William Johnson, described by James Goodenough as a man of cultivation and ability. Mr Johnson, having had enough by this time, one suspects, took the opportunity at the next captain's inspection to inform the captain that Markham's conduct was 'extremely unsatisfactory.' He further stated that he was 'very conceited and at times most impertinent'. [11] Clements was punished by being made to 'toe the line', by standing on the poopdeck from 8 am until sunset. He was furious at this public humiliation, and had all day to seethe and internally rehearse his case and solidify his hatred of Mr Johnson, and dislike of the Navy in general.

The next difficult event took place a few days later, when Clements burst into the captain's cabin, without so much as knocking, in order to deliver a passionate plea on behalf of a sailor who was scheduled to receive a flogging the next morning for repeated drunkenness. The captain was outraged and sent Clements packing. The sailor in question was duly given 36 lashes.

Clements sulked for some days after this, carrying out his duties in a careless and indifferent way, turning up late, and being generally passively aggressive. Lieutenant Bathurst, the son of a Naval officer famous for the respect and affection he inspired in his men, [12] attempted in a constructive and pedagogically sound way to cajole Clements out of his sulk by proposing a mock duel with 'single-sticks'. When Clements refused to defend himself, Bathurst warned him that he would hit him if he did not put his guard up. At this, Clements struck Bathurst across the shoulders as hard as he could with his stick. [13]

We will never know who witnessed the incident, but they are unlikely to have been alone on deck, and the shock must have been palpable. This was now a serious matter and Clements was placed under arrest. The captain informed him that he would make a report in writing to the Commander-in-Chief (Seymour), as it was too serious a case for him to deal with. Bathurst was terribly perturbed about it all. Gossip is likely to have been all over the ship, and the atmosphere around Clements was probably tense and subdued for a few days. What the seamen thought of it can be guessed, as for them, a similar offence would have meant being clapped in irons and five years in prison, or worse. As a 'young gentleman', however, such a punishment was out of the question, although he could still have expected to be dismissed his ship and sent home in disgrace on the next available transport.

Bathurst, recovering from the shock, had probably begun to think of the repercussions, even for a favourite like Markham. It would hurt Seymour, and Clements' parents would be heartbroken. If Bathurst was anything like his own father, he would have been conciliatory, and would have hated the idea that he could be responsible for ruining Markham's career before it had properly begun. Before the captain had had an opportunity to inform the Admiral, therefore, Bathurst persuaded Commander Broadhead to intercede on his behalf with the captain, as a result of which the charges were quietly dropped. Clements was ordered back to work, and nothing more was said about the matter. Attempts were even made to placate the sulking Markham, who felt misunderstood and hard done by.

There is, however, an alternative way of interpreting the incident. Whacking an officer across the shoulders with a stick is no ordinary act of insubordination. It carries an implied lack of respect and an extraordinary lack of concern for the consequences – a sense of immunity even. It hints at a freedom of action and familiarity that would normally be unthinkable between a cadet and an officer. Normally, the social and professional gulf would have been too wide, the automatic deference too ingrained. One explanation for that lack of respect and sense of familiarity would be that the relationship between Bathurst and Clements had been an intimate one. If there had indeed been erotic encounters between Bathurst and Markham, it would explain why Bathurst was so extremely perturbed about the possibility of the matter being officially pursued. The fear that Clements might take revenge by spilling the beans might have been only too real. Either way, the episode caused 'a veritable revolution' in Markham's feelings towards the Navy, and things were never the same again for him. He baulked especially at the tyrannical way he felt that punishment generally was meted out. He hated to see men flogged, although some he hated to see flogged more than others, and it clearly didn't include him hitting an officer with a stick.

Life on board the *Collingwood* went on, however, and although he had in his own mind already decided a career in the Navy was not for him, he knuckled down and made the best of it. A cruise among the Pacific islands was bound to bring its consolations and, as time went on, he was reconciled to a large extent. Many 'delightful' excursions were made on Hawaii, Oahu and Tahiti, and Markham even indulged in a spot of unilateral spying (on the French), on behalf of the Tahitians, which he got away with – although, notably, a fellow conspirator did not, and was arrested, dismissed from his ship and sent home. He also worked for his examination for the rank of midshipman, and was duly promoted a month or two later.

Alive to the possibilities and opportunities afforded by the mission, Markham made good use of his time in South America. He took the opportunity to learn Spanish, taught by Mr Johnson, but uncredited by Markham. On their lengthy sojourns at Callao he explored miles inland, getting a feel for Peru and its people. He also established contacts and friendships. He would use this knowledge and experience later in life to make a name for himself, and help make a lot of money for the British Government.

As far as the Navy went, he had lived and worked alongside many who were to go on and attain high status and influence in the armed services. In addition to those already mentioned, these included – but were not limited to – Sir George Seymour's son 'Wilfred', afterwards General Lord William F Seymour GCB; Flag Officer Beauchamp Seymour, a nephew of the Admiral (with whom he spent many afternoons in his cabin), afterwards Admiral Lord Alcester GCB; Lieutenant Richard Quin, who married a sister of Clements' and died a Rear-Admiral; Lieutenant Reginald McDonald, died a Vice-Admiral and a KCB; Algernon De Horsey, later Admiral Sir Algernon De Horsey GCB; Sherard Osborn; Captain Kellett (later involved in the 1852 search for the Franklin Expedition under the disastrous Sir Edward Belcher), who gave Markham much instruction in nautical surveying; and Lieutenant M'Clintock, later Admiral Sir Leopold M'Clintock KCB FRS, who was on the Austin Expedition in search of Franklin with Markham. M'Clintock went on to make his name in Polar exploration, determining the way British Polar exploration was conducted until the death of Robert Falcon Scott and his team. If ever a man could be said to have known everybody who was anybody (certainly as far as the Navy was concerned), it was Clements Robert Markham. Without these connections he would never have got his Antarctic Expedition up and away.

Next was a cruise along the coasts of Mexico and California, during which Clements passed his exam for midshipman, and turned 16. A return visit to Honolulu followed, where some delightful excursions took place in the company of a batch of new faces who arrived in HMS *Grampus*, fresh in from England. Clements, always keen to make the acquaintance of new arrivals, quickly made friends with among others Lord Gilford ('an exceedingly good-looking boy'), later Admiral of the Fleet the Earl of Clanwilliam GCB, and John Baird ('a very nice youngster') later Admiral Sir John Baird KCB. The entertainments culminated in a very jolly picnic for 40 young men from the combined gunrooms of the *Collingwood* and the *Grampus*, described by Markham as a very memorable event. The ship then took 69 days to sail from Honolulu to Valparaiso.

On arrival they were greeted with the news that Commander Broadhead and First Lieutenant Hankey, who had both been good to Markham, had been promoted out of the ship. Somerville was made First Lieutenant with a promise of being appointed Acting Commander, which he trusts was '... ordained by the Almighty, who only knows what is good for us'. Sherard Osborn was promoted to Lieutenant; and many new officers joined, among whom was Count Ladislav Karolyi, educated at Eton, and described as a charming Hungarian. He and Markham became great friends. Ashore, Markham did the social rounds until they reluctantly took their leave and sailed once again to Callao. On the way Markham was promoted to midshipman of the foretop.

The promotion rekindled his interest and enthusiasm for the Navy – for the time being, at least. He immediately set about making a list of the hundred or so foretop men, who were among the elite sailors on the ship – young, fit, agile and brave. In what was to become a habitual activity, Markham wrote a full description of each one, including their

> ... personal appearance, their zeal, activity aloft, family histories, and any little incident connected with their lives ... especially any particular accomplishments in which they individually excelled.

He never reported them to the commander. If they had misbehaved, they would be summarily dealt with during a night watch by the captains of the foretop. This was apparently very efficacious, and the men preferred it to being reported to the commander. History does not record what form these summary night-time punishments took.

Back in Callao, the usual picnics and excursions to the banks of the Rimac were again on the menu, facilitated this time by the renting of a house for their convenience. Captain Kellett frequently took Clements across to the island of San Lorenzo for practical training in nautical surveying. Clements' real interests, however, lay in another direction. He had by now decided to become an explorer and a great geographer – twin ambitions which he undeniably achieved in his lifetime, although some might interpret the word 'great' as enthusiastic, rather than historic. They stayed at Callao for four and a half months, after which they set sail again for Valparaiso for the last time. There they waited a further seven months – plenty of time for excursions and trips through magnificent countryside, staying at local inns and sharing the enjoyment of rudimentary facilities with a favoured few.

As light relief and in order to keep everyone from getting too rusty, the Admiral took the ship to the islands of Juan Fernandez. 'Robinson Crusoe Island' was avidly explored, in the course of which Goodenough fell down a wooded precipice searching for Alexander Selkirk's lookout point. Clements would use this adventure later in life to entertain the cadets on the training ship *Conway*. Goodenough survived the fall, eventually dying of tetanus in 1875.

Their relief ship appeared at last – bills were paid, farewells wished, and the *Collingwood* was homeward bound. They anchored at Spithead on 3 July 1848, after an absence of nearly four years. Looking back, in spite of his difficulties, Markham was to refer to his time in the *Collingwood* as having been among the happiest of his life, and she remained for him a '... beau idéal of what a British man-of-war should be'. In spite of the occasional tedium and the darker aspects of ship-board life, these had been halcyon days, packed with unforgettable experiences and exciting adventures. What better way to spend one's teenage years but to make friends and contacts, explore and enjoy exotic locations and fascinating cultures, and to have a great time partying, picnicking and reading. It was one of Markham's peak experiences, and fostered the nostalgia that would later influence his vision of the *Discovery*, the ship Scott took to the Antarctic for the first time.

References

1   B.R. Burg. *Boys at Sea*, Introduction

2   Admiral Sir Albert Markham. *The Life of Sir Clements R. Markham*, p. 26

3   [Unattributed writer]. Mid-Victorian RN vessel HMS Collingwood, www.pdavis.nl

4   Admiral Sir Albert Markham. *op. cit.*, p. 21

5   Michael Lewis. *The Navy in Transition*, p. 158

6   Alison Kay (ed.). *H.M.S. Collingwood*

7   Michael Lewis. *op. cit.*, p. 151

8   Alison Kay. *op. cit.*, p. 4

9   *op. cit.*, p. 57

10   Michael Foldy. *The Trials of Oscar Wilde*, p. 120

11   Admiral Sir Albert Markham. *op. cit.*, p. 49

12   Michael Lewis. *op. cit.*, p. 170

13   Admiral Sir Albert Markham. *op. cit.*, p. 51

3

THE ROYAL NAVY IN THE ARCTIC;

THE ENTERTAINMENTS OF WINTER

Markham's portrait was again painted when he came home from the Pacific. The beautiful boy has matured into the beautiful young man. Aged 18, he brings to mind Camille Paglia's observation that [1]

> ... divine charisma separates the hierarch from communality by a zone of privilege.

His uniform is expertly tailored. The collar and cravat flatter his effeminate looks, and his lips are set in a fastidious pout. There is a precision in the detail of his clothes and the styling. The averted gaze is coquettish, seductive but at the same time remote and exclusive. Everything about the pose suggests a conscious awareness of his own allure; he impresses, but from a distance, without engaging with the viewer. Sophisticated for his age, urbane and aloof, he looks like he knows very well how the world works, and already has plenty of experience in using that knowledge to his advantage.

After a couple of desultory years in the Mediterranean on a succession of different ships, in which he nevertheless met many 'charming fellows', Markham got a midshipman's berth on the *Assistance,* one of Horatio Austin's Arctic Squadron. The Navy as an authoritarian and often brutal taskmaster might have palled on him, but the men and boys who manned it had not. They had helped pass the service time needed to (eventually) qualify for the rank of Lieutenant – a thing much desired by his father, who although comfortable in his living, knew he would not be handing down a fortune to his sons on his demise. It was an insurance policy, a fall-back position.

Rife with blatant nepotism and *de-haut-en-bas* whim, the Navy resembled a private club and a milch-cow for people with 'interest'. It seemed to be run for the convenience of the incumbents who thought they knew best, went by tradition, and resented interference by the Government. At a time when the Admiralty was making deep cuts in ships and personnel due to the cessation of large-scale wars at sea, the officer class went on as usual, gaining automatic promotion and, for favourites like Markham, cherry-picking commissions.

It was Captain Horatio Austin's 1850 mission to the Arctic in search of the missing Franklin Expedition that laid the foundations for Markham's views on how best to conduct Polar expeditions. It set in stone a faith in the ways of the Royal Navy that rendered him incapable of giving due credit to any other institution, nation, or private individual – however experienced – in matters of exploration or maritime endeavour. This sudden enthusiasm for Polar work had been kindled in Markham by Sherard Osborn, whom he had first come to know on the *Collingwood*. Osborn had been promoted to Lieutenant during the Pacific mission. Eight years older than Markham, very different in character and outlook, and already forging a glittering career in the Navy, Osborn and Markham nevertheless shared a literary proclivity. Both produced a narrative of the Arctic mission which was published afterwards.

They had met again in Cork in early 1850. Delighted at his appointment to the command of the *Pioneer*, one of the two steamships commissioned for the Austin mission, Osborn's enthusiasm swept away Markham's *ennui;* and within days, with Osborn's help, he set in motion a comprehensive campaign, involving his father, and anyone else he could call on to pull strings for him, to get him a berth on one of the ships. He succeeded, in spite of the fact that there wasn't an obvious role for him, and was appointed as one of only two midshipmen in the squadron.

Before he left, and while in London getting kitted out for the journey, he met up with his original *beau idéal*, William Peel. Things were probably all very different this time. Time had passed and circumstances had changed. They were both preoccupied by work and life in the present, and they were probably in a hurry. There is never any going back to the past and no rekindling of the old magic is likely to have taken place. It was in any case a hectic week for Markham. Bad news had arrived about the state of his brother David's health. His parents decided to leave for Madeira at once in order to be with him, and would have been making urgent preparations. Clements probably busied himself with his kit, which would have been a major preoccupation, considering where he was going. He would not have wanted to be cold.

Nothing had been heard of from the *Erebus* and the *Terror* under Sir John Franklin since they were last seen tethered to an iceberg in Baffin Bay in the summer of 1845. It was now spring 1850 and, although hopes of finding survivors must by now have been slim, Lady Franklin made sure no stone was left unturned in the efforts to establish the fate of the expedition. The Admiralty seems to have taken a complacent view of things until this time, even after James Ross returned, having drawn a blank in 1848 in his attempts to locate Franklin. The Government and the Admiralty belatedly stirred in 1850, spurred by the fact that the Americans had put together an expedition to find Franklin – privately financed but manned by the American navy. Clearly, it would not do for Americans to succeed where the British had failed. It stung the Admiralty into prompt action – commissioning four ships: two sailing ships and two steam tenders. In addition, two fast brigs were commissioned, commanded by Captain William Penny, an experienced whaling captain. Penny, with 16 years' experience commanding Arctic whalers, and whose expertise and competence was widely acknowledged, was the choice of tireless and expert campaigner Lady Franklin, wife of Sir John.

The Admiralty was not impressed, however. Without pressure from Lady Franklin and the public support she enjoyed, the Lords Commissioners of the Admiralty would never have commissioned commercial vessels to form part of a Naval expedition. And certainly not whalers. Admiralty sages considered it 'an experiment fraught with danger', and especially if it succeeded, the results '... would prove inimical to the strict rules of government service'. [2] Clements Markham also took a dim view, observing caustically that

> The Government ... deemed it expedient to employ two brigs under Mr.
> Penny, a whaling captain.

Notably, he spells captain with a small c in this case, and calls Captain Penny *Mr* Penny, pointedly, throughout his account entitled *Franklin's Footsteps.* [3] As far as Markham was concerned, whalers were all very well in their own sphere, but not in conjunction with the Royal Navy. This was not to be the last time irritation at whaling captains being brought in to support a 'national' enterprise led him to downplay their importance. Those same feelings were to be in evidence too in 1903, when (whaling) Captain McKay, in the *Terra Nova*, accompanied the *Morning* on its mission to rescue Scott and the *Discovery.*

Austin, described by Markham as a short, stout, florid complexioned man of 50, seems to have been irritated by the situation from the start – no doubt frustrated and annoyed by the autonomy and non-subordinate status of Penny and his brigs. Penny was a thorough seaman, accustomed to dealing with Arctic conditions. The risk that he might outperform the Royal Navy was therefore very real. In any case, to Markham's orderly and controlling mind, an autonomous civilian seaman would have been a loose cannon, a potentially dangerous nuisance they could have well done without. He undoubtedly felt that if there were any discoveries to be made they should be made for the nation, officially, with due credit going to Her Majesty's Royal Navy.

A lot of money had been spent on fitting out the Squadron, and Austin felt that due precedence should be given to status and seniority, as was the iron rule in the

Navy. Most importantly, any conspicuous success for Penny would detract from his own record. The dislike was mutual. Penny distrusted Austin from the start, and suspected him of keeping information from him after the *Assistance* was the first to find traces of the lost expedition on Beechey Island. The gritty Scot Penny, in response, swore to scour the area like a bloodhound. [4] As it happened, Franklin left no messages on land, but Penny's suspicions – in addition to the lack of trust they showed in Austin – were a measure of how hard everyone found it to believe Franklin had not left any information whatsoever concerning his progress, nor in what direction they were headed.

Polar biographers and historians often describe in general terms the cumbersome and overmanned nature of the Polar expeditions sent out by the Admiralty in that era. What they tend not to do is explain in detail just what made them so cumbersome, even to a contemporary observer like Osborn, who was in command of one of the steamships. The Austin Squadron consisted of two large, bluff-bowed sailing ships, the *Resolute* and the *Assistance*; in addition to two steamships, the *Pioneer* and the *Intrepid*. Incredibly, the steamships were there to *tow* the sailing ships. The *Pioneer* was to tow the *Resolute*, the *Intrepid* towed the *Assistance*. Markham was a midshipman on the *Assistance*, captained by Erasmus Ommanney. Manpower in Austin's Squadron totalled 180, i.e. 30 in each of the steam vessels and 60 in each of the sailing ships.

Osborn [5] gives lengthy accounts of the efforts involved to get the *Resolute* and the *Assistance* moving along, both with steam and manpower. The times when wind and water were favourable for actual sailing were few and far between. When they were not being towed, the ships had to be physically hauled, with men heaving on ropes alongside on the ice, or 'warping' them (carrying out anchors by boat or manpower, fixing them in the ice, and winching the ship forward by turning the capstan). As well as tow it, Osborn, in the *Pioneer*, had to cleave channels through the floes for the *Resolute*. One day, watching the *Resolute* sagging to leeward in the company of a tough old Hull quartermaster, Osborn quotes him: 'Oh! Lord, sir! we have some rum craft in the whaling ships, but I don't think any thing so sluggish as the *Resolute*.'

Elsewhere, Osborn paints a vivid picture: [6]

> ... the majority of the officers and men laboured at the headmost ship, to move her through the ice. Heaving ahead with stout hawsers, blasting with gunpowder, cutting with ice-saws, and clipping with ice-chisels, was perseveringly carried on; but the progress fell far short of the labour expended, and the bluff bow slipped away from the nip instead of wedging it open. Warping the 'Resolute' through a barrier of ice by lines out of her hawse-holes, put me in mind of trying to do the

same with a cask, by a line through the bung hole: she slid and swerved every way but the right one, ahead ...

Osborn realised that the age of the sharp-fronted steamer had arrived. The ease with which he cut through the ice in the *Pioneer* contrasted with the 'ante-diluvian' (his word) bluff-fronted ships which formed a buttress that pushed the ice before it. Alternately going forward and being beset, they could be brought up short by just a few inches of ice. These ships were not built for the ice. They had been strengthened for Arctic service but, other than that, they were actually *expected* to have to claw their way through the Arctic as John Ross, and after him William Edward Parry, had done more than 30 years previously. A drawing by John Sacheuse dated 1818 shows one of Ross's ships being warped into the ice with three ice-anchors.

Although, as always, the commanders got the credit for any successes, the real heroes of this and other feats of strength, loyalty and endurance in the face of appalling conditions, were the crews. In a later narrative, Parry describes similar difficulties: [7]

> ... which it is our business to overcome rather than to discuss, I am convinced that no description of mine, nor even the minute formality of the logbook, could convey an adequate idea of the truth.

Parry urged them on with extra rations of rum and meat. It was hard on every-one, of course; but although the bulk of the work, and the injuries suffered in the course of it devolved mainly on the crews, they have passed anonymously into the dust of history. Osborn, exceptionally, gives credit where credit is due: [8]

> Captain Ommanney, myself, and Mr. Webb of the 'Pioneer' ... were the only three officers; we were consequently thrown much into the society of the men, and I feel assured I am not singular in saying that that intercourse served much to raise our opinion of the character and indomitable spirit of our seamen and marines. On them fell the hard labour, to us fell the honours of the enterprise, and to our chief the reward ...

Internally, however, the *Resolute* and the *Assistance* were fitted for comfort, with hot-air heating, a big and well-equipped kitchen, and a large Captain's cabin. Markham enthusiastically claimed that the *Assistance* was [9]

> ... the happiest, the healthiest, the cleanest, the dryest, and the most efficient ship that ever wintered in the Arctic regions.

Among stores calculated to be enough for 60 men for three years, the *Assistance* alone had on board 1,455 gallons of rum 40 over proof, which did not include the officers' stores of wines and spirits, 3,467 lbs of tobacco, and an astonishing 13,500 lbs of sugar. Mindful of the entertainments required to accompany these comforts during the long dark winters, they also shipped a printing press and a store of theatrical accoutrements, including dresses, wigs and make-up. The use of printed magazines, theatricals and balls had been pioneered by Parry and his officers in the 1820s to maintain mental and, as it was thought, physical health on board during the long dark winters. He rightly thought that being trapped in a Polar winter, surrounded for hundreds of miles by impassable ice, with only the howl of the wind and the hissing of snow for company, could play havoc with the minds of those with too vivid an imagination. He therefore made sure his officers and crews were too busy having a good time to allow anxiety and depression to gain a hold – not to mention personal animosities and boredom. Alcohol, in large quantities, had of course been considered necessary on board Her Majesty's ships since time immemorial.

Elisha Kent Kane (also in the Arctic at the time, as surgeon on the American Grinnell expedition to search for Franklin) wrote that the British even had sheets on their beds: [10]

> Winter, if we may judge of it, by the clothing and warming appliances of the British squadron, must be something beyond our power to cope with; for, in comparison with them, we have nothing, absolutely nothing.

The officers of the Royal Navy would not have been expected to rough it. Markham made special mention of having met Dr Kane in his grand overview of Polar history, *The Lands of Silence*. It is possible that the handsome, dashing Dr Kane was an inspirational figure to him. Markham, as well as admiring the charismatic Kane, might have felt an affinity in that Kane was bold and adventurous, in spite of a delicate constitution. Markham himself, although fit, was slight, and not an obvious candidate for a physically arduous career.

Osborn, clearly an exemplary officer himself, and in possession of a more generous spirit than his friend Markham, has nothing but praise for Captain Penny. Penny had fine bowed ships, and a hard, experienced crew. He also had a team of dogs on board who showed Osborn what they could do. Penny even found time to help Osborn refloat the *Pioneer* when it ran aground. Penny had the advantage of not having to spend a lot of time lugging and being lugged, and was therefore in a position to actually do the exploring they were there to do.

In consequence, it was one of his men who breathlessly ran up to him on Beechey Island one day to announce the discovery of three graves. Graves! Penny happened to be in the company of Dr Kane at the time, which must have made it doubly galling for Austin. Although they also discovered other important relics, among which were the remains of a workshop and an observatory, the graves, with their dates, formed the first incontrovertible evidence that Franklin's ships had wintered there. To Austin it must have felt like the upstart Penny was stealing the thunder he felt rightly belonged to the Navy. Suffice to say it was a further step in the worsening of relations between them.

Having come by way of Lancaster Sound, the Austin Squadron wintered beset in the pack in Barrow Strait, between Cornwallis and Griffith Islands, while Penny wintered about 20 miles away in a better situation, sheltered by land, at a place known as Assistance Harbour. Before they settled into their winter routines, a series of short journeys was undertaken in order to establish depots. The establishment of depots in advance of the next season's sledging was part of the M'Clintock method. It made a lot of sense – so much so that it was still used by Scott and Amundsen 60 years later. Markham's participation in these autumn journeys is unclear. In his *Arctic Navy List 1773–1873*, published in 1875, he credits himself with having been out altogether 40 days, presumably including his 19 days sledging in the spring. If he had been on any of these journeys, however, you would not expect him to have omitted the fact in his *Franklin's Footsteps*, but there is no mention of it. The 40 days he claims to have been out need therefore to be taken with a pinch of salt.

From the early days at sea the routine on the *Assistance* had been enlivened by '... social diversions of a somewhat convivial nature'. [11, 12] Captain Ommanney, commanding the *Assistance*, held weekly entertainments in his cabin, consisting of

> ... coffee, sweet biscuits, and cakes, an organ, a tambourine, sherry, brandy and water, a flute, a fiddle, chess, backgammon, and singing.

The officers on the *Assistance* also decided to bring out a weekly news-sheet, the *Aurora Borealis*, to which Markham was a frequent contributor. [13] In addition, Markham also wrote a series of geo-historical articles on Griffith and Cornwallis Islands, and he was a frequent contributor to the magazine of the *Resolute:* the *Illustrated Arctic News*. When the *Resolute*, in addition, brought out a humorous magazine, *The Gleaner*, Markham responded by doing the same on the *Assistance*, calling his publication, with typical young fogeyishness, *Minavilins*. [14] (Albert informs us that 'minavilins' was a term well known and frequently used in the Navy to designate odds and ends lying about on the deck.)

Both magazines were suspended after Markham went too far with the 'scathing satire' and the 'humorous' illustrations, in retaliation for a 'scurrilous' attack on one of the officers of the expedition. The officer(s) concerned evidently did not share the joke and, as well as suspending both magazines, confiscated the offending number. Later, at the *Grand Bal Masque* (about which more later), Markham gave evidence of continuing to harbour a grudge about this unjustified treatment, as he saw it. Interestingly, a very similar thing had happened on the *Superb*, the ship to which he had been appointed, against his wishes, in the summer of 1849. Here also Markham had brought out a magazine, which was suppressed 'by order', after a paragraph was 'inadvertently' inserted reflecting on the personal appearance of the senior officers of the ship. A flavour of what that might have sounded like can be had from his unflattering description of Sir Charles Napier, then in command of the Mediterranean fleet: [15]

> ... a short, broad-shouldered man with a large face and staring eyes, his legs too far through his white duck trousers, his cocked hat athwartships (in imitation of Nelson), and his nose and upper lip covered in snuff.

With the onset of winter, and the Austin Squadron safely beset in a floe, the festivities began in earnest. A 'very jovial' soirée with plenty of music was given by Captain Austin, who was described as 'the jolliest old Englishman', and on Guy Fawkes Day the Guy was burnt in a large fire by torchlight on the floe. One of the great events of the season was the opening of The Royal Arctic Theatre, under the Royal Crest of the Prince of Wales, complete with Fleur de Lis and the motto *Ich Dien*. Lieutenant William Browne of the *Resolute*, a competent watercolourist, created the 'brilliant and artistic scenery' cooed over by Markham, and displayed 'to the admiration and delight of the whole expedition'. Snow statues of the Prince of Wales and the Princess Royal, sculpted by Charles Ede, assistant surgeon on the *Assistance*, were placed on either side of the orchestra.

The theatre opened on 9 November 1850, and did not close until almost four months later. Markham was in his element on the stage with its costumes and make-up, impassioned melodrama, arch ripostes, and outré humour. And so, the 'beautifully arranged and artistically realised' Royal Arctic Theatre opened on the *Assistance* on the Prince of Wales' birthday, with a performance of 'Bombastes Furioso', a burlesque operetta with plenty of scope for stentorian and declamatory hamming, which would have suited Markham's talents admirably. Another production was the 'Grand Historical Drama: Charles the Twelfth'. The playbill shows that Captain Ommanney too enjoyed his hour on the stage, as both he and Markham are shown to have taken lead roles. We are informed that the production has 'Entirely new scenery and dresses!' Never short of performers, the men as well as the officers participated in the repertoire of plays, which were frequently repeated, with variations. The ships vied with each other in the popularity of these entertainments. The level of inward focus of the expedition is evident from the number and length of the rehearsals that must have preoccupied them: casting, costumes, make-up, scenery, script, arrangements for the auditorium, printed playbills and so on. At its height, the expedition turned into a competitive theatrical frenzy between the ships. The focus on parties and dressing up certainly helped to pass the long, dark, cold winter very 'happily and cheerily'.

However, the event which eclipsed these already highly entertaining pastimes was, without a doubt, the *Grand Bal Masque*, given in the Royal Arctic Casino, on board the *Resolute.* The scene on board was of 'unequalled magnificence'. They must have spent days discussing their costumes and making them. On the night, much fun was no doubt had getting ready; getting dressed, shaving off whiskers and putting on make-up, doing the hair. Who would want to be a sourpuss and deny them their fun? Nevertheless, the whole idea of an entirely male *Bal Masque* is intriguing. Arctic Naval masquerade balls were originally suggested by Henry Parkyns Hoppner, a lieutenant and later captain, on the Arctic expeditions undertaken by Parry, from 1819 to 1825. Captain Austin had been Hoppner's first lieutenant on the *Fury* – one instance of the strong social and professional network of relationships that formed the human core of the Navy. Hoppner never married and died in Lisbon at the age of 38.

Parry, himself an early *beau idéal* of a Naval officer, had loved music since childhood and played the violin. He also had a public-school-induced faith in the British ability to overcome any obstacle through sheer courage and perseverance. The values of the heroic amateur were always preferred to those of the skilled professional – not surprising in an age where professionals of any description were always considered inferior to 'gentlemen'. Parry's ideas about how to create a happy ship were carried forward with enthusiasm by Austin, especially Hoppner's *Grand Bal Masque.* All three decks were available, due to the topdeck being housed over with canvas, as was standard practice in Polar winters.

A very competent painting of the scene appeared in the *Aurora Borealis*, probably by Lieutenant Browne, [16] showing a cross-section of all three decks of the ship. The decks are hung about with swags and chandeliers, and 'young ladies', arm in arm with their various escorts, together with Turks, farmers, clowns, dominoes and dandies, can be seen crowding the stairs and the dance-floor. In the foreground is M'Dougall, fetchingly dressed as a *vivandière*, putting a particularly dainty leg forward. The 'restaurant', which looks more like a bar, is open, and staffed with 'barmaids'. Markham's dress was designed to illustrate his indignation at what he felt was unjust treatment with regard to the suppression of *Minavilins.* No one understood what it meant, even after he had informed them in 'sepulchral tones' that it was meant to be 'an allegory'. Markham harboured his grudges and nursed his grievances. He had done since he was a little boy, and he never got out of the habit. In the meantime, however, he tells us that

> The band played lustily until midnight; and the delights of that jovial evening were varied by punch and polkas, whisky and waltzes, cake and quadrilles.

Being cooped up in the middle of nowhere with all those men sounds like a gay man's dream scenario in itself – never mind the opportunity to let one's hair down at a big fancy-dress party with plenty of alcohol, and plenty of men in drag. Shipboard diaries and later narratives never contained controversial material, for obvious reasons, but events took place in the context of a rich and complex network of relationships. Living together for months on end in such a restricted space meant that relationships would have become more intimate than usual on an ordinary voyage, and professional boundaries were correspondingly looser.

As in Parry's day, officers and men alike would have been free to come to the party. He relates that although all seem to have entered into the spirit of the parties (Parry held masquerade balls once a month), nothing occurred to weaken the respect of the men towards their superiors. The crew are likely never to have forgotten their place. In any case, they probably gravitated towards their own groupings. Nevertheless, when the instruments came out and the dancing started, things probably became very lively. Masks and costumes provide an opportunity to step outside usual roles and behaviour, giving further permission for liberties not normally considered acceptable. Although Parry asserts that his were '... masquerades without licentiousness – carnivals without excess', the temptation must have been there, especially as these events were of course well oiled. So many fit young men, deprived of female company a long way from home, with nothing to do but have a good time. It is not surprising that Markham, for one, thought back to that winter with dreamy nostalgia.

The last production of the winter was a pantomime written by Charles Ede, called 'Zero, or Harlequin Light'. Markham thought enough of it to include the entire script in *Franklin's Footsteps*. Markham played a prominent part it seems, particularly displaying that 'great histrionic talent' which he undoubtedly possessed. In later life, his speeches and orotund oratory, where the front of his shirt was said to billow like a ship in full sail, were used to great effect. Much was asserted about the necessity of keeping up morale, legitimately of course, but doing it by way of theatricals and *Bals Masques* in an all-male environment is guaranteed to set speculation going. Days and weeks were spent in preparation for these extravaganzas, all no doubt accompanied by much hilarity and conviviality.

Interestingly, scurvy does not seem to have been an issue on this mission. Polar missions were especially vulnerable because of the lack of ports-of-call where fresh provisions could be taken on board. None of the ships reported cases of scurvy; and although Osborn states that they were all looking pale, all seem to have been fit to start sledging when the time came. This did not go unnoticed by Markham, who drew his conclusions, based on the conditions and conduct of the expedition. The ships were kept dry and clean, and as comfortably warm and aired as possible. This in itself will have kept infections and respiratory complaints to a minimum. Based on an apparent correlation between damp, unhygienic and cold conditions and the incidence of scurvy, a lot of care had been taken to equip the ships with adequate heating arrangements, and cleanliness routines were conscientiously maintained. Parry, the *eminence grise* of Arctic exploration, wrote in 1823 about having been over two years in the Arctic before signs of scurvy showed themselves, without having had access to fresh plants or vegetables. He had [17]

> ... begun to hope that with a continued attention to their comforts, cleanliness, and exercise, the same degree of vigour might ... [continue] at least as long as our present liberal resources should last.

Morale was also thought to play a part in warding off scurvy; the implied assumption being that it was in part a psychological problem, although they may not have put it that way. What they did understand, however, was that melancholia, anxiety, and depression needed to be kept at bay, whatever its role in antiscorbutic medicine. The theatricals and balls succeeded brilliantly in that.

The cure for scurvy was discovered many times, and yet, because vitamin C or ascorbic (antiscorbutic) acid is so easy to destroy, it was cast doubt upon again and again, as theories about the effectiveness of lime and lemon juice were successively hailed and discredited. The confusion was understandable, due to the fact that lemon or lime juice ceases to effective after it has been boiled, piped through copper, and stored for weeks, months, or even years, as it was by the time it was consumed. It was taken on the sledging sorties, but by then, it hardly contained any vitamin C at all. Markham was one of those who, in addition, drew attention to the fact that the Inuit did not consume lemon or lime juice, nor fresh vegetables, but did not suffer from scurvy. When, 25 years later, the Nares Expedition returned from the Arctic riddled with scurvy in spite of the consumption of lime juice, it provided the final nail in the coffin for the lemon/lime theory, certainly as far as Markham was concerned.

Nevertheless, fresh food continued to be acknowledged as useful in keeping the dreaded scourge at bay. Live cattle had been taken on board in Upernavik, in Greenland. Along the way, thousands of birds were shot, many for sport, but also for the pot. Loons and little auks were shot *enfilade*, killing 10 or 12 at a shot. If they had had more time, Osborn believes they might have killed tons of birds. [18] The Victorian Navy's automatic response to the sight of an animal, any animal, was to reach for their guns in a way that today we would find horrific, but which was normal for them. Rabbits, bears, foxes and narwhals were shot; for example, 'A shower of balls poured into the narwhales.'

The hares and the ptarmigans had begun to arrive by the spring of 1851, and they made excellent eating. M'Clintock and his party came across a herd of musk-oxen on their sledging sortie, '... the meat of which had helped to bring back his crew in wonderful condition'. [19] Around June, Osborn found good quantities of sorrel and scurvy grass, which contains high levels of ascorbic acid when fresh. They ate of it voraciously, '... for the appetite delighted in anything like vegetable food'. All this goes a long way in explaining why there had been no scurvy on the Austin Expedition. The only time they had been without fresh food intake had been over the winter months. If vitamin C levels had been normal at the beginning of the winter, the sorrel and scurvy grass they found in early summer must have come just in time. Scurvy grass was found in abundance and was used as a 'by no means unpalatable' salad. ('Scurvy grass', scientific name *Cochlearia*, is a small cress-like plant, tolerant of saline conditions and rich in vitamin C.)

But now spring was in the offing, and although it had been very much in abeyance, the serious business of sledging was beginning to take centre stage.

References

1   Camille Paglia. *Sexual Personae*, p. 523

2   Pierre Berton. *The Arctic Grail*, p. 171

3   Clement [*sic*] Robert Markham. *Franklin's Footsteps*

4   Owen Beattie and John Geiger. *Frozen in Time*, p. 61

5   Lieut. Sherard Osborn. *Stray Leaves from an Arctic Journal*, p. 47

6   *op. cit.*, p. 38

7   Sir W.E. Parry. *Journal of the Third Voyage*, pp. 4–5

8   Lieut. Sherard Osborn. *op. cit.*, p. 101

9   Pierre Berton. *op. cit.*, p. 186

10   Ken McGoogan. *Race to the Polar Sea*, p. 89

11   Admiral Sir Albert Markham. *The Life of Sir Clements R. Markham*, p. 112

12   *op. cit.*, p. 113

13   E.C. Coleman. *The Royal Navy and Polar Exploration*, p. 61

14   Admiral Sir Albert Markham. *op. cit.*, p. 120

15   *op. cit.*, pp. 104–5

16   E.C. Coleman. *op. cit.*, p. 63

17   Kenneth Carpenter. *The History of Scurvy and Vitamin C*, p. 138

18   Lieut. Sherard Osborn. *op. cit.*, p. 42

19   *op. cit.*, p. 105

4

MESSAGES IN BOTTLES AND SPRING SLEDGING

Markham, having from an early age established an antiquarian approach to his writing, sets his narrative in a historical context. The first 45 pages of his cumbersomely entitled *Franklin's Footsteps: A Sketch of Greenland Along the Shores of which His Expedition Passed, and of The Parry Isles, Where the Last Traces of it Were Found* are devoted to a résumé of Arctic history. Conflating the 'known' world with the world as known by Europeans, Markham starts by taking us back to 864 CE and the Norsemen's exploits on the shores of Greenland, followed by an overview of the mixed fortunes of early settlers and missionaries. His second chapter covers the development of the whale fisheries. The third chronicles the early Naval expeditions of Ross and Parry and, of course, their own mission in search of the lost Franklin Expedition.

It could well be argued that the most disastrous mistake Franklin made was to omit to leave written notes of his progress and intentions. He could be forgiven for not knowing that Peel Sound, at the southern end of which they became fatally beset, was only intermittently free of ice, but omitting to leave progress reports or plans seemed incomprehensible to Austin's men. They searched in vain within the cairns and detritus left behind on Beechey Island, where Franklin overwintered in 1845–6. No message was found there, nor anywhere else in the regions they searched. One theory has it that they must have been in too much of a hurry to leave a message because of a sudden break-up of the ice. This does not explain, however, why there were no messages left anywhere else either, when there must have been opportunities to do so if the intention had been there.

A careful reading of Franklin's instructions gives an insight into his thinking. He wrote those instructions himself, together with Barrow and Ross. They reveal that [1]

Once 65 degrees North had been passed, copper cylinders or bottles containing details of their position and the date were to be "frequently" thrown overboard.

How experienced sailors – or for that matter anyone with an ounce of common sense – could have surmised that messages in bottles or even copper cylinders would survive and be found months or even years later, especially in Polar seas, is incomprehensible. Presumably based on the fact that large bodies of water are relatively static, it nevertheless ignores the fact that subsequent ships would have to take the same line, and that the actions of winds, tides and ice over months and years would have had wide-ranging effects. Needless to say, there are only rare instances of these messages being found, and certainly not in this context. Did the officers stand mutely by while they watched the bottles being thrown overboard, seeing them disappear into the vastness, with never a doubt as to their efficacy? Was their faith in Franklin and the Admiralty so strong that it overrode any misgivings? Or were they, and Franklin himself, such slaves to the letter of their instructions that they shrank from broaching the matter at all? Maybe they were so fond and in awe of Franklin that it seemed disloyal to question his judgement. Or perhaps it simply never occurred to them to leave messages on land. We will never know.

While scarcely believable to us now, throwing messages overboard was standard Naval practice. The Franklin document(s) which were eventually found on King William Island confirm this, as they were printed on standard 'bottle paper'. This includes the second document found, which was actually left earlier by Lieutenants Gore and Des Voeux in May 1847 while on a reconnoitring trip the summer before they abandoned the ships. Both documents contained the same error concerning the dates of their overwintering at Beechey Island. [2, 3] The earlier paper is seldom mentioned because it contains no new information; whereas the message found at Victory Point had additional information, dated 11 months later, scribbled around the margins. Both messages, however, were written on bottle paper.

Standard bottle paper contained instructions in six languages, taking up more than half the space available: [4]

> Whoever finds this paper is requested to forward it to the Secretary of the Admiralty, London, *with a note of the time and place at which it was found:* or, if more convenient, to deliver it for that purpose to the British Consul at the nearest Port. [italics in original]

At the top of the paper is a space for identification of the ship, the date, the latitude and longitude, and space for a short comment, to be signed by the commander. Clearly, it is intended for whoever happens to find it, and not specifically for any relief or rescue party. The wording may explain why Captain Fitzjames (one of the signatories) went to such lengths to explain the whereabouts of the cairn under which the canister containing the final message was placed.

Being the one ultimately in command, Franklin must take responsibility for the absence of onshore messages. Clearly, he did not order them to be left. There seems to have been an almost wilful neglect, considering the number of opportunities there must have been on various points in their voyage. Astoundingly, it seems a real possibility that it simply did not occur to them to leave messages on land, on ordinary notepaper. The fact that they were still using bottle paper for their final messages suggests that they may never have thought beyond messages in bottles. In fact, the only reason they left any on land at all might only have been because there was no sea to throw them in, as it was all iced over.

In addition to their apparently blind faith in messages in bottles, a further explanation might be provided by a glance at the psychological state of the officers. One of them, writing home for the last time, actually thought that they would find the North West Passage (which had been their main objective) in their first season. The ships were lavishly equipped and fitted, and abundantly provisioned. They were reckoned to be able to spend up to seven years in the ice, providing their diet was supplemented with local game. The size and construction of the ships would have given an additional sense of security, as would the accoutrements for a civilised life and the maintenance of standards at the dinner table.

Psychology researchers have found evidence that people in general exhibit an optimistic bias when considering possible risks in the future. It is likely that Franklin's officers would have emphasised this bias in the tone and the content of their communications. Optimism would have been a defence against anxiety, as well as setting the tone for the morale of the crews. The fact that they were so well equipped and provisioned would have given them a sense of control. Perceived controllability seems to be a key determinant of our levels of optimism bias – even in situations that are not, objectively speaking, under our control. [5]

Blithely – or even cautiously – assuming that they were equipped to handle anything the Arctic could throw at them, and dismissive of hand-wringing Jeremiahs, they omitted the one thing that might have saved them, and which was under their control; namely, a land-based trail of progress reports and intentions for sailing.

The lesson, however, was well learnt. When Scott went to the Antarctic in the *Discovery*, he was under strict instructions to leave messages on all reachable onshore prominences and outcrops on the way. One of the first jobs he put in hand when they arrived was to send out a party to update the message left at Cape Crozier. If anyone has ever wondered why that job was given such priority they need look no further than the Franklin disaster.

Back on the Austin Expedition, if anyone was looking forward to the end of the winter theatricals and parties, it will have been Leopold M'Clintock. A tough, taciturn, resourceful man who never showed his feelings, M'Clintock was the second-in-command on the *Assistance*. He was also in charge of the sledging. In an earlier search for Franklin in 1849, M'Clintock had, in the company of James Clark Ross and 12 men, sledged along the northern and western coasts of Somerset Island and discovered Peel Sound. They were out for 40 days. Only M'Clintock himself returned well; but still, according to Markham, it was the greatest Arctic sledge journey that had ever been made up to that time. Since then, M'Clintock had made a study of Arctic sledging, based on that experience, and devised a structure for man-hauling that stood the test of time until Scott's Last Expedition, in spite of the brutal labour it required. It involved the laying of depots in advance of the sledging season, and support teams to accompany the long-distance sledgers part of the way, establishing depots for the return journey for both the support sledges and the long-distance teams. M'Clintock felt that this time, putting his hard-earned knowledge into practice, he could better his record, and planned to be out for 80 days.

Two main divisions departed on a cold and murky day in April, with the wind drifting the snow in fitful gusts around the hummocks of ice. Austin gave a farewell speech, after which the men took their places on the traces, and set off, a hundred hoarse voices joining in loud cheers. They were soon lost to one another in the snow and mist as they diverged on their different routes. The sledges had been given names like *Reliance*, *True Blue*, *Succour*, etc, and heraldic banners fluttered, each bearing a heroic motto or sentiment. Romanticised images of the scene show sails rigged on the sledges billowing faultlessly and cheerfully in the wind, some depictions even showing kites behaving themselves perfectly and towing the sledges along. Although sails were later shown to be of limited use in the Antarctic, there is no record of them having been used successfully in the Arctic. Kites must surely have been worse than useless.

The teams were to go broadly west and south, subdivided into eight more detailed directions. The sledges were heavy and the ice rough. The sledging outfits, also on advice from M'Clintock, consisted of layers of flannel shirts, waistcoats and drawers, box-cloth trousers and a box-cloth waistcoat with chamois leather sleeves. Over this they wore a monkey, or pea jacket, also of box-cloth, and a white cotton duck jumper with chamois leather shoulders and large pockets for ammunition, a watch and a notebook. Box-cloth is a kind of boiled wool or felt traditionally used by military outfitters. On their heads they wore so-called Welsh wigs: closely fitting knitted helmets with a fringe of faux curls at the back of the neck for extra warmth, with an optional sealskin cap or hat on top, and beaver mitts. A scarf over the face provided some protection against the risk of frostbitten noses and cheeks. Their footwear consisted of a pair of woollen socks, with a square of blanket folded over them, within boots made of canvas with leather soles. Leather is a notoriously poor insulator. Unsurprisingly, cold injuries to the feet predominated. The sledging suits weighed between 16 and 20 lbs dry weight. This would have increased significantly with the weight of the ice accumulating in the woollen garments, as the sweat from the toiling men froze in the fibres. Their frozen garments became perfectly hard soon after they emerged from their tents. Against this, the only remedy was to start the march promptly and briskly. The water bottles, covered with flannel, which were carried next to their flannel waistcoats, froze, at least until the summer. The first thing they did in the tent after dragging all day was to inspect their feet: [6]

> ... for it was only by ocular proof that one could be satisfied of their safety, sensation having apparently long ceased. I shall not easily forget my painful feelings, when one gallant fellow of my party ... exclaimed, "Both feet gone, sir!" and sure enough they were, white as two lumps of ice, and equally cold ... With returning circulation the poor fellow's agonies must have been intense; and some hours afterwards large blisters formed over the frost-bitten parts ...

According to Osborn, the total number of frostbites for the expedition amounted to 18, including several cases in which portions of injured feet had to be amputated. Richard B Pearse, however, Mate in the *Resolute* who, Markham helpfully informs us, acted the part of Lydia in 'Done on Both Sides', and Ulrica in 'Charles XII', was away 24 days and came back severely frostbitten, eventually losing a leg; and one man died, apparently of hypothermia or frostbite or both. [7]

Although all sledgers must have been nursing painfully inflamed feet on their return, it is surprising that they got off comparatively lightly so far as cold injuries were concerned. This must have been partly due to morale, which was high, as they all felt they were on a mission of mercy. Shared labour and hardship generates camaraderie; and all, including the officers, kept hypothermia at bay by sheer physical effort and mutual solicitude. Up steep and irregular hills of ice, and down into 'pygmy' ravines, in which the men sank deeply into soft snow, it was a struggle described by Osborn as heart-breaking. The thought of dinner, grog, a pipe, and a chinwag after the day's labour probably also went some way in keeping them going. They will not, however, have wasted any time getting into their tents as soon as they were up.

In Osborn's party, a healthy irreverence with regard to the heraldic accoutrements of the sledges was in evidence among the crew in the after-dinner hour, in spite of his presence: [8]

> Now a joke about our flags and mottoes, which one vowed to be mere jack-acting; then a learned disquisition on raising the devil, which one of the party declared he had seen done, one Sunday

afternoon, for the purpose of borrowing some cash to play skittles with.

One imagines them getting snuggled in, chuckling, in those brief after-dinner interludes where Polar sledging did not perhaps seem so bad after all. Indeed, history shows that many went back for more. However hard and painful it was, these were still peak experiences, and Markham wasn't the only one who looked back on them fondly. Scott himself later declared that it beat staying at home in 'too great comfort'.

Before the main search got under way, however, an early team had been sent to inspect the condition of the depots left the previous autumn. Markham was of this party, which left on 4 April, led by George F M'Dougall, Second Master in the *Resolute,* and one of the editors of the *Illustrated Arctic News.* Markham emphasises that they went out more than a month earlier than any travelling party of former expeditions, with the temperature almost constantly below zero Fahrenheit, dragging over much uneven ice. Their sledge was called the *Beaufort;* their motto, typical of the heroic, boyish optimism so beloved by Markham: 'That future pilgrims of the wave may be / Secure from doubt, from every danger free.'

It was a comparatively undemanding task, but it does not take Markham long to start complaining about what he perceives to be the 'real miseries' of Polar travel. The morning after their first night on the ice starts with '... the frightful agony of forcing the feet into boots frozen hard as iron'. Drinking half a gill (an eighth of a pint) of rum out of a tin pannikin risked taking the skin off the lips. In seriously young-fogeyish fashion, he has with him a copy of 'Hudibras' (a seventeenth-century mock-heroic narrative poem by Samuel Butler) and quotes: 'Ah me! What perils do environ – the man that meddles with cold iron.' It seems he was not required to do any dragging himself, however, as he mentions that it was 'the men' being harnessed to the sledge when ready to go.

The first depot they came to had been shredded by bears. At the second depot three cases of pemmican, 12 cases of chocolate and two potato cases had been torn to pieces and left quite empty. One of two bears that approached them was shot after a long chase and converted into fuel. They had their lunch while running up and down to escape being frostbitten, and suffered regularly from painful and disabling snow-blindness. On the 14th, they were confined to the tent by a gale of wind, on which occasion Markham found solace in his 'Hudibras'. On 16 April they found they had left their spirit lamp, on which they did all their cooking, behind. Sailors are renowned for their resourcefulness, and they made another one out of an old *bouilli* tin. Meanwhile, Markham takes the opportunity for a walk and concludes that it was the most desolate part of Cornwallis Island that he had yet seen, describing his surroundings as of unequalled wretchedness and isolation. The mist obscured everything except Markham's pocket handkerchief flying from a staff. That night they sang until midnight. There is a poignancy about the image of that small tent in the cold remoteness, enveloped in mist, with the muffled sound of a male voice choir emanating from within. Markham may well have felt a touch emotional on poking his nose out of the tent while listening to the brave songs of his homeland. Nowhere is there a suggestion that anxiety was a problem; no treacherous crevasses or thin ice to worry about, there was no shortage of food or fuel, no serious cold injury, no scurvy, no excessive tiredness, and no undue psychological pressure or responsibility. Even the sights were taken not by him, but by M'Dougall.

Next day, Markham finds the time to pick up some fossils and some corallines, later in the afternoon taking a walk over the top of a high point and finding much moss and hare-dung. The tent was 'delightfully comfortable', owing to its crowded state, '... two of our company being obliged to lie upon the rest, and thus producing considerable warmth'. It is interesting to note that his berth was always at the furthest end from the door. This tends to be the privileged position in the etiquette of tent-dwellers. Even though he was an officer, he was a very junior one, in age as well as status, and a commanding position in the unconscious hierarchical psycho-geography would not necessarily have been a given. A more modest junior officer might have preferred the anonymity of a berth along the side. Markham, with his automatic sense of entitlement, and finely tuned instinct for precedence and hierarchy, gravitated quite naturally towards the best positions, probably in all situations, and regardless, or perhaps because of, the nature of his relationships with senior officers.

The rest of the trip passed pleasantly enough, with plenty of leisure for Markham to reconnoitre and update his diary. They were back at the *Resolute* by 1.30 in the afternoon on 23 April, having been out 19 days. None suffered from frostbitten feet, for which he credits the carpet boots they wore with blanket wrappers and stockings. They had travelled an average of just over seven miles a day, and covered 140 miles. Markham asserts that 'this journey may be taken as a type of those which followed during the remainder of the season'. Many would surely have argued with that.

Osborn credits M'Dougall with having (erroneously) discovered that Bathurst and Cornwallis are not separate islands. He writes: [9]

> ... [M'Dougall] had to replenish the depot formed for Lieut. M'Clintock, and then to connect the search round a deep bay, which connected Bathurst and Cornwallis Lands, for separate islands they were proved by him no longer to be.

That they are indeed separate must have been clear later in the season, when M'Clintock returned with a more accurate survey, and it is puzzling that Osborn did not correct that statement in *Stray Leaves from an Arctic Journal*. M'Dougall seems to have mistaken a 'long point' (now known as Markham Point), which they found on the far side of a large bay on the southwest coast of Cornwallis, for Bathurst Island. He is now, however, credited with the discovery of the Sound which separates Bathurst and Cornwallis islands, and which bears his name. Interestingly, Markham, in *Franklin's Footsteps*, writes: [10]

> Another party from Captain Austin's ship discovered the deep bay dividing Cornwallis and Bathurst Lands, and which is terminated on the west by Markham Point, and on the east by a narrow inlet …

At the time, he wrote in his journal: [11]

> Reached the end of the bay, and landed on the same kind of beach, the bay being about six miles deep. 5 p.m. Reached a long point, which we supposed to be part of Bathurst Island, and encamped there.

Current maps show a large bay on the southwest corner of Cornwallis Island, with a deep narrow inlet to the east of it. This accurately represents what Markham asserts, apart from the fact that they are both on Cornwallis Island. Both Osborn and Markham fudge the issue. Osborn quietly calls Cornwallis and Bathurst 'Islands' throughout the rest of his subsequent narrative, without correcting his earlier statement. Markham, for his part, seems to have forgotten that he was on the team that made the mistake. Both must have realised they had been wrong when Lieutenant Aldrich returned after two months, having explored 70 miles along the unknown (to them) shores of eastern Bathurst Island.

When the message from the Franklin Expedition was eventually found in 1859, it transpired that the *Erebus* and the *Terror* had in fact circumnavigated Cornwallis Island before setting off on their fateful journey down Peel Sound. In *The Arctic Navy List 1773–1873*, published in 1875, Markham [12] fudges the issue even more by listing McDougall Bay under the entry for Mac Dougall [*sic*], and placing it between Bathurst and Cornwallis Islands – surely the only place on the globe where two islands are separated by a bay. Especially considering he was one of the honorary secretaries of the Royal Geographical Society at the time, it is safe to assume he would not have got away with that in a climate of more rigorous scholarship.

Even for an age in which snobbery and racism were part of a common discourse, Markham's comments on the Inuit stand out as particularly sniffy. Parry, in contrast, having spent almost ten months in daily contact with them in 1822–3, writes at length about the 'esquimaux' of Melville Peninsula, Igloolik, and the adjoining islands. He minutely studied their daily lives, their clothing, their hunting methods, their method of transport, boatbuilding skills, their ethics, their home life and their relationships with each other and with their animals. He participated in many of their entertainments and rituals with a mixture of bemusement and pleasure. Most of his gentlemen even had themselves tattooed.

It was not realised until much later that his observations, together with those of his second-in-command, George F Lyon, formed an important anthropological account of an aboriginal population in an uncontacted state. Although Parry and his men found the native diet of raw blubber disgusting (prompting some mischievous Inuit to run after them gleefully holding up pieces of it, inviting them to eat), the Inuit in return found European food equally revolting. In spite of this, and many other differences in culture and the way they conducted their personal relationships, Parry and Lyon respected and liked the 'esquimaux'. They also admired their 'huts' (igloos), describing how they were built, and that a soft and pleasant light was admitted into them by a circular plate of ice, four inches thick and two feet in diameter, let into the side: [13]

> It may, perhaps, then be imagined how singular is their external appearance at night, when they discover themselves only by a circular disc of light transmitted through the windows from the lamps within.

Osborn too, while still judging the 'Innuit' [*sic*] by British standards, is nevertheless capable of appreciating their skill in dealing with their environment, observing that their winter abodes are well adapted to afford warmth, and that their canoes are perfect models of beauty and lightness. Their clothing, too, is [14]

> ... vastly superior to anything we could produce ... We gladly purchased all we could obtain of their clothing.

Osborn befriends them, and sees nothing 'horrible' in their diet or their homes; in contrast to Markham, who, although crediting their amazing celerity in their canoes, writes of them: [15]

> Their appearance, with coal-black long coarse hair, broad shoulders, fetid odour, low foreheads, sunken eyes, flattened noses, stupid expression, and dwarfish stature, is very repulsive ... Their winter habitations are low huts ... Several families live together in one of these miserable abodes ... the smell [of their seal-oil fuel], when combined with raw seal's flesh, fish, and fat, is overpowering ... Their habits are filthy in the extreme; water never touching their skin except by accident; while they do not hesitate to eat offal which would disgust a starving European.

In his opinion, bears and foxes betray far more intelligence than the 'lords of creation in this part of the world!', and 'their stupid and insensate minds' form a striking contrast to the beautiful scenery. [16] It seems not to occur to him to credit the fact that these people managed to live tolerably well, purely on what nature provided, in one of the harshest environments on earth.

Amundsen tells an amusing anecdote about the 'Eskimos' when they became his teachers on his *Gjoa* Expedition (in which he, incidentally, did discover one of the North West Passages, although not a commercial one). A jocular old man showed them how to build snow houses. Amundsen, in his memoirs, describes their early attempts: [17]

> They, no doubt, hardly thought that a 'Kabluna' (foreigner) could manage a piece of work, which was their own speciality. But they did not wait very long before very audibly expressing their views on the point. Hansen and I did something or other they were not used to, and in a trice the whole crowd burst into noisy exultation. Their laughter was uncontrollable; the tears ran down their cheeks; they writhed with laughter, gasped for breath, and positively shrieked. At last ... they took the whole work in hand, but had to stop now and then to have another laugh at the thought of our stupidity ...

The Admiralty had this to say on the subject of Polar natives: [18]

> The prime consideration of fox-hunting is not the killing of the fox, but the observance of good form during the pursuit and at the kill. The objective of Polar explorations is to explore properly and not evade the hazards of the game through the vulgar subterfuge of going native.

If the British considered themselves superior to the Inuit, however, they in turn felt the same about the British. Parry notes that [19]

> ... they certainly looked upon us in many respects with profound contempt ... One day, for instance, in securing some of the gear of a sledge, Okotook broke a part of it composed of a piece of our white line, and I shall never forget the contemptuous sneer with which he muttered in soliloquy the word "Kabloona!" in token of the inferiority of our materials to his own.

The teams returned one by one, none of them having found a trace of Franklin. The ice, which had started to melt as the summer advanced, finally released the ships in early August. After a final foray by the steamers into Jones Sound, Austin, feeling that there was nothing further to be achieved, took his squadron home. Markham, [20] always to be relied upon for an uncritical overstatement of any achievements by the Navy, eulogises:

> The whole coast of the Parry Islands, from Beechey Island (where Mr. Penny had discovered the winter-quarters of the missing

Expedition) to the extreme western point of Melville Island – a distance of 350 miles – had been carefully searched; besides this, vast tracts of land, extending over more than five hundred miles, had been thoroughly examined by Mr. Bradford and Lieutenant Aldrich. To the southward also of Cape Walker four hundred miles was discovered, and as far as possible surveyed and explored. Jones's Sound was then examined, and both sides of Wellington Channel had been traced by Mr. Penny to a considerable distance ...

They were in for a rude awakening when they got home. Osborn writes that their self-importance as Arctic heroes received a sad downfall when asked what the deuce they came home for, and why they had deserted Franklin. Lady Franklin was disappointed, and the expedition was branded a failure by the public and the press. [21] *The Times* asked why the ships did not spend a second winter in the Arctic when they were provisioned for three years, commenting: [22]

> We shall never attain our end by sailing up to the ice and then sailing back again.

A Naval Inquiry was held. Unsurprisingly, Austin's word was taken over Penny's, putting the bulk of the blame for any disputes on Penny. Neither was, however, invited to participate in subsequent searches, nor did Ommanney ever return to Arctic waters.

There had been a fair bit of bad blood on the expedition. The Penny disputes were on the record, but Osborn too had had his grievances. In addition to his exasperation at having to drag the unwieldy *Resolute*, he also had a problem with the spirit of competition that had crept in over the distances achieved by the different teams, which he took no interest in [23]

> ... having gone to the Arctic regions for other motives and purposes than to run races for a Newmarket cup, or to be backed against the field like a Whitechapel game-cock.

He seems to have had his differences with Austin, too, writing to Penny: [24]

> I am young yet and have room and time enough to win a Post-Captain's commission in spite of Captain Austin or any other Liar in buttons.

Strong words indeed, and surely not entirely due to his failure to gain promotion on the back of the expedition.

The upshot of the Naval Inquiry into the Austin Expedition was that a second, even larger, expedition should be sent to look for Franklin. Osborn was again put in command of the *Pioneer* in the expedition of 1852, commanded by Edward Belcher. Belcher was a controversial figure, and opinion is divided. Some considered him to be competent, resourceful, energetic and brave. Others report that he was irritable, quarrelsome, hypercritical, and difficult to get on with. His wife left him, accusing him of twice having infected her with venereal disease. Markham wasn't a fan either, noting that Belcher was the most unpopular man in the Navy, from whom people would do almost anything to get away. He criticised him for being too old (at 53, only two years older than Austin, however), in bad health, and with no Arctic experience.

Whatever the case, his reputation was dealt a mortal blow by his decision to abandon the entire squadron that had made up the Austin Expedition only three years earlier. Belcher had taken the *Assistance, Resolute, Pioneer* and *Intrepid* again to the Arctic, again hoping to discover what had happened to Franklin. However, after almost two years in the ice, Belcher's nerve seems to have failed. It seems to be the most plausible explanation for the sudden, panicky decision to abandon all four ships – much to the appalled astonishment of his officers – and in the course of which Osborn was placed under arrest for resisting Belcher's order.

After carrying out the order, called 'a crime', and 'disgraceful' by Markham, [25] the entire crew hitched a passage home on the *North Star* (the supply ship that was also part of Belcher's flotilla), and two other ships that happened to be near Beechey Island at the time. Markham must have been especially upset to hear that the ship on which he had enjoyed such a special year had been left to the elements, despite being in seaworthy condition. In the subsequent Admiralty Inquiry, Belcher was cleared of any wrongdoing, although his sword was handed back to him in icy silence. He was never offered active employment in the Navy again. Osborn, on the other hand, was promoted soon after their return.

The *Resolute* eventually worked free of the ice, drifting Marie Celeste-like into Davis Strait, where she was picked up by whaling Captain James Buddington. An 1856 *New York Journal* reports: 'Finding everything in eerie good order, they entered the Captain's cabin, where they struck a match and lit a candle', and [26]

> ... before the astonished gaze of these men exposed a scene that appeared to be rather one of enchantment than reality. Upon a massive table was a metal teapot, glistening as if new, also a large volume of Scott's family Bible, together with glasses and decanters filled with choice liquors.

They towed the ship home to America, where she was repaired. She was sailed back to England, and handed back to Queen Victoria with due ceremony. HMS *Resolute* did not leave home waters again until she was retired and broken up in 1879. A number of her timbers were made into a large finely carved desk, which was presented by Queen Victoria to US President Rutherford B Hayes in 1880, and remains in use in the Oval Office to this day.

For Belcher, the appearance of the *Resolute* in Davis Strait, having made it out of the Arctic intact, even without men and sails, must have been the final humiliation. Although he never recovered his standing as a Naval officer, he was nevertheless knighted in 1867, and promoted to Admiral in 1872.

References

1   E.C. Coleman. *The Royal Navy and Polar Exploration*, p. 17

2   Owen Beattie and John Geiger. *Frozen in Time*, p. 129

3   E.C. Coleman. *op. cit.*, p. 183

4   Owen Beattie and John Geiger. *op. cit.*, p. 84

5   Dorothy Miell, Ann Phoenix and Kerry Thomas (eds.). *DSE Mapping Psychology*, p. 90

6   Lieut. Sherard Osborn. *Stray Leaves from an Arctic Journal*, p. 99

7   Clements R. Markham. *The Arctic Navy List*, p. 41

8   Lieut. Sherard Osborn. *op. cit.*, p. 102

9   *op. cit.*, p. 95

10   Clement [*sic*] Robert Markham. *Franklin's Footsteps*, p. 100

11   *op. cit.*, p. 87

12   Clements R. Markham. *op. cit.*, pp. 32–3

13   Sir W.E. Parry. *Journal of the Third Voyage*, p. 87

14   Lieut. Sherard Osborn. *op. cit.*, p. 11

15   Clement [*sic*] Robert Markham. *op. cit.*, pp. 52–3

16   *ibid.*, pp. 52–4

17   Pierre Berton. *The Arctic Grail*, pp. 539–40

18   E.C. Coleman. *op. cit.*, p. 146

19   Sir W.E. Parry. *op. cit.*, p. 122

20   Clement [*sic*] Robert Markham. *op. cit.*, p. 124

21   Pierre Berton. *op. cit.*, p. 203

22   *ibid.*

23   Lieut. Sherard Osborn. *op. cit.*, p. 104

24   [Unattributed writer]. Dictionary of Canadian Biography: Osborn, Sherard. www.biographi.ca

25   Sir Clements R. Markham. *The Lands of Silence,* p. 269

26   [Unattributed writer]. HMS *Resolute*, Wikipedia, www.e.em.wikipedia.org

5

TRAVELS IN PERU, CINCHONA, AND MARRIAGE

On a personal level, Austin's officers and crew did of course receive a warm and hearty welcome home. Markham was the returning hero and was made much of, being feted like a minor celebrity and being asked to give lectures on his Arctic experiences. His father drew diagrams, maps and pictures based on Clements' descriptions, providing visual aids for his lectures. He notes that Clements was [1]

> ... in excellent health and spirits ... He is looking handsome and well,
> not a jot the worse for all his hardships.

The hardships had in fact been few and far between. When not engaged in theatricals, parties and soirées, he had spent much of his time in the Arctic reading and writing. In addition to Shakespeare and the good-looking and inspirational Southey, he had read every book on the Arctic the well-stocked libraries of the expedition provided, and made use of them in *Franklin's Footsteps*. He also found time to translate the first of Virgil's Eclogues and wrote an essay on pastoral poetry. Peru continued to fascinate him, and he wrote a tragedy in blank verse on the fate of Tupac Amaru, the last of the Incas.

By coincidence, Dr Donnet, the surgeon on the *Assistance,* had a Quichua grammar with him, which Markham studied assiduously, enabling him to acquire a smattering of Inca. He was longing for the time he could go back to Peru and, apparently confident that he would find a way of fulfilling his wishes, was preparing himself accordingly.

There was, however, a serious difficulty in the offing. Clements wanted to leave the Navy; partly because he couldn't stand to see men flogged, especially not the boys and young men, but also because he wanted to become an explorer. More specifically, he wanted to explore the relics of the Inca civilisation. It would require a carefully planned approach, however, and he waited until the time was right. His father, knowing that on his death the well-paid Windsor Canonry would come to an end, and that there was no great fortune in the family for Clements to fall back on, was concerned that he should have a profession that would guarantee him at least a subsistence income. He therefore urged his son to stay on and make a career in the Navy. Getting his father's consent to leave it was the first hurdle. Clements himself said of his father, 'he never refused me anything', and he didn't now, agreeing to his leaving the Navy on condition he took his lieutenant's exam. That way, he would at least have something to show for his six years of service. This, Clements agreed to do.

He did, however, had a difficult confession to make. It rather suddenly transpired that the box containing his logs for the five years covering his whole *Collingwood* and Mediterranean service had been lost in Woolwich in 1850, while they were fitting out the *Assistance* in preparation for the Arctic. As these logs were essential for any midshipman wanting to take their lieutenant's exam, it would have been inconceivable for any young man, barring death or shipwreck, to have lost documents as important as these. They would have been secured as a priority in any shifting of gear. Perhaps he hadn't been as careful as he might have been. He was by nature impulsive, and he had a penchant for making derogatory comments about his superiors. It is entirely plausible therefore that those logs would not bear scrutiny by the examiners, and that they had been lost accidentally on purpose. He must, of course, be given the benefit of the doubt, as his father would have done, but an eyebrow is inevitably raised.

Nothing was said about this serious loss in the reports of his fitting-out at Woolwich. Indeed, he hadn't been at Woolwich long, having obtained leave almost immediately after having reported himself, and been introduced to Captain Ommanney of the *Assistance*, and Austin. The rest of April of 1850 had been taken up in a whirl of visits to friends and relations, getting kitted out in London, and meeting his old friend and *beau idéal*, Captain Peel. Presumably he had had some duties at least, in making sure everything was ready for departure. There had been a lot of hullabaloo and upheaval preceding the departure of the Austin Squadron, and it was certainly possible for things to get lost. Nevertheless, one would expect such a calamity as the loss of all his logs for his time in the Pacific and the Mediterranean to merit a mention in Clements' diary of the time. In turn, one would surely expect to be informed of it in his biography. As it is, there isn't a squeak until it suddenly comes out when he is supposed to take his exam. The episode suggests an already well-developed level of ethical plasticity and a fine calculation of what he could get away with that were the prerequisites for his rise to social prominence. Certainly no naive or overscrupulous man could have hoped to succeed in a national campaign for an Antarctic expedition, as he did in his later years, and certainly not in setting it up to reflect his (very) personal preferences, which were nothing to do with Polar knowledge or experience.

As far as his lieutenant's exam was concerned, Clements found a way around it by taking the gunnery exam – for which logs were not required – ending up with the required certificate, as he probably knew he would. The ins and outs of exams, paperwork, and qualifications are likely to have been well known among young men on a career trajectory. As an alternative, a career in the legal profession was briefly considered; instead of the Navy, the Rector thought that perhaps Clements might like to go to Oxford to study law. Clements, who had for some time been secretly working out the details of his trip to Peru, did not have the slightest intention of becoming a lawyer, and unforeseen obstacles duly arose to scupper the project.

In the meantime, in the spring of 1852, the Belcher Expedition left Woolwich with many of his old shipmates on board. Markham, seeing them off, and feeling depressed and disappointed at being left behind, worked instead on his narrative of the Austin Expedition. Motivated in part by indignation at the critical assessment by the press, he was keen to set the record straight, as he saw it. There was, however, a further reason for his restlessness and depression. He had yet to broach the subject of Peru with his father. He bit the bullet one afternoon during a long walk in Windsor Park, and told his father about his wish to go exploring in Peru. It was the age of the Victorian gentleman explorer, as epitomised by Livingstone, Speke and Burton. There were worse ways for a young man to make his mark, and it would be no surprise if that was the angle he took with his father. By the time he'd finished putting his case, the Rector had been won over, and agreed to give him £500 (about £44,000 today) to finance the project. Clements' depression vanished as if by magic. He left Windsor for Peru on 20 August 1852, seen off by his father who, still not entirely convinced, wrote in his journal, '... it is a long lonely business, and I have not much heart about it'. It was the last time Clements saw his father. The Reverend David Markham died just over six months later.

One result of having been in the Navy – and at a public school, for that matter – was that Markham, even at 22, already knew a lot of people, some almost like family. Wherever he went, especially in seaports, there was a good chance that he would run into men he not only knew, but knew intimately, having lived and worked together night and day in close proximity for years on end. It was the depth of these relationships that facilitated Markham's lifelong access to the Navy and influence within it. Another secret of his success was his knack for conviviality. His presence seemed always to be an excuse for a party. Accordingly, he was always popular, or at any rate well received. At anchor at Halifax, Nova Scotia, his first stop on his way to Peru, he found HMS *Cumberland*, commanded by his old boss, Sir George Seymour, together with a number of his old *Collingwood* shipmates. Invited to stay on board, he dined frequently with Seymour, and had a jolly time about town with his old friends. Everyone will have wanted to hear about his forthcoming adventure, and he is sure to have enlightened them accordingly.

Beyond the Navy also, Markham lived on that charmed social level where an introduction could always be obtained, and an open door expected, from almost anyone who was anyone. Accordingly, he went to Boston and was the guest for ten days of WH Prescott, held to be one of the greatest living American intellectuals and historians. Picking the brains of an acknowledged authority was one of Markham's ways of preparing for an expedition. Almost half a century later, Markham arranged a similar visit for Scott with Fridtjof Nansen, as part of Scott's preparation for his first expedition to the Antarctic. It was the amateur gentleman's way, characterised by the assumption that nothing but a few pointers are needed. Prescott had already written about the history of Peru and the culture of the Inca, based on academic research in the library, rather than work in the field and the study of archaeological remains. Prescott was, however, an *eminence grise*, and an accomplished writer. He was one of Markham's main literary influences and professional role models.

However, the preoccupation with written accounts, the focus on charismatic leaders and dynastic, military, and political structures of Inca civilisation may have cost Markham the coup and kudos of revealing to the world the citadel of Machu Picchu, which he almost certainly glimpsed, but of which he failed to realise the importance. But then he wasn't an archaeologist, and his journey into Peru was essentially a pilgrimage.

One possible explanation for Markham's avid enthusiasm for the Incas may be found in their apparent veneration of the heroic male, and their sexual mores and customs. Before the European conquest and the imposition of Christianity, attitudes towards sexuality generally – and male homosexuality in particular – seem to have been relaxed among the Inca. Some historians claim that it was the preferred practice among men. Certainly it was not viewed as the abomination that the invading Christians held it to be. Evidence can be found in the antique pottery artefacts that survived destruction by the Conquistadors, especially the well-known erotic Moche figurines now to be seen in the Larco Museum in Lima. What stands out from this collection is the prevalence of anal sex and fellatio. Androgynous couples are seen engaged in either same-sex, or heterosexual, acts – the males frequently shown with an oversized penis, often in doggy-style postures. Some figurines show grotesquely priapic males. Markham's visits to the museums of Lima when stationed there on the *Collingwood* may have given him the opportunity to view these artefacts, even though they were only accessible to a select few at the time. His social contacts and his status as an educated westerner are likely to have opened doors.

It is entirely possible that if he did see these artworks, they would have been a revelation. They may even have constituted at least part of the reason and the motivation that fired his longing to return to Peru and his desire to learn more about the culture and practices of the Inca. There was also likely to have been a residual tolerance of male homosexuality in nineteenth-century Peru, despite the inroads made by Christian missionaries. The freedom enjoyed by Markham and the boys in their frequent bathing sessions in the Rimac is consistent with the presence of a permissive social environment. Certainly, Somerville writes of the 'low' establishment near the embarkation point in Callao.

Exposure to foreign cultures and religions has a mind-broadening effect on most people. Although Victorians referred to pre-Christian peoples as heathens, a sophisticated culture like the Inca couldn't simply be dismissed as a proliferation of godless savages. In spite of the fact that they worshipped different gods, and that their religious rites went to progressively more bloody extremes, their system of government and their social and religious organisations force an acknowledgment of their sophistication. Markham would undoubtedly have mused on this; especially as, his clerical background notwithstanding, his education had not been especially evangelical. It might have strengthened a latent moral, religious and ethical relativism.

When Markham did eventually get to Lima, people appeared to fall over themselves to entertain him, and provide him with letters of introduction to all the important people, including the president of Peru. A box at the opera was placed at his disposal, as were a groom and a horse. He seems to have been regarded – again – as something of a celebrity, and clearly had credibility as a British gentleman explorer, with a book already in the pipeline (*Franklin's Footsteps*), and plenty of money at his disposal. Armed with letters of recommendation to the prefects of the departments through which he would pass, he eventually got under way.

His journey was by turns a challenging and dangerous trek through the mountains, and a triumphal procession. He spent a month in Ayacucho, as guest of the prefect, particularly enjoying the evening parties given by his host, where the wit and beauty of all Ayacucho assembled. On the road to Cuzco, his main destination, he was joined by a cleric, Dr Taforo, an 'earnest and popular missionary' whose acquaintance he'd made in Ayacucho. They were received with tumultuous hospitality everywhere – people running out from the villages, girls showering them with roses, and strings of dollars suspended across the road.

Cuzco was eventually reached – the ancient city of the Incas, '... the hallowed spot where Manco Capac's golden wand sank into the ground!' His ambition to visit the city he'd read about in Prescott had been realised at last. He wasted no time getting to know the eminent men of Cuzco, who not only entertained him, but assisted him in his researches. He devoured every book to be had on the subject, drew maps and diagrams of the palaces, forts, and other important buildings, compiling an exhaustive history of Cuzco and its rulers, later to be published as *Cuzco and Lima*, in the recapitulative style that was to become his signature approach. He made one major foray out of Cuzco, at least as far as Ollantaytambo (where one of his fictional heroes, Ollantay, was said to have had his palace-fortress), and which is not far from Machu Picchu.

Other historical sites and towns were visited, sometimes by way of difficult paths, made even more dangerous by the presence of hostile Indians. Whether through innate pluck or a minimisation of the risks, or both, he declined the offer of an armed escort, and eventually reached the place where he first discovered the cascarilla trees, of the genus *Cinchona*, from which quinine is obtained. It was a fateful occasion. The smuggling of cinchona seedlings out of Peru on behalf of the British Government was in later years to become the basis for his financial security and, together with his writings, his status within geographical circles. Throughout the trip he received nothing but generous hospitality, and he pays tribute to the unaffected kindness of the warm-hearted Children of the Sun. He writes that it had been the most enjoyable expedition he could possibly have undertaken.

Back in Lima, he finds HMS *Portland*, the current flagship of the Pacific Station, with many old shipmates and friends on board. He was invited on board, and made an honorary member of the wardroom mess, where he regaled them with his tales of adventure, needless to say, at once becoming the resident expert on all matters Peruvian. An irrepressible fun-loving livewire is hard to keep down, and soon Markham is up to something, instigating a 'mad prank' ashore, which involved racing in a straight line across the town over walls, roofs and backyards, without making use of streets or roads.

A great number of the officers entered the race, one of whom was handicapped by having to carry a live kitten. The appalling lack of respect and consideration for the inhabitants is to our eyes obvious, but this was a time when patronising and superior attitudes (not to mention racism) towards indigenous populations were accepted as being in the natural order of things. No criticism or punishment for the prank was therefore forthcoming. On another level it was the sort of escapade that allows young men to exhaust themselves in a physical rampage that the rules of formal relations prohibit. Events like these provide an outlet for pent-up energies and frustrations, and break down physical reserve – exactly the sort of thing that played into Markham's agenda.

But there was a shock in store. Clements' father had died on 31 March 1853. Clements had arrived back in Callao on 23 June, almost three months later. There had been no letters or papers from home for him on his return, which seems odd, as it was the custom to send a contact address. As it was, the first he heard of his father's demise was its announcement in an old copy of *The Times,* brought to him by one of his friends, presumably after the fun and games ashore. There could have been any number of perfectly ordinary explanations for the absence of letters from home, of course, and one must be wary of reading anything into it. The news, however, when it did come, must have been instantly sobering. Apart from any- thing else, the Bank of Dad had been peremptorily ripped away.

Overnight, everything changed. No more homes in Great Horkesley or Windsor to come back to, and no more financial, practical and moral support. An immediate return was called for, and Markham left Callao on 12 August, arriving back in England on 17 September 1853. Having had plenty of time to think about the implications on the way, he was ready to assume his new role as head of the family when he got home.

Shortly after his return, he completed and privately published a *History of the Markham Family* which his father had compiled, and worked on a paper he was to read at the Geographical Society. He was also doing background research for the book he later published entitled *Cuzco and Lima*, which came out in early 1856, and was well received. Prescott, to whom he had sent a copy, was (somewhat predictably) fulsome in its praise.

Franklin's Footsteps, Markham's first published work, came out in 1853, and sold well. His writings were not going to provide a steady income for the time being, however. He could not afford to be long without a regular salary, so he set about trying to get a job. A job in any sort of trade or commerce would have been unthinkable. Bad enough that the discoverer of Peru and the darling of the Navy should have to get a job at all! At length he succeeded in getting employment as a junior clerk in Somerset house. His office is straight out of Dickens: [2]

> ... [it] was begrimed with the accumulated dust of ages, the windows were impervious to light owing to layers of London dirt, the floor was unwashed and uncarpeted, the ceiling was black with decades of congealed soot, and the shelves round the room groaned under the weight of massive tomes smothered in generations of dust, containing the wishes of those long dead.

But all was not as bad as it seemed. The job was a foothold in the Civil Service. Six months later he was offered a better job at the Board of Control, copying 'absorbingly interesting' secret and confidential branch letters and despatches. Things got even better when in November 1854 he was proposed by Sir Roderick Murchison as a Fellow of the Royal Geographical Society, thus inaugurating a connection that came almost to define Markham in later life. Throughout, he also kept up his friendships in the Navy, making frequent journeys to Portsmouth. Evidence that he continued to be influential in Naval circles, even as a civilian, comes in the form of his cousin and biographer Albert's commission. Albert

Markham, 11 years younger than Clements, had followed his elder cousin's career choice, and had by that time been accepted as a cadet in the Royal Navy. In 1856 he had been appointed to a ship in which, for a variety of reasons, he did not want to serve. He wrote to Clements, asking for help. Within two weeks Albert was transferred to his ship of choice, the *Camilla*. [3]

Another portrait of Clements was painted that year. He has grown the side whiskers, the 'Piccadilly weepers' that were to become an essential part of his image for the rest of his life. The 'kiss-curls' on the temples are again in evidence, but the overall impression is more measured and less flamboyantly confident than his image at 18, reflecting his change of status from carefree gilded youth to (temporarily) impecunious responsible adult.

By the time he was 26, it seems to have been generally felt that it was time for Clements to find a potential wife and get married. It must have taken an effort of will for him to have turned his attention to women, as friendships or youthful romances with girls are conspicuous by their absence. He will have sensed the necessity for marriage himself, however, and when Miss Minna Chichester came along, daughter of the Reverend JH Chichester, Rector of Arlington, and niece of Sir Bruce Chichester of Arlington Court in Devonshire, he was quick to act. Her background was good enough and, more importantly, she was intellectual rather than sensual, bookish rather than coquettish, and spoke Dutch and Spanish – skills that would have further recommended her. They got on well, and married in April 1857. Minna was to become his lifelong companion, general amanuensis, linguistic resource, housekeeper, and occasional mother to their only child, May, born on 4 October 1859.

Theirs was a working partnership – unusual for the time. Far from staying at home, which would have normally been expected, Minna accompanied Markham to Peru only ten weeks after giving birth, on 17 December 1859, leaving the baby with a nurse. With the exception of a brief stopover between journeys, they did not see their daughter again until she was a year and seven months old. It is hard to escape the feeling that poor little May was conceived with an eye to convention which, thus satisfied, left Clements and Minna free to devote their attention to the things that really interested them – in neither case children nor domesticity.

Markham went back to Peru with the intention of obtaining and smuggling out cinchona shoots, to be planted in colonial India, for the production of quinine. Quinine was much in demand for the treatment of malaria. The Dutch had already transplanted cinchona in 1852, and were experimenting with farming it in Dutch colonial Java. Cinchona proved difficult to cultivate, however. Markham, certain that the British could do better, formulated his own plan for the collection of seedlings, and put it before the Revenue Committee of the India Office. A plan was adopted whereby three separate parties were to go to different locations in South

America, headed by Markham, Richard Spruce, and GJ Pritchett, each collecting the local variety of cinchona. As it happened, it was Spruce and Pritchett's seedlings that survived the journey and went on to form the basis of the Government's plantations in India. Unfortunately, these strains were found to yield low quantities of quinine, and it was not until 1865 that London-born Charles Ledger found the high-yielding species which was eventually to destroy the South American monopoly on quinine. To his credit, it was Markham who initially forced the Government to make a cheap cinchona product available to the poor of India, instead of reserving it exclusively for British personnel. However, the Dutch bought some of Ledger's smuggled seeds, and by 1910, Java was producing more than ten times the volume of quinine as India, at a fraction of its original price, making it widely available.

Whereas Ledger died poor and unrecognised, Markham maximised his involvement by claiming to have been in sole charge of the enterprise from its inception. When Markham and his wife got back from Peru in 1860 he was promoted to private secretary to the Secretary of State for India. He also wrote an account of his travels. By way of rest and recreation, he and Minna made trips to Spain and Denmark, before returning to India to supervise the cinchona plantations. Not only had he personally collected and smuggled out a number of seedlings, but he also supervised their transportation, selected the sites in India for planting, and personally supervised everything connected with them for the next 15 years. According to him, that is.

Crucially, he also happened to be a prolific and proficient writer, who kept a journal wherever he went. He was able to make his expeditions to Peru pay many times over. In addition to receiving a payment of £3,000 from the Government for his cinchona operation – over a quarter of a million pounds in today's money – he also profited by writing about Peru, putting out a seemingly endless series of histories and travelogue narratives, as well as lectures and magazine articles. An intangible, psychological, but nevertheless vitally important outcome of his cinchona operation was the boost it gave to his credentials, his credibility, and his influence.

Markham was a very public man who loved nothing better than to cultivate friends in high places. He was his own publicist, PR man and spin doctor. He had an impressive capacity for work, publishing over 50 volumes in his lifetime, not counting translations and official reports. He was not omnivorously social, however. He was not part of a wider social scene. He understood and felt at home within the traditions, politics, and assumptions of the all-male worlds of the Navy, clubland, and the Societies. In the course of events he also attended endless functions and dinners, and never lost his love of the theatre. Always in his element on stage, he enjoyed public speaking – like John Dalton, 'he possessed a resonant voice and much enjoyed listening to it'.

Away from the crowds and the meetings, however, Markham sought sequestration in the libraries of the Royal Geographical Society and the Hakluyt Society, and his study at home, immersing himself in arcane texts, translating historical volumes that very few would ever read. Meanwhile, Minna performed her role as Mrs – later Lady – Markham perfectly. Shrewd, cultured, self-effacing, and clearly fond of going abroad, she was by Markham's side on most of his travels. They had a harmonious arrangement. The existence of a list of plants collected by Lady Markham in Portugal is evidence that she had her own pursuits, suggesting a level of intellectual and personal freedom and independence. She must have done a lot of Clements' research, and certainly assisted with his translations. Their daughter, May, is reported in adulthood to have immersed herself in good works among the poor in the East End of London, leaving hardly a trace of her existence.

References

1   Admiral Sir Albert Markham. *The Life of Sir Clements R. Markham*, p. 127

2   *op. cit.*, p. 165

3   M.E. Markham and F.A. Markham. *The Life of Sir Albert Hastings Markham*, p. 6

6

Clements' career progresses, and Albert attains a scorbutic furthest north

M arkham tended to think he knew best how to do just about everything, and reeled off solutions with all the confidence of ignorance and inexperience. It was a habit he retained all his life, and it started early. Informed by his short sojourn in the Arctic, he wrote a detailed footnote in *Franklin's Footsteps* (published when he was just 23), on how to get to the North Pole. Although attempted many times, and claimed by a few, the feat was not verifiably attained until 1926, when Roald Amundsen needed a balloon to get there, and could still only fly over it – which gives an idea how difficult it was. But perhaps he hadn't read Markham's footnote.

True to form, without having grown so much as a blade of grass in his life, he submitted elaborate reports and suggestions to the Government on the cultivation of not only cinchona, but also coca (which he chewed himself during the arduous episodes in his treks through the Andes), cotton, coffee, pepper, caoutchouc (natural rubber) and ipecacuanha (a medicinal emetic). Similarly, when it came to infrastructure, no training or proper study of engineering was necessary to qualify Markham to report on the condition of the roads in the districts where he travelled in Peru and India, with suggestions by which improvements could be made (at little expense, in his estimation). He further designed and drew a bridge to convey goods across swollen rivers during the monsoon.

Some of his suggestions may have had merit, of course, but apart from his own lack of training, the central weakness in all of his schemes was that he never credited local knowledge and expertise, gained over generations of on-the-spot experience; nor did he acknowledge the social and political assumptions inherent in his world view. He was a living embodiment of the colonial attitude that conflated technological advancement and intrinsic merit, and that regarded other people's homelands as their 'possessions', primarily to be exploited for profit.

The India Office bought Markham's theories, predictably, as they shared the same mindset and background. After a short fact-finding trip to the Colne oyster fisheries, he was sent back to India to report on the Tinnevelly pearl oyster fishery at Tuticorin on the southeast tip of India. Pearls had been cultivated there for hundreds of years. The fisheries had been successively colonised by the Portuguese and the Dutch, and they were in British hands in Markham's time. It doesn't seem to have taken very long for him to assess and report on the situation, because while he was there, he also prepared a long report on the subject of coolie [*sic*] immigration. He also addressed a long memorandum on the subject of irrigation in the Madura district of India. Similarly, memoranda were submitted to the India Office on public works in the district of Travancore, the new dock at Suez, an alternative route to India, a proposed scheme for the improvement of the anchorage off Aden, the desirability of increasing the dock accommodation at Bombay and Mazagong, and a highly technical report on the tides in the harbour of Bombay.

The usefulness or otherwise of his activities and copious and wide-ranging reports is now impossible to verify, but they illustrate exactly the same kind of blithe know-all confidence when it came to exploring Antarctica. But it all served Markham in one important respect: it kept his name in front of the eyes of the decision-makers. Hence, after trouble had been brewing for some years in Abyssinia (now Ethiopia), in 1867 he was asked to accompany General Sir Robert Napier's punitive expedition to Magdala as a supernumerary geographer. He was away for almost a year and, as usual, made extensive notes on every aspect of the country and the campaign, later turning it into another volume, *The History of the Abyssinian Expedition*, which came out in 1869. Suffice to say here that Napier's forces routed those of King Theodore (Tewodros), and the King committed suicide rather than be taken alive. Commenting on the appearance of the King's body, Clements writes: [1]

> The body was that of a man of medium stature, well built, with broad chest, small waist, and muscular limbs. The hair was much dishevelled, crisp, and coarse, and done in three plaits with little stumpy tails. But it had evidently not been dressed or buttered for days. The complexion was dark for an Abyssinian, but the features showed no trace of negro blood. The eyebrows had a peculiar curve downwards and over the nose, and there was a deep-curved furrow in the centre of the forehead. The nose was aquiline and finely cut, with a low bridge, the lips very thin and cruel, the face, though thin, rather round than oval ...

There is more than a hint here of the connoisseurship of masculine attributes and beauty that so often characterises Markham's assessment of men. The romance of the mythos and the worship of the hero are also in evidence when later he states that [2]

> ... [Theodore] preferred death to lingering out a contemptible exist-
> ence after his true career was over, and he died like a hero.

Markham's bias in favour of beautiful male heroes seems to have escaped the attention of historians even to this day – but it ran through all of his schemes, and in the end it helped set in motion the train of events that culminated in the failure of the British to be first at the South Pole.

Overall, the 1860s were a time of work and consolidation for Markham. Throughout the decade he worked on his public and professional profile. In 1863 he accepted the position of Honorary Secretary to the Royal Geographical Society. Assisted by Minna, he produced a continuous stream of translations for the Hakluyt Society, of which he had been a prominent and active member since 1858. This Society, named after a sixteenth-century English clergyman (who, like Markham, had been a pupil at Westminster), had been set up in 1846 with a view to publish translations of primary records of historic voyages, travels and other historic material. According to a memorial tablet in Bristol Cathedral: [3]

> ... [Hakluyt's] studious Imagination discovered new Paths for geo-
> graphical Science, and his patriotic Labours rescued from Oblivion
> not a few of those who went down to the Sea in Ships, to be Har-
> bingers of Empire, descrying new Lands, and finding larger Room
> for their Race.

Markham's association with the Hakluyt Society, a sister organisation to the Royal Geographical Society, lasted well into his old age. In 1861 he had also become a Fellow of the Society of Antiquaries, and served on its Council for many years.

He received the War Medal and was created a Companion of the Order of the Bath for services rendered in the Abyssinian campaign. The gathering of honours continued. In 1867 he received the Grand Prix of the Paris Exhibition of that year. He was elected a Fellow of the Royal Society, Commendador of the Portuguese Order of Christ, and a Chevalier of the Order of the Rose of Brazil. He was also made a member of the Imperial Academy of Germany and of the Royal Society of Gottingen. Honours, awards, appointments, memberships and honorary doctor-ates continued to be heaped on him throughout his life. The establishment always obliged when it came to bolstering his social and professional standing. They helped confer the unassailable status that protected him from the scandalous gossip and damaging rumours that may otherwise have curtailed his power to shape events.

A formal photographic portrait of Markham from around this time shows further reasons why people did not mess with him. Although conventions around posing for portraits were different then – and one would not expect the ingratiating smiles that are standard today – he looks defiant, arrogant, and intimidating. The oblique gaze is there again, and again there is no doubt about his confidence, sense of self-worth and entitlement. There is the suggestion of a Sadean sneer around the mouth. Looking at him here, it is hard to believe that he had ever worked as a clerk in a dingy office, among ordinary men who were not 'gentlemen'. For Markham, however, it had only ever been a means to an end.

According to Markham himself, it was Sherard Osborn who was the prime mover behind the 1875 Nares Expedition to the Arctic. Osborn had been on the *Collingwood* as a gunnery mate and lieutenant in Markham's time. As we have seen, he had been in command of the *Pioneer* on the 1850 search for Franklin, of which he had also played a prominent part in promoting. He and Markham worked together within the Royal Geographical Society to keep the Arctic pot – if not exactly boiling – at least simmering. The Admiralty had lost interest in Polar exploration after the flurry of the Franklin searches. Osborn, however, consistently advocated the resumption of Navy efforts.

The discovery of the North West Passage had been abandoned as impractical, and the quest for the North Pole had been downgraded as useless. The proper objects of Arctic exploration were now considered to be of a scientific nature: to find out as much as possible about the Arctic's geography, geology, zoology, botany, meteorology, magnetism and oceanography. Of prime importance to both Markham and Osborn, however, was the view that Polar exploration gave worthy employment to the Navy in peacetime. As far as Markham was concerned, there was nothing to beat it for teaching officers and men about courage, endurance, constant vigilance, determination and prompt action. Englishmen, in his view, should never '... abandon that career of noble adventure which has done so much to form the national character, and to give our country the rank she still maintains'.

At the same time, he disingenuously subscribed to the view that reaching the North Pole would be an utterly futile achievement, of no commercial value – adding that the main objective had to be that of accurately mapping the Arctic. Geographical discovery and map-making are good covers for Pole-bagging, and were traditionally carried out by the Royal Navy. If it didn't aid national prestige, geographical discovery or maritime navigation, Markham had precious little interest in science. The only reason any science other than geography and magnetism were practised on the *Discovery* Expedition was in response to pressure from the Royal Society, which disdained any vulgar rush for the Pole, however disguised, and whose support any venture of this nature would require. It also, serendipitously, provided a face-saving hedge in the event that the Pole was not reached.

The Admiralty, on the other hand, professed no such scruples, and made the attainment of the highest possible latitude its main objective when Sherard Osborn finally, on 17 November 1874, got the go-ahead from the Government. Prior to this, cousin Albert, then a commander in the RN, had been on a reconnoitring trip to Arctic waters on board a whaler. He was now appointed commander of the *Alert*, one of the two ships of the 1875 North Pole Expedition led by Captain George S Nares FRS.

Albert looked up to Clements all his life, even though he himself had a long and distinguished career in the Navy, ending up as an admiral and a KCB. Inherently different from Clements, and having been much less indulged as a child, he was honest to a fault, active, robust, diffident and full of faith in God and his superior officers. Indeed, he could be said to have had too much faith in his superiors – as demonstrated by the fact that in 1893 he sunk a Royal Navy battleship, taking with it his commanding officer, Sir George Tryon, and 357 officers and men, rather than disobey an order from that same commanding officer. The *Camperdown* disaster is well known – details can be found in many accounts, and need not be repeated here, save to say that it subsequently became the event that defined Albert's career, but not in a good way.

Even though Albert tended to hero-worship Clements, it was Clements who benefited from Albert's position in the Navy, frequently taking advantage by getting himself invited as a guest on board Albert's ships. The first example of this was the Nares Expedition, where Clements accompanied the expedition as far as Greenland in the *Alert*. In spite of the discomforts of having to sleep in a small, leaky space, Clements is said to have been supremely happy and, true to form, became an '... immense favourite with everyone on board'. It was not long before he made the acquaintance of every man on both ships of the expedition, the *Alert* and the *Discovery* (another *Discovery*, not Scott's), regardless of rank or rating, and soon had a complete history of every soul on board, entering [4]

> ... so sympathetically into every little incident connected with their lives, that they soon confided to him all their woes and all their troubles, just as they would do to a father or brother.

To Albert, who informs us of all this in his biography of Clements, it would have been literally unthinkable that there may have been more to these activities than met the eye. The fact that Clements fostered feelings of trust and confidence in the men and boys is taken by Albert at face value – as wholly benevolent and disinterested. The legitimate aspect to the writing of all these *curricula vitae* was the resource they might constitute for historians and researchers. It is, however, also evidence of a preoccupation well beyond the level of ordinary human interest.

Clements' notes were not just brief records of Naval life, but complete accounts of ancestry and careers in the Navy, giving full descriptions of each man's appearance, weight, chest capacity, and all particulars connected with them, no matter how trivial. One of the men is actually recorded as having a cicatrix (type of scar) on his left big toe. He records when, and to whom, they were married, the dates of the births of their children, and in some cases even their children's names. The officers' coats of arms and sledge flags are emblazoned in correct colours over their respective histories; while in the case of several of the men, Markham has painted some device typical of their surnames or of the special duties allotted to them. Nares has no fewer than ten pages devoted to a recapitulation of his services; another officer is accorded nearly 24 pages; while in several instances some of the seamen have been given two, three, or even more pages. This kind of obsessive documentation is reminiscent of Marcel Proust, who also took a keen interest and, like many homosexuals, prided himself on his knowledge of all the prominent, undiscovered inverts of Europe. 'His documentation was remarkable.' [5] It is also a plausible explanation for Markham's extraordinary level of interest.

Compiled from the amassed notes at the time, and added to and brought up to date later, Markham's *Arctic Navy List* was brought out as a separate volume in 1875. While more concise, it does meticulously record all the roles played by the officers in the various shipboard theatrical productions over the years, the songs the men and the officers sang and the instruments they played – as does the list in his later volume, *Antarctic Obsession*.

Clements took a passage back home in the supply ship, but not before he had sight of the sledge dogs, brought on board the *Alert* before his departure. It is easy to imagine his response to their odour which pervaded the entire ship, and especially that a number of them were later found to have rabies. In the event, they were only used for rescue missions; the heavy work being done in traditional Navy style, by the men. And heavy work it was. Nares had warned them before leaving England that the sledging would be no sinecure. He told them that [6]

> ... if they could imagine the hardest work that they had ever been called upon to perform in their lives intensified to the utmost degree, it would only be as child's play in comparison with the work they would have to perform whilst sledging!

While they probably relished the challenge in theory, the reality must have brought many to their senses. Heavy wooden boats, loaded on heavy wooden sledges, were dragged along in case water had to be crossed. With memories of the grim discoveries of the Franklin disaster so fresh, the obstinacy of the Navy's belief in its own way of doing things seems doubly unjustified. Misquoting Talleyrand, '... they learned nothing and they forgot nothing'. In 1859, just 16 years prior to this, remnants of Franklin's doomed crew had been found dead in and around the boats they dragged along the desolate coast of King William Island. The possibility of having to cross water is academic if dragging a boat is going to kill you.

But they would have had their work cut out, even without the boats. The tents and equipment were heavy. The provisions were heavy. The ice was hard and uneven. They often had to carve a path through hummocks reaching a height of 10 to 20 ft. Sometimes they marched up to their waists in the snow. Few activities are more exhausting. But the men never complained, and '... the harder the work the more the mirth and merriment'. Perhaps there was nothing to do but to laugh; their clothing became heavy with frozen sweat which was impossible to dislodge, and their tents and sleeping-bags shrank after having been wet. Their overalls, intended as outer weatherproofs, were too small to be worn over their duffels and jumpers, which meant that the snow froze into their jumpers and thawed in their bags at night.

During the last three nights on the way back, sleep was impossible due to the extreme discomfort, amounting to positive pain, of frozen sleeping-bags. The risk of severe hypothermia and frostbite was ever present. One man collapsed from sheer exhaustion and nearly froze to death before they could get him back to the ship. The entire party only got back by the skin of their teeth. Albert, having gone on alone to get help, collapsed near the ship utterly spent and wet with perspiration which rapidly froze. And these were just the preliminary autumn reconnoitring and depot laying trips.

The Austin Expedition in the search for Franklin had been remarkably free from scurvy. Having overwintered in a locality where game and 'scurvy grass' were comparatively abundant, their winter had been bookended by the availability of fresh foods. This is the most plausible reason why they had, apparently, not suffered the so-called explorer's sickness. They were very likely to have been vitamin C depleted, however. They were reported to be looking very pale. They were probably more than just vitamin C depleted; a deficiency of vitamin D is likely after months of darkness, as well as deficiencies in a further range of vitamins and minerals. The difference that modern nutritional knowledge has made to the health of latter-day explorers and adventurers cannot be overstated. Fortunately for Austin and his men, and for Austin's reputation, fresh foods came in time to prevent overt signs of scurvy. To Clements, however, it was evidence that a happy, clean, dry ship was a healthy ship. Although he cannot have been expected to have had this level of scientific insight, it is now accepted that correlation cannot be used to infer a causal relationship between variables.

Nevertheless, everyone at the time seemed to know that 'green foods' and fresh meat cured scurvy. Although it seems obvious now, at the time it was far from clear that it was the absence of those foods that were the cause. As a result of his experiences on the Austin Expedition, Clements formed the opinion that lime juice was useless in preventing scurvy.

We now know that lime juice contains far less vitamin C than lemon juice, and that nineteenth-century methods of bottling and preserving it destroyed most of what may have been present to begin with. It still seems surprising, however, that was so difficult for people to accept the notion of a deficiency disease, and that it was the lack of the type of foods that cured it that caused scurvy to arise in the first place.

Although it must have been known about, and suffered, throughout human history, it was not until Europeans started to make long sea-voyages in the late fifteenth century that scurvy came to be described with any kind of consistency. The causes were thought variously to be lack of cleanliness, cold, damp, want of exercise, bad air, contagion or infection, a diseased spleen, bad food and/or water. It was thought to affect grudging, idle malcontents and those deprived of 'marital comforts'. It was thought to be the effect of [7]

> ... eating excessively of salt food and vegetables, which heat the
> blood and corrupt the internal parts.

However, it was also known, and often demonstrated, that the consumption of citrus fruits, green vegetables, fresh meats and fresh provisions generally cured the condition almost immediately.

An influential view which held sway for many years – especially towards the end of the nineteenth century, and right up to and including Scott's Last Expedition – was that scurvy was caused by a toxin or putrefying agent. It was an example of the seductive powers of plausible-sounding scientific terminology and academic endorsement. At that time it was Clements' view also; and another adherent, Reginald Koettlitz, was duly selected as medic on Scott's 1901 *Discovery* Expedition (albeit under pressure from Alfred Harmsworth). The belief was that scurvy was caused by a bacterium in tinned foods, sufficient to cause the disease, although not enough to make the food appear to be obviously off. As a result, Koettlitz carefully sniffed all the tinned food before it was consumed. This precaution was of course useless, and scurvy duly appeared on Scott's *Discovery* Expedition.

Similarly, Atkinson, medic on the *Terra Nova*, Scott's Last Expedition, believed that scurvy was caused by 'acid intoxication' – a view promoted by Sir Almroth Wright (nicknamed Sir Almost Wright), a much-honoured bacteriologist and immunologist who played his part in the obfuscation and blind alleys that characterise the history of scurvy. In a talk given in the Cape Evans hut on 17 August 1911, Scott reports Atkinson as stating that '... [acid intoxication] is due to two salts, sodium hydrogen carbonate and sodium hydrogen phosphate; these cause the symptoms observed and infiltration of fat in organs, leading to feebleness of heart action'. Scott adds: [8]

So far for diagnosis, but it does not bring us much closer to the cause, preventives, or remedies. Practically we are much as we were before ... he [Atkinson] holds the first cause to be tainted food, but secondary or contributory causes may be even more potent in developing the disease. Damp, cold, over-exertion, bad air, bad light, in fact any condition exceptional to normal healthy existence.

Not much seemed to have changed in half a century.

The persistent conviction that it was the presence of something rather than the absence of something – together with the fact that the substance we now call vitamin C is so easily destroyed – were the two factors that condemned so many to die such an agonising but preventable death. In spite of James Lind's famous experiment in 1746, hailed as the first controlled experiment in science, which seemed to show unequivocally that oranges and lemons cured scurvy, people continued to sicken and die at sea and on land. The problem, again, was Lind's theory on the *cause* of the disease, which he held to be due to 'blocked perspiration'. It is of course understandable that the humid and fetid conditions between decks, where hundreds of men slept in close confinement, might lead one to conclude that these were not conditions conducive to health.

Lind's later studies and treatments of the disease at Haslar, the Royal Navy Hospital, only served to confuse the issue further, as different cures were put forward, and different foods were tried in combination. Possibly due to mis-diagnoses, or a failure to comply with their prescriptions, some people did not get better even when allegedly fed fresh vegetables and fruits. In fact, the trouble with early studies in general is the lack of what we would now regard as essential scientific rigour. The presence of what are now known as confounding variables made the outcomes meaningless. In an apparent switch of cause and effect, a further cause proposed by Lind was lack of exercise. Fatigue and lassitude are some of the first effects of vitamin C depletion, and can be found as much as six weeks before the more obvious signs appear. [9]

Overall, it seems Lind confused the issue with his 'blocked perspiration' theory, obscuring his own observations, and neglecting his own earlier findings. Although he died in 1794, in relative obscurity, his experiments and his *Treatise of the Scurvy* have nevertheless withstood the test of time and remain pioneering work in the field – mainly as a result of his early attempt at a controlled experiment, and the finding that fresh citrus fruits reliably cured scurvy. Unfortunately, however, it could be said that lemon/lime juice was a victim of its own success (the terms were used interchangeably, although lemon juice has more vitamin C content than the West Indian limes that were then used).

By 1875, the year the Nares Expedition set sail, it had started to be processed and bottled in bulk for consumption by the Royal Navy. By the time the limes arrived from the West Indies they would already have been weeks, if not months, old. The juice was then stored in settling tanks and pumped through copper pipes before being bottled or decanted into large stoneware jars, neither of which were suitable for taking on sledging journeys. Copper is known to destroy vitamin C. If the juice had then also undergone reduction through heat, it can safely be assumed to have lost virtually all of its antiscorbutic properties.

The Nares Expedition had, allegedly, enjoyed good health throughout the winter of 1875–6, although they all looked very pale. In all likelihood, everyone, except the officers, were seriously vitamin C depleted by the end of the winter, having had only 1 lb of fresh meat per man on two consecutive days every three weeks. Although 'lime juice' had been distributed on a daily basis, it won't have made any difference. By the spring, vitamin C levels must have already been critically low. The result was that very shortly after the start of the first sledging trip on 3 April 1876, one by one, the men started to complain about pains in their ankles and knees.

Stoically and by a sheer effort of will, in view of the lethargy and malaise they must already have been feeling, they had set off in the usual British way, with prayers read by the Chaplain, a hymn, and pennants flying. Albert Markham was in charge of the northern division, with two sledges, named *Marco Polo* and *Victoria*, charged with reaching as high a northern latitude as possible. Due to the perceived danger of the pack suddenly shifting as the season advanced, it had been considered necessary, once again, to take boats with them. For the same reason, it was too risky to lay depots, which meant they had to drag all their provisions there and back. This meant taking an extra sledge, which obliged them to relay, dragging two sledges, and returning to drag up the third. The usual hardships of frostbite, dehydration, sleeplessness, sunburn and snow-blindness were suffered. They had to cut a path with pickaxes and shovels, making painfully slow progress. On one occasion they made only a mile in ten hours of 'marching', as they called their desperate struggle over banked, fissured, and snow-covered ice. They spent Easter Sunday tied up in their bags, freezing cold, sheltering from a fierce gale, spending what they all agreed was the most miserable day of their lives.

Unfortunately, however, this was not the worst of it. By 7 May the working force was reduced by one-third due to scurvy, with five men now having to be carried. The larger boat was abandoned. Still they went forward over snowdrifts and hummocks, the sledges with the invalids being regularly overturned in dragging them over almost insurmountable barriers. Albert had taken a couple of small bottles of lime juice with him, which he tried to thaw by holding them between his thighs in his sleeping-bag. Even then, it did not thaw sufficiently for it to be remixed, or homogenised, in the bottle. By 10 May, nine men were prostrate, with the rest steadily deteriorating. Albert tried to keep the truth from the men, but they cannot have been in much doubt as to what was the matter. Reluctantly, he called a halt, realising it would be madness to try to go any further. Still they did not turn back, however. They stayed where they were for a further two days, during which sights and soundings were taken, marine specimens collected, and seawater temperatures noted. On 12 May, Albert, together with all those who could still walk, marched to within 399.5 miles of the Pole, a record at the time. There, three cheers went up and songs were sung, ending with the National Anthem. Flags were flown, and back at the camp the event was celebrated with a special supper consisting of a hare shot some time before.

They struggled manfully back towards the ship, weakening as they went. Albert was afraid to look at his own legs in case he might see the tell-tale red spots and discolouration around the knee joints. The fact that he and Lieutenant Parr, in charge of the *Victoria* sledge, did not go on to fully develop the disease was attributed, in part, to their having taken more exercise during the winter than the men. It seemed commonly to have been the case that officers were spared for longer than the men. There is a certain amount of individual variation in the development of scurvy, but it wouldn't be surprising if the officers enjoyed a better diet in some respects than the men, although it was often protested that everyone ate the same, and not just on sledging journeys. Nevertheless, the officers tended to bring their own additional supplies, and may well have had first pick at anything freshly shot or snared. But to give him his due, Nares turned over what he had left of his private stash to the worst of the scorbutics.

With everybody except the two officers and two of the men now affected, Albert's team was forced to abandon the second boat. He had begun to fear they might not make it back to the ship, at times losing their way, and floundering through waist-deep, sometimes neck-deep, snow. The situation was critical. Lieutenant Parr, being the fittest, volunteered to go on alone to the ship to get help, and walked 40 miles in less than 24 hours without a break, foreshadowing Tom Crean's heroic walk some 36 years later. When he got back to the ship, he was so ravaged by the ordeal that Nares at first failed to recognise him. For Albert, [10] left with the sick men in the cold, dank, fetid and cheerless tent, the awful moment came the next day, on 8 June, when one of the men, George Porter, died in his arms:

> Pathetic indeed was that little funeral procession of feeble, crippled men, most of them in tears, as they laid the body of their late comrade ... in its last icy resting place ...

In another echo of events 36 years later, relief came at last in the shape of a dog-sledge. By the time they got back to the ship, after an absence of 72 days, only Albert and three of the men were able to walk – and that with great difficulty.

Nares, alarmed by the state of Albert's party, sent another rescue team, also by dog-sledge, to meet the western division, which had gone to explore along the north coast of Ellesmere Island. They were found in a similar condition to Albert's.

By the time everyone was back on the ship, it resembled a hospital, with only a few men able to do the work of getting the ship ready for the return home. The crew of the second ship of the expedition, which had been left to explore the northwest coast of Greenland, had succumbed to scurvy also, with most of the men laid up sick, and two fatalities. With both ships now riddled with scurvy, another winter in the Arctic was out of the question, and Nares had no option but to return home as quickly as possible. That there were not more fatalities was in large part due to the relief sledges pulled by dogs, and the hunting skills of Hans Hendrick, a native of Greenland who had accompanied the expedition as Inuit interpreter. Hendrik was a skilled Arctic hunter and, together with his expertise in handling dogs, is credited with almost single-handedly saving the expedition. Although this is surely overstating the case, it is nevertheless another example of the Navy's wilful blindness regarding the use of dogs, and the value of appropriate knowledge and skills.

It must have taken a heroic effort to get the ships home with so many sick; but after a difficult voyage, the two ships, which had been 'cheered by 200,000' out of Portsmouth Harbour 17 months earlier, were back – at first, to an enthusiastic welcome. The senior lieutenants were promoted, and Albert was made a captain at the early age of 35. The RGS presented him with a magnificent gold watch in appreciation of his having reached the furthest north. Nevertheless, there was disappointment in the air. They had come back too soon and they had not succeeded in getting anywhere near the Pole. And then there was the scurvy for which Nares bore the brunt of the criticism. Clements, however, sprung to his defence, in his usual verbose way.

By a quirk of fate, Sherard Osborn had died on 6 May 1875, 23 days before the Nares Expedition set sail. As Osborn's collaborator in getting the expedition off the ground, and also as secretary of the RGS, it now fell to Clements to submit a *Report* on the results, which was published as *The Royal Geographical Society and the Arctic Expedition of 1875–6*. After a lengthy recapitulation of the background, he enumerates the successes of the expedition. They had crossed the threshold of the known world, had established a base of operations beyond it, had reached the furthest north, had explored and put 300 miles of coastline on the map, and studied the frozen sea and its movements. They had discovered a sea of ancient ice and had named it the 'Palaeocrystic Sea', had gathered hydrographic data, and made observations of the fauna, flora, and geology of the region. Turning to the conduct and management of the expedition, he concedes the advantage of having two steamers, rather than sailing ships towed by steam tenders. Sledge equipment and clothing were identical to the Austin and Belcher Expeditions, and the provisions, with the exception of the salt beef, were equally good. Disadvantages were the fact that the ships had not been as warm and comfortable, and that the Nares Expedition had been seriously undermanned, in his view, numbering 'only 120 men, including chaplains'.

Clements eulogises the way the sledging had been conducted, and how the longest and most severe winter ever spent in the Arctic had been endured and admirably managed in all respects, including the daily drinking of lime juice. He notes that the Admiralty Instructions were gallantly and successfully complied with, by reaching the highest north under conditions beyond anything that been formerly experienced. In addition, [11]

> They fully, completely, and with heroic self-devotion, fulfilled the objects of the Geographical Society, by exploring ... to the farthest extent possible with the means at their disposal.

He continues by marshalling the views of his old pal, Captain Richard Vesey Hamilton, who had been on both the Austin and Belcher Expeditions. Hamilton: [12]

> Surely nothing finer was ever recorded than this advance of three sledges ... laden down with sick and dying men, in obedience to an order to do their best ... nothing more touching was ever penned than the narratives, full of tenderness and simplicity, in which the sailor-writers tell their story. These gallant seamen have failed to reach the Pole, but they have won a proud place in their country's annals. They have done Englishmen good.

The similarity to the way Scott's failed Last Expedition was later to be presented is striking.

Now, finally, we arrive at the 'unprecedented and most unexpected outbreak of scurvy'. Quixotically, in view of his later adherence to the ptomaine theory, Clements here states that the cause of scurvy is very generally believed to the absence of fresh vegetables, and that this 'exciting' cause existed in all previous Arctic expeditions. However, what he considered the predisposing causes, which included intense cold, darkness, damp, and confined air, were all endured for much longer than on previous expeditions, having wintered so much further north. This, he states with unconscious irony, could not possibly have been foreseen. He states that Nares adopted the same sledging diet recommended by M'Clintock, which did not include lime juice, and whose crews had never suffered from scurvy. (M'Clintock and his men had eaten fresh musk-ox – a crucial detail that had not been taken into account, evidently.) He states that the contents of bottles become frozen, and if they do not become useless by bursting the bottle, they take a lot of energy to thaw.

According to Clements, the great objection to taking lime juice on sledge journeys is the additional sufferings it imposes on the cook who has to thaw it. He confidently asserts that [13]

> It is, I believe, the unanimous opinion of all Arctic sledge travellers
> that Captain Nares did not commit an error of judgment on this

point, and that he had no reason to deviate from the lessons of former experience.

He goes on to refute further criticisms before stating that the outbreak of scurvy was the one single calamity in an otherwise successful expedition. As far as he was concerned, the fact that scurvy had also broken out on sledging trips where lime juice *had* been taken constituted conclusive proof that the outbreak was not due to the want of lime juice, but to causes '... which were in operation, though undetected, before the sledges started, causes due to the unparalleled duration of winter darkness'. Once more the cause seemed within grasp, but was destined to slide away again, maddeningly.

A further thundering and encomiastic enumeration of the achievements of the expedition winds up this part of the *Report.* The last word is given to the matter which was nearest to Sherard Osborn's heart: namely, that Polar expeditions were the training ground (albeit in the old ways of the Navy) for a new generation of Arctic experts. Clements' *Report* is a masterclass in spin and justification, achieving its ends by a comprehensive inflation of the achievements and a commensurate minimisation of the problems. The tone is orotundly authoritative and magisterial, and as formidable, defiant and entitled as he himself was.

Importantly, it showed how scientific gains could rescue a flawed and ultimately near-disastrous expedition. For Pole-baggers, science provided a fall-back position, or fail-safe, in case the said Pole was not bagged. The message was clear, and well heeded by Scott, especially when he had full control over the make-up of his own Last Expedition. On it, Scott made sure there was a large scientific group and agenda.

In the Betting Shop of the South Pole, he placed an each-way bet on himself. He did not play to win: he played not to lose.

References

1   Admiral Sir Albert Markham. *The Life of Sir Clements R. Markham*, p. 218

2   *ibid.*

3   Sir Clements R. Markham. *The Lands of Silence*, p. 110

4   Admiral Sir Albert Markham. *op. cit.*, p. 234

5   George D. Painter. *Marcel Proust*, p. 426

6   M.E. Markham and F.A. Markham. *The Life of Sir Albert Hastings Markham*, p. 103

7   Kenneth J. Carpenter. *The History of Scurvy and Vitamin C*, p. 11

8   Robert Falcon Scott. *Journals: Captain Scott's Last Expedition*, p. 270

9   Kenneth J. Carpenter. *op. cit.*, p. 241

10   M.E. Markham and F.A. Markham. *op. cit.*, p. 130

11   Clements Robert Markham. *The Royal Geographical Society and the Arctic Expedition of 1875–6: A Report*, p. 21

12   *op. cit.*, p. 22

13   *op. cit.*, p. 23

7

BOYS BOYS BOYS

Although Markham was a writer, he was not an artist, intellectual, or philosopher. Tightly buttoned up in his narrow house in Eccleston Square, scratching away in his cheerless study producing an interminable series of wordy histories, translations, reiterative biographies and narratives, he embodies a Dickensian archetype. He did not relate to, much less identify with, his contemporary arts scene. Although he enjoyed camping it up in his beloved theatricals, there was nothing in his everyday appearance that carried the slightest hint of bohemianism or effeminacy. It was a happy coincidence of personal preference and social expediency, and if it had been up to him, the world and everything in it would have stayed the same forever, especially with regard to sex. Deeply conservative and bourgeois, it is easy to imagine him sourly disapproving of avant-garde art and literature, especially in the decadent and homosexual genres that flowered in the second half of the nineteenth century. He would not have thought it was to his, nor anyone else's, advantage to bring things out in the open.

Under the more liberal Napoleonic Code, homosexual activities were not a crime in France, and Paris was not very far away; change was happening on his doorstep whether he liked it or not. However intellectually and artistically remote Markham may have been from Baudelaire, the Goncourts and Huysmans – and at home, from Swinburne, Pater or Wilde – he shared their moral and sexual ambiguities. But he was no social reformer or philosopher. His efforts on behalf of the education of boys had its merits, but they were also a cover for an ulterior motive, and concerned only Naval cadets. Unlike some contemporary writers such as John Addington Symonds, he never acknowledged, justified nor took responsibility for his proclivities.

We would not have known it from his socially constructed persona of a 'man's man': controlling, hierarchical, conservative, and busy. He projected a version of masculinity which, by its very conservatism, pre-empted doubts about its legit-imacy. Although his fun-loving side appears to contradict the dry archivist and chronicler, at a deeper level, his literary activities were also escapes into other worlds, into the lives of men and boys, into homosocial and chivalric realms. In the popular literature of the time, the male quest romance represented [1]

> ... a yearning for escape from a confining society, rigidly structured in terms of gender, class, and race, to a mythologized place else-where where men can be freed from the constraints of Victorian morality. In the caves, or jungles, or mountains of this other place, the heroes of romance explore their secret selves in an anarchic space which can be safely called the 'primitive'.

For Markham this space was not in the steamy jungles of Africa, nor the mysterious East, but in the Apollonian purity of the Poles. To him, the aloof, frowning (his word) cliffs of the Arctic suggested the remoteness and indifference of majesty, before which he felt both awed and exalted, and which activated his instinct to worship. All his life he was notably deferential to the point of obse-quiousness – especially in relation to the royal family, whom he sought to cultivate. He never neglected the well connected, whom he impressed and entertained with his archaic erudition. In spite of never having risen beyond junior lieutenant rank, he aligned himself with admirals and sea-lords, and gossiped with the establish-ment elite in the sanctuaries of the RGS and the Atheneum.

Meanwhile, in the streets of London, dramas and scandals played themselves out – notably the Cleveland Street scandal in July 1889 in which a homosexual brothel was busted, outing at least one member of the aristocracy (Lord Arthur Somerset), and rumoured to have involved Prince Albert Victor, grandson of Queen Victoria, and heir-presumptive to the British throne. This in itself must have guaranteed it a hearing in Clubland. The word 'homosexual' gained currency for the first time in the *fin de siècle*. Foucault argues that language changes everything. Equally, one could argue that art changes everything. In France and Germany particularly, intellectuals, philosophers, writers and artists contributed to the birth of a new social identity; and overtly effeminate, artistically flamboyant poses were experimented with. Joris-Karl Huysman's hugely influential novel *A Rebours* explores the sensibilities of a reclusive, rarefied, hypersensitive intellectual who shrinks from the chthonian horrors of nature in fastidious sequestration. Markham may never have heard of it, much less read it, but his world was similarly self-circumscribed by a narrow run of interests and activities. He used avoidance and diversionary tactics to keep the modern world at bay. He was often abroad and, when in London, he associated with men of like mind, mutually reinforcing each others' commitment to tradition, and deploring change and innovation. And of course in his partying with the boys, with whom he could enter into Neverland.

He had privileged access to the boys of the Merchant Navy training schools, which meant that he had no need to resort to the murkier corners of the London *demi-monde*. From the early 1880s, Clements had involved himself in the education of cadets on the training ships *Conway* and *Worcester*. It had happened to come to his notice that candidates for the navigation exam for the merchant service were 'lamentably' ignorant of geography. Backed by his status as Secretary of the RGS, Markham was able to propose, and succeed in improving, the education of these cadets – in the process appointing himself as a kind of supernumerary, providing general advice, looking out for their welfare, and giving lectures on a popular level about heroes of the past. These boys were aged between 14 and 18, and were 'fine, well-conditioned lads'. [2] The *Worcester*, in particular, was favoured with Clements' attentions, as it was moored near London. He went further than simply visiting the ship and giving lectures and advice: [3]

> His house soon became the resort of the *Worcester* boys. They loved running up to see him, and he for his part as dearly loved to have them about him ... We strongly suspect that the wildest ones were his especial favourites! ... There was nothing Markham would not do that could conduce in any way to their pleasure, their happiness, or their instruction. He would spend whole afternoons in their company, taking them to the Tower of London, the Zoological Gardens, Westminster Abbey, the Aquarium, or any Exhibitions that might be open; then home to tea and dinner, winding up the day with a theatre.

In fact, on at least one day, in addition to all the above delights, he also took one of his favourite *Worcester* boys to a hatter, a hosier and a tailor, before he took him home to dinner and the theatre.

At the same time, he had been in the habit of making regular visits to Portsmouth to meet old friends – keeping in touch. By an odd coincidence, in November 1882, Albert had been appointed – much to his astonishment – to command HMS *Vernon*, the Naval torpedo training establishment at Portsmouth. Albert, being a gunnery man, felt himself to be a 'square man in a round hole', and the three months it took him to acquaint himself with his new duties are a measure of the inappropriateness of the appointment. He had been offered the command by Sir (Astley) Cooper Key, First Naval Lord from 1879–85, a Fellow of the RGS, and well known to Clements. Albert was at first hesitant about accepting the command, but his objections were set aside by Sir Cooper. In fact, it set Albert's career on a trajectory involving the training of young sailors for the next nine years. If Clements had by now become the skilled manipulator many believe he was, then perhaps Cooper Key had had a little word whispered into his ear. It certainly seems an extraordinarily happy turn of events as far as Clements was concerned. In addition to his run of the Merchant training ships, Albert's appointment provided Clements now also with a ready-made pass on to the Royal Navy training ships – a facility of which he took full advantage.

He had to work like a demon to pay for his lifestyle, which involved many trips abroad, combining work and pleasure by lecturing and spreading bonhomie where he could. Unsurprisingly, his work has been criticised for showing signs of haste, and that he '... was in all things an enthusiast rather than a scholar'. [4] He was also [5]

> ... capable of intentional mis-translation or omission of inconvenient facts.

In 1886 he went on a trip to America, accompanied by Minna. To relieve the tedium of the long voyage across the Atlantic, he took the lead in organising entertainments, which included charades and theatricals. He devised a competition in 'graceful walking', for which he was one of the judges. Both men and women were presumably expected to take part. It sounds like a lot of fun, in a camp kind of way.

Albert's command of the *Vernon* had ended in the same year. However, after a six-month leave, he was again put in charge of a training establishment. This time it was the seaborne Training Squadron, which included the *Active*, the *Volage*, the *Rover*, and the *Calypso*. They had left by the time Clements was ready to join them in January 1887, but he did not allow that to stand in his way. He caught them up by taking a mail steamer for the West Indies, whence the Training Squadron had preceded him. Picking up the Squadron at Grenada, he took a berth in the *Active*, Albert's flagship. He soon became friends with all on the *Active*, and also all the other ships. In the gunroom, as usual, he was an especial favourite. He loved to be on board when it was blowing hard, watching the men reefing topsails, just like they did in the old days. He had brought his books and papers with him and worked in the mornings in the forecabin, where a dozen or so midshipmen would be doing their lessons under the tuition of the Naval Instructor: [6]

> Not infrequently the ... [Instructor] would be absent temporarily. Then, chaos reigned supreme, and would continue until summarily put a stop to by the Commodore, or other high official. Although it would not be fair to assume that their guest was the instigator of these somewhat irregular disturbances, yet it was generally conceded that there was never any cause to complain of their unseemly conduct when they were entirely by themselves! He loved the midshipmen, and they loved him; there was nothing that gave him greater pleasure than being with them in the gunroom mess, or going for a trip with them either on shore on some boating expedition.

Further, [7]

He adored above all the young midshipmen ... [and] encouraged them in some of their minor and harmless delinquencies!

At St Kitts, the famous boat race took place where Markham first became acquainted with Robert Falcon Scott, who was at that time a midshipman on the *Rover*. Although Scott famously won the cutter race, he was not an immediate favourite. Scott was not the type of disruptive, hell-raising boy of which Clements was especially fond. This dubious honour fell to Tommy Smyth, a reckless, hard-drinking and impulsive boy with a 'pedigree' – always so important to Clements. During an uproarious supper in the wardroom one evening, Smyth, who was seated between Clements and the Captain of Marines, had his head forced under the table whenever he got too excited. Whatever that may have meant. In later years, according to Huntford, [8] Smyth forfeited his candidacy for leadership of Clements' Antarctic Expedition by disgracing himself, mainly through drink. This supper had followed the performance of a play for which Clements had been on shore to buy 'ladies attire'. Entitled 'Too Clever by Half', or 'The Diary of a Scoundrel', it is a broad comic satire in which a young man who starts an affair with a married woman gets engaged to a young girl without telling his mistress. Clements revised the play considerably, inserting jokes that many felt were a great deal too personal. His tendency to ridicule surfaced again, evidently. Not everyone will have been amused, and there must have been those who heartily detested him but would hesitate to mess with him because of who he was and who he knew.

In early 1888 he accompanied the Training Squadron on another cruise to the West Indies. Clements: [9]

> As compared with the glorious old crowd of last year, the midshipmen are smaller, weaker, more quiet, less up to larks, more good: and not a patch on the old set!

He was nevertheless soon on intimate terms with them. In spite of his professed encouragement of education, and rather making a mockery of it (or maybe showing it up for the sham it was), he was irritated by recent orders that had been issued regarding increased school hours for the midshipmen and, as he terms it, other 'harassing folly'.

Markham did not have affairs or relationships, nor even casual sex with men his own age. Markham was a pederast. He covered his tracks very skilfully, however, and took care to emphasise his role as benefactor. He was an experienced man of the world, and knew how to judge situations to the optimum. He would have considered the abuse consensual, even with underage boys.

There were rumours among the men on the *Discovery*, but it would have been unthinkable to openly accuse Markham, a pillar of the establishment, of anything considered so abominable. Besides, who would the boys have turned to? The police? We have had to wait until well into the twenty-first century for victims of this kind of abuse to be believed, taken seriously, and to have action taken on their behalf. Not only that, but the Establishment takes care of its own; and the police would have been reluctant, to say the least, to have risked the outrage from on high that an accusation like that would have engendered. The very frequency and apparent lack of secrecy around his contact with boys would have militated against suspicion. He hid in plain sight. Virtually all heroic-age biographers up to now have taken the 'not a shred of evidence' line. He was careful not to leave any. Nevertheless, Markham's behaviour fits the classic profile of the predatory sex offender. Lack of concrete evidence is not an adequate refutation in the face of the weight of circumstantial evidence present in his case.

Clements cruised around the Mediterranean, the West Indies and the Baltic for almost the entire three years that Albert was in command of the Training Squadron. As the honoured guest of the ever-obliging Albert, Clements not only had the run of the ships, but was also invited to all the events, visits, functions and entertainments on shore, wherever they went.

Back home, at 21 Eccleston Square, Minna held the fort, doing translations and research work and running the home. Albert also lived there when on leave. Clements' and Minna's daughter May will have been in her late twenties around this time. She apparently dedicated herself to doing church work among the poor in London's East End – an occupation which shows a self-effacing religious turn of mind. There is no record of her ever having married; in fact, it is almost as though she never existed.

Minna, being not especially maternal or domestic, but scholarly, and fond of foreign travel, got her reward when in the spring of 1889, she and Clements went on a long visit to Rome, returning via Perugia, Assisi, Florence, Bologna, Parma, Genoa, San Remo, Marseille, Lyon, Dijon, and Paris. It is tempting to speculate about the nature of their marriage. When they first met, Clements must have seemed attractive. Good-looking, interesting, lively and well connected, he fit the bill for Minna, a vicar's daughter, even though he was not particularly well-off at that time. He seems to have knuckled down and paid attention to his career and marriage through his late twenties and thirties; the comparatively 'straight' period in his life. Minna stayed in the background, helping him with his work, a little like Dorothea, happy to be amanuensis to Will Ladislaw, discovering too late that she'd married Casaubon.

Considering the hypocrisies, lies, denials, frustrations and constant irritations that are said to have characterised most marriages at the time (and still often do now), she might have remained in ignorance of Clements' real nature, certainly in the beginning. Their relationship seems to have been one of friendship rather than lovers; he certainly had his own bedroom when he set fire to the bedclothes. They both needed a home base, and Clements needed a secretary, a companion, and a socially respectable front. All of these Minna provided. On the other hand, she was no fool; frequent foreign travel and a lot of reading would have given her a broad education. Clements' constant preoccupation with boys might have aroused her suspicions. There is no reason to suppose she wasn't clever or worldly, however, which means she would have realised that it was in both their interests to maintain a respectable front, and profess to believe that all was above board and genuinely philanthropic.

Minna seems to have appreciated the value of a harmonious and stable home, a comfortable life doing what she enjoyed, exempt from the serial pregnancies and confinements that characterised most Victorian women's lives. She enjoyed more trips abroad than the average Victorian wife even dreamt of. And later in life, a title: Lady Markham. It's not a bad deal, especially for the time. Beyond the occasional infatuation, Markham never seems to have formed any lasting or meaningful relationships with any of the scores of boys who passed through his hands. Even if he had wanted to, he could not afford it. He wanted his boys, but he wanted them without sacrificing his respectability, social standing or income – as, after all, many of his acquaintances were able to do, including members of the aristocracy. He made no secret of his affection for young men. He disguised its true nature with an elaborate show of benevolence, a tactic we now know to be effective in forestalling suspicion.

Alcohol flowed freely at every opportunity, however, and he consistently encouraged riotous behaviour. The boys loved those things, predictably, and as he knew full well. His boundless energy and infectious enthusiasm will have helped him gain their trust. At the same time he represented power, influence, and connections. He took advantage of the unequal power relations between him and the boys. A lot of boys would have wanted to be 'in' with him, and to be especially favoured. If the price was allowing themselves to be groped, well, alcohol would have made it easier. Much of it might have passed as raucous behaviour which 'accidentally' went too far on occasion. How far will never be known, but too far was undoubtedly a given. He cultivated the most amenable boys – those most 'up for a lark', but if they thought they might get something out of it, they were bound to be disappointed, beyond the odd boozy and riotous dinner and a ticket to the theatre.

As for complaining about it, we know even from recent times that they would have been wasting their time, or worse. What chance would a mere cadet have against the stentorian indignation of an outraged Markham? They stood to lose their cadetship, the support of their families, the regard of their friends. They would have been branded a liar, and their entire future would have been at risk. Can anyone be surprised that no boy ever came forward?

Nevertheless, if any doubts do remain about the nature of Markham's relationships with boys, then the Taormina connection must surely put paid to them. In the spring of 1890, Markham and Minna went again on a tour of Italy, paying a long visit to Taormina on the way back.

Taormina, situated on the southeastern coast of Sicily, is a balmy idyll – famous for its natural beauty and the ruins of the *Teatro Greco*, an ancient Greek amphitheatre, set into the hills overlooking the glittering sea. Markham was always enchanted by Taormina, and went there again and again. He is said to have made many friends among the country people. Albert claims they revered his memory, and children are said to have followed him around wherever he went.

In 1878, Taormina had become the home of Baron Wilhelm von Gloeden, a Prussian national who had travelled there for his health, fell in love with the place, and lived there the rest of his life. Von Gloeden was a photographer, specialising in photos of nude Sicilian boys, posed languidly in quasi-rustic or classical Greek styles. Von Gloeden's house and studio are reputed to have been one of the sights of Taormina, and by the 1890s they had become a magnet for the rich, famous, artistic, and hedonistically inclined. A constant stream of visitors included de Maupassant, Anatole France, Gabriele d'Annunzio, Oscar Wilde; bankers and industrialists like Rothschild, Krupp, and Vanderbilt; and even King Edward VII and the King of Siam (Thailand). Some built houses there; and Florence Trevelyan, an Englishwoman with a passion for gardening settled there and lived there for the rest of her life. She loved nature and planting, and she added to the charms of Taormina by creating exotic pleasure gardens – famous now for the whimsical pavilions, or follies she built, using salvaged materials. With their decorative verandas, balconies, flights of steps and walkways, lit by many lanterns, these added to what must have been an enchanting setting for twinkling soirées and grown-up games of hide-and-seek.

An unfortunate rumour has it that some of those materials were salvaged from the ruins of the *Teatro Greco*. Be that as it may, that garden – which still exists – was part of what made Taormina a chic and exotic tourist destination. And, according to Harold Acton, 'a polite synonym for Sodom'. Italy had long had a reputation for being permissive with regard to male homosexuality. Combined with the poverty of most Sicilians, this meant that any residual disapproval that may have been felt by the locals was soon overcome by the money that sex tourism brought in. In any case, patronage by the rich and famous had a legitimising effect. Even in Victorian England, surprisingly, von Gloeden's photographs were exhibited in public galleries, characterised as 'ethnographic studies of young natives of the island of Sicily': [10]

> Von Gloeden's more evocative nudes were avidly collected. Their
> suggestion of ancient places, use of artifacts and classic com-

positions helped to divert or at least excuse their sexual impact. Von Gloeden's photographs of lightly-clad or naked boys were circulated among the extensive coterie of the "Uranian School" of homosexual poets, as well as in many of the "physique and health" magazines spawned by the German Korperkulture (physical health/naturalism/nudism) and Wandervogel (boy scouts/hiking) movements. His theme of love for the adolescent boy, inspired by the *paiderasteia* of the ancient Greeks, was extremely erotic for the upper class of Victorian Europe.

Albert tells us repeatedly that Clements loved Taormina. Although it is theoretically possible that he and his wife were ordinary tourists, it isn't likely, given Markham's enduring and enthusiastic involvement with boys. Minna must have acquired some kind of awareness of her husband's proclivities, even if she held herself aloof and looked the other way. It is even possible that over time, she might have come to terms with what is likely to have been a light-hearted, benevolent version of what her husband got up to. The fact that there is no suggestion of the devastating effect that revelations of a similar kind had on other wives seems to point in that direction. There was no breakdown in their relationship, no apparent discord, no suggestion of any interruption to their apparently devoted companionship.

It was not entirely unknown for wives to retain their affection and concern for homosexual or pederastic husbands. Constance Wilde, for example, wrote to Oscar in prison to say there was forgiveness for him, went to see him in prison, and dropped divorce proceedings against him. [11] Another example is Catherine Vaughan, wife of the headmaster of Harrow School, the Reverend Charles John Vaughan, who had had an affair with a pupil, who [12]

> ... flung herself on her knees before Dr Symonds, [John Addington's father] confessing that she knew of her husband's "weakness" but begged the doctor to have mercy upon him because it had never interfered with his useful service to the school.

There is no evidence that Minna was in love with her husband, nor that she was especially protective of him, but there would have been no benefit for her in outing her husband as a pederast. Quite the opposite.

By the end of 1892 Markham was again in the Mediterranean, again as a guest of his cousin Albert, who served as Rear-Admiral on board *Trafalgar*, his flagship. He met many old friends in almost every ship in the squadron, and was promptly made an honorary member of the wardroom mess. An idyllic cruise around the Aegean followed, after which he travelled home via Sicily and Rome. He wasn't home for long. He and Minna went on another trip to Italy, ending up at his beloved Taormina, for a long stay. In fact, they were there for months.

Albert visited Clements and Minna in Taormina in April 1893. They were still there when news came through in the summer that Clements had been elected President of the RGS. There had been trouble over the admission of women as Fellows of the Society. The council had been in favour but the motion was rejected by the general membership, which led the incumbent, Sir ME Grant Duff, to resign. As a result, Markham, who could presumably be relied upon not to be in favour, was unanimously (according to Albert) elected as President. Women were not admitted as Fellows until January 1913.

Then, In April and May 1895, the Oscar Wilde trials took place. It made gay blood run cold, and many fled to the continent: [13]

> Every train to Dover was crowded, every steamer to Calais thronged with members of the aristocratic and leisured classes ... The truth was that the cultured aesthetes ... had been thunderstruck by the facts which the Queensberry trial had laid bare. For the first time they learned that [homosexual brothels] were under police supervision ... Never was Paris so crowded with members of the English governing classes; here was to be seen a famous ex-Minister; there the fine face of the president of a Royal society; at one table on the Café de la Paix, a millionaire recently ennobled, and celebrated for his exquisite taste in art; opposite to him a famous general.

Paris – so civilised, so adult, so basically honest – such a stark contrast to what they knew were the entrenched hypocrisies of the British establishment. As Edward Carpenter, the socialist sociological writer, commented: [14]

> The Wilde trial had done its work ... and silence must henceforth reign on sex-subjects.

The Wilde trials may have contributed to raising public awareness, but they also made it clear just how hostile society really was. But was that hostility against homosexuality *per se*, or was it against the version of it projected by Wilde? Through him, homosexuality became linked with [15]

> ... leisure, idleness, immorality, luxury, insouciance, decadence, and aestheticism.

One effect of the trials, which dominated the newspapers for months, was to bury any attempts that might have been made to promote a less-confrontational model of male homosexuality – one that emphasised individual freedom of choice and responsibility. As it was, Wilde may have set back the integrative process by alienating public opinion through his own arrogance and egocentricity. History has veered between casting Wilde as a disgusting pervert and at the other extreme as a martyr. A more nuanced view has it that he sabotaged his own case, mainly by attempting to sue Queensberry in the full knowledge that what he was accused of was basically true. He compounded the damage by being flippant and condescending in court and, by extension, to the public at large.

Throughout the trials in April and May, Markham seems to have been extra busy with events, functions, and drumming up interest and support for an Antarctic expedition. The newspapers cannot have been comfortable reading for him at this time. Wilde's speech about 'the love that dare not speak its name', and the exposition of the 'noblest form of affection that exists between an elder and a younger man', must have held a special charge for Markham. He would have been appalled, dismayed, angry and worried, and he must have feared that his own behaviour with the boys would suddenly be seen in a less innocent light.

Markham went to Norway soon after the Wilde trials, in June and July, when he would have been expected to be preparing for the Sixth International Geographical Congress, due to be held on 26 July 1895. He pleaded exhaustion from a series of events, including the commemoration of Franklin's departure 50 years previously on 19 May, and a week later the anniversary meeting of the RGS [16]

> ... and all it entailed – namely, the address, the presentation of awards, and the official reception in the evening at Prince's Hall, to which some 600 guests came.

On account of these busy and fatiguing events and [17]

> In order to obtain complete rest, and as a precaution to avoid a threatened attack of gout, he went to Norway, to prepare ... [for] the International Geographical Congress the following month.

He arrived back in London only a few days before the Congress and, according to Baughman: [18]

> ... with most of the [organisational] responsibilities falling on J. Scott Keltie, the secretary, and H.R. Mill, the librarian.

Markham's absence in Norway would have been unremarkable if it weren't for the fact that he should have been in London. A Norwegian Spa does after all seem like the perfect place to hole up while the Wilde storm passed.

On 25 May 1895, Wilde was convicted of 'gross indecency' and sentenced to two years' hard labour – a draconian sentence, even by Victorian standards. Compared with Markham, however, Wilde was positively benign. To begin with, he drew his sex objects from a pool of older boys than Markham, and many of them were rent-boys – full-, or part-time. Wilde's sex partners tended to be wiser in the ways of the world and complicit, to the extent that they received payment for their services. While this still implies abuse in terms of power relations, financial as well as social, there is a degree to which these relationships are mutually exploitative. Markham's boys, on the other hand, tended to be younger, more naive, and unlikely to have entered into monetary agreements, beyond some tacit level of debt on account of having been entertained, or bought clothes for. Even the young men who had been paid by Wilde tended to feel ashamed and humiliated. How much more so would it have been for the boys who Markham left in his wake. We can safely assume that Markham left a trail of shame, self-loathing, revulsion, guilt, and anger. And also the next generation of abusers, considering that men who were abused as boys often become abusers themselves. Camille Paglia: [19]

> In Greece the beautiful boy was always beardless, frozen in time. At manhood, he became a lover of boys himself.

Wilde's actions and poses contained at least some element of a social critique, and were justified insofar as they have in our more tolerant society been de-criminalised and embraced by most of society. The same cannot be said for Markham, however. There was no moral, ethical, social or political justification for his behaviour, as it must often have involved minors. The only intellectual context within which it could have been debated was the Hellenic ideal and conception of pederasty, but that would not have been feasible in *fin-de-siècle* England, even if one had been able to separate it from the sordid reality. In any case, Markham wasn't interested in subverting or challenging the status quo; far from it. He supported [20]

> ... the characteristic Victorian arrangement in which the existence of a whole universe of sexuality and sexual activity was tacitly acknowledged and actively participated in, while at the same time (every)one's consciousness of all this was, as far as possible, kept apart from one's larger, more general, and public consciousness of both self and society.

Hence, while Wilde languished in Reading Gaol, Markham was made a Knight Commander of the Bath, becoming, on 18 May 1896, Sir Clements Markham.

References

1   Elaine Showalter. *Sexual Anarchy,* p. 81

2   Admiral Sir Albert Markham. *The Life of Sir Clements R. Markham,* p. 259

3   *ibid.*

4   T.H. Baughman. *Pilgrims on the Ice,* p. 10

5   *ibid.*

6   Admiral Sir Albert Markham. *op. cit.,* p. 276

7   *op. cit.*, p. 128

8   Roland Huntford. *Scott and Amundsen*, p. 125

9   Admiral Sir Albert Markham. *op. cit.*, p. 285

10 Otto Geleng. *Gay Travel in Sicily*, www.strangersguide.wordpress.com

11 Richard Ellman. *Oscar Wilde*, p. 457

12 H. Montgomery Hyde. *The Other Love*, p. 112

13 *op. cit.*, pp. 152–3

14 *op. cit.*, p. 107

15 Michael S. Foldy. *The Trials of Oscar Wilde*, p. 92

16 Admiral Sir Albert Markham. *op. cit.*, p. 315

17 *ibid.*

18 T.H. Baughman. *Before the Heroes Came*, p. 58

19 Camille Paglia. *Sexual Personae*, p. 114

20 Michael S. Foldy. *op. cit.*, p. 183

8

BEARDED SCIENTISTS NOT WELCOME

The earliest recorded attempt to get close to the last great undiscovered continent was Captain Cook's, when on 17 January 1773 he and his officers and
crew in the *Resolution*, together with Captain Tobias Furneaux in the *Adventure*,
were (as far as we know) the first humans in history to cross the Antarctic Circle.
By the end of his epic voyage, Cook had circumnavigated the Southern Ocean. This
was evidence that any southern continent, the existence of which was by no means
certain at the time, was unconnected to the known world. In Cook's view, any land
south of the Antarctic Circle could not be habitable because the further south they
went, the colder it got. It was also practically inaccessible and of no economic
value, in his estimation. This verdict, together with the political, social and
economic upheavals of the late eighteenth and early nineteenth centuries in the
exploring nations, meant that attention was diverted away from the far south for
almost the next half-century. At first, discoveries in the Southern Ocean happened
only in fits and starts, sometimes more by accident than design. In 1819 Captain
William Smith was blown off course and discovered a number of islands now
known collectively as the South Shetland Archipelago. He claimed them for Britain.
In January 1820, both English Royal Navy officer Edward Bransfield, and Russian
explorer Fabian Gottlieb von Bellingshausen, claim to have been the first to lay
eyes on Antarctica itself.

Money played a crucial role in the early exploration of both Poles. The land
may not have had apparent commercial value, but the seas near the Poles teemed
with life. In the case of Antarctica, the continent is surrounded by a belt of water
now called the Antarctic Convergence, where the cold Antarctic waters meet the
warmer waters of the Sub-Antarctic, creating a zone of very high marine product-
ivity. Although the convergence phenomenon was not yet understood, it had been
noted that wildlife was abundant in those regions. American mariners were quick
to see the potential and, as early as the 1820s, some 30 to 50 sealing vessels

destroyed around 320,000 fur seals, and at least 100,000 young, due to the removal of their mothers, thus ensuring their virtual extinction in the sealers' areas of activity. [1]

It was private enterprise and the profit motive that secured funding for further forays into Antarctic waters. In 1822, a British sealing expedition was organised under the command of Captain James Weddell. Chancing upon an exceptionally warm Austral summer, he was able to sail south and across the Antarctic Circle, becoming, together with his officers and crews, only the second humans in recorded history to do so – in the process discovering what is now known as the Weddell Sea. The firm of Samuel Enderby & Sons, a whaling and sealing company based in London, also sponsored some of the early explorations of the Southern Ocean. From around 1830, in search of new sealing grounds, two of their ships circumnavigated the Antarctic Continent – in the process charting a large coastal land-mass in East Antarctica, which they named Enderby Land. Further discoveries under the auspices of the Enderby brothers include Graham Land, Sabrina Land, Kemp Land and, later, the Balleny Islands.

In 1839, Government funds and Admiralty resources were made available for an exploratory expedition led by Sir James Clark Ross, in the *Erebus* and the *Terror.* The main object was to locate the exact position of the South Magnetic Pole, of great value for accurate navigation and therefore of benefit to trade and communications. Famously, Ross and his men were the first to set eyes on the volcanoes on Ross Island, naming them after their ships, the *Erebus* and *Terror* – themselves destined to carve their undying place in history along with the Franklin Expedition. Now known as the Ross Ice Shelf, the Barrier – a name resonant with dramatic meaning – also revealed itself for the first time to human eyes.

In the main, however, purely scientific initiatives, where no lasting economic benefit to the nation were likely to accrue, attracted little funding from Government. This meant that whatever was learned about the southern oceans during this period concerned mainly the ways in which they could be commercially exploited. One exception was the *Challenger* Expedition. In a rare piece of co-operation between the Government, the Royal Navy and the Royal Society, the UK treasury generously funded the world's first major oceanographic expedition, led jointly by RN Captain George Nares, and Professor C Wyville Thomson, in charge of science. It earned Thomson a knighthood. The *Challenger*, a combined sail-and-steam vessel, was extensively refitted with state-of-the-art laboratories and equipment, and left on 21 December 1872 on a journey that would last four years and cover 68,900 miles, including crossing the Antarctic Circle. Captain George Nares commanded the vessel until he was called away to command the 1875 Arctic Expedition (discussed in Chapter 6). Thomson was in charge of five full-time scientists from a range of disciplines and nationalities, which included biologist

John Murray and chemist John Young Buchanan, both of whom were later to become two of Clements Markham's many adversaries. The *Challenger* sounded and dredged vast areas, and discovered the Mariana Trench – at about 6.8 miles deep, the greatest ocean depth known. The combined quantity of biological and physical data they brought back took almost two decades to write up, and it set the standard for the age.

Although the importance of Antarctic exploration continued to be affirmed, the scientific community found it difficult to get funding, and started to look for alternative ways to get science done in the Antarctic. Hitching a ride on a whaling ship was one possibility. Hence, when in 1892 Robert Kinnes, a Dundee whaling company owner, decided to send four steam whalers to the Antarctic in search of whales, he was approached by the RGS and persuaded to keep scientific records. Through the efforts of Benjamin Leigh Smith, an Arctic veteran, and Hugh Robert Mill, librarian of the RGS, scientific equipment was made available, and training in its use provided for the captains and officers. Kinnes also allowed Mill to suggest suitable candidates for the scientific positions, with the aim of taking out naturalists in the guise of surgeons.

William Speirs Bruce, later to lead his own expedition in the *Scotia*, and *bête noire* of Markham, was one. However, Bruce found that Captain Fairweather of the *Balaena* was far from favourable to scientific work. Bruce: [2]

> Bird specimens whether entire or as skins and skeletons, seals' skeletons, and rock specimens were all alike recklessly heaved overboard. Tow netting was naturally impracticable when I was in the boats, and unsatisfactory also during heavy weather owing to the vast amount of seal refuse thrown overboard ...

Other members of the crew wrote about being literally up to their necks in blood, and about the boats down to the gunwhales in the water with the weight of dead seals. [3]

Although they succeeded in filling their ships with seal oil and skins before going home, the whales they encountered were of a fast-swimming type, which they were not equipped to catch. This all changed when in 1894 the Norwegian Svend Foyn, the inventor of the heavy-calibre exploding harpoon, funded an expedition to the Antarctic. Stromness, the whaling station on the island of South Georgia, now best known for its connection with Shackleton, was built to service the needs of the factory ships that came after Foyn had shown what strong, fast ships could do with an array of his harpoon cannons on the forecastle. Between 1904 and 1965 some 175,250 whales were 'processed' at South Georgia stations. In the whole of Antarctica some 1.5 million animals were killed between 1904 and 1978 – a figure that does not include the slaughter up to 1904. The upshot was that wildlife was depleted in the Southern Ocean in much in the same way it had been in the Arctic. [4]

It was scientific curiosity, and the feeling that it behoved mankind to know its home planet, that provided the inspiration for Sir John Murray's address at an 1893 RGS Council meeting. His address is generally accepted to have marked the moment when the exploration of Antarctica caught the general imagination. Markham, returning from Taormina as president ('dictator', according to HR Mill) of the RGS, at once embarked on a series of minor reforms, but it was not until November of that year that he was officially installed as President, on the same occasion on which Murray gave his famous address. It inspired the Council of the RGS to appoint a committee to report on the subject of an Antarctic expedition. It was the first of the committees to be packed with Markham's allies.

Apart from Markham himself, there were old Arctics Ommanney and Nares, and Vesey Hamilton, his staunch supporter through all the subsequent debacles. Markham and Hamilton had been great friends in the Arctic in 1850. How great is perhaps suggested by their foray one evening in a boat, in calm weather, until they were hidden from the ships, spending some hours allegedly shooting ducks. They got into difficulties on account of a change in the weather, and didn't get back to the ship until noon the following day. No search party seems to have been sent out for them, probably because it was not unusual for the men to wander off from time to time, [5]

> ... some of whom, pining for forlorn damsels at home, were led to sentimentalize in retired places.

Whether or not Markham and Hamilton sentimentalised together will never be known. What is clear, however, is that Hamilton supported Markham unconditionally for the rest of his life.

Markham himself, needing to supplement his modest salary from the RGS, was busy giving lectures all over the country. Never too busy to entertain the cadets, he gave a talk on board the training ship *Conway* in Liverpool on 'The West Coast of South America, Including the Island of Juan Fernandez' – made famous by Daniel Defoe's novel *Robinson Crusoe*. As we know, he had been there himself as a teenager during his halcyon years on the Pacific Station. He was also busy setting up events and celebrations: [6]

> ... overflowing with enthusiasm like a boy, [he] used to stage a series of brilliant evening meetings ... [and] annual dinners, where Cabinet Ministers, great ambassadors, poets and social lions of every kind did honour to the Society ...

This tended to result in a flaring-up of his gout – necessitating visits to, among other places, Norway. He kept up a busy schedule and was back in London attending meetings and lecturing into May 1895, when he planned and arranged the 50-year commemoration of the Franklin Expedition and the anniversary of the RGS which, as we know, resulted in another visit to Norway, allegedly for his gout (but as a 'precaution' this time), which happily coincided with the uproar around the Wilde trials.

Fully recovered and in good voice, evidently, he delivered the welcoming address on the first evening of the Sixth International Geographical Congress, and a 10,000 (!) word opening address the next morning. The following excerpt hints at Markham's melodramatic and ultimately whimsical agenda, for which exploration provided the perfect setting: [7]

> ... the greatest geographers in all ages have devoted close attention to the study of historical geography ... as well as to the life-histories of great explorers and [illegible]. It is these narratives which invest our science with an [illegible] charm; which clothe with flesh and blood, and richest and most costly drapery, the skeletons of our surveys and triangulations. The fact that the delicate operation of swinging the seconds pendulum was performed at a height of 17,000 feet above the sea is a scientific fact and nothing more. But it cannot be detached from the heroic conduct of Captain Basevi, and from the story of his death. Besides the pendulum, we see the light tent pitched amidst the snow, the wild scene among the Himalayan peaks, and the gallant young martyr to science; and we know that, when bravely striving to rise from a bed of sickness to recommence work, he fell back and died. This is one example out of many; recorded of men of all nations. Not for itself I tell the tale. I mention it to remind us that the work by which we benefit, the knowledge upon which we pride ourselves, was won by the blood and sweat, through the trials and hardships, of our brothers, whose glorious deeds ought ever to be held in remembrance. When we discuss the results of surveys and of exploration, geographers ought never to forget that the routes so painfully and toilfully laid down are strewn with dead; and that our noblest heritage, one that we should cherish with reverence, is the record of the life stories of the great worthies of geography, telling how most of them fought their way out of obscurity, how they overcame appalling difficulties, and how many of them died in the midst of their work, martyrs to science. Without its history, which gives it the undying charm attracting old and young of all ages and countries, geography is shorn of half its interest.

It seems odd for a President of the Royal Geographical Society to feel that without the camp theatricality of young men falling back into their sickbeds, and the corpse-strewn *Vias Dolorosas*, geography was only half as interesting. It contains the genesis of the romantic martyrdom that Scott was eventually to embrace. It certainly suggests that dying for science would be lauded for its own sake – regardless of the value of the discovery – and, in Scott's case, without a dispassionate evaluation of the decisions that resulted in his and his team's deaths.

Mill's observation that Markham was an enthusiast rather than a scholar hints at the subjectivity and emotional involvement that runs through Markham's speech and through his writing and endeavours generally. He was certainly interested in geography and exploration, but those were not the things that inspired him. It is impossible to imagine him fighting tooth and nail for a ship full of scientists, ice-masters, dog-mushers and Alpine guides. Objectively, these are the kinds of professionals who should have formed the core personnel of the expedition. It is abundantly obvious what kind of explorer fired Markham's passion. Scott fitted the mould of the romantic hero almost perfectly. But few would have had the sheer effrontery to raise money on behalf of a 'national' expedition that reflected the tastes and agenda of its progenitor with so little justification.

Raising the money was never going to be easy. Markham, being very much a man of the world, will have known that talk is one thing, money another. Initial feelers put out to the First Lord of the Admiralty (Goschen) duly drew a blank. In the meantime, he had plenty of other things on his mind, including a border dispute between British Guiana and Venezuela, about which he got on his high horse and with which he involved himself. Whatever the outcome, he knew it would serve to keep his name in front of those who mattered. Hence, in May 1896, the coveted knighthood duly arrived – the official seal of approval that put his status and legitimacy beyond question.

Never too busy for cruising, partying, and the cultivation of useful contacts, by a great piece of good fortune Markham and his wife were in Norway when the return of Nansen from his epic attempt to reach the North Pole was announced. In the second-most-famous encounter in the history of exploration, Nansen had bumped into the Jackson-Harmsworth Expedition in Spitzbergen, completely by lucky accident. Clements and Minna immediately arranged to be in Christiania (Oslo) at the time of Nansen's expected arrival. They went to a dinner given at the Palace. More dinners followed, at which Markham had further opportunities to make interest with royalty, while nurturing his relationship with Nansen and firming up his Polar credentials. The next day they went on board the *Fram*, which had also returned from the ice, where they were received by Nansen and shown over the ship. He and Minna were favoured with a quiet dinner at home with Nansen and his wife the next evening before they went home.

Clements' cruising had, in latter years, taken on a more sober aspect, not being either so lengthy or leisurely as those of the past. The writing continued apace, at the same time as he continued to press for an Antarctic expedition. The overall impression during this period is that the combination of his elevation to President of the RGS, his knighthood, and the fright of the Wilde trials, catalysed a focus of mind and ambition – especially as he must have been aware that if he was ever going to achieve his dream of an Antarctic expedition, his advancing age made it a case of now or never.

The role Markham played in the creation of the British National Antarctic Expedition is unique in the history of exploration. By the end of the nineteenth century, the era of Government-sponsored expeditions was all but over. The Royal Navy was in reluctant transition, being dragged into the modern era by dynamic reformers like Admiral John 'Jacky' Fisher who, interestingly, was only 11 years younger than Markham. In all other respects, however, he might have been from another age. Reinventing and rebuilding the Navy as a modern war machine most certainly did not include dilettante forays towards the South Pole, and Fisher is known to have scorned it. Increasingly, it was the explorers themselves who raised the funds, got the backing, and provided the will, the effort and the goals for their own expeditions.

One who did so was the Anglo-Norwegian Carsten Borchgrevink, who managed to get modest funding from magazine publisher George Newnes. His *Southern Cross* Expedition of 1898–1900 was the first to overwinter on the Antarctic mainland, in a hut built for the purpose. It makes no sense to put the expedition ship out of action, and in potential danger from ice pressure, merely to provide accommodation for the ship's company. It is now felt that Borchgrevink's expedition, which did important and pioneering work in many disciplines, did not receive the recognition it deserved. This was due entirely to Markham's ire, spite, bile and unbridled jealousy of anyone who came near his precious Quadrants. Markham himself had devised the plan, which had been accepted by the international scientific community (in spite of the obvious British bias), for dividing the Antarctic into geographical quadrants; the Victoria, Ross, Weddell and Enderby Quadrants.

The Weddell and Enderby Quadrants he didn't care much about; but the Ross and Victoria Quadrants were his, and woe betide anyone who presumed to set foot on them. For the rest of his life, Markham never failed to pass up an opportunity to rubbish Borchgrevink and his achievements, with the result that the *Southern Cross* Expedition did not get the credit it deserved, and that few lessons were learnt from it.

Enthusiasm for Markham's project was at first lukewarm, and by March 1899 he had still only raised £14,000. Markham might never had have had the opportunity to bring his vision to life but for a sudden quirk of fate in the shape of a wealthy businessman, Llewellyn Longstaff, a Fellow of the RGS who, out of the blue later that March, offered £25,000 (equivalent to about £1.8 million today). That sort of money gave Markham credibility and leverage, and legitimised his vision, even to himself – those gallant young heroes, going out in style and fighting against the odds, winning through for the glory (and profit) of the Nation and the gentlemanly way of doing things. Those 'fine conceptions', as Scott would later call them.

The leadership of the British National Antarctic Expedition was by Markham's personal appointment – the first of the many anachronisms that characterised this supposedly national expedition. Markham styled himself the 'managing owner' of the *Discovery* which, although it was registered in his name, really belonged to the RGS. The Government contributed half the total cost. Today we would expect the Government to demand a say in any venture to which it contributes half the funding, it being public money. As it was, they didn't get involved until the situation had got out of hand, almost four years later, with the *Discovery* stuck in 12 feet of ice on the coast of Antarctica. Markham must have seemed like a safe pair of hands at the time, backed up as he was (at first) by the Royal Society, as well as the Presidency of the RGS. Not to mention his special contacts in the Royal Navy.

A special Ship Committee was appointed, consisting of several admirals and sometime Arctic explorers; while the Chief Naval Constructor, WE Smith, prepared the plans and supervised the construction. [8] According to Markham himself, [9] he had been scouting for a potential leader from as early as 1887, when the famous St Kitts boat race took place. He certainly took note of Scott, among others. At the time, however, Antarctic exploration seemed the last thing on his mind. It has nevertheless passed into legend, encouraged by Markham's own assertions, that it was then that Scott was earmarked as a potential Antarctic expedition leader. It is hard to see why winning a cutter race would mark anyone out as a future Polar explorer but, as we have seen, Markham had his own agenda and criteria for selection. Scott represented what Camille Paglia [10] calls the 'Billy Budd topos', an

> ... enduring class of homosexual taste ... fresh, active, and ephebic.

He is likely to have been comparatively naive, not having been to public school. These qualities, together with Scott's earnest wish to please, doubtlessly made a charming package.

Markham put youth above all other considerations and regarded inexperience as a virtue. His justification for what should be seen as a fetishistic preference, considering the irrationality and hypocrisy embedded in his criteria, was that [11]

> Elderly men are not accessible to new ideas and have not the energy and capacity necessary to meet emergencies. How can novel forms of effort be expected from stiff old organisms hampered by experience!

However, for all his talk about the importance of young men being open to new ideas, in practice Markham made sure the young men under his control were imbued with his own philosophies and ways of doing things – unable or unwilling to see that those philosophies and practices dated back half a century, and that he himself blocked 'novel forms of effort' from gaining ground. He had his supporters. In cosy familiarity and aligned with the *eminences grises* of (North) Polar exploration, reminiscing over the port, mutually reinforcing each others' biases, the old guard conceded new ideas grudgingly, or not at all. Huntford: [12]

> The really able men were excluded from the [Old Arctics] clique, and carefully avoided the R.G.S. In other words, the R.G.S. was a typical moribund stronghold of institutionalized mediocrity.

It is generally agreed that William Speirs Bruce would have been one of the more rational choices – if not to lead, then to at least take an important part in the conduct and aims of any national Antarctic expedition worthy of the name. With Markham at the helm, this was never going to happen. Bruce wasn't Navy, and had none of Scott's charisma and looks. He was a serious scientist who made Polar research his life work. By 1900 he had already been on the *Balaena* to the Antarctic, he was on the Jackson-Harmsworth Expedition to Spitzbergen, on the *Blencathra* to Novaya Zemlya, and twice to Spitzbergen with the then Prince of Monaco (a keen oceanographer). He had trained himself to live in cold and isolated conditions on top of Ben Nevis, and was an enthusiastic skier. He impressed colleagues and patrons alike with his enthusiasm and indefatigable perseverance.

Hugh Robert Mill, then librarian of the RGS, relates the story of how Bruce got to go on the *Blencathra:* he (Mill) was offered a place on the yacht, owned by the Scot Andrew Coats, who was later to help fund Bruce's *Scotia* Expedition. Markham refused to give him leave, telling him that 'The proper place of a librarian is in the library.' As a result, Mill offered his place to Bruce, observing: [13]

> That insatiable naturalist seized the chance, and so the retention of the librarian in the library ultimately cost Markham the mortification of seeing a rival in the field to his cherished idea of one great national Antarctic expedition which then possessed his mind – it was Bruce who later led the rival expedition.

There is more than a hint of *schadenfreude* in this – not surprising, given the meanness of Markham's decision and its condescending justification.

Markham felt slighted when Bruce gave the results of work he'd done on Spitzbergen to the Scottish Geographical Society instead of his own RGS. Mill wrote to Bruce: [14]

> You are too unworldly, and have too high an idea of the unselfishness of the scientific societies. The RGS quite naturally wished to

have the first news of your Arctic work and as you went in my place
I had expected you would have given the paper to the society that
would not let me go! However I know you did not mean to slight the
RGS and I still take pleasure in seeing the Scottish Society getting a
good thing. But you don't realize how necessary it is to keep on
cordial terms with such powerful corporations as the RGS if you
hope to enlist their aid in helping you to subsequent expeditions.

Bruce was a keen Scottish Nationalist, however, so unworldliness probably
doesn't entirely cover it.

Bruce wrote to Markham in March 1899, [15] stating his qualifications and
experience – presenting his CV, in effect, and offering his services as a scientist on
the proposed *Discovery* Expedition. Speak [16] states that it was unlikely that there
was anyone else better qualified. A less-than-enthusiastic two-line acknowledgement was all Bruce got back from Markham, after which he heard nothing for
almost a year. Markham's lack of interest in someone with Bruce's qualifications
is very telling. Bruce represented that body of scientists who were interested in
meteorological and oceanographic observations, and the origins of the great global
energy systems that create climate and weather. But Markham was indifferent to
Earth sciences and dismissive of those who carried them out.

Bruce was a committed scientist – a bearded academic, the presence of whom
would have made the costumes, dresses and make-up the BNAE took to Antarctica
seem absurd and embarrassing. And it is hard to imagine Bruce in all seriousness
acquiescing to the heraldic pennants Markham insisted on burdening the sledging
teams with. But Markham had underestimated Bruce. Having belatedly approached him via Reginald Koettlitz, two letters from Bruce arrived in quick succession.
Having put him on the back burner all those months ago, Markham got the shock
of his life when he read the first one, dated 21 March 1900: [17]

> Dear Sir Clements Markham
>
> I have to thank you for the message you have conveyed me through
> Dr. Koettlitz. I have already lodged my application to become a
> member of the British Antarctic Expedition, which you were good
> enough to acknowledge on the 17th April last year. I forget if I gave
> any names as references so I now mention seven [*sic*] gentlemen
> who know me and whom I am asking to act as references, viz:
>
> H.S.H. The Prince of Monaco
> Sir John Murray, K.C.B., F.R.S.
> Dr. Alexander Buchan, F.R.S.
> Dr. Fridtjof Nansen
> Mr. Andrew Coats
> Mr. Alfred Harmsworth

I may say I am not without hopes of being able to raise sufficient capital whereby I could take out a second British ship to explore in the Antarctic Regions.

I remain,

Yours very truly

Wm. S. Bruce

Bruce's revenge for having been ignored! Not just the Prince of Monaco, Murray and the others, but Fridtjof! Markham's own Fridtjof! And the possibility of his own expedition! Markham tried to restrain himself but didn't quite succeed: 18

Dear Mr. Bruce

I am very sorry to hear that an attempt is to be made in Edinburgh to divert funds from the Antarctic Expedition in order to get up a rival enterprise. Such a course will be most prejudicial to the Expedition which is much in need of more funds. A second ship is not in the least required. It is not true that the whole area is not provided for. If the Germans do not undertake the Weddell Quadrant, it will be undertaken by our Expedition as a first object. I do not understand why this mischievous rivalry should have been started, but I trust that you will not connect yourself with it.

There is a suggestion that Markham is in denial of the fact that Bruce is talking about his own expedition. Either that, or it is a rhetorical device that bypasses Bruce personally, and in doing so gives Markham permission to be as accusatory and unreasonable as he likes. In his outrage about what he clearly perceived as a queering of his pitch, Bruce's likely success in raising capital for his own venture is interpreted as an attempt to divert funds. Quite apart from the implication that his own expedition is the only true one, and has a prior right to all funds, Markham is suggesting that Bruce is actively conspiring to take away money that would otherwise have gone to THE Antarctic Expedition, and that Bruce is setting up a rival enterprise. Bruce was not a game-player in that sense. He was human, and he may have quietly relished getting his own back on Markham – but rivalry was not what motivated him. Besides, if Antarctic exploration itself had been Markham's passion he would have welcomed Bruce's efforts. Instead, he throws a tantrum, in the same way he did with Borchgrevink.

In March 1900, when this letter was written, the money had already been raised and the *Discovery* was under construction. It was therefore not true that Bruce was prejudicing the BNAE. The suggestion that he was, was a completely unjustified and inexcusable guilt-trip on Bruce, and a belittlement of what he was trying to do. So far as a second ship was concerned, we are in confused territory. Was Markham suggesting that a second ship was not required for his own expedition, or for exploration of Antarctica generally? In the first case, it did not take long to transpire that a second ship was in fact essential. In the second, the suggestion that *Discovery* alone was enough to explore Antarctica was patently ridiculous. It is a defiant and rejecting statement, out of touch with reality, and evidence that his emotions were running away with him.

To reiterate Markham: [19]

> ... if the Germans do not undertake the Weddell Quadrant, it will be undertaken by our Expedition as a first object.

There was never the slightest intention that the *Discovery* should go to the Weddell Sea, or anywhere near it, whether or not the Germans planned to go there. 'The Germans', with whom Bruce was also in contact, sensibly took the view that there was room for more than one ship in an entire quarter of Antarctica. It had always been Markham's intention to go to his Victoria Quadrant, which is the nearest to Australia and New Zealand. Much of it had already been discovered by Ross, and was known to contain potential landing places and access to the interior, making it the best starting place that had yet been discovered for both the geographical and the magnetic Poles. Markham's second choice was the Ross Quadrant. He had decided on all this even before his meeting with the leader of the German *Gauss* Expedition, Erich von Drygalski, in September and October 1899, at which both agreed that the English would undertake the Victoria and Ross Quadrants. [20] Markham: [21]

> ... I do not understand why this mischievous rivalry should have been started, but I trust that you will not connect yourself with it.

It is as though he has not read Bruce's letter properly. Or perhaps by pretending it's all someone else's doing, he avoids actually calling Bruce a 'mischievous rival' to his face. Bruce's backers, who were shown the letter, must have felt a mixture of outrage and disbelief at this calumny. Markham was his own worst enemy. According to Speak, [22] the letter alienated many members of the joint committee of the RGS and the Royal Society, and strengthened support for Bruce. It is inappropriately self-referential for Markham to think that it's all about him, and that whoever is behind the alleged rivalry is deliberately trying to sabotage *his* expedition. He sees it as a pernicious attempt to steal a march on him by means of intrigue and betrayal. At the same time, the letter is an emotionally infantile tirade, unworthy of someone in Markham's position. It suggests an almost pathological need for control and a concomitant level of insecurity. He knew that the claims of science were the chink in his armour, and he was hypersensitive to the danger they posed to his plans.

There was nothing Bruce could have said that would have satisfied Markham (except perhaps a contrite admission of wrong-doing and an unconditional withdrawal), but he tried to be reasonable. Bruce: [23]

... I do not understand why you should look upon my Expedition to the Weddell Sea as a rival to the British Antarctic Expedition. If my friends are prepared to give me money to carry out my plans, I do not see why I should not accept it, neither do I see why I should not accept the patronage and advice of any of the scientific societies, in the event of my departure.

There are at present no less than five Scientific expeditions wintering in the very much explored Arctic Regions, working in friendly co-operation. I do not see how there cannot be room for my small expedition in addition to the German and British Expeditions, in the very much unexplored Antarctic regions. With regard to a second ship not being in the least required, this is a point upon which authorities differ, there are several who maintain that a second ship is highly desirable.

I am very sorry that you should look upon my efforts as mischievous rivalry. Perhaps my letter of the 24th inst, which has crossed yours will show that I am not working as a rival.

Ever, Yours very truly

Wm. S. Bruce

Markham's reply is again a mixture of spin, plaintive accusation and moral blackmail. Bruce wrote across it 'I wasted over a year with no remit'. Markham: [24]

... as you are a volunteer for the Antarctic Expedition, and as you know I was doing my best to get you appointed, I certainly had a right to think that you would not take such a step as you have done, without at least consulting me ...

The Weddell Quadrant has been fully provided for. If the Germans do not undertake it, as I understand from Drygalski, certainly the British Expedition will ...

Of course a whaler, fitted out for scientific work, may be useful; but it would be far better to have one expedition well supplied with funds, than two insufficiently supplied and I regret your action – suddenly sprung on me without a word of consultation.

And, in May 1900, still hot with indignation: [25]

When I said a second ship was not wanted, I intended to refer to an independent ship. Of course a second ship for the expedition would be, in the opinion of many people a great advantage; but I am afraid that is not what you intend. You will cripple the National Expedition which is actually on foot, in order to get up a scheme for yourself.

It was of course not true that Markham had been doing his best to get Bruce appointed. The appointments were not up to anyone else, and Markham had shown no interest in Bruce for nearly a year. He did not have a right to be consulted, especially not after having given Bruce the brush-off. He repeats the lie that he was planning to go to the Weddell Quadrant, together with the absurd statement that it had been 'fully provided for'. The letter ends with a parting-shot of childish resentment and a completely unjustified accusation. Today, we would expect a greater level of emotional maturity from someone in Markham's position.

Markham felt personally betrayed by Bruce. It is clear evidence that the 'British National Antarctic Expedition' was entirely personal to Markham. The irrational hatred he felt towards Bruce is evidenced by the lifelong denial of the well-deserved RGS Polar Medal to Bruce and his team for their Antarctic work, for which Markham is widely held responsible, and which is said to have contributed to Bruce's mental deterioration afterwards. It was an abuse of his position, and an inexcusable piece of personal spite.

He wrote to Bruce again in February 1901, eight months later, in a markedly conciliatory vein, possibly prompted by Minna, in view of the fact that he never forgave Bruce: [26]

> Dear Mr. Bruce
>
> I am afraid I replied rather angrily when you announced your expedition to me: for I feared that your proceedings would divert funds from the national expedition which was and is much in need. But I can now see things from your point of view; and wish you success. Mr. Armitage tells me that you have been married, and I send my congratulations on the happy event.
>
> I shall be at Dundee in March for the launching of the *Discovery;* and I hope I shall see you then ...

Markham's defensiveness and over-reaction are in sharp contradiction to his commanding exterior. The tears do not seem very far away. A more mature person, while they may have felt something of what Markham felt, would not have allowed themselves to get so carried away. Nevertheless, experience must have taught him that it often got results. In the committee wrangles that were to come, he used his temper to shock and intimidate adversaries. In fact, there were occasions when the meetings of what were supposed to be the learned societies deteriorated into unseemly and upsetting shouting matches. But he got what he wanted.

References

1   Sir Clements R. Markham. *The Lands of Silence*, p. 400

2   Peter Speak. *William Speirs Bruce*, p. 35

3   Hugh Robert Mill. *The Siege of the South Pole*, p. 375

4   [Unattributed writer]. Whaling – South Georgia Heritage Trust, www.sght.org

5   Lieut. Sherard Osborn. *Stray Leaves from an Arctic Journal*, p. 76

6   Hugh Robert Mill. *Hugh Robert Mill*, p. 88

7   John Scott Keltie and Hugh Robert Mill (eds.). *Report of the Sixth International Geographical Congress*, p. 19

8   Captain Robert F. Scott. *The Voyage of the Discovery*, p. 32

9   Sir Clements Markham. *Antarctic Obsession*, pp. 3–4

10 Camille Paglia. *Sexual Personae*, p. 115

11 Reginald Pound. *Scott of the Antarctic*, p. 18

12 Roland Huntford. *Scott and Amundsen*, p. 120

13 Hugh Robert Mill. *op. cit.*, p. 141

14 T.H. Baughman. *Before the Heroes Came*, p. 118

15 Peter Speak. *op. cit.*, p. 69

16 *op. cit.*, p. 70

17 *op. cit.*, p. 71

18 *op. cit.*, p. 72

19 *ibid.*

20 Sir Clements R. Markham. *op. cit.*, p. 11

21 Peter Speak. *ibid.*

22 *ibid.*

23 *op. cit.*, p. 73

24 *ibid.*, pp. 73–4

25 *ibid.*

26 *op. cit.*, pp. 74–5

9

GERRYMANDERING

Markham: [1]

The selection of the Commander of the Expedition involved the most important decision. I had never forgotten the cutter race at St Kitts, but had followed Scott's career, and on February 24th 1897 I had the pleasure of meeting him at dinner on board the *Empress of India* at Vigo. On June 5th 1899 there was a remarkable coincidence. Scott was then Torpedo Lieutenant of the *Majestic*. I was just sitting down to write to my old friend Captain Egerton of the *Majestic* about him, when he was announced. He came to volunteer to command the Expedition.

In February 1897 Clements had, once again, been a guest of the ever-obliging Albert – this time on a cruise with the Channel Squadron, which included Scott's ship, the *Empress of India*. Scott was ten years older than he had been that sunny day off St Kitts, when he had first been introduced to Markham. Markham: [2]

He was then 18, and I was much struck by his intelligence, information, and the charm of his manner. My experience taught me that it would be years before an expedition would be ready, and I believed that Scott was the destined man to command it.

We have to take this with a pinch of salt. We know that at that time it was a borderline delinquent young man called Tommy Smyth who figured most prominently in Markham's voluminous notes on the youths he befriended. Markham continues: [3]

At Vigo we were thrown together again, when my young friend was torpedo lieutenant of the *Empress of India,* and I was more than ever impressed by his evident vocation for such a command.

The *Empress of India* was a 'backward' ship, according to Scott, but fun, as suggested by the theatricals on board. Forty-five years after Markham himself trod the boards in 'Bombastes Furioso', it was again on the programme – this time with Scott as the principal lady. Scott wrote to his mother: [4]

> A gorgeous golden wig complete with a complete dress made on board, stays, silk stockings, buckled shoes, sleeves with lace – splendid – you should see – and also you should hear – the rich falsetto voice.

His mother may not have been entirely impressed, but she might have reminded herself that the Navy had an established tradition of cross-dressing. It is entirely plausible that Markham was present at the performance. Something certainly seems to have galvanised him. According to Albert, Clements, on his return to England, set to work vigorously raising money for the expedition. In fact, if theatricals were in the planning stages when Markham was with the squadron, he would naturally have been involved in them. Perhaps it was actually Markham who suggested that Scott should take the part. It certainly seems out of character for a diffident and reserved officer like Scott to have put himself forward at all, let alone for a female part. Certainly Scott impressed Markham with his 'evident vocation', and it can have had nothing to do with leadership ability or Polar knowledge.

Scott was predominantly heterosexual, as is suggested by his occasional infatuations with women (and the apparent absence of the same with men), and his later sexual fascination and love for Kathleen. But he was also emotionally vulnerable and, according to Apsley Cherry-Garrard [5]

> ... cried more easily than any man I have ever known.

Although well presented, his posture suggested an obedient energy held in, rather than an anarchic muscularity wanting to break out. The comparatively modest social standing of his family was a big factor in Scott's diffident bearing and lack of presumption. As a young man he was comparatively naive, upright, and intelligent without being particularly clever. If he knew about Markham's sexuality, there would have been nothing in Scott's outward demeanour to suggest it. On a semi-conscious level, however, he must have been flattered by Markham's evident interest, and probably responded to it in a semi-flirtatious way. He certainly would not have wanted to put Markham off. In a world in which 'interest' and string-pulling were crucial aids to advancement, an ambitious young officer like Scott is sure to have nurtured the connection.

He had, in any case, to manage his relationship with Markham with tact and discretion – as a delicate *pas-de-deux,* as Markham might have put it. Although it is unlikely that their relationship was ever overtly sexual, Scott was still a homo-erotically inspired choice. Markham idealised and idolised him, evidently believing that he was the man most likely to bring his dream to fruition, whatever that meant. As second-in-command for the *Discovery*, Markham chose 'Charlie' Royds whose praises he sang on account of his resemblance to a young Wyatt Rawson, the 'gallant' Arctic officer in the expedition of 1875–6. Clearly another appointment inspired by romance and nostalgia. Royds, although a big and capable man, had a distinctly 'girlish' side.

Scott had seen Markham in action among the boys in the Caribbean, and had himself been subject to his attentions. He must have had an inkling, especially after the Wilde trials, when [6]

> ... relationships previously considered innocent might suddenly be subject to suspicions of impropriety and unspoken doubts.

Markham responded to Scott's soft, boyish qualities, and instinctively sensed that behind the mask of the competent young officer there were was anxiety, doubt, and pathos. Markham's Greek ideal of a relationship was probably destined to be forever Platonic and to be somewhat characterised by [7]

> ... a wistful yearning which he had never found absent from any homosexual relationships.

Especially unrequited ones. According to Camille Paglia, however, 'Tutelary relationships are filled with sexual ambiguities' [8] – and in this case they undoubtedly were, however sublimated.

Most Scott biographers accept Scott's version of events concerning that fateful meeting on the Buckingham Palace Road on 5 June 1899. It was a couple of months after the £25,000 offer from Longstaff (see Chapter 8), and a few weeks before the offer from Government, but by this time Markham was confident that an offer would be forthcoming. Markham himself would have us believe that he did nothing to encourage Scott to apply; claiming instead, that Scott, out of the blue, and on his own initiative called at his house one day, volunteering to command the expedition. Scott's own version is very different. According to him: [9]

> ... I was spending my short leave in London, and chancing one day to walk down the Buckingham Palace Road, I espied Sir Clements on the opposite pavement, and naturally crossed, and as naturally turned and accompanied him to his house. That afternoon I learned for the first time that there was such a thing as a prospective Antarctic expedition; two days later I wrote applying to command it ...

Neither Scott nor Markham can be trusted to be telling the truth. Close reading of Scott's *The Voyage of the Discovery* reveals many half-truths, omissions and spin; and as far as Markham's respect for the truth is concerned, it was contingent on his advantage. Oddly, Huntford takes Markham at his word: [10]

> In retrospect, Scott maintained – against the evidence of Sir Clements Markham's diary – that he had met Sir Clements by chance in the street ...

Markham's diary isn't evidence of anything. Clements wrote his diaries with an eye to posterity, as is shown by Albert's biography of him. As Scott was also later to show, diaries can be extremely useful for manipulating history.

The differences in Scott's and Markham's accounts means that plausible answers have to be found in likelihoods and motivations. Markham certainly had a motive for obfuscating events around Scott's application. It was a bit rich even for him to have gone ahead unilaterally by pre-emptively engaging a leader without so much as a word to other interested parties, notably the RS, the Admiralty, and even his own Council at the RGS. Claiming that the initiative had come from Scott would have allowed him to deny that he had taken that particular liberty. And it is not so very far-fetched to imagine that Markham was loitering in Buckingham Palace Road with the express intention of bumping into Scott. Markham had eyes and ears at the Admiralty – Vesey Hamilton was around at the time, and it would have been very easy for him to have found out Scott's likely movements. He knew Scott was staying with his mother and sisters in Royal Hospital Road, and he knew his route to the Admiralty from there would take him along Buckingham Palace Road. It is entirely plausible that Markham was practised in pick-ups and solicitations, and knew how to catch someone's eye as if by accident.

Scott biographers, by and large, skim over the discrepancies between Scott's and Markham's accounts – too ready to find excuses for Markham by saying he wrote the diary years later and that his memory was playing him tricks. It is inconceivable that Markham, having made his decision on Scott in Vigo, would have sat at home, leaving it to chance whether he would come calling or not. At the same time, it seems unlikely that Scott had no inkling about the expedition. But if he did, would he have considered himself a candidate for the leadership? Unlikely, one might think, without encouragement.

On the other hand, if Huntford is right, and if we accept that the blind (and blinding) ambition later evident in Scott was already there, then hints would have been enough, and lack of qualifications brushed aside. Spotting Markham on the other side of the road may have tipped him into taking the plunge into what he had dared to think might be possible, given Markham's interest in him personally, and in the Navy in general. But the interruption to his career would have been a worry for Scott, and he would have wanted assurances about his continued progress up the promotion ladder. Markham must have reassured him on that account. He had his contacts, he knew who made the decisions, and he had plenty of leverage.

In *The Voyage of the Discovery* Scott deals rather summarily with the circumstances of his application. Why? The matter is unlikely to have been quite as simple and straightforward as he claims. If he had indeed been approached by Markham, he might have been wary of what might be expected of him in return, and a fair amount of equivocation is likely to have taken place. As far as his public image was concerned, his association with Markham, especially in the role of protégé, would require deft management. There would be those, then as now, who could see nothing untoward in the ostensibly kind old man, but there must also have been knowing eyes weighing things in the balance. Scott's summary treatment could be interpreted as a symbolic way of giving short shrift to suspicions of an unseemly nature. Nevertheless, he must have been flattered and not a little astounded to find himself earmarked for the command of a national expedition. Any worries he might have had about his lack of experience and his modest social and Naval rank would have been assuaged by Markham's soothing reassurances.

Their differing accounts probably covers a concatenation of nods and winks, circumstance, coincidence and opportunism, but in the end there was only one decision-maker – Markham. In the death-tent Scott wrote to Kathleen: [11]

> ... I haven't time to write to Sir Clements tell him I thought much of him & never regretted him putting me in command of the Discovery
>
> ...

This in itself suggests that Markham was the prime mover in Scott's appointment; a view confirmed by Scott's passive position *vis-à-vis* Markham throughout the preparatory stages. In fact, Markham took him in hand from the beginning; giving detailed instructions, hints and warnings, and bolstering his confidence. Markham writes to Scott: [12]

> I very well remember the way you won the service cutter race at St Kitz [*sic*] when you were in the "Rover", and with the same combination of good judgement, prudence, and determination you will win again.

Instructions followed thick and fast about who to 'make interest with' and get on side, which included the Admirals Kerr, Hoskins, M'Clintock, Vesey Hamilton – and of course Albert Markham, with whom the ground had already been prepared, unsurprisingly. Also, regarding George Egerton, who was Scott's commanding officer at the time, Markham wrote to Scott: [13]

> The great thing will be to talk it over with Captain Egerton and get him to recommend you. His opinion will carry most weight ...

In the beginning, the whole thing must have seemed somewhat unreal to Scott; coming, as it did, in the context of his day job, which continued for almost another year. In the meantime, Markham may have had his leader, but he still needed to convince the world at large – and specifically the Council of the Royal Geographical Society – that Scott was the right man for the job. He didn't decide to bring in the Royal Society until later, and he was confident that the Admiralty would pose no problem. His first aim, therefore, was to 'sell' Scott to the RGS. This was vastly aided by the fact that there was a preponderance of old admirals on its ruling Council. It meant that they were biased in favour of a Navy man, which in turn meant that the battle was more than half won from the beginning. All that was needed was for Scott to give them the final nudge on his own behalf. As in the course of his job he mixed in Admiralty circles, he was in a position to do so.

On Markham's instructions, therefore, he started to 'make interest' with the right people, and schmooze his way around the relevant circles. He was good at it: he said the right things, he looked the part, and he had charisma. It is well attested that he could be utterly charming when in the right frame of mind. To the 'Old Arctics', and old-school thinkers into whose hands Scott's fate had been randomly pitched, these were important qualities. The man was, after all, going to represent his country in a high-profile role, and had therefore to look and sound right, and know how to conduct himself.

Scott's appointment wasn't the only matter on which Markham had made unilateral decisions. As far back as 1897 he had written a set of formal and detailed Instructions covering the activities, personnel, priorities and conduct of his ex-pedition. He resented and denied legitimacy to any and all alterations or differences of opinion. He made out the Royal Society to be a bunch of tiresome and irrelevant nincompoops, who should have known better than to cause him inconvenience. He found himself having to deal with them, however, which he did by a nightmare process of attrition, fired by a *joie-de-guerre* which would have been entertaining if it hadn't been so obnoxious and overbearing.

The RGS did know better than to mount a serious opposition to its President. The Royal Society, on the other hand, feeling they had a responsibility to science, had their own ideas, which Markham resented from the beginning: [14]

> In the end of 1897 I made another serious mistake by inviting the Royal Society to join us … It was a fatal error, but I did so under the impression that the great name of the Royal Society would bring in funds. This was a complete mistake. The coalition has been a source of worry, delays, friction and danger; and no good whatever.

Clearly, the RS had been brought in purely to serve Markham's personal ends. And in spite of his claim, it had of course contributed to the success of his campaign by lending it weight and prestige.

Never having had the slightest intention of involving anyone else in his plans, the Royal Society had outlived its usefulness as soon as the money had been raised.

For the first few months, however, Markham kept up the pretence that matters were up for debate. A large Joint Committee, numbering 33 in total (17 for the RS and 16 for the RGS), was formed. [15] It met for the first time on 26 June 1899, exactly three weeks after Scott had allegedly surprised him by coming to see him about the expedition – or, in Scott's version, encountered him by accident in Buckingham Palace Road. Markham drew up the Minute, taking care [16]

> ... to state exactly each subject that was referred to it, so that when all were dealt with the functions of the Joint Committee would cease.

If they hadn't known it from the start, the Royal Society will quickly have realised that they were there simply to rubber-stamp Markham's decisions. Unsurprisingly, the squabbles (his word) began almost immediately. As a result, there must have been those who experienced a sudden shrivelling of enthusiasm, and so there was little opposition when Markham proposed the formation of an Executive Committee that would thrash out the issues before they were put to the Joint Committee. This Executive Committee, destined to be only the first of a long series of Committees, numbered four only, and was made up of himself and Vesey Hamilton for the RGS and Captain Tizard and Professor Poulton for the RS, with himself as Chairman. Their proposals were still to be approved by the Joint Committee, however, as well as being referred back to the Councils of both Societies.

Captain Tizard, Assistant Hydrographer to Sir W Wharton (Hydrographer of the Navy), is described by Markham as 'Wharton's jackal', as 'the villain of the piece', and having 'a most forbidding countenance'. Markham: [17]

> Good at his work and with some ability, he is very narrow minded ... One would have thought that a worse appointment could not have been made. But the R.S. officials were equal to the occasion. Poulton was then a close friend of Sir Michael Foster. He had been made a Professor at Oxford, his subject being mimicry of butterflies. He is a dull stupid man, with a genius for blundering, and totally ignorant on every subject that could possibly come before the Committee.

In fact, Professor Poulton was an evolutionary biologist, who is remembered for his pioneering work at a time when the idea of natural selection was denigrated by the scientific community. Wrongly, as it turned out. But why Poulton? It played directly into Markham's hands, as his area of expertise seemed so irrelevant to Antarctic exploration and tailor made for Markham's ridicule. Maybe the RS just didn't anticipate having to deal with a man who was still part schoolboy. Ironically, however, it was evolutionary biology that inspired Wilson's later quest for Emperor penguin embryos – in the process, together with Birdie and Cherry, undergoing one of the greatest feats of endurance in the history of exploration: *The Worst Journey in the World,* immortalised by Apsley Cherry-Garrard.

The lengths Markham went to in order to lay the expedition wholly and un-conditionally at Scott's feet are extraordinary. To some extent this must have been personal; but perhaps more importantly, Scott's absolute command meant that the expedition was going to be a Naval affair throughout, with Naval ways, Naval values, and Naval pastimes. In the beginning, Markham pretended to be amenable to a scientifically orientated venture. According to him, he had himself introduced Professor Gregory (Head of the Geology Department at the British Museum, and an experienced explorer) into the fray, originally because he had been asked to write a testimonial for him. While writing, it occurred to him that Dr Gregory D.Sc. [*sic*] might 'do' for the post of Director of the Civilian [*sic*] Staff. According to Poulton, however, Gregory was nominated by the Royal Society on the basis of his qualifications and ice experience. Poulton further states that, in the opinion of British scientific men, no one was more competent; and that with as free a hand as English law would permit, Antarctic science directed by Professor Gregory was bound to produce great results. [18]

Markham, as ever orientated towards the personal, describes Gregory as [19]

> ... a little man with a very low voice, always nervously pulling his moustache, and does not inspire confidence ...

Gregory did not help his case by immediately leaving for Australia, and writing to Poulton from Port Said a long letter in which he set out his ideas and proposals for the expedition. Markham, who was shown the letter, wrote irritably: [20]

> It was the letter of a very self sufficient person, and made me more doubtful.

Nothing could have been better designed to raise Markham's hackles than a suggestion of proprietorial control over even part of the expedition.

Over the next few months Markham developed an antipathy towards Gregory which, by January 1901, led him to the resolve that [21]

> ... under no circumstances, should Dr Gregory be a member of the Antarctic Expedition.

That it had everything to do with Gregory's attitude, rather than fitness, is confirmed by Markham's comment [22] in a letter to Scott dated 10 January 1901 that

> The impudence of Gregory's draft has taken my breath away.

It is easy to imagine Royal Society ire at the suggestion that they had been used as window-dressing and to give Markham's campaign scientific gravitas. Although some did not have the stomach for a fight, there was a core group who were sufficiently aggravated to mount a concerted opposition; the 'Hydrographic Clique', as Markham called them, tending to see the opposition in terms of the intrigues and conspiracies at which he himself was so adept. When Markham received word from George Goschen (First Lord of the Admiralty), consenting to the appointment of Scott (and Royds), Tizard remonstrated – predictably angry that Markham had gone behind everybody's back, and was now presenting them with a *fait accompli*. He promptly received a letter from Markham '... giving him a piece of my mind'. [23]

The introduction of Scott was finely calculated and managed in two stages. To begin with, Markham proposed that Scott would simply 'command the expedition', leaving it vague as to what exactly that meant. It seems that both Societies assumed he would captain the ship, in equal partnership with the Scientific Director. After all, Markham's averred intention had originally been to create an identical set-up to that of the *Challenger*, where that had been the case. But this was already too much for many. An obscure torpedo lieutenant, with no relevant experience? Scott had never seen an iceberg in his life. He had never had sole command of a ship. He had no experience of leading men in difficult circumstances. Outrage must have followed incredulity. Hence, when Markham moved the appointments of Scott and Royds at the Joint Committee meeting on 4 May 1900, in his words, 'a regular row began'. Professor Rucker of the RS got up and delivered 'a carefully prepared attack'. It boiled down to the fact that so far, Markham had got his way with everything, and was now also trying to exclude the RS from his correspondence with the Government. Rucker proposed that any letters to the Treasury and Admiralty should be countersigned by both Presidents. Markham's letter to Tizard, 'giving him a piece of my mind' was also read out. If it still exists, it should make entertaining reading. Markham says he [24]

> ... did not condescend to reply to all this insolence ...

Poulton, in a letter to Gregory dated 6 May 1900, marked 'Private', wrote: [25]

> Clements M is terribly difficult to work with. We had a fearful row last Weds & if he had not climbed down the R.S (Royal Society) would have withdrawn from the whole thing & the Treasury would probably have withdrawn their vote & the whole thing comes to an end. The other three members of the Exec C (executive council) all agreed that they wanted a naval commander, I always doubted. Well C.M (Clements Markham) on this alone wrote to the Admiralty what he says is a private letter & also a letter suggesting names no one else had ever heard of even as standing. Well Goschen took his letter as official (no doubt it was on RGS paper) and appointed the men – A Lieut Scott of the Majestic & a Lieut Royds as second in command. He brought this before the Ex C as an accomplished fact.

The impasse that resulted was broken by the suggestion that a Committee of Naval Officers, who were also on the Joint Committee, should settle the Scott issue. This did not satisfy Markham. He says himself that a more futile or unpractical suggestion could not have been made. It was indeed a waste of everybody's time. The 'Hydrographic Clique' (as opposed to his own 'regular line' officers, which comprised mostly the usual suspects) strove to secure the position for the hydrographic department with what Markham describes as 'obstinate perversity'.

Two meetings of this Committee took place, with M'Clintock in the chair. At the first meeting with Wharton and Tizard, Markham rubbished the candidates they put forward as alternatives to Scott, and issued a threat to the RS to the effect that if Wharton was allowed to continue the deadlock 'they would be responsible'. But, he said, 'they could do nothing with him' (meaning Wharton). It is almost comical the way Markham acts as though the objectors are the problem, and that he is the one who has reason on his side. In the end, M'Clintock held a second meeting, 'when both Wharton and Tizard heard some home truths'. Clearly, all mature, civilised, rational behaviour had gone out the window. According to Markham, some of the clique were 'ashamed', and stayed away. Ashamed? It seems implausible that anyone would have been ashamed of trying to resist Markham's appointment of Scott. Whatever their reasons for staying away, however, it worked for Markham. The 'Hydrographic Clique' was out-voted, as a result of which Scott was proposed at the next Joint Committee, on 25 May 1900, and [26]

... unanimously recommended to be Commander of the Expedition.

Much as some will have fervently prayed that matters were thereby settled, they were destined to be disappointed. The ordeal had only just begun. Next came what Markham entitled 'The attempt to wreck the Expedition'. It was the fight by the RS to retain Gregory's status as Scientific Director. Gregory assumed he would be in charge of a landing party, while the ship would continue working at sea, under the command of the captain. It was a reasonable assumption, and an arrangement that made sense. To Markham, however, anything other than the full implementation of his plans – and his plans only – was tantamount to wrecking the expedition. Really, he should always have called it *my* expedition, but that would have been too blatant. It was, however, only his plans that were at risk, not the expedition itself. What he really meant was that it would wreck *his* expedition; *his* ambition, *his* agenda, *his* instructions, *his* reflected glory and vicarious entertainment.

Because for Markham it wasn't about science. It wasn't about analysing rocks, fishing for marine life, sounding depths, or recording the weather. Those things were not passports to greatness as he conceived it. In a nation where duty, obedience, and gallant endeavour were everything, it was relatively easy to justify his chivalrous conception. Science is a grown-up endeavour in which egos take (or should take) second place. There is no obvious heroism in dissecting crustaceans or cataloguing rocks – the activities engaged in by 'mudlarkers', as he called the scientists. In fact, he consistently denigrated and lampooned them. The 'expert in the mimicry of butterflies' (a juvenile put-down of EB Poulton, reinforced and legitimised afterwards by many biographers), the 'bird of prey' (JY Buchanan), the 'clown' (also Poulton), the 'pantaloon' (WJL Wharton), and the 'villain' (TH Tizard), are all straight out of the Royal Arctic Theatre.

In theory, this could be interpreted as Markham's defensive attempts to resolve his own latent sense of inferiority with regard to academic status and legitimacy. It could also be the case that he was genuinely imbued with a sense of ascendancy and moral superiority. He clearly felt that nationalistic claims out-weighed the cause of science. He carried the standard of medieval chivalry, all the rage for much of the nineteenth century: the return to Camelot, a retreat from the 'black iron monster', shattering forever the comfortable certainties of the past. His views were shared by many of his generation, but his way of expressing them was very much his own. Mockery and derision took the place of reasoned argument. Emotional histrionics took the place of adult negotiation and compromise. It wasn't actually possible to negotiate with him in the normal way. It was like deal-ing with a spoilt child. They gave up in the end. At home, he probably rehearsed the case for his vision. Minna is likely to have been subjected to lengthy and detailed harangues and self-justifications. His view was that what the nation wanted was heroes and a celebration of British supremacy in everything. Anybody can do science, but the British are gallant conquerors, especially those of the Naval variety. And who does not love an adventure and a dramatic story.

In May 1901, after the 'attempt to wreck the expedition' was over, Poulton wrote an open letter to the Fellows of the Royal Society regarding the circum-stances of the resignation of Professor Gregory, which was printed in the journal *Nature*. [27] He states that as far as he was concerned, the debacle around Gregory had started when his [28]

> ... attention was called to a statement in the press describing Professor Gregory as "Head of the *Civilian* Scientific Staff". [his italics]

Smelling a rat, he wrote to Markham regarding this sudden inclusion of the word 'civilian'. He got together with Professor Rucker, who agreed that it 'was full of danger', and designed to reduce Gregory's remit and status. Unfortunately for him, when he sounded out the RS members of the Joint Committee, it became clear that the Naval element actually preferred the term, and that it would be impossible to resist its use without dividing those in favour of Gregory. It was of course a ruse by Markham. In his retrospective account of events, Markham is very careful to call Gregory Director of the *Civilian* Staff throughout, as he would – but there is no reason to doubt Poulton's version.

Professor Gregory arrived back from Melbourne on 5 December 1900, when what Markham calls the 'profligate intrigue' commenced, very quietly at first. According to Gregory, he (Gregory) went straight to Dundee, where the *Discovery* was being built, to meet Captain [*sic*] Scott. He showed him a copy of the letter from Port Said from almost a year ago; the letter which Markham had characterised as containing matters of which Gregory 'could know nothing', and 'which did not concern him', and that it was the letter of 'a very self-sufficient person'. Scott returned it the next day, without comment, leading Gregory to assume that Scott 'understood and accepted the general conditions therein stated'. He made the wrong assumption. Probably Scott hesitated to act without instructions from Markham. According to Gregory, he then submitted to Scott and Markham a draft of the instructions he expected to receive from the Joint Committee, which he had previously shown to Poulton. This was January 1901, showing that even at this late date, Gregory still thought he was going, on his terms.

Markham's version of events differs markedly. Characterising Gregory's talks with Scott as an 'attack', he claims Gregory wrote to him for advice, to which he replied that he (Gregory) '... had better state his own view clearly and explicitly'. He goes on to say that [29]

> For a long time I could not get any clear statement out of him ... At last he sent me the draft of what he thought the Instructions should be, on January 22d, 1901. It was quite inadmissible.

Markham quickly summoned the Executive Committee on 30 January, when he presented 'for consideration' the Instructions he had prepared himself years ago, in 1897. There were only three members present – Poulton being absent – which meant there were only Markham, Vesey Hamilton and Tizard, who was of course out-voted two to one. He then sent copies of his 'Plan of Operations' for consideration by the Royal Society, prior to another Joint Committee meeting on 8 February. The RS suggested two crucial alterations: not to winter the ship in the ice, and to establish a landing party under the control of Professor Gregory. Exactly what Markham didn't want.

At the Joint Committee meeting, the RGS (meaning Markham), objected that they had not had the same opportunity of considering the amendments. This was accepted and the meeting was adjourned for four days, until 12 February. This meeting, the 'attempt to wreck the expedition in order to gratify Gregory's ambition', according to Markham, was, by now predictably, another fraught one. Both camps accused each other of being inconsistent. No constructive dialogue took place. At one point Markham threatened to leave the meeting, at which he reports that Geikie shouted 'Then go!' at him in a rude tone of voice. Markham: [30]

> The next exhibition was made by the bird of prey, who was perched at the end of the table. He got up and informed the Committee that my word was not worthy of consideration. I thought this was about enough, so I left the room, with no intention of again taking part in the squabbles of this precious Joint Committee.

Subsequently, the Royal Society amendments were approved by 16 votes to six.

Markham records that Poulton and Geikie went upstairs to enact a 'ridiculous farce', by informing 'His High Mightiness' (Gregory) that his demands had been met [31]

> ... and to express a hope that he would not resign. Professor Gregory condescended to accept on his own conditions. He went out to Australia again, in a fool's paradise, thinking he had gained a complete victory.

Shortly afterwards, Admirals Hoskins, Vesey Hamilton and Albert Markham also withdrew – according to Clements because as honourable men they could no longer be associated with the 'proceedings and jobbing of this Joint Committee'. This was in addition to Clements himself, who claims his reasons for no longer attending were not personal(!). Markham: [32]

> Considering the gross irregularity of their proceedings, the way in which they made all the interests of the expedition subservient to the demands of their protegé, and their incapacity, I felt that a seat in such a Committee was no fit place for the R.G.S. President [himself], nor for any one who had the interests of the Antarctic Expedition at heart.

Jaw-dropping. And, of course, another ruse by Markham – this time intended to reduce the RGS contingent to an absurd minority. The day after this meeting, Gregory did sail again for Australia. Bad timing, to say the least, and something he can be legitimately criticised for: it hardly showed commitment, as the expedition was scheduled to sail that summer, and of course it again played into Markham's hands.

On 17 February, Markham wrote a confidential memo to the RS urging them to consent to the abolition of the 'mischievous' Joint Committee. They declined, and there were further Joint Committee meetings on 19 and 26 February at which the RS had the field more or less to themselves. Although on the face of it an ideal situation for the RS, the absence of the RGS members had a delegitimising effect. Ideally, the RS would have wanted this to be a harmonious piece of co-operation between the two societies. This might have been what motivated Major Darwin (son of Charles, and RGS Secretary at the time) to try and smooth things over. Markham was irritated. To him, Darwin seemed to have an 'idolatrous veneration' for the RS. As far as he was concerned, there was no question of negotiating with them.

As it turned out, he did Markham a massive favour by muddying the waters with a set of contingency provisos. Sir Michael Foster (RS Secretary) supported them, much to the consternation of Poulton, who maintained that the arrangement with Gregory as it stood was already the minimum Gregory would accept. Foster, however, was of the opinion that there should be 'give and take'; and at the next meeting, on 5 March, not only Foster, but Geikie too, supported Darwin's changes (in the interests of peace, as he said) – as did others, including George Murray, who was there as Gregory's representative. Battle fatigue seems to have set in, which left Poulton with just a grimly determined core group, which included Buchanan and Tizard.

Gregory should have been there, showing an interest in the preparations (which were all this time going ahead, with Scott much in evidence), and he should have fought his corner. His absence must have had a demotivating effect on his supporters. Unwilling to sacrifice the Melbourne professorship he'd been offered, he spread himself too thin and paid the price. At the next meeting, on 5 March, Darwin's amendments were carried.

Poulton wrote to Gregory relating events, adding that he thought Darwin's provisos were accepted in order to keep the RGS on board, and that they would not interfere with his plans. Markham had other ideas: [33]

> The R.G.S. Council was not prepared to do anything of the kind. I should have positively refused to sign them. The Instructions of the Joint Committee represented the schemes of jobbers watered down by subsequent vacillation and compromise, and were in abominably bad English.

Enter Sir George Dashwood Taubman Goldie. Patrician, ruthless and arrogant, this small, wiry man, in status and influence sometimes compared to Cecil Rhodes, was a veteran of many years of colonial rule and exploitation. At one time *de facto* Governor of Nigeria, he ended up in control of the lucrative Niger trading route through a combination of financial muscle and intimidation. If anyone knew how to force a deal through, it was Goldie. As men of the world, Markham and he might have felt an instinctive affinity, as both had a potentially scandalous past to hide. Exactly what this entailed for Goldie is not known, as he destroyed all his papers before he died, forbade the writing of his biography, and is said to have threatened his children with a curse if they disclosed anything about his past. He is known to have lived a louche and promiscuous life for much of his time in Africa.

Markham was tickled pink to get him on board, and waxed theatrical, quoting from an 'Old play':

> Want you a man! / Experienced in the world and its affairs. / Here
> he is for your purpose.

Goldie wasn't the slightest bit interested in Antarctica, but eventually yielding to Markham's solicitations, the 'ablest man on our Council' was [34]

> Cool and collected, seeing his adversary's moves as clearly as his
> own, great as a diplomatist as well as an administrator, quickly tak-
> ing the measure of all with whom he has to deal, absolutely
> impartial, [!] mastering his brief rapidly and never losing a thread,
> he would turn the R.S. officials round his finger with perfect ease.

According to Markham, Goldie became as 'keen as a hound' once he'd consented. What was the payoff for Goldie? Not the sort of man to do something out of the goodness of his heart, the suspicion has to be that Markham promised him something. Was it the Presidency of the RGS? Certainly, Goldie's rise within the RGS was meteoric, becoming its President on Markham's abdication in 1905. Given the fact that Markham's power within the RGS seems to have been more or less absolute, it seems likely.

On 10 April 1901 there was a conference at the Royal Society. Present were Markham, 'Pilot' Goldie and M'Clintock for the RGS; and for the RS, Sir William Huggins (President), Sir Michael Foster (Secretary), and Mr Kempe (Treasurer). Markham took the initiative:

> I began by explaining the points on which we must insist. McClin-
> tock added some weighty remarks on the importance of the ship
> wintering.

After hearing what the RS team had to say, Goldie [35]

> ... began to twist the professorial tails very courteously but with
> marked effect. They had to learn the absurdity of wanting to have
> two Heads to one expedition.

Regardless of their academic standing and their illustrious careers, and in spite of the merits of their case, the RS team allowed themselves to be browbeaten and cowed into submission – not by reason or logic, but by force of personality and iron determination.

They must also have been forced to admit that Markham had raised the money, and that that made his claims hard to deny. Hence, Huggins, Foster and Kempe promised to be neutral when Goldie proposed that Markham [36]

> ... should write to the Joint Committee, informing them that their
> version of the Instructions was inadmissible, and asking them to

request the two Councils to appoint a Special Committee of six, to prepare Instructions which should be final.

Clearly, Foster had ceased to back Poulton, and had withdrawn his active support from the RS militants. The cohesion of the RS had been breached. It is what Markham had been trying to achieve for months. Markham was jubilant, and crowed that Foster would have to 'eat his leek', and that Goldie intended that they 'should be a good deal more than neutral'. Goldie drafted the letter, which, according to Poulton, 'clearly indicated that the real intention was to escape from the conditions proposed to and accepted by the scientific leader'.

The Joint Committee met again on 26 April 1901. It was by now a rather ragged, heterogeneous affair, and with important early figures like Wharton, Geikie and Nares having backed out (in Markham's words). This, added to the neutrality (by default, pro-Markham) of the three men at the top (Foster, Huggins and Kempe), left Poulton with only Tizard and Buchanan still interested in the fight. Accordingly, after what Markham called 'a very able and conciliatory speech, though perhaps a little sarcastic', from Goldie, Goldie proposed the motion and Foster seconded it. Foster even went so far as to give a speech which satisfied 'the best friends of the Expedition', which left any waverers in no doubt which way the wind was blowing.

The motion, whereby a Select Committee of six would prepare the final Instructions, was carried by an overwhelming majority. Poulton was outraged. Markham, with his usual blend of contempt and sarcasm, describes him as being 'up and down like a Jack in the box'. Poulton felt a deep sense of betrayal by his own Society; both on his own behalf, and that of science and Gregory. He said he'd write to *The Times,* which he did. His letter also appeared in the magazine *Nature,* as previously mentioned. Markham said of it: [37]

> It is full of incorrect statements and untruths, but written from ignorance and dullness rather than from intention. The involved rigmarole would be unintelligible to outsiders. Its main object is to attack the R.S. Officials, especially Foster, for deserting science represented by Gregory.

The mercifully final 'Select Committee' was appointed there and then, and met on 26 and 28 April – effectively restoring Markham's Instructions to what they had originally been, including the commander's option to winter the ship in the ice, and Gregory's subordinate position to Scott. Gregory was informed by telegram, and promptly resigned, exactly as Markham and Goldie expected and intended. Markham: [38]

> The Royal Society, with its preposterous Joint Committee, has been a curse to the Expedition ... a tale of dullness, intrigue, and spite; of

malignity luckily mated with incapacity, finally and completely thwarted; thanks to 'The Pilot that weathered the storm'.

Mission accomplished.

As this story shows, Markham was prepared to do whatever it took to put Scott in sole command. Considering the fact that he was almost comically under-qualified, the fact that Scott's appointment was of such passionate concern to Markham means he had an ulterior motive, which could only have been inspired by an attachment to Scott as a man and *ingenue*. In a letter to Scott he writes: [39]

> You remind me of Mecham to an extraordinary degree, not in face but many characteristics and ways. In face you are just like Sherard Osborn. Combine the two, with the tenacity of McClintock, and you will be, as I feel confident you will, the greatest of polar explorers.
> [Ferrar's typographical errors corrected]

Markham knew Frederick G Mecham from his time in the Arctic on the *Assistance*, on which Markham was a midshipman, and Mecham a second lieut-enant. In a lengthy entry in his *Arctic Navy List*, as well as detailing his sledging prowess, Markham gives us a run-down of Mecham's activities in the Royal Arctic Theatre. To Markham, details of men's theatrical activities were important parts of their *curricula vitae*. His *Arctic Navy List* is peppered with references to parts played and productions put on. Mecham, however much an exemplary officer he appears to have been, did not escape this treatment. Markham's priorities ensured that, whatever else Mecham achieved in his life, posterity will always know that he was Mr Honeybun in the production of 'Did you ever send your Wife to Cam-berwell?', and Brownjohn in 'Done on Both Sides'. He was promoted to Com-mander at the early age of 27, and died in Honolulu three years later.

It turns out that one of the reasons Scott went to the Antarctic was because he kindled nostalgic affection in Markham for men he'd known in the past. Scott must have read the letter, and must have been ready to accept that, if that's what it took.

Meanwhile, the building and fitting-out of the ship had been going on apace: supplies and equipment were tested and bought, officers were sent on crash courses in meteorology and ballooning (yes, ballooning), a few scientists were sel-ected, and Naval crew obtained.

With regard to the Naval crew, there was another man with a dubious reputation to whom Markham was indebted for putting flesh on the bones of his dream. That man was Sir Anthony Hiley Hoskins. Hoskins, a Fellow of the RGS, had been on the Joint Committee, and had resigned at the same time as Vesey Hamilton and Albert Markham. Hamilton and Hoskins knew each other well: Hamilton had preceded Hoskins as First Naval Lord from 1889 to 1891, after which Hoskins became First Naval Lord until 1893. Clements also knew him well: he and Minna had stayed at Admiralty House in Malta as guests of Sir Anthony and Lady Hoskins when Hoskins was Commander-in-Chief in the Mediterranean. [40]

Born in 1828, Hoskins was a contemporary of Markham's, and from a similar background. His father was a rector, and he went to a 'public' school, Winchester, where boys lodged together and were taught the Classics in the usual manner of elite schools of the time. He joined the Royal Navy at 14, taking with him a proficiency in classical learning unusual for his age, and is said to have acted as Greek coach to one of the officers (whatever that may have meant). Markham was just in time: Hoskins was retired and didn't have long to live. He died in June 1901, missing the departure of the expedition by about six weeks. As well as having had a reputation for harshness bordering on severity in his treatment of his 'inferiors', he seems to have been generally obnoxious.

To those he considered his social or professional equals or betters, however, he was said to be the most genial of men. He was certainly a friend to Markham. Hoskins may have retired from the Navy, but he evidently retained an impressive measure of influence at the Admiralty. Through Hoskins, Markham obtained the services of no fewer than [41]

> ... three first class petty officers, six petty officers, nine able seamen, five stokers, two Marines, and a steward to join from the navy making, with four officers, altogether 30 naval men: with time to count for pensions, full pay and allowances, and all borne on the books of the *President.*

Markham's contacts seem once again to have worked their magic. At the same time, the Admiralty, while keeping a low profile in case of failure, would not have wanted to pass up the opportunity to take credit for success in the event of the Pole being attained. It may have been a long shot, but as Gordon remarks: [42]

> Sporadically, for almost a hundred years, the Admiralty was entwined with polar exploration in unofficial partnership with the Royal Society and the Royal Geographical Society. As an expedition leader, Parry was followed by George Lyon, John Ross, James Ross, John Franklin, Frederick Beechey, Erasmus Ommanney, Robert McClure, Edward Belcher, Francis McClintock, George Nares and Robert Falcon Scott. All were naval officers and nearly every one was knighted (in Scott's case, his widow was entitled). It is difficult to be precise about their motivation. They assumed the roles of surveyors, meteorologists, biologists, naturalists, hydrographers, astronomers and physicists (it was vital to study the Earth's magnetic field near the poles, they said); but above all they wanted to be first.

Besides Markham's hidden agendas, and in spite of his outdated ideas, mismanagement, wasteful extravagance, and later lies and obfuscations, pioneering a route to the South Pole, and being the first to get there, was always the main aim of both Scott's expeditions.

References

1   Sir Clements Markham. *Antarctic Obsession*, p. 13

2   Sir Clements R. Markham. *The Lands of Silence*, p. 447

3   *ibid.*

4   Elspeth Huxley. *Scott of the Antarctic*, pp. 18–19

5   Apsley Cherry-Garrard. *The Worst Journey in the World*, p. 206

6   Michael S. Foldy. *The Trials of Oscar Wilde*, p. 131

7   H. Montgomery Hyde. *The Other Love*, p. 116

8   Camille Paglia. *Sexual Personae*, p. 320

9   Captain Robert F. Scott. *The Voyage of the Discovery*, p. 33

10   Roland Huntford. *Scott and Amundsen*, p. 125

11   Heather Lane, Naomi Boneham and Robert D. Smith (eds.). *The Last Letters*, p. 25

12   David Crane. *Scott of the Antarctic*, p. 85

13   *op. cit.*, p. 86

14   Sir Clements Markham. *Antarctic Obsession*, p. 8

15   *op. cit.*, p. 126

16   *ibid.*

17   *op. cit.*, p. 128

18   *op. cit.*, p. 164

19   *op. cit.*, p. 133

20   *op. cit.*, p. 134

21   *op. cit.*, p. 135

22   Sue Ferrar. 'Paths are Made by Walking', p. 7

23   Sir Clements Markham. *op. cit.*, p. 129

24   *ibid.*

25   Aubrey A. Jones. *Scott's Forgotten Surgeon*, p. 120

26   Sir Clements Markham. *op. cit.*, p. 130

27   *op. cit*, Appendix 2

28   *op. cit*, p. 165

29   *op. cit*, p. 134

30   *op. cit*, p. 138

31   *ibid.*

32   *ibid.*, pp. 138–9

33   *op. cit*, p. 141

34   *ibid.*, pp. 141–2

35   *ibid.*

36   *op. cit*, p. 143

37   *op. cit*, p. 145

38   *op. cit*, p. 147

39   Sue Ferrar. *ibid.*

40   Admiral Sir Albert Markham. *The Life of Sir Clements R. Markham*, p. 300

41   Sir Clements Markham. *op. cit*, p. 17

42   Andrew Gordon. *The Rules of the Game*, pp. 161–2

PART 2

1901 TO 1910

THE *DISCOVERY* TO THE *TERRA NOVA*

10

BORCHGREVINK AND THE

DEPARTURE OF THE *DISCOVERY*

William Speirs Bruce wasn't the only one to elicit Markham's infantile posses-siveness with regard to the South Pole. Markham saw to it that neither Adrien de Gerlache nor Carsten Borchgrevink, both of whom achieved significant 'firsts' in the exploration of Antarctica, were properly recognised by the RGS while he had anything to do with it. Borchgrevink belatedly received the RGS Patron's Medal in 1930, but de Gerlache went to his grave in 1934 without receiving his, in spite of his major achievement.

De Gerlache and his crew (among whom was a certain Roald Amundsen), on board the *Belgica* Expedition (1897–9), were the first humans to spend a winter in the ice inside the Antarctic Circle – a true step into the unknown – dark, cold and terrifying, not knowing if they'd ever get home. Borchgrevink and his *Southern Cross* Expedition (1898–1900) were the first to spend a winter on the continent itself. Whereas de Gerlache merely got the cold shoulder, Borchgrevink was bad-mouthed by Markham as '... impudent and stupid but cunning and unprincipled', and vilified for taking money which, as with Bruce, Markham felt should have gone to his expedition. [1] As with Bruce also, it brought out the same kind of hysterical calumny, with Markham claiming that Borchgrevink had paid too much for the ship, suggesting that it cost less than the stated price, and that he had pocketed the difference. He further averred that this had been hidden from Sir George Newnes (Borchgrevink's financial backer). Baughman states: [2]

> ... even to the point of providing a certificate of seaworthiness that
> Markham believed was a forgery. The reason for refitting the boat
> in Norway was not that a strike prevented the work from being
> done in England, as Borchgrevink had asserted, but to cover the
> sorry state of the vessel before and after refitting.

There is no suggestion anywhere else that there were problems with the *Southern Cross*.

De Gerlache hadn't had the temerity to go to the regions Markham claimed owner's rights over, and he'd been financed by the Belgian Government. Borchgrevink, on the other hand, was mainly Norwegian; and as far as Markham was concerned, should never have been financed by an Englishman. After he had, in addition, the nerve to plan to overwinter at Cape Adare, in the Victoria Quadrant, the full force with which Markham sought to deny others the right and the means to explore Antarctica came down on Borchgrevink's head.

Carsten Egeberg Borchgrevink had given an address to the 1895 International Geographical Congress, where he impressed Hugh Robert Mill with his dynamism and purpose, in spite of his blunt manner and abrupt speech. Borchgrevink [3]

> ... stirred the academic discussions with a fresh breeze of realism ...
> that struck some of us as boding well for exploration.

He spent the next two years trying to raise money for an expedition, succeeding at last with Sir George Newnes, a leading British magazine publisher. He fitted out the *Southern Cross* Expedition for a total of £40,000 (about £4.75 million in 2018) – less than half of what Markham considered the minimum for his own venture. Although civil in his public stance towards Borchgrevink, in private, Markham warned Mill not to have anything to do with him – calling him incompetent and criticising the ship for being rotten.

Behind the scenes, Markham intervened where he could to deny support for the *Southern Cross*, as a result of which Borchgrevink wrote, 'It was up a steep hill that I had to roll my Antarctic boulder.' Mill, however, again showing the maturity and integrity so lacking in Markham, helped Borchgrevink as a private individual, and was a guest at the send-off lunch on board the *Southern Cross*, together with Sir Erasmus Ommanney – which must have galled Markham. Mill proposed a toast, and 'In the name of British geographers he wished the expedition God speed, useful work, and a safe and quick return.' [4] It was what Markham should have done, but Mill was reproached by him for doing so.

Markham treated the RGS as his own personal fiefdom. Under his presidency, favouritism and personal 'interest' flourished – so much so that in later years the Society found itself having to make good on Markham's more egregious omissions. Nevertheless, historians continue by and large to indulge him, even to the extent of campaigning for a blue plaque to be fixed to 22 Eccleston Square – so far without success. For many, even today, his heroic vision seems to cast a rosy haze over the means by which he fulfilled it. The values with which he sought to imbue his vision were conspicuously lacking in his everyday behaviour, however, which was characterised by arrogance, bad temper, jealousy and meanness. Ranulph Fiennes justifies many of Markham's hubristic assumptions by saying that the Victorians [5]

... thought, spoke and acted quite unlike us.

To a certain extent this may be true, but relevant experience has always been recognised as essential – especially in risky ventures – and the story of his gerrymandering of the committees and his behaviour within them provides evidence of his bad faith and vindictiveness. And it isn't as if he didn't have his critics at the time, beginning with the Royal Society. The Victorians might have thought about things differently from us, but not all Victorians thought, spoke or acted like Markham.

His interest in exploration came from a curiosity to see what was round the next corner. It had little to do with what that corner consisted of, how long it had been there, what caused it to be there, nor how it related to the rest of the planet. His was essentially an unscientific approach to exploration – really not much more than a schoolboy's conception, consistent with Markham's core immaturity.

The grown-up in Markham wanted a crowning achievement. He knew he could not aspire to be another Cecil Rhodes, nor even a George Goldie – both men whom he intensely admired – but the South Pole was a worthy object, and one which fell within his scope and professed experience. What made it doubly attractive was that it enabled him to recreate the conditions of his own Polar idyll, and relive it vicariously. If his ideas had led to success, the kid gloves of the historians could almost be forgiven. The sensational grief over Scott's eventual death has tended to mask the fact that his first expedition ship, the *Discovery,* almost didn't come back at all – and that when she eventually did, it was without the Pole nor anything like it, and with a comparatively thin haul of scientific data. Even this was more than Markham had any right to expect; and credit did eventually go to Lieutenant Royds, who achieved more than might have been expected from a non-scientist. Thomas Vere Hodgson, the expedition biologist, did important work, as did Hartley Ferrar in geology, and Louis Bernacchi as chief physicist.

At the last minute, Markham had tried to divert the *Southern Cross* Expedition by suggesting they should try to look for de Gerlache's *Belgica,* whose return was beginning to be overdue. There cannot be much doubt that it was an attempt to use moral blackmail to subvert Borchgrevink. He might have suspected as much as, after due consideration, he rejected Markham's suggestion, and went ahead with his plans.

Carsten Borchgrevink was unfortunate in three major respects: the timing of his expedition, the place he chose for overwintering, and his unaccommodating demeanour. The *Southern Cross* arrived back in London in June 1900, at a time when preparations for Markham's BNAE were in full swing, with the ship on the stocks and the arguments raging in the committee rooms. His return must have seemed like a side show – especially as he hadn't achieved anything obviously sensational; like a disaster, for example.

But Borchgrevink knew that in order to discover Antarctica you needed people who knew how to observe it and how to survive it. Out of the nine men he chose as his team, therefore, three were scientists, and a fourth (Colbeck) was a magnetician, navigator and surveyor. Two of his team were chosen for their experience of living in the cold: the Lapps Ole Must and Per Savio, who also possessed dog-driving skills. A further two men were highly qualified general support workers, and the ninth was the cook. With Borchgrevink himself, it totalled just ten men, supported by around 80 Samoyed dogs. A hut was built on shore, dogs pulled the sledges, and the ship went away for the winter. It represented a modern, intelligent and responsible approach to Polar exploration.

At the time, however, Borchgrevink's achievements were easy to ignore; as in addition to unfortunate timing, he picked the wrong spot to overwinter. His spit of land at Cape Adare turned out to be not only very exposed but, crucially, it lacked a route onto the Plateau and into the interior. Because of the open nature of the Ross Sea, the ship was needed to access the adjoining coastal regions. This meant there wasn't much time if the ship was not to overwinter, but still they made good use of what time they did have. Louis Bernacchi (one of Borchgrevink's scientists on the *Southern Cross* Expedition, and later on the *Discovery*), writing many years later, reports that [6]

> ... on the return of the *Southern Cross*, landings had been made for the first time on Coulman Island, Franklin Island and in Wood Bay ... Ross's Great Ice Barrier landed upon for the first time ... [and] the highest southern latitude so far attained.

On his previous visit to the Antarctic, as a member of the crew and part-time scientist on the whaling ship *Antarctic*, Borchgrevink had set foot on Antarctica at Cape Adare. They found lichen on the rocks there, thus becoming the first men in history to discover vegetation on Antarctica. It had also given him an opportunity to assess the site as a potential place for wintering. With hindsight, he must have regretted his decision not to venture further into the Ross Sea and to reconnoitre Ross Island for a place to overwinter. At the same time, however, it may have seemed a safer bet to land where he knew he could, and to assume that there would be a route into the interior from Cape Adare. There could have been no other reason for bringing 80 dogs other than a plan to venture into the interior and, if possible, attain the Magnetic Pole.

Also of prime importance was that when they left civilisation, de Gerlache's *Belgica* had not yet returned, and that as far as they knew, they were going to be testing the very survivability of an Antarctic winter. The fact that Cape Adare is about 400 miles north of Ross Island, and therefore a little warmer and lighter, shows appropriate caution in Borchgrevink's approach. It was, in any case, impressive enough to have established the first habitation of a continent, in a dwelling which survives, and is as such of greater historical importance than the hut at Cape Evans.

Apart from one death from causes unrelated to their situation, Borchgrevink's small, experienced, democratic team came through in good shape, vindicating his decision to overwinter where he did in spite of the fact that Ridley Beach is bleak and inhospitable and raked by hurricane-force winds. Given the limitations of their situation, it is to their credit that they returned with a respectable haul of observations.

The third problem Borchgrevink had was himself. Mill called him blunt and abrupt. Today we would say that he lacked people skills: he wasn't charming, he wasn't tactful nor accommodating, nor glamorous. He was not a good communicator, and his leadership skills left a lot to be desired. There were a good few nasty flare-ups during the expedition, centred mainly around Borchgrevink himself, apparently. Living month after month cooped up with nine other people in a hut 15 × 15 ft square, in hostile conditions thousands of miles from civilisation isn't easy for anyone – but for a leader, with the extra burden of responsibility, it is particularly stressful. Borchgrevink spent part of the winter away from the main station in a stone hut accompanied only by the two Lapps; according to some, spending his time there getting drunk – understandably perhaps.

But his poor social skills were a serious disadvantage. The fact that questions were raised about missing scientific data and notes in the months after his return to civilisation didn't help. In addition to all the ballyhoo around the forthcoming BNAE, those things tended to overshadow his expedition's achievements and successes, unwelcome as they will already have been to Markham. They made it easy for him to dismiss Borchgrevink, and for posterity to treat him as an also-ran.

But Bernacchi asserts that [7]

> Borchgrevink, in many respects, was not a good leader, but the expedition was as well equipped in regard to foods, dogs and sledges, polar gear and scientific instruments as most modern expeditions. What he did, he did alone, with no help from official bodies or committees, but his plans cut into those already being formed by Sir Clements Markham for the great *Discovery* expedition. Markham was ruffled and annoyed. It follows that Borchgrevink was not a "White-headed Boy" of the Royal Geographical Society. As a small pioneering expedition without influence or backing, beyond the very liberal finance of Sir George Newnes, that of the *Southern Cross* stands unchallenged. The results were of pre-eminent importance. We had passed the first winter ever spent on Antarctic land within the Circle, and the first

complete series of magnetic and meteorological observations were scientifically taken, and later published by the Royal Society.

Bernacchi's comment about 'white-headed boys' is telling. Bernacchi wasn't the only one who thought that personal favouritism determined who should command and, to a large extent, man the expedition. In his opinion, objective measures of relevant competence were of secondary importance to the Royal Geographical Society. Reginald Skelton, Chief Engineer on the *Discovery*, agreed with him. Referring to the appointments of Scott and Royds, he wrote in his diary on 8 September 1904: [8]

> Some people say he [Markham] isn't "straight". I don't know any-
> thing about that, but I do believe all his actions have been more
> controlled by sentiment, favouritism etc. than by practical, common
> sense duty towards the expedition as a national undertaking.

Although Bernacchi was taken on as *Discovery* Expedition physicist, he clearly never considered himself a 'white-haired boy'. Markham's reflection that Bern-acchi was 'always a grown up – never a boy' (in itself an inappropriate comment), suggests that he was a serious young man, at least where work was concerned, and that he did not try to ingratiate himself. Although blue-eyed rather than white-haired, there was no doubt that Scott was Markham's boy, and Bernacchi's wry judgement must have been shared by many.

The main reason why Markham learnt nothing from the *Southern Cross* Expe-dition was that Markham didn't want to learn anything from the *Southern Cross* Expedition. What he wanted was a pretext for rubbishing it, which is exactly what Borchgrevink gave him. The last thing Markham wanted was for Scott to start looking seriously at how Borchgrevink had run things. He wanted to preserve Scott's naivety, which had always been one of his charms. Scott is almost lasciv-iously described as 'A young officer, with everything to learn ...' [9] Not only did it give Markham control, it formed the basis of a relationship in which Markham could take the place of the elder, in the classical Greek relationship Oscar Wilde described at his trial. Rumour has it that Scott and Markham had Greek nicknames for each other, which would confirm that, as well as implying a degree of intimacy over and above what would be expected from a professional relationship. It also suggests a level of collusion on Scott's part.

The ship, and the issue of whether or not to let her freeze in for the winter, had been hotly debated in the committees. It was clear that Markham wanted the men to overwinter in the ship. Whatever he said publicly, in private, Scott was in no doubt about what Markham wanted. Pretending still to argue the point, Markham claimed that the decision must be made on the spot by the commander, as only he would be in a position to assess the situation. He also claimed that keeping the ship in the ice would extend the time available for exploration. It is true that overwintering in the ship would allow a larger number of men to potentially explore for a longer period. Otherwise, she has to go back before the sea freezes over again, taking the crew with her. But overwintering the ship in order to provide comfortable accommodation wastes the potential for carrying out the hydrographical work she was equipped to do.

Even more important is the fact that the coast of Antarctica is not a good place to overwinter a ship. Markham, with only his experience of the Arctic to go by, assumed that conditions in the Antarctic would be comparable. In his day, they had been placidly beset in the middle of a floe, free from the katabatic storms that batter the coastal regions of Antarctica. Even before they had properly settled for the winter, the *Discovery* weathered a storm which, if they had not been firmly encased in ice by then, would have blown them out to sea. As the engines were already dismantled, and the wind too fierce for anyone to venture among the sails, they would have been at the mercy of the elements – like the *Aurora*, the ship used by Shackleton in his later ill-fated Trans-Antarctic venture. She was ripped from her moorings at Cape Evans and carried out to sea: [10]

> ... broken wires whipsailed shrilly through the air as [the bosun] raced toward the bulkhead, hurricane lamp in hand, shouting, "She's away wi'it!"

The *Aurora*'s engines, too, had been dismantled ready for winter; and the crew were lucky to escape with their lives after 11 months adrift in the pack-ice. The *Aurora*'s anchor is still there, embedded in the beach at Cape Evans.

Today, Markham would excel as a publicity agent. He had succeeded in building an enhanced public profile for Scott. One of the ways he did this was by conflating and spinning experience and qualifications in unrelated fields into evidence of fitness for the task in hand. Personal qualities were also exploited to the maximum: Markham quotes Scott's past captains' opinions of him as 'A zealous and excellent officer', and 'Very painstaking and attentive' (among many other similar descriptions), as evidence of suitability. [11] He posed for many photographs. Scott was a good-looking man with a genial expression, as Nansen succinctly described him.

Markham had had the option of having the ship built along the lines of Colin Archer's *Fram*: bulbous and ungainly but known to be superior in coping with pressure because of her ability to rise above it, rather than be gripped by the ice. The *Fram* had been built specifically for Nansen's Polar drift, however – an essentially passive occupation, where the first requirement was the ability to cope with pressure. There is some justification for the lines on which the *Discovery* was built, therefore, but it will come as no surprise that a sleeker, more glamorous ship resulted. And, of course, not for Markham a hard, professional crew led by a hook-nosed civilian who took orders from no one. Never mind a hundred dogs fouling the pristine decks.

For Baughman, the *Discovery* was an extravagant monument to the ego of the President of the RGS, [12] and he describes her as looking like a rich man's yacht. She was more than that. It was the realisation of a narcissistic and decadent fantasy, an expensively fitted vehicle for the theatrical rendition of the drama of exploration. She was staffed by a hand-picked coterie of young men, naive but willing. Professor Gregory describes Scott as 'very prepossessing' in appearance. He combined a masculine posture with beautiful-boy looks and an obliging, sexually ambivalent, remoteness. His sister said of him that he could appear to be giving you his undivided attention, while being somewhere else entirely in his thoughts. Dressed in his uniform he became more than a man: a symbol, an *objet de culte*, the personification of everything Markham valued. In the science department, such as it was, inanimate instruments were favoured: clean, impersonal, and showy. Those sciences whose realm represented the messy chthonian world beyond the glamour and artifice were always going to be merely tolerated. To Markham, it was the outer world, rather than the inner, that mattered. It was all about surface and image.

The Polar landscape exerted its fascination for Markham because of its Apollonian perfection in aspect and mood. The 'grandeur' of icy 'frowning' cliffs, and sterile, remote silence is indifferent and amoral. It does not judge. It is an essentially masculine world. The Poles are symbols of perfected male exclusivity and misogynistic *hauteur*. Life neither rots nor decays here, it remains in icy stasis. Cadavers dug up after 150 years remain almost untouched by time, ageless and glassy. It is a clean world, pared back to aseptic essentials, free from the tumult of procreative nature. Here, inexperienced young men in their boyish sailor costumes meet iron-hard frozen water and absence of feeling – a decadent juxtaposition of soft, warm flesh and ice, of naivety and the cold stare of eternal indifference.

The ship had been built, fitted and finished in just one year – an incredible achievement in itself, but with the inevitable risk that expediency sometimes had to take precedence over quality. The infamous 'Dundee leak' may have been one result. Above the waterline, however, everything had been finished to a luxury standard, with plenty of 'bright work' and polished wood. To all appearances, she was designed for glamorous cruising rather than dangerous work in extreme conditions – all except the seamen's quarters, which were not at all luxurious. They were spartan and had for heating a stove so small it could almost have come out of a doll's house. But they were close to the galley, which made them warmer than the wardroom, in spite of the fancy brass stove which graced it. The difference in standards between the wardroom and the messdeck is illustrative of the virtually unbridgeable gulf which separated the officers and the men. Markham may have waxed lyrical about 'charming fellows', but it could never impinge on his bred-in-the-bone sense of personal and imperial hierarchy.

In describing the ship, Markham informs us that there was [13]

> ... a space between the main mast and the main hatchway where there will be divine service, but too small for a theatre.

The theatre was never far away for Markham. Performance and drama were integral to his public persona. He saw things in theatrical terms, and his speeches were wordy *tours de force*. His shirt-front billowed like a ship in full sail as he delivered his exhortations in stentorian tones – inspired and inflated by an imaginary righteousness.

Unfortunately, as it turned out, there was no one on board with his appetite for drama. Just one play, 'Ticket of Leave', and a racist musical abomination entitled 'The Dishcover Nigger Minstrel Show' were put on in the course of the expedition – both performed in sub-zero temperatures. The audience kept warm by stomping and raucously cheering the action along. The cast must have been on the verge of hypothermia in their costumes. The *Discovery* productions certainly lacked the artistry, comfort, and glamour Markham would have brought to them. Nor, perhaps, was the ambiance entirely what he dreamed about. And there would be no *Bals Masques,* no Turks and dominoes, no *vivandières*, and no Little Bo-Peeps.

There wasn't time for proper sea trials. If there had been, they would have known about the *Discovery*'s sailing qualities. Common sense suggests a heavy ship, reinforced against the ice as she was, with small sails, would be slow in sailing; and that her weight would demand extra effort from her engines, requiring concomitantly increased amounts of coal. Presumably these issues were known to her designers, as they seem elementary. But she sagged badly to leeward and was a poor sailer, not being capable of beating to windward; and having so little expanse of sail that according to Royds [14]

> It will be a mighty strong wind before we have to shorten sail.

Her heavy coal consumption meant that much of the voyage south would have to be done under sail alone. The resulting lack of speed was more than an inconvenience – it was going to be race against time to get to Antarctica before the autumn.

It didn't help that she needed running repairs along the way. In Madeira a set of mast fittings had to be replaced and, not long after, a floor had to be built in the hold because of the intractable leak – on account of which she went into dry dock in New Zealand. They never did find out where the water was coming in. Her short masts, ostensibly kept short to avoid whiplash in butting the ice, contributed to a tendency to roll excessively, ensuring a lot of sea-sickness. Too late to do anything about it, it was found that the floors of the wardroom and the messdeck had no insulation – which affected the officers particularly, as the wardroom was above the coal bunker, a particularly cold and dusty place. After the first winter, every-thing was [15]

> ... black with soot and streaked with the trickle and drip of the damp.

The ventilation was poor – not a trivial issue in a confined space with so many people living and working together constantly, and where a few coal fires were the only sources of heat. Condensation froze into crusts of ice underneath the bunks, in the chests of drawers, on bolts and around deck-lights. Nevertheless, she was strong, and 'a comfortable sea boat', and many of her problems were to be expected in a brand-new ship of that type. According to Markham, that is.

The Cowes stunt was a master stroke. They were heroes before they'd even gone anywhere. On 5 August 1901, the *Discovery* steamed into Cowes, into the glittering gathering that was the Regatta of the Royal London Yacht Club. It must have been one of the peak experiences of Markham's life – a *coup de théatre* and the culmination of his dream and his vision. In a triumph of style over substance, it was as though the success of the expedition had already been achieved from the look and the presentation. All eyes were on the sleek adventure ship as she slowly steamed into Cowes through a flotilla of luxurious yachts, two of which were Royal, and all of which were expensive. It was Markham's finest hour when the King and Queen came on board and, after much interested inspection and strolling about, presented Scott with a medal – presumably for having made it thus far, and wished the ship and her handsome complement a successful voyage.

It was like a state occasion. In a paroxysm of hierarchical subjugation, Markham kissed the King's hand. Camille Paglia might well be talking about Markham when she says: [16]

> ... part of the male-homosexual world still follows a vanished aristo-cratic code: class consciousness, racial stratification, amoral veneration of youth, beauty, and glamour ...

After the departure of the royals, families and benefactors, assorted well-wishers and dignitaries thronged the decks – all eager to express their con-gratulations, admiration and best wishes. And at the centre of it all was Markham, the diminutive puppeteer, watching his men and his ship coming together and creating, in Skelton's words, 'a rather good show'.

It was gratifying in a way, but all that prestige and fanfare also applied pressure. Scott, for one, would have preferred a quiet departure, reflecting that [17]

> ... we might start off with a flourish of trumpets and return with failure.

A quiet slinking-off was not Markham's style, however. A photo of the occasion, showing Scott flanked by Markham and Skelton, shows everyone looking very pleased with themselves. Markham seems to be looking at Scott's new medal and making a comment. Skelton stands rather fetchingly with a hand on his hip and a rakish smile on the face he knew was handsome. He perhaps protests too much when he writes that [18]

All along we have been much troubled with numberless ladies ...

Scott's smile has a rictus quality, however. Referring to the medal that had just been pinned to his chest, he writes to his sister Ettie: [19]

Whatever natural expansion my chest assumes under the small piece of ribbon, it is speedily deflated when I think of the very small deserving of it.

He played his part amid all the puff and flummery; but there was no escaping the fact that the only reason he was there was because Markham had put him there – that he was performing the lead role in Markham's show and that, deep down, he knew it.

Over the past year, Scott had worked very hard to gain a measure of psycho-logical ownership of the expedition. Having been immersed in the practical side of the business meant that he now had at least some idea of what he was about. He would have needed whatever confidence it gave him – being presented to the King, and generally being treated like a celebrity. He must have been conscious from the beginning of the need for impeccable appearances. He must have suspected that some – many perhaps – secretly wondered about him and Markham. He had always had to make unchaste suspicions unthinkable. He probably had to mentally ban his inner imaginings of mortifying crew gossip. The photographic record suggests that Scott was concerned to create distance between himself and Markham in public. Photographed with Markham, he appears sometimes stiff and formal, sometimes conspicuously breezy, but always diffident. Since he could not rebut any suspicions verbally, he had to use body language, focus, conviction, and a stiff upper lip. By and large, it seems to have worked – outwardly, at least. But, as Scott wrote: [20]

After all is said and done, it was Sir Clements Markham who conceived the idea of an Antarctic Expedition; it was his masterful personality which forced it onward through all obstruction; and to him, therefore, is mainly due the credit that at the end of July 1901 we were prepared to set out on our long voyage and eager to obey the behest:

Do ye, by star-eyed science led, explore / Each lonely ocean, each untrodden shore.

With the uncritical backing of the 'Arctic worthies', Markham had contrived to produce his perfect ship. Scientific priorities were plain in the infinite pains taken over the magnetic observatory on deck, while the rest of the scientists had to make do with small labs either side which got too cold to work in during the Antarctic winter. In fact, other than the two surgeons there were only three scientists on the *Discovery* – and their status in Markham's eyes can gauged from their inclusion in his list of 'idlers', alongside the cooks, the stewards and the wardroom servants. [21]

A great deal of time, money and attention had been given to the construction of that magnetic laboratory. In order to get the truest possible readings, elaborate precautions were taken that nothing made of iron or steel should be permitted within a 30-yard radius – which included the other science labs. Fittings had to be made of brass, ropes had to be specially made of hemp, and some of the officers had to forgo sprung mattresses and take the buttons out of their bedding. This went down very well with the public. As in the expeditions of the Franklin era, the sophistication of the equipment gave the illusion of competence. The no-iron rule was a vainglorious attempt, as nothing could prevent boxes of tinned food nor, as on one occasion, a parrot in an iron cage, from straying within the exclusion zone. One they'd moored in Antarctica, two huts taken along specifically for magnetic work were constructed on shore – rendering the lab obsolete.

Bernacchi was to hot-foot it straight to Potsdam after the send-off, to secure the instructions for the very latest 'Eschenhagen magnetograph', of which much was made. They had on board two hydrogen reconnaissance balloons capable of taking a man hundreds of feet into the sky – which must have seemed pretty impressive and cutting-edge – as was also the dredging, towing, and sounding equipment fixed to the ship's side. At a time when most people's homes did not have electricity, this luxury was going to be enjoyed by all on the ship courtesy of a windmill (turbine), currently packed away somewhere on board but ready to be assembled and switched on. A task easier said than done, as it turned out. But it provided another wow factor, as was doubtlessly intended, and served to deflect criticism of the tiny science laboratories. Wilson made the most of these by [22]

> ... putting our smartest bits of apparatus and our prettiest coloured solutions in prominent positions. Microscopes were set out, water bottles, thermometers, every thing arranged and tidied up.

The balloons and the windmill had found their way on to the *Discovery*, despite the considerable expense, in response to Scott's visit to Berlin. Both would have appealed to Scott's inner techie; and he and Markham probably agreed that the *Discovery* must not be out-done by professor Drygalski's *Gauss* in terms of modern equipment and technology. In the event, the windmill was an expensive failure, being blown to pieces soon after it was put up, and again after difficult repairs had been made – this time for good. The balloons were similarly a whimsical and expensive waste of time and effort. Laboriously got into the sky with a panicky Scott on board, they were able to claim a first in Antarctic aviation on 4 February 1902 on the Barrier, almost two months before Drygalski – although they too claim to have been first.

Contrary to the view of the *eminence grise* Sir Joseph Hooker, who thought a balloon would prove essential to the expedition's success, they gained no information from it that could not be had by far-simpler means. They could, in any case, only go up a maximum of three times, as it took 19 gas cylinders to get *Eva* up, and just 60 were taken. Apart from the dangerous business of going up in her, it required a major effort to get her airborne, plus a lengthy spell of ideal weather. In the event, neither the *Gauss* nor the *Discovery* used their balloons more than once.

Scott was undoubtedly in favour of overwintering the ship. Apart from the superior comfort and security she provided, she embodied the structure and context of his framework of power. That that was important to him, he himself acknowledged. But as Borchgrevink had shown, a sturdy hut can provide adequate accommodation for an Antarctic winter, albeit for a smaller number of people. A small group of men overwintering in the spartan conditions of a hut, with very little privacy and without space or facilities for theatricals or parties, was not, however, Markham's idea of an expedition. But, apart from the infinitely superior accommodation a ship provides, there is no advantage to be gained from immobilising her in the ice. In fact, with very little idea of the implications of allowing the ship to be frozen in, there was every reason to avoid it, as the *Discovery* herself was to show.

But Markham had always envisaged the ship remaining for the duration. He hadn't raised money and spent years fighting just to provide a ferry service for a bunch of 'mudlarkers'. Nor did he have much interest in hydrographical work. The *Discovery* had been fitted and equipped with overwintering in mind. There was a piano/pianola in the wardroom. There was a typewriter and a device called an Edison's mimeograph, on which stencils could be made for a print-run of magazines, which had been produced on Polar expeditions since Parry's time. There was a library stocked with novels and plenty of board games. The officers' living quarters were comfortable and elegant, the wardroom was panelled and carpeted, and the private cabins were well appointed and expensively fitted. Props, costumes, dresses and make-up were taken. Markham supplied Scott with a booklet listing every and all occasions for splicing the main-brace. In a later era, Australian explorers took this to another level by making [23]

> ... such effective use of *Whitaker's Almanack* that they staged a major feast to celebrate the Anniversary of the Lighting of London by Gas.

While they may not have gone as far as this, the stock of alcohol on the *Discovery* was enough to reassure those who enjoyed the odd celebration.

In the first year, there were 44 mostly unmarried men, with an average age of 25, living closely together thousands of miles from home (and prying eyes and interfering busybodies), in a well-stocked and well-appointed ship, with plenty of time for leisure activities. Markham had recreated the conditions he had himself so enjoyed on the Austin Expedition. The 'babes in the wood', as they were called by the ladies in New Zealand, didn't how to put up a tent in a blizzard, and they were not overly familiar with Primus stoves. The ability to put up a tent in a blizzard and get the stove going are both life-saving basic survival skills – as are the abilities to ski, mountaineer, run dogs, and keep a ship from being trapped and crushed in the ice. More importantly for Markham, however, the officers were comfortable in the social milieu which he loved to impress, and the crew were a fine bunch of men. Dismissive of the potential difficulties and, of course, mostly ignorant of the challenges to be faced in Antarctica, he condemned as 'disgraceful' any doubt that the Royal Navy would be up to any task assigned to it. Experience was for pedants, danger-mongers and foreigners, all of whom were anathema to Markham.

Among those who predicted trouble as a result of inexperience was Dr Reginald Koettlitz, who was to be senior surgeon on the expedition. In a letter to Nansen, referring to Scott's appointment he wrote: [24]

> The course and final result of this matter, as at present constituted, will, I fear, be much blundering, waste of time and money, as well as not half being done which should have been done, in a word, it will be muddled through 'a l'Anglais' as so much undertaken by the official class (in England at least) is muddled and blundered through.

In spite of the fact that even in 1875 Nares had taken dogs and drivers, an Eskimo pilot, and whaling men as ice-quartermasters, [25] skis and dogs got short shrift from Markham. Writing to Professor Gregory at a time when he was still involved, he asserts that [26]

> With Nansen very poor work was made with the dogs, they got weaker and weaker, were killed to feed each other and all perished. Over rough ground they are an intolerable nuisance, cause endless delay and are worse than useless. Nansen's skis were not much better: in soft snow and rough ground he longed for Canadian snow shoes. Better with neither. Look at what men have done without all these new-fangled contrivances.

Gregory, too, is likely to have read Nansen's *Farthest North*, which came out in 1897, of which the above is a cherry-picked and self-serving reading. Only

Markham could have had the barefaced cheek to use Nansen in an argument against dogs and skis. Gregory must have been incredulous – if, that is, he hadn't already realised what kind of man he was dealing with. In 1899, moreover, Markham had heard Nansen, in an address to the Seventh International Geographical Congress, state publicly that [27]

> I have tried with and without dogs; in Greenland I had no dogs; then in the Arctic I used dogs, and I find that with dogs it is easier ... I agree it is cruel to take dogs; but it is also cruel to overload a human being with work. Likewise, it is cruel to kill dogs. But at home, we kill animals as well ...

In fact, Victorian explorers shot anything that moved. And as far as skis are concerned, Huntford asserts that Nansen's most conspicuous achievement was the application of skis to Polar travel. Markham's passion for Polar exploration was fired by his own conception of it, and he was prepared to do and to say whatever it took to keep his fantasy intact. Markham: [28]

> The *Discovery* left Cowes at 11.45 A.M. on August 6th 1901, and proceeded down channel. May all success attend the gallant explorers. They are engaged on a glorious enterprise; fighting no mortal foe, but the more terrible powers of nature arrayed against them.

> Truly they form the vanguard of England's chivalry, and England's King gave them a farewell signal of good wishes from the *Osborne* as the brave ship steamed away.

At last the farewells had been made: the fluttering hankies had faded into the distance, and the *Discovery* was on her way. First stop Madeira. Ten days later, after leaving Madeira, Scott ordered the photograph of Sir Clements in the wardroom to be taken down. [29]

References

1   T.H. Baughman. *Before the Heroes Came*, p. 82

2   *ibid.*

3   Hugh Robert Mill. *Hugh Robert Mill*, p. 142

4   C.E. Borchgrevink. *First on the Antarctic Continent*, p. 26

5   Sir Ranulph Fiennes. *Captain Scott*, p. 9

6   L.C. Bernacchi. *Saga of the "Discovery"*, pp. 29–30

7   *ibid.*, pp. 28–9

8   Admiral Sir Reginald Skelton. *The Antarctic Journals of Reginald Skelton*, p. 222

9   Sir Clements Markham. *Antarctic Obsession*, p. 27

10   Kelly Tyler-Lewis. *The Lost Men*, p. 127

11   Sir Clements Markham. *op. cit*, p. 69

12   T.H. Baughman. *op. cit*, p. 120

13   Sir Clements Markham. *op. cit*, p. 37

14   *op. cit*, p. 62

15   Edward Wilson. *Diary of the Discovery Expedition*, p. 190

16   Camille Paglia. *Sexual Personae*, p. 557

17   Captain Robert F. Scott. *The Voyage of the Discovery*, p. 71

18   Admiral Sir Reginald Skelton. *op. cit*, p. 18

19   David Crane. *Scott of the Antarctic*, p. 126

20   Captain Robert F. Scott. *op. cit*, p. 69

21   Sir Clements Markham. *op. cit*, p. 67

22   Edward Wilson. *op. cit*, p. 30

23   Sara Wheeler. *Terra Incognita*, p. 127

24   Aubrey A. Jones. *Scott's Forgotten Surgeon*, p. 125

25   M.E. Markham and F.A. Markham. *The Life of Sir Albert Hastings Markham*, pp. 76, 82

26   Aubrey A. Jones. *op. cit*, p. 121

27   Roland Huntford. *Scott and Amundsen*, p. 130

28   Sir Clements Markham. *op. cit*, p. 43

29   Roland Huntford. *op. cit*, p. 140

11

SCOTT'S MANAGEMENT STYLE AND

FIRST EXPERIENCE OF ANTARCTICA

It is widely agreed that towards the end of the Victorian era the Royal Navy had, to a large extent, become self-regarding and complacent, and was commanded by officers to whom the appearance of things mattered more than the substance. As a result, among the qualities that were important for promotion and that moulded Scott's generation of 'advancers' were, as well as the usual fortuitous connections of course, a smart appearance and the right attitude. The mainly diplomatic and ceremonial duties that occupied the Royal Navy at this time made it imperative that a 'good show' should always be put on, to which end many officers became preoccupied with achieving a visual ideal of perfection. This meant spotless decks, gleaming brass, and a complement of smart, clean, sailors who instantly jumped to orders. It gave a convincing impression of efficiency, even to itself.

Universal admiration, and complacent assumptions regarding its fighting powers, affirmed and perpetuated an attitude of personal as well as professional superiority and entitlement in much of the Naval hierarchy. On large ships especially, on which Scott served, the top officers formed a kind of Brahmin class in a caste system where men were identified by, and with, their jobs. Individual merit was no guarantee of promotion; accidents of birth were the main determinants of the levels to which men could aspire. No matter how talented, an ordinary sailor could not hope to rise beyond petty, or warrant officer, status without a commission, for which one had to receive officer training. This meant a level of education which, in the real world, excluded those not at least middle class by birth, bar the odd exception.

For junior officers like Scott, promotion was the main goal, and Scott became a torpedo officer because he believed it to be a path to promotion. When putting on a show and gambits for promotion become the main preoccupation of the participants, the ultimate aims of the organisation have been lost sight of. This is very bad news when this happens in an organisation that is supposed to form the main bulwark of a country's defences. Markham never allowed the defence of the nation to interfere with his chivalric vision. He might have felt they were much the same thing, as to him change and innovation were invariably examples of the Navy 'going to the dogs'. He would have preferred the Navy to have stayed exactly as it was in the 1850s, the way he had most enjoyed it.

However anachronistic his ideas, Markham, with his unshakeable self-belief, the stentorian voice that carried all before him and, last but not least, his enduring influence at the Admiralty, had the credibility and the power to make his dreams a reality. And Scott was 'Ready, Aye Ready', as his sledging pennant proclaimed. Markham liked pedigree, vigour, good looks, and a cheeky attitude in a boy. He may have had to sacrifice the pedigree and the cheek, but together with his air of intelligent competence, his physique and his looks, Scott was the nearest Markham was going to get to his *beau idéal.*

Scott was a compliant career officer. He played the game, becoming something of a martinet in his readiness to do whatever was needed to stay on the path to promotion. To all appearances a conventional officer with unexceptional beliefs and feelings, the inner Scott was conflicted and prone to depression. The Navy was more than a career, it was a way of life. Sets of ethics, morals, and values came with the job. It's no wonder Scott, in his quiet moments, asked himself what it was all about. If the transition from boy to man is a time of existential searching for identity, for meaning, for truth, how much more so, and how much more poignant would that search be in the context of an institution which rewarded empty shows of pomp and circumstance, and which deferred to rank often attained merely through seniority. The bottom line, however, would always have been that there was effectively no choice for him. The Navy was what he knew, and he needed the job. His inner angst and self-searching seem to have faded as he himself became increasingly part of the command structure. Nevertheless, the obedient, vulnerable and often frightened little boy within lived on. It was a part of Scott's psychology that Markham will have instinctively recognised, and it was part of what made him so attractive.

Nothing so well shows up Markham's folly than the fact that he allowed his personal, emotional and psychosexual preferences to dictate his choice of leader. He would have denied it, of course, but there could have been few other reasons for choosing Scott. Markham must have mentally conflated his sense of the right man for the job and his personal feelings. The two might have of course have coincided, but in this case they did not. The very things that made Scott attractive to Markham made him unsuited to lead an expedition, or to command a battleship for that matter.

Scott's father had been a man who hid from the world and reality in his potting shed. This must have meant that there was little modelling of a confident social role for young Con, and few lessons in how to face unpleasant facts. His father had hidden away from them; and whether it was an innate trait, or something he subliminally took on from his father, or both, in later life Scott evinced an instinct for denial and avoidance that would have unnerved anyone serving under him, had they had prior knowledge.

It may not be fair to review Scott's performance in the light of modern management and leadership theories and practices. The fact that he was in the Navy means that many civilian criteria for competence are redundant. One might also say it is unfair to apply modern understandings to a bygone era, when cultural, social, and organisational practices and expectations were different; in short, that it is unfair to judge Scott's performance by our own, civilian, standards. If, however, it is all basically about intelligence, confidence, communication and presence of mind, then the difference between Scott's era and our own boils down to the amount of information on the subject available in articulated form. You can now read or be told that the golden rules of management are about being honest with yourself, understanding other people, confidence, communication, adaptability, and an ability to put things in perspective and motivate your team.

A hundred years ago, even though that knowledge may not have been explicit, the basic tenets were as true then as they are today, and it was available in the form of live role models and individual examples. In spite of the fact that Naval officers could easily manage without those skills – and many of them did – the difference between a popular and effective officer and his opposite would have been to do with the emotional intelligence inherent in those golden rules, and having the courage to face reality.

Markham liked to think that Naval training sufficed to equip men for Polar exploration (and vice versa). This harked back to the heyday of M'Clintock, and his cousin Albert, who had for a short time held the Furthest North record with the Nares Expedition – scurvy notwithstanding. It was also traditional for governments to sponsor exploration, as it potentially led to territory to be claimed. Frozen wastelands, however, held few attractions, especially after the theory of an Open Polar Sea had started to be discounted after about 1870. [1] Enthusiasm for Polar exploration had further waned after the unfortunate Nares Expedition; and by the end of the century it was scientific, rather than material advancement that inspired the call for renewed efforts. Nansen breathed new life into Polar exploration with his oceanographical discoveries. Globally, the direction Polar exploration was taking was scientific, and it was strongly argued that exploration should now be of a scientific, rather than a geographical, nature. It was a view to which Markham paid lip service for strategic reasons, but which he fought tooth and nail.

The Naval command structure and the virtually unconditional obedience from the men, as well as the formally subordinate position of the officers, meant that Scott did not face the same kind of challenges as he would have in a non-military organisation. The fact that he was installed as absolute ruler on the *Discovery* made it possible for him – a complete Polar novice with scant experience of leadership – to head up a major expedition. But only on condition that the officers and crew were predominantly Navy. He didn't have to earn their respect: it was automatically bestowed on him as the Captain.

No one but Markham would have chosen Scott to lead the British National Antarctic Expedition. Lieutenant (as he then was) Scott had the position thrust upon him, never having evinced the slightest interest in exploration, nor having had the command of a ship. He was no naturalist, and had no knowledge of geology nor glacial matters. He had no experience of ice navigation, snow travel, camping, mountaineering, nor even surveying and cartography. It is interesting to note that neither Scott nor Markham, the great map enthusiast himself, had thought to equip the expedition with a plane table – essential for surveying and mapping. Skelton had to make one on the spot in Antarctica. Curiously – but then perhaps not, given Markham's vision – they did have on board a number of small silver medals [2]

> ... specially made before we left England, to be distributed as prizes
> to the winners of any kind of competition that we might have.

Graceful walking competitions perhaps?

In spite of his soul-searching and introspection, Scott was deficient in emotional intelligence and the courage to face reality – both essential to successful outcomes in terms of exploration and his career in general. There is something tortuous about both his expeditions; there is something tortuous about his entire career – Naval as well as Polar – and even about his marriage and his life in general. He was at war with himself, and his letters to his wife reveal low self-esteem, especially compared to her. Minor crises tended to throw him into a panicky fuss, and a major crisis was liable to result in a level of depersonalisation, or 'autopilot' response (a stress-response hyperstimulation) – as occurred when the *Terra Nova* nearly went down (about which much more later). At other times he burst into shows of temper and irascibility, for which he was sorry afterwards. All these things are evidence of stress, and a concomitant inability to deal with matters constructively.

Shows of temper serve to intimidate, and help to obscure a lack of competence in a leader. They alienate colleagues and divert attention away from the fundamental objects of the venture – and they are punitive, reflecting the Royal Navy school of management by chastisement and bullying. Skelton, describing an incident aboard the *Discovery*, gives an example: [3]

... the Skipper was a bit sick & kicked up a deuce of a fuss about [a broken sledge]. Whitfield, like the sensible man he is, had already acknowledged he was entirely to blame, but that wasn't enough. The skipper must send for Dellbridge & give him a severe dressing down, although I was on board all the time. The thing is a case of tyranny to Dellbridge, an unkindness to Whitfield, after he has said it was nothing to do with Dellbridge, & an insult to me ...

It doesn't take a management manual to point out that this is an instance of tyrannical behaviour and poor leadership. Skelton's diaries weren't published until 2004. Before that, they were only available to scholars and biographers – and they, on the whole, chose to ignore passages such as that. Instead, Skelton tends to be cast as dour, and inclined to complain.

Scott got his leave from Navy duties at the end of July 1900, a month after being promoted to Commander, and about a year before the expedition was due to sail. [4] The step up from lieutenant to commander is known for the challenge it represents. He might have been secretly relieved at not having to face the daunting prospect of commanding a battleship. Compared to that, the expedition was more of a pleasure jaunt, which is in fact how many people saw it. He was helped enormously by having a year as transitional period, in which he could ease himself into his new role, nursed along by Markham. He had not only to find his commander's persona, but he also had to reinvent himself as an explorer.

A visit to Nansen in Norway was arranged by Markham as a priority. It was just so much window dressing, as Markham had already decided how the expedition was going to be run – and that owed more to Nares and M'Clintock than it would ever do to Nansen. Nevertheless, Scott listened to Nansen, and not just on the subject of sledges and cookers. He took on board some of what Nansen said about skis and dogs, although without appreciating the vital importance of either. It is to Scott's credit that although he himself did not recognise their true value until it was too late, he withstood Markham's disparagement of those 'new-fangled contraptions' and foreign ways, and took a number of dogs and skis – which was just as well.

The visit played well with the public and helped establish Scott's credentials – as did the visit that was next on the agenda, to Professor Drygalski in Berlin, who was setting up the German *Gauss* Expedition, scheduled to sail for Antarctica at about the same time as the *Discovery*. Although treating Scott with the 'utmost kindness and consideration', Drygalski showed him what an expedition in the making looked like. Hence, back in London, a flurry of activity ensued, with a whirl of testing and ordering supplies and equipment. In the meantime, the joining of other officers, and Markham's behind-the-scenes machinations to get the Navy to supply a full complement of sailors, went ahead. Much of this was managed, as we know, with the help of Admiral Hoskins, who died soon afterwards.

It was probably one of the most fun years of Scott's career. Portraits from around this time show him looking reassuringly confident and at ease. Apart from the many provisioning mistakes made due to inexperience, which he disarmingly admits to, the ship was well stocked, especially with regard to alcohol and tobacco. Those were the days.

Scott was never the type of leader who gathers a team around him. Collaboration was never high on his agenda. He enjoyed 'bossing the show', in spite of his many anxieties. His reticence in letting others know what he was thinking and planning suggests a level of psychological insecurity – as does his habit of enquiring into, and suggesting improvements in the work of, the scientists and technicians. Bernacchi: [5]

> With his quick brain he would analyse statements and theories in a very embarrassing manner, and the scientists on board soon learned to row cautiously in connexion therewith, even as applied to their own specialities. Any weakness in the argument was quickly pounced upon.

This is challenging and competitive behaviour. He is clearly establishing his power and dominance. It was a way of showcasing his intellectual abilities and technical acumen, affirming his fitness as leader. Only an insecure person would bother. On the positive side, he was also no doubt genuinely interested, and it would have been a useful strategy for engaging with his officers and scientists. They might, however, sometimes have felt they could have done without his input, and they might have wondered whose interests it served.

Scott was competitive by nature: he first comes to history's notice as the winner of a boat race. That he turned out to be a naturally strong man-hauler allowed him to compare himself favourably with others, and always to outperform them. It was an important aspect of the vindication he and Markham would have sought as evidence of his suitability. Skelton [6] confirms Scott's ingrained competitive trait on the occasion of the dispersal of the ship's library at the end of the *Discovery* Expedition:

> There was a slight hitch at the commencement owing to The Skipper thinking he was not getting a fair chance, & altogether it seemed to me very silly & small-minded, but it 'blew off'. That is one thing our Skipper cannot do 'play a losing game'. It is most noticeable, even in the trivial little games on deck of Cricket, in 'bridge' which we used to play in Winter quarters, in fact in almost any form of sport.

This little window on Scott's psychology suggest he wasn't just competitive: he was also prone to reverting to what Eric Berne [7] would call a child-like ego state. In Transactional Analysis (TA) Berne differentiates between parent/adult/child ego states, all of which are present in potential in everybody. The adult ego state is obviously the appropriate one for a grown-up, and it therefore provides the standard by which the others are judged. While Skelton takes an adult line (with somewhat parental overtones) in the above citation, Scott's behaviour as described by Skelton certainly suggests this child-like ego state. Scott lacked a sense of autonomy: the fact that he had to win every time suggests he saw losing as a loss of face. It indicates that he was dependent on the opinion of others – or the opinions he projected on to others – to sustain a kind of dominance, which he probably mistook for leadership. Domination is, however an immature form of leadership.

It is plausible to characterise many of his negative behaviours as being the result of a reversion to psychological childhood: his outbursts of temper, his tendency to blame other people when things went wrong, his self-serving manipulation of the facts and denial, bullying, and the need to be the centre of attention. All of these behaviours will be analysed in more detail elsewhere. For now, we will just note that his habit of sitting at the head of the table in a monarchical way (complete with head courtier Wilson) constituted a strong signal, reminding the wardroom every day who was boss. So far as his mistakes were concerned, he did not blame others directly, but he habitually spun things so as to evade responsibility. It is another major theme to which we will return. Nevertheless, the guilt he tended to almost immediately feel after an angry outburst show that he was aware that he had let go to an unworthy impulse. The nature of the ego state that gave rise to the outburst probably remained unacknowledged. It is clear from Skelton's observation that others did recognise it, however, which must have been detrimental to the respect he commanded.

Scott had prestige and influence thrust upon him, but once he had it, he rose to it and made sure he kept it. Although often genial and humane, he was moody, irritable and hypercritical, especially when under stress or pressure. In the early months, before he formed his special relationship with Wilson, command must have been a very lonely job for him. Unwilling to share his doubts and uncertainties, he spent many hours alone in his cabin, while keeping up the appearance of a competent captain in control of the situation. His own career up to that point hadn't included much beyond carrying out orders from on high, and he had no experience of high-level decision-making. The obvious person he should have consulted with was Armitage, second-in-command, with maritime as well as Polar experience. Their initial meeting may have been full of goodwill and bonhomie, but their relationship didn't mature into confidentiality and trust. As time went on, they grew further apart.

Scott's leadership style was autocratic, defensive and insecure. He lacked confidence in his own leadership skills because he did not have the inner strength that comes with knowledge and experience – of himself, of others, and of the demands of the task in hand. His defensive leadership style suggests that his position was as important, if not more, than the optimal welfare of the expedition. One could argue that he should have refused the appointment in the first place on the grounds of his own inexperience and lack of qualifications, of which he was only too aware. It was an offer he couldn't refuse, maybe, but he was Markham's ideological and moral heir – more so than is generally credited. Although Markham probably reflected parts of himself that Scott was reluctant to admit to, there was an implicit affinity between them in terms of world view and values. Scott may have been more introspective and less blatant, but he was as competitive and jealous of his power and status as Markham.

It is difficult to see what more could have been done to ensure success for Scott, and for someone with no experience he achieved fair results. If the *Discovery* hadn't had to be rescued, it would have been a reasonably satisfactory, albeit unspectacular, expedition. The results had, however, been achieved at a very high cost both in effort and hardship. Of course, endeavours such as these do require utmost effort and commitment; but a grown-up expedition leader would always aim for an optimum, rather than a maximum, effort. I say grown-up, because it implies an adult ability to take distance – to disidentify with the effort, and to take the whole of a situation into account, including the inconvenient bits. Instead, Scott's *modus operandi* was to deny the unwanted bits and push through doggedly, often demanding that bit extra which was usually just too much. He was lucky to get away with it on his first expedition.

In the short term, all he had to do was to sail a brand-new, lavishly equipped and accoutred ship to New Zealand. It was almost a pleasure cruise. It gave him and the crew an opportunity to shake down, and for Scott to find his feet as Captain – a new sensation for him. Commanding the ship was a comparatively easy task, and their sojourn in New Zealand confirmed him in his position without all the questions and doubts that had hung over him at home.

After an ill-omened departure from Lyttelton, when a seaman called Charles Bonner was killed falling from the top of the mainmast while waving farewell, it was not until they got amongst the icebergs that the risks made themselves felt, and presented Scott with his first tests as Polar explorer. They had a couple of lucky escapes when icebergs and currents threatened to trap them. Disaster was narrowly avoided: a storm near Coulman Island required all Armitage's seamanship skills in managing the heavily laden ship – although he modestly says little about it, and is not individually credited. Skelton also did a brilliant job, keeping the engines going flat-out for hour after hour. Meanwhile, nobody on the ship knew what they were aiming for from day to day, nor even hour to hour. While still off Coulman Island, Wilson writes: [8]

> The Captain is strangely reticent about letting a soul on the ship know what even his immediate plans are ...

He adds that this may be right, as it keeps everything ready at all times. It is actually a wasteful and inefficient use of resources and poor man-management. People prefer and respond better to well-defined goals and agendas – even more so when they are part of the decision-making process. That way, people know what they are doing and why, what to prioritise, and when to take time off.

In Scott's day, men were expected to pick up leadership skills as they went along. Many people thought that you either 'had it', or not. There was probably something in that. In the absence of formal management training, one needed emotional intelligence, an ability to connect with others in a meaningful way, self-knowledge, courage in facing up to reality, and the ability to see beyond one's own biases – or at least to acknowledge that one has them. Parents, teachers, and peers were important role models. In the Navy, where boys lived as though at boarding school, it was the officers who provided the most powerful role models. Scott was at a disadvantage in that many of his superior officers were haughty pedants rather than practical seadogs. He gives the impression of having tried to emulate those who impressed or awed him most, which may have served – after a fashion – in the normal run of Navy life, but was not suited to the job in hand.

Schooled from the age of 14 by the Royal Navy, Scott became and remained a conformist officer, apparently unable and unwilling to think or to act outside the Navy box. In any case, too much of his power and worth was vested in that box for him to seriously contemplate messing with it. He also needed the structure and the support it gave him. Not only was he excused from having to earn the respect of his men, if he chose to direct operations from his cabin it was his prerogative to do so, whatever the circumstances. Accordingly, he spent a lot of time alone in his cabin, planning, doing calculations, and writing his diary, as was to become typical of him. It presented a legitimate opportunity to be otherwise engaged, away from the constant social, professional and practical pressures his position brought.

Being always the last one in for breakfast, as he was, could be interpreted as a reluctance to face up to another day. Although he did participate in the wardroom activities, it was always with a sense of decorum. And although he did engage mostly good-humouredly, albeit competitively, in the games and pastimes, he would have suspected that echoes of London and the memory of being Markham's blue-eyed boy had not been entirely exorcised. He had tried to erase the memory of Markham by ordering his photo to be taken down, which was no doubt quietly noted by the wardroom. As it probably also was on the messdeck.

In accordance with his instructions, when they got to Antarctica, Scott steamed eastwards along the 'Barrier' (Ross Ice Shelf), and discovered the land that lay on its eastern boundary. They named it King Edward VII Land, but found it sufficiently inhospitable to turn immediately back towards McMurdo Sound. Certain now that that would be where they would find their wintering station, he presented an elaborate schedule of operations. It might have sounded impressive, but its very complexity and lack of provision for adverse conditions betrayed its naivety. Skelton: [9]

> In the forenoon the Captain held a consultation in the Ward Room & gave a general idea of our future plans, which are: to winter somewhere convenient in McMurdo Bay [*sic*]; explore there by sledge next spring & summer, as far South as possible; come out end of January, meet relief ship, coal & also leave a stock of about 100 tons on Franklin Island if possible; then send in a party with sledges from Wood Bay leaving relief ship to look after them; go North ourselves & explore between Cape North & Adelie island, which is at present quite unexplored; join relief ship at a rendez vous, probably Auckland Island, & go into Lyttelton together. During the winter we should: refit; come South, pick up our cargo of coal & push still further East than we have already been, trying to come out somewhere by Alexander Land or Peter Island; & go on to the Falkland Islands.

There is no indication that this was any sort of draft plan that was laid on the table as a basis for discussion and debate. It was 'Moses come down from the Mountain', and it provides further evidence of how Scott saw his role, which was not to conduct a co-operative venture, but to generate plans and issue orders accordingly. Ruling rather than leading. He had his own orders, of course, which were fairly detailed but, as though command itself had conferred on him the wisdom and knowledge to carry them out successfully, he took it upon himself alone to direct operations. Whatever the burden of responsibility, he guarded his power. The messdeck was probably philosophical. It wouldn't have been the first time, nor the last, that their lives were put in the hands of someone not promoted on merit but, by turn, nepotism, 'interest', and in this case because of romantic attachments formed by the Director of the Royal Geographical Society.

The unveiling of the plan seems to have taken the wardroom somewhat by surprise. It probably took a while to sink in and be properly understood. Wilson, in trying to explain it, makes it sound even more complicated. [10] Scott, like Markham, minimised and was in denial of potential problems and delays. Perhaps that's how explorers need to be in order to attempt anything at all, but the plan must have seemed extremely complicated, and therefore commensurately more likely to go wrong – even to some of the younger ears in the wardroom. Yelverton infers that the plan made sense to the whole of Scott's audience on the basis that Royds, in his diary, praised it as 'excellent'. [11] However, neither Wilson nor Skelton comment on it after describing the scheme in their journals. Armitage doesn't mention it at all. There is no mention of any discussion afterwards. Of course, any objections would likewise be based on supposition, as even Bernacchi's experience was limited. Nevertheless, it must have occurred to some that the plan was not only complicated, but left no discernible margin for error, nor unforeseen circumstances and/or events – which, realistically, were extremely likely in this environment.

In any case, it seems they kept their mouths shut – not just literally, but on paper too. Under the Terms and Conditions, all journals, diaries, data and reports were to be considered the property of the RGS for the first six months after their return. Hardly an encouragement to frankness, especially where criticism of the 'Skipper' or his plans was concerned. We cannot know what they were really thinking about Scott's plans; but the silence of Armitage, and the lack of comment from Wilson and Skelton, may be more significant than the sole commendation from Royds. And of course, if they did think it was overambitious, their views will have been vindicated. *Discovery* became hopelessly trapped in the ice, and went nowhere until matters were taken out of Markham's and Scott's hands, and put into those of an experienced whaling captain. In fairness, even an experienced Polar explorer would not necessarily have known the extent to which the ice in McMurdo Sound varies from year to year – although they might not have so readily assumed that it always cleared as far down as Hut Point.

In the absence of ideas of his own, the basic template for Scott's approach to sledging came from Nares and M'Clintock. Nares had run the 1875 North Pole Expedition mainly from the comfort of his cabin: orchestrating the teams and the journeys rather than sledging himself, and working out complicated logistics for support teams and depots, as pioneered by M'Clintock. Scott and Markham assumed that whatever approach worked in the Arctic would also work in the Antarctic. It was a self-serving assumption, as it allowed them to dismiss the concerns of the 'danger-mongers' and Jeremiahs so despised by Markham. It was, however, a hubristically complacent assumption which was amplified by Scott's tendency to rush things.

Having arrived at the place they called Hut Point and frozen themselves snugly in for the winter, according to Yelverton: [12]

> Scott saw the initial tasks for that season as learning to use the dogs and giving everyone a chance to gain some experience sledging.

According to Bernacchi, however, even months afterwards: [13]

> ... there were still unplumbed depths of inexperience. We did not know how to put up a tent in a blizzard, nor how to secure it in place

when it was up. We did not know how to manage the cookers effect-ively, nor even how to put on our sledging clothes properly. Possibly competitions in making camp, including all the multi-farious duties to be performed in a tiny tent before toggling down for the night, might advantageously have taken the place of moon-light football matches ... and competitions in dog driving would have taken the keen edge off our ignorance of that most important accomplishment.

Football matches on ice sound exactly suited to provide opportunities for injury, and Scott himself was duly laid up with an injured knee.

Impatience was one of Scott's most commented-on characteristics. Hence, skipping the tedious basics, one of the trips he conceived as a training journey – the infamous first Cape Crozier trip –involved a party of 12 men, including three officers and a scientist, four sledges, eight dogs, and rations for three weeks – over unknown terrain with the possibility of blizzards, whiteouts, frostbite and a good chance of getting lost. Hardly a beginner's task – especially as it was late in the season (March 1902), when bad weather could confidently be expected. The popular prejudice against skis, which Scott doesn't seem to have done much to counteract, meant that only Skelton, Royds and Koettlitz were on skis and there-fore better equipped to go on. All the others trudged laboriously through the deep snow found in the area that later became known as the 'windless bight'. It was so exhausting as to rob them of the will to continue, and three days after their depart-ure the majority voted to return to the ship.

Barne, the only officer not on skis, was put in charge of the returning party of nine men (including himself) and eight dogs. Aged just 24, according to Wilson, he was [14]

> ... but a child, and has still a great deal to learn and the more immed-iately he learns it, the better for the men put under his charge in such a dangerous climate as this.

All might still have been well if they had gone back the way they came; but they decided the walking would be easier along the top of Hut Point Peninsula, where the snow might not be so deep.

They had seen the dangerous slopes that formed the northwest boundary of the peninsula from the ship on their way in. The terrain had as yet only been sketchily mapped, and wrongly at that. The outcome is history; but it was a miracle that Taff Evans, Barne and Quartley survived, as they slid down a slope, at the bottom of which the ice-cold sea awaited. Saved by a little patch of snow, they escaped the fate of George T Vince, who did indeed slide to his death – but it was a very close thing. Not equipped with crampons, ice-axes or ropes, they had to crawl, furiously 'clinging with knives & toes & fingers' back up the icy incline. Quartley reports that Barne almost stepped into space: [15]

> The snow was so thick that you could not see more than 2 feet ahead & he only just saw the abyss in time ...

Meanwhile, Wild, Weller, Heald, Plumley and Vince, having become detached from Barne's party, proceeded along further slippery slopes – all of them, except the unfortunate Vince, narrowly escaping certain death in the icy water.

Scott's tranquil evening was rudely shaken by the arrival back on board of Wild's exhausted and overwrought party, now numbering just four. A search party under Armitage was quickly assembled to search for the others. Scott: [16]

> Hatefully conscious of my inability to help on account of my injured leg, my own mind seemed barren of all suggestion of further help which we might render; but, as was always my experience in the *Discovery*, my companions were never wanting in resource. Dell-bridge thought he could soon raise steam enough to blow the syren, and before long its shrill screams were echoing amongst the hills.

The worrying possibility that they might have a leader whose mind went blank in a crisis must have occurred to some then, if it hadn't already.

Barne, whose fingers had been badly frostbitten climbing up the slope, and who seems to have been in a dazed, probably hypothermic, condition on his return to the ship, later took responsibility for Vince's death, writing that he took [17]

> ... full responsibility for this sad occurrence, for which I am entirely to blame.

While Scott declined to criticise Barne, citing extenuating circumstances and praising his subsequent sledging leadership, he did not go so far as to take responsibility for having sent men out so fundamentally unprepared. On the contrary: in a lecture to the men afterwards, Scott impressed on them their responsibility for their own safety. Without suggesting that he should have nurse-maided them, it is nevertheless normal for the captain of a ship to take responsibility for the safety of his crew and his ship in the execution of their duties, and to make sure they are prepared and fit for the job in hand. The sad irony was that there had been no need to go to Cape Crozier at all at that time. No ship could be expected there until January 1903 at the earliest. They could have waited for a much more benign season. In fact, the relief ship *Morning* arrived at Cape Crozier on 18 January 1903, ten months later. [18]

Scott had an unfortunate and persistent tendency to avoid taking responsibility for his mistakes; noted by Huntford also. The Navy blame-culture had kept alive and nurtured the 'little boy inside' who was frightened of being told off. According to Weinberg, [19]

... the flow of blame in an organization is one of the most important indicators of that organization's robustness and integrity. Blame flowing upwards in a hierarchy ... proves that superiors can take responsibility for their orders to their inferiors, and supply them with the resources required to do their jobs. But blame flowing downwards, from management to staff, or laterally between professionals, indicates organizational failure. In a blame culture, problem-solving is replaced by blame-avoidance ... blame coming from the top generates "fear, malaise, errors, accidents, and passive-aggressive responses from the bottom", with those at the bottom feeling powerless and lacking emotional safety.

There are plenty of indications that fear, malaise, errors, accidents and passive-aggressive responses were present on the *Discovery*. They may not have been explicit, as they wouldn't be, but they were there.

The Naval tradition of catching 'em young ensured that most officer cadets hadn't had time to develop a sense of autonomy or independence of mind by the time they entered the Navy. And it picked up where school left off. In most cases this would have meant a continuation of a culture where mistakes elicit punishment and count against you, rather than representing opportunities for learning – although that of course did happen by default. It meant, however, that there was an incentive to disown mistakes and, preferably, avoid them altogether.

Many, like Scott, never really matured beyond the parent–child dynamic that underlies authoritarian cultures. The blame-shifting reflex, for many originating at home, continued at school and, reinforced by the Navy, was entrenched by the time these boys reached adulthood. In Scott's case, it was never really lost. Of course that wasn't the whole story, and there were supportive, humane role models in his life. But they were not in the majority. Blame-culture was institutionalised in Scott's Navy. Passing the buck and tongue lashings were common behaviours in an officer, and Scott duly conformed when sensing his own mistakes and their potentially corrosive effect on his authority. They may not have won him many friends, but those behaviours would not have seemed unusual, either to himself, his officers, nor his crew.

It was somewhat different for the scientists. Rude snubs were not what they were used to – and Bernacchi, writing some 36 years later, leaves us in no doubt about who was responsible for one of the more preventable mistakes made on the *Discovery* Expedition: the near-loss of all the ship's boats. Five 26-foot whaleboats and two Norwegian prams were stored on the sea-ice, against Bernacchi's advice. We can imagine his legitimate *schadenfreude* afterwards, when Scott's refusal to listen resulted in the boats becoming encased in ice. Bernacchi tells the story in *Saga of the "Discovery"*, published in 1938: [20]

As winter closed down and the canvas deck-covering was being fixed over *Discovery*, it had been found that the boats interfered with its fitting, and Captain Scott had ordered their removal to the sea-ice. It was then that I had my one and only experience with what seemed an unreasonable side of his nature. I had been through a winter before, and had seen the effect of the unbelievable weight of snow which accumulated upon the ice, pressing it down into the sea so that the water displaced flowed over it, making a top layer of slush, until that, too, froze. When I saw *Discovery*'s boats spread out upon the ice, I had indicated this possible danger. The result was an experience I did not care to repeat, for I was told, in no uncertain terms, to attend to my own speciality. Now the worst fears were realized. The driving winter blizzards had filled the boats and covered them, the weight of the snow upon the vast surface of bay ice had pressed it beneath the water. It had frozen, and the boats were embedded in the solid floe.

Scott puts an entirely different spin on things: [21]

What has become of our boats? Early in the winter they were hoisted out to give more room for the awning, and were placed in a line about 100 yards from the ice-foot on the sea-ice ... Although we had noted with interest the manner in which the extra weight of snow in other places was pressing down the surface of the original ice, and were even taking measurements of the effects thus produced, we remained fatuously blind to the risks our boats ran under such conditions ... At present all hands are removing the snow on top of the boats and for a distance of ten yards around, and are forming a snow-wall on the outskirts of this area. It is a long job, and will probably have to be repeated after every gale. Meanwhile our stupidity has landed us in a pretty bad hole, for we may have to leave this spot without a single boat in the ship ... we bowed to the inevitable whilst we heartily cursed the folly which had landed us in such a predicament.

Bernacchi was the only one on board with any Antarctic experience. He had been one of only ten men to have spent the pioneering first winter on the Antarctic mainland. He had experienced and coped with many of the problems and issues that entailed. He had seen the dog- and cold-weather adepts Per Savio and Ole Must in action. He had written a book about his experiences. After they vacated Cape Adare, the *Southern Cross* had sailed along the coast of Victoria Land. They had made landings on Possession, Coulman, and Franklin Islands. They had discovered and named Lady Newnes Bay, from the vicinity of which Bernacchi, together with William Colbeck, had worked out the position of the South Magnetic

Pole. They had steamed along the Barrier and had made a landing in the Bay of Whales, from which Borchgrevink set his short-lived Southern Record. If any man on the *Discovery* deserved respect for what he knew about Antarctica, it was Bernacchi. Any leader worthy of the name would have taken full advantage of his knowledge. Instead, Scott told him to mind his own business.

The next five months were for Bernacchi a daily vindication. It took an enormous amount of work to stop the boats from being swallowed up by the ice altogether and, as for getting them out, it was to Bernacchi a wonder that it was accomplished at all. It was, but not without a great deal of damage to the boats. It must have affected his relationship with Scott – never very close at the best of times.

Scott fails to mention that he'd been warned about the danger. Instead, he generalises the blame, using the word 'we' throughout his account – while at the same time pre-empting criticism by criticising the error himself. At the time, the only option would have been to brazen it out and pretend the incident with Bernacchi never happened. It is understandable that Scott hated to be given unsolicited advice. In any case, if the boats had already been put on the ice, what Bernacchi had to say would have been the last thing he wanted to hear. To defer to his superior knowledge would have been humiliating to a defensive leader like Scott, and might detract from his authority. He had his legitimising Navy culture to fall back on. Naval officers were not in the habit of listening to, much less accepting, advice from 'inferiors'. We can imagine Scott's inner discomfiture, however, as the wisdom of what Bernacchi had tried to tell him revealed itself.

In an early example of Wilson's tendency to make excuses for Scott, he tells us that putting boats on sea-ice [22]

> ... has always been the recognised thing to do with the boats in the
> Arctic during the winter.

As Wilson was never noted as an expert on Arctic exploration, and because Scott had an investment in justifying his decision, the likelihood is that Wilson picked up that information from Scott, consciously or otherwise. Inwardly, Scott would have marshalled as many justifications as he could. As well as the putative practices in the Arctic, he might have told himself that there had been no reason to act on Bernacchi's say-so; because they were not now at Cape Adare; that his speciality was magnetism and meteorology, not snow and ice; and that if he had had something to say about it, he should have done so before the boats were hoisted out. Those kinds of thoughts might have gone a long way toward taking the sting out the gaffe for Scott; so that by the time he wrote his book, it might have faded into insignificance. Aided by denial, he could plausibly pretend to have forgotten all about it. Especially as of course he had a motive to do so. Markham would have done the same.

Notably, and indicative of a self-defeating tendency to petty vindictiveness, Scott did not include Bernacchi's 1901 book (*To the South Polar Regions*) about his experiences at Cape Adare in the library he took with him later on the *Terra Nova*. Campbell's team, who spent nearly a year at Cape Adare as Scott's Eastern (later Northern) Party, would have been grateful for it, as there was precious little information available as it was. [23]

Bernacchi's 'one and only experience' of Scott's unreasonable side is invariably taken to mean that Scott was seldom unreasonable; but as Bernacchi himself implies, he kept out of the firing line after that, and certainly never ventured to offer advice again. But he never forgot it, and it still rankled after more than 30 years – enough to impel him to put the record straight, regardless of what Scott had written, and in spite of his iconic status.

References

1   Pierre Berton. *The Arctic Grail*, p. 436

2   Lieut. Albert Borlase Armitage. *Two Years in the Antarctic*, pp. 150–1

3   Admiral Sir Reginald Skelton. *The Antarctic Journals of Reginald Skelton*, p. 106

4   Captain Robert F. Scott. *The Voyage of the Discovery*, p. 33

5   L.C. Bernacchi. *Saga of the "Discovery"*, p. 212

6   Admiral Sir Reginald Skelton. *op. cit.*, pp. 220–1

7   Eric Berne. *Games People Play*

8   Edward Wilson. *Diary of the Discovery Expedition*, p. 98

9   Admiral Sir Reginald Skelton. *op. cit.*, p. 50

10   Edward Wilson. *op. cit.*, p. 110

11   David E. Yelverton. *Antarctica Unveiled*, p. 115

12   *op. cit.*, p. 120

13   L.C. Bernacchi. *op. cit.*, p. 63

14   Edward Wilson. *op. cit.*, p. 202

15   Admiral Sir Reginald Skelton. *op. cit.*, p. 69

16   Captain Robert F. Scott. *op. cit.*, p. 174

17   David E. Yelverton. *op. cit.*, p. 134

18   Reginald Pound. *Evans of the Broke*, p. 40

19   Gerald M. Weinberg . 'Beyond Blaming', AYE Conference, 5 March 2006. Blame, Wikipedia, www.en.m.wikipedia.org

20   L.C. Bernacchi. *op. cit.*, p. 57

21   Captain Robert F. Scott. *op. cit.*, pp. 253–5

22   Edward Wilson. *op. cit.*, p. 169

23   Meredith Hooper. *The Longest Winter*, p. 146

12

KOETTLITZ AND WILSON

Albert Armitage and Reginald Koettlitz were the most experienced in Polar travel and survival, having spent almost three years in the Arctic with the Jackson-Harmsworth Expedition. Armitage was appointed second-in-command and navigator on the *Discovery*, Koettlitz as doctor and senior scientist. They had been taken on at the behest of Alfred Harmsworth (later Lord Northcliffe) who had donated £5,000 on condition that two of his nominees were appointed. [1] Armitage had been selected for his seamanship skills, which had saved lives in the Arctic, and Koettlitz because there had been no general outbreak of scurvy at Cape Flora, in Franz Josef Land, in the three years that the Jackson-Harmsworth Expedition spent there. There had, however, been one death from scurvy. A 52-year-old crew member had died after having persistently refused to eat fresh bear and walrus meat. With hindsight, it seems extraordinary that the penny should still not have dropped. Even Nansen, an eminent scientist himself, was an adherent of the tainted food theory. [2] Something of a conceptual paradigm shift had evidently to take place in their thinking. Unfortunately, it meant that tinned food, devoid of vitamin C, still made up a substantial part of the diet that Koettlitz (initially) recommended for the *Discovery* Expedition.

Koettlitz was critical of Scott and the way the expedition had been set up. He wasn't impressed either with the last-minute rush and muddle; with stores and equipment having to be sent on, and officers still being trained to use scientific instruments on the voyage out. He was especially scathing of the decision to take only a token number of dogs. Having become friends with him at Cape Flora, Koettlitz knew Nansen well. In a letter to Nansen in which he gives his opinion of the 'muddling through à l'Anglais', Koettlitz writes: [3]

> To give you one instance, among many, it had been intended to take
> no dogs, or other animals at all, but to use men only, as traction
> power when upon sledge expeditions, and it was only, as a grudg-

ingly given concession to the representation of Captain Scott, who cannot explain their value, that permission has been given to take twenty (20!!) dogs and I expect that Captain Scott has done this only because of what you have said to him when talking to him!

To think that men can be such fools, after the remarkable object lesson which has so recently been given them, by the success which has attended the Duke of Abruzzi's expedition which took over a hundred of these animals!! Such blindness has indeed a tendency to disgust and weary one with the whole business, and would, if it were not for the hope that one may be able to do some good work in the south not withstanding.

(The Duke of the Abruzzi had organised an expedition to the North Pole in 1898, in which Captain Umberto Cagni led a team that established a new Northern Record, beating Nansen's by about 35 kilometres.) [4]

Koettlitz was not one of the boys, and he was not comfortable amid the competitive, often laddish, repartee and mickey-taking that went on in the wardroom. What made it worse was that he was often the butt of the jokes, and although he seemed to take it in good part, inwardly he is likely to have been hurt and angry. General behaviour patterns would have been laid down on the voyage to New Zealand; and by the time they posed for the famous group photographs taken in Lyttelton, on the afterdeck of the *Discovery,* Koettlitz seems to have formed an attitude. Tall and serious, he stands squarely in the middle of the Royal Navy command nucleus, in a position that is clearly anomalous. Although Koettlitz was regarded as somewhat eccentric, it is unlikely that he was standing in that position by accident – especially as he maintains it through two exposures.

He might have been feeling bloody minded that day, or superior, or simply lacking in tact and discretion; but it also suggests an awkward attempt to subvert the Naval hegemony of the expedition and claim priority for science and those with relevant knowledge and experience. Another, flawed, and therefore less used, photo of the same occasion, apparently taken a few minutes earlier from a slightly different angle, shows Koettlitz in the same position but with his hands behind his back, standing just behind Scott's right shoulder, partially obscuring Barne. In the second photo, Koettlitz has his hands in his pockets, suggesting that he dug in, in spite of what must have felt like an increasingly uncomfortable, and possibly embarrassing, situation. Scott stands somewhat tersely in half profile. The facial expressions and body language of those around him suggest that Koettlitz was seen as intrusive and slightly laughable. And irritating to Scott.

'Cutlets', as he was inevitably nicknamed, might well have felt that, other than navigation and knowing how to sail a ship, he outranked them all in terms of experience and training. He had spent over three years in Franz Josef Land, becoming an experienced Arctic traveller and practised skier; he had successfully fulfilled his role as doctor there, and had done useful geological work. He had many years' experience in general practice as a doctor; he had held positions of responsibility, and was a competent self-taught geologist. He had submitted a substantial and (eventually) highly regarded paper to the RGS on the geology and age of Franz Josef Land. After Nansen's arrival at Cape Flora, they spent a month happily geologising together, as a result of which Nansen became a treasured friend with whom he was in correspondence for the rest of his life.

It must have been a disappointment when Markham appointed the newly qualified and completely inexperienced Hartley Ferrar as geologist – geology being Koettlitz's passion. Instead, he took on the botanical and bacteriological work, in addition to his medical duties. Quite soon after departure it must also have been disappointing to realise that Edward Wilson ('Billy'), the junior medical officer, was never going to be his natural ally. Instead, Wilson made friends with Shackleton, and had begun to impress the rest of the wardroom and crew with his quiet humour, selflessness, and avuncular demeanour – starting the process by which he was eventually to become the power behind Scott's throne. Wilson, despite coming to the job entirely without relevant experience and virtually no knowledge of cold injuries and the dangers of life in deep cold, never attracted criticism – unlike Koettlitz, who struggled to be taken seriously. The worship of Wilson began on that journey, and it threw into relief the increasing marginalisation – and concomitant sense of injustice – undoubtedly felt by Koettlitz.

With certain important reservations, the ambiance in the wardroom was one of which Markham would have approved. It echoed that of the gunrooms so fondly remembered by him. Koettlitz to Nansen, in a letter dated 29 August 1904: [5]

> Personally, with regard to this (*Discovery*) expedition, I am far from satisfied. Though very good, as well as a considerable amount of work has been done by everyone, the spirit under which it has been done has, in a large part, been a frivolous and happy-go-lucky one. These naval and other officers look upon everything that happens and that they do as a 'bit of fun', as sport, and they do it in sporting style. There is no backbone in it, and much of it is carelessly done. There is also too much of the official tradition in it, and too much 'red tape'.

In the event, neither Koettlitz nor Armitage formed especially close relationships with Scott, and neither seem to have been called upon to impart their knowledge of sledging and camping. Koettlitz was a competent sledger, according to Skelton. It is hard to imagine Scott taking advice from 'Cutlets', however, the 'foreign', somewhat aloof and disdainful scientist. Predictably, he was routinely baited and made fun of. Barne rather cruelly played practical jokes on him. For his part, Koettlitz, in addition to not being able to understand how a man with no scientific training could be appointed scientific director (as Scott was), must also have marvelled at how the same man, with no Polar experience, could be appointed leader of a national Polar expedition. With his socialist political leanings, he was probably also critical of all the pandering to royalty and the *beau monde*, and would have felt that there were more important things to do – especially in a ship full of Polar beginners. Skelton tells us that Koettlitz could be amusing after a couple of drinks, however, and that he wasn't always so rigorous in his dedication to work – but the overall impression remains that he was marginalised, not least by Scott. When the expedition returned, the plaudits went to Wilson. Koettlitz was largely excluded from involvement in compiling the scientific reports: a snub which one commentator claims accounted for his sad demeanour for the rest of his life. In fairness, however, he seems never to have been the most cheerful of souls.

In the *Discovery* wardroom, personal relationships mattered more than professional excellence. Competitive power and status games would have been a continual sub-dynamic. Anyone who couldn't, or wouldn't, participate paid the price, and lost out when the credits finally rolled. Koettlitz's story is illustrative of this process, and he would have felt defensive from the beginning. His first line of psychological defence would have been to scorn 'these naval and other officers', and to watch them make a hash of things. For example, soon after arrival in Antarctica, Scott describes the sledging party about to set off on the first, hopelessly shambolic, journey to Cape Crozier, on which Vince lost his life. Scott: [6]

> The [sledging] party consisted of four officers, Royds, Koettlitz, Skelton, and Barne, and eight men ... I am bound to confess that the sledges when packed presented an appearance of which we should afterwards have been wholly ashamed, and much the same might be said of the clothing worn by the sledgers. But at this time our ignorance was deplorable; we did not know how much or what proportions would be required as regards the food, how to use our cookers, how to put up our tents, or even how to put on our clothes. Not a single article of the outfit had been tested, and amid the general ignorance that prevailed the lack of system was painfully apparent in everything. Though each requirement might have been remembered, all were packed in a confused mass, and, to use a sailor's expression, 'everything was on top and nothing handy.'

This disarming piece of self-confessed incompetence shouldn't have, but did, deflect criticism afterwards; but this level of unpreparedness was inexcusable by any standards. Not only was Koettlitz an experienced sledger, he had been the principal designer of the pyramid tents they were using, and he knew about sledging rations. It is hard to dismiss the possibility that he had stood and watched the shambles unfolding, while deliberately withholding any advice or input, to perhaps gain a grim satisfaction from the mess the much-vaunted Royal Navy would make of it. He had probably not been asked for his advice, and so he did not give it. If this was indeed the case, the implication is that there was an element of passive aggression in Koettlitz's behaviour. He is also unlikely to have enjoyed the command structure, in which he was expected to obey orders. On the face of it, he would have been happier on Bruce's *Scotia* Expedition; a more democratic set-up where work mattered more than dinner-table wit, and where his passion for science would have been valued.

Skelton: [7]

> He [Koettlitz] is a funny old chap, absolutely incapable of taking or understanding "chaff", but all the same he hasn't got many scruples about asking one to do things for him, which he doesn't care about himself.

Nevertheless, Koettlitz and Skelton got on well. It is a thousand pities and, frankly, suspect that Koettlitz's expedition diaries have been lost. The fact that Koettlitz tended to socialise only 'now and then', suggests a tacit rejection of the bonds of shared values, assumptions, and interpersonal protocols of the rest of the wardroom. There is the obvious possibility that his diaries might have contained a lot of criticism. With Markham as media and publicity manager, there was no chance that such a document would see the light of day. Even Skelton's mild criticisms were buried in the archives. His journals were not published for a hundred years.

Koettlitz's stand-offishness is bound to have coloured perceptions of his work, as his attitude would have suggested a lack of commitment and a remoteness from the goals of the expedition. He was a professional, cultural and social anomaly; not least in his apparent need for privacy and space, which was probably interpreted as rejecting, and slightly suspect. The group photograph taken on board the *Discovery* on their return to England shows Koettlitz in a very different mood from the Lyttelton photo. No longer within (although never part of) the command hub, his body language seems chastened and uncommunicative. His emotions must have been very mixed.

In addition to his personal difficulties, there had been scurvy on the expedition – a fact that would have mortified him and detracted from his record. Scott had, understandably, tried to keep the killing of animals to a minimum, and Koettlitz had done his best by sniffing the contents of tinned food in an attempt to eliminate 'scurvy taint'. It didn't work. His claim that it had happened because his advice to eat more fresh meat was not, or only partially, heeded wasn't enough. The subsequent eradication of scurvy by the increase in the consumption of fresh meat has invariably been credited to Armitage's strong interventions with the cook, and the improvement in palatability of seal and penguin that resulted.

There had also been the difficult issue of Shackleton's *de facto* dismissal after the Southern Journey. Scott laments the necessity of sending home an officer who, in his opinion, was not fit, and [8]

> ... ought not to risk further hardships in his present state of health.

Huntford's claim, and that of many subsequent biographers, is that Shackleton was sent home because he presented a challenge to Scott's authority – both because of his alleged insubordination as well as his charisma and buccaneering positivity. The suggestion of insubordination is based on reports of friction between Scott and Shackleton on the Southern Journey. Huntford quotes an angry confrontation between the two. This seems to be confirmed by Armitage who, in a letter to HR Mill almost 20 years later, claims that Scott told him at the time that [9]

> If he [Shackleton] does not go back sick, he will go back in disgrace.

The incident in question may have been the occasion on the Southern Journey when Scott discovered that one of the dogs had got loose and had eaten an entire week's supply of seal meat. In his book, he calls it a 'dire calamity' and, knowing Scott, he would have been extremely annoyed, and not seen the funny side of it – as he says he did – until much later. Wilson says nothing at all about it in his diary – which is odd, as it would have been the sort of event that would normally merit a mention. A plausible explanation is that it involved a confrontation, which he would have preferred to stay out of, and silent about. The relationship between Scott and Shackleton was never the same after that journey.

Nevertheless, the state Shackleton got into on that journey is likely to have given Scott a nasty shock, with symptoms which Wilson reports as being 'of no small consequence' so far away from the ship. Scott would have been genuinely worried in case it should happen again, or worse, and that Shackleton was therefore no longer fit for sledging. Equally plausible is the possibility that his endless poetic effusions had begun to pall, and his bonhomie to grate. Nevertheless, his talent for leadership, combined with his loquacious affability and rapport with the crew, must have made an uncomfortable contrast with Scott, whose behaviour was diffident and formal. Scott might have reflected that all this mattered only in a moral sense, as there could be no questioning of the chain of command – especially not on behalf of a sub-lieutenant, RNR. All the same, Shackleton is bound to have stimulated Scott's insecurities, and may have started to undermine his moral authority. Clearly, sending him home would rid Scott of a challenge. The idea of sending home an officer in disgrace was fanciful, however. It would have raised too many eyebrows. He knew that there were plenty of critics back in London who would seize on it as evidence as much of a failure on his part as on Shackleton's. Ill health was the obvious option, and Shackleton must have gritted his teeth at having handed Scott his excuse on a plate.

Scott's rather nannyish concern over Shackleton's health carries a hint of humbug when it is remembered that Wilson was taken on the expedition in spite of the advice of the Admiralty Medical Board. When x-rays showed scar tissue on Wilson's lungs from tuberculosis, they advised against him going. In his case, however, where there was a will there was a way, and Wilson came at his own risk with regard to his health. Presumably, Scott could have offered the same deal to Shackleton if he had wanted to. And of course events went on to show that Shackleton possessed great powers of recovery and endurance. The implication is that Koettlitz was Scott's patsy and did as he was told in invaliding Shackleton. Koettlitz hadn't been there when Shackleton got sick on the Southern Journey, and could only go by Scott's description, as he improved rapidly when he got back.

Wilson doesn't say much about Shackleton's invaliding in his published diary, other than to assert rather lamely that it was certainly wiser for him to go home. Wilson himself was in bed for the first two weeks after their return, and seems to have stayed out of the issue, in spite of the fact that he should have been the one to report on Shackleton's condition – being a doctor, and having been on the scene. 'Shacks' had been Wilson's friend and ally in the early days of the expedition. Since then, evidently, his loyalties had shifted. There was no advocacy on Shackleton's behalf from Wilson. If either he or Scott had wanted him to stay, he would have. It meant that sending him home was dirty work and Scott hid behind Koettlitz to do it. As Hodgson, a biologist on the *Discovery*, wrote in his diary: [10]

> I hear it is true, as I suspected, that personal feeling is the real reason for Shackleton's departure. We find our combined selves an awful crowd on board this ship.

Sub-Lieutenant George Mulock was taken on board in Shackleton's place – at first sight a most inoffensive creature, and the complete opposite of Shackelton. Skelton, however, had this to say about him: [11]

> ... Mulock, newly joined, is distinctly peculiar for such a youngster, a mixture of sulkiness, attempts at sarcasm, great readiness to take offence where none is meant, a little conceit, & a very unnecessary seriousness in general ...

It sounds like he struggled to hold his own – understandably in a wardroom full of more experienced scientists and officers, who had pre-established levels of familiarity and habituation, living and working together for almost a year and a half. It makes a big demand on a person's inner resources to cope well with being a newcomer and an outsider. But a surveyor and cartographer, as Mulock was, should have been present from the beginning.

Koettlitz's carefully preserved specimens were lost. His extensive studies of plankton and Antarctic bacteria, and his record of the health of the officers and crew, were not used in the final expedition reports. Nor was a series of 58 colour photographs of the region, which should have been of primary importance. They have now been lost, as has his expedition journal, an important historical document. Even a report in the *British Medical Journal* of 1905 on the medical aspects of the voyage was presented not by Koettlitz, but by Wilson. [12] And it raised a laugh, sadly, when Scott described, at a RGS dinner, how Koettlitz went daily to a thermometer on the floe to prove the temperature was 20 degrees lower than on the ship. [13] Nevertheless, he seems to have got on well with the laconic realist Skelton, one of the hardest-working officers on the ship, who wore out his gumboots in the engine-room after only three months at sea. Although not blind to his faults, Skelton liked and respected Koettlitz, and appreciated his sledging abilities – unlike Wilson, who wrote irritably: [14]

> Koettlitz is the main stumbling block. He gave out early in the voyage that he preferred to differ from every one else and he has rarely failed to do so.

Earlier, Wilson had noted that [15]

> Koettlitz as usual never put a finger to it [arranging the drugs], though I was down there at it from after breakfast till dinner time. He does less work in the general way than anyone on the ship.

And: [16]

> Koettlitz had his hair cut. The refuse filled all the townets and fouled both logs.

The sanctification of Edward Adrian Wilson happened on Scott's Last Expedition. On the *Discovery* he was still 'Bill the Critic', and 'Bill the Cynic', whose tolerance had not yet attained the heights of which Cherry-Garrard was later to write: [17]

> ... though maybe you could not reach his standard, he was immensely tolerant of your shortcomings: he treated you as an equal even if you were not so.

Poor young Cherry. It sounds as though Wilson brought out Cherry's sense of his own inadequacy. Gurus become gurus because they allow themselves to be put on a pedestal. They have to collude, however subtly, with their admirers' estimation of them in order to create and maintain their status. Undoubtedly, whatever Wilson said or did, he did with the best of intentions. Many gurus profess only to have others' welfare at heart, and claim that they are responding to a need. And of course Wilson was a man of his time. It would be unfair to expect him to have had the levels of insight and psychological range that we would now expect from a trained counsellor.

Both Wilson's and Skelton's *Discovery* diaries have been published more or less as they were written, rather than in later narrative form, as for example those of Scott and Armitage. They are useful to historians in more ways than one because they allow a day-by-day comparison of the same events, however trivial, and are therefore a window on the otherwise hidden dimensions in both. While in New Zealand, before departure for Antarctica, the warship HMS *Ringarooma* had been sent to assist the *Discovery* in any way it could, which of course included invitations to dinner on board. One, on 4 December 1901, is described by Skelton as a 'good show'. Wilson, however, says: [18]

> It was not a pleasant show to my mind, but I got hold of one nice man, who was known as Bug Walker ... a most interesting man. I felt very sorry for him in a mess made up of such men as the officers of that ship.

The dislike was undoubtedly mutual. Wilson's later reputation delegitimised all criticism, but there must always have been those who resented him for being holier than thou.

There is comparatively little self-disclosure in Wilson's diaries. They are full of observations and descriptions of the natural world, but we often have look for the things he does not say in order to get some sense of his feelings and opinions. He was well known to abhor 'impure' talk. The following reveals a distaste for what sounds like a harmless but well-oiled all-male occasion. The day after the dinner on the *Ringarooma*, there was a dinner at the 'Canterbury Club', about which all Wilson has to say is 'I sat between Rhodes, the Mayor and a dentist.' From Skelton on the other hand we learn that [19]

> Dinner [was] rather a good show. Sat next to Hobson & opposite an old chap called Appleby, who was great fun. When the King was proposed he started singing "God Save the King" all by himself in enormous voice. Everybody roared with laughter. The President, an old chap called Peacock, also made rather a 'faux pas'. Instead of saying at the end of his speech that the King deserved all the respect he got, he said "he needs all the respect he can get" ... There were one or two more speeches & then old Appleby got up again & wanted some others to join in a glee with him. He was of course 'tight' & so there was plenty of sport. The President told a whale yarn with no point but everybody cheered, & then we started Snooker pool, finishing about midnight. Altogether very good show.

Wilson hated what he called 'impurity' in every shape, having imbibed a 'first-class' morality at 'that wonderfully high-toned' Clifton Preparatory School, where he says he never heard a dirty word or a doubtful tale or jest. It will not have taken long for his companions on the *Discovery* to learn not to indulge in such banter while Wilson was around. When offended in that manner, he would 'silently rise from his chair with a look of contempt and walk away'. Sir AE Shipley wrote of him in *The Cornhill* magazine of March 1913 that [20]

> He had always a very pleasant smile and a very expressive face which could, by a swift change of look, let it be known whether he approved or disapproved of a word or act, and this without uttering a syllable. He never obtruded himself, but he could never be overlooked.

Wilson was 29 when the *Discovery* set off, and was already a veteran of many internal battles with his emotions. The fifth of ten children, he was described by his father as a child as [21]

> ... a broth of a boy, a regular pickle, open about his faults but tearful and ready to cry on very slight provocation.

As well as being the 'jolliest' child, he had also been prone to violent temper tantrums and screaming sessions. His mood swings were described as more marked than those of his siblings. One incident in his childhood seems formative, and could have been a precursor to what developed into a life inspired by the idea of submission to a higher power. One day, in response to one of his childhood tantrums his father gave him 'a few good slaps' which, according to his father, had [22]

> ... the most beneficial results, he became as good as gold and went to bed calling out, "Dood night, Dod bless you".

Little Ted idolised his father. It is a truism that to a child a father is like a god. Certainly to the child of a Victorian head of the household he would have had god-like powers, although this would have been sensed, rather than rationally understood. The slapping seems to have been an unusual punishment. Presumably if it had been a common occurrence it would not have been singled out for a mention. It is likely, therefore, to have been a significant event in Ted's childhood. His father, a successful doctor and civic activist, seems to have been the epitome of a benign *pater familias*.

Ted was, according to his mother [23]

> ... his Father's boy, and his love for him is most beautiful.

It points to the likelihood that he was primed from an early age to worship a father figure. Certainly he seems to have made a smooth transition from earthly to heavenly father, evidenced by his habit of praying to God like a child: [24]

> I like the expression "child of God" immensely, for it was just as a very child that I was always speaking and praying to Him.

School put the finishing touches of Christian high-mindedness to him, and where many children rebel, he conformed. But not without a struggle.

The mood swings that were a feature of his childhood continued in adulthood: 'Alternations of abject misery, almost suicidal' ... 'with feelings of extraordinary freedom and happiness'. He hated 'society' (in the sense of social occasions) so much that he [25]

> ... had a physical reaction of a painful kind necessitating the use of
> a sedative whenever he had an unusually trying social ordeal to
> undergo ...

The mood swings might have had a genetic component, but not the social anxiety. A certain amount of nervousness is normal; but for him to have developed this almost debilitating anxiety, there are likely to have been shaming and/or humiliating experiences, either at home or in the schoolroom, or both. His childhood was not as ideal as it is made to sound, nor as he himself probably regarded it. Often no doubt with the best of intentions, he had been criticised at home and at school. Putting children on the spot and using them as examples was a popular teaching method, and probably still is, in spite of its sensitising effect. As so often happens, the critics of his childhood will have been introjected, making him critical in turn, while reserving his harshest criticism for himself.

Photos of him in his teens and as a young man show him in a variety of settings. At 15 he poses for a formal portrait looking pale, pious, tight-lipped and serious, perfectly attired and slightly arrogant. At 18 he is shown with his family in a less-formal mood, looking robust and independent. They illustrate two sides of this complicated character: both the high-minded seeker after 'God's own Truth', and the ordinary boy who mucked in and took part in the action. He eventually came to embody a kind of rugged, or 'muscular' Christianity – effectively masking the extent of his religiosity by his sportsmanship and his love of nature, especially birds. He worked hard to keep himself from temptation, however, as his years at Cambridge suggest.

While channelling his emotionality into the religious fervour that shaped his adult persona, his life as a student seems to have accelerated into an almost manic level of activity. In addition to membership of numerous undergraduate clubs and societies, he also participated in a fencing and boxing club where they beat each other black and blue with single sticks. There were medical lectures and discussion groups, rugby, swimming and charity work. He read, walked, drew, and painted. He rowed for his College and won the University prize for diving in his final year. A photo of him diving around this time shows a tall, athletic figure with especially well-formed, long muscular legs. However discreet he was about his religious feelings, there could be no doubt in anyone's mind after a visit to his room at Cambridge. Over the mantelpiece, a smallish but centrally placed crucifix in a sea of framed photographs seems to symbolise the ideal he set for himself: the integration of the religious and the secular – although always with that symbol of ultimate submission to a 'higher power' at its core.

There are no reports of any interest in, nor dalliances with, women in Wilson's life as a student and beyond. Not until the appearance of Oriana Souper, at any rate, and that was never a dalliance. Along with most of his contemporaries within the exclusively male cloisters of elite higher education, he had only male friends. In spite of having been brought up among a crowd of sisters, Wilson had am- bivalent feelings about women – influenced no doubt by the male supremacist assumptions of the Bible, and its conflation of 'sin' and sex. A few years later when his younger brother Jim went to Cambridge, he warned him to stay away from the town women, writing, 'Our family is a bit above that sort of thing, even in fun it is not a sign of superiority or manliness – rather a sign of true manliness is to have the greatest respect for even the most degraded woman.'

In *Civilization and Its Discontents*, Freud proposes the existence of what he calls the 'inhibited aim': [26]

> [some people] ... avoid the uncertainties and disappointments of genital love by turning away from its sexual aims and transforming the instinct into an impulse with an *inhibited aim*. What they bring about in themselves in this way is a state of evenly suspended, steadfast, affectionate feeling, which has little external resem- blance any more to the stormy agitations of genital love, from which it is nevertheless derived. Perhaps St. Francis of Assisi went furthest in thus exploiting love for the benefit of an inner feeling of happiness.

The question arising in many people's minds must be whether Wilson's *de facto* rejection of his sexuality was because he was gay. Here is no doubt that he was genuinely offended by ribaldry; and that even in his relationship with Oriana Souper, whom he was later to court and marry, there is no suggestion that it ever contained 'stormy agitations'. He spent most of his life in the company of men and in the great outdoors. His relationship with Scott was arguably the most important of his life. Whatever his temptations may have been, the iron will with which he kept them under control can be glimpsed in his pencil sketches. A street scene in Rouen is drawn with a discipline that is almost painful. The architectural details are meticulously hatched in complex interplay of light and shade, while in the background the Cathedral looms over all, ghostly and ephemeral, as though to suggest its presence in spiritual form – albeit with Gothic embellishments. A later drawing of St Francis of Assisi shows a similar intensity of focus. Wilson's drawings are self-imposed trials of patience and self-discipline, a form of meditation which no doubt also provided welcome interludes of therapeutic quiet and absorption. His hatching was perfect and his washes were immaculate.

If Wilson conceived of his art as a homage to God, he would not have been the first. In his own recent history, the Pre-Raphaelites had sought to return to the 'Age of Faith', and the 'honest to God' craft of painting before the triumph of style over substance that Raphael came to epitomise. They did their best to represent nature through the honest depiction of 'Truth', while thinking not of earthly glory, but of the glory of God. Rossetti (1828–82) wanted to emulate the attitude of the medieval masters; to read the biblical narrative with a devout heart, and to approach art with a renewed naivety and unselfconsciousness. According to Gombrich, however, [27]

> The longing of Victorian masters for innocence was too self-contra-
> dictory to succeed.

There is no returning to innocence, as indeed there is no getting away from one's time. Looking at Rossetti's 'Ecce Ancilla Domini' (the Annunciation), it is immediately apparent that this a painting of its time – Pre-Raphaelite, reminiscent of Mantegna if anything, and no more inherently valid than other attempts to arrive at a definitive Truth. Across the Channel the more experimental, radical, and unconventional artists of the *Rive Gauche* were starting to face the problems posed by the shifting, dynamic nature of reality. Anyone who has picked up a pencil or a brush knows the problems inherent in translating a life-size animated scene on to a much smaller two-dimensional piece of paper or canvas. A process of reduction to essentials has to happen, and a way has to be found to make it look convincing on some level, often by counterintuitive means. That's why it's called art. What Wilson thought was true to nature was actually a simplified version that accorded with the conventions of his time. He seems to have flirted with an impressionistic style now and again in an effort to catch movement, but he never tried anything new, much less radical or challenging. Although extravagantly admired, he was an illustrator, not an artist.

Religion was Wilson's passion, but he was a very private, non-disclosing type of man. Again and again, those who knew him state that they had no idea his faith was so important to him. Apart from his family, many of whom were similarly devout, the only person he could ever open up to about it was Oriana, whose religious devotion was equally deep. They understood each other and they reinforced each other's faith. It would fit Wilson's philosophy generally for him to want to be taken as an 'ordinary' man. The archetypes he sought to emulate, Jesus and St Francis, were similarly saints in disguise or, perhaps more accurately, men who had complicated relationships with the 'ordinary'. Wilson's faith gave him an inner strength that we would now call personal empowerment. There would have been a sense of inner calm and assurance about him which, combined with his readiness to help, singled him out from others, in spite of his claims to be just like everyone else.

In an increasingly secular world, Wilson seems to have wanted to guard his faith. Not everyone was inclined to wax lyrical about 'God's Creation' as fervently as him – especially in the new Darwinian age, when the hitherto-accepted truth of the Bible had come under unprecedented scrutiny. Somewhat illogically, Wilson accepted the theory of evolution, and by implication that the Bible could not be taken as literal truth, at the same time continuing to believe in the literal divinity of Jesus, and the sanctity of St Francis of Assisi.

The idea of being of service to others inspired him. The Rousseauist notion of a connection to God without the intermediaries of the Church is evident. Although Wilson was a close student of the Bible, he was critical of formalised religion, and agreed with Ruskin that sermons were often tantamount to '... sitting patiently under a piece of dead Talk'. [28] Carlyle had struck a chord when he said that '... the Church of England was nothing else than a vast machinery for maintaining religious decorums'. [29] Wilson found God in nature, and believed that every living thing was from God. Nevertheless, he must also have believed that man had dominion over the animals, because he killed many – often merely for museum collections.

He may not have shared his religious ardour with those around him, but he did find kindred spirits in the world at large. One such, and a role model to some extent, was Charles Kingsley: clergyman, Christian Socialist, Darwinist, writer (and chain smoker, as Wilson was in his early 20s). Writing to Darwin, Kingsley says that he had [30]

> ... learnt to see that it is just as noble a conception of Deity, to believe that He created primal forms capable of self development into all forms needful *pro tempore* and *pro loco*, as to believe that He re-quired a fresh act of intervention to supply the lacunas which He himself had made.

In fact, Wilson felt that the ultimate result of evolution would be the perfect human, which he seems to have interpreted as God's master plan.

God was by definition benign and infallible. Doctor Pangloss (Voltaire, *Candide*) couldn't have put it better when Wilson says: [31]

> ... having once given your life and your will to God as a reasonable offering, *everything* that happens to you is sanctioned by Him be-cause He allows only such things to happen to you, when once you have put your life in His hands, as can do you some good ... Only be quite sure that you have not given up your will to Him merely in so many words, but in reality, and then you will have every reason to

take things exactly as they happen to come and find a blessing in the worst of them.

And further: [32]

> This I know is God's own Truth, that pain and trouble and trials and sorrows and disappointments are either one thing or another. To all who love God they are love tokens from Him. To all who do not love God and do not want to love Him they are merely a nuisance. Every single pain that we feel is known to God because it is the most loving and the most pathetic touch of His hand.

It is conceivable that Scott and Wilson implicitly recognised the martyr in each other. It could have been one of the reasons why Wilson related so strongly to Scott, and that it formed the basis for his unconditional support.

If Markham had imagined that he'd sent away an outfit unencumbered by irksome God-botherers, he was mistaken. The presence of both Scott, who had something to prove with regard to Markham, and Wilson, who had, on top of all his other fortifications, got married a fortnight before departure, virtually ensured a wardroom free of the hanky-panky Markham might have fondly imagined. Wilson was a priest in tweeds. His influence in the wardroom was similar to what a vicar's presence would have been, and probably set the moral tone for both Scott's expeditions – at least when within earshot. It cannot have been what Markham preferred, but then who knew Wilson was so religious? From Markham's point of view, it was also a bad idea to appoint Wilson as wine-caterer. He wasn't only teetotal himself but seems to have derived a sneaky pleasure from denying it to others: [33]

> A case of very special King's champagne and whisky were sent on board by some thoughtful person for the King's special use, but other things so engaged our Commander's attention that the two cases were completely forgotten and we sampled them much to our satisfaction a few days later, until I as wine-caterer impounded the whole for medical purposes.

And when it was Wilson's engagement day, [34]

> They badgered me as the wine caterer for an extra glass of port, but they didn't get it!

Markham would not have been happy.

References

1   T.H. Baughman. *Pilgrims on the Ice*, p. 30

2   Roland Huntford. *Nansen*, p. 562

3   Aubrey A. Jones. *Scott's Forgotten Surgeon*, p. 125

4   [Unattributed writer]. 'Prince Luigi Amedeo, Duke of the Abruzzi'. Wikipedia, www.en.m.wikipedia.org

5   Aubrey A. Jones. *op. cit.*, p. 178

6   Captain Robert F. Scott. *Voyage of the Discovery*, p. 164

7   Admiral Sir Reginald Skelton. *The Antarctic Journals of Reginald Skelton*, p. 11

8   Captain Robert F. Scott. *op. cit.*, p. 488

9   Roland Huntford. *Scott and Amundsen*, p. 173

10   Elspeth Huxley. *Scott of the Antarctic*, p. 105

11   Admiral Sir Reginald Skelton. *op. cit.*, p. 183

12   Aubrey A. Jones. *op. cit.*, p. 181

13   *op. cit.*, p. 180

14   Edward Wilson. *Diary of the Discovery Expedition*, p. 275

15   *op. cit.*, p. 37

16   *op. cit.*, p. 55

17   George Seaver. *The Faith of Edward Wilson*, p. 45

18   Edward Wilson. *op. cit.*, p. 83

19   Admiral Sir Reginald Skelton. *op. cit.*, p. 31

20   George Seaver. *Edward Wilson of the Antarctic*, p. 6

21   Isobel Williams. *With Scott in the Antarctic*, p. 23

22   *op. cit.*, p. 24

23   George Seaver. *Edward Wilson of the Antarctic*, p. 2

24   *op. cit.*, p. 10

25   *op. cit.*, p. 29

26   Peter Gay (ed.). *The Freud Reader*, p. 744

27   E.H. Gombrich. *The Story of Art*, pp. 404–5

28   Simon Heffer. *High Minds*, p. 228

29   *op. cit.*, p. 229

30   *op. cit.*, p. 225

31   George Seaver. *The Faith of Edward Wilson*, p. 14

32   George Seaver. *Edward Wilson of the Antarctic*, p. 71

33   Edward Wilson. *op. cit.*, p. 30

34   *op. cit.*, p. 61

13

SCOTT, WILSON AND SHACKLETON: THEIR SOUTHERN JOURNEY

Scott asked Wilson to accompany him on the main Southern Journey in June, more than four months before they were due to start. Wilson's diary entry for 12 June 1902 has the details: [1]

> ... before the relief ship comes, Armitage will be surveying the land westward with Barne, Ferrar and others and the men, making a depot camp at the Bluff ... Then the Skipper told me he had taken the long journey towards the South Pole for himself ... that it must consist of either two or three men in all and every dog we possessed, but he hadn't decided whether two men was best or three, but in any case would I go with him? My surprise can be guessed. It was rather too good a thing to be true it seemed to me. Of course I reminded him that I hadn't got a clean bill of health ... He said some nice things and also that he didn't feel more certain of himself than he did of me and that he had quite decided to take me if I would go.

> I then argued for three men rather than two ... "Who then was to be the third?", he said. So I told him it wasn't for me to suggest anyone. He then said, he need hardly have asked me because he knew who I would say, and added that as a matter of fact he was the man he would have chosen himself. So then I knew it was Shackleton, and I told him it was Shackleton's one ambition to go on the southern journey. So it was settled and we three are to go.

Scott says nothing at all in *The Voyage of the Discovery* about this important discussion. There is quite a lengthy entry for 12 June, but not a word about Wilson, nor what they discussed. In fact, mention of Wilson is very sporadic over the whole of the rest of the winter, and never in connection with sledging. There is not the slightest indication that Wilson is going on the main Southern Journey. Instead, months later, in the introduction to the spring sledging plans, Scott writes: [2]

> I had decided in the very early winter months to undertake the southern work myself ... For a long time I contemplated taking only one companion, thinking that two persons would be sufficient to manage the animals ... but in considering the difficulties which might arise from the unknown nature of the route and the risk of sickness, I finally decided on increasing the number to three. Long before this my two chosen companions, Barne and Shackleton, had been training themselves for the work.

He then goes on to discuss other matters.

Barne and Shackleton? He means Wilson and Shackleton, doesn't he? He told Wilson on 12 June that Barne was going westwards with Armitage and Ferrar. He makes a further ambiguous reference to 'my two comrades, Barne and Shackleton', when he mentions the Spring Reconnaissance Journey. If there had been no attempt to mislead, there would have been more-or-less frequent mention of either Barne, or Wilson, as they prepared themselves and discussed what was to be the main event of the season – as Wilson did in his diary. Of course, Scott couldn't mention Shackleton either; Barne wasn't coming, and Wilson wasn't supposed to be coming. He therefore avoided mentioning Shackleton because that would have forced the naming of his second companion. Scott seems not to have been able to bring himself to repeat the lie, or was it literary sleight of hand? Either way, the truth was that throughout the winter it was Wilson, not Barne, who trained with Shackleton, often going walking and skiing together.

In *The Voyage of the Discovery*, the first time Scott mentions Wilson in connection with the main Southern Journey is when they are more than three weeks into it. An attentive reader would have noticed Barne's subtle syphoning-off into the support party, but would have been left without a clue as to who his replacement could be, until Wilson appears as if by magic, over three weeks into the main Southern Journey, on 26 November.

Neither Armitage nor Skelton mention any surprises in connection with the Southern Journey. Wilson talks matter-of-factly about it in his diary without mention of Barne, nor does he question further about who was to go. When writing his narrative of the expedition, however, Scott himself says nothing about Wilson in connection with the Southern (projected Pole) party. As we have indicated, he gives the reader to understand that Barne is going with him. This is especially notable in view of the fact that Wilson was Scott's first choice, that he was booked early on, and that there was never any doubt that he would go. The discrepancy seems to have gone mostly unnoticed. LB Quartermain mentions it in *South to the Pole*, but surmises an explanation. When Scott's book came out, it was illustrated with photographs. Together with some prior knowledge, the reader will have been primed to mentally fill in the gaps without realising it, and the passing mention of Barne would have been easy to overlook and forget.

The absence of Wilson in Scott's account, not only throughout the rest of the winter but also during preparations for the Southern Journey, and even when already on it, must be more than an oversight or mistake. While some might contend that this could still be the case, there is no getting around the fact that the manner and timing of his approach to Wilson was not mentioned in Scott's book. In fact, it was known only to a select few until Wilson's diaries were published in 1966 and 1972.

At the time, the outside world would have known who went south, and how far, from the report brought back to New Zealand by the relief ship *Morning* in March 1903. Markham would have been one of the first to hear that on the bid for the Pole, the ultimate goal, Scott was the only representative of the Royal Navy. If Scott had any fears about Markham's reaction to the news, he might have been relieved that he would have had plenty of time to get used to the idea by the time they got home. Markham's dream team would probably have consisted of a party of RN sailors led by a couple of RN officers, as it had been in his day. A team of only three, comprising Scott, the assistant doctor/scientist, and a junior Mercantile Navy officer can't have been what he had in mind for the heroic conquest. But Markham was a long way away, and Scott was irritated by the memory of him. He tried to reject his sledging banner with the motto 'Ready, Aye Ready', so beloved by Markham. Perhaps it carried unwanted reminders of creepy flatteries and innuendoes. Here in Antarctica, he could please himself. Ironically, this meant that he chose his main man, Wilson, for personal reasons – as Markham had done when he chose him.

On board the *Discovery*, it probably slowly leaked out that Wilson and Shackleton were going on the Pole Journey. It isn't possible in a small enclosed community to keep a secret like that for long. On 2 July, a couple of weeks after he was asked, Wilson spent the whole morning talking with Scott about the Pole Journey and its arrangements. In Scott's book, there are detailed discussions regarding just about everything else pertaining to life in Antarctica, but nothing about those important discussions that morning. On 15 July, Wilson is again in Scott's cabin all morning:[3]

> ... talky, talky, but necessary, having to arrange daily food to the half ounce for three months, no simple job. Also one dog lasts 17 dogs how many days? One dog lasts 16 dogs how many and so on, till one dog lasts four dogs how many days?

Feeding the dogs to each other appears to have been part of the plan from the beginning – another thing about which Scott was discreet to the point of silence. There is not a word from Scott about this meeting either, nor anything to do with dogs.

Scott's early, almost casual, mention of Barne as his companion without further elaboration, feels like an uncomfortable lie, hastily shuffled off. It nevertheless explains why Wilson isn't mentioned. Again on 6 September, Wilson writes: [4]

> ... some notes for the Captain and had a two hours yarn with him and Shackleton over the improvements possible for our long southern journey.

Again nothing from Scott. Perhaps the reason Barne was mentioned at all in connection with the Pole attempt is because Scott wanted to give the impression that he *intended* to take Barne, but that some last-minute incapacity, such as frost-injured fingers, had prevented him. Perhaps that's what he gave Markham to understand, and perhaps that's what the rest of the world was intended to assume. To an extent, it worked. In a piece of creative history-making, Reginald Pound states unequivocally that [5]

> Severe frost-bite put Barne out of the running. Wilson was asked to take his place.

Many Scott biographers have assumed the same, but it wasn't true. As already pointed out, Barne was scheduled to go to the west with Armitage from the beginning, as Wilson's diary entry for 12 June 1902 confirms.

The 'Barne frozen fingers fallacy' probably originated from his presence on the first of two preliminary reconnaissance trips Scott made before embarking on the main journey. Barne and Shackleton were with him when they ended up having to hang on to their tent for 36 hours in a blizzard due to it not having been properly secured. This resulted in a second dose of frostbite in Barne's fingers, the first having been suffered on the disastrous first foray to Cape Crozier. As a result, he was replaced by Feather, the bosun, on the second recce. (Wilson had asked to be excused these preliminary trips on account of his zoological work.) On both occasions, Barne's fingers recovered quickly. There seems to have been nothing preventing him starting out with the Southern Support Party a few days before Scott's own departure – and not only lead this, but also a major subsequent journey, to the western mountains, with never a mention of any disability.

Pound's assumptions were easy to make, however, as was probably intended. The narrative drama of the journey itself and the rest of the expedition soon leaves the faintly raised eyebrow behind, and we are eating out of Scott's hand again. Even Markham would have been swept away by the vicarious experience of the 'beastliness' they endured. It was a clever little piece of literary footwork of which Markham himself might have been proud.

Departing from the Royal Navy script would not have been Scott's only concern. People might ask, 'why Wilson?' Why indeed? It would have been difficult to argue that there were objective reasons for not just asking him but asking him so early on, and as his first choice. Although a decent sledger, there were others as good as Wilson, and some were better. He had no previous experience, he had a known medical history and, above all, he was nothing to do with the Royal Navy. 'Uncle Bill', was the man people went to for personal counselling. He was patient, understanding, and conciliatory. Wilson bridged the God-gap for Scott, allowing him to benefit vicariously from Wilson's Panglossian trust in the rightness of things.

He wasn't just God's vicar, he was Scott's too. His presence ensured a certain standard of decorum in the wardroom, thereby subtly imposing an orderliness and conformity that supported the status quo and, hence, Scott. He counter-balanced Scott's impatience and irritability and poured oil over troubled waters. He was his confidante. He calmed Scott's anxiety and steadied his nerves. He was not in competition with him, and did not judge him. Of all the people on board, Wilson was the most unconditionally supportive; and although sometimes critical, his loyalty to 'The Skipper' was beyond doubt. When they got back from the Pole Journey, it was almost painfully clear from their body language who had bonded, and who had been left behind. A long way behind Scott and Wilson, Shackleton limped in on his own, until supported by Koettlitz, Royds, and Mulock.

To Scott, his options for companions on the main journey might have looked something like this:

Armitage, second-in-command, was ruled out because he expected to lead a significant journey of his own, not play second fiddle to Scott on his. They never made a team. On the contrary, they were in competition with each other. Although they seem to have been able to maintain an acceptable working relationship, it was short on mutual respect. Both Armitage and Royds were critical of Scott, although both paid elaborate lip-service. Royds could have been the main contender, but seems not to have been too keen on excessive hardship, which he may have correctly guessed would be part of any journey with Scott. Although Scott had made his choice months before, he may have already formed an opinion of Royds' general attitude towards sledging, which was that he would rather not. Later, Skelton made damming comments about Royds' behaviour on the second Crozier trip. He thought him too 'girlish', by which he presumably meant that Royds didn't adapt well to roughing it. It is something of a mystery why Royds volunteered for the expedition in the first place. The fact that he was in charge of meteorology also made it difficult for him to be absent for long periods. The same went for Bernacchi, in charge of magnetics.

Apart from the 'men', of course, that leaves Barne, Skelton, and the rest of the scientists. Of those, Koettlitz was the main contender. He was at least as strong a sledger as Wilson – and vastly more experienced, both as a doctor and as a Polar explorer. Objectively, he was a better choice than Wilson – but then objectivity was seldom allowed to interfere with the running of Scott's expeditions. On a personal level, Koettlitz and Scott were separated by an unbridgeable gulf of social, cultural, and emotional difference. Of the other scientists, Hodgson was not a distance sledger, and the very young and rather goofy Ferrar can never have thought of himself as one of the favoured few.

That left two officers, Skelton and Barne, either of whom would have been good choices. Although both of slight build, they were wiry and tough, and men to be reckoned with. Skelton had, on his own initiative, become proficient on ski early on. Always at a disadvantage in the Naval hierarchy for being an engineer, he nevertheless ended his career as a vice-admiral and engineer-in-chief of the Fleet, as well as receiving a knighthood – which says something about his competence and professionalism. However, those might have been the very qualities that ruled him out. Both Skelton and Barne would have had a lot to say for themselves. Scott wasn't the type of leader who welcomed suggestions or tolerated argument. He was very controlling. While Armitage might have been given some say over his own sledging journeys, all others were planned and controlled exclusively by Scott. Skelton was one of Scott's more trenchant critics, which hints at a coolish relationship. In the event, Skelton and Armitage teamed up better with each other.

That left the boyish, lively, willing and young Michael 'Mik' Barne. Scott is likely to have understood from Markham's attitude that Barne was to be looked upon favourably. He was a great-grandson of Markham's old Admiral, Sir George Seymour. His father was MP for East Suffolk, and his mother was Lady Constance Adelaide Seymour, daughter of Francis Seymour, Fifth Marquess of Hertford. Markham was charmed: [6]

> Barne is very popular all round, always ready to help any one, full
> of good humour, the most unselfish of mortals with moreover great
> undeveloped probabilities of performance; to be entirely trusted
> and given responsibility.

Later in life, Barne was awarded the DSO for his service in WW1, and retired from the Navy with the rank of Captain, returning in WW2 to command an anti-submarine patrol ship. On the *Discovery*, he was well liked on the messdeck. Skelton: [7]

> Very evident that Barne is popular with the men. They gave three
> very hearty cheers. He seems to be able to work them very well.

There is evidence in Wilson's diary pointing to a further underlying reason for Barne's exclusion from the Pole Journey. Significantly, in view of Markham's proclivities and love of the theatre, Barne also organised the expedition theatre. About a week before Scott asked Wilson to accompany him on the Southern Journey, it became common knowledge in the wardroom that Barne was planning to put on a play. Evidence for this is that Skelton reports that on 14 June, only two days after Scott asked Wilson to come on the main journey, Barne came to him with a request for footlights. The play itself was performed 11 days later. This means that it must have been in the planning stage in the week(s) prior to 12 June. It is therefore entirely plausible that Barne's theatrical initiative was what finally decided Scott not to take him on the main journey.

Barne had a lot going for him with his impressive 'pedigree', *retroussé* nose, feminine mouth, blond hair, and bright and courageous attitude. He was Markham's type, and already close to his *beau idéal*. If, as well as having organised the theatricals, he performed well on the Pole Journey his star might, on their return, burn a little too brightly. At the same time, Scott might have suspected that the theatre initiative was a ploy by Barne to ingratiate himself with Markham. If so, it would have left Scott feeling morally free to leave him out and invite Wilson. Scott was a Royal Navy man and he always calculated his best interests. It was how the system worked, and one would be a fool not to play it.

This interpretation of events would explain the timing of Scott's invitation to Wilson, whom he was clearly keen to engage in any case. It was the timing he would have wanted to obscure. He would not have wanted his rejection of Barne to be associated with Barne's theatrical initiative. On board, he probably obscured it by asking Wilson and Shackleton to keep the plan under their hats for the time being – which would have been in character anyway. Although he might have felt morally justified, he would not have wanted his manipulations, if such they were, to be too obvious – neither to the men in the ship nor to posterity. On their own, the casual mention of Barne and the absence of Wilson could be explained as unintentional oversights; but together, especially when factoring in the theatrical element, they gain in significance.

With regard to Shackleton, when Wilson suggested Shackleton as the third man, Scott asserts that he had had Shackleton in mind himself. If true, it would have made sense for several reasons. Strategically, Shackleton could not be a rival to Scott because he was not RN, but on a personal level, he was a strong and positive character. Scott might have wanted those qualities at his own disposal, in his own support, and under his own control, rather risking their potentially undermining influence in his absence.

And then there were the dogs. It was Scott's negative bias and ignorance of dog-sledging that condemned his expeditions to drawn-out pain and hard-won disappointments. In Scott's view, the dogs were an adjunct, not the main means of propulsion. Their role was not seen as crucial. That's why there were too few, and why those they did have did not receive the training, food, and attention they needed for optimum performance. Bernacchi: [8]

> Snapping dog teams, untrained and during the whole winter un-accustomed to the feel of harness, went off more or less unwillingly under the guidance of unpractised drivers.

Some modern explorers, such as leading Scott apologist and fan Ranulph Fiennes, assert that because modern Antarctic sledgers use man-haulage, Scott was justified in his preference for it. This is a complete fallacy. First, modern sledge journeys to the South Pole are made for sporting and charitable reasons, support-ed by communications systems (and a space-age installation at the Pole itself), which ensure a level of safety unknown in Scott's day. Second, modern equipment, clothing, and nutrition have changed the conditions of man-hauling out of all recognition. While still no sinecure, it is now a vastly different proposition, as Fiennes knows perfectly well. In any case, dogs are no longer allowed in Ant-arctica, so it is not as though modern travellers have the choice. As it was, Shackleton probably did as well as was humanly possible at the time without dogs, when a few years later he got to within 100 geographical miles of the Pole (and back, crucially).

Scott's dogs appear to have been fed some seal meat over the winter, but their main food was dog biscuit. These were, however, of decent quality, and the dogs were in reasonable condition when the time came for them to work. They had been looked after, and mostly made pets of by the crew. Neither Scott, Wilson, nor Shackleton had had much to do with them until the spring sledging began in September 1902. Scott asserts that he had intended to take ordinary dog biscuits, but that [9]

> ... in an evil moment I was persuaded by one who had had great ex-perience in dog-driving to take fish.

He didn't name names, but he must have been referring to Nansen. Later, in a letter to his mother, he connects Armitage with the tainted stockfish. The Nor-wegian stockfish (dried cod), intended for the dogs on the march, was bought in the northern summer. It was shipped through the tropics in an unrefrigerated hold and arrived in New Zealand in the southern summer, where it was again stored unrefrigerated while the *Discovery* was overhauled. This meant it was stored in warm or hot temperatures for six months. It eventually froze of course, and it was then almost another year before it was used. By then it was lethally toxic. It is heart-breaking to read how well the dogs performed at the start, pulling up to 2,100 lbs between 19 of them, and making over 11 miles in a day. Scott assumed they were going to keep that up, and sent back half his support party earlier than planned. [10]

It was another mistake. Too much had already been asked of the dogs, and they were already unwell. By comparison, Amundsen's dogs pulled individual sledges weighing 880 lbs each, with a team of 12 to 13 dogs. That works out at between 68 and 73 lbs per dog. Scott's dogs were expected to pull about 1,850 lbs in a four-sledge train, with one team of 19 – which works out at 97 lbs per dog, or at least 24 lbs more per dog than Amundsen. [11] Scott planned for his human team to pull alongside the dogs. It didn't work out.

In spite of Nansen's personal advice, and the results he obtained, most of the ship's company and crew, with few exceptions, remained prejudiced against dogs. Equally inexperienced, they pronounced them to be as much of a hindrance as a help. The prejudice originated with Markham – curiously, in view of his admiration for Nansen. But for Markham, it will always have been about Nansen's looks, charisma and heroic pose. It was for those qualities that he was intended as a role model for Scott, not specifically for his *modus operandi*. It was probably only because of Scott's tendency to hedge his bets that a quantity of skis and a few dogs were taken at all. If it had been up to Markham alone, they would have gone without either.

On 15 November, less than two weeks into the Pole Journey, within the span of a single day, the mood changes from bright optimism to dejection and pessimism. Early in the day, [12]

> Confident in ourselves, confident in our equipment, and confident in our dog-team, we can but feel elated with the prospect that is before us.

Later that same day,

> The day's work has cast a shadow on our highest aspirations, however, and already it is evident that if we are to achieve much it will be only by extreme toil, for the dogs have not pulled well today ...

The elementary error of the rotten stockfish had started to extract its toll. Notably, they had seen that it disagreed with them from the beginning. Every day the dogs became more and more listless and obviously sick. 'Poor Snatcher' was the first one to die, on 8 December. Wilson's diary informs us that on opening him up he diagnosed acute peritonitis – a fact not mentioned in Scott's narrative.

Even without the benefit of hindsight, one might have thought that someone would have taken a closer look at the stockfish – if not before, then surely when the problem first became apparent. A cooler head would have acknowledged the potentially devastating effect on the dogs who, whilst having been regarded as merely an adjunct, were turning out to be essential to the party's progress. Instead,

Scott's response was to persuade himself that the effect was only temporary, and due to the fact that their diet had changed radically overnight – itself not a brilliant idea. After all, he had been advised by Nansen, the best authority in the world, which should have been good enough. The stockfish had looked all right on the outside, and that had been enough for Scott, who could never bear to go looking for trouble. Instead of approaching the potential problem head-on, he resorted to his habitual avoidant coping strategy – denial, in a word. Denial sacrifices long-term benefits in order to prevent short-term losses. It is generally considered to be maladaptive; acceptance and reappraisal is generally more effective, and constitutes a form of active, as opposed to passive, coping.

It was a passive-destructive weakness. In this case, instead of facing the problem when there was still a possibility of doing something about it, Scott chose to carry on, hoping that things would resolve themselves. With each day that passed, however, the dogs became progressively sicker – while at the same time it became more difficult for Scott to extract himself from his own complicated web of arrangements.

One of the reasons Nansen was so keen on stockfish was because, being dried, it was comparatively light. While it would have been too much to expect Scott's crew to dehydrate an adequate amount of seal meat, there were plenty of decent-quality dog biscuits left at the ship. While not ideal, anything would have been better what they were given. Scott makes no secret of the horror of whipping and shouting at dying dogs in an attempt to get them to perform work they were no longer capable of. The saga of the dogs is truly heart-rending. As he spins it in his book, however, it was easy to be wise after the event, and the dog-food issue constituted a lesson for future travellers. But would others have been as complacent as he had been about their food? Not if they had valued them more highly to begin with. The grim task of euthanising and butchering the 19 dogs with which they had started had fallen to Wilson. He says nothing about what it took, but it can't have been easy. On 14 January, just under three weeks before they got back to the ship, he killed the two remaining dogs, and threw away what was left of the stockfish.

Scott's faith in the powers of theory and calculation to make up for a lack of practical experience had probably helped him to overcome any initial doubts he might have had regarding his fitness for the command. It also puts in context his approach to the *Discovery*'s schedules and the sledging activities within it. He spent a lot of time at his desk making complicated projections and devising ambitious plans. He did this, moreover, with little or no consultation; while at the same time expecting top performance from men thrown into the field without appropriate training, instruction or experience.

This approach dovetailed neatly with Markham's, which was to downplay the potential difficulties. Both assumed that whatever Antarctica threw at them could be overcome by a combination of British guts and a sense of mission – an assumption that can be explained but not excused by their wilful ignorance of the reality. There was enough information about the nature of Antarctica to suggest that very different challenges would be met from those previously encountered in the Arctic. But Markham had to be dismissive of the difficulties. A realistic assessment of what they were going to have to deal with would make his choice of leader seem all the more incongruent and, frankly, suspect.

Markham and Scott accepted and reinforced each other's hubris, albeit for reasons of their own. Hence the seamless co-operation in terms of learning, for example, where a few chats with Nansen were deemed to suffice, and a trivialisation of the real-world experience that would have been commensurate with the scope, prestige and cost of a so-called 'national' expedition.

There was a lot of the good little boy inside Scott. He was predisposed to make his way by winning favour through pleasing his superiors. Gordon: [13]

> ... with no combat opportunities to establish reputations and disrupt the social certainties, the only plausible way to progress in the service was to obtain the patronage of the Establishment by gratifying and reaffirming its values.

Scott lacked the core autonomy that would have freed him from the grip of the Establishment and his dependence on it. He projected an image of the perfect officer; and when his turn came he relished his autocratic – and ultimately ego-centric – position on board the *Discovery*, which was itself a reflection of the Establishment and its power.

Gordon convincingly argues that the development of sophisticated signalling methods catalysed a tendency towards central command and control in the Royal Navy. It made it easier for individuals to add to their power, which in turn made them more intimidating to those under their command. Within the largely punitive culture of the Navy, this predictably led to a reluctance on the part of subordinate officers to risk making their own decisions, preferring to wait for instructions (poor old Albert and the *Camperdown* again spring to mind). While acknowledging that a co-ordinated approach demands a measure of central control, it carries the potential for becoming a straight-jacket for everyone involved, with those lower down the chain of command covering their backs and those at the top being overinvested in their original plan – however deficient it may turn out to be. Their reputations are at stake, and the temptation to yield to short-term expediency is strong.

Scott had seen within days that the stockfish disagreed with the dogs; but not only was it what they had with them, it was also what they had stored at the Bluff

Depot. There was nothing he could do, short of throwing the whole shebang out of kilter with the support parties and Barne's plans – not to mention the disruption to the tight overall schedules and the extra demands on the men and resources. Barne would have to be kept waiting, consuming food and fuel, curtailing his time as support for the southern thrust. Meanwhile, everyone would have had plenty of time for grumbling and criticism as they awaited further instructions. If Scott even considered the option of going back to replace the dog food there is no mention of any such thing.

In all Scott's journeys, extreme effort, pain (both physical and mental), and risk had always to make up for lack of expertise and management skills. The Southern Journey was no exception. Scott, Wilson, Shackleton and the sick dogs spent an agonising month relaying, having to go three miles for every mile of progress. They made about 100 miles progress in this stage. The 200 miles lost would have seen them to the foot of what Shackleton later named the Beardmore Glacier, in roughly the same period of time. The Pole had been the primary object. Scott had had to be discreet about it because of Markham's disavowals of the value of getting there first, but there can be no doubt about the aim of Scott's initial trajectory. When it became blindingly obvious that they were not going to get to the Pole, nor anywhere near it, they turned westwards, to where they expected to find land – partly as a concession to Wilson, but in reality the only rational choice in the circumstances. It meant they could get some bearings and leave a depot, which had been considered too easy to miss on the featureless plain, but which was rapidly becoming essential.

Scott was forming a habit of overstretching his resources; pushing to and beyond the limits of safety. For him, it wasn't enough until it was borderline suicidal. After having turned back at last, by now ravenous, scorbutic, haggard and worn physically and emotionally, they were lucky to find their depot on 13 January, and had that which had become a rarity, a satisfying meal. Far from being a reassurance that they would get back alive, it was but the prelude to a plan for a further extremity of effort. Scott: [14]

> All things considered, without knowledge of what may be before us, it is safer not to increase our food allowance for the present, more especially as in going north I want to steer inwards so as to examine more closely those masses of land which we have seen only in the far distance.

Scott never knew – or didn't want to know – when it was time to go home. It took Wilson's concern that Shackleton might actually die to persuade him at last to head for the ship without further delay.

When they got back, they found that the relief ship *Morning* had arrived at Hut Point, or rather at the ice-edge some nine miles north of Hut Point, on 23 January

1903. Scott had been expecting her: he had incorporated her into his plans for the season. But did anyone remember that she was to take a party to Wood Bay and wait for them to go inland for the Magnetic Pole, and afterwards take them back to Lyttelton? It might have been politic not to remind him of these plans, made a year ago, and now shown up as having been naively overoptimistic.

A relief ship would not have been needed at all if the *Discovery* had landed a shore party and returned to New Zealand. Markham was fond of saying that the Franklin disaster would never had happened if a relief ship had been sent out as early as the first year. This would be true if they had been expected back in the first year. The same was true for the *Discovery*. Markham knew perfectly well that Scott was going to keep the ship in Antarctica for the winter. An awning, like those beneath which such brilliant parties and theatricals had been enjoyed in his day, had been taken. There was no reason to assume they needed relief, although the snag was that they might.

Markham was in any case committed to the idea of a relief ship, and planned it from the start. What he did not do was budget for it. It would have meant economies, or even a complete rethink in terms of the expedition ship; and this, evidently, he was not prepared to do. He had styled the expedition as a national one, the latest in a long line of famous ships called *Discovery*. He identified his own and his ship's interests with those of the nation, and as such, make-do would simply not do. So he left the issue of finance for a relief ship for another day.

The euphoric interlude of the *Discovery*'s departure had soon, therefore, been over for Markham. More money now had to be raised. He had tried to pressurise the Societies by getting Scott to write a letter just before the ship left Lyttelton, which sounds a lot like it had been dictated by Markham. It was an obvious attempt to morally blackmail the Societies by implying that a refusal to provide a relief ship would be tantamount to abandoning the *Discovery* to her fate. Scott: [15]

> Gentlemen, – It is with great satisfaction I learn that it is intended to send a relief ship to the Antarctic regions in the Southern summer of 1902–3. I had contemplated writing most urgently to you on this subject, knowing how absolutely our retreat would otherwise be cut off, should any accident result in the loss of the *Discovery* ... It will be a great relief and satisfaction to me to leave Lyttelton, confident that such efforts will be successful and that a line of retreat is practically assured to us.

It was no such thing.

Markham made a public statement in October 1901 to the effect that in all great Arctic expeditions, except that of Franklin, a relief ship had been sent out in the second year. [16] It wasn't true, but then this was Markham. He cleverly got the King to start the ball rolling by squeezing a further £100 out of him. It was another

PR coup, but in spite of it he had to work hard for the money, and he only just made it.

The Admiralty had also been less forthcoming in terms of officer-class manpower, and it is perhaps surprising that they lent anyone at all. The two who went were Edward Ratcliffe Garth (Russell) 'Teddy' Evans, of the later Last Expedition, and *Broke* fame, and George Mulock the surveyor. Markham had been very lucky to secure the services, as Captain, of highly regarded William Colbeck, 'a fine Yorkshire sailorman'. The *Morning* was small and underpowered, but she would do for establishing contact and for delivering mail and fresh supplies. By today's standards, the *Morning* would not be considered viable for the seas around Antarctica. According to Armitage, if it wasn't for Colbeck's fine seamanship they would not have made it to Antarctica at all.

Markham recruited for the *Morning* on the same basis as he had the *Discovery.* Top of the list of requirements was that the men, especially the officers, appealed to him personally in looks and demeanour. Colbeck was a young, handsome man; Evans and Doorly were also young and nice looking. In fact, the officers and men of the *Morning* were altogether a good-looking bunch, and notably younger than their eventual *Terra Nova* counterparts. Markham had been lucky this time – at the very least regarding Colbeck and Evans, in whom, as well as good looks, he had, respectively, a Merchant Marine master mariner and veteran of Borchgrevink's *Southern Cross* Expedition, and an energetic hard nut who kept his head in a crisis.

It was in the summer of 1901 that Evans started to take a serious interest in Antarctic exploration. He had met Scott a few times when he was torpedo lieutenant in the *Majestic* and had followed the progress of the *Discovery* until she left New Zealand. The next spring, when he heard that a relief expedition was being planned, he wrote to Markham asking to be considered for it. His name can't have meant much to Markham because a brief acknowledgement of his letter was all he received. Undeterred, a week later he presented himself to Crease, Markham's 'splendid' butler, who seems to have known exactly what to do when a likely lad presented himself on the doorstep of 21 Eccleston Square. Accordingly, young Teddy Evans was promptly shown into the great one's little study. Full of bonhomie and eagerness to serve, photos show a strong neck and the suggestion of a hard musculature underneath the uniform. He'd served his time as a 'snotty' by this time, and was doing his sub-lieutenant's exams.

Really, he had nothing but his physical strength, his energy, and his boyish enthusiasm to offer, but that would have done nicely as far as Markham was concerned. It is easy to imagine Evans' discomfort at being made to feel too warmly welcome in Markham's oppressive little study, and it may have been this that prompted him to suggest a walk in the park. He writes of his enjoyment of the atmosphere there, and if he was feeling relaxed, he would have shown himself to

best advantage. The upshot was that Markham agreed to appoint him without further ado, saying (according to Evans, writing years later as Lord Mountevans): [17]

> Yes, I will go to the Admiralty now and see the Second Sea Lord. He
> is a friend of mine and I don't anticipate much trouble ... I shall see
> your record. I hope it's not too black!

Evans was duly appointed to HMS *President* for special service with the
Antarctic Relief Expedition. HMS *President* was a training ship of the Royal Naval
Reserve, and the Second Sea Lord at the time was Vice-Admiral Archibald Douglas.
The *President's* criteria for service were clearly suitably elastic, and cronyism was
taken for granted in Markham's world. Hence, after a series of interviews with
Colbeck, Evans found himself promoted to Second Officer before they even sailed.

Markham has been whitewashed, and Teddy Evans has not been given his due.
Both of those things have helped maintain the image of Scott as a great explorer
and man. If Markham's dubious behaviour and irresponsibility had been brought
more to the fore, it would have legitimised questions over Scott's appointment.
And if Evans had been given his due, Scott's shortcomings as a leader would have
been more starkly delineated.

Third officer was Evans' friend Gerald Doorly, at the time a junior officer with
the P&O line, who Evans had been successful in 'introducing as a desirable volunteer' (Evans). Before he was taken on, Doorly was obliged to undergo the
rigours of an interview in Markham's little den, in a way that is by now becoming
somewhat familiar. It would have been more appropriate as an absurdist sketch
in a comedy show, or as a slightly decadent version of the Mad Hatter's Tea-party.
Doorly relates: [18]

> The interview ended in this remarkable way. Turning round from
> his desk Sir Clements said:
>
> "Do you know a man named Heyden?"
>
> "Heyden? Yes, sir," I said, "there was a Heyden in the *Worcester*
> with me." ...
>
> "Yes; he's your age, too, I see. And what sort of a man is he?" the old
> gentleman asked.
>
> This seemed to be an awkward question to put to me; however, I
> replied that I hadn't known him very well – not as a chum, but I
> thought he was a good man.
>
> "H'm," mused Sir Clements. "Well, I think his upper lip is *too short!*"
> he said, and promptly stroked his pen across a paper lying on his
> desk.
>
> Strange! Then he asked again:

"Do you know a man named Frater?"

"Yes, sir; he was also a cadet in the training ship with me."

"I thought so; and what sort of a man is *he*?"

Another poser; but I answered as before – that we'd not been particular friends, but as far as I knew he was a good man.

"H'm," mused the old gentleman again. "Well," he said abruptly, "I
think his upper lip is *too long!*" And running his pen across another
sheet, he added, "I shall write to these two gentlemen and inform
them that the position is filled. ... You will be advised by the Council
in due course. ... Good-bye, m'boy!"

I ran down the steps and out into the square as happy as the
proverbial sand-boy, with a feeling of intense gratification that my
upper lip, at any rate, had not let me down!

Markham had clearly made up his mind there and then to take Doorly on,
inventing frivolous excuses for crossing out Heyden and Frater. On one level,
upper lips were as good a criterion as any: there probably wasn't that much to
choose between them, as they had all had the same training, and all lacked relevant experience. Nevertheless, this was going to be a dangerous journey on which
lives could depend, and which carried a tremendous amount of responsibility.

It is interesting that Doorly chose to report the details of that strange interview
– not in his 1916 book *The Voyages of the 'Morning'*, but in the later *In the Wake*,
published 1936. Perhaps he chose not to publish those details while Markham was
still alive, or too recently deceased. Markham died in 1916, and it could well have
been Doorly's own doubts that prompted him to wait for a later time. It didn't
make much difference. Doorly was always a peripheral figure and hardly gets a
mention before or since Reginald Pound's Scott biography of 1966.

One of the many ways Scott biographers have failed to do a service to history
is the way they have ignored Markham's 'eccentricities', or urbanely dismissed
them as rumour and gossip and ultimately irrelevant. Our view must be that
Markham's so-called eccentricities, and the way they determined his selection
procedures, are an important part of the history of British Antarctic exploration,
and had a direct bearing on how it all turned out. Evidence that does not suit the
established narrative of Scott's greatness and humanity has effectively been
pushed to the sidelines by the juggernaut of the Scott industry – accreting over the
years into a top-heavy body made up of layer upon layer of mostly repetitive
hagiographies.

Markham always indulged his boys, and they in turn were always generous in
their praise of him. But if Doorly had been somewhat bemused by this odd interview, it seems Evans had grasped the origins of Markham's beneficence, and

understood the leeway it gave him. When on the eve of departure of the *Morning* it was suggested that she should have a piano on board, Evans dashed up to town to see Markham about it, even though it was late in the evening. Markham was just going to bed when he rang the doorbell. What emergency was at hand? What last-minute calamity had brought Evans breathless and apologetic to his door? Why, there was no piano on board! Markham would have quite agreed with him that this situation could not be allowed to continue, and no doubt warmly reassured him that a piano would be forthcoming. It was delivered just in time the next day. The ship was so small, and the accommodation so cramped, that they had to saw it to pieces to get it below.

She may have had a piano on board, but the *Morning* was hardly fit for the job she was expected to do. She was a leaky old sealer: small and badly underpowered. No one could have faced the journey they were expected to undertake in her with any degree of equanimity. It was borderline irresponsible to send that ship to Antarctica, even at the time. Today, only powerful icebreakers venture into those waters, equipped with all the weather and communication aids modern technology can provide. Even before the *Morning* got to New Zealand she was forced to weather a storm that Evans described as 'probably my roughest sea'. A squall caught the helmsman off guard and the ship broached to in heavy seas and storm-force winds. Doorly, who was below, heard Evans shouting for help: [19]

> It was pathetic. Here was poor Evans all on his own, struggling with practically the impossible under such conditions.

Lord Mountevans: [20]

> The rattle of the sails as they flapped and shook in the wind, the wreckage and debris being carried about on the flooded decks, threatening to break away the bulwarks, and the smashing white-crested waves looking every minute like overwhelming us, these things I shall never forget!

Doorly: [21]

> After this night's experience I never needed to consider Evans's resources, which were quite equal to anything that might befall a ship even with a limited crew.

Doorly was right. As will be related later: without Evans, Scott's Last Expedition might never have made it to Antarctica in the first place. If it hadn't been for his cool head and muscular initiative, the expedition could well have been lost within days of having set sail for Antarctica.

After a few narrow escapes, the *Morning* did at last arrive at the ice-edge in McMurdo Sound. About nine miles to the south was Hut Point, and the object of their mission. The trucks of two of *Discovery*'s masts were visible [22]

... looking like a couple of match-sticks in the midst of the vast desolation of ice and snow.

With feelings of relief and joy we cheered the welcome sight, and as Eight Bells (midnight) struck, we saw, through the quivering mirage, a large flag fluttering up to the top of the staff on Hut Point. The *Discovery*'s people had seen us.

References

1   Edward Wilson. *Diary of the Discovery Expedition*, pp. 150–1

2   Captain Robert F. Scott. *The Voyage of the Discovery*, p. 346

3   Edward Wilson. *op. cit.*, pp. 161–2

4   *op. cit.*, p. 185

5   Reginald Pound. *Scott of the Antarctic*, p. 74

6   Sir Clements Markham. *Antarctic Obsession*, p. 78

7   Admiral Sir Reginald Skelton. *The Antarctic Journals of Reginald Skelton*, p. 163

8   L.C. Bernacchi. *Saga of the "Discovery"*, p. 58

9   Captain Robert F. Scott. *op. cit.*, p. 396

10   *op. cit.*, p. 390

11   *ibid.*

12   *op. cit.*, p. 392

13   Andrew Gordon. *The Rules of the Game*, p. 594

14   Captain Robert F. Scott. *op. cit.*, pp. 442–3

15   Reginald Pound. *op. cit.*, p. 52

16   *ibid.*

17   Admiral Lord Mountevans. *Adventurous Life*, p. 45

18   Captain Gerald S. Doorly. *In the Wake*, pp. 94–5

19   Captain Gerald S. Doorly. *The Voyages of the 'Morning'*, p. 46

20   Admiral Lord Mountevans. *op. cit.*, p. 48

21   Captain Gerald S. Doorly. *The Voyages of the 'Morning'*, p. 48

22   Captain Gerald S. Doorly. *In the Wake*, p. 103

14

THE SECOND WINTER AND THE

WESTERN JOURNEY

Scott, Wilson, and Shackleton returned from the Southern Journey on 3 February, ten days after the arrival of the *Morning*, and finding *Discovery* still beset in thick ice. At first, the bliss of home comforts and the need for rest obliterated all other concerns. All three had returned in a fairly advanced state of scurvy; resulting, among other things, in a tremendous feeling of lassitude in which Scott found it hard even to think. They were also ravenously hungry. Some idea of what this means can be gleaned from a description of their behaviour given by Doorly, who had come over and was sleeping on board the *Discovery* as a guest. To celebrate the occasion of their return, a 'banquet' was held that evening. Doorly: [1]

> Scott, weather-worn and lip-plastered, managed to take his place at the head of the ward-room table; Wilson and Shackleton were too played out to leave their bunks, but they did extraordinary justice to the supplies of mutton and fresh potatoes brought by us from New Zealand.
>
> The three explorers devoured at least three platefuls of food to our one, and still craved for more! Of course, after the long drawn-out weeks of starvation the digestive organs could not cope with such an orgy of gorging, and they were violently sick; But they persistently shovelled lavish helpings of food into themselves, and repeatedly lost the run of most of it! Indeed, even in the early hours of the morning they were still at it! I was awakened by hearing Captain Scott rousing Shackleton, whose cabin was next to the one I was in.

"Shackles!" I heard him call. "I say, Shackles, how would you fancy some sardines on toast!"

The smell of toasting bread at the ward-room fire soon filled the place; and with one eye out of my sleeping bag, I could see Wilson in his cabin opposite stoking up like fury with the supplies Scott kept passing in to him. This awful ravenousness, which struck me as being at once humorous and pathetic, lasted for two or three days.

One wonders where Koettlitz was all this time. He had returned from a satisfactory trip in good condition seven days before Scott arrived back at the ship, and must have been ready for duty. He was supposed to be the senior medic. Shouldn't he have taken charge of the sick men and confined them all to their bunks and had them nursed on a 'low' diet until they were well enough to eat normally? Shouldn't Scott have placed himself and his companions in the doctor's care? Nothing was further from his mind, it seems. There is no mention of Koettlitz – it's as though he wasn't even there. No longer relevant to what was happening in the wardroom, Koettlitz might have derived a grim satisfaction from seeing and hearing all three of them repeatedly gorge and vomit. It can hardly have been an edifying spectacle. As Doorly says, it was somewhere between humorous and pathetic. Although it provides further evidence of Koettlitz's marginalisation and loss of authority, shouldn't he have stepped in regardless? After all, it was his duty as a doctor.

The deterioration in Scott's and Koettlitz's relationship must have already reached an advanced stage. Apart from one or two friendly relationships, Koettlitz was excluded from the main clique around Scott. It can be impossibly difficult to break through that barrier. Being frozen out, or just elaborately tolerated, are guaranteed to cause feelings of rejection and anger. At a certain point he would actually not have wanted to be part of that in-group any more, and in his turn he would have rejected them also. Besides, wasn't Wilson supposed to be a medic too?

Meanwhile, Scott must have soon heard that Armitage had made a good journey. A very good journey. As things stood, it rivalled, if not outshone, his own. Armitage had led a team, which included Skelton, up the western mountains and had established that on the far side was a snow-covered plateau that seemed to stretch into infinity. It was a major discovery. Not only had he discovered the South Polar ice-cap, he had pioneered a route through mountains comparable to the Alps, all with an inexperienced team. He had brought everyone back safely – one man being carried on a sledge after falling ill, but otherwise without undue suffering or hardship. It was an achievement of which could be justifiably proud, and he was.

William Colbeck, Captain of the *Morning*, brought orders for Scott from the Societies to return that year. Still confident that the ice would clear, as it had evidently done the year before, Skelton, Dellbridge and the engine-room men had been busy getting the engines ready for departure. In the meantime, fresh provisions and supplies were sledged across from the *Morning*. Visits were paid, dinners enjoyed and yarns told. The days, and then the weeks, passed with no sign of a major clearing of the ice and, apart from a couple of token efforts, with no concerted attempts to get the ship free. All, except the men who were going home, had probably already got used to the idea of spending another winter. It had been on the cards from the beginning. Apart from Royds, most found the life bearable, in spite of the deprivations and hardships. Certainly Scott did. He looked forward with equanimity to another winter. Another sledging season would give him the opportunity to beef up his results.

As their first winter had passed in comparatively leisurely fashion, with a magazine, football, shove-ha'penny, etc, as well of course as the scientific work and the ongoing digging out of the boats, the differences on the messdeck had become clear. The faultline seems to have been mainly between the civilians and the Naval men. All the messdeck civilians wanted to go home, and four of them did. The fifth, Charles Clarke, had wanted to go, but could not be spared as he was the only baker on board.

Ten men went home in the *Morning* in March 1903; two of them invalided, the rest voluntarily. The list, with comments from both Scott and Markham, reads: [2,3]

> Ernest Shackleton. Lieutenant, Merchant Marines, RNR. Invalided.
>
> William Macfarlane, RN. Invalided. 'A thorough hypochondriac'.
>
> William Peters, RN. 'A young skulk'.
>
> William Page, Royal Marines. 'Skulk', 'undesirable' and 'an idler and at bottom a bad sort of man'.
>
> William Hubert. Listed under Royal Marines. 'Artificer (*not naval*)'. 'An ignorant Poplar cockney and a bad hat altogether'.
>
> James Duncan. Merchant seaman. 'never got on with the rest'.
>
> Clarence Hare. Civilian.
>
> John Walker. Civilian (previously RN).
>
> Henry R Brett. Civilian. Cook. 'that dirty little rascal'.
>
> Horace E Buckridge. Civilian. 'A rolling stone & a queer character strongly suspected as a bad influence in the ship but too intelligent to misbehave himself.'

Scott regarded it as serendipitous that the very men he'd earmarked to go were the same as those who volunteered. The antipathies were evidently reciprocal, although he didn't seem to have expected that. It suggests that in spite of having opinions about them, he was remote from the messdeck. Scott is described repeatedly as being aloof, and it is confirmed again by Buckridge in an interview on 15 April 1903 to the *Otago Witness* quoted below. The civilians, less accustomed to the instant and unquestioning obedience expected in the Navy, left almost *en bloc*. Presumably expecting similar conditions as in ordinary employment, the absolute power of the captain over their lives, and his freedom to dish out punishment at will, must have come as a rude shock. Brett may not have been the easiest of men, but reducing him to 'a condition of whining humility' after spending eight hours chained on deck as a punishment [4] is not something that would be acceptable in the context of civilian employment.

In any case, however recalcitrant Brett, Page, Hubert and Peters may have been, the fault cannot have been exclusively on their side. They were the guys who did the donkey-work, confined to the ship most of the time, taken for granted, and low in the pecking order. There were plenty of triggers for the resentment which doubtlessly motivated their behaviour. And not all who chose to leave were 'objectionable'. Clarence Hare is said to have been liked by everyone (although 'above his station', according to Scott). PO MacFarlane, a 'capital man', according to Armitage, was invalided home, much to his disappointment.

There is a note of condescension in Scott's comments about the men, which, while generally unlikeable, feels especially out of place with regard to Horace Buckridge. Buckridge (who played Mrs Quiver in 'Ticket of Leave'), became a minor celebrity on his return to New Zealand. He had joined in Cape Town as a laboratory assistant after having fought in the Second Boer War, volunteering purely for the adventure. He was in the avant-garde of a new breed of entrepreneurs who try to make a living from deeds of derring-do. Described as a remarkable man, he had been a prospector, trooper, explorer, seaman and pearl fisher. He had found his time on *Discovery* 'boring and monotonous', and after he came back he became involved in an attempt to circumnavigate the globe in a small yacht, the *Kia Ora*. He gave an interview to the *Otago Witness*, 15 April 1903. In it, he claimed that his reason for returning had been the fact that he had been confined to the ship for much of the time, and that his request for more outdoor employment had been denied.

He told the reporter that he thought the men on the *Morning* had been much better and more cheaply provided for in terms of clothing, while they had been forced to alter nearly all their 'apparel', including having to make mitts out of blankets: [5]

> All the fur apparel brought had to be cut up and altered, and we had
> to re-make the sleeping bags, although these goods were bought, so
> it is understood, by one who had experience of polar expeditions ...

[Scott] had his own apparel altered, and left it to everyone else to do so or not, as suited them ... Not only did Captain Scott alter the apparel, but also the sledges themselves and details in connection with their loading – in fact, he appeared to acquire knowledge in a week or two that some would have not acquired after years of experience.

One example is Scott's alterations on the harnesses for the dogs, only to find that they chafed so badly they had to revert to the original design.

Regarding Captain Scott: [6]

Mr Buckridge expressed the opinion that he is the right man in the right place, and the only thing that the men under him complained of is that he does not look after the internal arrangement of things sufficiently, taking very often his officers' opinion of the men rather than forming his own opinion of them. Mr Buckridge does not think that having a crew composed partly of naval men and partly of civilians has proved altogether a success in the Discovery's case. At any rate, he states that quite a different state of things was apparent on the Morning as compared with those on Discovery.

The implication is that Buckridge found life on the *Morning* much more congenial – and so it might have been with Evans on board, and a confident Captain Colbeck who was working within his capabilities.

In the almost certain event of their having to remain a second winter, letters were being written, to be taken home in the *Morning*. Scott wrote a long letter to his mother, dated 24 February 1903. It was not published until 1966, the same year that Wilson's *Diary of the Discovery Expedition* came out. It included: [7]

For myself, I have enjoyed the whole thing amazingly, and have remained throughout in better physical condition than even I expected. I had expected the sledging to be hard work, but I confess I did not fully appreciate the strain it would bring and the test it must be of a man's constitution.

Our own journey to the South was, of course, the severest, the distance travelled was the longest, the time longest, and our food allowance the least. For Wilson and myself, saddled as we were with an invalid for three weeks at the end, it was especially trying. After our return, Wilson was in bed for 10 days, but as to myself, after the first day or two, when the reaction set in and I felt a bit done, I was quite myself again. I hope this will banish from your mind all fears for my health or fitness to stand another winter.

... I have gone on with this rather dull subject [scurvy] because I can see excellently intentioned persons gathering about you with gruesome tales and prognostications until you may be led to regard us as a number of sickly persons, imprisoned in great discomfort and desperately dreading the prospect of another winter ... All the "crocks" I am sending away, and am much relieved to be rid of. Except Shackleton, who is a very good fellow and only fails from the constitutional point of view.

... Royds has improved wonderfully. His bumptiousness has entirely vanished, and the really solid good nature of the man has come up to the top, for which I take to myself much credit. Michael Barne is always in the front rank in health and spirits. Nothing daunts him, nothing dispirits him, and the more work he gets the better he seems pleased. When we spent 36 hours together holding on to the corner of a tent in a temperature of minus 40 degrees, whilst his fingers were being badly frostbitten, he was quite in his most cheerful frame of mind.

Wilson is another splendid fellow. Our Southern trip naturally brought us very close together and as we got into some pretty tight places I know there is no bottom to his pluck and endurance.

Skelton is an all-round sportsman, just the man for this sort of work, which he thoroughly enjoys, always ready to do or to make anything. He is also something of an epicure and we have to thank him for dishes which we might very well have missed ...

[reverting to the Southern Journey with Wilson and Shackleton:] We really had great times on that trip. For 95 days I never took off or put on a garment, except to change my foot gear at night. Your flag, my dear, has been to the farthest South! ...

[about the dogs:] I don't like to talk or think about them.

[about Armitage:] ... an excellent chap but *entre nous* a little old for this work. It wants men with the fire and dash of Barne and Skelton ... Do you remember Hodgson? He has turned out the most solid, sound old person imaginable. He is out and about all day long, winter or summer, and doesn't care a hang what happens next. We delight in him. Bernacchi is an awfully nice little chap too, full of quaint conceits and foibles, but also full of pluck and a hard worker.

Ferrar was a conceited young ass to begin with and it took quite a long time to bring him to his bearings. I sent him on some of the hard spring journeys in which he was worse than useless. This he had to have pointed out to him, so I did it very plainly, finally producing tears. Since that, he is a changed youth and I think would do most things for me. He was objectionable. He is now a nonentity and knows it, therefore in time he will be an acquisition to our little band.

So, my dear, taken altogether you can scarcely imagine a happier or more contented little company than ours. There is very rarely any friction and never a quarrel, and we are all far better friends than when we started even from New Zealand and that is saying a good deal after a polar winter.

Huntford also quotes Scott as telling his mother that 'Armitage was the man who got the stockfish for the dogs.' [8]

Scott's relationship with his mother was caring, affectionate and personal. The whole family was close, and financially interdependent after the brewery money was gone. Hannah Scott seems always to have been at the centre of her children's concerns. They nearly all contributed to her needs and comforts. Scott, his brother Archie, and his brother-in-law (husband of Scott's sister Ettie) contributed financially; while his sisters Kate (Kitty) and Grace (Monsie) kept her company and sewed her clothes. It is, in all likelihood, their work in which Hannah can be seen in her full-length photograph: the ensemble, for which no expense or effort seems to have been spared, is topped off with an expensive-looking hat. Her facial expression suggests something of the martyrdom of Christ.

Her ailing parents lived with them at Outlands, bringing the total number of people living in that house to 17. She was, apparently, constantly preoccupied with looking after her parents, which put additional strain on her husband. Overwhelmed as he must have been by being expected to provide for such a crowd, he carried the burden of gradual financial deterioration alone. Hannah did not share her husband's worries, preferring to stay in ignorance, even though she was, according to Seaver: [9]

> ... pretty, clever, and of great personal charm, was the more remarkable personality of the two. To the finenesses and defects of a highly strung over-sensitive nature she added that moral strength and sound judgment which are the reward of selfless devotion to others. In her case it was given too exclusively to her ageing and ailing parents, at the expense not only of her own strength but also of attention to the welfare of her children, who however loved and admired her the more in spite of it. Indeed it was this very deprivation of his mother's company that roused her son's tender chivalry for her when he was a boy, and deepened it into a love amounting to veneration as he grew older ... From her too he

inherited a strong strain of tragic feeling, an undercurrent of sadness which was stoical; for she always met disaster with a smile ...

What characterises the martyr is their choice to suffer rather than take
positive steps to change their situation. Hannah Scott tyrannised her family with
her smiling martyrdom. In her children it fostered an almost neurotic concern for
her welfare, but for her husband it seems to have been a source of inarticulate but
no doubt guilty rage, which expressed itself in volcanic outbursts when it all
became too much. It is indicative of a man who was struggling to keep his head
above water, and hints strongly at the rows his son became known for – probably
for similar reasons. Scott's parents suggest early role models for him: a martyr for
a mother, and a father who tried to assert his authority with counterproductive
outbursts of temper, for which he was no doubt instantly sorry.

Scott wrote to his mother often and copiously, and always affectionately, while
she in her turn doted on him. She was 'My own dearest Mother', and he was 'My
own dear Con'. He liked to entertain her, and always included anything unusual,
gossipy or sensational in his letters. As well as revealing of his relationship with
her, his letters show a side of him that we don't see in his book – very different
from the avuncular narrator of *The Voyage of the Discovery*. Always keen to
reassure his mother, his reassurances are nevertheless marbled with boasts and,
when talking about others, he is patronising, sadistic and complacent by turns. We
knew already that he used angry tirades to stamp his authority, but we did not
know that he boasted of them to his mother. If we accept that he always tried to
please her, it follows that he thinks she will think well of him for his treatment of
Ferrar. There was more to her saintliness than met the eye, perhaps. It also strikes
a hard edge when he talks about being 'saddled with an invalid' in reference to
Shackleton on the Southern Journey. It doesn't quite hit the tone of Christian
charity one would expect him to take with his pious mother.

To us, Scott's treatment of Ferrar sounds like bullying behaviour, reminiscent
of Markham's dictum that new recruits to the gunroom had to be 'sat upon' to
make then into acceptable mess-mates. Reducing the expedition's geologist to a
'non-entity' is dismissive; not only of Ferrar, but also by implication of his role and
his work. True, the fact that Ferrar was fresh out of Cambridge probably meant
that he retained some of the arrogance of that milieu, but he was also low in the
wardroom hierarchy, and this was what made him vulnerable. Set in the context
of Victorian attitudes towards subordinates, it is perhaps not as objectionable as
it seems now, but it still makes uncomfortable reading. All the more curious,
therefore, that he should choose this sort of incident to write about while
apparently ignoring the enormity of having been one of the first humans to
experience Antarctica, and having set eyes on landscapes never before seen by
mankind.

Another interesting aspect of the 24 February 1903 letter to his mother is the way Scott focuses on his physical prowess and his ability to withstand the work and the climate. Apsley Cherry-Garrard was later to say of him that [10]

Sledging, he went harder than any man of whom I have ever heard.

It was with his strength on the traces that Scott proved his worth as an expedition leader, and as a man. All his major journeys have this hard driving of himself and his companions at their centre. But he made it count for too much. It helped establish him as a hero, but it counted against him as an explorer. It masked the true level of hardship his way of sledging represented, which was always bound to increase the potential for failure.

In a confidential, gossipy, almost conspiratorial tone, he says nice but patronising things about the officers and scientists. Koettlitz seems to have slipped his memory altogether. The man was reduced to a mere cypher long before the expedition was over. He is especially patronising about Bernacchi; interestingly, in view of the boat fiasco. In *Saga of the "Discovery"*, Bernacchi asserts that even in 1902, man-hauling was already considered an old-fashioned way of travelling over snow and ice, and that the starvation diets on the march could only be described as fantastic. He kept these criticisms to himself until much later, evidently.

Regarding Armitage, Scott is both patronising and critical. Armitage, in spite of 'being a little too old for this work' (he was only four years older than Scott), had climbed 9,000 feet up uncharted glaciers and discovered the Polar ice-cap. This he seems not to have remembered to tell her about. Instead, he connected him with the 'tainted' stockfish.

After telling his mother that he reduced Ferrar to tears, he goes on without a hint of irony to say what a happy little company they are: by implication, due to the strength of his leadership. The statement wraps up the letter with a reassuring, up-beat message, as is the way of letters; but it was a gross oversimplification, if not a fantasy.

Koettlitz wasn't the only one who had a hard time on the *Discovery*. Hartley Travers Ferrar did not have an easy time either. Young, naive and, by the sound of it, not very assertive, he tended to be (another) butt of jokes, and even an object of ridicule. According to Skelton, [11]

Armitage talks to him [Ferrar] in a most absurd way, a sort of bullying or ridiculing tone, in front of the men.

Eight months into the expedition Ferrar reports that he was [12]

... not able to get on properly with my ship-mates ... [and receiving] frequent rude rebuffs quite against the spirit of the Expedition.

He suffered frequent headaches, which stayed with him for the rest of his life. [13] Barne's cartoon of 'Our Junior Scientist', shows a pigeon-toed, rather hapless young man. Like 'Muggins' Hodgson the marine biologist, he chose to spend a lot of time away from the others, and was frequently out geologising. Scott remarked that it seemed wherever he went, he found that Ferrar had been there before him. It seems an incongruous level of ignorance for Scott, who was supposed to be the scientific director, and who should presumably have been aware of what the scientists were up to.

Nevertheless, Ferrar, in a letter to his mother referring to what he claims is the good atmosphere in the wardroom, writes: [14]

> It is entirely due to the Captain ... for his friendliness & the example he sets of how to pull together. It must be a difficult position for him, but he's practically one of us, & we have all been as jolly as Sandboys.

Scott's moods ruled the wardroom, which should come as no surprise. Undoubtedly Ferrar is being selective and prefers to ignore those occasions when Scott was not in one of his charming moods. Being 'as jolly as Sandboys' sounds clichéd and artificial; but then he was writing to his mother, whom he would have wanted to reassure. He was putting a brave face on it. In any case, it would not have done for a junior member of the expedition to write critically about the Skipper, even in the privacy of a letter home. It would no doubt have worried his mother, and it may have reflected badly on himself.

Scott was capable of projecting a charismatic bonhomie; no one in the world was more charming than he when he chose. There are many hints, however, that the wardroom was a hard, competitive place; and that Wilson, for one, felt called upon to [15]

> ... "suffer fools gladly". I have *never* realised to such an extent the truth that "familiarity breeds contempt" ... I have seen a little of the inside of the "Royal Navy". God help it.

Wilson is known to have been critical of Barne, who was a bit of a know-all; but Armitage wasn't always light entertainment, and might sometimes have been responsible for what Wilson describes thus: [16]

> There is a very unhappy element of spiteful ill temper knocking about which damps most efforts at any innocent pleasantry.

Unlike Scott, who had *carte blanche* to rage about as he chose, Armitage and everyone else had to be careful what they said, and who they said it to. Inevitably anger and irritation seeped out at the edges. In Armitage's case this sometimes took the form of overloud or crude repartee, or poorly disguised derision, according to Skelton.

While Scott was ahead of himself most of the time, Armitage was slow and deliberate. One of seven brothers, he was sent away to school at an early age; and it can be confidently assumed that he was on the receiving end of standard Victorian pedagogy, which tended to inhibit, if not destroy, confidence and spontaneity. Frank Debenham later wrote of him: [17]

> For polar work his mind was perhaps not quite flexible enough or his aims were not sufficiently ambitious to make him lead an expedition of his own.

AGE Jones, however, states that Debenham himself lacked leadership qualities and is therefore not a reliable judge. Jones adds, referring to Armitage, that a man who could rise from apprentice to commodore in the competitive world of the Merchant Service must have been more able than he perhaps appeared. [18] Armitage had been second-in-command on the Jackson-Harmsworth Expedition, and he was second-in-command again on the *Discovery*. He could be charming: Nansen, referring to his meeting with him in Franz Josef Land commented: [19]

> ... a cordial welcome in Armitage's soft voice warmed my soul, and I looked into the open smiling face of a man with a noble heart.

Well built, albeit on the heavy side, and pleasant looking, although lacking the electric blue eyes and sensual appeal of Scott, he faces the camera looking honest and open.

Scott is often described as having been a dreamer, but he chose career over wanderlust. It was Armitage who watched the ships go by on their way to exotic far-away lands, and was inspired by the romance of a life at sea, unconstrained by the demands of the military. Lacking the usual class entitlements, he might also have preferred not to put himself at the mercy of the institutional snobbery of the Royal Navy. He had few natural allies in the wardroom, and gravitated towards the warrant officers' mess and the crew. He writes about the 'men' individually and with appreciation. He clearly cared about them, related to them, and appears to have been more relaxed in their company than in the wardroom.

When he and Scott first met all had seemed well. Armitage states that he was charmed with Scott from the start. [20] Nevertheless, it is asking for trouble to put a less experienced man in command over a more experienced one. Especially if, like Scott, he was not inclined to consult or discuss. Armitage was given several sops to his pride by being given to understand that he was there to nursemaid Scott, and that although second-in-command, he would be given a piece of exploration of his own, almost equal to Scott's. It won't have taken long to transpire that Scott wasn't inclined to take advice from the likes of him; and before the expedition was over, he will have fully realised that however important his own journey might be, it would never be allowed to outshine Scott's. But Armitage's loyalty was uncompromising and not necessarily dependent on the worthiness of its object. It was more a matter of personal honour. When, during the wrangles with the Societies prior to the expedition he was asked if he would be willing to take over if Scott resigned, he indignantly refused, affirming his loyalty to his commander. His account of the expedition, *Two Years in the Antarctic*, is a model of grace and circumspection. In it, we read nothing about the anger and hurt which he is widely believed to have been left with afterwards – as had Koettlitz, Ferrar, and of course Shackleton, who in the end got his own back, with interest.

The second winter passed in much the same way as the first. Although everybody worked very hard to keep things pleasant and easy, the wardroom atmosphere must have been borderline oppressive at times. Its denizens often went for walks, no doubt returning in a better frame of mind. On the messdeck the men settled their differences in their own way. It didn't really matter if there was sometimes verbal hostility or even fisticuffs among them. It was the behaviour of the officers that mattered in terms of how the expedition would be perceived by the world at large. So the wardroom got out a bit, tended and read the instruments, pottered, and retreated to their cabins, immersing themselves in novels, or diary writing, or dozing, probably, more often than they cared to admit. Scott will have based his sunny view on the appearance of things, but underneath there were all the interpersonal strains that are inevitable in those circumstances.

In Armitage's case, these were aggravated by Scott's questionable claims to leadership. His irritation broke through publicly on that account on at least one occasion, of which Skelton has this to say: [21]

> Armitage made rather a fool of himself & took unfair advantage in
> his speech of making a covert sneer, referring to The Skipper & one
> or two others as "Great Experts". Singularly bad taste, but he will,
> of course, get 'in the soup' if he does much of that.

Scott seems to have let it pass, but it must have been another nail in the coffin of their once promising relationship. They were never a team, and that will not have been a secret to the rest of the wardroom. When Scott leaves for the Southern Journey, the sense of relief in Armitage's account is almost palpable.

As Scott's achievements have been put more in perspective over recent decades (by some, at any rate), Armitage has started to be given more his due as the discoverer of the Antarctic Plateau, the existence of which had not been confirmed until he reached it. At the time, many thought that the mountains formed a series of islands, on the basis of what looked like straits running between them. They were in fact fjords, as Armitage's discovery proved.

It is often stated that Scott tried to send Armitage home on account of worrying rumours brought back in the *Morning*, about his wife, and that Armitage refused to go, suspecting a ruse by Scott to get rid of him. Whatever the truth of those statements, Armitage was not given any further opportunities to explore, apart from a token trip. In the second (sledging) season he had wanted to sledge south over the Barrier. Somewhat naively, he had asked Scott to be allowed to try and get further south than Scott had last year. Wilson thought he was quite rightly refused: [22]

> The Captain worked the possibilities out on paper and showed them to me and I agreed with him in thinking it was far better to apply all our sledging energies and equipment to new work, rather than to covering old ground to that extent, with the chance of doing so little at the end of it. The upshot of it all is that Armitage is now off the list of sledging for this year altogether, though whether this is due to himself or any one else I cannot say.

It seems surprising that Armitage thought he had a chance with this scheme. It wasn't true that not much could be done at the end of it: he could have broken Scott's record. Wilson, in his turn, seems naive to have bought Scott's line. Or perhaps we are seeing early evidence of his role as legitimiser in chief for 'The Skipper'.

Scott himself was planning a trip over 'old ground', but that was different of course. The difference was that he was the boss and Armitage wasn't – and the problem was that Armitage had had a successful journey and that he and his team had been the first in history to set foot on the Antarctic Plateau. It rivalled, if not outshone, his own achievement. Scott wasn't the magnanimous type, and too insecure to allow anyone else, especially not stolid, unimaginative Armitage, to shine at his expense. Scott: [23]

> If we could do all that I hoped in the Ferrar Glacier and beyond, during a second season's work, I knew that the value of our labours of the first year would be immensely increased. As I have said before, the interest centred in this region; there were fascinating problems elsewhere, but none now which could compare with those of the western land. It was such considerations that made me resolve to go in this direction myself, and I determined that no effort should be spared to ensure success.

It should be noted that Scott refers to a 'second' season's work because he does not include the season in which they arrived. That is because it was not a 'sledging' season. To Markham and those in London, however, what Scott calls his second season was, to them, his third.

So while Scott went off to repeat and beat Armitage's performance on the icecap, Armitage was ordered to stay and organise ice-sawing operations, intended as an aid to freeing the ship from the ice. Armitage: [24]

> This was, I must confess, a sore disappointment to me, for I had set my heart on sledging over the barrier to the south. However, I

resigned myself to the inevitable, and felt somewhat consoled by Captain Scott's kind permission to make a short journey to the south-west portion of McMurdo Sound, and complete that portion of the map as soon as I had seen the [sawing] camp established.

What he really felt is probably better expressed by his handling of the sawing operation, which was going on round the clock, officers and men working side by side. Skelton: [25]

I had already gathered from reports that [the sawing camp] was not doing much, but I didn't think it was so bad as it was. It was certainly the most fearful waste of time one could possibly think of. One would think Armitage was entirely devoid of common sense, & that his only idea was to say that he had carried out orders ... He also seemed to have been making himself particularly unpleasant to all hands, especially Royds, absolutely tactless.

Armitage was not a happy man; and the absurd exercise of sawing ice eight or nine miles away from the water's edge has all the hallmarks of an act of passive aggression. Irritable behaviour would confirm that. When he also heard about Scott's journey over the ice-cap, besting him by about 150 miles, his feelings can be imagined. He consoled himself with the thought that it was concern for his sick comrades that stopped him going further on the Plateau, and that Scott had been ruthlessly out for himself only.

Scott arrived at the sawing camp exactly a week after his return from the Western Journey, having enjoyed Christmas on the ship, and getting indigestion from eating too much. Doorly's description of the scenes on the return of the Southern Party springs to mind. In the meantime, he had written an extra-ordinarily long letter to Armitage who was at the sawing camp, about nine miles away, half-way between the ship and the ice-edge. The letter went into lengthy detail about his adventures. He asked Armitage to make the contents known to everyone at the camp. It focused on how tough the journey had been and the dangers they had encountered, and ends with a plea for recovery time. Scott: [26]

I have gone into some detail in this matter because I think, as does the doctor, that the men [Taff Evans and Lashly] not only deserve, but require a day or two of rest and full feeding before going down on the saws; and, for myself, I am particularly anxious to work out my sights and ascertain how far we got, and, roughly, what the variation was at different points.

Nobody would surely begrudge him a few days' rest after a journey like that; and besides, he was the Captain, and didn't owe anyone an explanation. So it seems odd that he goes to such trouble convincing them of its legitimacy. In fact, the sheer volume of the letter seems designed to obscure, or perhaps soften, the meaning and impact his achievement would have on and for Armitage. As such, the core motivation was probably defensive. Requiring Armitage to read out the contents of the letter to everyone there would, while hard on Armitage, undoubtedly cause collective admiration and wonder to drown out Armitage's chagrin, and force him to join in the general approbation.

The distance to the camp was only about nine miles, however, and it would have been no big deal to get there. One of the men, James Dell, had made a functioning dog team out of the previous year's puppies, and was making a regular run to the tent one day, and back the next. Scott could have hitched a ride, but he seems to have been reluctant to cut short the euphoria of having completed what he thought was his best journey; he was tired and enjoying the comforts of home, but he might also have been reluctant to face Armitage, whose achievement he had effectively buried.

Back at the sawing camp, Skelton was getting tetchy: [27]

> We hoped that The Skipper would come down to the sawing in a day or two, but he did not turn up for a week. Although Armitage had given him glowing accounts of the (good?) that the sawing was doing, he must have gathered from various other sources, what a waste of time it was.

It is possible that Skelton felt caught in the middle of an unspoken feud between Scott and Armitage. Armitage had, on previous occasions, shown a tendency to carry out to the letter orders that he knew were ill-advised. Skelton hints at Armitage's hidden agenda with the observation that Armitage's methods were 'not always genuine'. [28]

Scott had ordered the camp to be made just behind the Dellbridge Islands. He assumed that the ice would extend to about there as it had done the previous year. It was an assumption based on too little information. Armitage chose to follow Scott's orders regardless: with the result that they were sawing in the middle of the ice-sheet. Loose ice in the channel they were sawing could not be removed, and tended to freeze up again as they moved forward. There seems to have been something of a carnival atmosphere at the camp – not surprisingly, as the effort was laughable. Although the work was strenuous, Scott tells us that everyone agreed that it has the most splendid picnic they had ever had, and when he did eventually get there, he gave them all a day off for New Year's Day, 1904.

Scott seems to have been in an expansive and indulgent mood when he returned from his Western Journey. He could look back on another hairy epic and conclude that, against all odds, he now had an impressive store of results to go home with. He was proud of this journey, on which he thought they had reached the limit of possible performance. He and his team had penetrated far onto the ice-cap: the first men in history to do so – and, in spite of not having attained the magnetic South Pole, he had sledged to somewhere south of it, showing that he would have reached it if he'd had the right equipment with him. The expedition had achieved something like its potential. Much more was now known about the nature and composition of Antarctica, and the fact that it was a continent had all but been established.

The Western Journey had started well. The party, including Scott, numbered 12 in all: Skelton, Feather, Evans (Taff), Lashly and Handsley in Scott's team; the geologist Ferrar with Kennar and Weller; and the third, the general support team, Dailey, Williamson and Plumley. [29] Scott, feeling confident that his experience was now a thing to be counted upon,

> ... determined that from first to last of this trip there should be hard marching.

Chilling. It was almost too much for some of the men, but within six days they were 6,000 feet up and a long way into the mountains. Here things came to a halt. Dailey, the carpenter, had warned Scott about the state of the sledge runners the day before, but he hadn't wanted to know. Now the situation had become critical. The 'German silver' lining on the runners had, according to Scott, worn thin from the previous year's sledging but, as with the stockfish issue, they had seemed on the face of it to be all right. In spite of his assertion that rarely had more attention been devoted to the preparation of a sledge journey, the runners had not been further examined. Now they were in ribbons. The experience he thought he had, was not after all enough to have taught him the wisdom of bringing spare runners, nor an adequate repair kit for what he knew was often going to entail sledging on hard ice and rough terrain.

It meant a return to the ship for repairs. Scott tells us that on the following days they came as near to flying as is possible with a sledge party. They had 87 miles to cover. On the first day they sledged 27 miles, down the glaciers and moraines, taking all obstacles in their stride. On the second day they did 24 miles. As if those two days had not been hard enough, he then he decided to test to the utmost his own party: Skelton, Feather, Evans, Lashly and Handsley. They were away on the third day at dawn, and arrived back at the ship in the semi-darkness at 8.30 in the evening, having covered 36 miles in the day. It was manic, or panic, or both. It was brutal and they must have been utterly spent when they got in. Scott was proud of having set a record for a day's march, but it wrecked not only his own team, but also the support team which limped in some time later. This party included Dailey, who had now to begin work on the sledges.

Three men had had enough. Dailey, Williamson and Plumley did not start again when Scott left with eight men five days later. Again the pace was fast, crossing the Sound in two days at an average of over 25 miles per day. Scott's driven pace was hard on the men and hard on the equipment. Soon the runners were split and damaged again. Scott complains that from then on they had constant worries with 'these wretched runners'. Skelton and Lashly had to tinker away for hours after marching all day, cobbling together bits and pieces to somehow keep the sledges going. Although in the previous year Armitage had had damaged sledge runners to deal with, it was nothing like as severe as this. The equipment had been newer, of course, but he had also taken things much more easily, which must have been a factor.

The punishing race up the mountains was halted again when they became tent-bound for five days by what Scott thought was a blizzard. It was borderline intolerable to him, but it must have provided some welcome relief to the rest. Soon after they got going again they passed suddenly out of the wind, while behind them it could be seen still sweeping the valley. As it turned out, the one time he should have kept going he ended up spending the best part of a week in the middle of what was probably a localised weather phenomenon. These are not uncommon in the mountains – but not being a mountaineer, he wouldn't have known about them.

Scott's thoughts seem to have habitually been in the future. Always thinking ahead, he seems not to have been entirely present in the here-and-now, with the attendant lack of attention to what was in front of him. The cursory inspection of the stockfish and now also, as it turns out, the sledge runners, are just two examples that suggest this. His habitual impatience confirms it. His attention was on the next thing, while the present constituted merely a barely tolerable delay.

There is a fine line between necessary effort and driven behaviour. Nobody would deny that hard effort was necessary for Scott and his team. The question is at what point it becomes self-defeating and potentially dangerous. Scott had the choice. He and his team could continue on to the ice-cap at a moderate pace, keeping something in reserve, and with special caution in view of the loss of a booklet entitled *Hints to Travellers* (containing a set of astronomical tables by which their observations could be calculated), which is too well known to need reiteration here. A moderate pace with the whole team would inevitably be a loss in distance achieved, but they would have achieved it together, in relative safety.

It was never going to happen. After some 70 miles of back-breaking sledging in brutal conditions, Feather and Handsley began to show signs of overwork and probable altitude sickness, and were sent back with Skelton. It was hard lines on Skelton, as he told Scott, who agreed. It didn't change anything, and from there Scott went ahead with the two strongest men, Edgar 'Taff' Evans and William Lashly, giving himself the best chance of a high mileage, and initiating a bond with Taff Evans that would eventually cost him his life.

If it had been risky to venture so far on to the ice-cap with the whole team, it was positively dangerous to carry on for as long as he did with Evans and Lashly.

One can be temperamentally inclined to risky behaviour, but most people would presumably have baulked at taking such chances on the Antarctic Plateau. The three of them went on day after day until they reached the date at which Scott must have decided was the point of no return. They were now a very long way out on the ice-cap, at 9,000 feet altitude. Scott, in spite of the fact that he himself had led them out this far, was starting to get spooked: [30]

> The scene about us is the same as we have seen for many a day, and shall see for many a day to come – a scene so wildly and awfully desolate that it cannot fail to impress one with gloomy thoughts. I am not an imaginative person, but of late all sorts of stupid fancies have come into my mind. The sastrugi now got on my nerves; they are shaped like the barbs of a hook with their sharp points turned to the east, from which direction many look high and threatening, and each one now seems to suggest that, however easy we may have found it to come here, we shall have a very different task in returning.

Lashly and Evans kept his feet on the ground by maintaining a homely atmosphere inside the tent. They helped him keep his demons under control while he pushed on, in spite of the fact that with each day the risks became greater. When they did at last turn back, they had three days to make up on the outward journey with regard to food, and five with regard to paraffin. They could not afford a single delay, not the slightest deviation on their course, not the slightest breakdown in the weather, nor health, nor strength.

Scott's blood ran cold every time the sky became overcast with the threat of bad weather. Setbacks of any kind were not to be contemplated. He had again led himself and his companions in a race for life they would be lucky to get away with. He contemplated the horror of not recognising where they were when they got to the coastal mountains. As he lacked the data with which to work out their exact position due to the loss of the *Hints to Travellers,* they would not know which way to go, and they had no time to spare. It was a nightmare scenario. It doesn't sound like he was in any great state of denial about the dangers. He seems to have been rational throughout – although given the conditions and their situation, they must all have been to some extent in an altered state of consciousness.

It would be easy to attribute Scott's reckless behaviour to a manic, irrational, hyperactive mental state – perhaps even to extrapolate that he was bipolar, citing his black-dog moods. Or sadomasochistic, as his punishing approach to sledging, and his sub/dom style of relationships, suggests. While those elements were certainly present in his psychological make-up, there were also strong real-world pressures to which he was undoubtedly responding. Back home, the Admiralty was waiting, and expecting results. Not to mention Markham, the Press, his mother, his sisters, his peers and, perhaps especially, his detractors.

Scott knew this journey might be the last one on which he could achieve something that would put his entitlement to lead the expedition beyond doubt. He kept going because right up to the last minute he hoped to discover something spectacular. He writes about getting to the top of the last incline, and feeling a sense of disappointment to see only a continuation of the vast plateau. He had been hoping for a coastline, or a mountain range perhaps, or who knew what.

The Southern Journey had undeniably been a disappointment. The bunting had been out, but it had not been the triumphant return of his dreams. He was under pressure from his many critics back home, who had predicted unsatisfactory results, and whom he must have wanted to confound. He wanted to impress the Navy Brahmins who held his career in their hands. Overlooking the possibility that they might consider his behaviour reckless, he staked everything on the last roll of the dice. If nothing else, he could claim to have established the continuity of the Plateau, and a stunning mileage would probably nullify any quibbles about the defensibility of the risks he had taken. As would the entertainment value and the fact that it was hardly heroic to play things safe.

They were on a knife-edge the whole way, until by an incredible stroke of luck they tumbled blindly off the ice-cap, and emerged unhurt on the road home. Incredibly lucky to have avoided serious injury, they set off for the depot that awaited them half-way down the glacier. But they were not out of the woods yet. Coming to an icy surface, the sledge began to skid; and after telling Lashly to pull wide, the next thing Scott knew was that he and Evans were dangling by their harnesses in a crevasse with 'a very horrid looking gulf below'. Evans was hanging just above Scott. Fortunately, the sledge had become wedged over the crevasse. Lashly, instinctively pulling back on his rope, kept the sledge steady, and managed to slide a pair of skis under it to make it more secure.

Meanwhile, by another stroke of luck, Scott had found a ledge at about knee level. He hoisted himself on to it, and got Evans to lower himself down beside him, his harness tucked up well under his arms. With Lashly occupied in holding the sledge, Scott now tells us: [31]

> There remained no other course for Evans and me but to climb out
> by our own unaided efforts ... It is some time since I swarmed a
> rope, and to have to do so in thick clothing and heavy crampons and
> with frostbitten fingers seemed to me in the nature of the
> impossible. But it was no use thinking about it, so I slung my mits
> over my shoulders, grasped the rope, and swung off the bridge. I
> don't know how long I took to climb or how I did it, but I remember
> I got a rest when I could plant my foot in the belt of my harness, and

again when my feet held on the rings of the belt. Then came a mighty effort till I reached the stirrup formed by the rope span of the sledge, and then, mustering all the strength that remained, I reached the sledge itself and flung myself panting on to the snow beyond.

Consciously or otherwise, he primes his readers with the suggestion that they both got out unaided. It might have been true in a sense; but they did have each other, and if you had to fall into a crevasse, someone like Taff Evans would be the ideal man to fall into it with. Evans was even then a physical training instructor: actually trained to help people up and over obstacles. In the end, Evans himself got out with the help of both Scott and Lashly – but Scott, if we are to believe him, got out entirely unaided by Evans, who happened to be standing beside him. It is very hard to believe that Evans did nothing to help Scott as he climbed past and over him. It is inconceivable that he would not have given Scott whatever assistance it was in his power to give, even if it meant nothing more than acting as a stepping-stone. If Scott was still comparatively strong, then Evans would have been; and unless his harness prevented him from releasing one of his arms, the probability must be that Evans gave Scott a leg up, and then the almighty shove which enabled him to reach and grab hold of the sledge. Lashly might very well have been in a position to give Scott the final haul that landed him back on the surface. This could have been possible because much of the weight pulling down on the sledge had been put on the ledge inside the crevasse.

Scott remembers slinging his mitts over his shoulders, and everything else pretty much but, tellingly, nothing about what Evans or Lashly were doing all this time. Scott habitually spun things to his advantage. And of course his version must have been partially true – but to accept that he did what he himself describes as the impossible is a big stretch. Claiming amnesia was a convenient way of obscuring the more undignified aspects of the scramble, and Evans and Lashly were sufficiently subservient to accept anything Scott chose to say about it. The way Scott told it certainly made him look good. The flourish with the mitts is worthy of d'Artagnan – as is grasping the rope and swinging off the bridge. A case of too much Dumas, perhaps.

References

1   Captain Gerald S. Doorly. *In the Wake*, p. 104

2   David Crane. *Scott of the Antarctic*, p. 238

3   Sir Clements Markham. *Antarctic Obsession*, pp. 70–105

4   Roland Huntford. *Scott and Amundsen*, p. 146

5   [Unattributed writer]. 'Life on Board the Discovery: the Great Sledge Journey'. *Otago Witness*, 15 April 1903. Papers Past, www.paperspast.natlib.govt.nz

6   *ibid.*

7   Reginald Pound. *Scott of the Antarctic*, pp. 91–3

8   Roland Huntford. *op. cit.*, p. 175

9   George Seaver. *Scott of the Antarctic*, pp. 6–7

10   Apsley Cherry-Garrard. *The Worst Journey in the World*, p. 204

11   Admiral Sir Reginald Skelton. *The Antarctic Journals of Reginald Skelton*, p. 138

12   Sue Ferrar. 'Paths are Made by Walking', p. 10

13   *op. cit.*, p. 2

14   L.B. Quartermain. *South to the Pole*, p. 117

15   Edward Wilson. *Diary of the Discovery Expedition*, p. 173

16   *op. cit.*, p. 177

17   D.W.H. Walton. 'Profile: Albert Borlase Armitage', p. 511

18   A.G.E. Jones. *Polar Portraits*, p. 15

19   Lieut. Albert Borlase Armitage. *Two Years in the Antarctic*, p. v

20   David E. Yelverton. *Antarctica Unveiled*, p. 56

21   Admiral Sir Reginald Skelton. *op. cit.*, pp. 92–3

22   Edward Wilson. *op. cit.*, p. 271

23   Captain Robert F. Scott. *The Voyage of the Discovery*, p. 519

24   Lieut. Albert Borlase Armitage, *op. cit.*, p. 217

25   Admiral Sir Reginald Skelton. *op. cit.*, p. 192

26   Lieut. Albert Borlase Armitage, *op. cit.*, p. 280

27   Admiral Sir Reginald Skelton. *ibid.*

28   *op. cit.*, p. 109

29   Captain Robert F. Scott. *op. cit.*, p. 520

30   *op. cit.*, pp. 548–9

31   *op. cit.*, pp. 561–2

15

THE RESCUE OF SCOTT AND THE *DISCOVERY*

Still aglow from the Western Journey, and appearing satisfied with his achievements so far, Scott decided he had earned a little R&R. Free from his usual anxieties for once, he had long since decided that if necessary, they could comfortably survive a third winter – and although he claimed that the 20 miles of ice separating the *Discovery* from the open water hung heavily upon him, he did not seem unduly perturbed about it. After relieving the men of the absurdity of sawing ice in the middle of the ice-sheet, he and Wilson had gone on a little camping trip to Cape Royds. Relaxing after breakfast on the morning of 5 January 1904, enjoying the sunlit view over the sound, suddenly a ship hove into view, shortly followed by another. Scott could hardly believe his eyes: [1]

> ... what in the name of fortune could be the meaning of this second
> one? We propounded all sorts of wild theories of which it need only
> be said that not one was within measurable distance of the truth.

The previous year, after having waited in vain for the ice to break up, the *Morning* had arrived back in Lyttelton alone. While the *Discovery* settled down to her second winter of hockey, novels, chess, and more-or-less comfortable domesticity, back in London a Markhamian hell was breaking loose. In a letter to Colbeck he sounds pretty relaxed about the possibility of the *Discovery* not returning with the *Morning*. [2] But the reality of it meant raising more money, and quickly. He had only just scraped the money for a single relief voyage. The original sum of £93,000 he'd raised (around £11 million in 2018) had mostly gone on the ship and its refined accoutrements. He had had his work cut out to wangle even one winter, and one relief mission, in the teeth of opposition to overwintering the ship in the ice at all. Now the *Morning* had returned bearing news of miles of ice separating the *Discovery* from the open sea.

From looking forward with pleasurable anticipation to the return of the *Discovery* with news of heroic deeds and impressive results, Markham was ripped back into reality by the news that she hadn't come home at all, and almost certainly wasn't going to that year. For the first six weeks after the return of the *Morning*, all he had were the cables from Lyttelton. The bare facts were that *Discovery* was beset in miles of ice and unlikely to get out any time soon, that ten people, including Shackleton, had come back in the *Morning*, and that money was needed immediately. It sounded worryingly like the shambles his enemies had predicted. He must have instinctively known that he had to get on top of the situation immediately. He did this by making a lot of noise. The panic and histrionics were both real and manipulative. He was, after all, suddenly faced with having to raise yet more money, and that was going to be more difficult than ever, especially as there wasn't much time.

Hastily pre-empting legitimate criticism, he put it about that the expedition was in grave danger, that all lives could be lost, and that it was everybody's duty to help them. Any cavilling about unqualified command and naive crews would seem callous and insensitive in light of the danger he claimed the brave pioneers were facing. There seems to have been a suspicion that his claims about danger were exaggerated, as no Longstaff came forward this time; and apart from a few small donations, neither did anyone else. He was forced once again to turn to the Government. In a move which was rich even by Markham's standards, he suggested that the Government would be responsible if the expedition was lost. It didn't go down well.

Scott was counting on ongoing visits by the *Morning*, but as he thought, only for communications and extra supplies. Indeed, it was all she was capable of, being no ice-breaker, and in fact seriously underpowered. Six weeks after the first cables, Scott's report arrived in London, addressed to 'those authorities at home who were responsible for the despatch of the expedition', mainly Markham, of course. He informed them that the *Discovery* was preparing to spend a second winter in the ice, and [3]

> ... perhaps rather unfortunately [I] referred to the return of the *Morning* in the following summer as a foregone conclusion and enumerated the stores which it was advisable she should bring ...

Scott, worried that his Southern Journey might seem a bit underwhelming for such a trumped-up and expensive enterprise, and that Armitage's achievement might outshine his own, had thought only about what he could do, given another sledging season. As far as he was concerned, there was no need to panic; all were well, and they had enough provisions and fuel. As far as getting home was concerned, he must have assumed that they were experiencing exceptional weather, and that the ice would break up as far as Hut Point again – if not this year, then the next. We now know enough about ice conditions year on year in McMurdo Sound to suggest that he could have been there for five years or more.

It had obviously been to his advantage to stay for a second sledging season. It seems a big statement to make that Scott subverted the expedition to serve his own ambition, but he certainly nudged events in that direction. There would not have been the motivation to stay that second winter if Scott had had something to be jubilant about, and had not needed to out-do Armitage. If he had really wanted to go home, he would have tried harder to get out. After the *Morning* left, according to Armitage, [4]

> The regular routine of our ship-life continued as before. Captain Scott considered that it would be useless waste of material to make any serious attempt to free the *Discovery* by means of the explosives that we had on board ...

An excerpt from Scott's original orders reads: [5]

> If you find it impossible to return to Lyttelton at the time specified above, [March or April 1903] a ship will be sent to take you back in the next season.

> There are other possible courses that events may have taken which we, in England, can neither foresee nor provide for. Much must therefore be left to Captain Colbeck's discretion.

> We are aware that you were, and probably still will be, very anxious to continue your exploring and scientific work after your return to Lyttelton, during a third navigable season. This would certainly be very desirable if the funds are sufficient.

> As at present informed, we are of opinion that a third season is not feasible from a financial point of view. But matters may have a different aspect in April, 1903, and we will be in communication with you on these points when you return to Lyttelton.

> But, as now advised, we think that the work of the expedition cannot be prolonged to a third year.

They were signed by W Huggins (President of the Royal Society), and Markham. These orders assume that he would come back with the *Morning* after the second southern summer season (the first having been that in which they had arrived, according to Markham and London), and that if there was going to be a third season at all, it would be after spending the winter in Lyttelton. In reality, he had, of course, spent a second winter in the ice (the first having been the winter already setting in on arrival), and had carried out his Western Journey over the ice-cap in his second *sledging* season (the season London calls his third, confusingly). It also states that if he finds it impossible to return, a ship will be sent to take him back the next year. Scott must have interpreted this as meaning that the *Morning* would come back a second time. It was hardly feasible that the entire

Discovery's company should ship home on the *Morning*, however, and he wasn't seriously considering it. As a last resort, maybe, but Scott did not think they would be in anything like dire straits, and thought they could easily survive a third, or even a fourth, winter in the ice.

He must have assumed Markham would simply raise the money as before, no problem, and as we know, he settled down to a second winter in the ice, looking forward to the prospect of another sledging season on which to beef up his results, which he did with the Western Journey. He in no way anticipated the crisis his failure to return with the *Morning* would cause. Not in his wildest dreams did he imagine that Markham would lose control of the expedition as a result. He had not envisaged Markham resorting to apocalyptic histrionics to get further money raised, and he never quite forgave him for it.

Markham's attempts to morally blackmail the Government was patently a step too far. It was sufficiently outrageous to raise the ire of Prime Minister. Balfour, in another instance of him getting his own back on Markham, it would appear, made the following statement in the House of Commons: [6]

> The Government are prepared to contribute to the relief of the officers and men on board the *Discovery* which is now ice-bound in the Antarctic seas. The course taken by the two learned Societies responsible for the expedition in respect to the contribution of money (Government had already contributed £45,000) and men made by the Government is greatly to be regretted. I have always leaned towards the principle of extending the very limited aid which the British Government have been accustomed to give towards the furtherance of purely scientific research. But such action can only be justified so long as the Government are able to feel absolute confidence that the scientific bodies approaching them have placed before them all the information in their posses-sion as to the estimated cost of their proposed action, and the limits within which they intend to confine it. That confidence has been rudely shaken by the present case.

It was shocking for both the Royal Society and the Royal Geographical Society to be accused in effect of misleading the Government – especially as the statement was made publicly, in the House of Commons. Markham claimed it was all because of an intrigue by some malicious person in the corridors, but it had actually been Balfour who, as Chancellor of the Exchequer, had dealt with the matter originally, and knew perfectly well what the facts were, and who he was dealing with. The Royal Society protested and managed to distance itself. The RGS Council knew only too well who to blame. Markham's manipulations, spin, lies and bluster were in danger of damaging the integrity and standing of the RGS. There are suggestions that he became erratic and confused during this time – and indeed, that sort of censure, from the Prime Minister no less, must have been hard to endure, even for a 'pachydermous' old man like Markham. Worse, they were hardly going to give yet more money to a man and a society they no longer trusted. Instead, the Admiralty was ordered to take the matter in hand. Immediately.

The Admiralty, clearly inspired by the tone of Balfour's statement, was pleased to appoint an Antarctic Relief Committee of three Admirals, of whom two had been Markham's opponents in the long fight over the plans for the expedition. One, Sir William Wharton (aka 'Pantaloon', head of the 'Hydrographic Clique'), had been one of his bitterest enemies. Admiral Aldrich, who had been in the 'Party of Wrecker Poulton' had been another. The third Admiral, Boys, seems not to have been actively involved at any stage. Wharton and Aldrich must have felt quietly jubilant at seeing their criticisms vindicated and their dire predictions come true. If relations had been amicable, a way might have been found to soften the spirit of the exercise; but as it was, they saw their chance to get even with Markham and took to the task with relish.

Described by Markham as a blundering time-waster, Wharton now wasted no time at all and, together with Aldrich, managed to deliver a ship fit for purpose (the whaler *Terra Nova* enters into history), and engage a captain renowned for blasting ships out of the ice. All in record time. However, even though engaging a whaling outfit was a neat snub to Markham, appointing a whaling captain to command an operation to rescue a Naval officer was going a bit far. So Colbeck, who was at least a respectable Merchant officer, was put in command of both relief ships, sparing Scott (and through him, the Royal Navy) the ignominy, as they would have seen it, of being got out of the ice by a whaling captain. They would also have foreseen the embarrassment for the Royal Navy in having their officers brought back in a whaler. It was another reason the *Morning* went: a whaler might do for the men, but not for the officers. However, if for any reason Scott did find himself having to coming home in the *Terra Nova*, Captain Henry McKay had orders to hand over command of the ship to Scott. It would have been interesting to see what the outcome of that might have been.

The order was simple: Scott and his company were to come home, with or without their ship. It was as if grown-ups had been sent to order home a bunch of skiving schoolboys. Markham had been brushed aside, and it almost looked like the expedition wasn't being taken seriously any more. In fact, the *bona fides* of the expedition had early on been compromised by Markham's outdated and inappropriately personal approach. The allegations of financial misrepresentation were just one more way in which this showy confection of an expedition fell short.

Markham launched into a storm of personal abuse. His opponents were 'malignant curs', 'wretched obstacles', 'sneaks' and 'jackals'. Probably on advice of the more level-headed Minna, he decamped for a while to Norway. While he was away, the RGS Council signed away the *Morning* to the Government, eliciting an absurdly theatrical flight of literary fancy from Markham: [7]

> After scuttling the ship the crew have left her in the long-boat and have abandoned the captain to resist the Royal Society, and Treasury pirates boarding her over the bows, quite alone. For the sake of Scott and the other dear friends, I will save the ship or go down with her. I am not the owner of the *Morning* to do what I like with her and give her to Mr Balfour or anyone else merely because he points an empty pistol at my head.

He was right: the RGS owned the *Morning*, whatever proprietorial airs Markham gave himself. How was it possible that someone so out of touch, so cavalier with the truth, so abusive and so irrational, could ever have been in a position to organise a supposedly national endeavour? One of the reasons was that it took only one man, Longstaff, to start the ball rolling. Longstaff was a well-meaning paint manufacturer. What did he know. He must have trusted the director of one of the most prestigious learned societies in the country to know what the right thing was, and to do it. Another reason was that Markham's directorship of the RGS had itself come about mainly because he could be trusted to maintain their ban on women. Quirks of history put Markham in a position to organise this expedition. The whole floundering progression towards Scott's eventual apotheosis was conceived here, as a random event, a quirk of history.

And so it was not just the *Morning* that hove into view that sunny morning off Cape Royds, but also the *Terra Nova*. Whatever Scott might have wanted to believe, he was no longer in command of the situation, because Colbeck had been ordered to stay in command of the relief ships. The *Terra Nova* had, for much of the way from England, been towed by a relay of warships – an emergency procedure, but necessary if she was going to get south in time. The thoughts and comments of the captains of these ships are unfortunately not known, but it must have been considered a 'rum do', reflecting poorly on Scott, whose defence was to make light of it.

But it shook him out of his euphoria – especially the order to abandon ship if *Discovery* could not be got out of the ice. Both Scott and Markham must have assumed that the Navy would continue to play ball with regard to the *Discovery's* company, which included a complement of RN officers, warrant officers, petty officers, quartermasters and able seamen – a significant body of trained men. Scott writes about their sufficiency of provisions, fuel etc, but never the continued services of the Navy personnel. These he must have taken for granted, as there is nothing to indicate that he ever even gave it a thought.

It took Scott a long time to understand why a second ship had been sent and he could '... scarcely realise the situation fully.' [8] When he did realise it, he was very down in the mouth. Everything must have turned to dust for him at first. All his achievements, lately so gratifying, were diminished by the peremptoriness of the order. Apart from the order to transfer specimens, records, and equipment to the relief ships, whatever he had done or was in process of doing was of no concern, and no consideration was given to his prestige. Suddenly, from having been in command of the whole show, he was now being given his orders by Colbeck, a Merchant seaman who had previously been under his command.

Scott had been talking to Wilson about a third winter in the ice. When they first spotted the *Morning*, Wilson wrote that their first thoughts were that [9]

> ... at any rate we knew we were relieved and so safe at any rate for the coming winter if we had to stop, and our whole conversation yesterday was about the next winter. I was to stay if my home letters didn't make it impossible. The Captain practically asked me to stay and I said I certainly would if I could.

But it wasn't up to Scott any more.

He was reluctant to face the music, and took five days to get back to the *Discovery* and read out the following order to the ship's company assembled on the messdeck: [10]

> If the "Discovery" cannot be got out of the ice, you will abandon her and bring your people back ... in the relief ships ... as ... My Lords cannot under existing circumstances consent to the further employment of officers and men of the Royal Navy in the Antarctic Regions.

It was an emotional occasion. All Skelton tells us is that Scott spoke about reports of Chamberlain's Fiscal Policy and the tremendous reforms taking place in the service. His selective silence suggests that he had mixed feelings about the way Scott spoke, with tears in his eyes, and as Williamson wrote: [11]

> ... in clewing up his yarn he heartily thanked us one & all for having stuck to him through thick & thin, & after reading out his different orders he seemed to be quite greaved so we gave him 3 cheers to buck him up a bit & there's no doubt he deserves it if ever a man does.

The obvious point to make here is that things are the wrong way round (again). It's a captain's job to buck up the crew.

Scott had had five days in which to think about how to present the order. In the light of his habitual secrecy, his first instinct was probably to be economical with the truth, informing people on a need-to-know basis only. He would risk un-controlled speculation with this strategy, however, a thing which his letters show he was always concerned to avoid. He discussed the situation with Wilson, who is likely to have advised a frank approach. In order to divert attention from any adverse reflections on his leadership implied by the uncompromising nature of the order, he reminded everyone how much they loved their ship, and what a wrench it would be to have to leave her. Who would not have willingly spent another year in the ice, rather than leave her at the mercy of the elements?! Quite a few, judging by the jubilation shown by the men on the arrival of the rescue ships. Royds, for one, couldn't wait to get back to civilisation. But it succeeded, and there was hardly a dry eye in the house as he wound up his speech.

Honesty, for Scott, although perfectly genuine in the moment, was something he chose to use or not, as the situation demanded. Judiciously employed, it was a great way of winning over his audience, and he carried on using it very effectively throughout his Antarctic career, on paper and in person. His handling of the men on the messdeck that day foreshadowed his later 'Message to [the] Public', and it had a similar outcome. Scott had an instinct for pathos, reminiscent of his mother. They were very close, to the point of being soul-mates. His mother's martyrdom was expressed through a kind of Victorian version of Rousseauist *tendresse*, whereas Scott's was more the style of an honest victim of undeserved bad luck and circumstance. With Markham he shared a penchant for melodrama and the romanticisation of struggle and longing. They both milked the gallantry of the struggle 'all alone' for what really mattered – which was in reality nothing but their own vision and their own ambition, and which depended for its power on hardships which were mostly of their own making.

After the arrival of McKay and Colbeck, Scott spent most of the ensuing weeks in his cabin. It is unclear what he did in there, but it is likely he spent a lot of time wracking his brains how to safeguard his reputation. The atmosphere in the wardroom must have been more than ever tense and edgy. Royds, itching to get home, was at the ice-edge making himself useful in whatever way he could. It's where Scott should have been too, if his priority had been to get the ship out. Instead, he was agonising over what it was all going to look like. It appears he even went so far as to order McKay and Colbeck to stop blasting. The motivation for this must have been at least twofold. One, if he was going to get out that year, he didn't want McKay to be responsible. Two, if explosives were now seen to be effective, it meant that if he had made more of an effort, and had known what he was doing, then he might have freed his own ship the year before. Having not seen much result from the few blasts he had tried then, he must now have clung to the hope that he had been right, and that whatever McKay was doing was a waste of time. And if the ice went out by itself, well, then he could claim that the entire rescue mission had been unnecessary. The irony was that it had taken a considerable effort to get the ship iced in in the first place. She was still afloat well after the hut (the *Discovery* hut, at Hut Point) had been constructed, meaning that a party could have been landed, leaving the ship free to continue other work.

For almost a century, Captain McKay and the job he did – almost certainly saving Scott from an ignominious return without his ship – has been minimised and written out of history. The weeks of unrelenting work at the ice-edge – blasting away and slowly but surely clearing floes, and by doing so destabilising and helping to break up more and more of the miles of ice separating the *Discovery* from the open water – have been quietly ignored. Instead, Scott's version of events has been uncritically accepted, and continues to be so by nearly all biographers. Scott claims that it was primarily the silent doings of nature that cleared the ice. On careful reading his own journal, however, it becomes clear that he did not see the ice-sheet starting to break up until after the *Morning* and the *Terra Nova* were in sight of Hut Point. They had been 20 miles away when they first arrived. McKay and his crew (and Royds) had been working at the ice-edge for six weeks, detonating charge after charge, butting and clearing the ice day after day. The rescue ships had arrived on 5 January. It wasn't until 14 February, more than five weeks later, that Scott wrote: [12]

> ... in the midst of this peaceful silence was an awful unseen agency rending that great ice-sheet as though it had been naught but the thinnest paper.

Without McKay the 'awful unseen agency' might never have got near enough to Hut Point to make a difference.

If the ice had stayed in, the *Discovery* would have remained encased in 15 feet of ice, sinking lower and lower by the stern – as photos show she was already doing, ending up entombed, just like the boats. Scott should have been eternally grateful – but instead he complained about the amount of coal McKay had used. Don Aldridge, in *The Rescue of Captain Scott*, provides a very well-researched account of how *Discovery* was got out of the ice. When the chips were down, the Admiralty had brought in an acknowledged expert and seasoned professional. And it was that man who had seen to it that before the advent of the 'awful unseen agency', something like 18 miles of ice had gone out. Not only the date, but also the fact that Scott saw the floes breaking up from the deck of *Discovery*, provide evidence that this was something that happened in the last few hours of the operation, within visual range of the ship.

It is interesting to note Scott's change of mind regarding explosives after an evening with McKay. Entry for 4 February:

> Spent the evening with Captain MacKay, [*sic*] who is excellent company for a depressed state of mind.

Sounds like it was McKay's turn to buck him up. Then, 5 February: [13]

> I did not want to begin explosions whilst the distance was so great, but on considering the stagnant condition of affairs I decided to

make a start today. It has been evident to me for some time that if explosives are to be of any use, they must be expended freely, and so today we experimented in that direction.

He says nothing about the talk on explosives McKay must have given him; but he was suddenly not only a convert, but an expert, on explosives, who had decided that the time had come for some proper blasts.

After explaining how nature and explosives together help break up the ice, which must have come straight out of McKay's mouth, he is soon superintending operations while his moods go up and down – hopeful one day, despondent the next. Good leaders are steady and level-headed. They do not depend on emotional support from others. They make sure they are involved in whatever is happening from the beginning and they don't shut themselves away like an offended prima donna. The way in which Scott biographers, including recent erudite and scholarly ones, have overlooked not only these but all the other obvious failures in Scott's leadership, and have continued to add to the myth of the great explorer, is worthy of a study in itself.

No order to get the *Discovery* ready for sea was forthcoming, even as the rescue ships came nearer by the day, increasing the probability of their release. Then, suddenly, everything went from stasis to frenzy: 'The rapid passage of events has caught us unprepared', writes Scott, and five days after their release they were almost dropping with fatigue, having had no rest due to coaling and watering, but also that [14]

> We never quite appreciated what a lot of work there was to be done till we got to sea, but what with the bending of ropes and sails, the securing of movable articles, and the constant chipping away of ice from every conceivable place, there has not been a moment's peace ...

Skelton blames Scott's impatience for what happened next. After the ship had been blasted out of the ice there had been a panicky scramble to get steam up, and a hasty attempt to get out into the Sound in the teeth of a rising gale. Scott knew there was a shoal off Hut Point which they would have to get past. They had run aground on it when they arrived, but with far less dire consequences. Cutting things too fine, he was caught by a tide-race and ran the ship aground on the same shoal. Typically, his response was to try and force her over, ordering men into the freezing rigging in the howling gale to make sail, with the result that the ship swung round till her bowsprit almost touched the rocks of the peninsula. By his own admission, he had only made things worse. The ship now listed heavily to port, and seemed to be 'hopelessly and irretrievably ashore'. [15] They spent a nightmare eight hours crashing on the bottom so hard it distorted the shape of the ship, all the while awash with surf and edging closer to the ice-foot. Wilson describes it as a day none of them would forget as long as they lived.

Whatever excuses Scott and others may have made, they were never going to win any prizes for seamanship. Many thought the ship would break up, and were probably thinking somewhat anxiously about the boats, and hoping the carpenter had done a good-enough job on them after Royds and his team had blasted and hacked them out of the ice. There must have been meaningful looks and rolled eye-balls behind Scott's back as seasoned sailors wondered how many more crises they were going to have to endure, and whether they would survive to tell the tale at all. If it is surprising that there were a few who did make excuses for him, perhaps it is worth remembering that from the vast majority, there was no comment. Better to say nothing if you can't say anything good. The ordeal gave Scott a taste 'something very near akin to despair', and aged him visibly.

When, thanks to the turning tide, they were once more afloat, one would think he'd have been eternally grateful to have gotten away with it and would have head-ed for home without further ado – especially as he'd already stayed longer than he was supposed to, and was under orders to get back to Lyttelton immediately. That would not have looked good, however. Coming back in convoy with his rescuers would have looked too much like the bunch of schoolboys they had been treated as, who were now being escorted home by the grown-ups. It was psychologically important that he should reassert his authority, and take command of the exped-ition once more. To demonstrate this, he proposed to carry out a further part of what he claimed was their original programme. Scott: [16]

> I have already mentioned that I had determined to try to penetrate
> to the westward around Cape North, and now that it had become
> necessary to promulgate my plans ...

A few weeks earlier, his plans, or their 'programme' had consisted of another winter in the ice, and there was nothing necessary about it. Quite the opposite, in fact. But it was a way of putting the rescue in another context, reducing its signifi-cance by making it part of, rather than the final, act in the history of the expedition. Being got out of the ice and escorted straight home could not have been the note Scott wanted to end the expedition on.

Back in control, he once again organised matters to play to his own advantage, with apparently little regard for the burden it placed on others, nor the danger it put them in. After the *Discovery* had been set free, it would have been reasonable to conclude that it was time to go home. Coal was in short supply and they did not have a fully functioning rudder. It was broken at, or soon after, they left Hut Point, and had been replaced at Cape Adare with a spare, or 'jury' rudder. The nights were dark and the sea full of dangerous icebergs and pack-ice. Now, instead of heading for home, Scott gave the order to steam westwards to the Balleny Islands, at appalling risk. It was hard and insensitive to everyone's needs but his own, as surely everyone else must have been aching for warmth and civilisation after more than two years in the ice – not to mention their hopes of a safe return.

He took coal from both ships, and more from the *Morning* than he should have. Colbeck deferred more readily to Scott than McKay, who resisted Scott's demand for more, for which – if he was mentioned at all – he was criticised by Scott and his besotted army of biographers. McKay sensibly refused to endanger his ship, or even inconvenience himself on account of a non-essential detour in aid of Scott's career and face. In a letter to his old captain, George Egerton, Scott asserts that [17]

> ... Terra Nova ought & in fact could have given us a good deal more
> than they did – old McKay the captain is a very good sort but there
> is no doubt that he was thoroughly upset by the Antarctic and had
> only one desire, to get out of it as soon as possible.

Crane concludes from this that it was McKay's 'parsimony or nerves' that spelled an end to Scott's more ambitious exploring plans that season. In fact, it is just about the only thing Crane does have to say about McKay, whose activities he entirely ignores from the moment he arrived in McMurdo Sound to the moment the *Terra Nova* broke through to Hut Point. Apart from successfully enabling – or at the very least aiding – the release of the *Discovery*, McKay's crime seems to have been an indifference to the risk of a tantrum from Scott, and independence from any judgement from him. Unsurprisingly, there was never less than an arm's length between them. The subtext in Scott's letter to Egerton is that he would not have had to take so much coal from the *Morning* if McKay had come across with what Scott thought he 'ought' to have given. It subtly shifted a measure of responsibility for the plight of the *Morning* on to McKay.

Scott was not a hands-on captain. He spent a lot of time at his desk, remote from the bowels with their bilges, inlets, pumps, donkey boilers and muck. Dirt, and probably coal-dust, had accumulated in the frozen bilges for two years, and now it was blocking the inlets to the suction pipes. No one seemed to know exactly where the water was coming from except Wilson, who wrote that it was a result of watering the ship in Wood Bay, overfilling the tanks above the engine-room. Emerging from Wood Bay, the ship had started to roll badly which, according to Wilson, had caused large amounts of water to spill out of the tanks, flooding the stoke-hold. In addition, water that had been frozen in the bilges might now have been back on the move again.

In a notable foreshadowing of another occasion in which water would be rushing backwards and forwards in the stoke-hold, Dellbrige was set to work taking apart the steam pump, while steam was raised in the donkey boiler in record time. To no avail. Dellbridge was seriously worried, and Bernacchi thought they were going to sink.

Scott: [18]

> Then, and not till then, someone thought of examining the bilge
> suction, and here in a moment was found the cause of all the
> trouble. The pump, we discovered, had never been out of order, but
> the rose which drew the water from the bilges was quite choked up
> with fine ashes.

One would expect that it's a captain's job to be familiar with the workings of
their ship, but officers like Scott expected to be informed through the proper channels. His somewhat critical tone implies that he held other people responsible for
the belated diagnosis. Nothing had changed six years later, when the same thing
happened, and the *Terra Nova* narrowly escaped going down with all hands.

Next was the turn of the rudder. Despite the fact that there had been severe
crashes at the stern on several occasions, Scott seems mystified, telling us that he
could not guess how it had come by such an injury. Then, however, he hints that it
may have happened on freeing the ship or on collision with a submerged spur of a
glacier. His efforts to free the *Discovery* had included exploding a massive charge
only 15 yards from the ship. It shook the whole bay, and Hodgson is said to have
been tossed out of his bunk by it. The shock wave was said to have had the
potential for destroying a lesser ship, and that he had been lucky to get away with
it. He had exploded another charge the next morning just beyond the stern. There
had already been a big crack in the ice there – suggesting potential damage to the
rudder, as it had been completely encased in that ice. This explosion caused the
ship to shoot up the two feet by which it had become depressed. The *Discovery*
had been built with an overhanging stern in order to protect the rudder. Nothing,
however, could protect it from high explosives in the hands of an impatient
commander with only a very sketchy knowledge of explosives. They are not the
same as torpedoes. One would think it would have been prudent to order a damage
report after this – and if not then, then certainly after Armitage, manoeuvring the
ship at the Erebus ice-tongue, struck the ice violently at the stern. No notice was
taken of it. Later, when Armitage had pushed astern against some loose ice, he
heard creaking and splintering sounds coming up from the rudder well. He seems
not to have thought it necessary to inform Scott, however. In what perhaps was
another instance of passive aggression, he seems to have waited to see how long
it would take for Scott to become aware that they were sailing with a broken
rudder.

And this was not until the carpenter came to see him with a 'serious face',
informing him that there was something wrong with the rudder. If it had been up
to Scott, it might not have been discovered until it was too late, as he himself
admits. But again it shows Scott's old-fashioned and inflexible attitude. His mindset was stuck in big-ship mode, where inlet pipes and rudders were the responsi-

bility of someone else. Nevertheless, common sense would suggest that a thorough inspection should have been made and a damage report ordered after the ship had been subjected to two severe shocks on her release from the ice, and an eight-hour pounding on a gravelly shoal. Never mind after the crunch at the glacier tongue. Scott's fatal tendency to bury his head in the sand at the first hint of trouble is suggested by the fact that the only damages that were noted were the superficial ones; sections of the false keel had been seen floating away while the ship was being pounded on the shoal, and several deck-lights had cracked on the same occasion. Other than [19]

> ... diligently sounding our wells for signs of extra leakage

... it seems that there were no further inspections ordered nor made. A very diffi-cult job was completed by Royds and a team in replacing the broken rudder. The jury rudder was half the size of the original. It was designed to get the ship home, and not much else.

On their way again, accompanied by the *Terra Nova*, all must have heaved a sigh of relief when Scott resisted the temptation to enter 'a mighty field of pack-ice dotted with numberless bergs', with only enough coal for 16 days and a poorly performing rudder. Even as it was, they had their work cut out forcing their way through the heaviest pack they had seen – this 'wretched' pack, according to Scott, which was inconveniencing him by not being where it was supposed to be. They lost sight of the *Terra Nova* in a snowstorm, after which a rapidly rising sea made the ship kick and plunge in a 'most objectionable' manner, making nearly everyone seasick.

They were navigating some of the most dangerous seas on Earth with a lightly ballasted ship, and little idea of her current manoeuvring abilities. Scott was be-latedly realising what he should have known from the beginning: [20]

> Altogether it has been a very unpleasant day, but perhaps the most serious thing it has disclosed is the uselessness of our small rudder under such conditions; it had so little effect on the ship that we could only keep our course by constantly trimming our sails. Had we met an iceberg, we should have had no choice but to throw the yards aback. This is really a grave matter, as the nights are long and we may fall across bergs at any moment.

It might be remembered that they were on an entirely elective detour. While it didn't take them hugely out of their way, after what had already been an overlong stay and a traumatic departure, *any* detour should have been considered *de trop*. On a human level, to say that he was insensitive to his company's wishes, or even their safety, is understating the case. As for what we would now consider their right to expect responsible leadership, it wasn't even an issue.

Fortunately, they soon found themselves in an open sea where they had been expecting pack, enabling them to obtain a more accurate position and description of the Balleny Islands. Scott, pushing his luck as usual, writes: [21]

> We have only sixty tons of coal remaining, a bare sufficiency to take us north; no doubt the wisest plan would be to turn north now, but I have decided to go on as we are for another day in hopes that fortune may favour us with one clear sight of our surroundings.

Fortune did favour him. 'Eld's Peak', and 'Ringold's Knoll', land the discovery of which had been claimed by Captain Wilkes of the US Navy in 1840, were part of a whole series of discoveries claimed by Wilkes, many of which had already been found not to exist. That 'Eld's Peak' and 'Ringold's Knoll' were likewise mistakes, deliberate or otherwise, will have surprised no one. But to Scott it represented a result and it would do as a justification for the detour. He could now head for home, albeit reluctantly. It was in fact imperative that he should, as they had barely ten days' coal left, and the ship was unmanageable under sail alone with their jury rudder. Even as it was, they were going to have to rely on favourable winds just to get them to their pre-arranged rendez-vous with the *Terra Nova* and the *Morning*. The unnecessary risks that had been taken to achieve these minor aims were appalling – especially when one factors in the inadequately ballasted state, not only of the *Discovery*, but also of the *Morning* after Scott had taken so much of her coal.

Neither the *Terra Nova* nor the *Morning* were at the rendez-vous, the Ross Harbour, aka 'Sarah's Bosom', in the Auckland Islands; although they had been expected to arrive there before the *Discovery*. It caused Scott some anxiety, but that soon passed and, certainly in the case of the *Terra Nova*, concern wasn't especially warranted. The *Morning*, however, was a different matter. Nevertheless, Scott's thoughts were on the manner of his arrival into Lyttelton, to which end the ship was freshly painted, scrubbed, and polished. Many of the officers and scientists went on extended trips inland, Wilson shooting birds, and others hunting for pigs.

It was while setting out for a picnic that Scott saw the masts of the *Terra Nova* coming into harbour. [22] Much to his relief, no doubt: not only on account of her safe arrival, but also because he needed more of her coal. He had cut things too fine, by now a habit, and had arrived at the rendez-vous with insufficient coal for steaming to New Zealand. One way or another, Scott was going to get coal out of McKay, and in the end he succeeded.

Scott himself describes the state the *Morning* was in when she finally made it into the Auckland Islands, five days after he had himself arrived. Scott: [23]

> The little *Morning* had had an especially dismal experience. She had been nearly a month fighting this terribly hard weather, with

all sorts of added troubles in connection with her ramshackle engines and pumps, and her ill-ballasted condition. Captain Colbeck will no doubt tell of the adventurous incidents of this month, but none of us is likely to forget the utterly worn-out condition in which his small company arrived at Ross Harbour, or the universal testimony of officers and men that disaster had only been averted by the consummate seamanship with which their small vessel had been handled.

Presumably this was meant as a compliment. Colbeck later wrote that [24]

In our unballasted condition the ship was, to say the least of it, not seaworthy.

Considering the condition of the *Morning* after Scott had helped himself to her coal, the responsible thing would have been to order the *Terra Nova* to escort her, rather than the *Discovery*. As it was, the *Morning* was left to face the elements alone, while Scott took the *Terra Nova* for his own support. And this was before he knew about the state of the rudder. Nowhere is there a hint that he felt the slightest doubt or perturbation, nor that he felt in any way responsible for what the *Morning* had been through.

Colbeck probably berated himself for having acquiesced to Scott's demand for extra coal, especially as it was in aid of a non-essential detour. By writing that the unseaworthy state of the *Morning* was saying the least of it, he must have meant that that was putting it mildly, and that it had been positively dangerous to put to sea in her. He was right. Today we would consider it complete madness. Scott covered himself by pre-emptively describing the state the crew of the *Morning* was in when they came into Ross Harbour. He was clearly expecting Colbeck to tell his story. In the event, Colbeck never wrote his memoirs. It would not be surprising if this was because he was demotivated by the tsunami of uncritical support for Scott, in the face of which any adverse reflections would seem like unworthy carping and griping.

In *The Voyage of the Discovery*, Scott does not mention any doubts about the wisdom of having sent Colbeck off alone in a too lightly ballasted, underfuelled and underpowered ship. One imagines this was because it would have shown up the dubiousness of his judgement and tacit denial of the risks. Simply ignoring the question of responsibility implied that he had nothing to answer for. The ship herself was blamed – having somehow found herself with too little coal, ramshackle engines etc, having to face bad weather and heavy seas. Instead of taking responsibility, he sympathises with the ordeal they were forced to undergo. With this, he turned the event to his own advantage by impressing his many uncritical readers with his apparently caring empathy. The facts are, however, that he had taken potentially fatal risks with both the *Morning* and the *Discovery* to little purpose other than to bury McKay's intervention and to recover his legitimacy as the head of the expedition.

So by putting McKay's activities in the context of further exploration and thereby casting him as merely an enabler of the 'real' work of the expedition, Scott regained the initiative and the high ground. The findings relating to Wilkes were pieces of luck that played perfectly into his agenda by justifying the detour and adding to his tally of achievements. Meanwhile, McKay had been suitably reminded of his place by being forced to wait on Scott's convenience and to act as a supply ship for coal. By the time they were ready for the final leg to Lyttelton, Scott had made sure the expedition was going to come home in style – fresh from a successful voyage of exploration, looking good, and with him securely in command of what he called their 'imposing little fleet'.

References

1   Captain Robert F. Scott. *The Voyage of the Discovery*, p. 586

2   Dundee Heritage Trust. 'Letter from Sir Clements Markham instructing Colbeck'. www.dhtcollections.com

3   Captain Robert F. Scott. *op. cit.*, p. 588

4   Lieut. Albert Borlase Armitage. *Two Years in the Antarctic*, p. 208

5   *op. cit*, p. 204

6   L.C. Bernacchi. *Saga of the "Discovery"*, p. 111

7   Elspeth Huxley. *Scott of the Antarctic*, p. 124

8   Captain Robert F. Scott. *op. cit.*, p. 588

9   Edward Wilson. *Diary of the Discovery Expedition*, p. 332

10   Roland Huntford. *Scott and Amundsen*, p. 177

11   David Crane. *Scott of the Antarctic*, p. 281

12   Captain Robert F. Scott. *op. cit.*, p. 604

13   *op. cit*, p. 598

14   *op. cit*, p. 620

15   *op. cit*, p. 612

16   *op. cit*, p. 617

17   David Crane. *op. cit*, p. 292

18   Captain Robert F. Scott. *op. cit.*, p. 622

19   *op. cit.*, p. 615

20   *op. cit.*, p. 629

21   *op. cit.*, p. 633

22   Edward Wilson. *op. cit.*, p. 349

23   Captain Robert F. Scott. *op. cit.*, p. 637

24   Don Aldrich. *The Rescue of Captain Scott*, p. 137

16

COMING HOME, AND SCOTT'S BOOK
THE VOYAGE OF THE DISCOVERY

And so, on Good Friday, 1 April 1904, the prodigal son returned at last to Lyttelton to a warm and admiring welcome. Waiting for them when they finally came on shore was a telegram from Markham: [1]

> To Scott and Colbeck: How to deal with the press: It is advisable not to accept Reuter's offer. At the earliest possible moment after your arrival cable not more than 500 words giving main results of expedition address it to President 1 Savile Row. Better keep off all reporters and interviewers and give information to no one for at least 48 hours after you send off telegram, even after that as little as possible.

Markham evidently did not regard McKay as relevant, nor worthy of inclusion in his instructions. The assumption, that only what Scott and Colbeck might say was important and would be taken notice of, speaks volumes – not just about Markham's values, but also the kind of newspapers he was accustomed to dealing with. And these he had virtually sole control over – courtesy of his standing as President of the RGS and his family connections. And of course this meant rapturous reports of their achievements, whatever they were. Everyone was pleased to see them back, naturally, and it would have been churlish to have denied them their moment in the sun. Nevertheless, the sun did not shine on everyone equally, and McKay and the crew of the *Terra Nova* found themselves in the shadows almost from the beginning.

McKay was excluded from invitations after a farewell banquet given for the Governor, Lord Ranfurly, to which the officers of all three ships had been invited. Wilson's verdict was that the evening had been '... by no means a success'. [2] He had

had a similar opinion of the dinner on the *Ringarooma* during their first visit to Lyttelton, and it is not hard to guess why this one was not to his taste either. It had undoubtedly been similar in spirit, and it was probably McKay's idea of a jolly evening which drew the disapproval of both Wilson and Scott. It might also have had something to do with McKay's attitude and his inconvenient yarns about his activities in McMurdo Sound. Whatever the case, Scott instituted a week's moratorium on further festivities, and McKay was discreetly omitted from official functions and dinners after that.

Back in London, Markham was laying the groundwork for how the *Discovery* Expedition was destined to be almost universally perceived for almost a century. He had already made sure of the diaries, data, specimens and photos, by forbidding any unauthorised publication for the first year. That telegram was also meant as a warning to Scott and Colbeck not to say too much. He was right not to trust Scott's discretion or even intelligence.

Scott had come back bristling with irritation about having been 'saved' – a totally unnecessary expedient, as far as he was concerned. At first, his anger centred on the Government and the Admiralty for overreacting and causing unnecessary fuss and expense. Stupidly, he expressed what amounted to a censure of the Admiralty in an interview with a reporter. The Admiralty held Scott's future in their hands, but he made free with his criticisms to a journalist, who instantly wired it to London where it was headlined in the *Daily Mail* as 'Blunder Made in Sending Relief Ship!' It was reported that Scott emphatically protested against the despatch of the *Terra Nova*, and declared it to have been a wasteful expense of money. Belatedly realising that he was queering his own pitch, Scott hurriedly backtracked, and in a flurry of letters protested that he had been misrepresented and had never said anything of the sort. It rings rather hollow, however, as it happened to be exactly what he thought.

In a damage-limitation exercise, he wrote to his brother-in-law, William Ellison Macartney MP, Parliamentary Secretary to the Admiralty, and an important ally to keep on his side: [3]

> I have always been most careful to point out that we thoroughly understood the reason for the Admiralty's action ... There is here a dear old gentleman who is a brother-in-law of Sir Clements Markham. With the best intentions in the world he has promulgated the doctrine that the *Terra Nova* was a waste of money. I found everyone ready to tell me so on arrival, but I always replied that the Government could do nothing less than make a certainty of the relief by sending a second ship ...

Scott happened to be staying at the home of the dear old gentleman in question, who was Markham's brother-in-law, the Hon. CC Bowen, and who also happened to be proprietor of a local newspaper and a correspondent for another, *The Press*. The old man seems to have been keen to proclaim his views, which sound remarkably like they had been dictated by Markham. The article was published in *The Press*, New Zealand, on 2 April 1904: [4]

> There was really no need at all for her (Terra Nova) and, pecuniary, she had only been a burden on the expedition. The expenditure on her was quite useless ... As matters stand, the Home Government will not get out of it under an expenditure of £60,000 – ten times the amount for which the Geographical Society was prepared to do the work. Nor were the English Government by any means un-exacting as they insisted upon the Geographical Society making over to them the ownership of the Morning, and even tried to secure possession of the Discovery. This, however, was a little too much and the Society made a determined and successful stand against so unreasonable a demand. In addition, there should be reckoned the cost of the unnecessary voyage of the Morning to Hobart to meet the Terra Nova there, in order that Captain Colbeck, who had thus to go considerably out of his way, might assume command of the expedition there. There would, of course, have been no necessity for this loss of time and extra expense had the Morning alone been commissioned to go to the relief of the Discovery. Then also should be borne in mind the expense and the annoyance caused by having to take to Hobart the sheep presented to the expedition. It was almost incredible in Mr Bowen's opinion that the English Government could have been so obstinately persistent in acting as it did, against the remonstrance of those well acquainted with what had to be done, and one was at a loss to imagine what object the ruling powers could have had.

Scott had not understood the reasons for the Admiralty's actions, much as he might claim that 'the Government could do nothing less than making a certainty of the relief by sending a second ship'. The real reason, which was that he had Markham to thank for it, only became clear later. It wasn't until they were on their way home from New Zealand that Scott wrote to his mother: [5]

> I fear there is no doubt that our old friend Sir Clem started this.

He was right. It was all because Markham had gone round shouting about an emergency.

If the survival of Scott and his men had been Markham's real concern, he should have been delighted and grateful for the generous way in which the Government stepped in. He should have been only too pleased to hand over the *Morning* if it was going to help his boys. The fact that he wasn't suggests that his very public panic had been a ploy designed to raise money for what he wanted to keep as his own expedition – the 'British National' appellation notwithstanding. If he had genuinely believed lives were in danger he would have been grateful for the Government's intervention. Now it had backfired by actually succeeding, Markham's response was that the *Terra Nova* had been a most scandalous waste of public money, and that the [6]

> ... whole wretched story of Treasury insolence and malignity will
> have to be made public before long.

The Government was eloquently silent when the expedition finally returned to London.

In the event, the inconvenient truth of the exit from McMurdo stayed by and large in New Zealand. It must have been clear to McKay that his presence was surplus to requirements and he left, apparently without fuss, as soon as his ship was ready. Job done, as far as he was concerned. He knew, and his men knew, what they had done. The *Morning* on her own could have done nothing to help the *Discovery* out of the ice. It is likely that she would have spent a third winter in the ice, and who knows what her fate would have been in that event. Scott had been quite happy about the idea, and had wanted only fresh supplies and mail from the *Morning*. But then what? Was he thinking the *Morning* should come out for a third time, or did he simply assume that after the third winter the ice would clear and he would simply sail back to New Zealand? None of this was clear, and it is surprising that he thought the authorities back home would find it acceptable.

Perhaps significantly, Wilson says nothing at all about the politics of the situation – but then he was greeted by his wife, with whom he was very soon off on intensive sight-seeing and ornithological trips, punctuated seemingly only by attendance at church services. He seems to have been in a state of euphoria when he wrote to Scott's mother about the expedition. Scott combined outward strength with inner vulnerability – a potent combination, and it drew from Wilson a paroxysm of feeling the intensity of which he might have instinctively known was more prudently expressed to Scott's mother than to Oriana: [7]

> My dear Mrs Scott, – ... How happily everything has turned out after
> all! We feel as though the whole thing has been a great success, and
> I am quite certain that every soul on board agrees that the success
> is due wholly and solely to the splendid way in which your son has
> acted towards us all as our leader, from start to finish. Without a
> doubt he has been the making of the Expedition, and not one of us
> but will feel more and more grateful to him for the way he has acted
> throughout.

Notwithstanding that it is a difficult thing, at least I imagine it is, for the Captain to make intimate friends with anyone, I feel as though we were real friends, and I need hardly say I am proud of it.

I am glad indeed for your sake, and for my wife's and parents' sake, and for everybody's, that the thing is so nearly finished. We have had a most interesting experience, but to you it has been a very trying time. May you never be quite so completely cut off from your son again!

Believe me, Yours very sincerely,

Edward A. Wilson

Many biographers have taken letters such as this as providing evidence that Scott was a great man and a great leader. Coming from Wilson, widely regarded as a reliable authority, testimony such as this is persuasive and credible. Scott did hold the show together, he was genial and benign when it suited him, and the expedition did achieve some notable results. But Wilson seems overcome by an almost worshipful emotion, heaping a level of global praise on Scott that is extravagant by any standards. Scott was an emotional man and he drew an emotional response. Wilson was especially taken with him, and it is clear that his view is entirely subjective. Not everyone waxed lyrical – not then, and not now.

'Billy' and the 'Captain' were psychologically complementary. Scott infantilised Wilson by calling him Billy, and it heightened the sense of intimacy between them. Privately, Wilson might have called Scott Con, but in front of other people it was always Captain, or Skipper. And Billy was flattered to be addressed in such familiar terms by the man who was now being hailed as a hero, and made much of by all the most important people in New Zealand.

Without making any facile assumptions about sublimated romantic feelings between Billy and the Captain, Scott's predilection for hard, if not brutal, effort and self-denial was inspiring to Wilson. They shared a certain disdain for the comforts of life in the normal world – both found enjoyment in doing without, and both had an instinct for self-denial and martyrdom. We never hear anything like the same levels of passion from Wilson when he is referring to his wife. Ory was the 'brick', who inspired a tender affection – but not, as far as we know, the flights of near-worship that Scott drew from him. Ted and Oriana never had children, and there is no suggestion that she ever became pregnant. If they had any sort of sex life together, or at all, they hid it extremely well. What we do know is that they shared an ardent religiosity. There were three in that marriage: Ted, Ory, and God.

Oriana, *née* Souper, was a vicar's daughter and had never been far from a Bible or a crucifix. Ted once told his sister that he felt you could do more good in the world by being in it, rather than hiding away in a monastery. Wilson had an inner monk, and Oriana an inner nun. There seem to have been few, if any, flirtations in either of their lives before they met. But even that seems to have been more about a meeting of spirits than sexual attraction. There was an air of chastity about their relationship. Notably, they got married two weeks before Ted's departure for Antarctica. They spent the most unromantic of honeymoons staying with relatives and seeing to a hundred and one things before departure. They had known each other for some time, and in the context of an ongoing chaste relationship it could have been just business as usual. According to Birdie Bowers, Oriana was [8]

> ... coldly genuine to a fault, impatient of nonsense & without a particle of frivolity ... [a] woman of strong will & fertile brain [and] thoroughly good.

There could of course have been a medical reason for Ory's lack of pregnancies, of which neither was aware at the time. In this case, they might have been sleeping together and got married just before the departure of the *Discovery* in case Ory should turn out to be pregnant after he'd left. It seems unlikely somehow – but either way, they must have wanted to make sure of each other.

Either way also, the marriage seems to have worked. Both seem to have got what they wanted from it. Ory obviously admired Ted tremendously. She was his companion, housekeeper and general amanuensis. Ted's work always took priority, of course. Ory had worked as a matron at a boarding school, and had several temporary jobs in Ted's absence – but her most important calling, after God, was as Wilson's wife. Their itinerary on his return to New Zealand was demanding and social, giving them little time alone together. As a second honeymoon, it sounds about as unromantic as the first. Much of what leisure time Wilson did have seems to have been taken up with writing his diary. He was the breezy tweedy type, apparently asexual and forever opening windows. She was good looking and somewhat delicate, although she gamely trekked along with Ted when the occasion arose. She was close to her sister Constance, who must have been a great support to her after Ted's death on the Barrier.

Heroics aside, the expedition could claim a number of clear successes. Hodgson in particular seems to have been conscious of the opportunity, and hardly wasted a day. Treated like an old duffer, his achievements have never been properly acknowledged. Today, a biologist can only dream of the number of new species he discovered and brought back. Bernacchi did important magnetic work and brought back a series of seismic observations. He was also one of Royds' team which helped establish that the Ross Ice Shelf was afloat. With the 'brevity he reserved for the achievements of others' – to borrow a memorable phrase from AGE Jones [9] – Scott dispenses in three paragraphs with Royds' Southeastern Journey. As well as that journey, and taking charge of essential practical work, Royds organised two-hourly meteorological observations for the whole time they were there, doing much of it himself. In those conditions, it was perhaps one of the more truly heroic achievements. His piano and harmonium playing were important in maintaining a harmonious and civilised atmosphere. He has not generally been given the credit he deserves.

Wilson, whose contribution to the social harmony on board ship is more widely celebrated, had killed, skinned, preserved and painted the wildlife, and had made a special study of the emperor penguins and their chicks. He had also painted the colours of sea, sky, ice, and rock – the atmospheric phenomena and the auroras. He also kept an extensive descriptive diary. Ferrar had done solid geological and glaciological work, bringing back important plant fossils and rock samples from many locations. Koettlitz, undervalued as a sledger and as a scientist had, together with Wilson, kept the men in good, mostly scurvy-free condition. His diaries, notes and observations were lost – an inexcusable and highly suspect event, which meant his work could neither be appreciated nor validated. Barne had led a major journey to what subsequently became known as the Barne Inlet, but had until that time been thought to be a strait, running between the mountains beyond the Bluff (Minna Bluff). Scott gave it no more than a passing mention in his book. Mulock had made extensive and accurate maps. Scott, together with Wilson and Shackleton had discovered hundreds of miles of mountainous coastline, and together with Taff Evans and Bill Lashly had penetrated far into the ice-cap. It was better than many had anticipated, but not as good as it might have been.

The return to England of the BNAE was noisy and cool at the same time. The public was enthusiastic but the Government virtually ignored it. They famously had their welcome-home lunch in a dockyard shed. Markham had styled his own pet project as a national expedition, but this humbug was exposed after the Government took control. The nation had supplied more than half the cost, including the use of Admiralty personnel and the very expensive rescue operation – all of which they had been reluctant to provide. To say that Markham was not popular in the corridors is probably putting it mildly.

The washing of official hands of the affair left the field free for Markham, however, who spun the expedition into a triumph. Many would have felt it was just as well – if not because of vested interests, then for the sake of the nation. Markham's mental conflation of his own vanity project and a national endeavour culminated in a feeling of self-righteous indignation at the lack of official enthusiasm: [10]

> People do not understand the greatness of the achievement ... nor the greatness of the results ... Our people have done a great work, and it will be shameful if it is not officially, as well as generally recognised ... Scott ought to have the freedom of the city.

But, as Koettlitz wrote to Nansen about the Southern Journey, it [11]

... might have been much further had the Captain [Scott] been a man of more experience.

The scientific results were trumpeted after all, because they were useful in adding lustre – albeit of the scholarly kind – to otherwise somewhat underwhelming achievements.

It was therefore largely thanks to Markham's PR skills and hyperbole that Scott and the expedition were celebrated to the extent that they were. Scott was soon knee-deep in medals and honours, a guest of the King and Queen at Balmoral, and speaking to large audiences in halls and theatres all over the country. He was also writing a book, and it was this which was to become the expedition's most enduring popular legacy. According to Scott, by the time they came home, most of the Society adversaries seem to have been reconciled. Wharton had now 'showed his deepest sympathy with the objects of the expedition'; and Buchanan, Tizard and Poulton – Markham's bitterest enemies in the fight over the leadership – are mentioned in connection with the committee work they put in, and for their contributions to *The Antarctic Manual for the Use of the Expedition of 1901,* which Scott had taken with him.

Further, if anyone could still be in doubt about the origins of the Scott way of exploration: [12]

> Not less valuable to me, starting as I did with no experience of polar work, was the kindly advice and assistance I received from those officers who had taken part in Arctic Expeditions; and for my guidance in numerous respects I have to thank many a conversation with such eminent travellers as Sir Vesey Hamilton, Sir George Nares, Sir Albert Markham, Sir Leopold McClintock, Admiral Aldrich, Admiral Chase Parr, and perhaps most of all with my old Captain, now Admiral G. Le C. Egerton ...

A Polar *tabula rasa* had been engraved with the convictions of an institutional and hierarchic tradition, where plenty of workers were always available to do whatever their leaders demanded. The old expeditions were not overmanned, as normally claimed. They were manned to provide a sufficiency of human traction. The fact that many required hospitalisation and lengthy periods of recuperation is testament to the severity of the task. Sailors did the hauling because sailors did as they were told and didn't foul the decks. Above all, it was the British way. For the old guard at the RGS, dogs and skis were all very well for foreigners, but not for us.

It is reliably reported that the library on board *Discovery* contained nothing that was likely to challenge these attitudes. There was a copy of Nansen's *The First Crossing of Greenland,* but that had been accomplished without dogs. He had experimented with Canadian snow-shoes and ways of using skis for hauling sledges, but with mixed results. If anything, it reinforced the idea that skis were only partially useful. There were plenty of novels and stirring adventures (Dumas, among others), showing it was mainly intended to entertain rather than educate. Incredibly, Scott seems to have been content for someone else to choose the contents of the library. He must have had too many other things to think about. Not until they were into their first winter in Antarctica did he start to realise the level of his own ignorance and the grave disservice the compiler of the library had done them. Scott: [13]

> I find time also to read up Arctic literature, of which I am woefully ignorant; most unfortunately, our library is deficient in this respect ... Nordenskjold, Nansen (*Farthest North*), and Peary are absent, and two of these at least would have been amongst our most valuable books of reference. Yesterday I was pleasantly astonished to find that Wilson had some notes on Nansen's *Farthest North*, giving extracts of his sledge weights, &c ...

Good old Billy, but no relevant narratives, and therefore no detailed input from some of the world's most successful Polar explorers.

Scott's own experience with skis led him to assert that [14]

> ... since Nansen's journeys it has been very generally thought that they have revolutionised the methods of polar travel. I have mentioned ... how delighted we were with our ski practice, and I have also called attention to an incident where some officers were able to push on with a journey because they possessed ski. [the first Cape Crozier trip] The latter is really an extraordinary exception, and it is still more extraordinary that it should have been our first experience of Antarctic travelling. It naturally biassed us all in favour of ski, so that although a few remained sceptical, the majority thought them an unmixed blessing. Bit by bit, however, the inevitable truth came to light: it was found that in spite of all appearance to the contrary, a party on foot invariably beat a party on ski, even if the former were sinking ankle-deep at each step; while, to add to this, when the surface was hard, ski could not be used, and had to be carried as an extra weight and a great encumbrance on the sledges. The ski party still made a stand in their favour by stating that they saved labour, but even this could not be admitted when the facts were thoroughly known. It stands true to some extent for a party out of condition, but the fact we gradually came to appreciate was that after a week's marching our legs got so hard that it troubled us little to plod on throughout the day whether the snow was soft or hard. It will be seen, therefore, that our experience has led me to believe that for sledge work in

the Antarctic Regions there is nothing to equal the honest and customary use of one's own legs. Progress may be slow and dull, but it is steady and sure. On my western journey, having no knowledge of the inland surface, I took ski. They remained on the sledge from start to finish. As we were contemplating them just before our return to the ship, one of my companions remarked, 'They've had a nice cheap ride', and that about summed up the situation.

There are conditions wherein it is indeed easier to walk than to ski. Will Steger, who crossed Antarctica on skis, tells us that he sometimes found it less tiring to walk than to ski. The vast majority of the time, however, he and his companions went on skis, as do all Antarctic travellers today. For an impatient man like Scott, it would have been easier just to get going without the bother. But he expected to be able to carry on on his own two feet indefinitely, assuming adequate levels of strength and vitality however long the trip might take. Will Steger and Jon Bower-master, in *Crossing Antarctica*, state that what makes Antarctica different from other challenges is that it is so big, and that the journeys are so extended. This means that conserving energy, which may at first seem unnecessary, is in fact vital. Most of the time, skiing is more energy efficient than walking. Scott was not finally converted to the use of skis until he was well onto the Plateau on his Last Journey. But even that was not until he had tried leaving them behind, and had as a result been forced to admit they needed them. Antarctica had caught up with him at last. It was not the last, nor the most painful, realisation he was to have when it was already way too late.

As far as dogs are concerned, in *The Voyage of the Discovery* Scott asserts confidently that [15]

> ... on steep slopes and over uneven country the dog is practically useless.

As Amundsen was to show, that statement was probably based on nothing more than what Markham had told him. Scott himself didn't know enough about it to even venture an opinion. Even if there was some excuse for not knowing what dogs were capable of until after Amundsen had taken them up the Axel Heiberg Glacier, there was plenty of material attesting to the value of dogs for Polar travel available to Scott at the time. Von Wrangel, Astrup and Peary, and Nansen, had all successfully used dogs over all kinds of terrain. In the 1820s, Ferdinand von Wrangel, an admiral in the Russian navy, had explored Siberia and its seas north of the Arctic Circle using hundreds of dogs, travelling up to 30 miles in a day. His *Narrative of an Expedition to the Polar Sea* was available in translation from 1842. In it, von Wrangel gives details of distances, loading, and the feeding of dogs, and information about their management, training and behaviour. It must have been in the library at the RGS, as Markham wrote about von Wrangel's journeys in *The Lands of Silence*. Peary and Astrup had crossed Greenland in 1892 using dogs. Astrup had learned how to run 'Eskimo' dogs from the Inuit themselves as, notably, had Parry, back in the 1820s. Astrup asserted that [16]

> Were it were it not for these remarkable animals ... [he] and Peary would never have completed [their] journey. [the crossing of Greenland at a very high latitude]

And then of course there was Nansen himself, who had taken them on his bid for the North Pole, where the sea-ice is notoriously hummocky. Scott was not given publications such as these to read, nor did he seek them out. Even M'Clintock, in a piece that somehow got past Markham, wrote in praise of dogs in an essay included in *The Antarctic Manual*. M'Clintock, restricted in the number of men he could take on his journey in the *Fox*, in 1857, had taken 24 dogs. On one of his journeys he went 420 miles in 25 days with 15 dogs, a driver and an interpreter, in very low temperatures. This works out at an average of just under 17 statute miles per day. [17] If this was impressive, it was modest in terms of what dogs were capable of.

Both Markham and Scott must have realised that using human traction alone to get to the Pole would strain the limits of human capability. Even with unlimited manpower, you could only ever go at the maximum speed humans dragging sledges can attain. This means that it was always going to take at least four months of solid dragging to get to the Pole and back from Ross Island, always their favoured point of departure. To get enough food on the trail for the journey would take careful planning, and for the size of operation required, the logistics would be daunting. Scott did not have the required number of seamen at his disposal and so, copying M'Clintock, he took 23 dogs on the *Discovery*, but without anyone on board who knew how to manage, train or drive them. He took them in case they might prove useful, but not as a main traction force. As far as running them was concerned, he must have assumed the men would learn. They did, but the dogs would never be used optimally because no one had the expertise.

For a long time they experimented. Men tried pulling alongside the dogs, with indifferent results. In Scott's first venture into the snows, they harnessed a team in front of a sledge, expecting them to simply go ahead and pull in an orderly fashion. Scott was irritated and annoyed by the ad-hoc mess that developed, having apparently assumed the dogs would know what was expected of them and perform. Dogs need skilled management, and teams need selection and training for orderly and effective pulling. Kelly Tyler-Lewis, in her well-researched *The Lost Men*, states that [18]

The prevailing view is that inexperienced dog drivers need to begin with two or three dogs and train over a period of weeks or months, building up to a full team once authority is established.

Scott was too impatient for that, even if he had had the necessary instructions available. The relevant books had been left behind, deliberately or otherwise. In any case, all was nullified by the failure to inspect the stockfish. One of the sailors, James Dell, did eventually get a team into what Scott, with just the slightest whiff of patronage, called 'capital working order'. It might have been taken more seriously if one of the officers, or Wilson, had achieved it.

There was an ontological incompatibility between dogs and the Navy. It went beyond working practices: encompassing world view, values, culture and nationality. Parry and Ross may have learnt about Polar travel from the 'Esquimaux', but that was taken no further. When M'Clintock took dogs to the Arctic, it was on the *Fox*, a non-Navy venture. It was more than a prejudice: it was about their collective identity, and what they represented. Markham, champion royalist and conservative traditionalist, could hardly be expected to feel any different. Yet the dogs' ideal food, raw meat, was in abundant supply on the coast of Antarctica, and Arctic breeds are adapted to the cold. Von Wrangel and his drivers had sat on the sledges, but Nansen had discovered that men on skis can travel at the same rate as trotting dogs – thus saving weight and increasing the amount of provisions it was possible to take. Crucially, dogs, used in this way, increased speed, and therefore the distances that could be achieved. It also relieved the sledgers of backbreaking work, conserving energy and thus making a successful outcome more likely. In modern parlance, dogs were a no-brainer. The expedition had wasted a valuable resource, even in the few they had.

The reason both Scott and Markham (and Fiennes) most often gave for their reluctance to use dogs was that it was cruel. This was, and remains, absolute humbug. Markham had no experience whatever of working with dogs. Scott had not much more, but nevertheless considered himself an expert after the Southern Journey. Scott: [19]

> I have endeavoured to give a just view of the use of dogs in polar enterprises. To say that they do not greatly increase the radius of action is absurd; to pretend that they can be worked to this end without pain, suffering, and death is equally futile. The question is whether the latter can be justified by the gain, and I think that logically it may be; but the introduction of such sordid necessity must and does rob sledge-travelling of much of its glory.

Generalising from his own experience, he implies that sledging with dogs is sordid because it involves pain, suffering and death. Wilson diagnosed acute peritonitis in the first dog he opened up, and the stockfish was green with toxic mould.

The same symptoms were present in all the dogs, and they had started when their diet had changed to stockfish. What more evidence did he, or anyone, need that the pain, suffering and death of their dogs had been due to their own negligence?

Markham, commenting after their return: [20]

> The sledge journeys *without dogs* are quite unequalled. Easier for Peary or Nansen to make the dogs do the work while they stroll along or guide the sledge from behind. [his italics]

Claiming that Peary and Nansen had 'strolled along' was ridiculous of course, but a common strategy for raising one's own status is to reduce that of one's rivals. Some years hence, Amundsen was to suffer the same treatment. And so it became the level of hardship endured that defined one's true worth. Scott was very good at doing hardship. It was a brilliant cover for failure. Coming through an ordeal is a triumph in itself, regardless of what has actually been achieved. Important also was the fact that the Establishment and the nation in general had a vested interest in portraying Scott and his exploits as heroic. Markham found his friends in the enclaves of unelected power, and together they made sure the side was not let down.

But however perverse it is to do things the hard way, it is also entertaining. Scott would not have been half so much fun if he had known what he was doing. Arguably, the best thing to come out of the expedition was *The Voyage of the Discovery* (1905). Although Scott said he found the writing of it hard work, he was fairly practised, having all his life written letters and reports. He produced a lengthy narrative, which came out in two substantial volumes, lavishly illustrated with artwork, photographs and maps. The first edition sold out almost immediately. It was at least as successful as Markham's orchestration of awards and medals in elevating him to the exploring elite. He took his readers with him on an adventure. Starting slowly with ice upon ice, the story comes to life with a dramatic disaster, and goes on from there, relating dangers, difficulties, shocks, and hair's-breadth escapes from certain death. In an encomiastic letter to Scott, Admiral Sir Lewis Bayly wrote: [21]

> I had no idea that you had been through such trials and escapes. I held my breath as you shot down the ice following the sledge and your two companions. I trembled when you were down the crevasse.

The adventures are interspersed with cosy vignettes about life in the wardroom, eliciting in the reader nostalgia for the times when they too had enjoyed companionable evenings round the table or in front of the fire, toasting bread with long forks.

Markham's influence is clearly present in the résumés of historical expeditions with which Scott embarks on his tale. At a certain point, sandwiched between two mentions of the Balleny Islands we read that [22]

> The necessarily bald outline of fact which it is alone possible to give in these pages can convey no idea of the extraordinary hardships and difficulties successfully overcome by these men. In the smallest and craziest ships they plunged boldly into stormy ice-strewn seas; again and again they narrowly missed disaster; their vessels were wracked and strained and leaked badly, their crews were worn out with unceasing toil and decimated by scurvy. Yet in spite of inconceivable discomforts they struggled on, and it does not appear that any one of them ever turned his course until he was driven to do so by hard necessity. One cannot read the simple, unaffected narratives of these voyages without being assured of their veracity, and without being struck with the wonderful pertinacity and courage which they display.

Was linking this passage with the Balleny Islands coincidence or design? Either way, it prompts a re-examination of Scott's final foray to the Balleny Islands. Was it justified after all? Was it not these men from whom he took inspiration, and weren't the risks simply the occupational hazards which all explorers were bound to accept? In any case, to some degree all explorers hope to make their name and fortune. Scott can hardly be blamed for being no exception. The answer lies in what was at stake. It was certainly not their survival. In fact, that would have been better served by a direct return to New Zealand. Nor was this final flourish a voyage of discovery. They didn't have enough coal to go very far, and certainly not beyond the parameters of the (albeit imperfectly) known world. Scott got lucky through mistakes made by Wilkes, but he could not have predicted even that modest result. One might be forgiven for failing to see the object of that last detour. Unless the hypothesis – that it was undertaken to save face – is true.

Scott was a great story-teller. He fulfilled the creative writing essentials such as showing, rather than telling. Comparing Scott's and Armitage's narratives, it is immediately apparent that this is one of the great differences between the two. Scott gives us the feel, the sight and the sound; he shares his emotions, he makes us feel the pain. The horrors of camping in deep cold are vividly evoked through detailed descriptions of what it is like when bits of you literally freeze. He furnishes our imagination with the sensory particulars that allow us to enjoy a rich vicarious experience.

But he is reticent about the less heroic aspects of life on board and on the trail. Armitage is more informative about the dinginess of the wardroom and the general domestic squalor, with damp laundry hanging on lines festooned around, the soot from coal fires, the stale smell of dinners past, pipes, mildew, and the combined whiff of 11 men before the invention of underarm deodorants and washing machines. But even he stops short of telling us about how and where they went to the toilet. It's one of the first things people want to know, but one of the last anyone wants to tell us about. Explorers in general avoid writing about the basic functions, but they are anything but trivial. More-recent explorers are a little more forthcoming, but certainly when it comes to heroic-age narratives we have to make do with hints and chance remarks.

Scott washed his own clothes on this, as well as his Last Expedition, even though there was always a servant available to do it for him. He claimed it was in order to save the man the trouble. It might have won him brownie points in some circles, but his apparent altruism probably hid a sense of mortification at letting another man see (and handle!) his dirty underpants. The drawback of course was that it meant he had to wash *all* his clothes. On board ship there were the 'heads' (toilets), and the officers appear to have had chamber pots in their cabins. Presumably they also used the heads, but considering the fact that they were open to the outside air, and that snow would have been bound to drift into them, it must have been an issue.

Presumably they found ways of dealing with impossibly cold and windy conditions, but we are left wondering how. Sledging, Scott 'went to the lavatory' outside the tent, and expected everyone else to do the same, whatever the call and whatever the weather. Other expeditions found ways of mitigating the ordeal. In Shackleton's case, a hole with a flap over it was made in the floor-cloth, and on the call 'heads under!' everyone turned away for the person in question to do their business inside the tent. On some expeditions everyone would be given a few minutes inside before taking the tent down. Amundsen went one further and dug a channel to the outside, where the dogs ate the men's excrement with relish. Scott found the idea revolting, and was once driven to exasperation by puppies running around the *Discovery,* forever gorging themselves on the midden heap.

For those wishing to know how to cope should they ever be caught short in Antarctica, the basic guidelines are to loosen clothing while in the tent, find some-where sheltered if you can, face the wind, and do it as quickly as possible. Un-surprisingly, many Polar travellers develop piles and constipation, or its opposite. But what about toilet paper? Modern expeditionaries learn to make do with as little as possible, and for many it becomes something of an obsession. In Scott's case, there is a single reference of toilet paper being stored at One Ton Depot on the Last Expedition, but nowhere is it mentioned as an item carried on the sledges. So who knows? Scott never touched on the subject, and neither did anyone else. They probably had to make do with snow, at least part of the time. What is certain is that it was a very chilling process, and that it didn't always go smoothly. It is, apparently, only a matter of time before a little accident occurs. On Scott's expeditions most must have experienced agonising struggles at times and risked, or even suffered, actual frostbite on account of social delicacy. Similar hardships were endured on Scott's Last Expedition, as we shall see.

On long journeys they took extra finneskoes and socks, and most of them will have taken extra underpants. Even if they did take their dirty laundry home with them (there is evidence to suggest that Scott did so on his Last March), the heroic age of sledging left behind it a trail of waste. In fact, this has been the case for all sledging epics in Antarctica until recently. Currently, travellers are required to bag up their waste and bring it back, but the once-pristine wilderness was polluted with trails of human and canine detritus by all the early so-called heroic treks and sojourns. It is no particular consolation that it is now buried in many layers of ice and snow. The midden heap *Discovery* left behind when she broke out of her ice-prison was impressive. Sadly, this was still very small beer compared to what has been dumped there since.

If it hadn't been the intention from the beginning, the *Discovery* Expedition certainly ended up with the feel of a preliminary foray, a learning experience. It was arguably too soon to think of a focused effort – how to do what needed to be done took a while to become clear. Scott pre-empted criticism of his inexperience by frankly acknowledging, and lamenting, it. Undoubtedly influenced by Wilson in his ostensibly honest approach, he took the weapons out of his critics' hands. The irony is that people related to him *because* of his inexperience. It brought them closer to him than they could ever be to Amundsen, for example. And the greater the horror, the greater the thrill in reading about it. And the greater the risks and the hardships, the greater the heroism for having faced them and overcome them.

Scott kept very quiet in his book about the interpersonal challenges: the snide remarks in unguarded moments, the intimations of criticism and gossip behind his back, the personal antipathies, the explosions of temper, the dressings-down, the hidden tensions and the suppressed resentments. And whatever their private feelings, no one would have risked a negative report or a howl of derision over the telling of tales, no matter how justified or true. It allowed a perception to arise of an expedition unsullied by rows and resentments, and superior to other expeditions – certainly the ones that were not British, and not run on Royal Navy lines. This probably elicited many a wry smile, not least on the *Terra Nova*. Common sense would suggest that the general atmosphere on *Discovery* was no better or worse than on any other expedition.

Some of the crew went on to achieve a degree of renown in the years ahead; namely, Tom Crean, Frank Wild, Edgar Evans, William Lashly and Ernest Joyce. We will hear a lot more about Crean, Evans and Lashly, because they were on Scott's Last Expedition; but Wild and Joyce went with Shackleton, with whom they had evidently formed a bond, and who must have been impressed enough to take them on the *Nimrod*. His judgement was vindicated. Wild, who had showed early promise on the first abortive trip to Cape Crozier, was cool-headed, resourceful, and with a natural talent for leadership. By the time Shackleton set off in *Endurance*, Wild was second-in-command. Markham wrote of Wild that he was 'no more good', after having liked him at first. He must have made a special point of amending his biographical notes later, in order to add 'Went with Shackles – Swollen head – No more good.' [23] Bad enough to go with Shackles, but getting ideas beyond his station made him no longer good.

Petty Officer Ernest Joyce, so unremarkably lined up in the second row in the homecoming photo of the *Discovery*'s company, co-led one of the hardest journeys ever made in Antarctica. He was one of Tyler-Lewis' *Lost Men* who, in 1916–17, sledged to the foot of the Beardmore Glacier and back to Cape Evans to lay depots for Shackleton's Trans-Antarctic Expedition on which his ship, the *Endurance*, was crushed. This led to two of the most harrowing stories of survival against the odds in the Antarctic literature. The first, Shackleton's boat journey, is of course legendary; but the journey on which Joyce helped save the lives of two of his companions, and attempted to save a third, is less well known, but equally agonising.

The *Gauss*, which had set off at roughly the same time as the *Discovery*, had returned to Kiel on 23 November 1903, after having spent only one winter in the ice (literally), beset about 50 miles from land. Drygalski was a scientist, and the expedition had been primarily a scientific one. Their results were impressive. Venturing into an entirely unknown region, they had discovered strong evidence for the Antarctic Convergence, surveyed 600 miles of coastline, and described 1,440 organisms endemic to the Antarctic. The expedition received high praise from the scientific community, but it seems the Kaiser was not impressed. In spite of having a piece of Antarctica named after him (now called the Wilhelm II Coast), there was little to excite the popular imagination. When Drygalski asked for a second season, it was refused. The Kaiser will have already heard about Scott's more spectacular exploits. The news of his Southern Journey and Armitage's discovery of the Plateau had been brought back by the *Morning* after her first visit. By the time this news had passed through Markham's hands, it will have sounded like no one's discoveries could ever aspire to the greatness of Scott's, and that everyone else might henceforth save themselves the bother of going to Antarctica at all.

References

1   Don Aldridge. *The Rescue of Captain Scott*, p. 142 (Colbeck Private Papers, Dundee Industrial Heritage Archive DH1097)

2   Edward Wilson. *Diary of the Discovery Expedition*, p. 357

3   David Crane. *Scott of the Antarctic*, pp. 299–300

4   Don Aldridge. *op cit.*, p. 143

5   David Crane. *ibid.*

6   *ibid.*

7   Reginald Pound. *Scott of the Antarctic*, p. 113

8   Anne Strathie. *Birdie Bowers*, p. 81

9   A.G.E. Jones. *Polar Portraits*, p. 259

10 David Crane. *op. cit.*, p. 303

11 Roland Huntford. *Nansen*, p. 491

12 Captain Robert F. Scott. *The Voyage of the Discovery*, p. 68

13 *op. cit.*, p. 215

14 *op. cit.*, pp. 309–10

15 *op. cit.*, p. 318

16 Roland Huntford. *op. cit.*, p. 195

17 George Murray (ed.). *The Antarctic Manual for the Use of the Expedition of 1901*, p. 302

18 Kelly Tyler-Lewis. *The Lost Men*, p. 321, n

19 Captain Robert F. Scott. *op. cit.*, p. 318

20 David Crane. *ibid.*

21 Reginald Pound. *op. cit.*, p. 122

22 Captain Robert F. Scott. *op. cit.*, pp. 21–2

23 Sir Clements Markham. *Antarctic Obsession*, p. 94

17

THE PERIOD BETWEEN EXPEDITIONS

Command of a battleship is not for the faint-hearted, even in peacetime. It was six years since Scott had last set foot on one, and two years since he had been promoted to Captain, on the day of his return from Antarctica. He had spent much of the interim living out of a suitcase, writing, and giving illustrated talks on a tour that almost sounds like a penance – given that he hated public speaking – and denied himself what comfort he might have had from staying in decent hotels and travelling better than third class. Having said that, he was no especial lover of comfort, and might have preferred it that way. Much as he might profess hatred of the limelight, it had its compensations and, as an explorer celebrity, he was more popular socially than he would have been as an ordinary officer. His mother and sisters had high hopes that with his rank and extra glamour as an explorer and author, he might marry money and status. As we know, they were destined to be disappointed.

As far as his career was concerned, far from having benefitted from Polar service as he was supposed to, according to Markham's theories, Scott now found himself out of the run of things and assigned to a desk job at the Admiralty. Eventually, an apparently convenient solution to his anomalous position as a Captain without experience (again), was found when his old Captain and admirer, now Rear-Admiral George Egerton, offered to take him under his wing as Flag Captain, at first on HMS *Victorious*, in August 1906. Within days Scott was writing to his friend JM Barrie, sounding nostalgic about Antarctica, evidently, as it prompted Barrie to reply on 8 September: [1]

> I chuckle with joy to hear that all the old hankerings are coming
> back to you. I feel you have got to go again.

Hankering after one's old job so soon after having started a new one doesn't suggest much enthusiasm for the new job. Although he was an officer in the Royal Navy, Scott was not by nature a sailor, nor a fighter.

All officers want to further their careers but, as the following episode shows, Scott was more inclined to do this by engaging with, and fussing around, superior officers, rather than by interested involvement with his ship or the military role he was supposed to fulfil. After his stint in *Victorious*, Scott had arrived at Chatham on 1 January 1907 to take command of the 14,000-ton battleship *Albemarle*, still as Egerton's Flag Captain – which must have been a relief to many, including him. That he was stressed nevertheless is evidenced by BM Peck, a sub-lieutenant at the time, and 'Captain's Clerk' to Scott. Many years later, Peck, by now a retired captain, wrote: [2]

> I got no thanks for my slow and imperfect typing of Captain Scott's letters. He was an ardent and impatient man. I knew him to be kindly at heart. Doubtless for my good, he concealed that part of his nature from me.

It sounds like Peck's resentment lived on, however veiled, even after all those years and Scott's posthumous sanctification.

On 11 February 1907, the *Albemarle* was in collision with HMS *Commonwealth* during a manoeuvring exercise. Briefly: eight ships were sailing in right echelon: closely following, and slightly to the right of each other. The fleet commander in the lead ship gave an order to increase speed, but did not do so himself. The next ship in the line, in order to avoid coming too close up beside him, veered off to the right, as did the next three ships, and the *Albemarle*. On the *Commonwealth*, however, the next ship in line, everyone on the bridge must have been enjoying a quiet after-dinner nap, as they failed to see what was happening in front of them. They steamed straight on ahead, therefore, colliding with the *Albemarle*, which had turned directly into their path. It is not known at which point the bridge of the *Commonwealth* woke up and had a collective heart-attack. Fortunately, it wasn't a repeat of the *Camperdown*: no lives were lost and neither ship was damaged beyond repair. Clearly, the fault lay both with the lead ship, which should have increased speed, and the *Commonwealth*, which had not noticed what was going on in front of them. No one was court martialled afterwards, and the matter was put to bed as an occupational mishap.

The issue for Scott biographers is that he was not on the bridge when it happened, and whether or not he was justified in being absent. It tells us something about his attitude to his job and his fitness for command. Perhaps because no one can prove it one way or the other, two of Scott's most recent and admired biographers take the opportunity to show Scott in their preferred light – one for, the other against. They give versions regarding the circumstances which directly contradict each other. David Crane (for), states: [3]

> Like all other captains in the formation, Scott was below ...

Roland Huntford (against), states: [4]

It was one of those crises of command, when the instinct of every captain ought to be – and indeed of every other captain in this fleet was – to stay at his post. Scott alone deserted it.

Crane asks us to believe that all the other captains were below. On the basis of probability, and in spite of the shambolic nature of how the event unfolded, it seems unlikely that *all* the captains in a fleet of eight large warships would have been below during manoeuvres in the dark, in heavy seas, as they are reported to have been. The lights of the ships could be seen clearly, as Scott himself tells us in a letter to his mother. [5] Crane claims that the *Albemarle* was steaming without lights. [6] If so, she must have been the only ship without lights, which is vanishingly unlikely. In summary, Crane asks us to believe that the fleet was on manoeuvres in close formation in the dark, in heavy seas, without lights, without a single captain being present on the bridge. It simply can't have been the case. Even if it was, it wouldn't excuse Scott; just because no one else was at their post does not mean that it was OK for him not to be at his.

It seems odd that he didn't appear to sense that his ship had swerved quite suddenly and sharply while he was below. He says in a letter to his mother that he did not notice anything was amiss until he was in Egerton's cabin, and [7]

> ... felt that the engines had stopped suddenly and the next moment that they were going astern.

On the bridge, his officers had been busy in his absence. Taking direct charge of the ship, the navigator – 'the coolest and most excellent officer' – had swerved in order not to crash into the ship in front. They had also seen that the *Commonwealth* was heading straight for them, and had tried to avoid the collision. They had not, however, sounded their warning siren. Scott claims that none of the other ships had sounded theirs either. As he was below, he might not have heard them if they had. Huntford claims that all the other ships had sounded theirs, and blames Scott for the collision because he assumes it wouldn't have happened if the *Albemarle* had sounded hers. Ironically, he pays Scott a backhanded compliment by assuming the siren would have been sounded if he had been on the bridge. But again, which ships did and did not hoot is one of those details now impossible to verify.

Scott admitted to his mother that he was on the bridge when a change of speed was ordered, and that he should have stayed there until the fleet had settled down to its new speed. Instead, he left the bridge to go and fetch an incoming message, leaving the ship in the hands of the officer of the watch and the navigating commander. Normally, one would expect the captain to order one of the lieutenants to go on an errand like that and bring any message to him, deciphered, on the bridge. While it is true that Scott did not know that a situation was about to develop, it was still a bad idea to leave at that time, which he admits himself. Why go then? We know he was prone to fussing when things got a little bit hairy.

Crane, in a piece of temporal inexactitude and creative history-making, states that Scott wrote his sister Ettie the following letter around the time of the collision, which was about six weeks after he joined *Albemarle* on 1 January. Crane, however, in his own notes, [8] lists this letter as being dated 21 March 1907, nearly six weeks *after the accident*, not six weeks after Scott joined *Albemarle*: [9]

> ... the dearest nicest man, [Egerton] is always worrying over trifles and frittering away my time and his own over details which might be left to subordinates – can you understand – he has no notion of his mission as an Admiral which is essentially to take a wide grasp of fleet affairs and the larger organization ... his mind, forever remaining on the minute pros & cons of a question, is incapable of decision until it recalls some obsolete precedent on which it dwells with mulish obstinacy utterly devoid of reason ...

It looks like another of those tweaks, bumps, omissions and happy errors so often evident in the biographies and diaries concerning Scott. If it had been Scott's intention to shift the blame for fussing at the time of the accident on Egerton, he is getting a helping hand here from Crane, who leads one to believe that he wrote the letter at that time, when he actually wrote it six weeks afterwards. The irony is that Scott might have been describing himself when he wrote that about Egerton.

But what did his officers think about it in the privacy of their own minds? The whole context Scott was working in was one where everyone knew how he had got where he was – that he was more experienced in pulling a sledge and writing a book than commanding a battleship. He was a celebrity who dined with royals, but he lacked a solid track record of warship command. Whatever respect his officers and crew might have had for his Antarctic achievements, and however much leeway they might have given him, they would at least have expected sound judgement. In fact, given the way he was hyped and celebrated, his crew might have been expecting Superman. If he himself recognised that he should not have left the bridge when he did, his officers are sure to have recognised it too. It would not have been a comfortable thing for him to reflect on.

In the above letter to Ettie, Scott is harsh and ungrateful to Egerton, a man who had supported and promoted him in both his Naval and Antarctic careers. He is severely critical, almost contemptuous of him, which is evidence of irritation and rejection. Was it that Scott felt he had outgrown both Markham and Egerton? In the latter part of 1906 all three had been on the *Victorious*, on a cruise in the Mediterranean, just before Scott took command of *Albemarle*. Scott was Flag-Captain to Admiral Egerton, and Markham was Egerton's guest. In terms of power relations, there would have been a delicate balance. In a sense, he was still their protégé, and it is perhaps something he became increasingly to resent. It is also possible that he was irritated by seeing his own weaknesses reflected in Egerton.

As always, one of Scott's first concerns at the time of the *Albemarle* incident had been how his mother might react to the news. After sending her a reassuring wire as soon as they got to Gibraltar, he wrote her a long letter a couple of days later, explaining the collision in detail. He was always anxious to reassure her, which suggests that she worried, and that this in turn worried him. It was one of the ways she exerted her hold over him, although this was undoubtedly un-conscious on both sides. Hannah Scott dreaded poverty. We take the welfare state for granted now, but it was only after WW2 that it came into existence. Before that, someone in Hannah Scott's position would have been entirely dependent on her relatives, especially her children. This was abundantly clear to Scott, and all his adult life he felt the responsibility very deeply. It was part of what motivated him to succeed, and if that meant exploiting his personal attractiveness, it would have felt natural for him to have done so.

Inevitably, his charm worked better on some than on others. Among those on whom his charm worked most strongly were Markham and JM 'Jimmy' Barrie, with whom Scott had become friendly after his introduction to the London literati by way of *The Voyage of the Discovery*. These men were important figures in Scott's life: Scott named his son Peter Markham, after Peter Pan and Clements, and made both godfathers to the boy. Barrie and Markham had a striking number of things in common. Both were diminutive and earned their living by the pen but, above all, both had an obsessional love of boys, which many maintain was completely innocent. The evidence to the contrary is similarly by the accumulation, and the reaching of, a critical mass of indicators. Important here is the fact that even at the time, there were those who disliked what they saw in Barrie. One wrote that [10]

> ... one or two people were rather disturbed about Barrie, though of course it was never talked about openly. There was something very sinister about him, rather shivery.

The way Barrie invaded the Llewelyn Davies family and almost took over with regard to their boys is aberrant and damaging in itself – quite apart from any sexual dimension. The blatant eroticism in some of his writing, which was never talked about openly is, however, a strong indicator that there *was* a sexual ele-ment in his love for the boys. There are also the hundreds of photographs he took of them, many of them nude or in costumes designed by him, in poses directed by him, acting out fantasies dreamed up by him. Even at this level it was exploitative, but the many nudes and languid studies further suggest prurience and romantic longing.

To this day, many people more or less angrily refute the idea that any kind of impropriety was ever indulged in by Markham and Barrie in their relationships with adolescents and pre-pubertal boys. But we know for a fact that they both actively sought out their preferred objects and that their preferences were enduring and borderline, if not actually obsessional. They both used their status and connections and, in Barrie's case, also his wealth, to facilitate their entry into gunrooms and nurseries, where they proceeded to charm, entertain and cajole. In Markham's case, set as it often was on board ship, in the context of rowdyism, escapades, alcohol and testosterone-fuelled omnisexuality, the abuse is likely to have been physical and possibly gross. In Barrie's case the entertainment was more childlike, in accordance with his preferred age group, and the abuse more subtle. Both made sure it was deniable, and both benefitted from the fact that these things were not talked about, and that they were too celebrated for anyone to dare to accuse them.

To our twenty-first-century eyes there is obvious decadent and erotic content in Barrie's work. Are we seeing something that isn't there, or did they, at the time, not see something that *was* there? We now have a trained eye, so to speak, but back then many people were ignorant of the more esoteric reaches of sex and sexuality. Even if the idea had occurred to them, they would have self-censored, and almost by conditioned reflex turned away from a recognition by which they themselves might be incriminated. Barrie's fame, money and literary status, and his undoubted gifts as an entertainer of children, as well as his benevolence towards them, made suspicions of impropriety seem unworthy and inappropriate. Many of the forces that protected Markham were in place also in Barrie's case. There was a conspiracy of silence around them, which endures to this day.

Both Markham and Barrie hid in plain sight, and seemed to be popular with the children. They were also careful not to leave any evidence. In Barrie's case it is known that quite a lot of written material was destroyed after his death because it was 'too much', showing that others actively covered up for him. A very good case can be made for the claim that they were both invasive and controlling paedophiles. It isn't surprising that biographers in general have shied away from these unsavoury backstories. One is more likely to have abuse heaped on one for calumny and misinterpretation than praise for shining a light into murky corners, but when abuse remains hidden it allows it to continue. It has been rife throughout history, and there is therefore nothing fanciful in the suggestion that the most likely impulse behind Markham's and Barrie's predilection was an erotic one.

That these men found Scott attractive tells us something fundamental about Scott, as it does about those who didn't find him so attractive. Neither Markham nor Barrie could ever have responded to men like Bruce or Amundsen, or even Shackleton, like they responded to Scott. And they in turn could not have responded to Markham and Barrie the way Scott did. The contrast shows not only how pliant and obliging, how soft-featured and 'femininely sensitive' (in Cherry's words) Scott was – at least in relation to Markham and Barrie – but also suggests a subtle sense of psychosexual reciprocity that must have been there for these relationships to have worked. Scott may not have been a boy, but he had boyish attributes and there is evidence that he responded to Markham and Barrie as mentors. He had always been Markham's pupil and protégé, as we know. In Barrie's case – according to Barrie's introduction to Scott's *Journals* – on the evening they met they walked each other home over and over into the small hours, Barrie unable to leave this 'entrancing' man. During it, Scott had poo-pooed the worth of his own work and contrasted it with Barrie's. It is worth remembering that Barrie was a huge success and made a lot of money in his time – principally but not exclusively with Peter Pan, a whimsical archetype popular to this day.

In addition to their love of boys, Barrie and Markham shared a love of the theatre, and both tended to project theatrical fantasies and roles on to others, based on outward appearances, demeanour, and their emotional responses. Both were romantics with a penchant for escapist fantasies. Markham's love of heraldry and knight errantry was part of that, as was Barrie's Neverland and stories at bedtime. Both had an inner boy who never grew up. Dressed in his immaculate uniform, dapper, clean and fit, Scott was the living embodiment of a schoolboy hero. He provided the obliging blank(ish) canvas for Markham and Barrie to project their hopes, ideals, and fantasies onto. Anything untoward or unseemly was literally unthinkable, and Scott, like so many others, had a vested interest in turning a blind eye. Besides, he could hardly be expected to refuse their support and friendship on the basis of something nobody talked about.

There are reasons to suppose that Scott had a hazy notion, if not from hearsay, then from his own adolescent experience. The written record suggests he was a 'good' boy; only minor misdemeanours are recorded, which means that he wasn't involved in any of the more dubious goings-on among the cadets, which are likely to have been kept hidden from him. There seems to be little reason to suppose that he was any more naive than the next boy or man, having lived cheek by jowl with them for most of his life. He probably tended to stay aloof, together with most of the others who knew instinctively what things were about, and that it was extremely dangerous territory. Nevertheless, if he was in any way bemused by the near-veneration he elicited from Barrie and Markham, it must have been out of modesty, rather than mystification.

But there wasn't anything like the rapport he had with Barrie to sustain his relationship with Markham. After the writing of *The Voyage of the Discovery*, Scott's and Markham's lives started to drift apart. Scott seems to have found it hard to forgive Markham for having cried wolf and brought the entire *Discovery* rescue effort down around his ears. It had risked making him look incompetent and had suggested a need where, as far as Scott was concerned, there wasn't one. It had threatened his reputation as a captain and explorer. Markham had, in any case, ceased to be President of the RGS in 1905, handing the position over to George

Goldie. Goldie seems not to have been interested when Scott came calling, and handed him over to the Secretary, John Scott Keltie.

Scott had come to the Royal Geographical Society wanting to sound out the possibility of any support they might offer for another Antarctic expedition. Goldie rather airily dismissed him with a promise that he would keep his eye out for a likely millionaire, after which Scott wrote on 28 January 1907 to Keltie: [11]

> ... I don't think he [Goldie] has any heart in the matter ... He will need little reminders and this is a service in which you can assist me ... you must do the very best you can to enlist general sympathy. There cannot be a doubt that the thing ought to be done. There is the finest prospect of a big advance in latitude that has ever been before a polar explorer.
>
> Rub all this into Goldie – it's essentially the thing for a Geographical Society and remember what a future generation will think if you lose the experience combined with the will to go when these are at your command. It will soon be on record of course that I want to go and only need funds. I am pretty certain that I could do the whole thing for £30,000. It won't look well for the Society if an inexperienced foreigner cuts in on the thing while we are wasting time. There really is a splendid chance.

There are suggestions that he is taking Keltie's goodwill and efforts on his behalf for granted, and there are hints of moral blackmail and threat. If Keltie was somewhat offended by this letter, it would explain his subsequent behaviour which, although correct, lacked the partisan zeal Scott expected. Scott had, as always, wanted to keep his plans secret, both on account of his Naval career and because things were at a very early stage. Keltie was duly sworn to secrecy.

A couple of weeks later, Keltie had a visit from Shackleton, who informed him he was about to make a newspaper announcement about a proposed Antarctic expedition, and of course also wanting to sound him out regarding support. Back in the real world after his return from the *Discovery* Expedition, Shackleton had not found it easy to carve out a career for himself. He had conceived the bold notion of setting up his own Antarctic expedition and had, crucially, found a backer. During this visit, at which (coincidentally) Amundsen and Nansen were also present, Keltie said nothing about Scott's plans. Perfectly fair, one would have thought. Keltie had been sworn to secrecy by Scott, and kept his mouth shut accordingly. The result was that it left the coast clear for Shackleton to go ahead and make his plans public. Keltie knew this, and one wonders whether there was not a tiny part of him that relished getting his own back on Scott, who was acting as though he owned him, and the RGS.

When Scott heard the news, the shock must have made the blood freeze in his veins. He can't have been expecting a threat from that quarter. It seems that he had thought if he was going to get competition from anyone it would be from Michael Barne, who had been at Lautaret at the same time as Scott, testing his own design for a motor tractor. Scott had effectively neutralised him by offering to take him as first lieutenant on any expedition he might put together, which Barne had agreed to. He didn't go in the end, nor did he ever mount his own expedition.

As far as Scott was concerned, the first problem was that Shackleton had been making plans without informing him. There were of course reasons why Shackleton may not have felt especially concerned to take Scott in his confidence as a first priority, but he also seems to have genuinely believed that Scott had no plans for another expedition, none that he knew of, at any rate. Scott now sought to justify himself for having kept his plans secret, uncomfortably aware, no doubt, that this was how he had himself contributed to the situation. He had been trying to have his cake and eat it by looking after his Naval career at the same time as keeping his paw on McMurdo Sound. To Shackleton he wrote: [12]

> ... you know that I support my mother & family, it is therefore essential for me to have an assured income ... I therefore decided to be very quiet about the matter to go back to my profession & accept appointments which would give me a chance of getting quite up to date in Naval matters ...

> Of course my intention was to go to McMurdo Sound our old winter quarters again! I cannot but look upon this as my area until I signify my intention to desert it ... after all I know the region better than anyone, everything concerning it was discovered by our expedition and it is a natural right of leadership to continue along the line which I made ... The foreigners always conceded this when I was abroad ... Surely if a foreigner has the good taste to leave this to the country which has done the work there, the English must admit the same argument to apply amongst themselves ... it never entered my head that you had a wish to go on. I have imagined you as very busy ... I had naturally no object in keeping any of our old company in the dark, you know how attached I am to all and how gladly I would take anyone who cared to come again.

Why, if he felt entitled, did he feel the need to justify himself? There is a hint of a little boy in a grown man's world, pleading to be understood and accommodated. But this is what Markham and Barrie both sensed, and were attracted to. It was the boy in Scott they loved, it was his very lack of true independence and self-belief that melted their hearts. He was almost as emotionally immature as they were, and as unreasonable and vindictive.

The problem was that Keltie's silence had allowed Shackleton to go ahead and publicise his plans. As far as Scott was concerned, this was either Shackleton's fault for ignoring what he thought Keltie must have told him, or Keltie's fault for staying silent, when a word from him would have forced Shackleton to at least delay going public until he had spoken with Scott. Keltie downplayed Shackleton's chances, presumably in an effort to mollify Scott. But Scott was having none of it and, in a way reminiscent of Markham, wrote to Keltie on 2 March 1907, rubbishing and lashing out at Shackleton in the hope, presumably, of diminishing his chances of support: [13]

> ... on the one hand he [Shackleton] has lots of energy & he may select his people well – on the other I personally never expect much in this sort of work from a man who isn't straight – it is the first essential for the co-operation necessary for such a venture – of course also Shackleton is the least experienced of our travellers and he was never very thorough in anything – one has but to consider his subsequent history to see that – he has stuck to nothing & you know better than I the continual schemes which he has fathered.

The accusation that Shackleton wasn't 'straight' is presumably based on Scott's belief that Keltie *must* have told Shackleton about his plans when he came to see him that day, and that Shackleton had therefore deliberately gone ahead and forestalled him: [14]

> ... I would not have believed it of any of my own people – and since it is so I cannot express my condemnation of such an act too strongly.

It is tempting to think of Scott's readiness to believe the worst of Shackleton as a projection of the vindictiveness he himself might have felt in Shackleton's position. Why else would he be so ready to impute vengeful motivations to Shackleton? Perhaps he had not trusted the gentlemanly way Shackleton had behaved since he got back, and how he had been one of the first to come on board and congratulate him on his return in *Discovery*. Shackleton may have been a bit of a buccaneer with the gift of the gab, but he had a strong sense of honour. And he was his own man.

Meanwhile, it was bad enough to be calling both Keltie and Shackleton liars by implication. Keltie wrote back to say that he thought Scott had wanted to keep the matter secret, and that he was now sorry he hadn't said anything, but that he had been in an impossible position having been sworn to secrecy. As it was, Shackleton had not only stolen a march on Scott in having impressed someone enough to bankroll his expedition, but had also gained the tacit support – as Scott saw it – from the man who mattered at the RGS.

Eventually, after much persuasion, he grudgingly accepted that Shackleton had known nothing about his plans. It was now Keltie who was accused of acting in bad faith. In a letter to Shackleton: [15]

> His [Keltie's] silence seems to have been deliberately calculated to make trouble – he must have known that I should protest and think evil things of you and that you would be deeply troubled, as I gather you are.

And to Keltie: [16]

> I confess your silence appears to me inexplicable ... Now that I know the facts I must of course acquit Shackleton of want of loyalty but I cannot think that you acted a friendly part ... It is beyond me to guess what was in your mind ... I confess I am at a loss to find your motive and being a plain dealing person I have been exceedingly hurt by your act.

In a court of law he wouldn't have had a leg to stand on; but clearly, Scott felt a sense of betrayal, and he may have been right to a certain extent. Nevertheless, Keltie would have felt he had every right to feel aggrieved by these reproaches, as he had merely done what was asked of him. As if to add insult to injury, Scott proceeded to tell Keltie his business, what his and the RGS's duties were, and what their policy should be. [17] It is high-handed, prescriptive and, in the end, threatening:

> The attitude of the RGS should be noncommittal altogether. It is their duty to encourage exploration but it must be also remembered that an ill-conducted expedition tends to ruin the cause of true exploration ... Whilst the experience of the "Discovery" remains available it is a question how far the Society should condone an act of disloyalty. As to the King I shall of course explain the case in the proper quarter.

Considering any support the RGS might give Shackleton's as an act of disloyalty is vintage Markham. The conceit inherent in the assumption of authority, and the insulting implication that Shackleton's would be an ill-conducted expedition, are also straight out of Markham's book. Scott seems to be thinking he is the Explorer Royal, by Appointment, and entitled to threaten Keltie with the King's displeasure. It is a hissy-fit happening on paper, a bitchy lashing out with whatever weapons come to hand. Shackleton had always been a threat to him. It was the underlying reason he was sent home from *Discovery*. Shackleton was a grown-up, and in response, Scott could only jump up and down and make absurd threats.

He just couldn't leave it alone, and rubbed it into Keltie one more time, presumably in case Keltie would for one moment forget how deeply he had been hurt.

Flipping from child into parent, it is now his internalised mother who seems to be doing the talking: [18]

> ... indeed you mistake me altogether ... if you suppose that I have ever attributed any malicious motive to you – in my angriest moments I never did that – no the case was this, I cherished a warm feeling of friendship for you on account of many kind things you had done ... Then the time came when it seemed to me you might have done something which a friend should have done and you didn't do it. – That's the whole case. I've no claim that you should have treated me differently from a hundred others that came to your office – it is only that I thought & expected that you would and therefore I was deeply disappointed & hurt when it seemed to me that you did not.

The self-exoneration, the disappointment, the faux self-effacement, the moral blackmail and the whiff of martyrdom are all reminiscent of mother. Keltie was something of a family friend to Scott's mother and sisters, and had taken an interest in their welfare while Scott was away. With this in mind, Keltie might also have been motivated by an extra vigilance against a conflict of interest when it came to his professional role. As far as Scott was concerned, however, it should have been the other way round.

In spite of all that, there was nothing Scott could do stop Shackleton going to Antarctica. But if he couldn't altogether stop him, he could do his utmost to make it as difficult as possible for him. Wilson was brought in to mediate and, after first advising his erstwhile friend to throw the whole thing up in favour of Scott, ex-tracted a promise from Shackleton not to use McMurdo Sound, nor to cross the 170 meridian to westward, which Shackleton confirmed in a letter to Scott. It left thin and almost impossible leftovers in the form of the inhospitable edges of the Barrier and King Edward VII Land, where the *Discovery* had found it impossible to land.

It did not deter Shackleton. He and everyone in the *Nimrod* got a tremendous boost to their morale when they were commanded by the King to Cowes for a royal inspection. Scott and Markham will not have been pleased. They will have privately trashed and shredded the *Nimrod* and all who sailed in her, and reas-sured each other that nothing would come of it. In the event, Shackleton, having arrived in Antarctica, was faced with three unenviable choices: to set up base on the Barrier, to go back, or to break his word to Scott. It would have been absurd for him to turn around and sail back with a shipload of supplies, equipment, people, and animals – to abandon the expedition he had worked hard to raise the money for, and on which his future depended. He had the choice of letting down his backers, his crew, his family and himself; or letting down Scott, the man who had sent him home from the *Discovery*. He must have pictured himself arriving back in New Zealand with his ship and everything in it. All because Scott wanted to keep Ross Island for himself, to use as a base for a future attempt at the Pole. Shackleton must have felt that he did not owe Scott his future. No man could ask it of another. So, having done his best in a struggle with pack-ice and bergs to reach King Edward VII Land and failed, and having found the Barrier edge apparently unstable, they had landed on Ross Island, at Cape Royds, about 40 miles north of Hut Point. Shackleton had gone where he had given his word he wouldn't go.

When the *Nimrod* came back to New Zealand with the news that the expedition had set up its base in the forbidden zone, Scott was livid. He had multiple copies typed up of the letter Shackleton had written, and sent them to fellow explorers and people of influence. He did what he could to damage Shackleton's reputation, and Bernacchi is unlikely to have been the only one to be told that he could now '... have nothing more to do with [Shackleton] when he returns[,] whatever he does'. Markham was entirely in agreement that they would also now 'find it impossible not to doubt any result he claims'. And the final appalling insults from Scott in a letter of 25 March 1908 to Bernacchi: 'I am sure [Shackleton] is prepared to lie rather than admit failure and I take it he will lie artistically. The whole thing is sickeningly vulgar.' He wrote to Kathleen also of the 'terrible vulgarity' that Shackleton had '... introduced to the Southern field of enterprise', which had been 'so clean and wholesome' till then. [19]

All this tells us more about Scott than Shackleton. Superficially, Scott behaved like a gentleman, but behind the mask there was vitriol and spite. Too resentful to contemplate reasoned argument, he used character assassination and sneering contempt to make his case – again very much in the manner of Markham. He did his best to make sure that whatever results Shackleton obtained would be under a cloud of dishonour and of dubious value. Markham had been both a role model and a permission-giver for bitter, childish and unreasonable missives that found their way to Dr Napier Shaw, Director of the Meteorological Office. In response to criticism of some of the scientific data brought back by the *Discovery*, Scott had written a letter which Shaw described as [20]

> ... very painful reading ... the asperity of Captain Scott's letter goes beyond the limits of ordinary criticism ... [and] displays a resentment under *bona fide* criticism that would put an end to all scientific progress if it were indulged in by all observers.

Judging by this, the accuracy of the scientific data was less important to Scott than his *amour propre* and, by the same token, Shackleton's results would be rubbished regardless of their validity.

But it was all in vain. Shackleton had a level of emotional maturity, and an adult sense of autonomy and independence against which Scott was powerless. He was a man, not a boy; an adult, not a child or a parent. He didn't need the Navy, nor a Markham, nor a Wilson to prop him up. He was less of a snob, and martyrdom was anathema to him. He was by nature and ability more suited to manage an expedition than Scott could ever be. That is not to say he was any kind of angel, however, nor even that Scott's suspicions were entirely unfounded. Shackleton's claim to have come within 100 geographical miles of the Pole hardly needed to have been literally true. What really mattered was that it was close enough. Doubts do, however, surround the claim by Mackay, David and Mawson to have reached the South Magnetic Pole. It is now known that by the time they got to the region where it was known to be located, none of them were in a fit state, nor did they have enough time to accurately determine their position. They plonked their tripod and took a photo more or less arbitrarily where they were, which some claim might have been as far as 85 miles away from their goal. [21]

The so-called Heroic Age of Polar Exploration was all about personal gain. It was another Klondike. Borchgrevink, Scott, Shackleton and Mawson were all motivated by the same thing, and they took risks, not only with their own lives but also with others', in the icy gold-rush that was fashioned as the Heroic Age. The exception was Amundsen who, although equally ambitious, did at least train and equip himself for the task, thereby offering his comrades a better chance of a safe return.

Neither Scott nor Markham ever forgave Shackleton. According to Fundamental Attribution Error, in apportioning blame we tend to attribute blame to circumstances when we ourselves are to blame for something, but tend to hold personal internal dispositions responsible when it concerns the actions of others. Shackleton undoubtedly blamed circumstances for his decision to land on Ross Island, whereas Scott blamed Shackleton's lack of personal integrity. Shackleton had done his best, which was the most any reasonable person could ask in the circumstances. The public evidently felt the same, as on his return in the *Nimrod*, Shackleton was wildly celebrated and admitted at once into the ranks of the *bona fide* explorers.

Markham predictably exploded in a paroxysm of rage, exceeded only by his later excoriation of Amundsen. Scott's only consolation was that final 100 miles or so that Shackleton hadn't managed. It was at the same time the most pointless and the most crucial distance left to be covered. Shackleton had shown that beyond reasonable doubt the Pole was located on a vast snow-plain. This meant that attainment of the exact spot could now only have symbolic meaning. It was nevertheless true that whoever was first at that exact spot would enter the history books and stay there forever.

References

1   Reginald Pound. *Scott of the Antarctic*, p. 125

2   *op. cit*, p. 127

3   David Crane. *Scott of the Antarctic*, p. 333

4   Roland Huntford. *Scott and Amundsen*, p. 220

5   Stephen Gwynn. *Captain Scott*, p. 103

6   David Crane. *ibid.*

7   Stephen Gwynn. *op. cit*, p. 101

8   David Crane. *op. cit*, p. 601

9   *op. cit*, p. 327

10 Andrew Birkin. *JM Barrie and the Lost Boys*, p. 214

11 David Crane. *op. cit*, pp. 332–3

12 *op. cit*, p. 336

13 *op. cit*, p. 338

14 *ibid.*

15 *op. cit*, p. 339

16 *ibid.*

17 *op. cit*, p. 342

18 *op. cit*, pp. 342–3

19 David Day. *Antarctica*, p. 135

20 Elspeth Huxley. *Scott of the Antarctic*, p. 177

21 David Day. *Flaws in the ice*, p. 21

18

KATHLEEN

Edith Agnes Kathleen Bruce was born in the Rectory at Carlton in Lindrick, Nottinghamshire, on 27 March 1878, the eleventh and last child of the Reverend Lloyd Bruce and his wife Janie. She weighed 11 pounds, and had hands the size of a two-year-old. It can't have been easy; and for Janie, having now borne 11 children, including two sets of twins, in the space of 15 years, it was the beginning of the end. Two years later, weakened and exhausted by not only bearing but raising so many infants, she died, finally succumbing to pneumonia on a trip to the seaside. Subsequently, the Reverend rose in the church hierarchy and remarried, but the marriage failed and he died not long afterwards. Kathleen was eight years old at the time. After rejecting the offer from her stepmother to live with her, preferring to stay with her siblings, she ended up being taken in, along with her sisters Hilda (Presh) and Janie (Podge) and their brother Wilfrid, by their Great-Uncle William Forbes Skene, Historiographer Royal of Scotland. [1]

Great-Uncle William, although unmarried himself, was well set up for the children. He had always taken an interest in them, and seems to have provided a relatively benign, if rather impersonal, home for what was already a bright and lively bunch. The deaths of their parents are not much commented upon in any published material. It gives the impression that however upset they might have been at the time, they recovered quickly. All of Kathleen's siblings were older than she was, many significantly so. Apart from her sister Hilda, who was only about two years older, they will have had the benefit of a full set of parents for longer, and are likely to have been less badly affected by their loss. Rosslyn, for example, seven years older than Kathleen, and her favourite brother, was also one of the wackiest – becoming, in his daughter's words, the 'last of the great eccentrics', a breeder of terrier dogs and green mice (allegedly). In his case, however, the eccentricity seems to have been part of an otherwise stable and neurosis-free life as a caring cleric and beloved family man.

264

He had loved the baby Kathleen, calling her Kiddy, and had nursed her 'as tenderly as though she were a newly-hatched chick'. It was unfortunate that he happened to be away at boarding school when their mother died. He mourned his mother deeply, which gives a hint of the sadness that must have enveloped the family. In later life the loss of her parents was so little felt by Kathleen, apparently, that according to Rosslyn she [2]

> ... thanks God seriously and constantly that she has no parents because so many of her friends have suffered from misunderstandings and restrictions and she remembers nothing at all of hers.

She probably didn't consciously remember her mother, but she must have had some recollection of her father, as she was eight when he died, in March 1886. It sounds like a typically Kathleen type of statement – made on the spur of the moment and hinting at denial and bravado.

Kathleen's history of childhood bereavement starts with the death of her mother when she was two and a half. Views differ as to the impact of such an event on a child that young. John Bowlby's Attachment Theory emphasises the importance of a stable relationship to the developing child – both for emotional and psychological well-being, as well as for healthy cognitive and physical progress. A Freudian would point to the importance of object relations, and the way a child's individuation process is linked to its relationship with its mother, or primary caregiver. Any radical interruption to this process therefore results in disorder, with deleterious consequences to the healthy ego-formation of the child. The question is to what extent those consequences are mutable – do they lead inevitably to permanent damage, or does adequate subsequent care make up for, or at least mitigate the effects of such a loss?

Clinical psychologist J William Worden [3] has made up a checklist of risk indicators, of which several are shown to be consistent and long lasting (over two years), and therefore strongly predictive of negative affect. In this category are perceived stress of surviving parent, parents' passive coping style, additional family stressors, and low self-efficacy (the belief that one has little control over events in one's life). All of these risk indicators were present in Kathleen's childhood, as the following analysis shows.

It is fair to assume that life was stressful for the Reverend Lloyd after Janie died. He had 11 children under 18, a home to run, and a parish and church to serve. Comparatively poor, he could only have afforded a limited number of household servants. While they fulfilled many of the household tasks and nursing work, they also added to the crowd that needed to be managed and provided for and, together with the known stressor of bereavement, it seems inevitable that he was stressed. He found it difficult to talk to his children about their mother. The children probably helped themselves by talking and consoling each other. For Kathleen, however, too young for reasoned understanding, it must have been a bewildering time.

The Reverend didn't cope very well with the death of his wife, who was 'all gentleness and humility', according to Elma, one of his eldest daughters. After an absence on church business, Lloyd writes in a letter to his sister-in-law: [4]

> I got home last night to find everything as comfortable as poor Sarah could make it but very very dreary. The children I find well and I am happy to say that they do sometimes ask about 'poor mama' though I find it impossible to respond as I should wish.

It was healthy for the children to want to talk about the death of their mother, but the fact that Lloyd found it impossible to respond as he would wish suggests he wasn't well equipped to help his children through their grieving process.

As far as his coping style is concerned, after he had remarried somewhat in haste, Elma tells us that she felt more sorry for her father than for their new step-mother, a formidable lady, quite unlike poor Janie. The fact that the new Mrs Bruce got up from the table one day and slapped her husband's face over an enquiry about the fish suggests he was unassertive, and that he almost certainly had a passive coping style.

It is clear, from the unsettled nature of the years following Janie's death, that additional family stressors were present. There was the clearly disastrous experiment with the new 'Mama', nurses came and went, the children were farmed out in an ad-hoc fashion – variously being sent to boarding schools, staying with relatives from time to time, and so on. So far as a lack of control over events is concerned, if Kathleen ever had it at all, it must have been shattered when after not many years her father also died.

If Kathleen had not been at risk before, she was certainly at risk now. Evidence that Kathleen was affected – if not by her mother's, then certainly by her father's, death (in spite of her claim to remember nothing) – is clear from her sister Janie's recollections dating from their time at Great-Uncle William's, where she says that for some years Kathleen's prettiness was obliterated by a perpetual frown. Elma, one of the eldest twins, had to all intents and purposes taken the role of female head of the family after their mother died. She remained in a position of authority *vis-à-vis* Kathleen, as the following anecdote shows. Kathleen was about nine, and Janie (Podge) around 11 at the time. Janie: [5]

> I think you can't have been at all well ... From this age onwards you had no one to mother you or shew you any affection of any kind and more and more you shut yourself up and became reserved and chary of shewing any feeling whatsoever, partly due to our somewhat spartan bringing up but more I think from fear of being

laughed at. Once however you began to cry and nothing and nobody could stop you, you sobbed and sobbed, no one knew why and no one could console you, you lay on the bed inconsolable. At last Elma came in and Hilda told her. I shall never forget seeing the determination in her quick walk as she went to your room and came down like a thunderbolt. 'Get up AT ONCE, wash your face and stop this minute.' Implicit obedience and not another sound!

Kathleen, clearly already isolated, withdrawn and emotionally sensitive, far from receiving understanding and support in working through her grieving process, was summarily dealt with. It may have been a watershed moment. After years of a relatively affectionless and rootless existence and the loss of her one remaining parent, the finality of which she was now of an age to understand, she was vulnerable and at risk of enduring emotional and psychological damage. Elma's summary intervention may have had a devastating effect on what remained of Kathleen's emotional and psychological health. If she had already been in the process of turning inward, it must have exacerbated the process. With this background of bereavements and 'spartan' upbringing – evidence of a bleak and affectionless home life – Kathleen would today be considered at risk from a range of emotional and psychological disorders, one of which would be Narcissistic Personality Disorder.

Sam Vaknin takes a Freudian psychoanalytical approach: [6]

> ... the very delicate construction of the mental apparatus [the healthy ego] can be tampered with by traumatic deficiencies and by object losses right through the Oedipal period [age 3 to 6] (and even in latency and in adolescence) ...

> Pathological narcissism is largely a defence mechanism intended to deflect hurt and trauma from the victim's "True Self" into a "False Self" which is construed by the narcissist to be omnipotent, invulnerable, and omniscient. The narcissist uses the False Self to regulate his or her labile sense of self-worth by extracting from his environment Narcissistic Supply (any form of attention, both positive and negative) ...

> Such a person possesses a set of values and standards, but he is always on the lookout for ideal external figures from whom he aspires to derive the affirmation and the leadership that he cannot get from his insufficiently idealized superego.

Apart from being grateful that she had no parents to argue with or place restrictions on her, Kathleen doesn't seem to have thought or talked much about the effect their deaths might have had on her. The fact is, however, that she was orphaned at an early age, and lacked proper parenting after that. It seems that subsequent to the episode of uncontrollable sobbing there was a steady refusal to admit to any sense of loss or abandonment. Similarly, any feelings of low self-worth are utterly contradicted by her showy confidence. Nevertheless, her history is predictive of a flight into a false self and a bravado denial of the grieving little girl inside. If Kathleen had enough narcissistic traits to be diagnosed as suffering from Narcissistic Personality Disorder, then the trauma of losing both her parents at such an early age, the lack of understanding and mature emotional support afterwards, and at least one instance of harsh if not abusive treatment (in this case from Elma), provides amply sufficient cause. For Kathleen, having been the last of her mother's babies, there may have been an extra element of distress in that she might have had a hazy notion that she bore some responsibility for her mother's death.

Children's reactions to bereavement are considered to be qualitatively different from those of adults, and often lead to a negative shift in their self-concepts and self-esteem. Underlying the narcissist's cover of blithe confidence, there is always a deep – and utterly denied – sense of shame and/or worthlessness. To adults, it seems puzzling that children should have those feelings in response to events for which they bear no responsibility, but feelings of having been deserted often lead to a belief that they are unlovable and result in low self-esteem. Vaknin: [7]

> There is a whole range of narcissistic reactions, styles, and person-alities: from the mild, reactive and transient to the permanent personality disorder ...

> The interpersonal relationships of patients with Narcissistic Personality Disorder are typically impaired owing to their lack of empathy, disregard for others, exploitativeness, sense of entitlement, and constant need for attention (Narcissistic Supply).

> Though often ambitious, intelligent, and capable, inability to tolerate setbacks, disagreement, and criticism make it difficult for patients with Narcissistic Personality Disorder to work in a team or maintain long-term professional achievements.

Considering Kathleen's constant need for attention and affirmation, her frequent indifference to other people's needs, her sense of entitlement, her hostility to criticism, and her insensitive and counterproductive interventions in collective endeavours (the preliminaries of Scott's Last Expedition for example, to which we will return), her adult history presents ample evidence for a diagnosis of a moderate, but evident and life-long, case of Narcissistic Personality Disorder.

The full effects of these types of emotional disturbance tend not to manifest until early adulthood, and so for the next decade or so Kathleen's behaviour seems not to have been unusual. When Great-Uncle William died, in 1892, his estate was divided between the Bruce children, and Kathleen was left an income of £72 a year – enough to live on, frugally. She was 14, and was sent to a convent boarding school where she spent the next two years participating in teenage religious ecstasies – in her case mainly involving babies. She also got an education, and a job as a teacher was duly envisaged for her. The Church was the main employer for the Bruces. Six of Kathleen's siblings ended up as clergymen or the wives or companions of clergymen. Kathleen was similarly expected to perhaps spend some years teaching, as her sisters had done, and then marry – presumably another cleric or academic.

But on her mother's side of the family, there was a streak of unconventionality, and even rakishness. On a visit to the ramshackle, happy-go-lucky London home of her cousin William (another William Skene, whom Kathleen calls Colin in her autobiography), a whole different direction was suggested for her. Her convent schooling seems to have all but destroyed her religious faith, but she had been free to draw and paint. She must have taken some work to show her London relatives, because on the strength of a few watercolours she'd done, Willy suggested she should go in for art.

She was a beneficiary of an opening-up of opportunities for women at that time. Not long before this, it would have been impossible for a respectable girl to go, if not to art school, then to Paris to study sculpture with no other company than that of two young women her own age. It still raised eyebrows; but the emancipation of women and their fight for equal rights had progressed thus far, although Kathleen was the last to appreciate it. Kathleen's attitude to women and women's rights was illiberal and contrary, and seemingly out of character for such an independent-minded woman. It was incongruent with her own assumptions of freedom and autonomy, but she was against women's suffrage – a live issue at the time – and remained so all her life. It was based, ostensibly, on her view that women did not deserve the vote because they were silly and irresponsible.

A general irritation and impatience with the culturally approved airhead image of women at the time was given intellectual gravitas, substance and legitimacy by Schopenhauer. The writings of philosopher Arthur Schopenhauer (1788–1860) were popular in the early twentieth century. Another of Kathleen's cousins, Hener (Henry) Skene, had brought her 'a couple of volumes of Schopenhauer' during her early days in Paris, and it is possible to see a number of ways Kathleen's negativity towards women was legitimised and reinforced by him. His '... contempt for, and rage against, women struck a sympathetic chord in me'. [8]

Schopenhauer claimed that women are directly fitted for acting as the nurses and teachers of our early childhood by the fact that they are themselves childish, frivolous and short-sighted. He also claimed that women are by nature meant to obey. In later life he added the caveat that he believed that if a woman succeeds in raising herself above the mass, she would grow more and more like a man.

Both Kathleen and Schopenhauer ascribed an ontological and global inferiority to the female sex, neither apparently open to – or even aware of – the possibility that they were basing their views on a female stereotype, created by prevailing societal and cultural assumptions. The get-out clause as far as Kathleen was concerned must have been that she could cast herself as one who had risen above the mass – which is undoubtedly how she saw herself. To a female narcissist, giving other women power would have the unwanted effect of levelling the playing-field. Keeping down women in general allowed her to maintain her place above the common herd. Identifying with women in general would have reflected on her. She must have felt that she would be devalued by association, and thereby less worthy of the admiration she needed. Last but not least, there may have been a residual hatred, especially towards assertive women, left over from her treatment by Elma.

Kathleen's ideas on heredity and eugenics also appear to have been facilitated by Schopenhauer, as it was around this time that she conceived the grandiose idea of breeding a hero. Schopenhauer believed that personality and intellect were unalterable and inherited: the intellect through the mother and the personal character from the father. According to Schopenhauer: [9]

> [The] final aim of all love intrigues, be they comic or tragic, is really of more importance than all other ends in human life. What it all turns upon is nothing less than the composition of the next generation ... it is not the weal or woe of any one individual, but that of the human race to come, which is here at stake.

For Kathleen it was more important to find the right material for breeding a hero than to fall in love and have a child as the natural outcome of a loving relationship. That means she wanted a child who would be admired, primarily. Her fulfilment would come through the social status of the boy, rather than in the quality of her relationships with both the father and the project son. To a narcissist, the reflection is more important than the substance. Being the mother of a prodigy was a potential source of high-grade narcissistic supply by proxy. There seems to be a complete absence of any desire for personal fulfilment other than idolisation in the eyes of other people and the world in general.

The hero was by definition male, of course. In a conversation with her flatmate Hermione about men, and Kathleen's judgements about who was worthy to be father of her son, Hermione asks her if she thinks she's such a very unusual person, and she replies, [10]

> Can't you see? It's not me I'm thinking about, it's my son.

She presumably means that it is not that she is so special that only a hero would do for her, but that she is the vessel through which one hero would beget another. It's actually a piece of humbug, designed presumably to deflect criticism of her apparent conceit. It seems never to have crossed her mind, however, to doubt her fitness to pass judgement – and there is no acknowledgement, and probably not even conscious awareness, of her own subjectivity in the matter.

Kathleen lived in Paris on and off for almost five years – frugally, but with seldom a dull moment. Within weeks her two English friends started to drift away and men started to hang around her front door. Kathleen: [11]

> ... the two other girls would go on with a glance of mockery. This made me feel incredibly ill-bred. I wanted the nice boys to walk home with me; I wanted them to because I liked them and it was fun; but I would tell my two dignified friends that it was a good way of learning French. I thought their expressions accused me of behaving like a kitchen-maid. In any case, no young men hovered around them, I had no notion why; and I thought them very nice and well behaved, and myself very inferior. The nuns would approve them and reproach me, but it was all so exciting, so stimu-lating, and so sunshiny.

It is noteworthy that she wrote this passage in her autobiography many years after the event. It seems extraordinarily naive, but it is beguiling, and easily passed over as a charming little anecdote about life in Montparnasse. But did she really still not realise why those young men hung around her, and not her friends? Or is she trying to show posterity how naive she was in those days? There are good reasons for claiming that she was then, and ever after, in denial about her own flirtatiousness. Of course it was fun – who would deny it, or her? – but there was more to it than that. The references to her popularity with men follow thickly on each other; in fact one would be justified in saying that her entire autobiography is about how much attention she got from men and how strongly they felt about her. It is a sustained narcissistic affirmation of her own desirability. Nowhere is there a hint that it was anything to do with her behaviour. She seems to assume that posterity will simply marvel at how irresistible she must have been.

Kathleen studied sculpture at Atelier Colarossi, receiving occasional lessons from Rodin; befriending, and almost certainly 'vamping' him. Her looks were handsome rather than pretty. She was about 5 ft 5 inches, had a big nose, good teeth, a vertical forehead, masses of hair, a slightly cleft lower lip, and a sturdy rather than svelte body. She hated jewellery and make-up, dressed mainly in sacks, improvised her hats, and never had sex with her boyfriends. She writes that some of her fellow students were her 'entire slaves' nevertheless. But it didn't always turn out well. It isn't unusual for men to turn nasty if they feel they have been led on, and there were times when she had to run – almost for her life (if she is to believed). She tells us that a great giant of a Swede, a fine-looking creature, waited for her with a revolver. Hener told her (and she made sure we would know about it by telling the story in her autobiography) that the Swede had said she was so lovely that she'd better be killed before she got less so. Kathleen: [12]

> I'll bolt to Chartres for a few days. Tell him I've gone to England. It's
> not the first time I've had to bolt to Chartres. He'll soon get over it.

There was a small hotel at Chartres called *Le Chariot d'Or* which was getting used to short visits from *une jeune Anglaise toute seule*.

The surprising thing is not the narcissism inherent in her recollections, and the way she presents them, but how long it has gone unrecognised for what it was by historians and biographers. More than anything else, Kathleen's life is defined by her need to be noticed, valued and wanted – which was expressed in both the quality and the quantity of her relationships with men. A huge procession of them wandered in and out of her life: writers, poets, painters, sculptors, soldiers, sailors, academics, explorers, politicians and statesmen, financiers, wits, and sweet boys in general. She needed their attention and their admiration – and by emotionally seducing them, they gave her what she needed. According to Vaknin, in his 'Proposed Amended Diagnostic Criteria for Narcissistic Personality Disorder (NPD)': [13]

> ... one of the nine criteria for NPD is: 'Requires excessive
> admiration, *adulation, attention and affirmation, or, failing that,*
> *wishes to be feared and to be notorious* ... [his italics]

Aleister Crowley, who had of course his own way of looking at things (and his own issues with narcissism), makes an interesting comment on Kathleen, whom he first met in 1902: [14]

> She was strangely seductive. Her brilliant beauty and wholesome
> Highland flamboyance were complicated with a sinister perversity.
> She took delight in getting married men away from their wives, and
> the like ... Love had no savour for her unless she was causing ruin
> or unhappiness to others. I was quite ignorant of her intentions
> when she asked me to sit for her, but once in her studio she lost no
> time, and 'The Black Mass', 'The Adepts' and 'The Vampire' describe
> with ruthless accuracy our relations. She initiated me into the
> torturing pleasure of algolagny on the spiritual plane. She showed
> me how to intensify passion by self-restraint ... She made me
> wonder, in fact, if the secret of puritanism was not to heighten the
> intensity of love by putting obstacles in its way.

Ignoring the hocus-pocus occultism and hyperbole, Crowley provides evidence of the flavour of Kathleen's interactions with men, and how she used her sexuality to get what she needed. It would no doubt have been much to Crowley's chagrin had he learned that he, on this occasion, was nothing more than a source of narcissistic supply.

Genital chastity seems to have been the only criterion by which she judged the propriety of her relationships. In her own mind she was clear that she was going to remain a virgin, and this freed her from inhibitions she might otherwise have had about flirting, going vagabonding, dancing, or dining with whomever she chose – regardless of their, or her, marital status or prevailing social norms. Her ultimate chastity was the thing that made it possible.

She was anything but the stereotype of demure womanhood of the time. Autonomous, clever and creative, in later life she used her work and her connections to influence and network – becoming a kind of Edwardian English Mme de Stael, the confidante of prime ministers and diplomats, the social lubricant, introduction agency, advisor and political fixer. With people she liked, she was spontaneous and unguarded. While it made her prone to the occasional gaffe, her letters and diary show that she had an engaging turn of mind and a lively way of expressing herself. The rollcall of her friends, admirers and acquaintances reads like a who's who of Edwardian society. When she tired of politicians she entertained artists, writers and poets. When she needed rest, she would go to a cottage on the beach, and when she needed a change of scenery she would go abroad. She may well have taken on board something of Crowley's Sadean dictum 'Do what thou wilt shall be the whole of the law.'

Kathleen, or 'K' as she was known to her family, managed to beguile not only Scott, but over many years also his countless biographers and their readership. Her behaviour has been accepted without much comment or reflection. Her biographer (her grand-daughter Louisa Young), doesn't try to hide Kathleen's constant flirtations, but she does so without comment and without making value judgements. While this is admirable, it means there is a psychological and moral vacuum. The fact that Louisa is also biased in her grandmother's favour means that Kathleen once more evades critical scrutiny. In her lifetime people didn't dare. She was critical and had an intimidating aura. Kathleen herself wrote about her endless interactions with men, but the fact that she wrote about them as though they were the most natural thing in the world has blinded people to their significance. They weren't the most natural thing in the world. They were evidence of a neurotic and obsessive hunger for attention and admiration which would be pathetic but for the way her own defences forbid such an interpretation.

Part of the reason she loved men was that she identified with them – they, not women, were her allies. Novelist Mrs Humphry Ward, Founding President of the

Women's National Anti-Suffrage Movement, opined that constitutional, legal, financial, military, and international problems could only be solved by men. Apart from the total lack of evidence – not to mention the ethical, moral, and human-itarian problems with this view – the assumption that only men are naturally endowed with an ability to handle such matters is an affront to women. Mrs Ward's confident pronouncements must have been welcome to Kathleen, who must have found her rejection of women's suffrage hard to defend – especially as she was so emancipated herself, as was Mrs Humphry Ward.

But her anti-suffragism had its roots in emotional needs which she could never acknowledge, least of all to herself. She once told her second son Wayland (by her second husband Edward Hilton Young), that any woman worth their salt could communicate her wishes through her husband – whereupon he replied that not every woman was married to a cabinet minister. As women won their last battle about voting rights in 1928, and Wayland's father wasn't a government minister until 1931, it appears she defended her position even after the event. Never being able to admit the real, personal reasons for not wanting women to have the vote, she had to find plausible pretexts for justifying her position. She wrote that she didn't think women deserved the vote, setting herself up as arbiter, in spite of being a woman. The internal contradiction didn't seem to occur to her. And as for communicating her views via her husband, one wonders whose views were then to prevail at the ballot box.

Lees-Milne describes her face as [15]

> ... more masculine than feminine. She was totally unconcerned with her appearance; her clothes were abysmally dreary. She wore sack-like garments with no adornment of any kind beyond a straight band across her [by then] abundant iron-grey hair, close-cropped at the back of the neck like a man's.

George Bernard Shaw famously described the feelings he had for her as being the nearest he came to homosexuality. She was, nevertheless, heterosexual – which is what gave her relationships with men its edge, and which facilitated the getting of narcissistic supply. If any of her objects ever felt somehow used after having been left behind, as nearly all of them were, they would have been right.

Knowledge of her condition was in its infancy at the time, and it is safe to say that even today, there would be outrage at the mere suggestion that there was anything wrong with this brilliant, creative, strong and independent woman. But none of the Scott biographers, nor her own, have paid enough attention to the conditions of her childhood which, although obviously traumatic, have been skipped over as though they weren't important. It's as though Kathleen wove a web of enchantment that all have been caught up in – in her own lifetime as well as for posterity.

While her autobiography gives the impression that she lived a hectic life, there were frequent gaps and some quiet periods. Some of these gaps cover interludes which either she or her editor considered too controversial for the record, or for publication. *Self-Portrait of an Artist* is notably silent about some of her more controversial relationships. This is because the book is, in large part, an edited collection of diary entries compiled by her second husband Edward Hilton Young. For some of the more controversial entries, therefore, short of accessing the actual diaries, we have to refer to research done by Louisa Young and others.

Crowley was probably right when he suggested that Kathleen took particular pleasure in seducing a married man – especially a highly regarded one. It was high-value narcissistic supply. Her relationship with Douglas Mawson is a case in point. Married with a baby, he was besotted with her, and she indulged him by inviting him to her cottage near Sandwich, and spending nights with him in a tent on the beach.

A photo (not included in *Self-Portrait of an Artist*, nor Louisa Young's biography) shows Kathleen and Mawson with Peter (Scott's son) on his shoulder, paddling in the sea at Sandwich. Intriguingly, it has been neatly cropped, taking out Kathleen's body up to chest level. We will probably never know what it showed, but the fact that she (or whoever else) cut it out seems odd. It looks remarkably like a family group, showing an intimacy, which even if not fully consummated, implies a familiarity well beyond that of ordinary friendship. Kathleen had known Mawson for some time, and he is mentioned her autobiography, but never in the context of the beach at Sandwich. Her editors must have felt it would be hurtful to Mawson's wife Paquita, who lived until 1974, well after *Self-Portrait of an Artist* was published. This is evidence, if any were needed, of a consensus that her behaviour was controversial at the very least, and open to a variety of interpretations, none of them congenial to Paquita.

Even more valuable narcissistic supply came from Nansen. He was another of the famous men she worked to a pitch of amorous intensity – this time while Scott was still alive and on his Last Expedition. At a certain point it seems Nansen asked Kathleen to book a hotel for them. Whether she did or didn't – or indeed spend a week in a hotel room with him – has been raked and speculated over many times. Years later in a letter to her second husband Hilton Young, she wrote this, apparently with reference to the much-disputed week with Nansen: [16]

> I was going to remain a completely faithful wife, only I was not going readily to throw aside such a divine friendship.

Whether or not she spent time in a hotel with him is in a sense immaterial, as she would not have slept with him if she had. The romantic tenor of Nansen's letters confirms that their relationship was in the nature of an *amitié amoureuse*, but it was firmly under her control and on terms that suited her agenda.

Scott's first official biographer, Stephen Gwynn, whom she also sculpted, was another of her admirers. She allowed him access to a huge number of Scott's letters – many of them intensely personal and never intended for anyone's eyes but hers. It is unusual for anyone to allow such intensely personal letters to be published. Scott would have been mortified. One cannot help noticing, however, that many of these letters show him throwing himself at her feet.

It took a long time for her letters to him to be published, however, and even longer for revealing material such as the following, referring to her feelings for Hilton Young: [17]

> I'm now experiencing what I've let hundreds of men experience about me. I am mad crazy in love ... I know he's no better than plenty of men who have been equally mad and crazy in love with me.

The narcissism in this statement is multi-layered: not only have hundreds of men been mad crazy in love with her, she has *let* them be mad crazy in love with her.

In the light of her true motivations, i.e. the getting of narcissistic supply, it doesn't seem so remarkable that she was able to maintain her virginity. Sex wasn't her ultimate objective – unlike her idol and friend Isadora Duncan, one of Kathleen's early and lasting artistic and personal inspirations. Both in her life and her work, Duncan aspired to a new and radical freedom of expression. She showed that the whole body could be used as a way of expressing emotion – an idea Kathleen had already become familiar with through Rodin.

Isadora brought to her performances a strong sense of the heroic. It was an age in which it was much in evidence. Schopenhauer, Nietzsche and Wagner inspired students, artists and thinkers of all kinds to reach beyond the domestic ideals modelled by Queen Victoria and the Church in matters of individual freedom and morality – conceptually and emotionally at least. In practice, it was hard to live a superhuman life, and Kathleen was an example of one who had exalted ideas but who turns out to have had conventional moral standards – she was deeply shocked by Duncan's unmarried pregnancy.

Isadora's heroism as theatre gained strength and emotional impact from dramatic gesture and movement. Duncan gave form to the abstraction of heroism, imbuing it with passion and significance. It was a kind of balletic rhetoric – a semi-conscious choice to abandon reason and logic in search of an ideal, a condition where all that mattered were instinct, courage, and an exalted notion of Truth. Kathleen wrote to Hilton Young that she and Isadora [18]

> ... were both soaring artists subject to terrifying elations.

When it came to her plans for a hero, however, Kathleen seems to have made her moves in a more sober frame of mind. The findings of the early geneticist

Gregor Mendel had been rediscovered and were given a lot of attention at the time. In a nutshell, he had discovered that heritable traits were passed on whole and were not blends of parental traits, as had been assumed, but separate physical entities passed from one generation to the next. Kathleen, who would have been *au courant* about such matters, is likely to have read about it. It dovetailed neatly with Schopenhauer's philosophy, and it would have firmed up her belief that making a hero was a case of finding a sire with the right characteristics. She seems to have taken it for granted that nature would be selective on her behalf and pass on exactly those traits that conformed to her idea of a hero – whatever that was.

This essentially adolescent and morally questionable ambition began to be fulfilled when she met Lieutenant Robert Falcon Scott. As it turned out, it was celebrity-explorer status, broad shoulders, a trim waist, a 'rare' smile and 'eyes of a quite unusually dark blue, almost purple' that were eventually to satisfy her. In spite of her high-flown ideas, the things that determined her choices were naive and conventional. If she fancied her scheme to have been some kind of valid eugenics experiment, she ran it on undefined aims and subjective parameters.

The pseudoscience of eugenics was at its peak of popularity in the early twentieth century. Many prominent people supported the idea – among them Winston Churchill, Marie Stopes, HG Wells, Havelock Ellis, Theodore Roosevelt and GB Shaw, among others. If eugenics is taken to cover the broad spectrum of control and manipulation of our reproductive capacity, then of course mankind has been practising it since time immemorial. Also, every parent who cares about their offspring wants them to be happy, well, and preferably successful. Nevertheless, the implications were not realised at the time, nor the ethical minefield, especially assumptions about hierarchies of worth among people.

Freud seems to have passed her by entirely. This means that she did not appear to consider the effect her eugenics experiment might have on the little hero, who would inevitably, as he grew up, become aware of the fact that he had been bred as a project to create a version of Superman. She may have been clever, creative, warm and seductive, but she was psychologically obtuse. In another example, when writing about her many boyfriends she says: 19

> It was odd. My son didn't seem to mean anything at all to any of them.

One wonders if she actually tried to console them by telling them she was reserving herself for a hero. She never saw past Markham's benign-old-man facade, and she fancied Charles Shannon was in love with her, and TE Lawrence – casting doubt on her ability to gauge the true nature of their, or even her own, feelings. She was friendly with Barrie for many years, and evidently saw not the slightest untoward element in his relationships with his boys. Her sculptures of nude boys are clearly reminiscent of Peter Pan.

History chose to push the boundaries of art through abstraction, concept, symbol, form and meaning. Especially meaning. Kathleen may have been bohemian but she was not avant-garde. It's extraordinary to think that Dada originated around the time of Kathleen's heyday. There's no evidence that Kathleen ever considered fundamental questions about what we call art, nor that she experimented with ideas, nor considered separating the craft from the concept. She was no visionary and she wasn't especially original. She never succeeded in bringing to her sculpture that extra dimension which separates the merely good from the great. And in terms of technical virtuosity, her work never attained the sustained mastery of, for example, Charles Sargeant Jagger, whose bronze of Shackleton can be found in a niche on the wall of the RGS headquarters.

An example of Kathleen's work is in the garden of the Scott Polar Research Institute, in the form of one of her slightly perverse naked boys, 'These Had Most to Give'. Whether or not they wanted it, it was a gift they couldn't refuse – another example of her psychological insensitivity, both in the subject matter and its incongruity in the context of the SPRI. Only her own opinion – and that of people she deemed qualified to judge – mattered to Kathleen. The sculpture is situated in front but to one side of the building – a compromise position, evidently.

More appropriately, she also made a bust of Scott, which is in a niche. Although a decent piece, it looks nothing like him. Although competently executed, this bust and all her other monuments to Scott (including the little-known bust at Stoke Damerel College, Plymouth) are idealised, imbuing him with a strength of character and steadiness of purpose – which are more her own projection than an honest portrayal of the conflicted and introspective man he was. She gives his face a chiselled ruggedness and unself-consciousness which were simply not there in reality. Her representations of Scott are based on the image she wanted posterity to have of him and, by extension, her. She had [20]

> ... [an] overweening desire, obediently and repeatedly echoed in
> press accounts, for recognition as Rodin's foremost British disciple.

But however dedicated she thought she was to her art, it was intermittent. It was, after all, only one of the ways she entertained herself and sought narcissistic supply. She was massively diverted by her (verbal) intercourse with statesmen and politicians. The Prime Minister HH Asquith (Squiff, or Squiffy as he was known, on account of his drinking habits), was an almost daily visitor after having sat for her in the summer of 1912. It's not clear how much she knew about his other relationships with women, notably Venetia Stanley, with whom he had a passionate – albeit mainly epistolary – relationship in the years leading up to and into WW1. Kathleen might have crowed about being party to state secrets, but she wasn't the only one. To have learned that she shared that distinction with Venetia

Stanley, whom she would not have considered her intellectual equal, would not have pleased her greatly.

That there was sexual energy in her relations with men is beyond doubt. She must have sailed close to the wind at times and, as far as Squiffy was concerned, she may have been a bit more circumspect if she had known about the liberties he was in the habit of taking with women. As she tells us herself, their conversations were sometimes of a most intimate nature, concerning the most private matters, confirming again her strategy for getting the ardour she needed. Things cooled somewhat, however, after Squiffy arrived one evening and overstepped the mark. 23 November 1916: [21]

> The P.M. came at 6. I didn't like him. He wanted to make love to me
> or something & wouldn't talk sensibly at all …

Fresh from the bar at the House of Commons, by the sound of it. But Kathleen's comment again suggests she was in denial about the way she got and maintained the interest of her admirers.

It was on the Asquith watch that militant suffragettes were imprisoned and force-fed. In view of Kathleen's lack of empathy with women and their cause, it wouldn't be surprising if she condoned it, however tacitly. Certainly one looks in vain for any hint of her having voiced opposition to the jailing of demonstrators and the force-feeding to which they were subjected.

Even more uncomfortable is the fact that Asquith was PM during the first half of WW1; since, while men were dying in their thousands on the Western Front, he was intimate friends with the wife of a man who had 'shown Englishmen how to die'. This helps to give moral weight to the lie that they died for their country, rather than because of the hubris and failure of their leaders in their response to Kaiser Wilhelm's pathology.

Kathleen had been very much involved in the glorification of her dead husband – including tinkering with his Last Expedition journal, taking out any bits that might detract from his heroic image, and nudging the temperatures to make it seem colder. She spent nearly a year publicising the Last Expedition. [22] Markham too had been busy, writing letters that were 'almost indecently eulogistic' about Scott. It is said that Scott's journal helped to spin the carnage in the trenches into something heroic. To the ordinary soldier it was anything but. A hint as to what *they* were thinking is in what Rosslyn Bruce, who had served at the front, told Colonel House during the war: [23]

> … Rosslyn told him [House] how he had asked at a front line service
> if there was any message he should take back. 'For God's sake tell
> them to care more' was the answer.

Kathleen's sometime friend Sybil Colefax, the socialite and interior designer, said that Kathleen was 'a snob who tried to vamp every distinguished man'. [24] According to art historian James Lees-Milne, she was someone whose presence in a crowd could not be ignored. And further: [25]

> She expected adulation, and she got it ... She fascinated men. Scott was a very great hero in those days, and she was in her own right a great sculptress, and everywhere she went people were agog.

It's amazing what she got away with. Kathleen, 26 December 1920: [26]

> Lord what a day! I entertained eleven Americans from one till seven-thirty. I took them in four cars to Hampton Court, went through the maze, gave them tea at Mrs. Scott's chambers, fed them on chocolates, and danced and did my damnedest to support the Anglo-American *entente*. One of them held my hand the whole way up in the car, which amused me mightily. He is nineteen.

She was 42, and any other woman would have been disapproved of, but she seemed to draw no adverse comment at all. Partially, this must have been to do with her air of entitlement and her status. It was also to do with the fact that narcissists can turn nasty when criticised. People might have instinctively shrunk from it. Behind her back, however, it might have been a different matter.

After Scott's death, Kathleen continued to live at 174 Buckingham Palace Road for many years, and although her neighbours must have known who she was, they must sometimes have wondered at the never-ending stream of men going in and out. Where other women might have had a salon and shared her guests with others, she had a studio where she had her guests all to herself, one at a time. A plausible scene is of her quietly working away while her sitter muses and extemporises, almost as if in a counselling session. The intimacy inherent in flirtation quite naturally elicited confidences and disclosures which, in any other context, would have been unthinkable. It was balm to the soul of many men, but most of all to those with inner struggles, existential perplexities, uncertain self-worth and depression.

Kathleen's 'god', Robert Falcon Scott, was exactly the complicated, pessimistic and insecure type of man who tended to be impressed by her. She called him her 'perfect man' – ostensibly because he wasn't jealous, but on a deeper level because he combined a heroic public image with private vulnerability. A self-willed, briskly managerial woman like her could only ever find her match in an accommodating man, and vice versa. Sometimes they swapped roles, and she would be his 'girl', and he her idol – but on the whole it is obvious who was dominant in this relationship. Cherry describes Scott: [27]

Temperamentally he was a weak man, and might very easily have been an irritable autocrat. As it was he had moods and depressions which might last for weeks ...

Similarly, James Lees-Milne found Kathleen's second husband ('Bill' Hilton Young, later Kennet), morose, supercilious, ungracious and condescending. [28]

There was sexual attraction between Kathleen and Scott, undoubtedly; but for her, this would not have meant anything special – if not for the fact that he brought into focus her necessarily vague imaginings of what her hero would look and sound like. Here was an explorer and captain of men with an impressive reputation, but modest withal. Clean and fit, with stunning blue eyes and a 'rare' smile, with what Camille Paglia describes as [29]

Charisma ... [that] flows outward from a simplicity or unity of being and a composure and controlled vitality.

At least, that was the impression he gave. They had met once before and noticed each other, but had gone their own ways. It must have had some kind of impact, however, as she instantly noticed him across the room, and he her, when they were both at Mabel Beardsley's again some nine months later. He walked her home that evening, laughing and joking and jostling each other as they went, and she allowed him to come up and see where she lived, at which point the narrative falls discreetly silent.

It is obvious they bonded quickly and, as she soon found out, there were certain advantages in a relationship with a mariner. Scott had to be often away at sea, which meant that In spite of the excitement of the developing romance, Kathleen's busy social and artistic life could go on much as before – apart from a little pruning of her entourage of would-be lovers and husbands, that is. Famously, Charles Shannon walked under a bus after she told him she was getting married. She took it to be the result of his devastation, but it could just as well have been a random accident.

She allowed yet another romance to go on simultaneously, with the lawyer and writer Gilbert Cannan. His letters to her are almost frightening in their intensity. She had tried to hint at her developing relationship with Scott by having dinner à trois. It didn't work. Cannan suggested she should have them both: [30]

... it seems perfectly ridiculous that you can't have both of us since you are so rapacious that the love of the one you love isn't enough for you.

She didn't finally end it until well after she had decided to marry Scott. In spite of the fact that she had already decided he was not her begetter of heroes, she had allowed Cannan to continue worshipping her. Perhaps she just kept putting off breaking up with him in the hope he would get the message – but she had worked him up to a frenzy while all the time toying with Scott, trying to make up her mind whether he now fulfilled her eugenic requirements.

Her relationships were always conducted on her terms – she was the one who called the shots. It was no different with Scott. There was sexual energy between them, and it would have been a stimulus for her to be her most flamboyantly confident self. For Scott, this was at times intimidating: [31]

> ... You know, I'm half frightened of you – and dear I'm very humble
> before you ...

She triggered, as well as assuaged, his sense of inadequacy and low self-esteem. On one level she couldn't be doing with it ('NONSENSE'), but on a more basic level it satisfied her vanity. She may write 'nonsense', in capitals, but it was a reprimand, not a rejection. Where Cannan had been high Wagnerian melodrama, Scott was Puccini's beseeching martyr. At times he sounds almost perversely abject: [32]

> ... – I've so little, so very little to offer ... and all the time I'm conscious
> of bringing unhappiness to you – it's *I* who make you cry – dis-
> appointment in me I think, though your sweet generosity wouldn't
> admit it – Kathleen dearest don't let your happiness be troubled ...

He gave her exactly what she needed and more.

Contrast this with a similar letter Shackleton wrote to Emily: [33]

> ... I have nothing to offer you: I am poor: I am not clever, it is as
> wicked of me to want you to keep caring for me when my name is
> "Nemo" as it is to make or do other wrongs ... when like today you
> spoke about him: something catches at my heart and I feel lost, out
> in the cold ... why did I not know you first? Why did you not tremble
> to my touch first of all the men in this world.

The difference in tone reveals a masochistic quality in Scott absent in Shackleton, even though both are equally rueful. Shackleton is romantically pleading, whereas Scott is martyrised and self-abasing. Again there are echoes of his mother: her self-pitying martyrdom and the way it drew – and was in fact a gambit to secure – solicitude, commitment and reassurance from her children. None of this was conscious, of course, and both she and her children would have been shocked and outraged to have such a thing suggested to them. But they did have a felt sense of it, and Kathleen felt it too. When writing of her reluctance to get married she tells Scott: [34]

> I know dear that you will be lonely without me for a little while, but
> the relief of knowing that you need not worry or uproot your sweet
> little mother will soon compensate ...

The irony is hard to miss. Although she didn't analyse and identify the pressure, she sensed the effect it had on the Scott family. It might have contributed to the cold feet she got on and off as she contemplated the likely realities of wedlock.

She must have felt the moral pressure there would be on her to place her needs secondary to Scott's and his mother's, and to fulfil his family's expectations. She must have foreseen endless trouble in case she failed to knuckle down to being a more-or-less conventional wife. Who could imagine 'mummy' ever being reconciled to her going out dancing alone or with other men, entertaining whom she liked, when she liked, and having a life and work of her own? There had already been tensions in the family over Scott's plan to marry her because she had no money. It didn't take much imagination to see that a continuation of her vagabonding would only be grist to their mill. Nevertheless, when she wrote 'Don't lets get married ...', the 'Don't lets' isn't a unilateral gambit for breaking up, it is rather a plea for co-operation in an amicable re-orientation of their relationship. Unlike Cannan, Scott wrote back soberly, saying he wanted to marry her 'very badly', but that he felt under obligation to his mother.

The appeal to her understanding and indulgence worked better than Cannan's attempt to force her to see (his) reason. Scott went on in this vein in his next letter also, spelling out their modest circumstances and predicting a drab future, living in poverty always. It may seem irrational to woo a potential bride with promises of a life of deprivation, but she knew it couldn't be true. It was a distortion of reality, but one that supplied her narcissism because it implied that he wasn't worthy of her.

But what about her conceptions of a hero? On the face of it, Scott seemed to be determined to prove to her that he was no such thing. As though to further make sure she knew what a poor specimen of humanity he was, he wrote: [35]

> Yet oh my dear, there is another side of me, born of hereditary instincts of caution, and fostered by the circumstances which have made the struggle for existence an especially hard one for me. Can you understand? I review a past – a real fight – from an almost desperate position to the bare right to live as my fellows.

For goodness *sake*, give that man a reality check! He had had a major expedition handed to him on a plate, he was internationally famous, he had been awarded more medals and honours than he knew what to do with, his book was a highly rated best-seller, and he was the captain of a battleship. Kathleen knew this, but he was so preoccupied with his inner torment that he lost his hold on reality and actually entered an almost-delusional state where all of that seemed immaterial. Ironically, it may actually have been Kathleen who triggered this particular bout of self-pity and depression. Her breezy confidence made him feel inadequate, stiff, old-fashioned and dull. He compared himself negatively with her, and put her on a pedestal. But at the same time as she was making him feel bad about himself, she was also the one from whom he sought – and received – solace.

Kathleen wasn't sure she wanted to marry him. Sometimes she did, sometimes she didn't. Perhaps as a set-up to test his tolerance of her escapades with other men, she arranged to go on a hiking trip to Italy alone with a man. Arty Paget may have been the husband of a distant cousin, but he was still a man. It would have been considered outrageous – scandalous even – for an unmarried woman (never mind a prospective bride!) to go off on an unchaperoned hiking trip abroad, sleeping rough, alone with another man. Clearly, she didn't think the rules that ordinary people lived by applied to her. She did it anyway, and she got away with it.

If she set it up to test Scott and to give herself a final chance to make up her mind, it succeeded on both counts – while enjoying herself, of course. Scott seems merely to have told her to write to him often and not stay too long. 'Perfect man!' It was, actually, pretty unusual behaviour. Scott marvelled at, and envied her for, her freedom and autonomy. How could he now possibly endeavour to take it away? It wouldn't have made sense, and he probably instinctively knew it would drive her away. Her attitude must also have reassured him – also that she had spent most of her life around men without losing her virginity. To Kathleen it must have meant that he was on her side, and that she would therefore have little to fear from his mother.

And so, a few weeks later, in Italy: [36]

> That morning, as my companion was sitting on a boulder in the middle of a stream with his feet in the water, shaving for the first time in his life in cold water, I, from the shingle on the bank where I was brushing my hair in the sun, called, "You know that lovely naval officer, Captain Scott? I'm going to marry him. Say you're glad!" He cut himself slightly, but save for a little musical whistle said nothing. 'Well, I've told him, anyhow,' thought I. 'Now we needn't say any more about it.'

Cutting himself shaving was not quite in the same league as nearly walking under a bus, but she just could not resist telling us about it.

References

1   Verily Anderson. *The Last of the Eccentrics,* p. 56

2   *op. cit,* p. 173

3   J. William Worden. *Children and Grief,* chapter 6

4   Verily Anderson. *op. cit,* p. 41

5   Louisa Young. *A Great Task of Happiness,* p. 14

6   Sam Vaknin. *Malignant Self-love*, pp. 78, 41, 79

7   *op. cit.*, pp. 41–2

8   Lady Kennet. *Self-Portrait of an Artist*, p. 41

9   Arthur Schopenhauer. 'On Women', 1851

10   Lady Kennet. *op. cit.*, p. 26

11   *op. cit.*, p. 27

12   *op. cit.*, p. 37

13   Sam Vaknin. *op. cit.*, p. 39

14   Louisa Young. *op. cit.*, p. 32

15   James Lees-Milne. *Fourteen Friends*, p. 2

16   Louisa Young. *op. cit.*, p. 137

17   Elspeth Huxley. *Peter Scott*, p. 27

18   Louisa Young. *op. cit.*, p. 221

19   Lady Kennet. *op. cit.*, p. 71

20   Mark Stocker. 'Young male objects', p. 122

21   Stefan Buczacki. *My darling Mr Asquith*, p. 186

22   Lady Kennet. *op. cit.*, p. 127

23   Verily Anderson. *op. cit.*, p. 234

24   Louisa Young. *op. cit.*, p. 241

25   *op. cit.*, p. 242

26   Lady Kennet. *op. cit.*, p. 187

27   Apsley Cherry-Garrard. *The Worst Journey in the World*, p. 206

28   James Lees-Milne. *op. cit.,* pp. 5–6

29   Camille Paglia. *Sexual Personae*, p. 521

30   David Crane. *Scott of the Antarctic*, p. 364

31   *op. cit.*, p. 360

32   *ibid.*

33   Roland Huntford. *Shackleton,* p. 39

34   David Crane. *op. cit.*, p. 358

35   Stephen Gwynn. *Captain Scott*, p. 118

36   Lady Kennet. *op. cit.*, p. 85

19

MEN, TRACTORS, PONIES AND DOGS

There was never any doubt in Kathleen's mind that her Con should go back to Antarctica. Kathleen, writing in summer 1908: [1]

> You shall go to the Pole. Oh dear me what's the use of having energy and enterprise if a little thing like that can't be done. It's got to be done so hurry up and don't leave a stone unturned.

Any doubts he might have entertained from time to time she instantly banished. She supported, reassured, and consoled him. She networked, lobbied, canvassed and vamped on his behalf.

As Scott was to write on the eve of departure for the Pole, however, he had not felt confident during the setting-up of his expedition. The spread and the hedged bets evident in the make-up of the expedition told the story: motor tractors, ponies, dogs, manpower, a fairly heavyweight scientific department, a separate mini-expedition (Campbell's Eastern Party), and an expert photographer. He'd covered all bases, but evidently it hadn't been enough to assuage his doubts and uncertainties. He'd thought of everything, but however much he told himself that it *ought* to make for success, it wasn't until it was just him against the elements that he truly relaxed. On the eve of his final departure from Cape Evans he wrote to Kathleen: [2]

> I am quite on my feet now, I feel both mentally and physically fit for the work, and I realize that others know it and have full confidence in me. But it is a certain fact that it was not so in London or indeed until after we reached this spot. The root of the trouble was that I had lost confidence in myself. I don't know if it was noticed by others consciously, but it was acted on unconsciously, as a dozen incidents in my memory remind me. Had I been what I am now,

many things would have been avoided. I can trace these things to myself very clearly and can only hope that others do not ...

Many explorers confirm that it is the preparation that is the hardest part of an expedition – unsurprisingly, when one thinks of the mountain of work to be done, the hundreds of things to be thought of, tested, ordered and made. And that's the easy part. It is the public speaking and fundraising that are by far the greater challenges, and there is plenty of evidence that Scott found those things stressful and depressing – especially his tour of the Midlands and Yorkshire, where he found money tight, and encountered scepticism about the point of getting to the South Pole in the chilly, half-empty halls where he spoke. Canny northerners might have had a suspicion that the main beneficiary of such an expedition would be the speaker himself. There was also a new-born baby at home, born almost exactly a year after he got married. The birth caused Kathleen to fall in love for the first time with her husband. Not so odd, perhaps, as she had only ever wanted to marry in order to have a male child, although hormonal fluctuations also probably played a part. Little Peter was earmarked not only for heroism, but was also destined to be the son of a national icon. It resulted in a rather agonised blend of conceit and self-effacement in the adult Peter Scott.

His father must, by this time, have started to suspect that the tractors were not going to be the answer to his problems and, as far as the ponies were concerned, all he had to go on was Shackleton's narrative of the *Nimrod* Expedition. On a psychological level it sounds like there were many things going unsaid and un-acknowledged. Scott only admitted conscious awareness of his lack of confidence months afterwards, as the above letter shows. Behind the facade of competence, understanding and co-operation, a whole different game was going on. The statement that many things could have been avoided, and the hope they were not going to be traced back to him, suggests that he felt guilty and wished to avoid blame for those things. At least one of those 'things' might have had something to do with the difficult issue around Skelton and Teddy Evans.

Edward Ratcliffe Garth (Russell) Evans (aka Teddy) had been making pre-liminary plans and had started to obtain funding for his own expedition. He had made the most of his connections in Wales, and had obtained the backing of the city of Cardiff – that's where the expedition's Cardiff connection came from. He gave all this up, and donated the funds to Scott when he agreed to go on the *Terra Nova* as Scott's second-in-command, but only on the condition that Skelton did not come on the expedition. He claimed that it would be intolerable for him to out-rank the more senior Skelton. From Scott's point of view, Evans not only brought money with him, he was good at fundraising, and was a gregarious live-wire. For Scott, it was a choice between the value Evans represented, and loyalty to Skelton, who had put in a lot of work on the motor project, and who was more experienced, having been engineering officer on the *Discovery*. Teddy Evans had only been on the relief ship *Morning*. Skelton seems to have wanted to go back, and had reasonable expectations of a berth on the *Terra Nova* in view of his close involvement with the tractors.

Teddy Evans, on the other hand, was reassuring in a way that Skelton wasn't – not only because of the money, but also because of his social skills, energy and boyish enthusiasm. Skelton was more reserved and, despite his advanced technical expertise, at least partially replaceable with a skilled mechanic. Teddy, on the other hand, might still have seemed capable of getting up a rival expedition if his demand was refused, taking his connections and his money with him. Skelton was also more adult and laconic, and gave the impression of being more judgemental than Teddy – representing therefore more of an interpersonal challenge. The letter to Kathleen might therefore have referred to feelings of guilt about not having put up a stronger fight on Skelton's behalf – and especially about a hidden self-serving agenda, in that he had allowed Evans to carry the can for a decision for which he himself was ultimately responsible.

Scott had started to think about another expedition very soon after going back to sea. His first problem was that of traction, having by now apparently divested himself of the romantic notions of his *Voyage of the Discovery* – itself a rather CS Lewis kind of title – in which [3]

> ... no journey ever made with dogs can approach the height of that fine conception which is realised when a party of men go forth to face hardships, dangers, and difficulties with their own unaided efforts, and by days and weeks of hard physical labour succeed in solving some problem of the great unknown. Surely in this case the conquest is more nobly and splendidly won.

Always assuming one wins the conquest of course, tautology notwithstanding.

Clearly, Scott had moved on from this idealisation by this time. A technological solution was the most obvious one for him, especially as – assuming he would be taking a similar route as before – a large part of the journey would be over a comparatively flat snow surface, which seemed potentially suitable for motor vehicles. He had been introduced to Howard de Walden, one of the richest men in England and a motor-boat enthusiast. Together with de Walden and his engineers, Skelton and Scott, but mainly Skelton, had put together an experimental design for a motorised sledge. The engine was made in France by the De Dion-Bouton Company, which had also been working on a design on behalf of Antarctic explorer Jean-Baptiste Charcot. As De Dion-Bouton was involved with both sledges, it had been agreed to test them together. In March 1908, the sledges were duly conveyed by train and horse-drawn vehicle to the Col du Lautaret in the French Alps. A third man and sledge were at the party in the form of Michael Barne, who also harboured plans for an expedition, and who had had a sledge built to his own design.

Scott, Skelton and Barne, together with Charcot and his wife, engineers from De Dion, and various other interested parties, were present at the testing of the three quite different prototypes.

Charcot wasn't intending to haul long-distance as he was headed for a different part of Antarctica. He tested and ended up with a lighter sledge, on ski runners; something in the direction of the skidoos of today. Of Barne's design, suffice it to say that it has slipped quietly into oblivion. Scott's sledge was an altogether heavier machine, already with a continuous track, but one which tended to dig itself into the snow rather than propel itself over it. The continuous track idea had been around for a while, but it wasn't until 1907 that it was being tried by the military, who gave them the name caterpillar tracks. Although never having been tried on snow, they had the potential, given the right kind of treads. So, encouraged by Skelton and Bernard Day, renewed efforts (and funds) were put into improving this sledge and building two more, all of them using continuous tracks. While promising in theory, it was a high-risk strategy, based as it was on new technology with no track record in Polar conditions, and that no one concerned had experience of in the field.

It wasn't until the 1950s, almost half a century and two world wars later, that there were tracked vehicles capable of long-distance travel in Antarctica. No amount of wishful thinking could have obscured the fact that Scott's cumbersome, complicated, temperamental machines could only have a limited range – and then only with constant nursing and expert attendance. These drawbacks, together with their cost and weight, should have ruled them out but for the fact that he must have felt committed by then. So he chose to listen to the optimists and decided to take not just one or two, but three.

In terms of time and money, what the design, development, manufacture, transport and trials cost, who knows. Certainly it was a very expensive business. Scott paid £1,000 each for the machines. Three thousand pounds was a large chunk out of the £40,000 expedition budget. Even so, Howard de Walden paid for much of the R&D, and the patents were granted to him. While it must have been gratifying to Scott that so much money and time was being invested on his behalf, it brought with it pressure to buy and use them.

They were actually motor tractors, not sledges. The rebuilt Lautaret tractor was tested twice – the second time in Fefor, Norway (where Scott and Kathleen first met Tryggve Gran), just three months before the *Terra Nova* was due to sail. A photo of the trial [4] shows the tractor pulling what appears to be a very small load over a flat, hard snow surface in pretty much ideal conditions. Even then it had needed a major repair. Kathleen was present on the occasion and can be seen in the photo, poking it with a stick.

If as a result of the trial this motor appeared in any way feasible, it can only have been by the omission of a vital real-life consideration; namely, that it would, as a priority, have to drag its own fuel before any payload was added. A delicate balance would have to be struck between the distance they could go and the amount of fuel this would necessitate. Their dragging strength dictated their range – unless further fuel was dragged by ponies or men, and this would have defeated the object. In order to arrive at any kind of viable prognosis for the performance of these machines, therefore, it would have been vital to attach a suitably heavy load, thus projecting more nearly the actual job it needed to do. Consistent with his history of refusing to face uncomfortable truths, Scott now failed to properly acknowledge this potentially illusion-wrecking reality. His habitual tendency to denial sabotaged his aims again and again, and made him fall for an entire range of biases and fallacies. Here, it was the Sunk-Cost Fallacy, causing him to stubbornly stick with the motors purely because so much money, time and effort had already been invested in them. He would have been much better off with a realistic appraisal and a review of his options. Instead, perversely, he decided to take not just two, but three, motors to Antarctica. It was as if he wanted to contradict his own misgivings – in the process putting up a show of defiance against the nay-sayers and Jeremiahs. His lack of insight was lamentable and utterly self-defeating.

The tractors were made at the Wolseley Tool and Motor Company's works in Birmingham, and were said to be very advanced for the time. There were two forward gears, no reverse, no steering and no brakes – a terrifying thought in connection with crevasses. Steering was effected by a man in a harness attached to a rope fastened to a shaft at the front. [5]

After the best of the three had broken through the ice and sunk shortly after landing at Cape Evans, the other two had chugged away merrily, hauling light loads backwards and forwards between the ship and the hut site. It was still not a real test of their ability to do what they were there for, however, and when that day came to pass, so did the real difficulties.

They constantly overheated. It is testament to their fragility that this could have been due to all or any of a number of causes: not enough speed for the airflow to the air-cooled engines, air too dry or, as Lashly thought, the engines were simply not powerful enough to pull the loads over heavy surfaces. According to Teddy Evans, they would not move over blue ice either: [6]

> We advanced under three miles after ten hours' distracting work –
> mostly pulling the sledges ourselves, jerking, heaving, straining,
> and cursing – it was tug-of-war work and should have broken our
> hearts, but in spite of our adversity we all ended up smiling ...

Good old Teddy.

In spite of their reportedly jaunty performance on arrival, by the time the main journey was due to start, the motors had sunk to the status of slowest mode of transport. Lashly's diary records that they were due to start on the Pole Journey on 23 October 1911, a week before the main exodus. Scott:

> ... but the inevitable little defects cropped up ... Day and Lashly spent the afternoon making good these defects in a satisfactory manner.

He commented that the weights seemed a good deal heavier than bargained for (!), but a fresh start was made the next day, shortly after 10 am. He was [7]

> ... immensely eager that these tractors should succeed, even though they may not be of great help to our southern advance. A small measure of success will be enough to show their possibilities, their ability to revolutionise Polar transport.

History shows that the thing which truly revolutionised Polar transport was aviation – Fuchs' and Hillary's Sno-Cats notwithstanding. In any case, it was thin enough reward for the fact that they were not capable of pulling more than their own weight and their own fuel – and that was taxing enough because they were always liable to break down, mostly seriously. When a payload was added they became virtually impossible, and the motor team had to work very hard to keep them going at all. By the time the overheated engines had cooled, the carburettors would have frozen and needed to be thawed out with a blowlamp. Looking back after many years, Teddy tells us that he thought of Amundsen as he glided along on skis one afternoon around that time: [8]

> Yes, Amundsen was over 150 miles farther South, and his sledge runners were slithering over the snow, casting its powdered part-icles aside in beautiful little clouds while I was rapidly overhauling the motors with their labouring, sorely taxed custodians ...

The first motor broke down irreparably on 29 October, six days after starting, the second four days later, after having [9]

> ... coaxed the wretched thing to Corner Camp and ourselves dragged the loads there.

Would an objective assessment at the time have necessarily condemned the motors, and if so, at what point? They had a lot of psychological value for Scott and the expedition. They not only represented potentialities and a glimpse perhaps into the future, they lent prestige and added a touch of glamour. They made the expedition seem cutting-edge, reminiscent of the balloons and the windmill on the *Discovery*. Surprisingly, Amundsen, normally such a shrewd cookie, was spooked by them. He allowed his imagination to run away with him, to the point where he made a premature start on account of the motors, which nearly cost him the Pole (what a result for Scott that would have been!). Clearly, Amundsen credited the tractors far beyond their actual capacity. And if they impressed Amundsen, they must certainly have impressed the public. Their power seems altogether to have been more in the psychological than the physical realm.

It was just as Scott was on his way to Lautaret that he heard the news about Shackleton's landing at Cape Royds. He instantly assumed that Shackleton had only made a pretence of trying elsewhere, and had always intended to land in the forbidden zone – which says more about him than it does about Shackleton. Shackleton returned to tremendous acclaim, and received a knighthood soon afterwards. For Scott, the contrast with his own rather subdued return in the *Discovery* must have been painful – as must the tally of achievements chalked up by the *Nimrod* Expedition. As far as Scott was concerned, however, the main thing was that the Pole had still not been reached, and that that particular plum could still be his. He could take the view that Shackleton had conveniently reconnoitred the route for him and had tested methods of haulage.

Scott's decision to take ponies was entirely due to Shackleton who had, in his turn, been influenced by Armitage and Frederick Jackson and their experience of ponies on Franz Josef Land. Shackleton, at this time, shared Scott's lack of confidence in dogs – ostensibly still as a result of their experience on the first Southern Journey – but really because they were both the victims of confirmation bias: the tendency to search for, favour, and interpret new information in a way that confirms one's preconceptions. It is a form of selective thinking whereby one not only tends to notice and look for what confirms one's existing beliefs, but also ignores or undervalues the relevance of what contradicts those beliefs. Scott had been prejudiced against dogs from the start. He was Markham's man, and Markham had a constitutional aversion to the use of dogs. In the event, Scott had allowed himself to be partially persuaded by Nansen, and he took a token number on the *Discovery*, but was predisposed to judge them negatively – and he interpreted the nightmare of the first Southern Journey as a vindication of his existing bias. Logically, he knew the food had been at fault (Wilson diagnosed acute peritonitis), but he still drew negative conclusions, in spite of the wealth of positive testimonies from Polar explorers far more experienced than him. It is surprising that Scott decided to take dogs again on the *Terra Nova* – a limited number only, however.

Ponies were more congruent with military styles of campaign – the M'Clintock-ian siege template that relied on support and backup, rather than expertise or speed. In view of the fact that ponies would have to be led on foot, and could there-fore go no faster than human walking speed, his priority was to get sufficient supplies on the route to support the time and the numbers required by this slow and labour-intensive system. Average human walking speed is about 3 mph under normal conditions, without dragging a heavy load. The Beardmore route to the Pole and back from Hut Point is approximately 1,760 statute miles – roughly the distance, there and back, from Land's End to John o'Groats. Scott planned for the journey to take 144 days, which means an *average* speed of 12.2 statute miles per day. This meant that bad weather, difficult terrain, or other unforeseen delays would all have to be made up for to keep up that daily average.

Scott planned to be out from 1 November to 22 March. This meant a journey of almost five months' duration for those going to the Pole and back. If successful, it would beat M'Clintock's Arctic record, which was set under less stringent conditions, and where there had been musk-oxen, providing extra nutrition and, crucially, vitamin C, on the way. It could not but be an ordeal of the most searching kind, but it must have seemed just about possible. And so it might have been if Scott had won the Pole and not taken two injured men with him on the last leg.

But to that, obviously, we will return in detail later. In the meantime, let's take a look at the pony issue and Scott's more-or-less infamous decision to order Meares to buy only white ones. Shackleton had been very enthusiastic about his ponies: [10]

> ... a Manchurian pony can drag a sledge over a broken trial at the rate of twenty to thirty miles a day, pulling not less than twelve hundred pounds ... compared with the dog, the pony is a far more efficient animal, one pony doing the work of at least ten dogs on the food allowance for ten dogs, and travelling a longer distance in a day.

There is almost a case to be made for hardy Siberian/Manchurian ponies as draught animals on the Barrier: not too many crevasses, and a comparatively straightforward run in summer. Anyone can lead a horse, so no special driving skills are required. But these positives are nothing compared to the drawbacks. First, they are large and heavy animals, which means that all transfers from ship to shore and vice versa involve cumbersome boxes and hoists, and specially adapted accommodation on board. Then there is their food, all of which has to be paid for and brought with them. There is also their vulnerability to breaking through snow-crusts and bridges because of the concentration of weight on small sharp hooves. They sweat through their skin rather than their tongues, as dogs do, and have to be protected from wind-chill with blankets. In spite of all this, Shackleton had pronounced them valuable, and this is what Scott went by. Not entirely irrational in itself, perhaps. But what certainly was irrational, and completely unscientific, was the idea that their being white had anything to do with their survival rate.

Shackleton had arrived at Cape Royds with eight surviving ponies. Four of these died within a month: three from eating sand, and one from eating a corrosive material. It must have been the little leprechauns whispering in his ear when he reckoned it [11]

... a rather curious fact that the survivors were the white or light coloured animals, while disaster had befallen all the dark animals.

If they had survived in a contest of fitness and endurance there might have been some excuse for thinking their colour had something to do with it, in spite of the plethora of variables involved. But the darker ponies hadn't died on the march, and the white ponies hadn't survived on the march. None of them had ever even been off site. Those that died did so from eating sand and a corrosive substance, as post-mortems confirmed. A rational mind must have been forced to conclude that, however curious, the survival of the lighter-coloured ponies was pure coincidence.

But for Scott it was enough to prompt the decision to take exclusively white ponies, regardless of age, condition, or tractability. It was a huge error, and it must have cost him a good deal of respect in certain quarters – never mind the loss in terms of survival, pulling power and ease of handling. Anyone who had carefully read Shackleton's narrative must have wondered at Scott's judgement. He had allowed a passing superstitious notion (or perhaps just Shackleton's observation of a curious coincidence) to precipitate him into making the most elementary of mistakes. It would have been better if he'd just allowed Meares to get on with it. One explanation is that perhaps, in his perpetual hurry, Scott had skim-read Shackleton's book, and was left with the impression that the white ponies had done better overall. His thinking might have been primed by the fact that much Polar wildlife is white, and extrapolated that it signified a better level of adaptation.

Unsurprisingly, it had the opposite effect from that intended. The thick vein of Establishment propaganda that runs through most biographical Scott material invariably characterises him as having a scientific turn of mind. In their view, he is the intelligent amateur going around mildly tying the scientists in knots. It is a very flattering picture. Even if he reasoned that the ponies were going to have a one-way ticket only, and that all he required of them was to drag sledges over a comparatively flat surface for limited periods of time, over limited distances, he must still have been interested in them doing well. It was the reason, however irrational, he'd ordered white ones after all. One wonders whether Oates had ever read Shackleton's book and found out exactly why he'd been saddled with a bunch of what he described as variously narrow-chested, knock-kneed, aged wind-suckers with doubtful back tendons, slightly lame, pigeon-toed, ring-wormed, worn-out ponies – with, as he was later to find out, their fair share of lice and tape-worms. Scott himself may have realised his error, as the ponies were picketed away from sand on arrival at Cape Evans without further comment.

And they were always destined to be killed at the end of their usefulness. Much as Ranulph Fiennes might insult Amundsen by claiming (on television) that his success relied on his ability to be cruel to animals, Scott's ponies ('The Baltic Fleet') were on a one-way trip to oblivion, just the same as most (but not all) of Amundsen's dogs. And let's not forget the first Southern Journey. Those dogs were never going to come home either. Remember the dog-eat-dog conversation between Wilson and Scott on the *Discovery*? On that same journey they took 12 weeks' provisions plus extra seal meat for the men, and about 40 days' food for the dogs, which speaks for itself. Fiennes is prone to equate his first-hand knowledge of Antarctic conditions with a superior entitlement to judge Scott and the quality of his leadership (and even his kindness!). It is of course a logical fallacy.

Cecil Henry Meares had applied to join the *Terra Nova* Expedition through a contact at the Admiralty. [12] He spoke some Russian and had learned to drive dogs. He had the credentials to go out and collect sledge dogs, which he knew about, but he didn't know much about ponies. It would have made little difference if he had, as his brief was to buy white ponies only. It is often claimed that Meares worked for British Intelligence in the Russo–Japanese war of 1904–5. He would certainly have fitted the bill: something of a linguist and adventurer, he was widely travelled, having gone abroad straight after school and gravitated eastwards from then on. Intelligence-gathering was in the process of becoming more organised, but journalists and 'observers', were still being used on an ad-hoc basis as sources of information. They had contacts at the relevant British Embassies and Consulates, as did Meares. Herbert Ponting's connection with Scott came through Meares. He and Ponting had met in 1905 and they had travelled together to India, Burma and Ceylon, Meares acting as interpreter and photographer's assistant. [13] They knew each other well, but seem not to have been especially close at Cape Evans. Here, Meares was closer to Atkinson and Oates, who were some of Scott's most trenchant critics.

In January 1910 Meares had gone to northern Siberia to obtain sledge dogs for the expedition. He wrote to his father that he had been [14]

> ... kept very busy collecting dogs, trying teams and picking out one or two dogs and making up a team and trying it on a run of 100 miles and throwing out the dogs which do not come up to the mark and collecting others ... I expect to be back in Vladivostok by the middle of June where I will collect the ponies ... It is a very big contract indeed to choose all these animals and carry them down to Australia single handed.

He recruited assistance in the form of Dmitrii Girev and Anton Omelchenko, dog driver and jockey/groom respectively, and eventually Wilfrid Bruce, Kathleen's only non-clerical brother, who 'always had a weather-eye out for the ladies'. It is unclear why it was Bruce, rather than Oates, who knew about horses, who was sent out to assist with the selection and shipment of the ponies. Scott to Kathleen, writing from the Barrier after 24 days of sledging: [15]

> ... we had a bad scare about the condition of the ponies last week. The animals are not well selected, I knew this in New Zealand though I didn't tell you. That they are going well now ... is entirely due to Oates. He is another treasure.

If Meares had the feeling that Scott held him responsible for the poor quality of the ponies, it is likely to have added barbs of resentment to the negative judgements he already held about Scott. Meares left the expedition at the first opportunity. There are no post-mortem eulogies of Scott from him: nothing survives, if indeed he ever wrote anything about Scott or the expedition at all.

The menagerie was not on board when the expedition left England. Neither was Scott, although he had posed for many photos on the occasion of the ship's send-off – one of several – among much fanfare and interest from the public, as had by now become customary. Some of the most famous photos taken at this time were those of Kathleen, Scott and Markham on the *Terra Nova*, sitting on and standing beside the capstan, with Markham perched on a barrel in front. A famous shot by Ponting shows the strain of a composition forced on more-or-less unwilling participants. Scott looks as though he wishes he were somewhere else – anywhere, probably – as long as it was away from Markham. Far from looking like the proud 'owner' of an important expedition, he looks like a business associate whose mind is on something else, and who is reluctantly going along with somebody else's idea. The hand on the boater is particularly awkward. Kathleen looks OK-ish, as she would, although even she has put out a finger for Scott to hold. Markham looks wistfully into the middle distance.

It was the last time Scott and Markham saw each other. Their relationship had never really recovered from Markham's *faux-pas* in going ballistic over the rescue of the *Discovery*. There were also the rumours around Markham's private life; and if Scott wanted to put distance between himself and Markham, at least in public, it would seem only natural. But on this occasion it was more than that. What we are seeing in Scott's body language is irritation. There is no comradeship, no standing together facing the world, no solidarity or affection, and no hint of Scott's legitimate pride or satisfaction in, nor even psychological ownership of, the expedition. By rights he should have been looking solid, present, and happy, but he looks equivocal and distracted. This was not just about his lack of confidence. It was irritation at once again being forced to acknowledge Markham's role in how he had got where he was. And again it was Markham who was being humoured, and who automatically stole the show. The show that should by rights have been his. If Markham had been the father of the *Discovery* Expedition, he was the godfather of the *Terra Nova*.

Another photo taken on the same occasion shows Scott, Markham and Minna (but not Kathleen), surrounded by the officers and men of *Terra Nova*, including many RN sailors whose faces and names are unfamiliar to history. It's easy to overlook the fact that in addition to the shore parties, the *Terra Nova* was manned by a crew who sailed the ship under the command of Harry Pennell. The photo can be found on the internet under 'Clements Markham, Images', and is captioned in German. As is the case with so much material about Scott, it shows glaring errors made at the time – although many are still being made today. Scott is listed as 'Christian Scott', and the man here listed as Oates is actually George Murray Levick, one of the medics, who was later to form one of Campbell's Northern Party. Scott, Markham, Minna and Teddy Evans form the quartet at the centre of this picture. Markham looks smug and in his element, with a slight suggestion of larking about going on in the background. Minna looks composed and tolerant. Scott has a tight little smile on his face, and seems to be reluctantly putting up with having to pose again for a photo. Especially alongside Markham. Teddy Evans, on the other hand, looks confident, relaxed, and happy.

The essential difference between Scott and Teddy Evans is suggested in this photo. Complicated, reluctant and uneasy, Scott's body language forms a poignant contrast to the expression of legitimate pride and confidence displayed by Evans. Perhaps this was another source of irritation for Scott, but then Evans was bound to feel an element of ownership – having cleaned and refitted the ship, hired the crew, and now about to take command of her on the first leg of the journey south. Altogether, the send-off from England seems for Scott to have been more of a trial of endurance than the celebratory occasion it should have been. The final departure from New Zealand made up for some of it, but the departure from England without him was an opportunity missed, and it sent out the wrong message.

There is an uncomfortable sense of hubris in Scott's decision to leave to others the mundane task of sailing the ship south. It may have been partially justified by the necessity to raise more money, but that is not entirely convincing as there were going to be further opportunities for that in South Africa and New Zealand. Perhaps it was Kathleen's idea. It would have been characteristic for her to dismiss as trivial or unnecessary issues such as being seen to be in command of the expedition leaving England – not to mention bonding, and the fostering of shared goals and mutual understandings. Most on board were strangers to each other, and many were going to be spending a long time together in intimate and challenging circumstances. Above all, leaving with the ship would have demonstrated a sense of commitment. As it was, it was Teddy Evans, Scott's second-in-command, who set off on the historic voyage, with Scott lagging behind somewhere, fiddling about with business that should by then have been concluded, and no doubt in thrall to the views of Kathleen and her self-serving psychological obtuseness.

Scott seems not to have been interested in the preparation of his ship. According to Evans, it was not until they were ready for departure from London that Scott even visited her. Evans tells us that it wasn't until sailing day, on 1 June 1910, that he 'proudly showed Scott his ship'. The *Terra Nova* had been handed over to Evans to manage and fit out from the day she came down to the West India Docks, stinking of whale oil and blubber, in Teddy's words. He had overseen the cleaning, refitting, purchasing, stowing and provisioning, and had 'wangled' (his word) many freebies. All in addition to the money he'd raised and turned over to Scott. He had also, along with Scott, been present at the RGS farewell dinner, attended inevitably by Markham, the [16]

> ... father of modern British exploration, [who] proposed the toast of
> the officers and staff in the most touching terms.

'Sailing day' has to be taken with a pinch of salt, since it wasn't until some weeks later that the *Terra Nova* finally left England. First there was the by-now-traditional procession along the Thames and the coast, stopping for visits from sea cadets, and the 'swinging' of the ship (adjustment of compasses). Scott was on board for the obligatory visit to Cowes, after which he had again gone ashore to attend to other business, coming on board again in Weymouth, in time to be seen on board steaming through the home fleet. The last stop was Cardiff, where Evans' friends and connections endowed them with extra supplies, including a large amount of fuel. It made the ship settle so deeply into the water that the seams, which had until then been above the waterline [17]

> ... leaked in a way that augured a gloomy future for the crew in the
> nature of pumping.

Ominously, in view of later developments, earlier in London, a quantity of patent coal briquettes had been stowed as a flooring in the lower hold, keeping their provision cases out of the bilge water [18]

> ... which was bound to scend ... to and fro if we made any quantity
> of water, as old wooden ships usually do.

Finally, on 15 June 1910, they departed, accompanied by a flotilla of small boats, and having enjoyed a 'rattling good time' in Cardiff. Bowers rather primly told Kathleen that there should have been [19]

> ... a little less of that spirit that did not do us credit on our departure
> from Cardiff.

But Charles Wright (Silas) noted that: [20]

> The day before I arrived there was a dinner for the officers of the
> *Terra Nova* at which fifteen hundred pounds was raised at one
> shot. One old chap who gave five hundred pounds ended up the
> evening by walking (with assistance) down the centre of the table.

Teddy thought 'It was a wonderful send-off and we cheered ourselves hoarse.' There must have been a sense of anticlimax as [21]

> Captain Scott left with our most intimate friends [wives] in the pilot boat and we proceeded a little sadly on our way.

The *Terra Nova's* almost triumphal procession stands in marked contrast to Amundsen's more subdued departure. Not quite the silent slinking off into the night that Huntford describes – presumably as a dramatic contrast to the *Terra Nova* circus – but certainly much less showy. Amundsen and his crew had had a visit from the King and Queen of Norway, however. Ships had been manned, and the band had played the National Anthem when the *Fram* had passed them on her way out to sea – first on what Amundsen called 'a little hydrographical cruise' around Ireland. This gave them an opportunity to test the ship's new diesel engine. No more shovelling coal on the *Fram*. On the way back to Norway, they struck a violent gale in the Pentland Firth and were lucky to come through with only the loss of a few boxes of cigars, which were wet through. Amundsen: [22]

> They were not entirely lost for all that; Rønne took charge of them, and regaled himself with salt and mouldy cigars for six months afterwards.

Amundsen took obvious pleasure in relating the odd amusing anecdote. The forbidding and dour look of his photo portraits is very much at odds with the way he comes across as a writer. Rønne, by the way, was the man who made the little South Pole tent immortalised by Birdie and his camera.

The most important thing, however, remained to be done. After about a month of trials and repairs, Amundsen and his crew returned for the embarkation of 97 Greenland dogs. They had been kept at Fredriksholm, a fortress island off the coast of southern Norway. The dogs had been on the island about a month, and [23]

> The usually peaceful island, with the remains of the old fortress, re- sounded day by day, and sometimes at night, with the most glorious concerts of howling.

It attracted a certain amount of attention, and the public was sometimes admit- ted to view the animals. At this time the men had not yet been taken into Amund- sen's confidence about their true destination. Arguments continue to this day about whether or not Amundsen was justified in his secrecy, and whether or not he was underhand in changing his original destination.

Amundsen was, like Scott, a very ambitious man. He was of course aware that Scott considered the Pole to be reserved for himself; and it is clear from his comments that he thought that was nonsense. The North Pole had been reached – or so Amundsen, along with everyone else, believed at the time. If not Cook, then Peary, had made a convincing claim – and it is completely understandable that

that, for Amundsen, took away all motivation to reach it. He knew there would be criticism, but if he reached the South Pole first, it would be a price worth paying. Besides, as he somewhat disingenuously claimed: [24]

> The British Expedition was designed entirely for scientific research. The Pole was only a side issue ...

Even though everyone knew that wasn't true, it was the official line, and Scott couldn't have it both ways. Even more disingenuously, and with a suggestion of self-serving sophistry it must be said, Amundsen went on to say that [25]

> ... I doubt whether Captain Scott, with his great knowledge of Antarctic exploration, would have departed in any point from the experience he had gained and altered his equipment in accordance with that which I found it best to employ. For I came far short of Scott both in experience and means.

To the extent that Amundsen hadn't actually set foot on Antarctic land when on the *Belgica* with de Gerlache, and hadn't raised as much money, he was right of course, but it was far from the whole story. He was right about one thing, however. Scott did not alter his plans one iota on account of him.

As far as Amundsen was concerned, Scott had an equal, if not better, chance of getting to the Pole. Scott had more resources at his disposal and was following a known route. It was up to him to make what he could of it, and let the best man win. Amundsen's was a bold decision, but all his men were behind him when they got to Madeira and he told them where they were going. All had the option of going ashore if they chose not to go on. All stayed. The venture was in the nature of a stealth raid, nipping in and stealing the prize from under the nose of the official candidate. Everyone on the *Fram* was up for it. If the nationality of the two expeditions had been the other way around, and if it had been an Englishman who did what Amundsen did, the English would have rubbed their hands and gleefully wished him every success.

The *Fram* had been specially adapted to provide optimum conditions for the health and comfort of the dogs, who took over the decks to the point where it was hardly possible for the men to move. A more comfortable *modus vivendi* was arrived at further into the voyage, as there seems to be plenty of room on the decks in photographs. The more docile dogs were given a free run, and it seems many crowded on to the bridge, a favourite place. The dogs always came first. 'We care for our dogs like little children', Amundsen wrote: [26]

> Dogs have rarely had such care ... Everyone is anxious to busy themselves with them. [Oscar] Wisting however wins first prize. He is tireless, and always on the go ...

Thorvald Nilsen, the Captain of the *Fram* ...

... had assumed supervision of all maternity establishments. Every afternoon at 3.15, he brings milk and pudding round to all the women who have just had their babies.

Of course, it was in their interest to look after the dogs; but Fiennes' comment – about Amundsen's success being due to the fact that he was able to be cruel to his dogs – is shown to be untrue, regardless of the authority a handful of missing fingertips can command. As J Gordon Hayes said even in 1928: [27]

> British explorers now realize that the inhumanity of dog-sledging is more imaginary than real; and that its extraordinary efficiency, when compared to hand-sledging, was never understood by the old British school ... dogs do not suffer when they are properly treated.

Amundsen's success was due to his confident leadership, focus, preparation, experience, commitment and intelligence – as well as his knowledgeable and humane, even affectionate, treatment of the dogs personally; and also to the hand-picked team of multi-skilled men he surrounded himself with.

Finally, on 9 August 1910, the *Fram* was on her way. After Funchal, they set course for the Bay of Whales. There were no half-measures in Amundsen's plan, no fail-safes, and no hedged bets. Obviously he could not go the same route as Scott (and never had the slightest intention to), nor set up base anywhere near him. He had to build his winter station on the Barrier, a long way away from land, and find his own route through the mountains. It was as well for their peace of mind that Amundsen thought the ice was aground under them, but he was mistaken: Framheim has long since dropped into the sea. But ultimately, as far as Amundsen was concerned, the Pole belonged to no man, and [28]

> ... the country would have to be difficult indeed to stop our getting on to the plateau.

References

1   Louisa Young. *A Great Task of Happiness*, p. 98

2   Stephen Gwynn. *Captain Scott*, pp. 207–8

3   Captain Robert F. Scott. *The Voyage of the Discovery*, p. 318

4   Serge Aubert, Judy Skelton, Yves Frenot and Alain Bignon. *Scott and Charcot at the col du Lautaret*, p. 100

5   Admiral Edward Evans. *South With Scott*, p. 191

6   *op. cit*, p. 192

7   Robert Falcon Scott. *Journals*, p. 306

8   Admiral Edward Evans, *op. cit*, p. 196

9   *op. cit*, p. 198

10   Sir Ernest Shackleton. *The Heart of the Antarctic*, pp. 108–9

11   *ibid.*

12   Leif Mills. *Men of Ice*, p. 134

13   *op. cit*, p. 116

14   *op. cit*, pp. 134–5

15   Stephen Gwynn. *op. cit*, p. 218

16   Admiral Edward Evans. *op. cit*, pp. 22–3

17   *op. cit*, p. 26

18   *op. cit*, p. 22

19   Stephen Gwynn. *op. cit*, p. 211

20   Colin Bull and Pat F. Wright. *Silas*, p. 8

21   Admiral Edward Evans. *op. cit*, p. 27

22   Roald Amundsen. *The South Pole*, pp. 98–9

23   *op. cit*, p. 101

24   *op. cit*, p. 44

25   *op. cit*, pp. 44–5

26   Roland Huntford (ed.). *The Amundsen Photographs*, p. 60

27   Gordon J. Hayes. *Antarctica*, p. 149

28   Roald Amundsen. *op. cit*, p. 52

20

TEDDY, AND ANOTHER DOSE OF KATHLEEN

Edward Ratcliffe Garth Evans was born in the West End of London on 28 October 1880. He was a sturdy little ruffian who regularly got into trouble for fighting and bunking off school. He and his two brothers formed a gang whom the neighbouring matrons forbade their children to play with. He writes about the frequent canings he received in punishment, although they do not seem to have bothered him unduly. His progress through life reads a lot like the archetypal Boys' Own Story about a wayward lad who ultimately makes good. The adult Evans wrote that in the process he learned how to survive and get out of tight corners, and thereby [1]

> ... developed quite an instinct ... which has often saved my life, and, no doubt, my reputation.

He was hyperactive and pugnacious; and although his parents clearly had a lot of patience, when the Evans brothers' escapades and misdemeanours culminated in them being hauled up in front of the magistrate, it was clear that things had got out of hand. When he was then also expelled from Merchant Taylors' for persistent truancy, he was sent to a school for 'troublesome boys' in Surrey. In spite of feeling homesick, he loved it there, as outdoor pursuits were encouraged and gave an outlet for his superabundant energies.

In London, his explorations had included the slums of the East End. These roamings gave him an insight into how 'the other half' lived. What he saw evoked his sympathies and, as he was later to say, kindled sparks of democracy. It gave him a lasting awareness of the contributions made by the men of the 'lower deck'. Writing of his experiences as Captain of HMS *Active*, a Royal Navy light cruiser doing convoy work in the Atlantic during WW1: [2]

> Looking back on those days I can picture it all so vividly, and re-
> member a still starlit night when I had 32 dreadfully slow ships

without any patrol craft to watch my flock ... I saw the wisps of smoke from the funnels, the phosphorescent bow-waves and wakes, the dim black hulls and so on, and heard the metallic clang of an iron door which meant that the Watch was being changed and that the black squad, engineers, greasers and firemen were coming up from their heated boiler-rooms and engine-rooms where they had been running the gauntlet of torpedo and mine perhaps for nearly four years of war. A great wave of admiration and affection surged through my heart, for I knew that if a torpedo or mine had exploded in the engine-room the great inrush of water would have drowned the occupants before they had a chance to reach the engine-room steps.

Socially, his knowledge of London's poor areas expanded his comfort zone beyond the middle-class milieus that would otherwise have circumscribed his experience. He was as comfortable with the officer class as he was with the 'men'. The fact that he bunked off school, got into scraps and was generally unruly would, in a different context and perhaps a different time, have been considered high spirits and indulged – encouraged even – by some. For example, he sounds a lot like Markham's favourite kind of boy.

When his parents moved to St John's Wood he was sent to a school known at the time as Warwick House School, where he carried on being the irrepressibly adventurous and rule-breaking boy he had always been. He must have had redeeming qualities, because he seems never to have lost the goodwill of his parents and teachers. In spite of having held up a fellow pupil at gun-point (!), in an inspired (or perhaps last-ditch) move, the headmaster made him a prefect. It had the desired effect. Teddy decided to give no more trouble, and started to win prizes for his school work.

It was clear, however, that a life among books and ledgers would never be for him. He tried for a cadetship in 'Her Majesty's Naval Service'. He was refused, and went to the merchant training ship *Worcester* instead. Here we can confidently assume he completed his education in how to survive in a psychologically, as well as physically, challenging environment. As a priority, he got himself the support of a best friend and sidekick, Gerald Doorly. Already a veteran of many street fights, he worked on his fitness, developing a muscular physique and a skill in wrestling. He could certainly look after himself, in street parlance. A favourite party trick was to lift someone up by the seat of their pants with his teeth. He possessed a relentless vitality that was sometimes tiresome to his companions.

As we know, Clements Markham took an interest in the *Worcester* boys, and Evans recalls listening to him giving a lecture on Antarctic exploration. Together with watching the *Windward* sail by on her return from Franz Josef Land (with

Albert Armitage on board, coincidentally), it touched on his love of adventure and provided a focus for his dreams. At the time, it was still possible for a few exceptional *Worcester* boys to try for the Royal Navy, so he worked hard and tried again, and this time was accepted for a Royal Navy cadetship. This confirms that when Evans was determined, he could deliver.

Whereas Scott and Markham are always ultimately found worthy of admiration by most biographers, Evans tends to be a peripheral figure. Crane credits Evans with having had the qualities that Scott and the expedition particularly needed, but he is not specific about what those qualities were. Conversely, he is very specific about what he sees as Evans' shortcomings. For example, he makes Evans carry the can for the painful issue around Skelton's rejection for the *Terra Nova* because [3]

> There was another and harder side to Evans, however, and Scott had his first unwelcome sight of it when his new second-in-command protested against Skelton's presence on the expedition ... If the only puzzle in all this is Evans's motives – the cavil over rank will not wash – it can have been small consolation to Skelton that Scott got all he deserved when he backed Evans.

What those deserved things might have been emerges through an ongoing drip-feed of criticisms and concomitant downplaying of Evans' strengths, especially those that involved facing a problem and dealing with it effectively. Socially relaxed and confident, Teddy Evans actually enjoyed his job and relished a challenge. He didn't need the rules to shore up his leadership. He led from the front, and wasn't afraid to get stuck in.

Scott and Evans were never really close. They hadn't spent very much time together, even back in London, where Evans had been working on the ship and Scott had been busy everywhere but. And then Teddy had taken the ship to South Africa while Scott and Kathleen had travelled there on a liner, together with Oriana Wilson and Hilda Evans, Teddy's wife. Kathleen, being a 'bad sailor', had probably spent much of the passage in her cabin, attended to by her husband. Even so, there were times when they had perforce to socialise, and it must have been clear from the start that Kathleen and Hilda were especially ill suited. Hilda may have been provincial by Kathleen's standards, but in photos she looks self-possessed and intelligent.

There are hints of trouble to come in the photo taken on the eve of departure from Cardiff. Scott and Kathleen, and Evans and Hilda are pictured together with the Mayor and Mayoress of Cardiff. It should have been a happy occasion, but they all look very glum. Kathleen in particular looks dissatisfied, and averts her face from the camera, while Scott looks tired and oppressed. The Mayor and his wife look stony-faced. Evans looks like he is trying to make the best of it, and Hilda looks composed and neutral, facing the camera. Teddy was popular in Cardiff. It looks like Kathleen was annoyed at all that admiration and praise for Teddy, which she would have felt belonged to herself and her husband. Narcissists cannot bear for someone else to be the centre of attention, and the body language in that photo suggests that it was Kathleen who turned what should have been a happy occasion into a trial of endurance. She was also no doubt irked by the fact that Evans was going to sail the ship out of Cardiff, which almost made him look like the leader of the expedition. And then there was Hilda.

Scott's party had arrived in Cape Town several weeks before the *Terra Nova*. Scott and Kathleen had gone up country fundraising by themselves. The ship was overdue, and Kathleen's 'poor Con' was very dejected, and having 'horrid' nightmares. She wrote that he imagined all the things that might have happened and even wondered whether another ship could be equipped in time. [4] Assuming the worst, it appears, his prime concern was how he might still cobble something together to take him to the South Pole.

When the ship did eventually arrive and they were all back in Cape Town, it must have soon been clear to both Scott and Kathleen that Evans had been a very popular commanding officer. Bowers mentions Teddy's 'unbounded popularity' and, according to Oates – although he would be sorry for the man who hesitated to obey an order from him – Evans led the ragging in the rowdiest mess he'd ever been in: [5]

> We shout and yell at meals just as we like and have a game called
> Furl Top-gallant Sails which consists in tearing off each others'
> shirts.

Debenham tells us that Evans would come down the companionway into the wardroom shouting 'Hello girls, what's doing?', and on seeing 'Farmer Hayseed' (Oates) still standing up, shout 'down with him', and get involved in the group scrap. Interestingly, according to Debenham, the reason why wrestling sessions were a frequent event on the expedition was not just because of Teddy. Debenham claims it was the normally circumspect Wilson who turned out to be one of the prime aficionados and instigators. The practice endured throughout the expedition.

Bowers was probably not wrong when he saw the hand of 'Mrs S' in Scott's decision to join the ship for the journey from Cape Town to Melbourne. It wasn't a popular decision, and to Evans it felt like a slight. The original plan had been that he should sail the ship all the way to New Zealand; so to him, it felt like a more-or-less peremptory dismissal, which sounds like Kathleen. Bowers thought that Kathleen was jealous of Hilda and Teddy, and had wanted to put Teddy in his place and, through him, Hilda. Even the comparatively naive Bowers thought that the usually so-independent Kathleen was jealous of Hilda Evans. No doubt Kathleen would have snorted her derision, but he was probably right. Bowers thought Hilda was marvellous: everything a man could desire in a woman. If Hilda was also generally admired, it would have severely riled Kathleen, who would have wanted – and was accustomed to receiving – all the male admiration for herself, including that of the physically unprepossessing Birdie.

In any case, Kathleen must have felt that it was time Scott reasserted his authority and, in reality, it was high time Scott got better acquainted with the members of his expedition. Of the 24 who wound up in the hut with him, he only knew Wilson, Teddy and Taff Evans, Lashly and Crean at all well. There was also a body of sailors whom he hardly knew at all. It was a big crowd: there were 59 in the combined shore and ship's parties. Scott may well have girded his loins to take command of an officers' mess that included Commander Harry Pennell RN, Lieutenant Henry de P Rennick RN, Lieutenant Victor Campbell RN (the 'wicked mate') – as well as, of course, Teddy Evans, with whom he would inevitably be compared. They had already 'shaken down' together and Scott must have felt like an outsider on his own expedition.

Meanwhile, Wilson had agreed to accompany the wives for the passage from Cape Town to Hobart on the liner *Corinthic*, and from there to Melbourne, where they all waited for the *Terra Nova* to arrive. Famously, when she did arrive, a seemingly puzzling but nevertheless disquieting telegram was waiting for Scott from Amundsen:

Beg leave to inform you *Fram* proceeding Antarctic. Amundsen.

The full meaning of it wasn't to hit Scott until months later, when Campbell returned to Cape Evans after having seen Amundsen's outfit in the Bay of Whales. It is perhaps fortunate that Scott didn't know earlier how many dogs Amundsen had on board. Alarm bells would have started ringing a lot sooner. It would still have been too late: Scott was committed to his tractors, ponies, and men; and it was now – and always had been – too late to do anything about it.

When the *Terra Nova* arrived in Melbourne, with their 'beautiful husbands' on board, Kathleen famously (or notoriously) insisted on going out to the ship and boarding her in the dark, with a heavy sea running. Kathleen: [6]

> ... Bill was furious with me & protested, the women were cold & hungry. It was very dark & very wet & humours were questionable; but I knew my man would expect me & in spite of a very difficult opposition I persisted – the little motor launch pitched and heaved horribly but I was far too excited to be sea-sick & it didn't occur to me to be frightened. Bill taunted me through the journey making me feel that the elements & everything else was all my fault, but I wouldn't have him turn back ... At last we arrived at the ship, & as we came along the weather side our little launch got in a bad swell

& the ladies thought it was capsizing, & wanted to return without going to the ship, but I had heard my good man's voice & was sure there was no danger so insisted, getting momentarily more unpopular. Bill said it would be very dangerous to go alongside in this swell but the launch man thought it all right, so after much toing and froing we at last got close to the beautiful Terra Nova with our beautiful husbands on board. The relief of getting back to some folk who understood one was more than can be written about. The others stayed in the launch but I went on board & Mr's Campbell and Rennick were so nice & I went down to the wardroom so snug it looked, filled with beaming brown faces & pipes – A cheery scene after the hours of coldness & churlishness. So I went to Con's & Teddy's cabin for they had all but finished changing to come ashore with us & I changed my drenched stockings with a pair of Con's socks, & so ashore – a very happy meeting.

It had only been a few weeks since she last saw her husband, and he was about to come ashore anyway, so why the mad rush in the face of so much opposition and good sense? As indifferent as she generally was to other people's wishes or even safety in this case, and as much as she might have been desperate to get away from Hilda, the impulse to fly to Scott in that manner suggests an unusually strong emotional motivation. The over-the-top drama of her insistence on clambering on board a ship in the dark, in a rough sea, for no good reason, may have been something to do with a dalliance she had conducted on board the *Corinthic*.

On the way over from South Africa to Australia she had flirted with a 'young South African', to the point where a little while later he actually took the liberty of sending her an amorous letter. An amorous letter to a married woman – the wife of the great explorer no less – must surely have been unthinkable, unless she had given him cause. Hilda must have been aware how much time Kathleen had spent on the *Corinthic* with her young South African, and aware of the general tenor of her demeanour with him. Wilson was preoccupied with his ornithological studies, and Oriana was always by his side, leaving Hilda at something of a loose end. It would have done nothing for her feelings towards Kathleen to be left alone on account of a young man.

Wilson says nothing about Kathleen's behaviour during the 'crank little motor launch' affair; although he describes the event in detail, leaving no doubt about how risky it had been. Nevertheless, volumes can be read in his final statement that, in future, [7]

> ... I hope it will never fall to my lot to have more than one wife at a time to look after, at any rate in a motor launch, in a running sea at night time.

Kathleen later provided a counterpart to this statement when she said: [8]

> If ever Con has another expedition, the wives must be chosen more
> carefully than the men – better still, have none.

The difference was that Wilson was talking about Kathleen, and Kathleen was talking about Hilda. Oriana must have tried to remain neutral, but there was no particular love lost between her husband and Kathleen. Her charm did not work on Wilson. She considered him a prig, and she probably resented his influence over Scott.

Kathleen was dismissive and patronising – borderline contemptuous – about Evans, and especially Hilda. What she wrote and how she behaved towards Hilda went beyond the boundaries of civilised behaviour. She was unpopular generally, due to her narcissistic disregard for other people's opinions and feelings, and her own convictions about her superior good sense. According to Henry Bowers: [9]

> Nobody likes her in the expedition & the painful silence when she
> arrives is the only jarring note in the whole thing. There is no secret
> that she runs us all now & what she says is done – through the
> Owner.

The thing that bothered Bowers most was the fact that it was no secret. He thought it was a 'crime' that it was generally perceived that Kathleen was in control. It suggests that he felt defensive against Kathleen on Scott's behalf. There is no doubt that Kathleen was an outspoken, controlling woman – but it takes two to tango, and Scott must have been in the habit of deferring to her opinions and suggestions, otherwise their relationship would not have worked. It seems, however, that it was more Kathleen's decisive influence that was disapproved of, rather than any lack of conviction it implied with regard to her husband.

As well as being provincial in Kathleen's eyes, Hilda did not have the requisite demureness appropriate to such a person. Hilda and Kathleen couldn't stand each other. On the eve of the expedition's departure from New Zealand, things got so bad that they had a fight, described by Oates in his frequently quoted simile as [10]

> ... there was more blood and hair flying about the hotel than you
> would see in a Chicago slaughter house in a month ...

It sounds like it might actually have been physical. Either way, it must have been vicious enough, and very upsetting for everyone involved – so much so that it threatened the whole expedition. According to Bowers, Teddy Evans was on the point of resigning. He maintains that Evans was always loyal and never had a bad word to say about Scott; but that that day, he had never seen a man so determined to throw up all his hopes and leave the expedition. Bowers wrote home: [11]

> May it never be known how nearly the "Terra Nova" came to not
> sailing at the last few hours.

The trouble with narcissists is that they make themselves very unpopular. As much as one ought to feel compassion and understanding, they make it impossible. Even a cursory look at the internet reveals a torrent of advice for people caught up with narcissists and how to survive them. In any case, any kind of compassion would have positively infuriated Kathleen, and indeed it is hard to feel it for her. It's just as well that narcissists don't care. They leave in their wake a trail of angry and hurt people, while they sail on regardless, wasting no time in finding replacements for the ones left behind.

It is no wonder that things reached breaking point between Hilda and Kathleen. It can't have helped that Hilda had been witness to Kathleen's flirtation with 'Mr Hull', the young South African, and that her wishes had been overridden by Kathleen's refusal to turn back from the mad and dangerous dash to the ship in Melbourne, which she would have been justified in considering hypocritical as well as selfish. Some vestige of good sense must have prevailed, however, as, in spite of the ongoing hatred between them, Hilda and Kathleen joined the others in going to see peacemaker Wilson. Bowers: [12]

> With hearts like lead we all went like children to that Man among men, the quiet unselfish & retiring Dr Wilson. 'Our Bill' was the turning point & nobly he did his duty. Things were undecided when with hearts far from gay we went to dance on our last night. A Mrs Edmund had got this up for us ... I was very half-hearted about filling a programme at all considering my already formed determination – However Mrs Wilson came over & simply said 'All's well' & without a word made for her husband & shook him so violently by the hand that our hostess must have thought us funny.

Perhaps Ory's and Ted's relationship really was platonic. We will never know, and he might rightly say it was none of anyone's business. Nevertheless, a sense of the limits to his openness can be gleaned from the fact that in his published diary there is no mention whatsoever of discord between Evans, Kathleen, Hilda, nor anyone – and no mention of any role Bowers tells us he played in sorting out the row. Only the gnomic [13]

> ... I had to go off at once with Nelson to Port Chalmers where the ship was lying. Ory knows, and knew then, why.

Kathleen's view of events is: [14]

> ... on the wharf we met the Evanses both in a tearful condition. Apparently she had been working him up to insurrection, & a volley of childish complaints was let fly. Such as that Con had cut his wife's dance! & many others too puerile to recount, & that therefore he must retire.

Considering Kathleen's habitual arrogance, it is highly unlikely that Hilda's grievances were as 'puerile' as she asserts. The ostensible reasons may have been unimportant, but the underlying antipathy and lack of respect had been festering for months, and was entirely mutual. The following quote from Kathleen leaves us in no doubt about the contempt she felt for Hilda and Teddy, and the patronising attitude she had in regard to both: [15]

> There is not a vestige of doubt that Mrs Evans is the root of most such troubles, poor little ignorant one. Once away from her the poor little man was soon brought to order.

A tragic footnote to the saga is that Hilda was to die suddenly from peritonitis on the way back to England from Antarctica with Teddy. It was in her memory that Teddy added 'Russell', Hilda's maiden name, to his forenames.

Kathleen's last words on the matter, still blaming everyone but herself, came after they had arrived at the ship for the last time, finding Evans [16]

> ... quite recovered – told me a string of lies or hot air & I believe as he told lies he believed them ... he's a rum little beggar, but there's something very attractive about [him].

She made light of her extra-marital flirtations to Scott, of course, but the sheer frequency of them, and the strength of feeling she evoked, are evidence of her constant narcissistic need for attention and admiration. She just couldn't, and wouldn't, leave it alone. There are arguably nothing but societal norms to say that her behaviour was unnatural or perverse. Sex is one of our prime motivators, and flirting is a lot of fun. Nevertheless, most women in love, as Kathleen says she was with Scott, aren't particularly susceptible to passing fancies and, if they do have them, tend to inhibit the impulse to flirt out of respect for their husbands. As for doing it in public, and then running off alone with the person in question into the bush for nearly a week, these days it would invite speculations as to the state of her marriage – especially if the husband in question was in the public eye. Today it would not be enough to say she was 'pagan', or 'bohemian', or an 'artist'.

'Mr Hull' had written Kathleen a clearly intensely personal letter which was received in Lyttelton in the days leading up to departure. Scott had walked in with it in the middle of a party, obviously having read it. To many of us it may seem odd that he had opened her mail and read it, but an anecdote in EJ Howard's memoir suggests a culture of opening other people's mail in Kathleen's world.

Elizabeth Howard (first wife of Kathleen and Scott's son Peter) was staying with Kathleen at the time. She tells us: [17]

> ... I came in to breakfast late; everyone else had had theirs. Pete was away at the time, and on my plate was a letter from him. It was addressed to me and it had been opened – quite carelessly, no

steaming of the gum from the envelope, but torn, and I knew at once that K had opened it and presumably had read the contents. The envelope was addressed to me; it was *my* letter.

For most people it would be an unthinkable violation of someone's privacy to do such a thing. As Elizabeth says, Kathleen didn't even bother to hide what she had done. The very blatancy of it is evidence of her overriding sense of entitlement and lack of respect for other people and generally accepted boundaries. She is even known to have been in the habit of peeking into Peter and Jane's bedroom at night. This, and her general possessiveness around 'Pete', suggests that she felt that he belonged to her, first and foremost. He seems to have been a willing participant.

It was appalling behaviour, as was the way she nullified any idea Elizabeth night have had about Peter having married her for love, and then actually threatening her with physical violence. According to Elizabeth, they had gone for a walk together in the woods at Fritton: [18]

> She was talking about Peter, and then she suddenly said, 'I suppose you've realized by now that Pete only married you to have a son'. I said, no, I hadn't, but my heart began to pound. She looked me straight in the eye and then said, 'If you ever make Pete unhappy I shall want to stab you. I should enjoy doing it.'

Later, when Elizabeth confronted Peter with the business about the letter, he took his mother's side, and told her that she always opened his letters and that he didn't mind. If Kathleen had no compunction about opening her family's mail, presumably she opened letters addressed to her husband; and he, taking his cue from her, opened letters addressed to her. It would explain why he opened Mr Hull's letter to her, which 'certainly did read stupidly', and Con 'didn't like it', she wrote, but she shrugged it off and went on dancing: [19]

> Con took my word. If he had not I don't know what might happen as it is I don't think I shall ever lie to Con in all my life.

Not counting lying by omission, presumably.

After the *Terra Nova* had finally left for Antarctica and Kathleen had, for what was to be the last time, 'watched his face radiating tenderness as the space between us widened', she was soon thinking about other things. 'Poor little Kathleen' crossed the Tasman Sea to Sydney, and was staying at Admiralty House while she waited for a liner to take her home. She was there as a guest of the organisation that employed her husband. Not that that carried any obligations as far as she was concerned. She couldn't wait to get away which, although perhaps understandable, was an urge most people in her position would have felt bound to resist. In any case, if she had merely wanted to visit the Blue Mountains, then presumably her hosts would have done their best to organise it. It wouldn't have had the same attractions for her.

If there was one thing Kathleen loved, it was going off vagabonding, invariably with a man, or men. The mackintosh sheet makes its first appearance in 1904, in connection with a certain 'Rex'; it must have been well worn by now. She wrote: [20]

> At night, after my kind hostess had left me, I wrapped myself in a rug and slept on the zinc of the balcony, and lay hour after hour under the stars, watching the lights of the ships in the harbour and taking the vagrant decision that I could not remain there and behave nicely and socially for a week. I must off and away some wild whither. The bush! How could one go to the bush? Very furtively I made my plan. I had better have an escort.
>
> On the ship coming out there had been a young South African, intelligent and adventurous, who could be trusted, without a doubt, to fall in with whatever plan I suggested. Fearful of disturbing the kindly circle at Admiralty House, with speed and stealth we packed a sack with a blanket, mackintosh sheet, and food for a few days, left a long letter for my hostess, and fled into the Blue Mountains.

This was the young South African Mr Hull, he of the 'stupid' letter. She must have kept in touch with him to know where to find him; that he was in Sydney at all may have been coincidence, but it was certainly convenient. They spent their time in the Blue Mountains 'out in the sun making love to wallabies', getting 'terribly' lost, and waking up to the sounds of the forest at dawn. She wrote 'It's the first time I had been anything approaching happy since Con left.' She had waved him goodbye only a few weeks before. She wrote: [21]

> Con said "Do anything you like but don't get talked about." I shall not be talked about this time anyhow.

This time? Sounds like she was no stranger to the 'blasphemies of convention', as she put it on a similar occasion. If she made sure she wouldn't get talked about she must have told a pack of lies about where she was going, and with whom. Apart from anything else, she wouldn't have had to leave stealthily otherwise. That letter would be historical gold if it ever came to light.

But it must have seemed strange, if not rude, to her hosts that Kathleen had disappeared so suddenly – however convincing the letter may have been. Presumably she returned as stealthily as she had left, and her hosts will have been confronted with her presence as peremptorily as they had her absence. Her hostess would have felt honour-bound to take her at her word. To do otherwise would be tantamount to calling her a liar. In any case, Kathleen knew exactly how to bury that sort of thing in a flurry of words and bravado. Down in the kitchen, however, they might have had a pretty good idea where all that bread and cheese had gone.

Part of Kathleen's appeal to a man like Scott was her blithe inability to find fault in herself. She extended that over him, and he took heart from her confidence; as far as she was concerned, she was always right, and justified. She reassured him and bolstered his confidence in a motherly way. He was her 'Lambie', and mustn't be upset at any little pinpricks – like Amundsen's plans, for example.

Narcissists are often highly successful, socially dominant and charismatic. They do not seek treatment because they fail to see that there is anything wrong with the way they are. They tend to have strong sex appeal and sexual appetites, and they put others down to bolster self-worth. They are unable to empathise, they are insensitive, seek praise, and are always right. Mental sadism, grandiosity, paranoia, and anti-social behaviour are common. At the same time they are often high-functioning, intelligent, charming, soft-spoken, seemingly emotional, gracious, kind, well-mannered, and able to form relationships. But they falsely accuse, lie, smear, dramatise, cheat, manipulate, and behave as though anything bad is always someone else's fault. Seeing nothing wrong in their actions, they justify them and bask in a sense of egocentric entitlement. Far from feeling remorse or guilt, they consider themselves the injured party. They are also deeply in denial of their true feelings and emotions, and will defend their artificially constructed persona to the end. [22]

Kathleen was dismissive of, and hostile to, criticism. She had no regard for, and did not concern herself with, other people's feelings. Scott admired her, and was pulled along in the slipstream of what he saw as her bold attitude to life. He actually allowed himself to be mentored by her. Some of what even Crane admits was a diminution of Scott's likeability since the *Discovery* days are likely to have been due to her influence. She did have the occasional bout of shyness, but she writes about these in a wheedling, narcissistic way. In a court of law she would be deemed responsible for her actions, even if she was in denial about the more heartless and compulsive aspects of her behaviour. The hapless Hull seems to have been efficiently dispensed with on their return from the bush, as nothing further is heard of him. Quite soon afterwards, she was in any case already preoccupied with another man.

Steaming home on a liner, journeying home, in her words 'as countless sad wives have journeyed before', her sadness was soon dispelled by the acquaintance of a Mr Wesche. Before they'd even reached Ceylon (Sri Lanka), she had inflamed his desires, evidently. Strolling around the lake at Kandy, she tells us she had to explain to him [23]

> ... very carefully and finally how very distasteful it is to me to have
> him make love to me. He was very nice about it and there should be
> no further difficulty.

She seems never to have doubted that her readers would simply assume that Mr Wesche conceived an infatuation with her spontaneously, and that she was nothing but a victim of her own devastating attractiveness. *Quel ennui!* The story nevertheless found its way into her diary. Not content with having her endless flirtations in the flesh, she also wrote about them, presumably so that posterity might also have an opportunity to know how desirable she had been, and how many men had thrown themselves at her feet.

References

1 Admiral Lord Mountevans. *Adventurous Life*, p. 7

2 *op. cit*, p. 128

3 David Crane. *Scott of the Antarctic*, pp. 403–4

4 Reginald Pound. *Scott of the Antarctic*, p. 194

5 Elspeth Huxley. *Scott of the Antarctic*, p. 195

6 David Crane. *op. cit*, p. 422

7 Edward Wilson. *Diary of the 'Terra Nova' Expedition*, p. 51

8 Reginald Pound. *op. cit*, p. 209

9 David Crane. *op. cit*, pp. 435–6

10 *op. cit*, p. 437

11 *op. cit*, p. 438

12 *ibid.*

13 Edward Wilson. *op. cit*, p.62

14 David Crane. *op. cit*, p. 436

15 *ibid.*

16 *op. cit*, p. 439

17 Elizabeth Jane Howard. *Slipstream*, p. 140

18 *ibid.*

19 David Crane. *op. cit*, p. 431

20 Lady Kennet. *Self-portrait of an Artist*, p. 90

21 Louisa Young. *A Great Task of Happiness*, p. 119

22 Sam Vaknin. *Malignant Self-love*

23 Louisa Young. *ibid.*

PART 3

1910 TO 1912

THE *TERRA NOVA* TO THE DEATH-TENT AND BEYOND

21

DEPARTURE, AND THE NEAR-SHIPWRECK
OF THE *TERRA NOVA*

The *Terra Nova* set sail at last from Port Chalmers, New Zealand, on Tuesday 29 November 1910. It was a disaster waiting to happen. Not only was the ship grossly overloaded, there was an undetected, potentially fatal, danger lurking below in the bilges. Teddy Evans cheerfully records that back in London they had taken on board a quantity of Crown Preserve Patent Fuel [1]

> ... which stowed beautifully as a flooring to the lower hold, and all our provision cases were thus kept well up out of the bilge water which was bound to scend to and fro if we made any quantity of water, as old wooden ships usually do.

According to the National Museum of Wales, Crown Preserve Patent Fuel was made by mixing and heating waste small coal with pitch, and ramming the mixture into moulds. This means that Teddy's lovely floor was made from small pieces of coal and coal-dust bound together with tar. The ship did make a lot of water, especially in rough weather. Blocks rub together and create a lot more debris than ordinary randomly shaped coal. This means that the Crown Preserve Patent Fuel blocks would have been abrading at the maximum at the same time as the water washed through and rose among them, thus creating the perfect conditions for quantities of tarry coal-dust to wash into the bilges. Unsurprisingly, the carpenter had already reported trouble with the pumps all the way from England.

Cherry informs us that prior to arrival in Australia, the patent fuel blocks were shifted farther aft and stacked against the boiler-room bulkhead, nearer the intakes to the pumps – the worst possible place for it. The floors in the hold were then swept, prior to the final fit-out. [2] According to Evans, the bilges were 'of course' washed out as part of the general overhaul in Lyttelton. If they had started off with clean bilges, it seems extraordinary that quite so much of the sludge formed in such a short time, as it had only been two days since they left Lyttelton when the pumps failed. Cherry reports that 40 gallons of oil had been spilled in rough weather. He thought this was what caused the coal-dust in the bilges to form into greasy balls. Evans blamed the build-up of sludge on the water coming down from the topsides during the storm, washing though the coal, and mixing with oil from the engines. 'Silas' Wright thought that barrels of whale oil had leaked into the bilges. One way or another, oil mixed with coal-dust allegedly made a habit of leaking into the bilges. Everyone had their theory as to exactly how and why the problem came about – but the most likely cause, the composition and shape of the patent fuel, seemed not to occur to anyone.

The *Terra Nova* was a sail-and-steam whaling ship, launched in 1884. This means that by 1910 she had seen 26 years of service, much of the time working as a sealer in Arctic waters. She must have always had coal in her holds, while there must have been ample opportunity over the years for seal oil, or engine oil for that matter, to seep into the bilges. Why then did the combination of coal and oil give trouble now, when those pumps had presumably been working OK in the past? If they hadn't, something would have been done about it by now; they wouldn't have gone 26 years with pumps that blocked after just a few days at sea. They wouldn't have been fit for purpose. The answer is that it wasn't the ordinary coal, or the whale oil, or even the engine oil. It was the Crown Preserve Patent Fuel: the 'small coal' held together with pitch; one of the stickiest, claggiest substances known to man.

The planks in the lower hold are unlikely to have been caulked. A confused and rising sea, which was reported, added a twist to the motion, exacerbating the grinding of the patent blocks against each other, increasing the shedding of tarry coal-dust through open seams in the floor. This claggy debris was being sucked into the pump inlets at an ever-increasing rate, coating the pipes within hours with a sticky build-up that got worse the harder they pumped. As the water rose among the blocks, more and more pitchy dust was being washed into the bilges. Within a very short time, the flow in the pump shafts would have been impeded by tar sticking to the sides in increasing volumes, combining with ordinary coal-dust, oil, and random debris, until the resulting mass of tarry muck blocked the inlet valves of both the steam pump and the hand pump, putting both of them out of action.

We have to assume that the ship left New Zealand with its bilges and pumps in reasonable condition. If she had actually sunk, there would have been plenty of people claiming to have predicted it – she was horribly deep in the water, and had a dangerous journey in front of her. But probably no one would have guessed the real reason, which would have been that the pumps had failed because of the Crown Preserve Patent Fuel. As it was, the story that follows is about as close as it is possible to get to what the last moments of a sinking ship look and feel like.

They did 110 miles in a light breeze on the first day out, and all seemed well. The barometer was falling, however, and the wind increased during the night. On Thursday morning Scott awoke to much motion, with the ship [3]

> ... a queer and not altogether cheerful sight under the circumstances.

By the afternoon, waves were beginning to crash against the side of the ship, sending heavy showers down on the decks. The sound of the wind in the rigging rose from a whistle to a shriek as the overloaded ship heaved and pitched ever more steeply over and into the rising seas.

Crucially, there was no engineering officer on board. In place of Skelton, Scott had taken on EG Riley, a Navy lieutenant who, although technically well qualified, made himself unpopular with Scott after just three weeks at sea, having insisted on a place at the mess table to which it was felt he was not entitled. He got on Scott's nerves, and before they reached Australia he had decided that that Riley had to go. [4] Simpson's journal, however, states that Riley had not been equal to the strain and, having been in bad health all the way out, was invalided out of the expedition on arrival in Australia. [5] Either way, he wasn't replaced, presumably because there seemed to be plenty of lieutenants on board. None, however were tasked specifically with overseeing the engine-room and associated mechanisms.

We already know that Scott was the type of captain who expected to be told what was going on rather than getting involved himself, especially regarding matters below the waterline. Apparently without taking account of the lack of oversight in the engine-room, he must have simply taken for granted that no news was good news. That's if he gave the engine-room any thought at all, amid the thousand and one other things claiming his attention as they started on their historic voyage.

It hadn't been until final loading in Lyttelton that the decks took the strain. The ship had been in dry dock; leaks had been stopped, and upper decks had been caulked. Scott had noted with some trepidation the many hundreds of tons of supplies and equipment being loaded on to the ship. His observation that she was still three inches above her load mark would not have convinced anyone, although he may have clung to the thought. The tractors had come by cargo ship to Lyttelton, where they were loaded on to the decks of the *Terra Nova*, together with the hundreds of gallons of petrol needed to run them. With the extra tonnage already on the decks, they were a strain on the planks, opening up the seams in spite of the recent caulking. Given ideal weather, they would probably get away with it. The problem was, they were heading into some of the roughest seas on earth.

So, by Thursday evening the wind had got up, and the waves had started to rake the decks ever more frequently and deeply. They may have dealt with the worst of the leaks in the hull, but now it was the decks that were leaking. The ever-increasing weight of the water, which must have been at least four feet deep at times, opened the seams even wider, letting in sheets of water almost continually. Everybody and everything got wet, while the levels in the bilges crept inexorably higher, necessitating ever more frequent pumping. The steam pump was the first to become blocked, as sludge built up in the valves below the footplates of the stoke-hold. Then the hand pump failed, producing only a dribble after hard pumping. Davies the carpenter must have had a sinking sense of *déjà vu* as he contemplated those pumps once again. They had been playing up, undoubtedly for the same reason, all the way from London to New Zealand. Under normal circumstances there was access to the inlet of the hand pump shaft through the main hatch on deck. Now, however, if they had opened that hatch they would have gone down within seconds.

As the weather inexorably worsened the ship started to be almost completely submerged at times. Green seas came in over the weather side, and still more disastrously on the leeward side, lifting whole banks of petrol cases. They gradually worked loose, becoming like battering rams slewing across the deck, a danger to anyone or anything in their path. Bowers: [6]

> ... I set to work to rescue cases of petrol which were smashed adrift. I broke away a plank or two of the lee bulwarks to give the seas some outlet as they were right over the level of the rail, and one was constantly on the verge of floating clean over the side with the cataract force of the backwash ... [The ship] sagged horribly ... Capt. Scott said to me quietly – 'I am afraid it's a bad business for us – What do you think?' I said we were by no means dead yet ... And then an awful sea swept away our lee bulwarks clean ... and I was soon diving after petrol cases. Captain Scott calmly told me that they 'did not matter' – This was our great project for getting to the Pole – the much advertised motors that 'did not matter'.

In the meantime, Lashly and Williams battled with the rising tide in the engine-room until four in the morning. They had been trying to clear the valves of the steam pump underneath the floor plates by themselves, until the water rose so high that it entailed getting under the water entirely. Wilson describes it: [7]

> Lashly ... spent hours and hours up to his neck in bilge water beneath the foot plates of the stoke-hold clearing these balls of oily coal dust ... until at last it was impossible to reach the valves ... There was now a huge wave of water in the engine-room stoke-hold, washing backwards and forwards, or rather from side to side, with a rushing roar at every roll of the ship. In this water the stokers stood and worked at the furnaces to keep the engines going – and the noise and steam and clatter of iron and rush of water down

there in the dark lamp-light and glare of occasionally opened furnace doors was fearsome.

The first thing that strikes us is how long Lashly and Williams were left on their own in the hellish stoke-hold grappling with the clogged valves. There seems to have been an awful void in the place where pro-active, purposeful leadership should have been. Perhaps if Riley, and certainly if Skelton, had been present, things might have been very different. By the time Scott made it down there the water was rushing across the floor plates in a way that gave it a 'fearful significance'. [8]

With an engineering officer on board there would have been regular reports coming up from the engine-room that would have been impossible to ignore. If Skelton and Dellbridge, the dream team from the *Discovery*, had been on board, it is tempting to think that the problem might have been diagnosed before it became a potential catastrophe. As it was, nearly everybody was busy on deck, Teddy Evans included, trying to cope with the havoc happening up there with supplies and animals, while Williams and Lashly fought a losing battle in the engine-room with what they assumed was coal-dust mixed with whale oil, diving beneath deeper and deeper water until the situation became critical, at 4 am, 12 hours after the beginning of the storm. Much valuable time was lost. Eventually they were forced to put out the fires when the water got too close to the furnaces. As nearly all the sails had already been taken in, this meant that the ship was now virtually without power. They must have had enough to keep her head into the wind, but that was about all. It was about as desperate a situation as it is possible to be in without actually going down. So what was Scott doing all this time? Good question.

According to Teddy Evans, it was he who ordered Williams to let fires out in the boiler. Evans: [9]

> It could not be otherwise. We stopped engines, and with our cases of petrol being lifted out of their lashings by the huge waves, with the ponies falling about and the dogs choking and wallowing in the water and mess, their chains entangling them and tripping up those who tried to clear them, the situation looked as black and disheartening as it well could be ... The poor ship laboured dreadfully, and after consultation with Captain Scott we commenced to cut a hole in the engine room bulkhead to get at the hand pump-well ... Meanwhile I told the afterguard off into watches, and, relieving every two hours, they set to work, formed a chain at the engine room ladder way and bailed the ship out with buckets. In this way they must have discharged between 2000 and 3000 gallons of water.

Writing about the event afterwards, Evans appears to give credit to Scott: [10]

The watch manned the hand pump, which, although choked, discharged a small stream, and for twenty-four hours this game was kept up, Scott himself working with the best of them and staying with the toughest.

Should we take this to mean that Scott worked at the hand pump? It seems plausible; in the grip of fear-induced cognitive impairment it might have been all he was capable of, but it isn't the sort of activity appropriate for the Captain. A hint to the effect that Scott was not actually in command of the ship comes from Debenham. Afterwards, in a letter to his mother he writes: [11]

> Capt. Scott is a thorough leader, tho' he has not commanded the ship, he is very humane too and has counteracted several orders of Campbell's ... The gale was a very thorough fright to us all.

Scott was the leader of the expedition and there is no doubt that he was meant to be in command of the ship. Pennell, who took over on the *Terra Nova* after Scott had been landed, is listed as the senior navigator. Teddy was second in overall command, which included the ship. Debenham's comment seems odd, sandwiched as it is between positive comments. He is clearly thinking of the gale, however, as we can tell from the context. If anything, it supports the view that Scott was, in effect, not in command of the *Terra Nova* during the crisis.

Psychological leadership in dangerous situations rests with the person who maintains presence of mind and who takes the lead in positive action. As we will see, Scott's own comments, made after the storm, imply that the initiative for cutting a hole in the bulkhead was Teddy Evans', while his own involvement was limited to giving formal assent. The bulkhead was made of steel, and a hole was cut through this with hammer and chisel: [12]

> It was a long job for Lieutenant Evans and a very small team which had to work in very close quarters.

The metallic clang of the hammering must have echoed through to the howling deck like a tocsin warning of imminent disaster. Thin strains of shanties came up intermittently from the ladders along which the scientists handed up buckets from the stoke-hold below in a desperate effort to keep pace with the ever-rising level of water. Bowers: [13]

> The water came chiefly through the deck where the tremendous strain, – not only of the deck load, but of the smashing seas, – was beyond conception ... we were dependent for our lives on each plank standing its own strain. Had one gone we would all have gone, and the great anxiety was not so much the existing water as what was going to open up if the storm continued.

The idea that deck planks might actually break seems almost incredible, but coming from Bowers we have to believe it. Scott must have spent a lot of time on deck, as he watched nearly all hands labouring for hours, mesmerised and unable to tear himself away: [14]

> ... heaving coal sacks overboard and re-lashing the petrol cases ... The seas were continually breaking over these people and now and again they would be completely submerged ... No sooner was some semblance of order restored than some exceptionally heavy wave would tear away the lashing, and the work had to be done all over again.

Bowers had felt called upon to buck up Scott – a familiar scenario – when he said 'I am afraid it's a bad business for us – What do you think?' Bowers replied that they were 'by no means dead yet'. And even he, always one of Scott's greatest champions, seems incredulous at Scott's apparent lack of concern for the petrol that was being washed overboard. Scott's lame response that they 'did not matter' is suggestive of the 'autopilot' state mentioned by Gordon in *The Rules of the Game* – a state of semi-paralysis wherein people mechanically go through the motions, unable to mentally disengage from the focus of their fear.

It is of course perfectly understandable for someone in that situation to become gripped by a paralysing dread. Immense seas ran over the ship every few minutes (in Wilson's words), at one point burying Scott up to his waist while standing on the rail of the poop. He seems to have been gripped by a sick fascination as he watched the waterlogged ship lifting agonisingly slowly out of each successive wave. Cherry reports that at a certain point during the storm [15]

> ... Bowers and Campbell were standing upon the bridge, and the ship rolled sluggishly over until the lee combings of the main hatch were under the sea. They watched anxiously, and slowly she righted herself, but 'she won't do that often,' said Bowers. As a rule if a ship gets that far over she goes down.

It is hard to imagine such terror. There were no fewer than 65 men on that ship, as well as dozens of animals. It was emergency stations everywhere, including at the wheel, where men fought to keep her head into the wind and into the walls of water. If she broached to, they would be lost.

By 10 pm on Friday the hole in the engine-room bulkhead was cut. Teddy climbed through it, followed by the smallest men in the ship: Bowers, Davies the carpenter, and Nelson. Teddy: [16]

> ... when we got into the hold there was just enough room to wriggle along to the pump-well over the coal. We tore down a couple of planks to get access to the shaft and then I went down to the bottom

to find out how matters stood. Bowers came next with an electric torch, which he shone downwards whilst I got into the water, hanging on to the bottom rungs of the ladder leading to the bilge. Sitting on the keel the water came up to my neck and, except for my head, I was under water till after midnight passing up coal balls, the cause of all the trouble ... I sent up twenty bucketfuls of this filthy stuff, which meant frequently going head under the unspeakably dirty water, but having cleared the lower ends of the suction pipe the watch manning the hand pump got the water down six inches, and it was obvious by 4 o'clock in the morning that the pump was gaining ... the seamen worked steadily at the pump until 9 a.m. and got the water right down to nine inches, so we were able to light fires again and once more raise steam.

To recap, the chronology of events was as follows: The wind starts to pick up during the night, becoming stormy at around 4 in the afternoon of Thursday 1 December 1910. Scott doesn't come down to the engine-room until 4 the next morning (Friday). Work starts on the bulkhead somewhere between 4 and 6 am, and the hole is finished between 10 and 11 that evening, Friday 2 December. This means that it must have taken around 17 hours to do. Heroic. The storm had abated somewhat by then, but if the shaft had been cleared just after midnight, they had pumped solidly for over eight hours through the night to get the water down to nine inches by 9 on the Saturday morning. It gives an idea how water-logged the ship had been.

Scott, reviewing the emergency afterwards: [17]

> The hand pump produced only a dribble, and its suction could not be got at; as the water crept higher it got in contact with the boiler and grew warmer – so hot at last that no one could work at the suctions.

Wilson says nothing in his diary about the temperature of the water, nor does anyone else. It was warm, according to the balers, but it could not have been so hot as to prevent them working at the suctions. According to Wilson, they couldn't carry on at the suctions in the engine-room because the water had become too deep. Scott continues: [18]

> Williams had to confess he was beaten and must draw fires. What was to be done? Things for the moment appeared very black.

If he thought the water was too hot, then he didn't have a grip on the facts of the situation, and if he asked himself what was to be done, he didn't know what to do. All the indications are that he was not in full control of his faculties and appeared to be just waiting for the ship to go down.

It was Evans who effectively took command. Scott: [19]

> The afterguard were organised in two parties by Evans to work
> buckets; the men were kept steadily going on the choked hand-
> pumps – this seemed all that could be done for the moment, and
> what a measure to count as the sole safeguard of the ship from
> sinking, practically an attempt to bale her out! ... Meanwhile we
> have been thinking of a way to get at the suction of the pump: a hole
> is being made in the engine-room bulkhead, the coal between this
> and the pump shaft will be removed, and a hole made in the shaft.
> With so much water coming on board, it is impossible to open the
> hatch over the shaft. We are not out of the wood, but hope dawns,
> as indeed it should for me, when I find myself so wonderfully
> served.

Certainly, if it had been up to Scott, one wonders whether they would have
survived.

Neither Evans nor Bowers mention any intention or attempt to cut a hole in
the actual shaft. Scott's attention seems still not to have been entirely focused.
Thinking it through, any hole in the shaft would have had to be below the water. It
would have been difficult, but for it to have done any good, they would have had
to make the hole under the water. It would also have meant repairing that hole for
the pump to be effective once the water level had gone below it. It was clearly the
sort of option a lucid mind would have wanted to avoid.

Again it is Bowers who, in his psychological naivety and predisposition to
interpret all his superiors' behaviour in a positive light, gives insight into Scott's
state of mind: [20]

> Captain Scott was simply splendid, he might have been at Cowes.

The point is, he wasn't at Cowes. The apparent calm was eerie and inappropriate. From Scott's own comments we can see that inwardly, he was feeling anything but the same as at Cowes. Rather, his comments and behaviour suggest his
mind was fixated on the imminent loss of the ship and all lives on board. Bowers
was no psychologist and he took Scott's behaviour at face value; but from Scott's
own comments, a more likely explanation is that he was in thrall to a mind-
numbing and semi-paralysing fear, unable to drag his attention away from the
imminent disaster, even if he might have been dimly aware that his obsessive
vigilance was useless.

What evidence is there for this claim? There are good reasons for believing
that Scott suffered from trait-state anxiety. Trait anxiety refers to an elevated
baseline level of anxiety, while state anxiety is an acute fear response. If an individual is generally inclined to be fearful, then they are also more vulnerable to

acute levels of high anxiety and panic reactions. They are primed, in a sense, and fright is more easily triggered. There is evidence to suggest that it is hereditary in many cases, which would fit well with Scott's father's reclusiveness, which was almost certainly anxiety-related. His mother was also a worrier, as is evident from Scott's frequent attempts to reassure her. There are plenty of references in his letters referring to his inner doubts about his own competence and worthiness, which show his anxious states of mind. There are some notable instances when 'ticklish' situations unnerved him to the extent where he was unable to resist the impulse to run. He tended to cope with acutely difficult situations by way of avoidance or denial strategies, and he tended to fuss and lose his head under pressure. A familiar-sounding comment comes from Royds to the effect that Scott was [21]

> ... continually on the panic, just the same as ever, expecting every-
> thing to be done at once and rows if nothing is done ...

And Oates later blamed him for the loss a pony that could have been saved if [22]

> Scott had not been fussing to the extent he was ...

Another indication that Scott had anxiety issues is the fact that he had a morbid fear of blood, amounting to a phobia. He must have been living with this phobia since well before the occasion when he fainted on the doorstep of his sister Ettie, who was giving birth at the time. This is unlikely to have been mere coincidence, as it is well attested elsewhere that Scott had a strong aversion to blood. It is likely that childbirth would have been associated with blood in his mind, which would explain the severe emotional reaction he experienced, resulting in a sudden loss of blood pressure and lack of blood to the brain, causing him to faint. It is a fairly extreme reaction. It must also be said that there isn't always a connection between a phobia and baseline anxiety. For example, Birdie Bowers had a spider phobia, but in all other respects he appears to have been pretty much fearless. Never-theless, it is unusual for someone to actually faint at the mere suggestion of blood. And you certainly wouldn't want to be on a warship in action under the command of a man who might pass out at the sight of it.

Anxiety tends to be associated with depression. Although no one knows exactly why, the vast majority of people diagnosed with depression are also diagnosed with anxiety disorder. It is well attested that Scott was markedly prone to depression. If for no other reason, it can be confidently inferred that Scott was also plagued by anxiety. His entire demeanour suggests it moreover: complicated, preoccupied, moody and self-doubting, his body-language is hunched and defens-ive, his smoking is almost constant, his sense of humour virtually non-existent. His angry outbursts are evidence of stress, which is itself fundamentally anxiety-related.

Depression tends to lead to withdrawal and apathy. Work must have been a trial of endurance for him when depressed, and he must have been grateful for any opportunity or excuse to retreat into his cabin, or cubicle, as at Cape Evans. According to Cherry, Scott cried more than any man he had ever known. It is another symptom of depression, as are irritability and impatience. And as we have seen, it interfered with his perceptions and judgements to the point where at times he could see nothing but his own imaginary suffering. He was depressed for days and even weeks at a time. He hid it under a veneer of *hauteur*, which fooled a lot of people, but it was tantamount to an altered state of consciousness, during which he probably had to force himself out of his cabin to do his job at all. That he did it at those times with bad grace and temper is well known, but the possibility that his full attention wasn't on it because of his preoccupation with his inner demons would have worried both those under, as well as above, his command.

He had a sense of himself as deprived and hard done by. Given the snobbery of the Navy and the pleasure they took in looking down their noses at each other, it is perhaps not surprising. But not every person treated that way ends up depressed. It suggests again a lack of autonomy, of agency, of a core of self-belief and self-possession. As a result, he lacked dynamism and positivity. He swung between being risk-averse to flinging caution to the winds. His basic *modus operandi* was to let others break new ground, and then to top them. The only times when he seems truly to have come into his own is in pitting himself against raw nature. When it was him against the Beardmore Glacier, for example, he was in his element. Generally, however, his leadership was not dynamic because he was self-obsessed and preoccupied with his fears, doubts and uncertainties.

Acute fear manifests in a variety of ways. We are all very familiar with the notion of the fight-or-flight response, but there are a variety of ways in which people respond to acutely threatening situations. A lot depends on the event, the level of danger, and individual differences in the underlying traits or predispositions of the person concerned. One of the fundamental differences between Scott and Teddy Evans was their response to a life-threatening situation. Evans' baseline anxiety was low. He writes that he certainly felt fear, but it is clear that his response was to mobilise appropriate action. Scott's baseline anxiety was certainly higher than that of Evans, and to that extent he was worse affected by acute danger. Although someone with high trait anxiety doesn't necessarily suffer a paralysis reaction when a crisis arises, the faint on his sister's doorstep suggests Scott's underlying potential for it in response to certain stimuli.

A 'freeze' reaction is thought to have its origins in an evolutionary strategy for playing dead when threatened by a predator. There is, however, a big difference between freezing and paralysis. Freezing is seen in animals as a defence against predators which respond to movement. It implies a retention of muscular tension and a mental alertness. Paralysis, or in an extreme case fainting, on the other hand, implies a loss of muscular tension, and a loss of cognitive function. Crucially, it isn't *playing* dead, or possum, it is to all intents and purposes *being* dead. I remain to be convinced that that is actually a good strategy for survival. There are, however, gradations in the paralysis response. Many of us have had frights in which we experienced our legs going to jelly, or felt something slipping from our hands, or struggled to control our bladder or bowels. And how many times have we heard people say they couldn't think straight – suffered level of cognitive impairment, in other words.

Whether or not Scott was weak and pigeon-chested as a child, as he was said to have been, it is eminently plausible that the 'hereditary instincts of caution' he mentions were handed down to him not only genetically, but also in the form of frequent exhortations to be careful, making him frightened of having an accident and resulting in a loss of confidence. Life as a cadet on a training ship from the age of 14 must also have held its challenges. Criticism and peer pressure would have had the effect of further sensitising him, causing raised anxiety levels in tricky situations and making him frightened of making a mistake. Anxiety causes people to avoid the triggers for that anxiety. Someone who has a panic attack on a plane will be reluctant to fly again. It will not always have been possible for Scott to avoid challenging situations, and he struggled to cope at those times. He was perfectly good at his job in a routine day-to-day context – charming, efficient and capable as far as it went, but sudden crises diminished his cognitive abilities and caused him to either flap around ineffectually, or slow down and almost shut down, according to the severity of the crisis.

Scott was heavily invested emotionally in the tractors. Not so much because he believed they would do great things, but because it would entail a loss of face to admit they were not worth the risk, and that the expense, the hype, the time and the effort had all been for nothing. He had painted himself into a corner. Leaving them sitting on the wharf at Lyttelton would have seemed like an admission of error – unthinkable after all they had been through just to get to this point with them. Scott is not known for his adaptability, nor the clarity of his vision. If he had been in denial about the risk he was taking with that overloaded ship and those strained decks, it would have been only one more instance of that dangerous habit. He was fortunate that his luck held again this time. Counting on luck may work as a short-term strategy (albeit a risky one), but the odds are against it in the long term. The problem with Scott was that he was dependent on it for success, and even survival.

For Bowers, the choice had been either to overload the ship, or suffer worse things down south. It isn't clear whether he included the motors in this assessment. Much credit has also to go to him for keeping that ship afloat, and keeping hold of some kind of order on deck. Scott's Last Expedition would not have been the same without this tough, indefatigable, loyal man. Bowers was one of the three who went down to the bilges with Evans, the other two being Davies the carpenter and Edward Nelson the biologist. It seems out of character for Nelson, generally not known for getting his hands dirty. And indeed, he wasn't the one sitting in filthy bilge water, scooping tarry muck out of the bottom of the pump shaft with his bare hands. When Teddy emerged from the depths, according to Huntford, [23]

> The men thought Evans had saved the ship, and cheered him when he came on deck.

Scott considered himself well served at the time of the storm. Indeed, one is at a loss to imagine what he would have done without men such as Evans and Birdie – not to mention the other officers, the scientists who lifted heavy buckets up the ladder for hour after hour, and a cohort of tough sailors. Any gratitude he might have felt did not stand the test of time as far as Teddy was concerned, however. In spite of having done him the honour of naming their home station after him, in a paragraph which was omitted from the published version of Scott's diaries, and which Kathleen thought Teddy should never be allowed to see, Scott revealed his private opinion of his second-in-command. His diary for 5 May 1911, well into their first winter at Cape Evans – and when the memory of the storm had evidently faded – reads: [24]

> Evans himself is a queer study – his boyish enthusiasm carries all along till one sees clearly the childish limitations of its foundation and appreciates that it is not a rock to be built upon – He is altogether a good fellow and wholly well meaning but terrible slow to learn and hence fails altogether to grasp the value of any work but his own – very desirous to help everyone he is mentally incapable of doing it – There are problems ahead here for I cannot consider him fitted for a superior position – though he is physically strong and fit for a subordinate one. It was curious to note how his value (in this respect) suddenly diminished as he stepped onshore – The ship's deck was his named? position – on the land he seems incapable of expanding beyond the limits of an astonishingly narrow experience.

All this is belied by Evans' colourful youth, the breadth of experience it gave him, and his brilliant subsequent career. It is more likely to be evidence of a deteriorating relationship between the two. In fact, the sourness of tone suggests jealousy, even if there might have been an element of truth in some of Scott's claims. They could not have been more different, but the main difference, as far as the expedition was concerned, was that Evans understood that a crucial element of leadership was 'the power to grasp a situation'. [25] Perhaps it was Scott's deficiency in that respect that prompted the pointedness of the observation.

Scott's own comments suggest he thought the ship was on the point of going down. This means that there was not only cause, but plenty of his individual history, to support my claim that Scott was in a state of mental, physical, and behavioural semi-paralysis during the storm. It would have waxed and waned, but much of the time he would have physically slowed down, while mentally he would have been in an altered state – glazed over and on autopilot.

By around eight on the Friday morning, after the ship had weathered the storm for 16 hours, Scott was back at his desk, making a start on his description of the ordeal. The wind had eased off a bit, and it must have reassured him tremendously to see and hear the concerted activity that was going on around him. He had stopped believing that the ship was going down. He hadn't had much faith in baling, but it was better than doing nothing, and in the end it may have been the margin that saved the ship. Eventually, things returned to normal, and the ragging in the wardroom resumed. 'As usual', Scott would have sighed as he quietly slipped away to his cabin and his pen.

It was in his silent communion with his diary that he revealed himself, more so than he probably realised. One of the elements that makes Scott an engaging diarist is his intimacy with his ghostly interlocutor. We feel closer to Scott than we do to Shackleton or Amundsen, for example. He is self-disclosing and vulnerable. This has always inspired an emotional following, where criticism is howled down with aggrieved righteousness, and mistakes are mostly airbrushed out of existence or justified by the difficulties of the job.

He had, from an early age, learnt to present himself in the best possible light: always well presented, affable, with an air of competence. His diary is no exception, and while apparently candid and comprehensive, there are lacunae and tweaks which suggest more than an element of calculation. Nevertheless, he can't really be blamed for spinning his diary in his own favour – many do the same, consciously or otherwise. The fact is, however, that Scott's diary was so much more than a chronicle of events and circumstance. Whereas Shackleton and Amundsen imposed themselves on the action, and wrote up events with a level of detachment, Scott was so much more subject to the vagaries of chance, and so much more personally invested in his presentation of events. Whereas others might make more-or-less perfunctory notes, serving merely as an *aide memoire* for future use, Scott was habitually at his desk. The fact that Ponting chose to photograph him in that pose suggests it depicted characteristic scene.

Whatever the pressures of time or circumstance, Scott always found time to write, and it is clear from his unhurried style that he was relaxed when he did it. For a man as busy as he allegedly was, his diaries are amazingly voluminous and detailed. Although the Last Expedition diaries were edited, they were published largely as written, unlike The *Voyage of the Discovery*, and retain much of the unvarnished vitality of the original. Like the hut, they represent a unique historical record, and will always interest admirers and critics alike. But it was more than just a historical record. Scott controlled the narrative of the expedition through his diary. Not only was his version of events the only one permitted to reach the public for many years, its dramatic *dénouement* meant that nothing else could touch it. For a long time it determined the way the expedition was perceived, while the fact that he spoke from the grave gave it a power and significance his living word could never have had. At the time, it also gave him a subtle measure of control over the behaviour of everyone on the expedition: as far as the community in the hut was concerned, all knew that they might be written about, and that one's words and deeds might, therefore, be revealed to the world one day. It is bound to have conditioned people's behaviour.

The diary was also a therapeutic tool. In the absence of a taste for alcohol, it gave him an emotional outlet and a chance to express his inner bitch. It was not unusual in the Navy for men to turn to drink. It must be the only institution where liberal rations of alcohol were served out on a daily basis – not least in order to take the edge off the rigours and dangers of the job, and not to mention the rotten food. Scott was never a drinker. One commentator claims that on one occasion he drank quite as much as was compatible with his dignity. It suggests he didn't hold his drink very well and he may not have trusted himself to overimbibe. Writing is therapeutic. It engages the mind on many levels through memory, attention, cognition and emotion. It shifts the focus away from the demons and it probably helped Scott more than he knew.

There is a quintessential Englishness and a reassuringly conventional set of values inherent in Scott's writing. He represents what many people feel is the best of British pluck, culture and society – the chivalric values of amateur sportsmanship and the superior value of playing the game, rather than playing to win. The thing is, however, that Scott did want to win. Badly.

Meanwhile, no sooner had order been restored after the storm and people's belongings begun to be dried out, when they hit the pack at a high northern latitude. It was a trial of endurance for Scott as it meant delays and inroads into precious fuel. It took three weeks to get through it. According to Wilfrid Bruce, writing to Kathleen, the weeks in the pack-ice worried Scott a lot: [26]

> He talked very little to anybody.

The general atmosphere on board seems to have been good, however. The stillness of the pack was a welcome relief for everyone. In spite of his impatience, Scott couldn't help but marvel at the fabulous scenery, and was moved to paint a vivid word picture: [27]

> The sky has been wonderful, with every form of cloud in every
> condition of light and shade; the sun has continually appeared

through breaks in the cloudy heavens from time to time, brilliantly illuminating some field of pack, some steep-walled berg, or some patch of bluest sea. So sunlight and shadow have chased each other across our scene ... The sun just dipped below the southern horizon. The scene was incomparable. The northern sky was gloriously rosy and reflected in the calm sea between the ice, which varied from burnished copper to salmon pink; bergs and pack to the north had a pale greenish hue with deep purple shadows, the sky shaded to saffron and pale green. We gazed long at these beautiful effects.

References

1   Admiral Edward Evans. *South With Scott*, p. 22

2   Apsley Cherry-Garrard. *The Worst Journey in the World*, p. 33

3   Robert Falcon Scott. *Journals*, p. 13

4   Reginald Pound. *Scott of the Antarctic*, p. 199

5   Colin Bull and Pat Wright (eds.). *Silas*, p. 27

6   Apsley Cherry-Garrard. *op. cit.*, pp. 52–3

7   Edward Wilson. *Diary of the 'Terra Nova' Expedition*, p. 66

8   Robert Falcon Scott. *op. cit*, p. 17

9   Admiral Edward Evans. *op. cit.*, pp. 48–9

10   *ibid.*

11   June Debenham Back (ed.). *The Quiet Land*, pp. 41–2

12   Colin Bull and Pat Wright (eds.). *op. cit.*, p. 45

13   Apsley Cherry-Garrard. *op. cit.*, p. 54

14   *op. cit.*, p. 50

15   *op. cit.*, pp. 57–8

16   Admiral Edward Evans. *op. cit.*, pp. 49–50

17   Robert Falcon Scott. *op. cit.*, p. 16

18   *ibid.*

19   *op. cit.*, p. 17

20   Apsley Cherry-Garrard. *op. cit.*, p. 53

21   David Crane. *Scott of the Antarctic*, p. 291

21   Departure, and the near-shipwreck of the *Terra Nova*

22   Sue Limb and Patrick Cordingley (eds.). *Captain Oates*, p. 148

23   Roland Huntford. *Scott and Amundsen*, p. 318

24   Robert Falcon Scott. *op. cit.*, p. 463

25   Reginald Pound. *Evans of the Broke*, p. 20

26   Reginald Pound. *Scott of the Antarctic,* p. 212

27   Robert Falcon Scott. *op. cit.*, p. 24

22

CAPE EVANS AND THE DEPOT JOURNEY

Considering what they'd been through, they got to the newly named Cape Evans in good shape, having lost just two ponies, a dog, and a quantity of petrol and coal – but otherwise unscathed. The sun shone and although there was much to do, the pressure, for the moment, was off. Scott was cheery, according to Cherry.

Originally called 'the Skuary', but renamed in honour of Teddy (perhaps in tacit recognition of his role in the saving of the *Terra Nova*), Cape Evans is a little triangle of land on the west coast of Ross Island, at the foot of Mount Erebus, the southern-most visibly active volcano on earth, first seen by humans in 1841. If anywhere could be said to be inviting in this environment, this spot is about as near as it gets. A gently shelving beach is backed by hillocks and ridges, providing shelter from the whirling blizzards that circle the continent. In the Austral summer, which runs from about November to February, it can seem almost benign – especially when sunny and almost clear of ice and snow, as it was on 4 January 1911, when the Scott Expedition first set foot on land there.

When they arrived, the floe skirting the Cape was still in, and formed an ideal wharf. The distance to the shore was only about a mile and a quarter. On closer inspection, the beach, made up of 'volcanic agglomerate with olivine kenyte' as Scott informs us, showed no evidence of flooding, nor signs of incursions by ice. It was an ideal site in many ways, except for the fact that it is cut off from the Barrier when there is insufficient ice in McMurdo Sound. There is no feasible overland route. Cape Evans is about 15 miles north of Hut Point, and therefore much more likely to become ice free as the summer progresses. This process was already gathering pace, as the story of the landing will show.

But they had arrived, and that in itself must have been a massive relief. There was almost a holiday atmosphere. The sound of hammering and men's voices echoed, and where only the squawking of skuas and penguins had been heard before, dogs barked and ponies neighed. Interestingly, Scott mentions picketing the ponies in a place where they could not eat sand – indicative perhaps that he had reread Shackleton's book, this time properly. Meanwhile, they were saddled with their white ponies, most of which had been on the market because they were incorrigibly difficult or because they were old and decrepit, or all of those things. However Oates might have pictured the expedition to himself, it is unlikely he ever considered the possibility that he might have a load of difficult old crocks to deal with – not on a national expedition on which, moreover, they were expected to perform in extraordinarily arduous conditions. But he took it on anyway, and no one could have done the job better.

We will never know if Scott acknowledged to himself how wrong he had been about buying white ponies only. Generally, people seem to have kept quiet about it – publicly at least. Presumably, opinions varied depending on how positive they felt about the 'Owner' and how much they knew about his white-ponies reasoning. It can't have been a secret what Oates thought. His concern was obvious. Those ponies were crucial to Scott's plan for the expedition, which was primarily about the Pole. A matter which should have been carefully researched was instead decided upon in a rushed, almost off-hand, way – on the basis of an improperly read account and a superficially plausible notion. Scott knew the Pole Journey couldn't be done by man-hauling alone. His mind had always been made up about dogs, and he was soon to lose what little faith he may still have had in the tractors. It must have taken a considerable amount of *sang froid* on Scott's part to maintain face, considering the white-ponies-only criterion – now seen to have been whimsical, to put it mildly.

The last tractor to be unloaded from the ship broke through the ice and sank. Scott wasn't there. According to him, he had 'stupidly given permission' for it to be got out. According to Cherry, Scott had ordered the motor to be hoisted out first thing in the morning. According to Campbell, who was in charge of unloading, Scott thought that the motor could be pulled safely across because of the big bearing surface. [1] Whichever the case, after it had been put on the ice, Scott had stood discussing the matter before setting off for the hut, leaving Campbell to it. The motor duly broke through and sank to the bottom, leaving the men stranded on dangerous ice. Raymond Priestley fell through and was only able to save himself by managing to get hold of a rope, while Pennell, lying flat, hooked him under an armpit and hauled him out, almost paralysed and unable to speak from the shock. It was a very close thing. [2]

Argument has raged along the usual partisan lines about the degree of Scott's responsibility, and to what extent his decisions were justified – not only to unload the motor on to that ice, but also to leave the scene. It would be in character for Scott to have been in denial about the state of the ice, and also to act on his reflex response to run away from a 'ticklish' situation. Considering the importance of the operation, it isn't good enough to say Campbell was in charge of unloading, and that therefore Scott bears no responsibility. Describing the incident in his diary, Scott starts disarmingly enough, appearing to criticise himself for having 'stupidly' given permission – but in a subtle way this assertion is still an attempt to shift responsibility. 'Giving permission' implies that it had been someone else's idea, contrary to Cherry's and Campbell's assertions. Either way, he should have been there until the motor was out of the danger zone. What in fact he did was set off for the hut with a single man load – a job that could have been done by anyone anytime – leaving Campbell to manage the more important and difficult job, and to carry the can for a disaster that had been getting increasingly more likely.

As the other two motors had by this time already started to show signs of wear, their limitations had become sufficiently obvious to suggest it wasn't any great loss. The main lament was not so much to do with the hauling power they had lost, but that so much money and effort had been expended for nothing.

As was made painfully clear by this incident, the motors would require a level route over thick ice to reach the Barrier at all. Right now, they were not going beyond Cape Evans. The ice was already becoming honeycombed and fissured when the ship first arrived, and before everything had been landed, the *Terra Nova* had to be shunted about again and again, chasing a safe ice-road to the beach. At a certain point in the process, she ran aground. Scott [3] was disconsolate (his word) as he walked towards the edge of the Cape to watch the grounded ship, writing later:

> Visions of the ship failing to return to New Zealand and of sixty people waiting here arose in my mind with sickening pertinacity, and the only consolation I could draw from such imaginations was the determination that the southern work should go on as before – meanwhile the least ill possible seemed to be an extensive lightening of the ship with boats as the tide was evidently high when she struck – a terribly depressing prospect ... Some three or four of us watched it gloomily from the shore whilst all was bustle on board ...

There is an odd sense of disconnect between Scott's gloom and the bustle on board. It should have been encouraging, but still he imagined the worst and became – as usual – preoccupied, anxious and depressed, brightening only at the thought that he would allow nothing to stand in the way of his ambition to be first at the South Pole.

Fortunately, she was got off, and Scott writes with palpable relief and appreciation for his officers and men, echoing his feelings after the gale: [4]

For here and now I must record the splendid manner in which these men are working. I find it difficult to express my admiration for the manner in which the ship is handled and worked ...

After the main expedition had been landed, the plan was for Campbell's Eastern Party to spend what was left of the season and the following winter on or near King Edward VII Land, geologising, surveying and generally exploring the land flanking the eastern edge of the Barrier. They were equipped with a hut, sledges, stores and two ponies. Having found it impossible to land anywhere near their intended location, those ponies were returned to Cape Evans, narrowly surviving a swim from the ship to the shore and a half-bottle of brandy. Victor Campbell, Raymond Priestley, George Levick, Frank Browning, Harry Dickason and George Abbott relocated to Cape Adare, where they built their own hut, which has since blown down. Borchgrevink's old hut, which is still there, was used mainly for work.

Ridley Beach is a triangular spit of land situated on the inside of Cape Adare overlooking Robertson Bay. It is a popular breeding-place for Adelie penguins. Levick made a ground-breaking study of these penguins – noting, among other things, their indiscriminate sexual behaviour. Those particular behaviours were censored from the published version of *Antarctic Penguins: a Study of Their Social Habits*. A four-page excerpt was privately distributed – partially translated into Greek, as Levick, although a scientist, considered those behaviours too depraved to be generally read about.

At the start of the following winter they found themselves marooned at Evans Coves, on the shores of Inexpressible Island, where they survived by living in an ice-cave. It is one of the great survival stories of Polar history. The site has now been designated a Historic Site, and a wooden sign, a plaque, and seal bones remain there.

There was therefore pressure to get the ship away in time to find a wintering spot for Campbell, and to unload and help establish him. It was never really likely. Scott himself had caught glimpses of King Edward VII Land on the *Discovery* and knew how forbidding it was, and how hostile the conditions. Shackleton hadn't even been able to get near the land in the *Nimrod*. If Scott had doubted Shackleton's word on this, as he did about most things, Shackleton will have felt quietly vindicated when he heard about Campbell's abortive attempt.

Another pressing issue was the unusually warm summer – the ice was fast disappearing. A depot needed to be laid as far ahead on the Barrier as possible in anticipation of next season's Pole attempt. Scott was relaxed in the thought that enough ice would remain south of Cape Evans, and on the inside of the bays either side of the Glacier Tongue, to make a passage to the Barrier with ponies feasible.

(The Erebus Ice Tongue is a mountain outlet glacier which, rather like a pier, projects about 11 km into McMurdo Sound.)

It was just as well that he trusted that enough ice would stay in. If he had known that his confidence was misplaced he would not have been so sanguine. From recent weather maps, we can see that the ice does go out quite readily just south of Cape Evans, especially along the coast. Neither Shackleton nor Scott found it expedient to leave a boat at base camp. Gran, for one, thought they should have had a motor launch at their disposal. It would have been a great comfort to anyone finding themselves adrift on a floe – as actually did happen – and it would have made possible ongoing communications, and the ferrying of supplies between places otherwise cut off by open sea.

As the Antarctic summer progresses, the ice clears further down McMurdo Sound until early March, when the gradual process of freezing starts over again. The extent to which the ice goes out varies from year to year – sometimes enormously, as Scott knew from his *Discovery* days. In 1908, Shackleton had arrived in McMurdo Sound almost a month later in the season than Scott. Finding open water around Cape Royds, he finally built his hut there, in spite of the fact that there would be no possibility of making a depot journey that season. For Scott, therefore, there was an opportunity to gain an advantage over Shackleton if he could lay a depot before the winter closed in.

With this in mind, Scott set off with Meares and nine dogs for a short preliminary recce to Hut Point on 15 January, 11 days after arrival. Crossing Cape Evans overland to the south side, they found the ice still in in the bay but already cracked and thawed in places around the Glacier Tongue and Hut Point – Scott getting wet feet as they neared the old *Discovery* hut. It had been used by Shackleton and his men in the meantime, and it was now filled with snow because a window had not been properly closed. The following is taken from the original text and reconstructed to include out-takes from the first editions. Scott: [5]

> It is difficult to conceive the absolutely selfish frame of mind that can perpetrate a deed like this ... There was something too depressing in finding the old hut in such a desolate condition ... To camp outside amidst confused debris and to feel that all the old comfort and cheer had departed, was dreadfully heartrending. I went to bed thoroughly depressed. It seems a fundamental expression of civilised human sentiment that men who come to such places as this should leave what comfort they can to welcome those who follow ... and to feel that such a simple duty had been barbarously neglected by our immediate predecessors disgusted me horribly.

Although this passage was extensively edited in the first published versions of the diaries, Emily Shackleton was upset about what had been left in, which included what she saw as Scott's hypocrisy. As she says, Shackleton's hut at Cape Royds which, together with all the remaining supplies, had been left at the disposal of future explorers, seems to have been taken more or less for granted – in spite of the fact that it, and the supplies, were made good use of by Scott's people. She also mentions the window at the *Discovery* hut, which Shackleton had tried to mend, but that time had run out. Most of all, however she was upset about the phrase 'civilised human sentiment', and wept bitterly over it. She considered writing to Kathleen, but 'she is so hard about Ernest'. [6] Kathleen did in fact use her influence to Shackleton's detriment. But worse news about the *Discovery* hut was to follow.

Twenty days after arriving at Cape Evans, the Depot Journey proper set off on 24 January 'in a state of hurry bordering on panic', according to Cherry. During the last two days, [7]

> ... provisions had been bagged with the utmost dispatch; sledges packed; letters scribbled; clothing sorted and rough alterations to it made. Scott was busy, with Bowers's help, making such arrangements as could be suggested for a further year's stay, for which the ship was to order the necessaries. Oates was busy weighing out the pony food for the journey, sorting harness and generally managing a most unruly mob of ponies.

It looks like the poor quality of the ponies had caused Scott to lose confidence in this Pole attempt. Oates had had a chance to properly impress on him what a poor lot they were, and it must also have been Oates who advised him that Indian mules would have been better. Although a second winter had been on the cards because the Pole Party were not likely to be back in time to catch the ship, there is no indication that Scott had also planned a second shot at the Pole. Now, however, this must have been what he had in mind when he wrote a pleading letter to Major-General Sir Douglas Haig, at the British Army HQ, Simla, asking for mules. Haig (himself known to history as the type of officer who doggedly persisted in the face of mounting evidence that he was on the wrong tack), duly obliged; and eight Indian mules (together with their food requirements, presumably) were delivered in the second season, being put ashore on 6 February 1912, together with a further number of dogs and sledges.

As it is difficult to imagine what else these mules might have been wanted for, they must have been intended for a second attempt at the Pole, in case the first one failed. It constituted another hedged bet, in effect, and a tacit acknowledgement that the white ponies had been a mistake. It also suggests that he was ahead of himself (as usual) and preoccupied with the future – while not paying enough attention to and, in a sense, writing off, the present. Muddle-headedness is suggested by the fact that these mules would arrive while he was part-way through his first Pole attempt, and that they would have to be stabled and fed for the winter, prior to a second attempt the summer after. This would necessitate in all probability a third winter at Cape Evans, and a fourth journey out for the ship to get them all home after that. Only fast travel and a return from the Pole before the beginning of March – which was extremely unlikely without dogs – could give them any hope of avoiding that third winter, and a fourth journey there and back from New Zealand for the ship. Unless, that is, it was decided for the ship not to bother making that third journey out because she would have to leave before they were likely to be back. If nothing else, it demonstrates how hurried and unthought-through the mule issue had been. There would, in any case, not have been nearly enough money for it all.

Back in the present, the logistics of the depot run were complicated by the fact that sledging infrastructure for 12 men had to be taken, and enough pony fodder, dog and man food for the journey there and back. There was also a potentially long spell of waiting for the Sound to freeze over in order to get back to Cape Evans. As will be seen later, Scott chose to ignore that particular issue. Last but not least, there were the stores to be depoted. All of this, including two teams of dogs, were loaded back onto the ship to be taken as far as the Glacier Tongue, down to which there was open sea.

The ponies had to be walked over the fringe of ice that remained on the inside of the bay between the south side of Cape Evans and the Glacier Tongue. It was going to be hazardous, as everyone will have appreciated. The ice was going out fast: indeed, it went out the day after they crossed it. Scott was well aware of the dangers. On the eve of departure he writes: [8]

> One breathes a prayer that the Road holds for the few remaining hours. It goes in one place between a berg in open water and a large pool of the glacier face – it may be weak in that part, and at any moment the narrow isthmus may break away. We are doing it on a very narrow margin.

Actually, the narrow margin was for the people on the ice. Scott was safely on the ship.

Wilson and Meares scouted the way, first across the rough rock and snow of the Cape, and then over about six miles of sea ice skirting the inside of the bay towards Glacier Tongue. Wilson tells us the ice was on the point of breaking up in places, and they had to go around large thaw-pools. Eight ponies were taken, led by Oates, Atkinson, Bowers, Cherry, Keohane, Forde and Gran (Blossom, Blucher, Weary Willy, Jimmy Pigg, Nobby, Uncle Bill, Guts and Punch). There was open sea at the far end of the Glacier Tongue, which meant that in order to get to the other side they had to cross over the heavily crevassed ice of the Tongue itself. The loads, sledges, dogs, etc were offloaded from the ship not far from where the ponies were picketed when they got to the south side of the Glacier Tongue. From there, everything was relayed by pony, dog, and human teams in the direction of the Barrier over the Sound between the south side of the Glacier Tongue and Hut Point, where the ice was at that time still safe.

In passing, the *Discovery* hut was again inspected. A party was sent over to see what could be done about digging out the hard-packed snow with which it was filled. An unpleasant surprise awaited. Scott: [9]

> Everyone was disgusted with the offensive condition in which the hut had been left by its latest occupants. Boxes full of excrement were found near the provisions and filth of a similar description was thick under the veranda & even in the corners of the hut itself. It is extraordinary to think that people could have lived in such a horrible manner and with such absence of regard for those to follow – It seems evident that in no case can we inhabit the old hut.

This entire paragraph was edited out of the first published journals – and it is interesting to note that, to date, the version of Scott's *Journals* held on the Scott Polar Research Institute website is the edited version. The Oxford University paperback edition (2005, see Bibliography) is the one that contains the out-takes.

To Scott, it must have felt like Shackleton had not only comprehensively beaten his record, but had also literally defecated all over his heritage. Not intentionally of course: Shackleton didn't know that Scott, nor anyone else for that matter, would be visiting the hut – perhaps ever again. Maybe if there had been latrines it might not have been such a temptation, but Scott was always reluctant to address matters pertaining to lavatorial convenience, and so there weren't any. Shackleton was less squeamish – and considering the condition his team was in after their near-miss of the Pole, it can have been only humane to allow a modicum of comfort to prevail over delicacies of taste and propriety. It wasn't a major problem of course, and the hut was subsequently cleaned up and used as the essential resource it was. It also contained a large store of biscuits left over from the *Discovery* days so, according to Scott: [10]

> ... we need not have any anxiety about provisions if delayed in returning to Cape Evans.

There was no 'if' about it, and they would require more than just biscuits.

The depot caravan wended its way laboriously over the Barrier – the pace dictated by the slowest pony. There was tension between Scott and Oates over snow-shoes for the ponies. Only one set had been brought. Oates was no fan. Nevertheless, the one set they had were tried and found to be surprisingly effective. Falling victim to the cherry-picking fallacy, Scott instantly assumed they were a panacea and was annoyed that not more sets had been brought. On the face of it, he may have had a point: snow-shoes for horses have a long history and appear to have been used with some success in the past – but not in the harshest conditions on earth, where sinking into snow could almost be said to be the least of their problems. Later that winter they experimented with different designs, but there wasn't an equine snow-shoe in existence that could perform to the level required. When they were used on the Last Journey, Scott referred to them as 'wretched affairs' as they racked and impeded even those ponies that had been persuaded to wear them.

Snow-shoes were not the only bone of contention between Scott and Oates. On 12 February, the three weakest ponies were sent back with Teddy Evans, Forde and Keohane, less than three weeks into the journey. There were approximately 70 miles still to go before reaching the 80th parallel, where Scott hoped to establish his fateful One Ton Depot. He might have blamed Oates' negativity with regard to snow-shoes for the way the ponies floundered in the patches of deep snow – but it was their age, their loads, the cold, and probably dehydration that told most against them. As they were to find out later, Oates' grim prognostications had already started to come true: two of the three ponies that had been sent back had died soon afterwards. Two days later, one of the five that had been taken on, poor old Weary Willy, broke down and was nearly torn to shreds by the dogs. By this time Oates was convinced that the weakest of the remaining ponies should be shot and cached as food, while the rest pushed on south.

The day after Weary Willy had nearly been eaten alive by the dogs, things came to a head between Scott and Oates. They had radically opposed views. Scott: [11]

> The more I see of the matter the more certain I am that we must save all the ponies to get better value out of them next year. It would have been ridiculous to have worked some out this year as the Soldier wished. Even now I feel we went too far with the first three.

Besides, as Gran reports, he had had enough of cruelty to animals. [12]

The fact was that the weakest ponies were dying on their feet: a point Oates squarely faced, but of which Scott was in denial. Prompt action could have put at least two failing ponies out of their misery – and made the most of by feeding the dogs, and butchering and caching the rest of the meat. It may sound harsh, but that was indisputably what they should have done, and it didn't take hindsight to know it. They would probably have made it further to the 80th parallel if they had. As it was, One Ton Depot was laid about 30 miles short of it. It was the occasion of Oates' famous, prophetic remark to Scott: [13]

'Sir, I'm afraid you will come to regret not taking my advice.' 'Regret it or not,' replied Scott, 'I have taken my decision, as a Christian gentleman.'

If he did actually use those words, it constituted an implicit moral judgement on Oates, and would have made another dent in their relationship.

The options were to kill, butcher and depot the failing ponies or, as Scott would have preferred, send the first three back earlier. Even if they had, two of these would almost certainly have died anyway. Teddy, who, together with Forde and Keohane, was leading Blucher, Blossom and Jimmy Pigg, tells us that Blucher failed immediately on starting the return journey. They decided to kill him for humanity's sake, and Keohane cut his throat with a knife – a gruesome procedure. There was hardly any blood to let out. This suggests that this pony was badly dehydrated. Teddy described their eyes as being dull and lustreless, another sign of dehydration. Being off their food, as they often were, is another.

The ponies were expected to eat snow for hydration. It wouldn't have been nearly enough. They were also sweating with the work. The sweat then froze close to their skin, encasing them in ice – yet one more reason why horses are fundamentally unsuited to that hostile environment. Further, horses sweat through their skin, while dogs sweat through their tongues – proof that dogs are so much better adapted to the conditions. Hypothermia and the lack of drinking water hastened the demise of the weakest ponies, and it weakened the rest. Blossom was nursed along for another 30 miles. He was kept going in spite of the fact that he showed much distress because Teddy was worried about how angry and disappointed Scott would be at the loss. Blossom finally fell and died in his tracks. The meat seems to have been wasted, as it seems Blucher and Blossom were simply buried where they fell. In any case, the cruelty was not in killing them, it was in bringing these animals to Antarctica in the first place. In trying to better Shackleton, Scott ended up merely amplifying his mistake.

After One Ton Depot had been made, Scott took the fast train back with the dogs, together with Meares, Wilson and Cherry, alternately sitting on the sledge and running beside it. Meares had learnt how to drive dogs in an orthodox manner, sitting on the sledge, which was [14]

> ... a very different thing to the beastly dog driving we perpetrated in the *Discovery* days.

Bowers, Oates and Gran were left leading the remaining five ponies back. According to Cherry, Scott was anxious to get any news that might have been left by the ship about Campbell's proposed landing on King Edward VII Land. Accordingly, he set a course for Safety Camp, the last stop on the Barrier before Hut Point. It should have been plain sailing, as they made brilliant mileages with the dogs, but it didn't turn out that way. Instead of taking the safe route around the turbulence surrounding White Island, Scott cut the corner and almost lost a team of 13 dogs down a crevasse.

The rescue of these dogs was a collaborative effort between all four of them. The way Scott tells it subtly suggests that he and Meares worked inside the crevasse together, hauling the dogs up two by two. Teddy states that they did, so he must have thought that's how it was. He heard the story very soon afterwards, and one way or another he was left with the impression that Scott and Meares had gone down on ropes into the crevasse together. Wilson, however, who was there, mentions only Meares hanging on a rope in the crevasse pulling up those dogs that were still on the trace. Scott didn't go down until afterwards to rescue the two that had gone to sleep on a snow-bridge about 65 feet down, according to Scott, 40 according to Wilson.

Things between Scott and Meares were going in the wrong direction. Scott: [15]

> Meares is excellent to a point but a little pig headed & quite ignorant of the conditions here ... Meares is loath to run & I think rather imagined himself racing to the Pole and back on a dog sledge. This journey has opened his eyes a good deal and mine too. It is evident that I have placed too much reliance on his experience.

On reaching Safety Camp, Atkinson and Crean also came in for criticism: [16]

> Atkinson and Crean have departed, leaving no trace – not even a note. A very thoughtless proceeding.

Atkinson had been left behind at Safety Camp because of a blister that had become infected, and Crean had been assigned to look after him. They should have left a note; but they had, on their own initiative, gone back and cleared the *Discovery* hut and made it ready for habitation.

Scott, Meares, Wilson and Cherry went on to Hut Point in search of Atkinson and Crean, and news of the *Terra Nova* – but finding nobody there, reasoned that their paths must have crossed, and so they made their way back to Safety Camp. Their paths had indeed crossed; and Atkinson and Crean were waiting for them with devastating news. The ship had returned from trying, and failing, to land Campbell on King Edward VII Land, and on the way back had come across the *Fram*, moored in the Bay of Whales. All hell broke loose at the news. Scott, in his own words, found the news 'startling'. They felt trespassed upon and morally outraged. But Scott had known about Amundsen's intentions since Melbourne. The telegram had been cryptic, however, and Scott seems to have told himself that Amundsen would land on the Weddell Sea coast – a supposition for which there was precious little justification, other than that Ross Island was obviously out of bounds. The last thing he seems to have expected was that Amundsen would make his temporary home on the Barrier.

It meant that Amundsen had a straight run to the mountains, without potential delays over sea-ice or awkward dog-legs around islands. It was also about 60 miles closer to the Pole. That, and the news of all those dogs, was profoundly disconcerting. It made what had been a rather vague worry into an acute threat. Cherry: [17]

> For an hour or so we were furiously angry, and were possessed with an insane sense that we must go straight to the Bay of Whales and have it out with Amundsen and his men in some undefined fashion or other there and then.

In Cherry's original Antarctic journals, held at the SPRI and researched by Sara Wheeler, he continues: [18]

> ... on 24 February Scott leapt out of his bag and said, 'By Jove what a chance we have missed – we might have taken Amundsen and sent him back on the ship.' ... Scott said we could go and fight Amundsen. There was no law south of sixty.

Further: [19]

> Wilson calmed Scott down, arguing that there might well be no law south of sixty, but at some point they would have to go north of sixty. 'We had hours of it ...' Bill said to me, 'we had a bad time with Scott on the *Discovery:* but never anything like this.'

This is confirmed by Pound, who states that Cherry told GB Shaw that [20]

> ... in a burst of temper, Scott wanted to go to the Bay of Whales and fight Amundsen.

What Amundsen thought is best expressed in his diary entry dated 26 January 1912, the day of his return to Framheim from the Pole: [21]

> A number of people seem to be indignant over our activities down here – a breach of 'etiquette'? Are these people mad? Is the question of the Pole exclusively reserved to Scott for solution? I don't give a hang for these idiots.

Scott calmed down eventually, but he had been trotting beside a dog-sledge for the last few days and had seen what a well-managed team was capable of. If doubts had already started to creep in, it would have added a sickening twist to his discomfort. He sought refuge in denial, as usual, and from here on we hear nothing but disparagement of the dogs. He felt an ever-increasing need to justify his decision – to himself as well as to others – not to design his transport around them. He must also have needed to reassure himself, to reduce the dissonance arising from the difference between the Polar expert's preferred mode of transport and his own.

It also meant that the wisdom of his choice depended more and more on the ponies doing well. The pressure brought on a spell of fussing up and down the line for the next six days. From Safety Camp, Scott set off in a southerly direction again, taking more stores to Corner Camp – also with the intention of meeting Bowers, Oates and Gran with their five ponies. With him were Crean, Cherry, Teddy Evans, Atkinson, Forde and Keohane, still leading Jimmy Pigg, the survivor from the first three that had been sent back. Jimmy was now going back south again dragging supplies, confounding all expectations. He ended up being one of just two ponies out of the eight to survive the Depot Journey.

Getting up one morning at 3 am, Scott saw Bowers' caravan pass by on the horizon, too far away to make contact. On arrival at Corner Camp, they cached their provisions, and Scott started back to Safety Camp on skis with Cherry and Crean, leaving the others to nurse Jimmy Pigg and bring him along in short stages. On 28 February, Scott, Cherry and Crean were back at Safety Camp, and found Bowers and everybody else there (except Teddy, Atkinson, Forde and Keohane, who were still leading Jimmy Pigg back). That meant that eight men, including Scott, and the five ponies that had been marched back from One Ton Depot, were now at Safety Camp, a few miles south of Hut Point peninsula. It was cold, and already late to be out on the Barrier, especially for the ponies. The wind-chill of the blizzards they endured was particularly damaging. It was now a matter of urgency to get those ponies into shelter, which meant the hut at Hut Point. When the blankets were taken off prior to marching, their tired and emaciated state was revealed, with Weary Willy in particular in a 'pitiable condition'. Almost dead on his feet, in fact.

Even the normally forgiving Wilson sounds testy when he gives us the background to the decisions that led to what followed, which became known as the Pony Disaster. Wilson: [22]

> We had a somewhat lengthy discussion on the advisability of going there [Hut Point] by the Gap or by the other way round Cape Armitage which meant round the large thaw pool off Cape Armitage. I was all for the Gap, for I didn't believe that the sea ice would still be safe the other way without making a very big détour round the Cape Armitage thaw pool – and this point I urged – but I was overruled to the extent of being told to go round Cape Armitage way if possible, but to feel quite independent and so far as the dog teams were concerned to be guided by my own judgment. As it turned out this freedom of movement saved Meares and myself from getting into great trouble with the two dog teams. With the ponies we had nothing to do, as Captain Scott was in charge when we left the camp ...

Without having scouted the route and guessing (wrongly, as it turned out), that any route via the peninsula would be impossible for the ponies, Scott gave orders for Bowers to take the sea-ice route. This, in spite of the fact that the water holes around Cape Armitage were, in his own estimation, the most enormous he'd ever seen. Guessing –wrongly again – that the ice would be safe if they made a large-enough detour around the water holes, he confirmed Bowers' orders via Cherry and Crean. Bowers' orders were 23

> ... to push on to Hut Point over the sea-ice without delay, and to follow the dogs; previously [he] had been told to camp on the sea-ice in case of the beasts being unable to go on.

It appears that Wilson and Meares had raced off with the dogs without specific orders to lead the ponies, whereas Bowers was told 'to follow the dogs', under the impression that they were meant to pilot him.

Bowers had gone on ahead with his pony, and had halted to wait for the rest of the party, which he expected would include Scott and Oates. To his surprise, only Cherry and Crean appeared, leading three ponies and sledges. In one of the most appalling decisions of his career – evidence of a pathological level of avoidance behaviour – Scott had chosen to stay, together with Oates and Gran, with a single, dying pony (Weary Willy), instead of leading the baggage train back to Hut Point. His presence was not required at Weary's last hours. Gran and Oates were well able to manage that between them. Bowers, on the other hand, was inexperienced on sea-ice and undermanned – with four ponies between three men, and four sledges loaded with six weeks' food and oil for 12 men, as well as a lot of gear from the depot, pony food etc. 24

Let us stop there for a moment to let that last point also sink in. Bowers was taking supplies *back from the Barrier towards Hut Point.* Why hadn't those supplies been left at or near Hut Point when they passed it on the way out? It was always the obvious place to wait for the Sound to freeze over. Even though Scott had, in a fit of pique, written off the hut, those supplies should still have been left there or thereabouts. Besides, even Scott must have realised quite soon that writing off the hut was madness.

In his journal, Scott says nothing about the disagreement with Wilson about the sea-ice. He offers a few vague remarks about the ponies following in the tracks of the dogs, and for his party to start off last and get ahead of the ponies because he was anxious about the water-holes. Passing over the puzzling idea of getting ahead of the ponies (after the death of Weary Willy presumably), let us focus on what he did next.

The obvious course of action would have been for Weary to be put out of his misery there and then; and for the three men, Scott, Oates and Gran, to go in support of Bowers. We can be certain that that was Oates' view. If he had been in

Scott's position he would have considered it his absolute duty to lead the main baggage train, whatever the state of Weary, and even more so as the pony was clearly dying. The awful truth lurking behind Scott's decision must have been that he was too frightened to undertake the mission himself. Staying behind to care for Weary Willy, as one of no fewer than *three* men, can't be considered appropriate by any stretch of imagination – especially not for the man who was supposed to be leading the expedition. Even if there had been a glimmer of hope that Weary might be saved, it was perfectly within Oates' and Gran's capabilities to do this without Scott's assistance. While perfectly genuine so far as his pity for Weary was concerned, one is forced to conclude that this decision must have been motivated by anxiety – and that staying behind, surplus to requirements, merely to witness the almost-certain demise of Weary, was a pretext for avoiding the leadership of the baggage train.

Meares and Wilson hadn't gone far with the dogs when they found themselves travelling over ice that was beginning to show ominous signs of cracking. Realising the danger, they veered off towards the pass called the 'Gap', the overland route to Hut Point, considered feasible for men and dogs but not for ponies. According to Wilson, there was enough of a commotion with the dogs to make his actions unmissable by the Pony Party. He assumed he had been seen and that his actions had been understood. After having practically arrived at Hut Point, he saw Bowers' party in the distance, carrying on beyond the point where he and Meares had changed direction. From that distance Wilson couldn't see it was Bowers leading. He naturally assumed it was Scott. Wilson: [25]

> I couldn't understand how Scott could do such a thing, and it was only the next day that I found out that Scott had remained behind and had sent Bowers in charge of this pony party. Bowers having had no experience of the kind before didn't grasp the situation for some time ...

Wilson assumed that Scott was in charge of the caravan he could see in the distance heading across the ice, as of course he should have been. But it was the hapless and trusting Bowers. Bowers thought that the dogs were meant to pilot him. As we can see from Wilson's earlier comment, this is not exactly what Wilson had understood ('With the ponies we had nothing to do, as Captain Scott was in charge when we left the camp ...'). Bowers saw the dogs in the distance wheeling off to the right in a landward direction, after which they disappeared in a 'black indefinite mist'. Misinterpreting their actions, he assumed they were disobeying orders to guide him, and went ahead over the ice as ordered.

When he also then came to visibly working cracks, it was obvious, even to the inexperienced Bowers, that to go on would be madness. So they turned around and began a 'dark, gloomy and depressing march' back, stopping frequently to rest the tired and emaciated ponies, who were still dragging supplies that should have been left at Hut Point in the first place. When at last they got to what they considered safe ice, they set up camp, fed the ponies, and went to bed. Wilson had seen all this with his field-glasses, and assumed that Scott – as he still thought – was camped on safe ice.

Two and a half hours later, Bowers woke up, went outside, and saw that they were in the middle of a floating pack of broken-up ice heaving up and down with the swell, with long black tongues of water all around. There was only a dark streak of water where one of the four ponies had been. The horror of the situation can hardly be imagined. His instinctive response was to save what he could. He, Cherry and Crean packed up and harnessed the ponies in record time, and started to leap from floe to floe, together with all the sledges and supplies, in the direction of the Barrier, drifting westwards as they went. They kept their nerve despite the arrival of a lively school of orcas; and to their enormous credit, managed to work their way back towards the Barrier, together with the remaining ponies and all the loads. It took them over six hours to get close to the Barrier edge, which itself had started to break down.

It must have been the warmest year in a long time. Hints to that effect had been obvious from the lack of snow which Scott had remarked upon on arrival both at Cape Evans and Hut Point, while apparently failing to realise the implications. When Bowers came to what he thought was the edge of the Barrier, he discovered that an entire fringe had calved, leaving a broad lane 30 to 40 feet wide, filled with heaving brash-ice in which orcas were cruising with 'fiendish activity'. The new barrier edge, beyond the brash-ice, was a sheer cliff of ice up to 20 feet high.

Both Cherry and Crean volunteered, as always, to do whatever was necessary. Bowers' first priority was to communicate with Scott, the alleviation of whose anxiety seems always to have been uppermost in everybody's minds, and to get help. It was decided that Crean should go, so he set off over the floes and the bergs; while Cherry, Bowers and the remaining three ponies had to wait for what turned out to be the entire day – until 7 that evening – for help to arrive [26]

> ... knowing as we did that it only wanted a zephyr from the south to send us irretrievably out to sea.

The previous night, Wilson, feeling uneasy, had got up and gone outside and, looking out over the strait, had seen the Pony Party adrift on the floes. For him, the question was what he should do to help, as there was no one to consult with, [27]

> ... for everyone was on the floating floe as we believed, except Teddie Evans, Forde and Keohane [and Atkinson], who with one pony were on their way back from Corner Camp.

Early the next morning he and Meares set out through the Gap to try and meet up with Teddy and, seeing a tent in the distance, assumed it was him. When they got there they were astonished to find instead Scott, Oates and Gran, who had come on from Safety Camp after spending the night there and burying Weary Willy.

Earlier that morning, as Scott had approached Forage Depot, the nearest depot to the Barrier edge, he had seen what he had initially wanted to believe was a mirage. According to Gran: [28]

> We followed the horse and dog parties' tracks, and were dismayed
> to find these led to the edge of a cliff straight down into the sea.

The ice, over which he had insisted Bowers should go – and camp on if necessary – was broken up to the Barrier edge, and was drifting in pieces out to sea. Scott: '... fearful anxieties assailed my mind'. That was probably putting it mildly. It sounds more like he panicked, as he immediately set off in a fast march in the opposite direction: [29]

> We turned to follow the sea edge and suddenly discovered a
> working crack. We dashed over this and slackened pace again after
> a quarter of a mile. Then again cracks appeared ahead and we
> increased pace as much as possible, not slackening again till we
> were in line between the Safety Camp and Castle Rock.

This fast pace was in an easterly direction, *away* from what was obviously a potential disaster zone, and away from where any conceivable rescue attempt – or even an effort to ascertain what had happened to Bowers and his team – might have been possible. Of course it was entirely legitimate to consider his own safety; but a clearer head would have moved back to a safe distance from the Barrier edge and gone along it in a westerly direction – the only direction in which they had any chance of finding out what might have happened to the baggage train.

Scott had avoided the trip over the sea-ice in the first place, which suggests that his anxiety levels were already high. What he had come upon at the Barrier edge tipped him over into panic. His apparent inability to resist the impulse to run away from the scene, apparently for his life, overrode everything. It is as if he expected the whole line of Barrier on which he stood to collapse under him. Not until he got to a place where he felt safe did he stop, set up tent, and consider what to do. The first thing he did was order Gran to ski over to Safety Camp to see if he could find Teddy, ostensibly in order to warn him. At least that's what he wrote in his journal. He must also have been hoping for Teddy's support and input. It was while he was sitting with Oates disconsolately 'thinking out the situation' (not knowing what to do), when Wilson and Meares, having rushed down from Hut Point, found him. Scott had been thinking that they too might be adrift on the floes, and was in 'a dreadful state of mind', according to Wilson.

A short time after Wilson and Meares had appeared – to Scott's ineffable relief – an exhausted Crean arrived with his message from Bowers. He had given everything he had to get there in the time, and was badly affected by snow-blindness. The contrast between Crean's sense of urgency and Scott's response is striking. First, Wilson and Meares, when they arrived at Scott's tent with news of what they had seen happening on the floes, were sat down and given a hot break-fast. Wilson wrote that he saw Crean in the distance while he was eating. The discussion was then in terms of going to see if they 'could help Bowers and Cherry', with what Scott afterwards calls a 'mishap'. Then, no fewer than three men, Meares, Wilson and Gran, were ordered back to Hut Point to look after the dogs. Two would have been ample, one in an emergency, which this was. The reason given for this is that they only had three sleeping-bags between them. This was presumably because Crean had come without his. While sleeping-bags are important, the concern about them in an acute emergency situation was inap-propriate and suggests Scott's head was all over the place – especially as the desired outcome would presumably include the recovery of Crean's bag. A further result was that the three men at Hut Point had only two bags between them and had to spend a lot of their time trying to keep warm, something they might have done while helping with the rescue.

After setting off, Scott, Oates and Crean first made a detour to Safety Camp to load some provisions and oil. What was he planning, a picnic? Only then, taking an interminably long time, did they march 'carefully' around to the scene of the emer-gency, less than seven miles away. Bowers, Cherry and the ponies had waited on their floe all day, until 7 pm, according to Bowers, at imminent risk of being blown out to sea. Scott puts his time of arrival at 5.30 pm, an hour and a half sooner. Bowers wasn't likely to make a gross error like that. Not only was he a meticulous operator generally; someone who is waiting on tenterhooks tends to look at their watch every five minutes. Nor did Bowers have a motive to falsify the record. Scott, on the other hand, did.

A close analysis of events reveals the following: Crean must have set off on his rescue mission at about 10.45 am, going by Bowers' record of having discovered their predicament at 4.30, and having negotiated the floes for over six hours. Wilson and Meares arrived at Scott's tent shortly after noon. While they were eating they saw Crean in the distance, hurriedly approaching. [30] This must have been around 12.45 pm, if we take it that their meal took about three quarters of an hour to prepare and eat. If we allow another 15 minutes or so for Crean to actually reach the tent, that puts his time of arrival at around 1 pm, or soon after.

That means that Crean had covered the distance, jumping from floe to floe and having to find a place to climb up on to the Barrier – doing so with difficulty – in two hours and fifteen minutes. There is no reliable estimate of how far Scott's tent was from the disaster scene except the time it took Crean to get there. Scott, looking out a week later from Hut Point, which was at a similar latitude to the tent from which he set out, wrote that the distance was about 12 miles from where he was standing. It was a subtle attempt to justify the time it took for him to get to the scene, as Crean could not have covered anything like that distance in two hours and fifteen minutes. It was an instance of the 'stretched figures' of which he was so quick to accuse Shackleton.

Taking into account that he was having to negotiate his way among the floes, and had to spend time looking for a way on to the Barrier, it is unlikely that Crean achieved more than the average walking speed, which is 3 mph. That would indeed have been very good going under the circumstances. It means that Scott was at the most seven miles from the disaster scene. Corroboration for this can be found from Wilson's comment from the previous evening, when he had looked out from Hut Point with his field glasses and had seen Bowers' party around six miles in the distance. [31] When Crean got to Scott's tent, the first priority was evidently to give him a hot meal. There is no indication that Crean, apart from being tired and snow-blind, was suffering from acute malnutrition or frostbite. In the circumstances he would probably have expected a stick of chocolate and a hurried mug of tea, but not a fussy and time-consuming hot meal. Assuming everyone was given time to finish their meals, there could not have been any justification for hanging around until after 2 pm. In the absence of data to the contrary, we therefore estimate this to have been their approximate time of departure. This means that going by Bowers' report of Scott's arrival at 7 pm, Scott, the normally fast and hard sledger, took five hours to cover what was at the very most seven miles – well over twice the time it had taken Crean. Their sledge can't have been excessively heavy, and it was a level surface. Scott, well aware of how slowly he had gone, must have made up his own data, both with respect to his time of arrival at the disaster scene and his estimate of how far away it had been, to suggest they had gone faster than they had.

A Scott apologist might claim that for Scott to have gone out to the rescue without a full sledging kit and provisions would have constituted an unacceptable risk, and that the Barrier was in an unstable state, justifying ultra-cautious, and therefore very slow, progress. But who was more at risk: Bowers and Cherry on their floe, or Scott, well back from the edge of the Barrier? As far as sleeping-bags and provisions were concerned, it is highly unlikely that anyone would have starved or frozen to death, given the supplies and equipment they already had with them. It was Bowers' predicament that was acutely life threatening.

There wasn't just a lack of urgency from Scott: there was a sense of slow-motion, lack of focus and procrastination, indicating that he was in an altered state of consciousness and in the grip of another paralysing anxiety state. He seemed terrified that the whole area of the Barrier they were on might calve into the sea. His avoidance of leading the Pony Party, his panicky hurry to get away when he first saw the state of the Sound, his readiness to sacrifice the ponies, the sledges and the supplies in his near desperation to get away from the ice-edge when he did eventually arrive at the scene, all corroborate that view.

Meanwhile, by an incredible stroke of luck, by the time Scott arrived, a large piece of ice had wedged itself across the channel separating Bowers and Cherry from the Barrier, and they were able to make their way across it comparatively easily. Bowers: 32

> Scott, instead of blowing me up, was too relieved at our safety to be anything but pleased. I said: 'What about the ponies and the sledges?' He said: 'I don't care a damn about the ponies and sledges. It's you I want, and I am going to see you safe here up on the Barrier before I do anything else.' ... I was all for saving the beasts and sledges, however, so he let us go back and haul the sledges on to the nearest floe ... Scott knew more about ice than any of us, and realizing the danger we didn't, still wanted to abandon things.

Dear Bowers, always ready to credit Scott with superior knowledge and insight. The usual spin has been that Scott cared so much about the men that he didn't care a damn about anything else; but the truth was that he was desperate to get the hell out of there, and never mind the ponies and the sledges. Never mind, also, that by abandoning everything they would then have been *three* sleeping-bags short. The sleeping-bag issue had never been more than the irrelevant concern of an unfocused mind.

Bowers wouldn't hear of leaving everything behind. In a rare instance of resistance to orders, he remonstrated with Scott: 33

> I fought for my point tooth and nail, and got him to concede one article and then another, and still the ice did not move till we had thrown and hauled up every article on to the Barrier except the two ladders and the ponies.

It was true that as far as they knew the ice they were standing on might calve into the sea at any moment. Nevertheless, if Scott's orders had been given with lucid authority and had seemed the right thing to do, then it is fair to assume Bowers, Oates and Cherry would have complied without further ado. Scott's behaviour suggest a preoccupation with his own anxiety: vacillating and fussing, itching to get away and not in control of the situation. Oates, meanwhile, took matters into his own hands by starting to dig out a ramp for the ponies.

Unfortunately, by the time they were ready to start getting the ponies on to the Barrier, a lane of water formed between them and the floe, putting the ponies beyond reach. It was heartrending seeing them standing there, patiently waiting to drift – almost inevitably – out to sea. Much has been made of Scott's tenderheartedness towards the animals, but he had been in favour of abandoning those ponies from the beginning, and he made several more suggestions to that effect now. Of course it upset him to see animals suffer. It upsets most people (including Amundsen, in spite of Fiennes' repeated assertions to the contrary). That he was *still* prepared to abandon the ponies suggests that his anxiety was such that it overrode not just his concern for their welfare, but even the loss to his transport that their abandonment would entail.

Walking back to their temporary camp away from the edge, Bowers, in spite of his own grief, tried to console a mournful Scott by telling him that there would still be ten ponies left for next season. Scott responded that he had no confidence in the motors whatever, and – incongruously – that his confidence in the dogs had been 'much shaken', and that on top of all that, he had now lost the best of his pony transport. He told Bowers: [34]

> Of course we shall have a run for our money next season, but as far as the Pole is concerned I have but very little hope.

His primary anxiety for his life would have abated by this point, only for his second great anxiety to catch up with him: his chance of the Pole. Now that he had regained a measure of equilibrium he realised the threat to that chance the loss of the ponies represented; but rather than grieving over their fate, he grieved over his diminished prospects.

The next morning they discovered that the ponies' floe had, by another stroke of luck, drifted back towards the Barrier, and that another chance to rescue them had arisen. Bowers' account is worth quoting: [35]

> After our recent experience Captain Scott would only let us go on condition that as soon as he gave the order we were to drop every-thing and run for the Barrier. I was in a feverish hurry, and with Titus and Cherry selected a possible route over about six floes, and some low brash ice. The hardest jump was the first one, but it was nothing to what they had done the day before, so we put Punch at it. Why he hung fire I cannot think, but he did, at the very edge, and the next moment was in the water. I will draw a veil over our struggle to get the plucky little pony out. We could not manage it, and Titus had at last to put an end to his struggle with a pick.
>
> There was now my pony and Nobby. We abandoned that route, while Captain Scott looked out another and longer one by going right out on the sea-floes. This we decided on, if we could get the animals off their present floe, which necessitated a good jump on any side. Captain Scott said he would have no repetition of Punch's misfortune if he could help it. He would rather kill them on the floe. Anyhow, we rushed old Nobby at the jump, but he refused. It

seemed no good, but I rushed him at it again and again. Scott was for killing them ... but I was not, and, pretending not to hear him, I rushed the old beast again. He cleared it beautifully, and Titus, seizing the opportunity, ran my pony at it with similar success. We then returned to the Barrier and worked along westward till a suitable place for getting up was found. There Scott and Cherry started digging a road, while Titus and I went out via the sea-ice to get the ponies. We had an empty sledge as a bridge or ladder, in case of emergency, and had to negotiate about forty floes to get to the animals ... we brought them along with great success as far as the two nearest floes. At this place the ice was jambed.

Nobby cleared the last jump splendidly, when suddenly in the open water pond on one side a school of over a dozen of the terrible whales arose. This must have flurried my horse just as he was jumping, as instead of going straight he jumped sideways and just missed the floe with his hind legs. It was another horrible situation, but Scott rushed Nobby up on the Barrier, while Titus, Cherry and I struggled with poor old Uncle Bill [Birdie's pony]. Why the whales did not come under the ice and attack him I cannot say ... anyhow, we got him safely as far as the bottom of the Barrier cliff, pulling him through the thin ice towards a low patch of brash.

Captain Scott was afraid of something happening to us with those devilish whales so close, and was for abandoning the horse right away. I had no eyes or ears for anything but the horse just then, and getting on to the thin brash ice got the Alpine rope fast to each of the pony's forefeet. Crean was too blind to do anything but hold the rescued horse on the Barrier, but the other four of us pulled might and main till we got the old horse out and lying on its side. The brash ice was so thin that, had a 'Killer' come up then he would have scattered it, and the lot of us into the water like chaff. I was sick with disappointment when I found that my horse could not rise. Titus said: 'He's done; we shall never get him up alive.' ... In vain I tried to get him to his feet; three times he tried and then fell over backwards into the water again. At that moment a new danger arose. The whole piece of Barrier itself started to subside.

It had evidently been broken before, and the tide was doing the rest. We were ordered up and it was certainly all too necessary; still Titus and I hung over the old Uncle Bill's head. I said: 'I can't leave him to be eaten alive by those whales.' There was a pick lying up on the floe. Titus said: 'I shall be sick if I have to kill another horse like I did the last.' I had no intention that anybody should kill my own

357

horse but myself, and getting the pick I struck where Titus told me. I made sure of my job before we ran up and jumped the opening in the Barrier, carrying a blood-stained pick-axe instead of leading the pony I had almost considered safe.

They returned to the camp Scott had pitched on arrival, at what he thought was a safe distance from the edge. Now, even there seemed unsafe to Scott. Reasonable caution is one thing, but he walked nearly two miles checking for cracks. Only then did he feel safe enough to turn in for the night.

There was wasted time and opportunity in what might, with more speed, an extra man (or two), and a level-headed approach, have been a successful salvage operation. Oates: [36]

> We lost 6 ponies including mine (Punch) which was a long way the best pony we had I was very upset the more so as I think he could have been saved if Scott had not been fussing to the extent he was, this pony was one of the ones drowned, the loss of the ponies was Scott's fault entirely.

References

1   Meredith Hooper. *The Longest Winter*, p. 64

2   *op. cit.*, p. 65

3   Robert Falcon Scott. *Journals*, p. 100

4   *op. cit.*, p. 101

5   *op. cit.*, p. 91; *see also* Editor's Appendix III, p. 459

6   Emily Shackleton and Dr. Hugh Robert Mill. *Rejoice my Heart*, p. 115

7   Apsley Cherry-Garrard. *The Worst Journey in the World*, pp. 107–8

8   Robert Falcon Scott. *op. cit.*, p. 102

9   *op. cit.*, Editor's Appendix III, p. 459

10   *op. cit.*, p. 107

11   *op. cit.*, p. 125

12   *op. cit.*, Explanatory Note for p. 125 on p. 482

13   Geoffrey Hattersley-Smith (ed.). *The Norwegian with Scott*, p. 59

14   Edward Wilson. *Diary of the 'Terra Nova' Expedition*, p. 100

15   Robert Falcon Scott. *op. cit.*, Editor's Appendix III, p. 460

16   *ibid.*

17   Apsley Cherry-Garrard. *op. cit.*, p. 132

18   Sara Wheeler. *Cherry*, p. 95

19   *ibid.*

20   Reginald Pound. *Scott of the Antarctic*, p. 231

21   Roland Huntford. *Race for the South Pole*, p. 262

22   Edward Wilson. *op. cit.*, p. 108

23   Apsley Cherry-Garrard. *op. cit.*, p. 142

24   *ibid.*

25   Edward Wilson. *op. cit.*, p. 110

26   Apsley Cherry-Garrard. *op. cit.*, p. 147

27   Edward Wilson. *op. cit.*, p. 110

28   Geoffrey Hattersley-Smith (ed.). *op. cit.*, p. 64

29   Robert Falcon Scott. *op. cit.*, p. 139

30   Edward Wilson. *op. cit.*, p. 112

31   *op. cit.*, p. 110

32   Apsley Cherry-Garrard. *op. cit.*, p. 148

33   *ibid.*

34   *op. cit.*, p. 149

35   *op. cit.*, pp. 150–2

36   Sue Limb and Patrick Cordingley. *Captain Oates*, p. 148

23

THE HUT, OATES, AND THE HUT AGAIN

And so a dejected and tired little troupe slowly made its way back towards Hut Point – still in a state of shock, no doubt, and ruminating on what they had all just been through. And still having to drag the heavy loads that should have been left at Hut Point at the start.

It had been virtually certain from the beginning that they would have to wait for the sea to freeze over in order to get back to Cape Evans. The strait was already open north of the Glacier Tongue on the way out. They were certainly not going to be able to get any ponies back to Cape Evans without reliable sea-ice, even if Scott had imagined that men might wing it over the slopes of Erebus – an idea that was soon dismissed as unfeasible. The obvious place to wait was the *Discovery* hut at Hut Point. In another example of Scott's reluctance to face up to reality, no supplies were left there and, having kept everyone in the dark over his plans for the Depot Journey (as Debenham confirms), there were no irksome reality checks from any perhaps more grounded members of the expedition.

Scott's offhand and petulant rejection of the hut itself would, in addition, have condemned them all to spending the weeks or months of the oncoming winter in tents and/or snow-caves, while his proposed abandonment of the provisions at the scene of the Pony Disaster would have meant sledging more supplies back off the Barrier. That's if they had wanted a diet other than seal and penguin, cooked with blubber, augmented by biscuits from the *Discovery*, salvaged from those left in a hut they weren't using. Jimmy Pigg, being the only pony to have survived after the others had been abandoned on the floe, would almost certainly have died, and the men would have had to endure barely survivable hardship. All the while a perfectly good hut would have sat there unused. It would of course have been absurd.

Scott had been in denial over the needs of what would have included not only the whole Depot Party and the dogs, but also an unknown number of ponies, for what could be many weeks of waiting. The motivation for that denial must have been his urge to get as many supplies as possible on to the Barrier, while leaving all other considerations for another day. While understandable from an emotional point of view, it meant that a considerable weight of provisions and fodder were first dragged on to the Barrier, and then back again to Hut Point. If they had left those supplies at the hut in the first place it would have freed up the pulling power that might have got them to 80 degrees south, where it was originally planned to build One Ton Depot. This failure of organisation must have been painfully obvious to everyone.

A small team and a load of fodder and provisions should have been dropped off at Hut Point at the start, with orders to make the hut habitable, and to lay in a stock of seal and penguin. It would not have taken hindsight to realise this, and it is entirely plausible that those are exactly the kinds of thoughts that were going around in the heads of Meares, Oates, Atkinson, Teddy Evans, and anyone else who dared harbour a critical thought about the 'Owner'. While Scott was away on the Barrier, Atkinson and Crean had cleared the hut on their own initiative, which was just as well. Again and again, Scott is rescued by his company; and not just in terms of judgement, initiative, good humour and, dare one say it, intelligence. Even on a moral level, some found excuses for him. Bowers blamed himself for his predicament on the floe. And beyond that, both he and Wilson put down what happened to divine intervention. It was the kindest of all interpretations, but it couldn't have satisfied the critical thinkers of the party.

In the meantime, Teddy, Forde and Keohane, bringing up the rear of the Depot Party together with Jimmy Pigg, had arrived at water's edge where ice should have been, and had turned and found a way on to the Peninsula for their pony in the vicinity of Castle Rock. It had not turned out as impossibly difficult as Scott assumed, which must have been his reason for sending out Bowers over the sea-ice. Fiennes defends Scott by asserting that there was no reasonable alternative to the sea-ice for getting the ponies to Hut Point. [1] Clearly there was, when the assumption was tested (on Teddy's initiative, it seems), and Nobby, the only pony to have survived the floe predicament, duly joined the indefatigable Jimmy Pigg up by Castle Rock on the Peninsula, from where they were safely walked to the *Discovery* hut where they were comfortably accommodated.

There appears to have been silence around Scott's initial dismissal of the hut and the failure to leave supplies there. He was, throughout his career, the beneficiary of the gentlemen's code of not publicly criticising one's leader. It fed neatly into his fatal habit of denial, and made it easier for him to sweep his errors under the carpet. Superficially, that is. On a deeper level he must have felt an increased vulnerability in terms of his leadership. He must have known that his recent performance was open to criticism. It would have added to his residual feelings of self-doubt and insecurity. On top of all this was the shock news about

Amundsen in the Bay of Whales. Unsurprisingly therefore, Scott was a driven man on arrival at Hut Point. In an effort to reduce his mental and emotional discomfort he drove himself hard, and pressed everyone else to do the same. How stressful this was is illustrated by a *contretemps* with Gran just over a week later.

On 15 March (but written on the 17th) Gran had gone down with cramp in his legs, according to him. Scott thought he was shamming in order to get out of out-door work. He may have been right: Gran was a big, strong young man, who could be expected to walk off something like cramp – under different circumstances, that is. His lameness is likely to have been a non-verbal protest – refusal even – to be driven as hard as he was. It tipped Scott over from stress into barely controlled fury. Later that day, Scott unleashed a tirade against Gran that might have been understandable if not for the fact that he did it in front of everybody in the hut, which on that evening numbered 14, not counting Scott and Gran. Even if most of the others agreed with him (as Scott avers), it must still have been a painful spec-tacle to see a grown man publicly humiliated. The scene [2] does not appear in any of the (published) journals – not even Gran's. It is a sure indication that the inci-dent was painful and embarrassing, and probably not just on behalf of Gran. In a rare comment on the matter, Wright later remembered [3]

... thinking that Scott's public castigation of Gran was unfortunate.

However grubby and lazy Gran was at times, he was here used as a scapegoat and a dumping ground, as well as fodder for Scott's need to re-assert his domin-ance. Apart from in their private letters home, people kept quiet about unpleasant scenes, allowing Scott to get away with the fiction of universal harmony – in spite of the fact that he himself was often angry, irritated and critical. The fiction was maintained by the editors of his journals who cut out the entire tirade against Gran, and how it was delivered.

This wasn't leadership – this was oppression and tyranny. It is reminiscent of his public dressing-down of Hartley Ferrar on the *Discovery*, mentioned by Scott in a letter to his mother. Both Ferrar and Gran were the youngest men of the after-guard and therefore easy meat. Scott's RN training meant that all he knew about leadership was throwing his weight around – ruling rather than leading. This might have done for his captaincy of the overwhelmingly Naval *Discovery*, but it wasn't enough now. Not only was he vulnerable because of his mistakes, he didn't have military discipline as a safety net. He was under pressure to keep his hold on the company and the integrity of the expedition and, knowing no other way, resorted to a form of verbal and physical tyranny – both in overt form, as with Gran, and also in the form of his ongoing moodiness and irritability, around which a lot of tiptoeing went on.

Some of the most obvious evidence that there was criticism of Scott comes from Oates, who had by this time at least three documented cases against him: the poor quality of the ponies, disagreement on the march about euthanising those that were failing, and his behaviour and responsibility for the loss of the ponies in the Pony Disaster. Oates commanded a lot of respect. Not only was he higher up the social scale than most of the others, including Scott, but he also had a proven record of bravery in combat. Oates was a formidable adversary who, with his allies Meares and Atkinson, formed the nucleus of dissension that endured throughout the coming winter, a fact Scott must have been aware of but which he dealt with by ignoring it. And they weren't alone. Taylor had a heated argument with Scott about the quality of the mapping on *Discovery*, after which there remained a certain *froideur* between them; while Frank Debenham was, in his own self-effacing way, devastatingly critical, as evidenced by a letter to his mother, to which we will return. By the time they were half-way up the Beardmore Glacier on the Pole Journey, Teddy Evans was fiercely resentful and borderline mutinous, as evidenced by Birdie's comments, to which we will return also.

Conflict is common on Polar expeditions, of course. The environment is highly stressful for everyone, both physically and mentally. Even today, when we are so much more emotionally literate, there are occasions when people develop differences that only a parting of the ways can resolve. When this isn't possible physically, mental and emotional distance must suffice.

Waiting wasn't Scott's strong point, as we know, and he was soon itching to get over to Cape Evans. The ostensible reason was that a huge section of the Glacier Tongue had broken off, and there had been some heavy swells – with worrying implications for the hut, which wasn't much above the waterline. In the absence of a boat there was no possibility of communicating with Cape Evans. (A photo shows that a boat was left at Cape Evans by the *Terra Nova*, but not until she returned in the second season.) Some pre-arranged signals would have been invaluable, but in the rush to get the Depot Journey up and away it was not thought of, although they did use them later.

Meanwhile, Scott reiterates his view of the dogs and of Meares: [4]

> I am losing all faith in the dogs and much in Meares – I'm afraid neither he nor they will ever go the pace we look for. Meares is a real nice fellow but he hates exercise and doesn't inspire any confidence to see the thing through.

This is a puzzling statement, in view of the fact that the dogs were the fastest transport he had. Apart from the dogs injured in the crevasse fall, which wasn't their fault, they had rapidly recovered from the Depot-laying Journey. What was the pace he was looking for? It seems altogether a delusional statement, and suggests an attempt to reassure himself about Amundsen's prospects, rather than a realistic assessment of the dogs' potential. Not only had the dogs outpaced the ponies by something like a factor of three to one, they had nearly all survived, while the ponies had gone down like ninepins. It had devastating implications for the Pole attempt. He told himself that Amundsen would never get dogs through the mountains. What prompted him to think he knew more than Amundsen about what dogs could and couldn't do will forever remain a mystery. In reality, it was just one more attempt to reduce his mental discomfort, which, incidentally, would have been infinitely worse if he had known about Amundsen's version of laying depots. By 11 April, Amundsen and his teams had succeeded in laying three times the weight of depots, vastly better signposted, distributed over twice Scott's attained distance (up to 82 degrees latitude) on the Barrier, at a cost of less of a tenth of his dogs, against Scott's loss of a third of his ponies.

At Hut Point the sea-ice was checked daily. At that time of year the sea may freeze over and seem quite safe, only for it to break up and disappear without warning in a sudden blizzard – a not-infrequent event in those latitudes – or for any number of reasons to do with the dynamics of the Antarctic climate. The main danger was the unpredictability of these events. McMurdo Sound starts its process of autumn freezing early to mid March, into April. This means that the ice cannot be considered reliable in April, nor even through May. Evidence for this comes from the horrific fate that befell two men from Shackleton's Ross Sea Party five years later. On 8 May 1916, Aeneas Mackintosh and Victor Hayward set off from Hut Point over the sea-ice towards Cape Evans and were never seen again. Their footprints ended at water's edge, about two miles north of Hut Point. The rest of their team didn't consider the ice to be safe until mid July.

Scott, together with a team of no fewer than eight men, set off for Cape Evans on 11 April. The first part of the route was along the Peninsula, and down over an icy cornice, with ropes, on to the fast ice on the inside of the bay towards the Glacier Tongue. By the time they got to the Glacier Tongue it was dark, and they had some difficulty making their way across it. This accomplished, they stopped to have something to eat. Bowers wanted to stay where they were for the night: [5]

> It was after 8 p.m. ... it seemed to me folly to venture upon a piece of untried newly frozen sea-ice in inky darkness, with a blizzard coming up behind us. Against this of course we were only five miles from Cape Evans, and though we had hardly any grub with us, not having anticipated the cliff or the saltiness of the sea-ice, and having to set out to do the journey in one day, I thought hunger in a sleeping-bag better than lying out in a blizzard on less than one foot of young ice.

He must have kept his mouth shut as Debenham records that Scott took a vote on it, and that all voted in favour of going on. Never mind that five of the eight voters were complete Antarctic novices, whose votes can only have been based on supposition and compliance with what they probably thought was Scott's pre-ferred course of action.

And so they struck out towards Little Razorback Island, which is almost two miles from the shores of Ross Island, in the middle of what would have been ex-tremely vulnerable young ice, in the dark. The blizzard Bowers had seen coming overtook them, reducing visibility to near zero. Unable to discern the details of Little Razorback, they camped on the sea-ice near it and spent an uncomfortable, wet, stormy, and very insecure night on thin ice. Bowers didn't sleep that night, which is saying something. Teddy Evans was of the party and tells us what happened the next morning: [6]

> ... we were called at six to find a blizzard with a high drift making it impossible to move, so we remained in our bags until 4 p.m., when we shifted on to the narrow platform of rock situated on the south side of Little Razorback. We had one small meal here, but our con-dition was not a pleasant one, since little food remained and fuel was short. There was undoubtedly a chance that the sea ice would break up and drift away in this high wind. Had that happened we should have been left to starve on the tiny island. The position was not an enviable one.

Watching the ice breaking up around you on a floe half way to Cape Evans would have been worse. Much worse.

They were extremely fortunate that the ice stayed in, and the next day they made it safely to Cape Evans. It was, by any standards, a horribly dangerous journey. Scott may have thought he was an unlucky man, but that was because he noticed the bad luck and took the good for granted. A dispassionate assessment of the situation would have been unequivocal. Whatever had or had not happened at Cape Evans, there was no point in adding to the potential disasters by setting off so early to get there. Although the old ice along the inside of the bay between the Peninsula and Glacier Tongue would probably stay in, even that could not be taken for granted, as the Glacier Tongue itself had lost miles of its length a matter of days before – a rare event, which confirmed it was an exceptional year. It makes the decision to traverse the ice so soon afterwards even more risky than it would have been in a more typical year. As it happened, Scott's luck held, even to the extent of rounding the Cape on the sea-ice.

In the meantime, the nine men who had been left at Cape Evans had spent over two months together in the new hut, and would psychologically have 'shaken together' as a separate little community. Everything was up and running, and it ap-pears a comparatively relaxed atmosphere had been enjoyed. Scott's arrival, while said to have been welcome, must have felt like a whirlwind invasion. The boss was back, and suddenly the quiet life was over. The population of the hut doubled, routines were disrupted, and people would have had to re-adjust and re-integrate. There are echoes of Teddy Evans showing him over the *Terra Nova* in London when Scott was shown around his new hut.

In spite of the luxuries and the opportunity for rest and recuperation Cape Evans now provided, however, Scott couldn't wait to get back off to Hut Point. Hence, only four days later, on 17 April, he started back with seven men and two ponies dragging provisions. In an emergency, it would have almost have been justified. But knowing the men at Hut Point were doing OK, and not in any imminent danger, why the hurry? He must have known it was still early, and that there was a fair chance the ice could go out again. As we know, Scott had a complicated relationship with danger and risk. By any standards it was dangerous to set off again at all. With ponies it was hair-raising. Shackleton had written about McMurdo Sound having been open water as late as 11 April – information to which Scott had access. It is of course possible, with hindsight, to interpret all this as showing Scott's dynamism and good judgement, as nothing disastrous happened. Another interpretation is that he was driven by a need to make up for his mistakes on the Depot Journey, and that he was very lucky with the sea-ice.

He had been forced to face the fact that there were not enough supplies at Hut Point: the provisions that had been rescued from the floe due to Bowers' interventions weren't enough, and they had started to run out of things like sugar, butter and flour. As far as pony fodder was concerned, they had already been obliged to fetch loads back from the Barrier. This was in addition to an earlier trip that had been taken to Corner Camp for which the objects are not clear. Wilson writes that the trip was in order to fetch supplies back from Corner Camp, although others suggest it was to take further supplies there. Maybe it was both, as they had a surfeit of biscuit at Hut Point, which may have been used to offset what they were bringing back.

It was known from the beginning that there were going to be 12 men at Hut Point – 16 with the addition of Taylor's returning Geological Party – and an unknown number of ponies, all of whom would have to wait there potentially many weeks for the Sound to freeze over. The failure to cater for this explains Scott's hurry to get back there with groceries – a thing he was prepared to take tremendous risks to do.

Another consideration was that he had left behind a nest of critics – even Wilson sounds tetchy again in his journal around this time. Having to haul pony fodder back from the Barrier may well have elicited a wry remark here and there, while any post-morteming of the Pony Disaster might have been met with meaningful looks and eloquent silences between certain members of the party. Or worse. In the back of everyone's mind will also have been Amundsen, and the ominous news about his hundred dogs. Scott was probably right if he thought he needed to re-establish the credibility of his arrangements, and to re-assert his competence and authority to boss the expedition.

Meanwhile, with Scott away at Cape Evans for a few days, the *Discovery* hut had relaxed into a haven of peace and domesticity. Wilson certainly appreciated it, having time at last to darn his socks, get some rest, and sketch the fabulous sunsets. Cherry describes this little interlude as an immersion in a kind of Robinson Crusoe existence; hunting seals by day, enjoying camaraderie around the blubber stove in the evenings, and sleeping like babies. Spartan it may have been, but in later years he looked back on these days as some of the happiest in his life. [7] 'Professor Gregory's Bungalow', as it had been scathingly called, and which Scott had considered 'never likely to be of such importance as to be indispensable', was to prove a lifeline for them throughout the expedition – as it had for Shackleton, and would be for his Ross Sea Party after them. It still stands, and is a designated Historic Site, dwarfed by the current installations at McMurdo Base.

After a difficult and dangerous journey, when Scott did get back to Hut Point he wasn't especially welcome; they would rather he hadn't bothered. Cherry: [8]

> We had spent such a happy week, just the seven of us, at the *Discovery* hut that I think, glad as we were to see the men, we would most of us have rather been left undisturbed, and I expected that it would mean that we should have to move homewards, as it turned out.

Cherry was indeed ordered home, along with six others. Soon they were off again. Cherry miraculously kept up in a brutally competitive race – a dominance contest – back to Cape Evans. Bowers forced himself to carry on in spite of two nasty falls, and everybody arrived back at Cape Evans bathed in sweat and 'just about laid out'. [9] Scott himself describes the effect of sweating in super-cold conditions: [10]

> ... as we took off our wind clothes showers of ice fell on the floor. The accumulation was almost incredible and shows the whole trouble of sledging in cold weather ... assuredly a winter and spring party cannot afford to get so hot if they wish to retain any semblance of comfort.

On 13 May the ponies and dogs returned from Hut Point with Meares in charge, marking the end of the Depot Journey, three and a half months after it had started.

By this time the hut had been turned into the basic but comfortable abode so famous now from Ponting's photos. When they had first landed a cook-tent and a latrine must have been the first essentials to be set up on shore; anyone who has ever set up camp anywhere knows the priorities. Scott mentions the cook-tent but not the latrines. Scott shared his delicacy in such matters with everyone else, it seems. None of the published Cape Evans diaries contain details, and most of them nothing at all about what was, and always will be, an important issue. A latrine block, improvised from one of the motor crates, was built alongside the hut, a couple of metres beyond the similarly improvised stables. Getting to it entailed about a 12-metre walk out of doors. While we may all have experienced a chilly walk to the loo at times, surely most of us would draw the line at having to claw our way through a howling blizzard in the dark, in bone-chilling temperatures, risking a pelting from gravel and pebbles on a really bad day. Yet this is what they seem uncomplainingly to have subjected themselves to. Taylor's plan of the hut in the first year, [11] and Wilson's drawing, [12] show that there was only one door in and out of the main hut, and that access to both the stables and the latrines involved the same icy little hurry around the outside.

The latrines were, like the interior of the hut, segregated into men's and officers' compartments, and had trap-doors at the back, through which boxes were shoved in and out. It was probably Hooper's job, and it is only fair to give him credit for it. But the icy walk, and the enforced sojourn within, would have meant serious discomfort most of the time, while woe betide anyone with an upset stomach. It seems an entirely gratuitous, self-imposed hardship and inconvenience. Many people still had outside privvies in Scott's day, but one would have thought that Polar conditions might have inspired a rethink. Even when an extension to the hut was built during the (Austral) summer of 1912 along the western wall, incorporating the original lobby, there seems to have been no thought to build a loo inside it, as Shackleton had done at Cape Royds. Eventually a door was made at the end of this passage, reducing the outside walk to the latrines to a couple of metres. It is possible, however, that it wasn't until the members of Shackleton's Ross Sea Party inhabited the hut a few years later that the door that is there now was installed.

Toiletting aside, they were pretty comfortable inside the hut, which was roomy by Polar standards. It was arranged much like a ship: fore and aft, with the men in an open-plan service-cum-dormitory department forward, and the afterguard arranged in cubicles either side of the wardroom table. Scott had his 'Holy of Holies', with his co-leaders Teddy and Uncle Bill, in a separate compartment furthest aft.

The cubicles either side of the wardroom table housed the little cliques that formed – mostly on the basis of personal inclinations, but also reflecting their professions and status within the community. People naturally gravitated towards their allies and geopsychological comfort zones. Furthest aft, in addition to Scott and his co-leaders, was Simpson, with his important meteorological instruments, and 'camera artist' Ponting. Ponting turned out to have hitherto-unsuspected skills. He built his own darkroom with extraordinary speed, and to everyone's admiration. [13] He also furnished posterity with some of the most technically accomplished and evocative studies of life in Antarctica ever made – the only exception being Bowers' photos of the tragedy at the Pole.

While many accounts of life in the hut cite the prevailing harmony and good fellowship, the reality would, like any community thrown close together for any length of time, have been much more complicated than that. The frequency with which Wilson's counselling skills were resorted to is evidence of a fair amount of difficulty. Nevertheless, Scott's moodiness was out of step with the general sense of camaraderie, as evidenced by Debenham in a letter to his mother: [14]

> ... the marvellous part of it is that the Owner is the single exception
> to a general sense of comradeship and jollity amongst all of us.

There was without a doubt another layer of reality that played out in *sotto-voce* exchanges, meaningful looks and private conversations. For example, it must have been clear to everyone that Oates and Meares had an especially close under-standing, and what it was about can't have been a secret. Ponting's study of them hunched together over the blubber stove in the stables is one of his finest achieve-ments. It is alleged that this was the occasion when Scott overheard Meares telling Oates that Scott should get himself a shilling book on transport. True or not, there are no prizes for guessing the tone and the content of those conversations in the steamy semi-darkness.

Another of Ponting's famous photos is that of the Tenements, the prison-camp-style arrangement in which Oates, Meares, Atkinson, Birdie and Cherry, aka the Bunderlohg, had their bunks. In the middle was Oates' bunk, the most gloriously thrown-together mess of a bed ever to grace Antarctica, festooned – as it came to be – with a mixture of horse tack and Oates' personal gear. Taylor: [15]

> He brought in some boards from the stables ... and has built an
> erection which presumably satisfies him.

This somewhat facetious remark takes no account of the fact that Oates had been a busy man, and had had neither the time nor the materials to build himself a bunk until after his return from the Depot Journey. From the moment of his arrival on Quail Island, where the ponies were quarantined on their arrival in New Zealand, he had been expected, with only Anton as an assistant, to take charge of the entire training, management, and transport of what began as a string of 19 ponies. Everybody seems to have been quite happy to leave him to it; and Oates, not being one to complain or kick up a fuss, got on with the job and gave it his best.

On the *Terra Nova*, of the 63 other people on board other than himself and Anton, only one person, Atkinson, seems to have been available to help him look after the ponies during the gale. Atkinson gave him the help he sorely needed, but for which he was too stoical to ask. The fact that only two of the ponies were lost on that occasion was due to Oates', Anton's and Atkinson's unremitting care and hard work, under savage conditions. After landing them at Cape Evans, Oates had been constantly at work getting them as ready as he could for the Depot Journey on which, after having nursed them along for weeks and watching them falter one by one, he had been obliged to drive an ice-pick into a pathetically struggling pony's brain, and watch Bowers doing the same.

When he got back to Cape Evans after all that, he was expected to find his own materials and construct his own bunk. All there was for him was an empty space, and in his more cynical moments he may have thought that at least was something. Considering his importance to the expedition, and the debt of gratitude that was owed to him for his performance so far, and the rather leisurely time those at Cape Evans had enjoyed, it seems heartless for there not to have been the slightest consideration on his behalf – not even in terms of providing a few materials. When Scott was first shown over the hut on his return from Hut Point, he should have ordered a bunk to be constructed for Oates. But he was not a fatherly man, in Gran's words, and too preoccupied. If Oates experienced a slight sinking feeling when he was faced with a job that could so easily have been done for him, and which it would be fair to say he deserved to have done for him, he would never have shown it – overtly at least. It is, however, possible that there was an element of anger and passive aggression in the perfunctory way he built that bunk.

Maybe he was also somewhat reluctant to come in from the stables, and so built his bed in the hut as a more-or-less grudging concession to society, which in this case included a strong contingent of professional academics. Never having shone as a scholar, it would not have been the sort of company he would have chosen for himself. It probably made him feel at a disadvantage and put him on the defensive. He tended to hang back, as is suggested in photographs, and his taciturnity seems to have been more marked in this environment than it had been in the Army. He had his allies in the Bunderlohg, but apart from Debenham, he was out of his comfort zone among the scientists, among whom competitively erudite sparring went on for a pastime.

While there may have been an element of anger in the perfunctory way he built his bunk, the Spartan and unadorned look of Oates' bunk fulfilled a number of additional functions. It was also an assertion of his indifference to, and independence from, the values of the scholars. The Tenements as a whole were a material expression of traditional, idealised male values. The austerity and the macho scorn for the fripperies of the scholars' 'boudoirs', or 'opium dens' opposite which it implied, and which was voiced, laid claim to a purer and more potent conception of masculinity. In Markhamian terms, the boudoirs housed the 'mud-larkers', whereas the Tenements were home to the 'real' men: the enablers of the Pole attempt, the doers of derring deeds. As well as being a metaphor for his machismo, however, Oates' bunk also suggested precariousness and vulnerability. The ramshackle and rickety bunk, held steady by an ad-hoc nailed plank, may have expressed something about who he was and what he felt; but beyond the machismo, it was poorly constructed and lacked stability.

He had not been particularly robust as a child, and had been regularly taken abroad in order to avoid the cold and damp winters of England. While enriching in many ways, it disrupted his school work, which, although welcome to him, put him at a disadvantage in terms of his future career. 'Laurie' Oates was just 16 when his father died, after which the already close relationship he had with his mother Caroline became even closer. She was the type of woman commonly described as 'formidable', and it seems it was she who facilitated his entry into the Sixth Innis-killing Dragoons, as he writes: 16

> I shall not try to thank you in writing for all you have done for me but what I say is this, that if it had not been for you I would still be rotting in the old 3rd [Prince of Wales' Own] and knowing how keen I was to get a commission you must if possible try to realise how grateful I am.

She arranged his bank account for him and made sure he always had enough in it to pay his mess bills and buy the odd bit of prime horse-flesh. If his siblings resented him being the apple of his mother's eye they never showed it. Indeed, it was hard to be angry with someone like the 'Soldier'. He was the type of man whose sense of honour and devotion to duty transcended considerations for his own comfort and safety.

Frank Debenham admired him tremendously: 17

> The man I am the best of friends with is Soldier ... He is ... an Eton boy, of some independent means. Picture a very plain but yet splendid face rather wrecked by wounds (South African War) and smallpox (India), a big bluff figure always made the worst of by coarse clothes and a slow leisured manner of speaking. He is without the slightest pretension of any sort except to being a gentleman and the casual observer would take him to be the stable-man with unusual good manners ... We got to know one another very slowly but before half the winter was over I got into the habit of playing him chess every night and yarning with him for hours. He is not reserved in the ordinary sense and, though he loathes society, I fancy that when he does mix in it he is quite a brilliant member. His talk, though slow and measured, is brimful of wit and as straight as they make them. He has temper such as I never met. It is impossible to make him even testy! I should think if a man insulted him rankly he would merely smile, tho' he would also twist the man's neck.

But in spite of his cool image, his service record, his social status and his rugged physique, Oates was vulnerable. 'No-surrender' Oates had sustained a serious injury to his left leg in a Boer War confrontation, leaving it slightly shorter than the other. Under normal circumstances it didn't bother him, evidently, but for skiing hundreds of miles dragging a sledge it was clearly not ideal. It put him at risk, especially as his physique as a whole suggested strength – a perception he was happy to reinforce, but which made it too easy to overlook his susceptibilities. In addition to his leg, these included his lack of domestic skills. In the hut, for the first time in his life, he was thrown back on his own devices as far as his personal care was concerned. At home, at school, on his travels, and even in the Army there had always been someone to look after his domestic requirements. While having had to rough it in the field at times, those occasions were picnics compared to what he was now facing. But now there was no mother, no domestic worker, no adjutant nor aide to take care of such things as washing and darning his socks. The sock hanging over him in the Tenement photo must be the worst sock in history to be photographed, clearly having been worn long beyond the point where it needed attention. While happy – keen even – to do 'men's' work, domestic work was foreign territory to Oates. He would probably have argued that there were more important things to worry about than socks, but this was not England, or India, or South Africa. This was Antarctica, a dangerous place for feet.

While in many ways typical of his social class, Oates was also rebel who enjoyed confounding people's expectations with the way he dressed and his hands-on attitude to work. His relationship with Scott is perhaps the most fraught and poignant of anyone on the expedition. They both kept up the pretence of a good relationship, but under the surface Oates was angry and borderline contemptuous. For Scott, it would have been just one more item in a catalogue of buried discomforts, but for Oates it was central. In a letter to his mother he says: [18]

> ... myself I dislike Scott intensely and would chuck the whole thing
> if it was not that we are a British Expedition and must beat those
> Norwegians. Scott has always been very civil to me and I have the
> reputation of getting on well with him but the fact of the matter is
> he is not straight, it is himself first the rest nowhere and when he
> has got all he can out of you it is shift for yourself ...

He qualifies this statement by saying it was written in an angry moment, but it is evidence that his relationship with Scott was at best patchy, and that what motivated him was pride in his nation, rather than allegiance to Scott.

Oates' practical – and in some ways egalitarian – approach went down well on the messdeck, eliciting affection as well as admiration. Anton, the jockey from Vladivostok who, spooked by the perpetual dark of the winter, left cigarettes outside to propitiate the gods (surmising, evidently, that they enjoyed the odd fag), came almost to worship him. Always patient, skilful and persevering, Oates got more out of those ponies than probably either of them had thought possible.

From the moment he heard about Amundsen in the Bay of Whales, with his hard crew of expert sledgers and a hundred dogs, Oates had no illusions about the challenge they represented. But rather than criticising Amundsen, he gave him credit, and wished his own outfit was more like his. The Norwegian's approach was more Oates' style, if his admiration for Napoleon is anything to go by. Although his Russian Campaign was a disaster, and he was ultimately defeated of course, Napoleon still commanded a lot of respect, not only for his strategic nous but also for his sheer chutzpah and rational approach to politics. Not in England, however, where it became – and remains – a tradition to revile and belittle the 'Corsican upstart'. For Oates to have flown in the face of establishment orthodoxy by hanging Bonaparte's portrait on the wall hints again at Oates' individuality and defiance of convention. It put Scott at a double disadvantage in relation to Oates: not only was Scott a cut below him socially – an awareness which, for all his anti-establishmentarianism, was bred into Oates' bones – he was independent by nature, and judged people on their merits. To Oates, Scott was a dilettante who spent too much time in the office, and [19]

> ... would fifty times sooner stay in the hut seeing how a pair of Foxs spiral puttees suited him than come out and look at the ponies legs or a dogs feet ...

The Soldier had integrity. He might complain bitterly in private, and he might scoff at Scott's brand of leadership, but he would always do his duty, and do it well. Years later, Meares must have recalled the blubber stove sessions, and Titus' feats of patience and skill with the ponies, as he gazed at the photo of the blackened husk standing at the Pole which had once been his friend the Soldier. Whether Caroline Oates could ever bear to look at those photos who knows; but her heart, and those of many others, must have broken to recall Titus the Soldier, as he was, and be moved to reflect that he deserved better than poorly qualified leadership.

Ultimately, the blame must as always be laid at Markham's door. It was his homo-erotically inspired, vain and hubristic criteria for leadership – and his desire to control 'his' expedition – that led a man to be put in a position beyond his experience, leadership skills, emotional stability, knowledge and interests, and with an airy disregard for the potential human cost. It is testament to the irrationality of public opinion that in spite of the never-to-be-forgotten tragedy of Oates, Scott's responsibility for it should have been allowed to be played down in the tide of uncritical sentiment unleashed by his own carefully stage-managed death. How Caroline must have felt to see Scott sanctified after leading her son to such an abject and comfortless end can hardly be imagined.

Oates had, early on, found a friend in Atkinson. They had teamed up on the ship, finding each other congenially taciturn, and appearing to share a sense of laconic detachment. Atkinson was generally an enigmatic figure. He was a Royal Navy surgeon who specialised in parasitology. His work understandably attracted limited curiosity among the men at Cape Evans. It is a pity that, as mentioned before, he was an adherent of Almroth Wright's theory on scurvy as an 'acid intoxication', and it was probably as well that Wilson wasn't convinced, and continued to press people to eat fresh seal and penguin. It may not be too much of a leap to suggest that Atkinson and the Tenement boys shared Wright's views on women and women's suffrage. Almroth Wright wrote the notorious and im-passioned quasi-scientific treatise against the idea of votes for women, *The Unexpurgated Case Against Woman Suffrage*. His premise was that women are inferior to men in all respects (except childbearing and rearing), and that what-ever women have was given them by men, and that they should therefore be quiet and grateful, and do as they are told. It is sobering to think that at as recently as the start of the twentieth century it was still possible to present such views as legitimate. Without wanting to impute that level of crassness to the Bunderlohg, their creed was, nevertheless, 'Down with Science, Sentiment and the Fair Sex' – a decidedly laddish motto, and Oates was jokingly said to prefer goats.

There was no overt acknowledgement of the strains that the absence of women must entail. Scott missed Kathleen and wrote to her in amorous terms, but dealt only obliquely with the obvious issues arising from a prolonged, intimate, all-male environment. Many expeditions put curtains or doors on all the bunks in acknowledgement of a person's need for privacy in a crowded space. While the Ubdugs (Taylor, Debenham and Gran) were semi-private, and the other scientists had fairly sheltered bunks, it would have seemed antisocial and frankly suspicious to have curtained oneself off, especially in the Tenements. Instead, an ostentatious asexuality prevailed, especially among the lads. But the air in that hut must have been thick with hormonal body odour (and feet). Assuming they were no better or worse than people in general, and not especially saintly, Wilson notwithstanding, it is reasonable to suppose that sex, like bowel movements and conflict, was present in some form within the community. Historians have eschewed the subject entirely, apart from rubbishing allegations about Markham. It has no doubt been considered irrelevant and in bad taste in this context. This means, however, that, in addition to self-censorship on the part of the diarists, we have another example of historians' collusion in presenting an oversimplified and sanitised version of history.

Scott would have been well aware of the risks, and sensitive around any suggestion of impropriety – especially in view of his relationship with Markham, whose odium never really went away. Kathleen's near-ubiquitous presence in photos around his cubicle will have sent out a clear message. This time there were no theatricals, and absolutely no make-up or dressing up as women. Propriety forbade remarks like Sherard Osborn's in a more permissive era, about men pining for forlorn damsels and seeking retired places in which to 'sentimentalise' – although something like that probably happened here also. Weather permitting. There was no reflection on the 'Ladyless South', as there had been on the *Belgica*, where men held a beauty competition by cutting out pictures of women from magazines and rating them according to their attractiveness. Or a light-hearted little interlude on the *Fram* with one of the men in a tutu sitting on laps, fluttering a fan as they sat on deck with coffee and liqueurs on crossing the equator. [20] Discussions about women seem almost exclusively to have been about their political status. Even the ragging that had been such a popular pastime on the ship under Teddy was now against the rules, ostensibly to preserve the furniture. It happened anyway, occasionally.

Does the ragging – 'Furling Top-gallant Sails' as it was known – which included tearing each others' clothes off, wrestling, mock-boxing, and dragging each other about half- or even completely naked, constitute anything other than a fun way of letting off steam? Birdie wrote that 'Uncle Bill' Wilson made it all seem wholesome and above board, in a tacit admission that it could be interpreted otherwise. Cherry regarded Wilson as not far short of a saint. The Church has always taken a very puritan view of sex of course, although this has been much honoured in the breach. It is undeniable, surely, that at the most basic level the rough-and-tumbles satisfied a need for physical contact and, for Wilson, the kind of contact that his marriage probably didn't provide. One cannot imagine the rather etiolated, reserved Oriana chasing him around, ripping his clothes off and getting him in an arm-lock. Besides, they were always too busy doing other things.

It is nowhere recorded what the messdeck thought about 'Furling Top-gallant Sails', but it seems unlikely that men like Keohane, Crean or Lashly could have behaved in that manner without raising eyebrows. So why was it different for the afterguard? Or was it? It was of course differentially regarded and sanctioned along class lines. There was permission for it among ex-public schoolboys as a leftover from the ethos which had its roots in homocentric Greek culture, which wasn't anywhere near dead yet. Cherry, for example, had been to Winchester, where the classics had still been at the heart of the curriculum, and to Oxford, where John Betjeman once said 'everyone was queer'. At the same time there was tremendous guilt even around heterosexual sex in that era, let alone that of the gay variety. Gay sex, even between consenting adults, was actually against the law, which means that many upholders of the status quo must have been victims of their own repressive hypocrisy. So even if there was an element of sensuality in 'Furling Top-gallant Sails', which seems likely, they would have strenuously denied it, even to themselves.

But while the seamen were denied the delights of rough sensuality through horseplay, ordinary homosexuality was an everyday reality for them. There were positions – domestic mainly – that were traditionally filled by gays, and tacitly acknowledged as such. Frederick Hooper was here in that role. Gilbert Scott had been a domestic servant on the *Discovery*, where he played Mary-Ann in 'Ticket of Leave'. 'Mary-Ann' was slang for a gay male prostitute. Without wanting to suggest that either of them were prostitutes, the suggestion is obviously that both Hooper and Gilbert Scott could well have been gay. Clissold, the cook, good-looking in a boyish way, but camera shy, slept next to Hooper, apart from the others. It is certainly possible that they were something of an item, and that it was tacitly accepted by all as an ordinary part of life in the Navy.

There were a few female nicknames in the afterguard like 'Jane' (Atkinson), 'Marie' (Nelson), and 'Mother' (Meares). Not so well known is the fact that Debenham was known as 'Jessie'. According to Taylor, Oriana Wilson's sister Constance had provided the little presents for Bowers' Christmas tree, among which Taylor tells us every second present or so was a necklace or earrings. Most of these were given to Debenham, which he doesn't seem to have entirely enjoyed. The third edition of the *South Polar Times* featured some illustrations made by Wilson described by Taylor as [21]

> ... "The Ladies' Page", a record of Antarctic fashions, [which] were
> some of the best he had done; especially Madame Bowers and Miss
> Jessie Debenham, coyly proposing to Titus Oates!

Again, whether these characterisations had any deeper significance is a moot point. As far as the female nicknames are concerned, it seems hard to fathom why Atkinson was called Jane. 'Mother' Meares was presumably so called because of his role with the dogs, and also quite simply because it is alliterative. Things might not have been quite so straightforward with 'Marie' Nelson, however.

Nelson, also nicknamed 'Bronte' after the First Duke of Bronte, Horatio Nelson, committed suicide at the age of 39. The circumstances (see Chapter 27), suggest that there was torment and difficulty in his life relating to his relationship, or lack of it, with his wife. There was a strong suggestion of misogyny in his attitude to women. Taylor: [22]

> ... never have I had such amusing arguments (cags we called them)
> as during the Antarctic night. Woman's Suffrage I have known
> argued *ad nauseam* from dinner-time (7 p.m.) till midnight, when
> Nelson and myself were left still opposed, and still full of argument.
> Prayers for peace never deterred Nelson from preaching women's
> inferiority.

According to Kathleen, Nelson was a man who [23]

... spends all his time on shore being a man about town, which
makes him look exceedingly tired.

Debenham thought Nelson was 'weird': [24]

Its easy enough to get on with him as *he* won't lose his temper, but
it is very easy for the other man to do so. He is such an anomaly that
he is best described verbally.

It sounds like there were something about Nelson he didn't want to commit to
paper. Nelson was a complicated man with 'issues'. Always immaculately dressed,
Nelson was given a 'huge fan' at Christmas, according to Taylor: a hint that he
might in fact have been generally – if discreetly – regarded as effeminate.

Nelson had gravitated toward Bernard Day on the ship. He and Day shared a
love of methodical neatness and had, according to Scott, been greatly relieved not
to have to share their space with an untidy companion. Not only was their cubicle
neat and tidy in every respect, it was carefully designed and crafted, featuring a
set of much-admired veneered drawers, and pillars topped off with decorative
finials. They had even stained the woodwork mahogany brown.

Bernard Day had been with Shackleton on the *Nimrod* Expedition. He had
been an engineer with the Arrol-Johnson company who supplied Shackleton's
Antarctic motor car. Like Clissold, Day seems to have kept a low profile generally;
he is not often seen in photos, and there isn't much mention of him in the published
journals, apart from his activities with the motors and the acetylene lighting. It
does, however, appear that Nelson, Day, Hooper and Clissold often accompanied
each other in some combination on the jobs and journeys. None of them seem to
have been avid diary writers, although Day was given to periods of very deep
thinking, according to Debenham. [25] All of this is consistent with the idea that there
were hidden undercurrents and complicated relationships in that hut – which
shouldn't, after all, surprise anyone.

The ruling triumvirate was also sexually ambivalent. Scott himself had an
essentially passive nature and was diffident, soft-featured, and neurotic – qualities
which gave him an ambivalent sensuality. Wilson was a sexual enigma. Not
counting Oriana, his history is devoid of relationships with women outside his
family. Wilson made Scott's leadership possible: making excuses for him, protecting him and supporting him. In the end, he more or less laid down his life for
him. It would be no exaggeration to say that Wilson loved Scott with a passion that
transcended reason.

As for Teddy Evans, he was something of a connoisseur of male physiques, and
an enthusiastic wrestler. Together with Wilson, he was one of the prime instigators and participants in 'Furling Top-gallant Sails', as a fresh-faced young man
he had had a very close relationship with Doorly in the *Morning* days. Markham

liked them both. There was an omnivorous quality about Teddy, and it is not beyond the bounds of imagination that this extended over his sexuality. Much could be read into Debenham's statement regarding Teddy: [26]

> He is great fun in company but I don't like being alone with him –
> his confidences are too overwhelming and ill-advised.

Describing the 'Mayfair District', where he, Wilson, and Scott had their quarters, Teddy writes that Scott's part was [27]

> ... well illuminated ... and, although hung around with fur mitts, fur
> boots, socks, hats and woollen clothing, there was something very
> chaste about this very respectable corner.

Chaste? Very respectable? Surely it would have been unthinkable that it could be anything else?

There must have been sexual tensions under the surface, especially considering the circumstances. In conditions like those in the hut, it is well known that even normally heterosexual men not infrequently turn to each other in a behaviour known as situational homosexuality. One of the main facilitators for this is alcohol. Scott must have known it, and that is undoubtedly one of the reasons why there was so little of it around.

The exception was Midwinter Day, 22 June 1911. They had a 'Christmas' feast, accompanied by 'About 50 bottles of Heidsieck 1904!' according to a gleeful Gran. If true, that makes more than two bottles per man, as at least three were teetotallers. Scott made a spectacularly boring and inane after-dinner speech, and Bowers stole the show with his Christmas tree with little presents all over it, including a sponge for Oates. A quiet hint maybe? He must have been rank with the smell of horses and blubber. And he had sweaty feet. Things must have livened up considerably with a game of 'snapdragon', a game whereby they had to snatch raisins out of a dish of burning brandy (now banned because of health and safety). Then the table was upended and its legs removed, creating space for them to sit and watch Ponting's slides.

The evening had to be concluded with a dance, naturally, and those still standing put the music on and started off with what was probably a fairly hilarious and disorderly set of lancers (a type of quadrille), after which they danced with each other. Nelson, among others, had reportedly taken to his bed by now. Teddy gives an authentic-sounding flavour of the evening: [28]

> Few of us remember much about it for we were very merry, thanks
> to the wine, and there was considerable horseplay. I remember
> dancing with the cook whilst Oates danced with Anton. Everybody
> took a turn ... It was left to me to see the seamen turned in; they

were good-humoured but obstreperous, and not until 2 a.m. did silence and order once more reign in the hut.

It was a 'magnificent bust', according to Cherry, but Wilson says very little about it. He was on watch that night and entertained himself with Ponting's book on Japan. It would not have been a good show in his book, as he hated drunkenness. That didn't spoil the fun for Oates though, as Cherry tells us: [29]

> As we turned in [Oates] said, 'Cherry, are you responsible for your
> actions?' and when I said Yes, he blew loudly on his whistle, and the
> last thing I remembered was that he woke up Meares to ask him
> whether he was fancy free.

Clearly drunk, Oates was probably saved from worse silliness by Meares turning over and making him go away.

We will never know every detail of what went on in that hut – nor, for that matter, in any of the heroic-era huts or ships, but Scott seems to have done what he could to keep things chaste. Scott was only a light drinker and Wilson was tee-total, which more or less guaranteed a generally abstemious culture and a concomitant absence of disinhibited behaviour. In spite of his love of ragging, Wilson wouldn't have needed words to shame anyone tempted to go too far. The conditions would also have militated against it. There was no privacy to speak of in the well-lit hut, while the presence of a night-watchman must have discouraged nocturnal shenanigans.

So the evenings in the hut tended to take the form of a collegiate debating society and chess club, while a subfunction of the lectures must have been that they kept minds and bodies occupied. Scott was well schooled in the ways of avoiding ribaldry. People spent a lot of time reading: Scott was usually in his cubicle reading and writing (or doing arithmetic), while the scientists brought a sense of genuine enquiry and earnest intentions. Well aware of the unique opportunity afforded them – as evidenced by the large body of work resulting – they were determined to stay focused and make the most of it. Taylor gives us an idea of life in the hut on a quiet afternoon: [30]

> I am sitting on my bunk in the pose photoed by Ponting, using my
> little drawing-board as a table. Gran is writing one of his six diaries
> with Deb's nib, which he blunts ... Debenham is painting his third
> masterpiece ... Day also is busy elaborating his sketches. Marie
> Nelson is writing a voluminous lecture ... Dr. Atkinson is groping
> among encysted 'mully-grubs' at his half of the table, while Silas
> Wright wrestles with pendulum details on the other side. Simpson
> is writing up weather for S.P.T. [*South Polar Times*]; while, I
> believe, Dr. Bill has finished the 'hot-stuff' sketches of geology, etc.,
> for my S.P.T. article ... Cherry is flapping away at S.P.T. on the

typewriter and chortling muchly ... Teddy Evans is plotting a
graticule for the southern survey, while Ponting has just perpetuated the 'Teamsters' in the stable where Titus entertained
Meares to tea. Birdie Bowers is writing reams for his lecture on
sledge-foods – guess it will make a book! The 'Owner' is reading in
his cubicle as usual.

There must have been moments that winter that gave supreme satisfaction.
Not only was it an escape from all the usual demands and expectations at home, in
many ways it was a fantasy come true. They were marooned on a desert island,
albeit a cold one, yet cosily huddled together and safe in their hut. The hostility of
the conditions accentuated the comfort and warmth of the human companionship
within. When they laid back in their bunks listening to the tempest outside and the
voice of Clara Butt or Nellie Melba wavering through the rafters, they must have
contemplated the extraordinariness of it all, and felt privileged to be there. Which
they were.

References

1   Sir Ranulph Fiennes. *Captain Scott*, p. 226

2   Robert Falcon Scott. *Journals*, Editor's Appendix III, p. 461

3   Reginald Pound. *Scott of the Antarctic*, p. 236

4   Robert Falcon Scott. *op. cit.*, Editor's Appendix III, p. 462

5   Apsley Cherry-Garrard. *The Worst Journey in the World*, p. 174

6   Admiral Edward Evans. *South With Scott*, pp. 112–13

7   Apsley Cherry-Garrard. *op. cit.*, p. 180

8   *op. cit.*, pp. 178–9

9   *op. cit.*, p. 180

10   Robert Falcon Scott. *op. cit.*, p. 175

11   Griffith Taylor. *With Scott*, p. 212

12   Edward Wilson. *Diary of the Discovery Expedition*, p. 117

13   Robert Falcon Scott. *op. cit.*, p. 97

14   June Debenham Back (ed.). *The Quiet Land*, p. 125

15   Griffith Taylor. *op. cit.*, p. 227

16   Sue Limb and Patrick Cordingley. *Captain Oates*, pp. 30–1

17   June Debenham Back (ed.). *op. cit.*, p. 126

18   Sue Limb and Patrick Cordingley. *op. cit.*, p. 169

19   *op. cit.*, p. 132

20   Roland Huntford (ed.). *The Amundsen Photographs*, p. 58

21   Griffith Taylor. *op. cit.*, p. 317

22   *op. cit.*, p. 260

23   David Thomson. *Scott's Men*, pp. 151–2

24   June Debenham Back (ed.). *op. cit.*, p. 127

25   *ibid.*

26   *op. cit.*, p. 125

27   Admiral Edward Evans. *op. cit.*, pp. 122–3

28   *op. cit.*, pp. 135–6

29   Apsley Cherry-Garrard. *op. cit.*, p. 238

30   Griffith Taylor. *op. cit.*, pp. 248–9

24

THE WINTER BEFORE THE POLE

All nautical pride we cast aside
As we ran the vessel ashore
On the Gulliby Isles, where the poo-poo smiles
And the rubbily ubdugs roar!

From 'A Capital Ship', an old English folksong, with words by Charles
Carryl, 1896

An eerie silence may now impress itself on visitors to the hut but, at the time,
it was never silent. From Simpson's meteorological lab at the back a constant
ticking, clicking, whirring and pinging could be heard. The thinkers, too, made
quite a lot of noise with their conversations, Taylor providing a fair amount of it.
They also provided most of the lectures which, somewhat ambitiously, were held
three evenings a week at first – the *Universitas Antarctica*, as it became known. It
was an earnest programme of lectures which Scott, in one of his more charming
moments, proclaimed to be voluntary only [1]

> ... and neither the lecturer nor the chairman will feel aggrieved if
> any person prefers to read a novel or otherwise employ his time.

This quite often included the men of the messdeck, who had their own space,
partitioned off by provisions boxes. Apart from Anton and Dmitrii, they were all
Royal Navy, many of them petty officers. While they mixed socially with the
afterguard on special occasions like the midwinter party, they had their own
psychological space, culture and hierarchy. Taff Evans was dominant on the messdeck, as Ponting confirms. [2] Taff was a big, strong man. He and Lashly had been on
the Plateau Journey with Scott on the *Discovery* Expedition, and Taff in particular
had carved for himself a virtually indispensable role, especially in front of a sledge.
He had been the cause of a major row between Scott and Teddy shortly before
departure from New Zealand when, in a state of advanced inebriation, he fell into

the water between the ship and the quay. It must have been an ignominious spectacle, and dangerous. Teddy was furious about it but Scott 'smoothed him down'; he was never going to sacrifice muscle which he might have already have pencilled in for the final Pole push.

In social identity terms, the situation was complex and inter-related. While there was inter-group bias, there were crossovers, as for example between Taff and Scott. Where would Taff's primary loyalty have lain? With his mess-mates or with Scott? However finally balanced his loyalties were (and where he thought his best interests lay), there was no chance of social mobility nor inter-group permeability. The divisions were absolute, and there was therefore no point in competing on either a personal or a group level. There may have been a variety of personal relationships, but both Scott and Wilson, the *de facto* leaders, were social snobs. Wilson, for all his piety, was markedly racist – usually excused by historians as having been 'a man of his time'. He was also a social and intellectual snob, and patronising towards those he considered lower on the social scale than himself. It was Teddy who had the 'common touch', and it was to him the 'men' went for counselling, not Wilson.

Cherry's pen-sketch of Scott at this time [3] shows how Scott made life difficult for himself by his autocratic rule. Whatever the pressure, he *would* boss the show and, although he was reputed to be always open to new ideas, his own invariably prevailed, until in the end, people stopped bothering. But Cherry's insights go some way to explaining why Scott, in spite of his errors and issues, nevertheless elicited affection from at least some of those around him – some of the time. Those who felt differently are not so well represented in writing, and those who did keep diaries tended to self-censor and pass over difficult interpersonal issues.

But there was clearly a body of genuine feeling for Scott. Cherry's account suggests that people saw beyond the irritability, the depressions and the petty tyranny, and perceived the hidden agony – the nerves, the lack of confidence, the anxiety and the 'almost feminine' sensitivity, and possibly above all the martyrdom to his ambition. Wilson undoubtedly saw Scott as he really was, and loved him in spite of it or even because of it. Cherry was clearly compassionate, Bowers responded to Scott's needs unconditionally – and many of the others related to what were, after all, very human failings. But they did not crowd around him in spontaneous bonhomie. One might have expected at least one photo of the company arranged around him, glasses raised, with smiles on faces. If such a thing had occurred spontaneously, Ponting would undoubtedly have recorded it for posterity. As it was, apart from the Christmas party, the celebratory dinners seem to have been rather dour affairs, with Scott at the head of the table in a pose suggesting a hieratic tranquillity, impassive and condescending. Oates, Meares and Atkinson always look down at their plates, as do most of the others, while those around Scott appear to be making self-conscious conversation. Wilson is invariably by Scott's side, smiling and modest, but always as Scott's people-pleasing intermediary, ally and apologist.

A curious footnote here is that in Ponting's book, *The Great White South*, Scott's birthday dinner is not only wrongly captioned as the 'Midwinter Day Dinner', but also cropped to exclude Day and Atkinson. Eyebrows might not necessarily be raised at that, but they would by the fact that Gran has been 'disappeared' – reminiscent of Stalin's practice of erasing from photos those who had fallen out of favour. If Scott had been first at the Pole instead of Amundsen, whoever did it would presumably not have gone to the trouble.

Debenham too was caught up in the general mood of forgiveness and generosity in the aftermath of Scott's death, and was instrumental in setting up the SPRI, which has safeguarded Scott's heritage and reputation for more than a century. At the time, however, Debenham too was critical of Scott. In material that, similar to other critical material, has been slow to come into general public view (in this case not until 1992), Debenham writes this to his mother in a letter dated 14 November 1911: [4]

> The depot-laying, even apart from the loss of 3 ponies by drowning, was not at all a success. The loss of 6 out of 8 ponies was a big blow to the Owner ... and it is hard to blame him but things went rather wrong.

> I must tell you what I think of him. I am afraid I am very disappointed in him, tho' my faith died very hard. There's no doubt he can be very nice and the interest he takes in our scientific work is immense, he is also a fine sledger himself and as organiser is splendid. But there I'm afraid one must stop. His temper is very uncertain and leads him to absurd lengths even in simple arguments. In crises he acts very peculiarly. In one, where Atkinson was lost for 6 hours in a blizzard, I thought he acted splendidly but in all the others I have been quite disgusted with him. What he decides is often enough the right thing I expect, but he loses all control of his tongue and makes us all feel wild. His treatment of one or two of the officers has been very bad in my opinion but it is difficult to judge one's leader ... altho' I cannot say he is in the least popular, still we are all prepared to follow him. The whole thing is not a pleasant subject but one expects something to go wrong down here in tempers etc.

If only it had just been a question of temper. Scott would have got away with being the most irascible man on Earth if he had known what he was doing. It's not enough to say that he was unlucky, nor that circumstances came out against him. The fundamental basis on which he proposed to travel to the Pole was fatally flawed. He thought he could do better than Shackleton, but on what basis? He was proposing to use ponies and man-haulage like Shackleton. This meant that he would be subject to approximately the same weight:mileage ratios and levels of endurance per man, regardless of the number of support parties. The problem is that support parties have to be catered for too.

If Scott had been able to overcome his prejudice against dogs and had learned what they were capable of in time, would he have used them? Probably. Whatever his notions about man-hauling, he had mustered as much pulling power as his scattergun approach afforded, suggesting that his early idealism about unaided manpower had been dropped. His failure was always about his mistrust of dogs, which was based on his own ignorance and mistakes, bolstered by confirmation bias and denial. As far as his temper was concerned, it was not helped by the worry that Amundsen might snatch the prize from under his nose and, as though adding insult to injury, with the very method of transport he had persistently rejected. But he had nailed his colours to the mast and was committed to carrying on exactly as though Amundsen didn't exist. Well, try to, anyway.

A daily reminder of the Norwegian threat was the good-looking Tryggve Gran, taken on at Kathleen's instigation, who shared a cubicle with Debenham and Taylor. The skiing expertise he had been engaged to impart was underutilised and, as a result, it took him a while to find a useful role for himself. He helped create the 'boudoir' opposite the Tenements, complete with draperies and bookshelves with decorative trimmings. Here, the Ubdugs were more secluded than any other coterie in the hut, according to Taylor. [5] Taylor was very much a varsity man and had been friends with both Wright and Debenham from before the expedition. Cambridge University was well represented: Wilson, Taylor, Nelson, Debenham and Wright were all Cambridge men.

All the scientists had their bunks on the right-hand side of the hut, while the Pole enablers were on the left. It was an interesting dichotomy between thought and action, and two different types of exploration. In the end, the thinkers on the right suffered no casualties. On the contrary: for many, the expedition was a boost to their careers. On the left, death, illness and trauma cut a swathe through the men of action: the only men on the left not to die, or almost die, or suffer obvious PTSD, were Meares and Atkinson. As far as the messdeck was concerned, apart from Taff Evans, who is still on the move encased somewhere in the Beardmore Glacier, Antarctic service made little difference to their subsequent careers. The exceptions are Tom Crean, who went on to achieve legendary status with Shackleton, and William Lashly, who also achieved a measure of Polar fame and had his diary published (although heavily edited, much to its detriment). Crean ended up with a pub in Ireland, which is still there (The South Pole Inn, Annascaul, County Kerry), and Lashly ended up working as a customs inspector in Cardiff before retiring to Hambledon.

Of the Bunderlohgians, Cherry and Birdie were always loyal to Scott – out-wardly, at least. Birdie was imbued with an almost naive loyalty, apparently refusing to believe anyone or anything could be superior to Scott and the 'British way'; but Cherry lets slip a few mild criticisms in *The Worst Journey in the World*, to the effect that Scott was at times peevish, irritable, moody and depressed. Kathleen expressed her disapproval and thought he'd been put up to it by his neighbour GB Shaw (whom she 'vamped', nevertheless), who helped Cherry with the manuscript. Not only does this fail to give credit to Cherry, it also shows Kathleen's ongoing wish to suppress criticisms which she nevertheless knew to be justified.

Together with Wilson and Bowers, Cherry endured, at Wilson's behest, one of the most spectacularly cold journeys ever undertaken by man: the infamous mid-winter Cape Crozier bird-nesting trip. It really was the worst journey in the world. Not only were they lucky to survive it, it was a miracle that they came back without serious cold-injury. But Cherry asked too much of himself, and too much was asked of him. By the end of the expedition he had, by his own reckoning, done more sledging than anyone else. Even without the last dog-sledge journey to One Ton Depot, the expedition would have been a life-changing and defining event for him; but it was this journey, alone with Dmitrii and the dogs, which left him trauma-tised. On leaving Cape Evans for the last time he wrote in his diary: [6]

> I leave Cape Evans with no regret: I never want to see the place
> again. The pleasant memories are all swallowed up in the bad ones.

This was, of course, after the finding of the dead; and no doubt this was the event uppermost in his mind when he wrote it, but that wasn't what haunted him for the rest of his life.

Cherry's father, a retired Army major-general, was in his early fifties when he married and started a family. Cherry was the first-born, and only boy; and as successive sisters arrived, he must have felt the weight of expectation increasing at every sibling birth. His father, although no doubt a fair and kind man was, as an arch-conservative and a retired Army officer, likely to have had a habit of manner that was intimidating to a sensitive boy like Cherry. Evidence of the pressure of expectations on him can be seen in his father's refusal to believe that Cherry was permanently and seriously short-sighted, and denying him spectacles until he was 15 years old. He was duly sensitive about his glasses forever afterwards and always took them off whenever a camera was pointed in his direction.

At Oxford, George Mair, a fellow student, remembered Cherry as [7]

> a dark, lean, rather silent man ... remarkable only for a certain taste
> in natural history, an extreme shyness, and a nervousness which
> was not what we commonly call nervousness, but rather a sensitive
> imagination which made him see further round things than other

people, and, like a tightly stretched wire, made him react more quickly than other and duller men.

This suggests that anxiety was always close under the surface. Cherry's connection with Scott came through his cousin Reginald Smith, Scott's publisher, who had a shooting lodge near Kirriemuir – JM Barrie's birthplace, coincidentally. Here Cherry met and befriended Wilson, who became his conduit to Scott and the expedition.

Apsley Cherry-Garrard had been a young man in search of meaning and purpose, a *raison d'être*. His father died in 1907, leaving him heir to a considerable estate. Taking over where his father left off wasn't an option; he hated running his estates and the never-ending decisions to be made and issues to be dealt with. And yet, the question was what else he should do. The expedition was a chance to find out and at the same time to be part of a historic adventure. What wasn't there to like? The unfortunate upshot was that it landed him with a psychological burden he was ill-equipped to bear. There is a bronze of him in St Helen's Church at Wheathamstead, where he is buried. The sculptor was Ivor Roberts-Jones, more famous for his Churchill in Parliament Square. Roberts-Jones chose to depict the shy and vulnerable Cherry – pelvis thrust forward, sloping shoulders, one knee turned slightly inwards. It's Cherry at the start of the Midwinter Journey to Cape Crozier. He was only 25, and he was apprehensive.

But brave as it was, this hellish trip wasn't what broke him. Nor was it the blood and guts he sweated going up the Beardmore. It was the final dog-sledge journey to One Ton Depot, and the fact that he and Dmitrii were the closest anyone was ever to get to a living Scott and what was left of his Polar Party. When they found the location of Scott's last camp, the inevitable thought must have been that all he needed to have done to potentially save Scott's team was to have left a small depot of fuel and food between 15 and 20 miles south of One Ton – an easy day's journey for him and the dogs. He must have told himself over and over that he had no way of knowing where Scott was, nor what condition he was in; but in retrospect, putting a depot as far south as he could reasonably manage would seem the obvious thing to have done. The argument that he stayed put because he feared he might miss Scott didn't really wash because there were cairns and the remains of pony walls still marking the route. Predictably, the issue weighed heavily on him and was probably the main cause of the half-life of valetudinarian hypochondria and depression he sank into in later life – attempting to rid himself of his two albatrosses: his material inheritance, which he succeeded in divesting himself of, and the emotional burden he carried home from Antarctica, which never really went away.

While most of the Bunderlohgians' relationships with Scott were ambivalent, that wasn't the case with Henry Robertson Bowers, aka Birdie. A 'tough little square block of a man' (in Oates' words) with a superlative cardiovascular system, he defied the cold with his famous green hat until even his ears froze, which was way beyond the point at which a normal human ear freezes. He had lost his father at an early age and had strong and loving bonds with his mother and sisters – the only women he ever had the chance of a meaningful relationship with. While not a secular monk like Wilson, he nevertheless had a strong religious faith, as genuine and uncomplicated as was his entire approach to life and other people. If there were demons in his psyche (other than spiders), they didn't bother him. He was described as elemental, a force of nature. Intensely loyal himself, he inspired loyalty in others.

Birdie thought God had a hand in all things, but his presence on the expedition and in the Shore Party was due to his own merits as a worker and as a man. Henry had been a cadet on the training ship *Worcester* for two years from 1897 (a couple of years after Teddy Evans and Gerald Doorly, incidentally, and some ten years after Wilfrid Bruce, Kathleen's brother, and about 20 years after Albert Armitage). Markham was a regular visitor on the *Worcester*, as we know, and was on friendly terms with the captain-superintendent of the *Worcester* of Birdie's day, David Wilson-Barker. As a man, Wilson-Barker was said to make surprisingly little impact, being short and slight, with a little pointed beard, and giving the impression of being more of a scholar than the stereotype of a man in his position. Diffident, quiet, somewhat prim, he seems to have spent a lot of time at his desk writing, and engaged in the study of natural history and meteorology. As well as a friend of Markham's, he was a member of the Royal Geographical Society. To most of the cadets, however, he was a remote figure and was rarely seen among them.

Henry was an exception. He kindled a fondness in Wilson-Barker which, in spite of his professed reluctance to single out any particular boy, found expression in extra lessons in which Henry was taught the rudiments of photography, butterfly collecting and ornithology. He was the only cadet who ever took a real interest in natural history, according to Wilson-Barker, who described him as being an average type of boy who nevertheless distinguished himself by the quiet accumulation of knowledge and physical strength. Wilson-Barker's interest and solicitude on Henry's behalf went beyond his time on the *Worcester*. He had many times heard young Henry voice his fascination with Polar exploration; and when the opportunity came to meet Markham, shortly after the return of the *Discovery*, Henry was invited to lunch on the *Worcester*, when he was introduced to Sir Clements. The table talk inevitably centred on Polar exploration, and Wilson-Barker told Markham that he thought Henry was the type of man who would lead one of those expeditions one day. It seems extravagant praise, but it gives an indication of the strength of feeling Birdie (just one of his many nicknames) was capable of kindling, and not just in the heart of this rather solitary and diffident man.

Markham too found Birdie endearing, in spite of his unromantic appearance. Plausible reasons for this were that he submitted cheerfully and unconditionally to his superiors, was honest to the point of naivety, eager to please, fiercely loyal, and tirelessly devoted to duty. When Scott's Second Expedition came along, it clearly represented a unique opportunity for Wilson-Barker to fulfil his protégé's most cherished ambition, and he duly prevailed upon Markham to recommend Birdie to Scott in the strongest terms.

And so Birdie was plucked from the Royal Indian Marines in Bombay (Mumbai) and requisitioned for services in the Antarctic. In a letter dated 9 April 1910 to his mother, Birdie writes: [8]

> I had a short note from Sir Clements Markham last August saying this Expedition was under way; he remembered my keenness over the *Discovery* Expedition, and said he would recommend my name to Capt. Scott if I would like. Of course I said I would like ... My next letter was from Capt. Wilson-Barker, saying he had had a letter from Capt. Scott, but there were over 5,000 applicants then – December.
>
> Things were still in this state while I was away boat-cruising and I wrote my 3rd and last letter to Evans ... The list of applicants had swelled to 8,000 by this time, and I dropped the matter and did not apply.
>
> On arriving here the Director told me of my appointment and congratulated me, and now cables are flying about like smoke and your son has become a curio. ... Well, there is the plain unvarnished history of the greatest surprise I have ever had ... I know you will feel that your son has hardly been fair to his mother; but you will not I am sure blame my acceptance of the opportunity. I never really asked for it.

He may not have asked for it in so many words, but it was a wish come true all the same. Writing to Captain Wilson-Barker he said he didn't know how to thank him for getting him appointed to the expedition and that he was so surprised and pleased he could hardly realise it: [9]

> I was under orders to return to the Persian Gulf when Captain Scott's telegram arrived. I shall be leaving by the next French mail to Marseilles and should be in London by the 1st May. I shall look forward to seeing you then for what I consider to be the climax in a long succession of kindnesses you have done me. Needless to say I was never keener on anything in my life.

He wrote to his mother implying that he thought a higher power must have been at work on his behalf and, in order to reassure her, he wrote that [10]

It will all be over in a couple of years and then you will be glad I went.

Those words must have echoed painfully for Emily Bowers after the fate of her boy became known.

Birdie was multi-skilled, strong, tireless, and ready to do anything he was ordered to do without doubt and without question. It was not in his nature to question authority, divine or otherwise. It is clear from his analysis of the causes of the Pony Disaster that it was almost impossible for him to imagine those in authority could be at fault in any way. He was schooled from an early age to credit his superiors and to defer as though by conditioned reflex. This, together with his navigation skills and his physical and mental strength, secured him a place on the journey that killed him.

Birdie could find no fault in Scott, and Scott himself seems to have been unaware – or as seems more likely, in denial of – any negative feelings he engendered. A Scott diary entry dated 14 May purports to state the 'real truth', which was, according to him, that there was no friction at all, and that a universally amicable spirit prevailed at all times. It is often the case that people are not fully aware of the effect their behaviour has on others. Much as one ought to give Scott the benefit of the doubt, and while acknowledging he did have his charming moments, the picture is not enhanced by his childish need to be right and always to have the last word in debates, as reported by Debenham. The abusive outbursts were also extremely damaging, and while they may have forced a degree of compliance, they also alienated people.

Scott was an outsider. He was an observer of the amicable spirit, rather than an integral part of it. His core insecurity and diffidence precluded authentic man-to-man bonding and shared emotion. He was never able to let himself go, take his Owner's hat off, and be equal, real and truly at ease. There was always a defensive psychological shield and a certain distance between him and everyone else, apart from maybe Wilson and sometimes Birdie. Under the surface there were mixed feelings generally: yes, the Owner had his charming moments and everyone was outwardly loyal, but he wasn't popular. Further, opinions as to his competence as an explorer were not unanimously positive.

On 8 May, just six months before the proposed departure for the Pole, the company was informed of the way this most demanding and dangerous of journeys was going to be accomplished. Whether or not the timing of it was deliberate, it was just five days before the return of Meares and the dogs from Hut Point, which suggests Scott may have wanted to save himself the eloquently averted gaze he might have anticipated from Meares. After all, he had waited this long to put his plans before the company, surely another few days wouldn't have made any difference. It seems plausible, considering the fact that, as Debenham reports, he re-iterated his disappointment with the dogs, and expressed his doubts as to whether they would make it as far as the bottom of the Beardmore. With regard to the dogs, Scott reflected [11]

> ... ruefully on the misplaced confidence with which I regarded the provision of our transport. Well, one must suffer for errors of judgment.

Amundsen would have been dumbfounded. As far as he was concerned, the Barrier provided ideal conditions for dog-sledging; and if he had had the broad expanses of the Beardmore to look forward to, and the likewise pretty-much-known and safe route over the Plateau, he would have considered it a no-brainer, and must have positively marvelled at the opportunity that was squandered. Instead, Scott seems to have succeeded in fostering a kind of group-think with regard to the dogs, to the point where the touchingly credulous Birdie thought that Amundsen had *no* chance of getting to the Pole. [12] Debenham quietly thought otherwise.

In almost comical contrast to Amundsen and the select band of appropriate experts around him who had spent not just that winter, but much of their lives, in preparation for exactly this kind of endeavour; and who were, as he spoke, not just preparing but fine-tuning every conceivable detail for the challenges ahead, Scott chose the format of one of the evening lectures to set out his plans for the conquest of the South Pole. Debenham tried to give the salient parts of the lecture exactly as Scott said them. [13]

He drew a basic map, showing the three stages to the Pole: Barrier, Beardmore, and Plateau. Going by Shackleton's figures, Scott informed them the journey there and back would be 1,530 geographical miles (1,760 statute), and would take a total of 144 days. By this calculation they would be back at Hut Point on or about 22 March (1912), which meant they would almost certainly miss the ship, and would have to stay another winter. He then repeated his mantra that they would go ahead exactly as if Amundsen did not exist. Shackleton started from Hut Point on 3 November 1908 and arrived back there on 28 February 1909. This means that he had travelled to within 100 geographical miles of the Pole and back in 117 days. Scott allowed an extra 27 days – almost four weeks – extra for those extra 100 miles there and back, an average of 7.4 miles per day, including time at the Pole for establishing position. It must have seemed do-able.

As far as transport was concerned, he felt sure that the only reliable means were the ponies, calculating quite dispassionately that of the ten he hoped to start with, two would last for 18 days, three for 22 days, another three for 28 days, and the last two would be killed by the 34th day out. Men alone would be counted on for the last two stages. This did not take account of the return journeys. There was an emphasis on the detailed calculations of supplies and depots, ignoring the effect that months of savage exertion and deprivation were likely to have on the men. It was typical of the brute force and ignorance approach of the British 'gentlemen's' school, whereby the ruling class looked down on professionals, and even 'scientists' (one of the tribal divisions present in the hut too), and considered it unnecessary to educate themselves. In a culture which regards its leaders as born to rule, incompetence is by definition impossible.

Cherry, who, in spite of his occasional criticisms, was instinctively loyal to his conservative roots, sets out an apologia for the apparent lack of depth and sophistication of the plans for the journey. Something obviously struck him as incongruous, as he admits that the reader may ask why these plans weren't prepared until the winter previous to the journey itself. Without apparently seriously questioning the ad-hoc approach to the problem, he states that until the autumn (depot) sledging had been accomplished it was impossible to have more than a rough idea in terms of the performance of the dogs, sledges, ponies and men, and what transport would be available for the bid for the Pole. [14] While there must always be an element of uncertainty in an endeavour such as this, a competent leader would have had more than a rough idea; they would have calculated their chances on the basis of known variables and, leaving aside random, unpredictable events, would have a pretty good idea of the resources at their disposal.

The secretiveness to which Scott (by his own admission) was prone, was a defensive ploy, designed to protect his plans from scrutiny and criticism. It also allowed him to keep his options open in the face of his own uncertainty. In reality, he did not have options. While the whole expedition had been planned on the basis of fail-safes, hedges, and the availability of alternatives, it had become clear that the tractors were not going to do very much; and the most the ponies were only ever expected to do was drag supplies to the start of the Beardmore Glacier. There were not enough dogs to take them anywhere near the Pole, a possibility which he was in any case deeply invested in denying. In reality, for the vast majority of the journey, there was no option but to man-haul. Even the inevitable hardships of this might have been mitigated by a greater willingness to admit of the possibility of improvement in, for example, tents and equipment. Some tinkering around the edges did take place, but the basics were never critically appraised.

It was as though Scott was interested in all other science except how to get to the Pole and back. He made copious notes of all the science lectures, and took a great interest in the weather and local environment; but instead of making all those notes and impressing the scientists with his comments, he would have been better advised testing his equipment. It would have been consistent with his denialist approach for him not to have wanted to know about potential shortcomings. Instead, he preferred to believe that everything was perfect as it was, beyond perhaps a few minor adjustments, and after having gone round 'mildly tying the scientists in knots', he went to bed with *Tess of the d'Urbervilles.* There was no justification for this complacency, but the thought didn't seem to occur to him to experiment with tent design, nor clothing, nor other ways in which they might make the forthcoming journey more bearable – survivable. Scott was not interested in Polar travel, and never had been. It is clear from his diary that what interested him on a day-to-day basis throughout the winter was the meteorology and geology of Cape Evans.

This lack of interest in transport and equipment set the tone and the culture over the whole of the expedition – except for Meares and Oates, whose daily business concerned it, and who both seem to have felt inadequately supported or valued. Wilson, apart from the very risky Cape Crozier trip, spent much of his time sketching and painting. Between Scott and Teddy, nominally second-in-command, a chasm had opened up, destined only to get wider as time went on. For now it meant that Teddy chose to go out surveying much of the time, when they should have been putting their heads together for the benefit of the Southern Journey. But then, Scott didn't consider it necessary. He made a token effort after having perused Sverdrup's book *New Land: Four Years in the Arctic Regions,* which led to instructions for Taff Evans to make an experimental inner lining for the tents. Although many were sceptical at first, inner linings did make the tents feel warmer. This was probably due to the fact that there was less radiant heat loss in a lined tent. An interesting example of this phenomenon occurs in small stone churches which are only heated in preparation for Sunday services. Although the air may have been heated, the walls remain cold; and church occupants radiate heat to them, making them feel cold in spite of a comfortable ambient temperature. [15]

It was also left to Taff to design and make improvements to their ski-bindings and crampons. Taff supervised the maintenance and repair of all camping and sledging equipment; but apart from small improvements, it was obviously not his remit to suggest radical changes even if he had thought of them. Scott's lack of involvement with the practicalities also hints at that air of conceit affected by Naval officers of Scott's era, whereby work of that kind was the province of the 'men'. Much as he hated the snobbery among Naval officers, it had rubbed off on him, certainly with regard to what he considered suitable employment for an officer, which did not include practical work on sledges, cobbling, nor tinkering with crampons. Nor did he encourage the scientists to think about such things. It was another reason why there were no significant improvements in his equipment since the *Discovery* days.

There were certain problems that should have been addressed as a matter of ordinary competence. Scott has already been strongly criticised by Roland Huntford for his lack of remedial action with regard to the leaky paraffin tins, for example. On the journeys, the quantities were only just enough, with no allowance for spillage, wastage nor loss of any kind. On the way back from the Pole, Scott implied that the return parties were to blame for shortages, as he never evinced any sense of responsibility, either for planning depots without adequate margins, or for neglecting a known problem. But the buck stopped with him, however unwilling he was to own up to it. It was he who was to blame for having ignored what he dismissed as no more than an occasional nuisance rather than the 'great anxiety' (his words) it was to become.

The awful result of the lack of attention to the shortcomings of the oil tins made itself felt at what was, predictably, the most vulnerable stage of the Pole Journey: the last phase of the return. There are plenty of comments in the various diaries about paraffin having leaked into food supplies. It may have been due to more than just the perished leather washers on the stoppers, or the result of evaporation. The seams might have opened, for example. In an anecdote attributed to Atkinson, eight one-gallon tins had been put out at Cape Evans in September 1911. They were snowed up, and when examined in December 1912 showed three tins full, three empty, one a third full, and one two-thirds full. [16] There is no confirmation that these tins were in fact full when they were put out at Cape Evans; but they had presumably left their original supplier full, which means that either because of handling and transport, and/or exposure to Antarctic conditions, half the oil had been lost from the date of supply. One way or another, these tins were not fit for purpose, and may have failed in more ways than one. The leaky tins were a well-known issue throughout the expedition. It seems incomprehensible that with so many practical men and so much time to address the problem, nothing was ever done about it.

While paraffin-flavoured biscuits may have been a survivable unpleasantness, the loss of oil over a longer and bumpier journey was potentially disastrous – as it turned out. Scott knew that the sledges were going to be constantly jostled and hauled over uneven surfaces – sometimes capsizing altogether – with the result that the tins were going to be subjected to almost constant shaking and upset. Suffice to say that the most convincing evidence that the loss of oil was a serious – life-threatening – issue, is that Amundsen not only soldered his tins shut, but even went to the trouble and extra weight of carrying a soldering kit with him on his Pole Journey.

Scott's tents too could have been massively improved. They were difficult and cumbersome to put up, especially in windy conditions. They were heavier than they need have been, and not as warm as they might have been. A single-pole design with guy ropes and a sewn-in groundsheet would have been infinitely preferable. Amundsen, needless to say, used that design, which he said could be put up by a single man in any conditions. While that may have been a slight exaggeration, Scott's tents were undoubtedly less efficient and more difficult to put up in windy conditions. They had up to six poles, which had to be put in position before the fabric was hauled over them, which could be 'the dickens of a job' in a blizzard, risking frostbitten fingers, as Scott himself reports. They had loose, square groundsheets, which did not cover the whole of the floor, nor anywhere near, meaning those sleeping on the outer edges were mostly on snow. This was so that the groundsheet could be used as a sail when the wind was in the right direction, which Scott was hoping would be the case on the return from the Pole.

The tents were held in position by an outer valance, on which blocks or heaps of snow (which had to be excavated every time), were placed. It worked well in terms of anchorage, but it was extra work and more arduous than knocking in tent pegs. It also made the tent heavier because of the extra canvas required for the valance. It also meant that those sleeping around the edges were not only in direct contact with snow on the ground, but also indirectly against the snow piled up on the outside. With a sewn-in groundsheet, the saving on the fabric for the valance could have allowed for a purpose-made sail to be taken. A better sail than the unwieldy square one they were committed to could have been designed, yielding a saving in both weight and efficiency. None of this was particularly radical or innovatory, and they had all winter to test ideas.

The clothing could also have been improved. There is significant loss of heat around the neck, which is much reduced by sewn-on hoods. Tests were carried out with this but, as is clear from photos, not consistently put into practice. It isn't clear why not. The sledges might also have been improved. Amundsen's team found they could reduce the weight of the standard sledges hugely without a loss of strength.

Sleeping-bags were another major issue. Breathing inside the bag makes them wet on the inside, increasing their weight, and freezing them when not in use. Scott claims that carrying them open on the sledges kept them freer of moisture than rolling them up, especially on sunny days, obviously; but even so, people frequently report sleeping in wet bags. Scott simply accepted this as inevitable and, apart from trying to dry them on the march, made no effort to overcome the problem.

The answer was to have double bags with a drawstring around the neck, isolating the head from the body as, needless to say, Amundsen's team had. The fact is there was plenty of room for improvement almost everywhere. Oddly enough, Birdie's lecture on 'Evolution of Polar Clothing', given on 1 September, recommended making the tent floor-cloth wider, and that separating the head from the body of the sleeping-bags stopped them getting so wet, and also that the wind-helmet should be fastened to the blouse. [17] Scott commented on Birdie's lecture: [18]

> The points in our clothing problems are too technical and too fre-
> quently discussed to need special notice at present, but as a result

of a new study of Arctic precedents it is satisfactory to find it
becomes more and more evident that our equipment is the best
that has been devised for the purpose ...

In other words, Birdie might have saved his breath. Scott wasn't interested,
preferring to reassert his belief that no improvements were necessary.
Immediately after reporting Birdie's lecture, Griff Taylor's attention was also on
other things. This suggests that it was noted as interesting, but almost instantly
forgotten in the press of other matters, such as the compilation of the second
edition of the *South Polar Times*, which appeared on 8 September. Besides, Scott
was already getting ready for his Little Spring Journey, for which arrangements
had to be made, while in the meantime there were other lectures to be listened to
and discussed. Bowers himself was soon occupied, together with Scott, in learning
how to take photos, while Cherry was typing out sections of Shackleton's *The
Heart of the Antarctic* for Scott to take on the Pole Journey.

Sceptics like Oates and Meares probably kept their heads down because the
one issue that trumped all others was dogs, and they would have known better
than to open that particular can of worms. Meares clearly had views of his own
and would have considered it useless to address them seriously. Like Oates, he
appeared to have a cordial working relationship with Scott, but as time went on it
deteriorated to the point where he shipped out on the *Terra Nova* at the earliest
opportunity, leaving the expedition short-handed with the dogs. In fact, he had
already started to absent himself from Cape Evans by 1 September, two months
before the planned start for the Pole. One gets the feeling that Scott was somewhat
intimidated by Meares, as he seems to have acted unilaterally in choosing to take
frequent trips to Hut Point with Dmitrii and the dogs, eventually taking up
residence there altogether. Scott claims it was because he preferred to rough it;
but it could equally plausibly have been to do with getting away from him, and the
pressure to humour him and cater to his bouts of despondency and irritability. It
might also have grated on Meares to watch Scott chasing weather balloons instead
of focusing on his methods and equipment for getting to the Pole and back.
Whatever the case, Meares' actions do not seem to have depended on Scott's
permission or approval.

Scott's way of involving himself in the practicalities of life on the march was by
immersing himself in calculations. His multi-level transport arrangements guaranteed fiendishly complicated logistics – especially as two pulling resources were
uncertain quantities, namely the tractors and the ponies. In his diary entry for 1
September he tells us that he had been working very hard with Bowers on the
sledging figures, sounding confident that in spite of the immense amount of detail
and the uncertainty around the motors, their plans should carry them through. He
interpreted the absence of suggestions offered for improvement as meaning his
schemes had earned full confidence from everyone.

On 13 September, Scott gave another account of the programme for the Southern Journey, which was essentially a reiteration of the earlier one, but this time with figures. Wright notes that [19]

> It was certainly comprehensive, giving everything in the way of weights for each pony at every stage, and covering the contingency of the dogs or the motors breaking down or both.

No script of this lecture seems to have survived, unfortunately, but the reference to a 'Table VIII' in Scott's instructions for the dog teams gives an idea of the scope and volume. [20] Gran's comment was: [21]

> My goodness, it is an involved proposition. The thought behind it is no doubt marvellous, if only he can carry it out.

Scott was happy: [22]

> It is good to have arrived at a point where one can run over facts and figures again and again without detecting a flaw or foreseeing a difficulty.

Undecided about how long he would stay away, or exactly where he would go, he wrote: [23]

> Simpson, Bowers, and I are going to stretch our legs across to the Western Mountains.

In the event, he took Taff Evans as well. No one entirely understood the objectives of this journey, as Taylor was already planning to take a geological party to the same area. Scott claims he was brushing up on his sledging techniques and seeing what he could do with his cameras. They were away for 13 days, until 1 October, just one month before the main event. An explanation for this apparently pointless journey is explored in Chapter 27, Reflections.

At some point during October he must have come down to earth when he realised, or when it was pointed out to him, that his euphoria about the facts and figures was misplaced: and that there were not enough supplies at One Ton Depot to feed the returning parties, nor enough dog food to allow the dogs to come out and meet him on his return from the Pole. Hence the urgent instructions to Meares to take no fewer than five XS units, plus biscuits, oil and dog food to One Ton after his return from the main Southern Journey.

For now, Scott was in buoyant mood after returning from his 'remarkably pleasant and instructive little spring journey'. Almost immediately, according to Evans, [24]

> [He] set to work to put the final touches to his elaborate plans, drew up instructions, got his correspondence in order lest he should miss the *Terra Nova* through a late return from the Pole ...

On 20 October, four days before departure, Scott handed Teddy his instructions for the Motor Party. Clearly optimistic, in spite of the unpromising performance of the motors so far, Teddy's instructions were detailed and comprehensive, covering the pony food and biscuit he was to drag up to and beyond One Ton Depot. As will be seen, the motors broke down irretrievably within days, eliciting a sigh of relief from Lashly, for one, who evidently felt that even man-hauling was preferable to coaxing the wretched things along.

In addition to his instructions for the motors, Teddy was also handed all Scott's instructions for the various other parties to read. Teddy: [25]

> They are so explicit and comprehensive that I may well append certain of them here, for they clearly show how Scott's organisation covered the work of the ship, the base, the western party, the dog teams, and even the arrangements for Campbell's party.

This might have been a little disingenuous; Teddy's decision to reproduce all these instructions in his book *South With Scott*, published 1924, could be interpreted as an implied comment on the extent to which Scott micromanaged, and how preoccupied he was with paperwork in the months before departure.

The following are synopses of Scott's instructions, [26] starting with:

I. – INSTRUCTIONS FOR COMMANDING OFFICER, *Terra Nova*.

This forms an approximately 3,000-word set of instructions for Pennell, giving a résumé of the activities of the Southern Party, and informing him that the ship would in all probability have to return again next year. Details then followed about picking up Taylor's Geological Party, landing them somewhere else, and picking them up again and taking them back to Cape Evans before returning to New Zealand. Simpson was left in charge of the station (Cape Evans). The mules from India were to be landed at Cape Evans, together with additional equipment, stores and mails. There follows in great detail suggestions about how and where to moor the ship. Pennell was a competent commander and had been there in charge of the ship the year before. He could be expected to have a good idea already, but Scott's suggestions and recommendations were extensive. Then there were instructions what to do about Campbell's party, and further details of the behaviour of the ice in the Sound at considerable length, including a table of dates. Nevertheless, Pennell was assured these were suggestions only, leaving him to judge as he saw fit. Then follow instructions regarding repair of the galley stove, replotting the coast (evidently not convinced Taylor was right about the poor mapping on the *Discovery*, about which they had had a row). Instructions for leaving boot leather, stout nails and reindeer pelts, if available, followed, as well as a request for sheet metal for the blubber stove at Hut Point, extra coal, wood for extensions, and a meteorological hut. A depot of provisions was to be landed at Cape Crozier if possible, and rockets for signalling left. Then details of who would be returning with the ship and who would be staying.

Then:

> I am leaving with Simpson under separate cover a telegraphic despatch concerning the doings of this party, containing about 3000 words. I hope you will duly receive letters from me through returning sections of the Southern Party.

He instructed Pennell to remind everyone returning in the ship of the ship's articles. Worries about discipline seem puzzling, especially as Pennell was highly regarded and not likely to lose control. Regarding Ponting, who was returning, he had to be given every facility, but must not be allowed to run risks taking pictures. Finally, Pennell should not feel it incumbent on him to attempt to visit Amundsen's station, although he was to feel at liberty to rearrange this programme as necessary for the purpose.

> I am sure that you will do all that is possible under the circumstances. (Signed) R. F. Scott.

Next:

II. – INSTRUCTIONS TO DR. G. C. SIMPSON.

Approximately 500 words. Simpson was left in charge of the base after the departure of the Polar caravan. After Taylor had left for the Western Mountains with Gran, Debenham and Forde, he was there on his own with just Nelson and Clissold for company and Ponting, who was accompanied back by Anton from filming the start of the odyssey. He was told to see to a number of improvements to the hut and to carry out a variety of household duties including airing the mattresses. Concerning the safety of people going there and back to Hut Point, he was told to keep an eye on the state of the ice.

Next:

III. – INSTRUCTIONS LEADER OF WESTERN PARTY.

This was Griff Taylor's Geological Party. About 900 words, covering details of where he should go, what provisions he should take, where to leave depots, where he should concentrate his explorations, and where to rendez-vous with the ship. He was given a copy of the 3,000-word Instructions to Pennell, which he was at liberty to peruse.

> This should be left at your depot and the depot marked, so that the ship has a good chance of finding it in case of your absence ... Should the ship fail to appear within a fortnight of the date named you should prepare to retreat on Hut Point, but I am of opinion that the retreat should not be commenced until the Bays have re-frozen,

probably towards the end of March. An attempt to retreat over land might involve you in difficulties, whereas you could build a stone hut, provision it with seal meat ...

And so on. Further:

> ... it would be dangerous to be without shelter in such storms as that encountered by the *Discovery* off Coulman Island early in January, 1902.

> With camp equipment a party is always safe, though it is not easy to pitch tent in a high wind ... I wish you to show these instructions to Debenham, who will take charge of the party in case you should be incapacitated.

Et cetera.

IV. – INSTRUCTIONS FOR DOG TEAMS.

Approximately 650 words. An incredibly complicated and demanding set of instructions, about which there was destined to be much controversy. Meares, Dmitrii and the dogs were scheduled to accompany the Southern Train for a good part of the Barrier stage. He was expected to be back at Hut Point by 19 December at the latest. After a period of rest he was then to transport emergency stores from Cape Evans to Hut Point, and should, by 19 January, have made a second journey to One Ton Depot taking

> 5 units X.S. ration. [a unit was a week's supplies for four men]
> 3 cases of biscuit.
> 5 gallons of oil.
> As much dog food as you can conveniently carry (for third journey).

After that, he was expected to have nothing to do for at least three weeks and was to go back to Cape Evans and help unload the ship when it landed. Then he was to sledge out again to meet the returning Polar Party about 1 March in latitude 82 or 82.30.

> If you are then in a position to advance a few short marches or "mark time" for five or six days on food brought, or ponies killed, you should have a good chance of affecting your object ... of course you will not wait beyond the time when you can safely return on back depots.

> You will of course understand that whilst the object of your third journey is important, that of the second is vital. At all hazards three X.S. units of provision must be got to One Ton Camp ...

This third mission to the south was in order to hasten the return of the Polar Party to give it a chance to catch the ship. This was based on Scott's assumption that the ship would not have to leave until after the middle of March. In the event, however, she almost became beset on 22 February and had to depart soon after that. [27]

Next:

V. – INSTRUCTIONS TO LIEUT. VICTOR CAMPBELL.

In just over 500 words, Scott explains to Campbell that it looks like the ship will have to come back to McMurdo a third time, and that it gives him an opportunity to carry out a further season's work, should he wish to do so. However,

> ... it would of course be impossible for any of your party to stay at Cape Evans ... Being so much in the dark concerning all your movements and so doubtful as to my ability to catch the ship, I am unable to give more definite instructions ...

As we know, Campbell and his party were dropped off at Evans Coves, from where they were not able to be picked up.

In addition to all these instructions, from 1 to 24 October (from when he came back from the Little Spring Journey to when the motor sledges set off from Cape Evans), Scott wrote approximately another 6,700 words of diary material. This covered a résumé of his Little Spring Journey, the comings and goings from the base, the condition of the ponies, Clissold hurting his back while posing for Ponting, learning how to use a camera, the telephone (a line had been laid between Cape Evans and Hut Point), Forde's frostbitten hand, trouble with Christopher (the equine Manchurian demon), the comings and goings of the rest of the ponies, getting the motors out and one being damaged almost immediately, how the dogs were performing, the weather, minor accidents with the ponies and a football match for the benefit of the camera in which Debenham hurt his knee.

Towards the middle of October he held a meeting with everybody to discuss finances. The likely necessity for the ship to come down a third year, and the concomitant necessity for a number of people staying a second winter at Cape Evans meant a large extra financial outlay, necessitating an overdraft at the bank. Most people were willing to forgo an extra year's salary, but it involved a fair amount of paperwork, including a list of potential assets for the attention of Sir Edgar Speyer to use as security for monies borrowed. These included contracts with the newspapers and the Gaumont Film Company, proceeds from lectures and literary work, and so on. It seems odd that he had not addressed the issue of a second winter and a third trip down for the *Terra Nova* until now. He had decided to allow 144 days for the return trip to the Pole back in May, which had always meant a return on or around 22 March, by which time the ship would have to be out of McMurdo Sound. This conversation could, and should, have been had months before. All this was without mentioning the implications of a second shot at the Pole if the first one failed, which is why he had ordered mules, as discussed earlier.

There was also his correspondence, which included a fairly long discursive letter to JJ Kinsey (his agent in New Zealand), letters to his mother, his eldest sister, a nephew, a niece, his publisher, Taff Evans' wife, Oates' mother, and Admiral Egerton. His letter to Kathleen filled 17 pages. [28]

A seven-page letter dated 31 October 1911 was also written to Francis Drake (secretary to the expedition) with detailed instructions regarding diaries, mails, stamps etc. [29]

It was of course necessary for Scott to leave orders and instructions; but while a certain amount of anxiety would be normal under the circumstances, the above shows the frankly neurotic extent to which Scott retreated into paperwork as the day for departure drew near. No amount of procrastination, diversion, or fussing about everything under the sun could stop the moment of truth, however, and if he had ever had any doubts about it being a case of do or die, Kathleen effectively banished those doubts, as we shall see.

The rest of the Polar Party, with some exceptions, had taken Scott's little spring jaunt and apparent lack of concern as a cue for a similar nonchalance with regard to the imminent Pole Journey. For reasons he doesn't make clear, but which seem inspired by Scott's seemingly offhand attitude towards the approaching epic, Teddy went on surveying trip which was surely surplus to requirements at that late stage. It left him with a bare two weeks to rate chronometers, sew, pack, stow, make sundials, calibrate instruments, write letters home, and so on. Scott's behaviour seems generally to have been a cue for unfocused and irrelevant activities. It gave permission for time spent on *divertissements* in the form of humorous trifles, poems, artwork and associated material for yet another edition (the third) of the *South Polar Times*, which came out on 15 October, just nine days before the motor sledges were due to start.

Scott is silent about it. Perhaps he was somewhat embarrassed, as he himself – in addition to filming the 'camp doings' in a tent with Bowers, Wilson and Taff on the 4th – was also involved filming some sledge-hauling and camping scenes for Ponting – together with Taff, Wilson and Crean, on 29 October – which makes those last few days before departure seem almost unreal. It had been left to the men to overhaul the sledges and camping equipment; but although Taff made some useful improvements, the obsessive interest in what he was doing that prompted Amundsen to constantly experiment and search for improvements was notable by its absence in Scott. There were those, like Meares and Dmitrii, Oates and Anton, and Bowers, who were appropriately impressed with the demands of the forthcoming journey and grounded enough to address them. Meares was making dog pemmican at Hut Point, having overhauled the dog harnesses at Cape

Evans, Oates had his work cut out training the ponies to pull sledges, and Bowers had been occupied organising and packing the sledges.

Leadership of the Motor Party may have sounded like a fitting job for a second-in-command, and Teddy looks cheerful enough about it in photos, but the fact is that it was a difficult and thankless job. Details of the halting and sputtering inadequacies of the motors have been given in an earlier chapter. Now, Teddy's written instructions detailed the loads he should take on if the motors were successful. As the Motor Party, which included Lashly, Day and Hooper, left Cape Evans a few days before the main cavalcade, the dog teams were to follow him so that Scott could have the latest news of his success. In the event, the dog teams were too busy going up and down to Corner Camp hauling further supplies, which they did in record time. Meanwhile, there was a fuss getting the motors even as far as Hut Point, with Scott in the process making an unnecessary dash there and back on 26 and 27 October. [30] If and when they did finally get ahead, Teddy had instructions about what to do if they broke down irretrievably.

Scott writes that there was brief jubilation when Day became the first man in history to run a motor on the Great Barrier. Both motors had, however, irreparably broken down shortly afterwards – one just before, the other just after, Corner Camp, way before they were anywhere near One Ton. This meant that the Motor Party broke trail, man-hauled extra provisions, and put up wayside cairns the rest of the way, past One Ton Depot, to Mount Hooper (at 80.5 degrees, approximately 60 miles south of One Ton), where they waited six days for the rest of the procession to catch up. Lashly was pleased when the agony (his word) of the motors was over, but writes that well before they reached Mount Hooper, they were getting tired and hungry man-hauling. So soon after departure, it didn't augur well for the rest of the journey.

References

1   Griffith Taylor. *With Scott*, p. 229

2   Herbert G. Ponting. *The Great White South*, p. 112

3   Apsley Cherry-Garrard. *The Worst Journey in the World*, pp. 204–5

4   June Debenham Back (ed.). *The Quiet Land*, pp. 124–5

5   Griffith Taylor. *op. cit*, p. 228

6   Apsley Cherry-Garrard. *op. cit*, p. 585

7   Sara Wheeler. *Cherry*, p. 35

8   George Seaver. *'Birdie' Bowers of the Antarctic*, pp. 146–7

9   *op. cit.*, pp. 147–8

10   *op. cit.*, p. 148

11   Robert Falcon Scott. *Journals*, p. 196

12   June Debenham Back (ed.). *op. cit.*, p. 101

13   *op. cit.*, p. 102

14   Apsley Cherry-Garrard, *op. cit.*, p. 218

15   Gordon G. Giesbrecht and James A. Wilkerson. *Hypothermia, Frostbite and Other Cold Injuries*, pp. 31–2

16   Robert Falcon Scott. *op. cit.*, Editor's Appendix, p. 442, n. 26

17   Griffith Taylor. *op. cit.*, p. 302

18   Robert Falcon Scott. *op. cit.*, p. 283

19   Colin Bull and Pat F. Wright (eds.). *Silas*, pp. 168–9

20   Admiral Edward Evans. *South With Scott*, p. 186

21   Geoffrey Hattersley-Smith (ed.). *The Norwegian with Scott*, p. 128

22   Robert Falcon Scott. *op. cit.*, p. 284

23   *op. cit.*, p. 282

24   Admiral Edward Evans. *op. cit.*, p. 161

25   *op. cit.*, p. 167

26   *op. cit.*, pp. 166–90

27   Roland Huntford. *Scott and Amundsen*, p. 359

28   Reginald Pound. *Scott of the Antarctic*, pp. 255–60

29   Christie's. British Antarctic Expedition, 1910–1913, Sale 6409, Lot 100, www.christies.com

30   *ibid.*

25

THE POLE JOURNEY

A final note from Kathleen on a torn piece of paper, written in pencil: [1]
I left off just where I was going to tell you a very difficult thing. Look you – when you are away South I want you to be sure that if there be a risk to take or leave, you will take it, or if there is a danger for you or another man to face, it will be you who face it, just as much as before you met Doodles [Peter] and me. Because man dear *we can do without you* please know for sure we can. God knows I love you more than I thought could be possible, but I want you to realize that it won't [crossed out] wouldn't be your physical life that would profit me and Doodles most. If there's anything you think worth doing at the cost of your life – Do it. We shall only be glad. Do you understand me? How awful if you don't.

Scott appears to have carried this letter with him to the Pole. Most wives would tell their husbands that the most important thing is for them to survive and come home, regardless of the success or otherwise of their venture. One interpretation is that she is trying to get out of his way – setting him free of his responsibilities towards her and Doodles to do whatever he thinks worth doing, even at the cost of his life. But she also tells him his physical life would not profit her and Doodles most. It may have been just an unfortunate choice of words, but it appears to mean that his achievements matter more to her than his life. In that case, the pain of his failure must have been magnified.

We will never know how much it influenced his mood or his decisions, but to anyone but Kathleen it would have been an uncomfortable reflection. She made sure he understood her with the chilling 'Do you understand me? How awful if you don't.' Presumably, she doesn't want him to misinterpret what she is saying, but it isn't actually clear what she means, except that she is quite prepared for him to die. She ignores the fact that he wouldn't be on his own, and that other lives too would be at stake.

She was right about one thing: the drama of deaths in the wastes would create bigger headlines than the news of a bedraggled return by a bunch of also-rans.

'Do it – we shall only be glad.' Doodles wasn't of an age to understand any of it, yet she decided that it would be better for him to be orphaned rather than have a father who put his life before his ambition. If this Pole attempt had been of benefit to mankind in some way, one could understand it, but it was only ever about being the first man to stand at a certain geographical point on the globe.

The cavalcade set off on 1 November 1911. The pace was slow. Scott put the slowest and most decrepit ponies at the front of the column, and allowed them to dictate the pace and the daily distance up to One Ton Depot. Oates and Anton were wrestling daily with Christopher, a horse so intractable that it had to be brought to its knees before being hitched to the sledge. Then, according to Wilson: [2]

> ... his whole energies are spent in trying to bite. Then the sledge is drawn up to him and he is put into the traces. Now his forelegs are released – or one of them – while two men hang on to his head, and the moment he gets to his feet he rushes forward. If in this effort he kicks again, as he often does, he may again get his hind legs over the trace and the whole business has to be gone through again.

Bowers relates a similar story of ongoing struggles on the march, when it took up to five men to get that horse hitched to a sledge and away. Even Wilson doubted that there was enough in Scott's preference for white ponies [3]

> ... to warrant the cutting down of a very much larger selection in the Vladivostok market.

The distance between Hut Point and One Ton Depot via Corner Camp was approximately 118 geographical miles. They arrived at One Ton on 15 November, after 12 marches from Hut Point (13 days minus one march lost due to blizzard on the night of 6–7 November). This means that their average speed for the first 12 marches was 9.8 geographical miles per day. Clearly, there was a need to speed things up. Hence, their average mileage, still with all the weaker ponies, increased after 17 November to 13 geographical miles per day. Why couldn't this have been achieved from the start? All the ponies had been exercised in the run-up to the departure; and the fact that they achieved the improved mileage consistently after One Ton suggests that it was achievable from the beginning, as the surface conditions were similarly variable before and after One Ton Depot. The start of the epic was tentative, shambolic and inefficient. There were nerves where there should have been focused determination. It meant that after the first 12 marches,

38 miles had been lost – the equivalent of three days travel at the rate they were going.

On 25 November, Hooper and Day from the Motor Party started their return journey to Cape Evans, carrying a note to Simpson from Scott which read: [4, 5]

> My dear Simpson. This goes with Day and Hooper now returning. We are making fair progress and the ponies doing fairly well. I hope we shall get through to the Glacier without difficulty, but to make sure I am carrying the dog-teams farther than I intended at first – the teams may be late returning, unfit for further work or non-existent ... So don't forget that [*the supplies*] *must be got to 'One Ton Camp'*... somehow.

Those supplies were the five units XS ration, three cases of biscuit, five gallons of oil and as much dog food as they could carry, *or* a minimum of three units of XS rations. Simpson, having been left in charge at Cape Evans, should have been aware of all the instructions given to everyone, which included the instructions to Meares to take out the five XS units, etc. However, he seems to have had only a vague notion, or perhaps insufficient motivation to do more than send out the minimum requirement, as will be seen.

The dogs were kept on until 11 December, to a point slightly south of the Lower Glacier Depot – much further than planned and catered for, either in time or sustenance. It wouldn't be surprising if this unplanned extension elicited criticism (to say the least) in the already sceptical mind of Meares. It put a strain on the food supplies in terms of the extra return distance of the two men and the dog teams. Pony meat made up much of the deficit and fed the dogs, but the other teams had to give up part of their supply of biscuits and other sundries to supply Meares and Dmitrii over the extra return distance. It set Meares' timing back by at least two weeks, as he took until 4 January 1912 to get back to Hut Point. He had originally been scheduled to arrive back by 19 December at the latest.

It was another instance of Scott's autocratic leadership style in springing unexpected alterations on his teams without meaningful consultation. The already fragile relationship between Scott and Meares must have been further strained. Looked at from Meares' point of view, he had been sitting around twiddling his thumbs for much of the trek south because of the difference in pace between the ponies and the dogs, all the time knowing there was a shortage of supplies at One Ton which he had orders to rectify. That expectation was partially lifted when Hooper and Day turned back with the message for Simpson to get supplies to One Ton, which Meares was presumably told about. However, he also had orders to come out to 82 or 82.30 degrees south, more than 280 miles south of Hut Point, by 1 March, ostensibly to help Scott catch the ship, leaving Hut Point around the first week of February.

Scott's comment 'We are naturally always discussing possibility of meeting dogs', made on the Return Journey from the Pole on 27 February, when he was at around 82 degrees south, is evidence that this was still the hope, if not the expectation. However, for this to be possible it was essential that enough dog and man food for at least four weeks was available en route. This meant a depot of dog food. The alternative was to feed the dogs to each other. As this would have diminished the very pulling-power they were there to provide, it was obviously better to have dog food available on the way. Simpson, however, had been told that it would be enough to get just an extra three XS units to One Ton. The onus, therefore, must still have been on Meares to get the dog food and those other supplies to One Ton Depot.

In summary, Meares had been given a set of orders which were thrown into chaos by ad-hoc decisions which put extra pressure on the dogs, whom he already felt had not been used well. He had also had to listen to endless denigration of the dogs, when to him their value had been obvious all along, and certainly after the news about Amundsen. Meares had been expected to stay a second winter, depending on news from home. [6] He had left his options open, in other words. He might have had a difficult journey back to Cape Evans, as he claimed, but he is likely to have been demotivated by having had his schedule thrown hopelessly awry. When he also met Day, Nelson, Hooper and Clissold's party somewhere around Corner Camp, on their way to One Ton with the minimum three XS rations, he seems to have lost interest altogether. There were no further attempts to get dog food to One Ton, and no preparations by anyone for the 560-mile round trip to bring Scott home in time to catch the ship.

In the event that someone had gone out to meet the Polar Party with the intention of getting them, or their news, back in time with any hope of catching the ship, the return of 280 miles from 82 degrees would have meant an average speed of 20 miles per day, which would have been doubtful, even with the support of the dogs. Back at Cape Evans the thinking might have been that in any case the middle of March was an overoptimistic estimate as far as catching the ship was concerned, even if just for the news, and that there was no prospect at all of the Polar Party being in time for the ship on the 144-day schedule, according to which they were not expected back until 22 March.

When, at the top of the Beardmore, the first Supporting Party (Atkinson, Cherry, Wright and Keohane) was ordered back, Cherry claims that Scott instructed Atkinson to come and speed the Polar Party home with the dogs instead of Meares. [7] However, other than Cherry's word, and Atkinson's tacit concurrence, there is no evidence for this. It would imply that relations between Scott and Meares had broken down completely, as it would have constituted a *de facto* dismissal of Meares. As Atkinson had no experience of driving dogs and wasn't a navigator, it is hard to accept this claim without further corroboration, which doesn't exist. On the contrary, Scott's entry for 10 March on the Return Journey reads:

> The dogs which would have been our salvation have evidently failed. Meares had a bad trip home I suppose.

Although it isn't conclusive, it does imply that he was expecting Meares, rather than Atkinson, while of course Scott's original instructions were for Meares to come out.

The question, then, is why Cherry claimed that Scott ordered Atkinson to come out with the dogs. Wright says nothing about it. Although it sounds like Cherry was covering for Meares' failure to come out, there is no particular reason why he would want to do that other than to obscure the fact that Meares had stopped following orders – which would imply that Scott's authority had broken down, certainly with regard to Meares. This means that Cherry (writing after the events, of course), wasn't covering for Meares, but for Scott, and his failure to inspire people with the will and the loyalty to stay and perform. Both Meares' and Simpson's reasons for leaving prematurely (abandoning the expedition, in fact), were later found to be not particularly compelling, which implied a breakdown in their commitment to Scott and the expedition – it was an idea that Cherry might well have felt moved to contradict.

But the chickens of irritable, egocentric and capricious leadership had come home to roost, as efforts on Scott's behalf – if they existed at all – seem altogether to have been notably half-hearted back at Cape Evans. They chose to believe there was nothing to worry about and that there was a good chance that he would be returning home 'with the Pole on his sledge' without help from anyone. They also assumed Scott knew what he was doing when he deemed only three units of XS rations to be sufficient for the returning parties; and Simpson, who was in charge back at base, clearly took him at his word. Hence the rather fun-sounding party of Day, Clissold, Hooper and Nelson, who were not overburdened, and in no particular hurry to complete their mission to One Ton, as their rate of travel was leisurely, having met Meares who was on his way back from the Beardmore with the dogs.

There is a confusing set of reports based on an alleged entry in Simpson's diary as follows: [8]

> Meares intended to go out to One Ton Camp again taking a little more food, but chiefly to take out a stock of luxuries like Irish Stew, Marmalade and Tinned Fruits … On the 17th of January Meares had his sledges packed with the idea of starting that evening.

There was, however, an unexpected event: the *Terra Nova* had been seen on the horizon. Simpson: [9]

... Naturally, when the ship was seen Meares delayed his departure
in the hope of being able to take home news with him.

He was still there on 28 January, when Atkinson and his team returned. In the
end, Meares didn't just delay his departure, he didn't go at all – calling into
question whether he had ever seriously intended to go to 82 degrees south,
especially in view of the non-essentials he had on board instead of the further XS
rations, oil, dog food etc one would have expected in that case.

Sometime between 17 January and around the end of the first week of
February, Meares must have decided to hand over the dogs to Atkinson and go
home. The fact that Simpson also elected to go home may well have had a decisive
effect. They seemed to have wanted to emphasise their belief that all Scott needed
was luxuries – the ones Simpson enumerated and Atkinson confirmed – as: [10]

> ... two weeks' surplus supplies ... complete and certain delicacies
> which they had asked for.

If posterity could be convinced that all Scott needed was 'surplus supplies'
(whatever they were) and luxuries, it would make the failure to go out seem less
of a dereliction. Meares' and Simpson's actions are further discussed in Chapter
27, Reflections.

In the event, Atkinson, after a period of rest, went over to Hut Point with
Dmitrii and the dogs, presumably loaded with Irish stew, marmalade etc, and obviously with no intention of going anywhere near 82 degrees – the job that Scott
had said was important but not vital: [11]

> You will of course understand that whilst the object of your third
> journey is important, that of the second is vital. At all hazards three
> X.S. units of provision must be got to One Ton Camp ...

It had suited everyone at Cape Evans to quietly drop the non-vital order, and
reinforce the fiction that after Day, Hooper, Clissold and Nelson had taken the
three XS units to One Ton, everything else was either 'surplus', or a luxury.

Clearly in no hurry to get going, Atkinson was still at the *Discovery* hut when
Crean famously walked in on 19 February with the news that Teddy Evans was
dying of scurvy at Corner Camp. If Atkinson had been reluctant even to go as far as
One Ton, it may in fact have come as something of a solution to be able to go
instead on a mission to save Teddy's life. To an inexperienced dog-driver like
Atkinson, Corner Camp will have sounded a lot less daunting than One Ton and
beyond, while sickness was something he was trained to handle.

Teddy had not had a good journey south. The pull up the Beardmore had been
mostly a prodigious effort ('killing' work, according to Wilson), shifting heavy
sledges in deep snow. They were pulling around 180 lbs per man. This is the
weight of a muscular six-foot man. Imagine four of those sitting on each sledge to

get an idea what they were pulling uphill, sometimes through deep snow, and over constantly changing terrain. Initially they had been pleased to dispense with the horses, but that soon wore off as reality hit. Bowers: 12

> ... the sledges sank in over twelve inches, and all the gear, as well as the thwartship pieces, were acting as breaks. The tugs and heaves we enjoyed, and the number of times we had to get out of our ski to upright the sledge, were trifles compared with the strenuous exertion of every muscle and nerve to keep the wretched drag from stopping when once under weigh ...

It's easy to see why Amundsen regarded the idea of man-haulage with unmitigated horror. It sounds like Teddy didn't like it either, as Cherry wrote to Reginald Smith (Scott's publisher) a year later that 13

> ... I wish to put it down in black & white for being one who knows that Evans is no man to whom to entrust the account of this expedition ... That he has spoken when sledging continually disloyally of Scott, not only to officers but also before the men is the main reason why ... That he did not pull probably interested those who manhauled with him mainly – I was thankful that I was never on the same sledge as him. Bowers was the most loyal friend & companion that any friend or superior officer could have – he spoke to me once of Evans's behaviour as "sedition".

Scott was equally critical of Teddy. Writing on 11 December in a note omitted from the original published version of his Last Expedition diary: 14

> I had expected failure from the animals but not from the men – I must blame little Evans much – he shows a terrible lack of judgement ...

(The above quote was entirely edited out of the published diary.)

Teddy was feeling irritable and fatigued from having, along with Lashly, man-hauled from Corner Camp to the start of the Beardmore, whereas the others had been leading ponies. 'Silas' Wright, who was angry about being ordered home with the first Supporting Party, sounds like he felt he deserved to go on in preference to Teddy because he had pulled better than him: 15

19–20 December:

> Teddy, the damn hypocrite, as soon as he sees the Owner's sledge stopped and they watching us come up puts his head down and digs in for all he is worth ... Atch, Cherry, Keohane and I turn back tomorrow night. Scott a fool. Teddy goes on. I have to make course back. Too wild to write more tonight. Teddy slack trace 7/8th of today.

Teddy's attitude labouring up the Beardmore with those absurdly heavy sledges clearly brought out the worst in him, which was expressed in partial withdrawal of labour and harshly critical comments behind Scott's back. However justified he might have felt, it seems out of character for Teddy to act in such an openly disloyal manner. It could well have been that he was suffering the first effects of scurvy, as fatigue and lassitude can begin some six weeks before visible signs appear. [16] About six weeks later, on 22 January, Lashly reports that Teddy had stiffness at the back of his knees, and that he was convinced he was 'on the point of something anyhow' after he had 'watched to see' Teddy's gums. [17] Frank Debenham allegedly said years later that Teddy really was a very naughty boy and wouldn't eat his seal meat. If he had an aversion to seal he would have been low in vitamin C when the journey started, which would explain why he presented with scurvy at a time when the others still seemed free of it. There was, however, talk of it in Atkinson's team on their return to Cape Evans.

Scott was happy with his choice of men to go on, tipping over into near euphoria on 23 December: [18]

> I hung on to the S.W. till 6 p.m., and then camped with a delightful feeling of security that we had at length reached the summit proper. I am feeling very cheerful about everything to-night ... To me for the first time our goal seems really in sight. We can pull our loads and pull them much faster and farther than I expected in my most hopeful moments.

Plateau conditions were beginning to be felt, however. Breathlessness due to altitude seems almost to have been taken in their stride – not surprising as they were heaving and panting most of the time anyway, but now a searching wind had started, with the temperature hovering around 0 F, which is around -18 C. It was enough for their faces to start getting iced up, and for them to get mighty cold (Scott's words) during any break in activity.

Teddy's description of the little tents in the great white glittering waste is evocative and gives an idea of the desolation: little eddies of snow swept around the tents in which sleeping figures breathed heavily, but only until 4 am, waiting for the shout 'Evans' at 5 am precisely. Both Evanses would reply 'Right-o, Sir', and instantly all would be a bustle of activity and frantic haste as the cookers were filled with snow. The primus stove burned with a curious low roar, filling the tent with the unforgettable smell of paraffin, and then, what they always looked forward to: the savoury aroma of pemmican. In an incredibly short space of time both teams, now consisting of Teddy, Bowers, Crean and Lashly; and Scott, Wilson, Oates and Taff Evans, would swing southward, with every appearance of perfect health.

However, as Teddy wrote: [19]

... a close observer, a man trained to watch over men's health ...
would have seen something amiss ... The two teams, in spite of the
... "Happy Christmas" greetings they exchanged to begin with, soon
lost their springy step, the sledges dragged more slowly, and we
gazed ahead almost wistfully.

After a comparative feast on Christmas Day, the relentlessness of the march
had been felt again in a series of hard and tiring days. Then, on 30 December, they
made a depot at which Teddy's party left their skis, among other things, ostensibly
to save weight. This apparently irrational decision has been much debated and
questioned by historians, as it was bound to slow Teddy's party down and tire
them out more easily. That this in fact transpired is confirmed by Scott's own
comments to the effect that it was a plod for the foot people and pretty easy going
for his own party on skis. While none of the diarists expressly state that it was
Scott's order to depot the skis, it must have been the case.

The payoff for Scott would be that it would rule Teddy out for the Pole. Teddy
had a strong case for entering the history books along with Scott. He had given up
his own plans for an expedition, and had worked hard to make this one a reality.
He was second-in-command and had felt throughout that he had a solid claim. In
spite of the fact that he must have felt himself seriously tiring, he must also have
felt that he had a moral right to stand at the Pole alongside Scott. This was a private
expedition, not under the aegis of the Royal Navy, which meant that Scott had no
power in law to back up his orders. A simple refusal to go from Teddy would
therefore have been difficult for Scott to countermand. As in the above quote from
Cherry, Bowers reports that Teddy continually spoke disloyally of Scott, and
behaved in a 'seditious' manner. Sedition is a serious challenge to authority: an
incitement to mutiny and rebellion.

Scott probably caught wind of all this, and it is likely to have worried him. He
might have feared a difficult confrontation, at the very least. But on foot, an already
tired Teddy would have great difficulty making it to the Pole. The muscular and
usually lively Teddy had been tiring visibly and would himself have known he
would need his skis. Therefore, assuming the decision was a rational one, the most
plausible explanation for denying Teddy the use of his skis is that it would make
reaching the Pole impossibly hard for him. At the same time, unless the inclusion
of Bowers in the final party was an entirely impulsive one, it also suggests that
Scott considered it worth forcing Bowers to carry on on foot just to get Teddy out
of the way.

Next morning, New Year's Eve, they marched just over eight miles statute and
had lunch, after which a depot was made and work started on converting the two
12-foot sledges into ten-foot ones. Taff, Lashly and Crean spent the afternoon converting the first sledge inside one of the tents, warmed by one of the primuses. The

sun was shining and at first everything went smoothly. They made efforts to keep their hands from freezing, but at -10 F (-23 C), it can't have been an easy job. Meanwhile, the officers were snug in a double tent doing odd jobs, chatting, and writing up diaries.

After dinner the men started on the second sledge. It took longer than expected, and by about 11 pm, Taff, cold, tired, and impatient to finish, ripped at something with his knife and gave himself a nasty cut on the knuckle. Many historians have implied that he hid the injury. There is no evidence to support this. The story of the hidden cut has acquired a spurious factual status purely through repetition by successive Scott biographers. It is difficult to imagine how he could have hidden something like that, especially from his tent-mates who, in Taff's case, included Scott.

It is likely that he went to see Wilson right away because he would have been encouraged to do so by Crean and Lashly, both sensible men. Wilson's diary for 7 January, a week later, states: [20]

> Evans who cut his knuckle some days ago at the last depot – a week
> ago – has a lot of pus in it tonight.

While this is not proof positive that Wilson saw the injury at the time, it does sound like it. There are a couple of entries in Scott's diary, moreover, that suggest he knew about the injury when it happened. The first is an entry dated 7 January, the same day that Wilson made his: [21]

> Evans has a nasty cut on his hand (sledge-making). I hope it won't
> give trouble.

If this had been the first he knew of it, he would have said something to the effect that Evans revealed it, and there would surely have been expressions of surprise, dismay, and very likely irritation, rather than this matter-of-fact statement. The second hint comes on 30 January, a couple of weeks after the shock of the defeat at the Pole. Scott: [22]

> He [Taff] hasn't been cheerful since the accident.

The event that could have most plausibly have qualified as an accident was the incident with the knife, and the only way Scott could have known the date of the onset of Taff's lack of cheer is if he had known about it when it happened.

Not being a fatherly man, as we know, and being almost constantly stressed, Scott is likely to have been annoyed when it happened. It wouldn't have taken more than an unguarded glance to tell Taff how Scott felt. Not wanting to spoil a congenial evening, Scott might have stifled his anger, but Taff would have felt it anyway. Nobody breathed a word about the incident – typical of the tendency to remain silent around painful scenes generally. There is fulsome praise of Taff from Scott a week later, along with praise for his other companions, but nevertheless suggestive of a sense of guilt. Taff gave his heart and soul to Scott; his entire future hung on Scott's approval and success. Scott, for his part, had always relied on Taff's pulling power, and right now, he was not about to sacrifice that on account of a cut knuckle. Taff was no doubt also annoyed with himself over it, but it would have been Scott's displeasure that hurt and worried him most.

The wound should probably have had stitches. Unfortunately, unlike Koettlitz's medical bag, Wilson's does not appear to have included a suture kit. It might not have made much difference in the end, but it would have been preferable in the short term. As it was, Taff must have made light of it, and he strove to continue working as normal, which probably didn't help.

A plausible reason Scott did not mention Taff's injury in his journal at the time was because it might have called into question his judgement over taking not just one, but two, injured men to the Pole (the other being Oates) – in addition to putting more strain on the organisation by taking an extra man who was also at a disadvantage by having to walk hundreds of miles where the others skied. As it was Bowers, the one man strong enough to cope without skis, the decision could have been worse; but an objective assessment of the fitness of all eight on 2 January, when Scott made the final decision about who was coming with him, would certainly have ruled out Oates, and more than likely the injured Taff.

There was some reason to hope that Taff's hand would heal as time went on; but Oates had started to limp, which wasn't something that might be expected to get better. It isn't clear whether it was the old war wound on his thigh, or his feet that were responsible. It was probably both, but certainly his feet were already in poor condition, the hard ice on the Beardmore having made 'rather hay' of them. Oates' feet had been wet almost continually for weeks. That means it is likely that they had started to macerate, a process affecting soldiers and endurance athletes whose feet are wet for long periods. Maceration turns the skin wrinkly and then white; the skin is tender and can fold over itself, separating and creating problems. As layers of skin separate, the skin becomes pale and can split open and bleed similar to, but not the same as, a blister. Feet become so tender that every step is painful. It feels like the whole of the bottom of the foot is blistered.

Oates had an opportunity to dry his feet at night, but it would never have been for long enough to fully heal them, while day after day the process would start over. Even taking a mild view of it, there can be little doubt that Oates had very sore feet. He was visibly limping. Why did Wilson not advise against Oates going on? Partly it must have been because aches and pains and seemingly minor injuries had already become daily occurrences, and they had accustomed themselves to take these in their stride. Crucially, Wilson would not have been motivated to take a pessimistic (or even a realistic) view of things as he knew how

much it meant to Scott to be first to the Pole, and to reach it in style, with represent-
atives from both the Army and the Navy, and from science.

While the work on the sledges was going ahead, Oates had sat in the tent with
his fellow officers and had opened up, talking for hours about his life, his horses,
his regiment; anecdotes and reminiscences had flowed in uncharacteristic abundance. What happened? What caused his habitual reserve to fall away in that
manner? In large part, it must have been catalysed by sheer exhaustion. It takes
energy to keep up the defensive shield and the separation from others. It was as if
he didn't care any more. It sounds like he experienced a little epiphany, a moment
of understanding and forgiveness, when his defences dropped away and opened a
sense of direct contact with those around him. Everyone in the tent that night
shared the experience. When Oates wrote his last letter to his mother three days
later, the elegiac mood was still discernible in his parting words: [23]

> What a lot we shall have to talk about when I get back – God bless
> you and keep you well until I come home. L.E.G. Oates
>
> PS. ... I am afraid the letter I wrote to you from the hut was full of
> grumbles but I was very anxious about starting off with those
> ponies.

Teddy wrote a moving tribute to the 'Soldier' for *The Strand Magazine* in 1913.
Describing that New Year's Eve, he wrote: [24]

> This was the only occasion when we ever took a holiday on that
> memorable journey, and in that tent, high up on the King Edward
> VII. Plateau, in spite of the crisp coldness of that bleak, white
> tableland, we warmed to one another in a way that we had never
> thought of, quite oblivious to cold, hardship, scant rations, or the
> great monotony of sledge-hauling. Some of us passed round our
> diaries, with the little photographs pasted in them of our nearest
> and dearest, and somehow we cemented a new and even greater
> friendship throughout the little band, then so full of hope, so
> confident of success, and so happy together. As we said "Good
> night" we shook Captain Scott's hand and wished him a "Happy
> New Year and the South Pole." He had a cheery, affectionate reply
> for all of us, and we little dreamt that before three months should
> pass only two seamen and one officer would be alive out of the
> eight.

A few days later, on 4 January, Scott, Wilson, Bowers, Taff and Oates said good-
bye. Teddy: [25]

> The last farewell was most touching, Oates being far more affected
> than any other of the Southern Party. He handed me a letter for his

mother, and told me to write and let his people know how fit and happy he was. He asked me to send him out tobacco and sweets by the dog teams, and his last words to any man now living were words of consolation at our not going forward, and thanks for our undertaking the return journey short-handed ... Oates, who was pulling in the rear, waved his hand several times. We frequently looked back until the little group were but a tiny black speck on the southern horizon, and finally they disappeared.

There were multiple knock-on effects from taking an extra man. Cooking took a lot longer for five than for four. The consumption of oil was significantly higher than anticipated. Another effect was the overcrowding of the tent, which meant that those sleeping on the outside were pressed further against the sides than they would otherwise have been. In 1875 Albert Markham, while sledging in the Arctic, did an interesting little experiment to test the temperature inside his bag during the night. He found that on the side next to which someone was sleeping it was 74 degrees; on the other side it was 30. [26] This test doesn't meet scientific criteria on many levels, obviously, but it does suggest that sleeping on the outside makes a significant difference – which is in any case to be expected.

The floor-cloth was square, which meant that those sleeping on the outside in an overcrowded tent were probably mostly on snow. There is no indication that a system of rotation was practised, which means that certain people routinely slept around the edges, to some extent on snow, which must have had implications for the wetness of their bags. The most likely candidates are Taff and Oates – Taff because he was 'lower deck', and Oates because he was psychologically the most distant from Scott. If this was indeed the case, it is not surprising that it was precisely those two who succumbed to the effects of the cold before the others.

However much Teddy sometimes got on people's nerves, a little light had gone out for the five who set their course for the Pole. It is vital for morale for there to be at least one person in a team who is irrepressibly optimistic – someone who is not floored by the apparent hopelessness of a given situation. Of the five who went on, Taff had lost his usual cheerfulness, Wilson was never exactly a bundle of laughs, and Oates tended to laconic taciturnity. That only left Bowers to counteract Scott's oppressive negativity. It wasn't enough.

At the same time it would be surprising if some didn't feel surges of acute anxiety. It must have been as though the final link with the rest of humanity had been severed, and only complete isolation to look forward to. The first night alone they basked in a rare interlude of windless sunshine, when for a brief moment it seemed as though few things could trouble them except, perhaps, the surface. Almost as if on cue, the surface was as bad as could be on the next day, 5 January. Their rate of progress slowed to just over a mile and a quarter per hour. They were no longer strong enough to take bad surfaces in their stride. The next day it was a fearfully hard pull again. They dropped a sleeping-bag and had to go back for it, reducing their hard-won mileage for the day. The next day they lost another hour and a half by depoting their skis, changing their minds, and going back for them.

The 7th January was a slightly better day, and the mood seems to have lightened somewhat. Scott writes that Taff's hand was dressed; it was the occasion of Scott's matter-of-fact remark about it. He would surely have been less sanguine if he had just been confronted for the first time with a nasty cut filled with pus across the knuckle of his most 'invaluable assistant'.

Blizzard-like conditions obtained the next morning, prompting a doubtless much-needed day in bed, and a chance for Scott to write up his diary. They had a leisurely start next morning and didn't break camp until lunch time. On this day one of the watches was found to be 26 minutes out – potentially disastrous for navigation. These are hints suggesting a loss of vigour and a diminution of attention to detail. Scott had been looking forward to lightening their load by leaving a depot, and on 10 January they did so, but the benefit was negated by a surface that was 'beyond words', making the pulling distressingly hard. The day after was worse. Scott: [27]

> It was heavy pulling from the beginning to-day, but for the first two and a half hours we could keep the sledge moving; then the sun came out ... and the rest of the forenoon was agonising. I never had such pulling; all the time the sledge rasps and creaks. We have covered 6 miles, but at fearful cost to ourselves ... Another hard grind in the afternoon and five miles added. About 74 miles from the Pole – can we keep this up for seven days? It takes it out of us like anything. None of us ever had such hard work before.

And so it continued, day after day, with little to relieve the monotony and the grim effort. They were beginning to feel the cold more acutely and Oates and Taff in particular were getting cold and tired. Scott continued to regard the team as very fit, but it would not have looked like it to a ghostly observer. Without even the energy for the hopeful anticipation one would expect at this stage, their increasingly bony frames, bent over and panting in the thin air, heaved at the traces at half normal walking pace. A sliver of comfort was derived from the fact that they had seen no trace of Amundsen until now, but there must have been the worry that the Beardmore wasn't the only way through the mountains.

On the threshold of the realisation of the dream that had inspired years of effort and sacrifice, Scott was subdued. In his anticipatory fantasies he had probably chosen not to imagine the full effects of dragging heavy sledges almost 10,000 feet up the Beardmore, and the mostly heavy haulage on the summit. Desperate to shed what weight they could, they left behind anything not absolutely essential at the last depot and went ahead with nine days' provisions [28]

> ... so that it ought to be a certain thing now, and the only appalling possibility the sight of the Norwegian flag forestalling ours ... Only 27 miles from the Pole. We *ought* to do it now.

Then, Wilson's diary, 16 January 1912: [29]

> We got away at 8 a.m. and made 7.5 miles by 1.15. Lunched and then in 5.3 miles came on a black flag and the Norwegians' sledge, ski and dog tracks running about N.E. and S.W. both ways. The flag was of black bunting tied with string to a fore-and-after which had evidently been taken off a finished-up sledge. The age of the tracks was hard to guess – but probably a couple of weeks, or three or more. The flag was fairly well frayed at the edges. We camped here and examined the tracks and discussed things. The surface was fairly good in the forenoon – -23 temp. and all the afternoon we were coming down hill with again a rise to the W. and a fall and a scoop to the east where the Norwegians came up evidently by another glacier. A good parhelion and plenty W. wind. All today sastrugi have been westerly.

The matter-of-fact tone of Wilson's account gives no hint of the devastation, but it must have been impossible for Scott to look Oates in the eye, now that past criticisms were so blindingly vindicated. The 'shilling book about transport' jibe might have echoed in both their minds as they contemplated the black flag that spelled the end of their hopes and dreams.

Meanwhile, in another reality, concerned as usual with herself and her admirers, Kathleen was in Berlin on this day, visiting her cousin Benjie: [30]

> She went dancing, and found the German officers 'all spotty and poor-looking creatures' ... Nansen was giving some lectures; she went to an art gallery with him and modelled his head ... 'He really is an adorable person,' she wrote for Con, 'and I will tell you all the lovely times we had together when you get back. He thinks you are marvellous, and me still more!'

Scott had put himself and all those who dragged with him through all that backbreaking labour, day in day out, only to be comprehensively beaten. Hubris, impatience, denial, and confirmation bias had occupied the space at Scott's core where insight and the courage to face reality should have been. His initial resistance to dogs had been inspired by patrician disregard and because, *au fond*, he couldn't be bothered with them. He didn't have the patience. Preferring men because they do as they are told and are less of a nuisance, and stubbornly

419

resistant to advice – even from one of the world's leading authorities – he had continued to refer to his negative *Discovery* experience and disparage dogs at every turn; latterly for no better reason than simply to cover and reassure himself. Now the evidence of their capability was right there in front of his eyes, in the cruellest imaginable way. And no, Amundsen had *not* found an easy way up, as Scott surmised, still unwilling to give credit where credit was due and to accept, unconditionally, that he had been catastrophically wrong.

What Oates must have felt and thought, standing there on damaged and freezing feet, can hardly be imagined. For Taff, his hopes and his future crumbled before his eyes. Bowers and Wilson found solace in their God. Wilson's Panglossian equanimity came to his rescue: whatever is, is God's will, and therefore good. Birdie's solace was a mix of chauvinism and martyrised Christianity: as far as he was concerned, they had done the journey with good-old British manpower, regardless of the cost to themselves. Scott wrote that many bitter thoughts came and much discussion was had. The anger was deflected on to Amundsen, who was blamed for having made a deliberate effort to forestall them. But what else did they expect him to do? As far as Wilson was concerned, Amundsen only beat them insofar as he made a race of it. Scant consolation, surely.

While it was true that both teams had got to the Pole, it was the 800-mile Return Journey that would be the test by which the rival expeditions would ultimately stand or fall. A return is an imperative. There can't have been much probability that Amundsen would fail to get home, judging by his performance so far. For Scott, all that was left now was to fulfil their programme: to pinpoint as accurately as they could the exact location of the Pole, and to record the event for posterity. Wilson's and Scott's accounts differ as to whether they found Amundsen's little tent before or after they photographed themselves with their flags. Not that it mattered. In spite of the cold, Bowers' conscientious attitude ensured that their devastation was recorded for posterity in a series of technically brilliant photos. We can only wonder at the impulse that led to the multiplicity of poses with which they chose to record their defeat, with time taken to line up the shots, all while standing around in -30 C, with wind-chill. In those temperatures it is essential to keep moving in order to maintain even a semblance of comfort.

For Scott it was the ultimate humiliation. He kept up a facade of normality in his journal, but the photos reveal the inner pain as he stands in front of the camera, unable to look into the lens. His body language spells out his complete mortification at having brought his team and the expedition to this – not to mention the nation and the Royal Navy, of whom he was still a representative, in spite of it being his own expedition. And to think he had wanted the Army to be present.

It was the disaster of his life, and for someone already prone to depression, it must have been utterly crushing. Even the indefatigable Birdie looks pinched and tired. Taff looks deadly serious, as he had reason to be, while Oates' face suggests the tragic irony of a disaster foretold, combined with the ache of a man desperate to get into a tent and out of the perishing cold. Only Wilson seems relatively untroubled. But then he had made his peace with his Maker well before this. A valedictory note to Oriana had gone back with Meares, in what would have felt like an age ago: [31]

> ... It is good to have been loved by you, and oh, a privilege indeed to
> have been allowed to love you. God keep you.

It is as though he was already preparing to die before they were half way up the Beardmore.

No more Kathleen's hero – nor even her potential hero – the leadership Scott had so jealously guarded must have felt like a toxic albatross, dragging down not only his present companions, but the entire expedition and everyone associated with it. He had made it vulnerable to criticism and condemnation and, worse, scorn. The guilt at having brought his companions and his country to this defeat, having obstinately stuck to his own opinions regarding Polar travel over that of more knowledgeable and experienced travellers – his own hubris – must in those moments have been inescapable and excruciating. As far as his companions were concerned, from the moment of their arrival at the black flag, one of the effects must have been that henceforth they had to live with the psychological tyranny of Scott's guilt and devastation. From then on he must have become untouchable by virtue of his agony and the depression that emanated from him. On paper he sounded normal, but that wasn't the whole story, nor anything like it. In the flesh, he bore the imprint of a man crushed by defeat and the weight of a responsibility he could no longer shirk.

However dangerous and knife-edge the physical aspects of the Return Journey, it was now Scott's mental and emotional state that constituted the main threat to their survival. The urgency of getting back to base got more acute by the hour. 17 January, Scott: [32]

> Now for the run home and a desperate struggle [to get the news
> through first]. I wonder if we can do it.

Scott's editors removed the words 'to get the news through first'. Why? One can hazard a guess that the thinking was that the reading public would be better set up for the impending disaster if that part of the sentence was left out. In other words, they were anticipating Scott's dramatisation of the Barrier Journey, thereby assisting him in the job of legitimising the outcome. Wilson too seemed to think the priority was get the news rushed to the ship, although one wonders what the hurry would have been in view of their defeat. Nevertheless, it shows that he too was counting on the dogs coming out to somewhere between latitudes 81 and 82 to meet them. They all were.

Returning, they had to withstand Plateau conditions and soul-destroying pulling for 19 days, from 19 January to 7 February, before they reached the start of the Beardmore. In order to protect core body temperature, peripheral blood vessels constrict, virtually eliminating peripheral bloodflow, and skin temperature decreases from the elbow towards the fingertips and from the knees towards the toes. Heat delivery and heat loss in the limbs are decreased and the core temperature is protected. It decreases the ability to perform physical tasks and increases the risk of frostbite. [33] Taff had very cold hands on 17 January, and on the 20th he had developed blisters. A certain amount of rewarming must have taken place, as he was able to carry on, albeit while deteriorating incrementally. They were all getting colder, but Taff and Oates suffered more with frostbite, suggesting they were consistently the coldest. Not only were they both injured, they never had the chance to rewarm sufficiently at night, as they slept on the outer edges and, effectively, kept Wilson, Scott and Bowers warm.

Every morning they all got up feeling sore and stiff and it took an effort of will to get going again. There was stress too from having to make the distance between depots on the food in hand, which was only ever just enough, with scant margin for delay. Mountaineers know that the way back is when most fatalities happen. Modern treks to the South Pole do not normally include a return journey. Scott must have minimised the magnitude of the return in his mind, no doubt telling himself that they would hopefully have the wind behind them, and that success at the Pole would give them wings. 20 January, Wilson: [34]

> ... [sleeping] Bags and gear getting a bit wet and frozen up. No chance to dry things for some time now and temperature low ... Evans has got 4 or 5 of his finger tips badly blistered by the cold. Titus also his nose and cheeks – so Evans and Bowers.

20 January, Scott: [35]

> I shall be very glad when Bowers gets his ski; I'm afraid he must find these long marches very trying with short legs ... I think Oates is feeling the cold and fatigue more than most of us ... It is everything now to keep up a good marching pace; I trust we shall be able to do so and catch the ship.

They did 18.5 miles that day.

22 January, Scott:

> I think about the most tiring march we have had; solid pulling the whole way, in spite of the light sledge and some little helping wind

at first ... we have covered 14.5 miles (geo.) but, by Jove! It has been
a grind.

Although the mileages were heartening, they were also demanding. Day after
day walking and skiing, much of the time dragging, of distances between 15 and
20 miles is tough at the best of times. For undernourished, cold, tired men it is
unsustainable.

23 January, Scott:

> We came along at a great rate [with a sail] and should have got
> within an easy march of our depot had not Wilson suddenly dis-
> covered that Evans' nose was frostbitten – it was white and hard ...
> There is no doubt Evans is a good deal run down – his fingers are
> badly blistered and his nose is rather seriously congested with fre-
> quent frost bites. He is very much annoyed with himself, which is
> not a good sign. I think Wilson, Bowers and I are as fit as possible
> under the circumstances. Oates gets cold feet. One way and another,
> I shall be glad to get off the summit!

The only effective way people can keep warm in those conditions is by
muscular activity. Standing around waiting for the tent to be put up would have
reduced Taff's temperature in seconds. His survival was fatally impacted by
contemporary ignorance about hypothermia. His companions would have
assumed his power to generate his own body heat would continue unimpaired,
and that he would always warm up and recover, even if he did get very cold. It was
also unfortunate that altitude inhibits shivering, and that when a person's core
temperature drops below a certain level shivering stops. There are no comments
in the diaries about how much they shivered, or if they shivered at all, but it is an
important way in which bodies warm up, and a positive indicator. What should
have happened at this stage, when Taff was probably still in the comparatively
mild stages of hypothermia, was to put him in the middle for sleeping. There is no
indication that this happened. People knew you could freeze to death, of course;
but the stages and, crucially, the ways to recognise and treat a hypothermic
person, were unknown. It was Taff's death warrant. For the time being, however,
he was able to soldier on, evidently.

24 January, Scott:

> Things beginning to look a little serious ... At first Evans, and then
> Wilson went ahead to scout for tracks ... [Bowers and Oates] had a
> fearful time trying to make the pace between the soft patches. At
> 12.30 the sun coming ahead made it impossible to see the tracks
> further, and we had to stop. By this time the gale was at its height
> and we had the dickens of a time getting up the tent, cold fingers all
> round ... Is the weather breaking up? If so, God help us, with the

tremendous summit journey and scant food. Wilson and Bowers
are my standby. I don't like the easy way in which Oates and Evans
get frostbitten.

Generally, Wilson tends not to go into detail about the health of the party, and
he doesn't now. Partially this must have been because he has his own problems to
contend with, now suffering a bad attack of snow blindness.

The next day, to Scott's heartfelt relief, they found their Half Degree Depot.
Now it was (25 January) ...

> Only 89 miles (geogr.) to the next depot, but it's time we cleared off
> this plateau. We are not without ailments: Oates suffers from a very
> cold foot; Evans' fingers and nose are in a bad state, and to-night
> Wilson is suffering tortures from his eyes.

Only 89 miles?

28 and 29 January, Wilson: [36]

> We are all pretty hungry – could eat twice what we have ... Evans
> has a number of badly blistered finger ends which he got at the Pole.
> Titus' big toe is turning blue black ... We got in a very long march
> for 9 hours going over part good and part bad surface ... I got a nasty
> bruise on the Tib. ant. [Tibialis Anterior] which gave me great pain
> all the afternoon ... Temp. -25 ... very cold. We are now only 22 miles
> from our depot and 400 miles about to go before meeting the dogs
> with ship's news.

Distance for the day: 19.5 geographical miles, 22 miles statute.

Wilson was counting on meeting those dogs; all the more tragic that no one at
Cape Evans knew it. Scott's written instructions to Meares to come out with the
dogs had not carried the urgency they had now acquired. As for those disputed
secondary instructions to come out with the dogs, allegedly given to Atkinson on
the return of the first Supporting Party, these seem unlikely, as Atkinson wasn't a
navigator, nor a dog-driver, nor even an especially robust sledger. His team, which
included Wright, who *was* a strong sledger, and a navigator, arrived back at Cape
Evans on this day, 28 January, having collected a small number of geological specimens and having made good time on the homeward march.

On 30 January, Scott reports:

> ... another fine march – 19 miles.

Scott may have called it a fine march, but a more realistic word would have
been 'desperate'. They still had a long way to go just to get off the plateau. The
effort was too much and caused injuries.

Wilson has strained a tendon in his leg; it has given pain all day and is swollen to-night ... I don't like the idea of such an accident here. To add to the trouble Evans has dislodged two finger-nails to-night; his hands are really bad, and to my surprise he shows signs of losing heart over it. [which makes me much disappointed in him]

(The words 'which makes me much disappointed in him' were removed by Scott's editors.)

On 3 February, Wilson's leg had improved, but the day after that Scott and Evans fell unexpectedly into crevasses.

4 February, Scott:

... a second fall for Evans, and I camped ... The temperature is 20 [degrees] lower than when we were here before; the party is not improving in condition, especially Evans, who is becoming rather dull [stupid] and incapable.

(The editors removed 'stupid' and replaced it with 'dull'.)

Wilson's diary for the 4th contains a fairly lengthy description of the terrain, and ends with a short medical summary: [37]

Evans is feeling the cold a lot always getting frost bitten. Titus' toes are blackening and his nose and cheeks are dead yellow. Dressing Evans' fingers every other day with boric vaseline – they are quite sweet still.

Not gangrenous, is what he means. It gives an idea of the state of them. Distance for the day: 18.1 miles. Birdie stops keeping his diary.

There are many theories about what killed Taff Evans. Indeed, there were many deficiencies and hardships that could have been the cause, and certainly contributed. The fact that Scott makes the comment about Taff getting stupid and incapable just after they both fell into crevasses has almost invariably been taken as evidence that Taff suffered brain damage from those falls, probably due to scurvy. The use of Occam's Razor would lead one to conclude that hypothermia, which had been gradually worsening, would satisfactorily explain his symptoms, and that other explanations are superfluous. Some have suggested altitude sickness, septicaemia, an inability to come to terms with the loss of the Pole, mental breakdown, class difference, and Wilson's claim that it was because he had never been sick in his life before. One theorist has even suggested it was anthrax poisoning, on the basis that the knife with which he cut his hand may have been contaminated through an infected pony. Interesting, but very unlikely.

Taff must have been more vulnerable to the cold for several reasons. He is likely to have carried on pulling to the best of his ability; it was one of the things he could still do now that his hand was in such bad shape. On those long and punishing marches he is likely to have sweated, in spite of the cold. Scott writes that Taff could not help properly with the work, which means that while the others kept moving making camp, he would have been waiting around, his sweat freezing in seconds. Roger Mear and Robert Swan, retracing Scott's journey in 1986, wrote that [38]

> Each day, breaking and pitching camp were the two periods when we were most exposed to injury, and I cannot overstate the frantic urgency with which we set about the task.

5 February, Wilson: [39]

> We had a difficult day getting in among a frightful chaos of broad chasm-like crevasses ... Evans' fingers suppurating, nose very bad and rotten looking.

5 February, Scott:

> Our faces are much cut up by all the winds we have had, mine least of all ... Evans' nose is almost as bad as his fingers. He is a good deal crocked up. [and very stupid about himself]

(The editors removed 'and very stupid about himself '.)

Undated diary entry from Oates: [40]

> It is an extraordinary thing about Evans, he has lost his guts and behaves like an old woman or worse.

Distance for the day: 18.2 miles.

There was precious little sympathy for Evans. No one would have understood his behaviour for what it was, as a result of which he was blamed for not being stoical. Being 'stupid about himself', and behaving 'like an old woman or worse' suggests that there was more going on for Evans than anxiety, dehydration, scurvy, starvation, infection and exhaustion. It is evidence that Evans was affected psychologically in a way the others were not, and suggests the sort of personality change typical in a hypothermic person. The early stages are characterised by the 'umbles': fumbles, stumbles, tumbles, mumbles, and grumbles. The first three reflect impairment of motor function, the last two reflect intellectual impairment. [41] At this stage Taff evinced especially the last two. He was in sufficiently bad shape to have lost the ability to withstand the cold, and had started to succumb to advancing hypothermia.

6 February, Wilson: [42]

> Got in amongst great chasms ... Very cold march ... it [the wind] often falls in the evening to nil and then feels real warm.

6 February, Scott:

Food is low and weather uncertain ... but this evening ... the outlook is much more promising. Evans is the chief anxiety now; his cuts and wounds suppurate, his nose looks very bad, and altogether he shows considerable signs of being played out. Things may mend for him on the glacier, and his wounds get some respite under warmer conditions.

Relief of a kind came at last on 7 February. They had come to the end of the Summit Journey. The Beardmore Glacier now lay ahead.

The next day, the pace was allowed to ease off a little. It was a massive relief to be off the Plateau and they needed the rest, but it was the opportunity to geologise that seems to have tipped the balance. If sufficiently important geological specimens could be found it would go some way to reinstating the value and purpose of the journey. If they had been first at the Pole, geology would not have of been of more than passing interest.

The respite didn't last long, as by the 11th their situation changed from a balmy interlude on the moraines of Mount Buckley to the crevasse fields leading to the Cloudmaker.

11 February, Scott:

> The worst day we have had during the trip and greatly owing to our own fault ... half an hour after lunch we got into the worst ice mess I have ever been in ... my spirits received a very rude shock. There were times when it seemed almost impossible to find a way out of the awful turmoil ... It got worse, harder, more icy and crevassed. We could not manage our ski and pulled on foot, falling into crevasses every minute – most luckily no bad accident ... We won through at 10 p.m. and I write after 12 hours on the march ... Short sleep to-night and off first thing, I hope.

The next day, the 12th, they were in a very critical situation, as Wilson described it: [43]

> We had a good night just outside the icefalls and disturbances and a small breakfast of tea, thin hoosh and biscuit, and began the forenoon by a decent bit of travelling on rubbly blue ice on crampons – then plunged into an icefall and wandered about in it absolutely lost for hours and hours.

12 February, Scott:

> ... finally, at 9 p.m. we landed in the worst place of all. After discussion we decided to camp, and here we are, after a very short supper and one meal only remaining in the food bag; the depot doubtful in locality. We *must* get there to-morrow.

Scott had gone through moments of sick anxiety, and wrote on the 13th:

> Yesterday was the worst experience of the trip and gave a horrid
> feeling of insecurity.

The horror of getting lost and the critical importance of locating their depots
seems finally to have been felt. Other than Scott, Bowers was the sole navigator on
the team. Four out of five of Amundsen's team were navigators, which seems prudent in a place where you do not survive if you can't find your food. They also
marked their depots much more clearly. Bowers seems to have been the only one
who fully appreciated the ease with which they might miss their depots, and the
implications of failing to find their food. One of the reasons he tended to go out and
get sights, whatever the weather, is because he wanted to know where they were
– not only essential for locating their depots, but also for avoiding the waste of
time searching for them would entail.

Eventually, to everyone's profound relief, they found their way out of the ice-
falls and arrived at their depot the next morning. It only gave them three and a half
days' food, which should have lent a sense of urgency to their progress. In view of
this, it is surprising that Wilson was allowed to spend more time geologising, in
the process adding significantly to the weight on the sledge. At this point there
could still be rational explanations. These could include the fact that it gave Taff
an opportunity to recover a little, while there could also have been the chance that
Wilson might find something spectacular.

Vain hopes, as it turned out. Wilson and Bowers suffered bad attacks of snow-
blindness, and Evans continued to go downhill fast.

13 February, Scott:

> Evans having no power to assist with camping work is a great nuis-
> ance and very clumsy.

(Altered by the editors to read 'Evans has no power to assist with camping
work.')

It is clear that Evans' motor functions had now become impaired, indicating
worsening hypothermia. His drastic weight loss reduced the insulation to his core,
while the slowing of the pace while wandering around trying to find their way
reduced the brisk movement needed to raise his temperature. Meanwhile, his
ability to rewarm without outside sources of heat continued to deteriorate.

14 February, Scott:

> Started on crampons; one hour after, hoisted sail; the combined
> efforts produced only slow speed, partly due to the sandy
> snowdrifts similar to those on summit, partly to our torn sledge
> runners ... There is no getting away from the fact that we are not
> pulling strong ... Wilson's leg still troubles him and he doesn't like

to trust himself on ski; but the worst case is Evans, who is giving us serious anxiety. This morning he suddenly disclosed a huge blister on his foot. It delayed us on the march, when he had to have his crampon readjusted. Sometimes I fear he is going from bad to worse ... He is hungry and so is Wilson.

Evans' feet, as well as his hands and nose, were now frostbitten.

On 15 February they made 13.75 miles, but they weren't sure how far they were from the next depot and cut back on food again. Wilson reported that they were going to have to make one day's food last over two.

15 February, Scott:

> We are pulling for food and not very strong evidently ... We have reduced food, also sleep; feeling rather done. Trust 1.5 or 2 days at most will see us at depot.

Wilson had been on his skis again that day, for the first time since injuring his leg, but it was painful and swollen after nine hours on the march. The suspicion has to be that his injury was related to scurvy. It has been argued that it would not have got better in that case. In fact, it didn't consistently get better. Wishful thinking prompted by temporary improvements didn't make the injury go away. They had now been three and a half months on a scorbutic diet. Even under favourable circumstances this must have impacted on their overall health. As it was, stress, and a punishing daily routine, must have exacerbated the effects; while Taff's health, in addition, was acutely threatened by rapidly advancing hypothermia. We now know that the worst thing for him would have been to be forced to walk. Ideally, he should have been laid down and kept quiet in order to preserve cardiovascular stability, and external heat should have been applied, but that was obviously not going to happen. Somehow, and probably with assistance, he made it into bed that night and slept. The next two days chronicle Taff Evans' terminal decline.

16 February, Wilson: [44]

> Got a good start in fair weather after one biscuit and a thin breakfast and made 7.5 miles in the forenoon ... All the afternoon the weather became thicker and thicker and after 3.25 hours Evans collapsed – sick and giddy and unable to walk even by the sledge on ski, so we camped. Can see no land at all anywhere but we must be getting pretty near the Pillar Rock. Evans' collapse has much to do with the fact that he has never been sick in his life and is now helpless with his hands frost-bitten. We had thin meals for lunch and supper.

16 February, Scott:

A rather trying position. Evans has nearly broken down in brain, we think. He is absolutely changed from his normal self-reliant self. [and has become impossible] This morning and this afternoon he stopped the march on some trivial [*sic*] excuse. We are on short rations with not very short food; spin out till to-morrow night ... Perhaps all will be well if we can get to our depot to-morrow fairly early, but it is anxious work with the sick man.

(The words 'and has become impossible' were removed by the editors).

Wilson was a doctor, but he had little clinical experience. After qualifying he spent most of his time studying birds. He was also a social snob. To diagnose Evans' condition as being due to the fact he has never been sick in his life and because he could not use his hands is not only unprofessional, but also snobbish and condescending. Even Scott could see the man was sick.

17 February, Scott:

A very terrible day. Evans looked a little better after a good sleep, and declared, as he always did, that he was quite well. He started in his place on the traces, but half an hour later worked his ski shoes adrift, and had to leave the sledge. The surface was awful ... the sledge groaning, the sky overcast, and the land hazy. We stopped after about one hour, and Evans came up again, but very slowly. Half an hour later he dropped out again on the same plea. He asked Bowers to lend him a piece of string. I cautioned him to come on as quickly as he could, and he answered cheerfully as I thought. We had to push on, and the remainder of us were forced to pull very hard, sweating heavily. Abreast the Monument Rock we stopped, and seeing Evans a long way astern, I camped for lunch. There was no alarm at first, and we prepared tea and our own meal, consuming the latter. After lunch, and Evans still not appearing, we looked out, to see him still afar off. By this time we were alarmed, and all four started back on ski. I was first to reach the poor man and shocked at his appearance; he was on his knees with clothing disarranged, hands uncovered and frost-bitten, and a wild look in his eyes. Asked what was the matter, he replied with a slow speech that he didn't know, but thought he must have fainted. We got him on his feet, but after two or three steps he sank down again. He showed every sign of complete collapse. Wilson, Bowers, and I went back for the sledge, whilst Oates remained with him. When we returned he was practically unconscious, and when we got him into the tent quite comatose. He died quietly at 12.30 a.m.

While symptoms may vary in different individuals, a person with severe hypothermia is likely to have depressed vital signs, staggering gait, an altered level of consciousness with slurred speech, and no shivering in spite of being very cold. Muscular control also fails, as individuals progress from simply stumbling or falling to being unable to walk without assistance. Eventually they cannot stand upright, and collapse. As core temperature continues to fall and intellectual function deteriorates, individuals become disorientated and often behave in odd ways: [45]

> Paradoxical undressing is a bizarre event in which very cold individuals loosen or remove some, or all, of their clothing ... These actions result in more rapid core cooling, unconsciousness and, unless rescue occurs soon, death. [typically from ventricular fibrillation and cardiac arrest]

17 February, Scott:

> On discussing the symptoms we think he began to get weaker just before we reached the Pole, and that his downward path was accelerated first by the shock of his frostbitten fingers, and later by falls during rough travelling on the glacier, further by his loss of all confidence in himself. Wilson thinks it certain he must have injured his brain by a fall. It is a terrible thing to lose a companion in this way, but calm reflection shows that there could not have been a better ending to the terrible anxieties of the past week. Discussion of the situation at lunch yesterday shows us what a desperate pass we were in with a sick man on our hands at such a distance from home.

In the absence of knowledge about the process and symptoms of hypothermia, Scott and his team made various assumptions about what killed Taff Evans, but all of them reflected the knowledge and prejudices of their time. In the light of current knowledge, there is sufficient evidence to suggest that all the criteria for hypothermia were present. None of the others suffered altitude sickness, brain haemorrhage due to scurvy and falling, nor a fatal loss of confidence; and there is no reason to suppose Taff would have been the exception, in spite of him being 'lower deck'. This is not to say that he was not scorbutic, as all of them must have been, and as suggested by the fact that his hand refused to heal. He may very well have been shaken up by falls into crevasses, but while this may have caused some temporary confusion, it is unlikely to have been the cause of death. All the evidence points to the fact that, for reasons already outlined, he was more vulnerable to the cold than the others. Having been left behind in the snow for what may have been up to two hours was fatal.

Wilson's matter-of-fact account reads: [46]

He was comatose when we got him into the tent and he died without recovering consciousness that night about 10 p.m. We had a short rest for an hour or two in our bags that night, then had a meal and came on through the pressure ridges about 4 miles further down and reached our Lower Glacier Depot. Here we camped at last, had a good meal and slept a good night's rest which we badly need.

Whatever they wrote in their diaries, the shock of Evans' death must have been profound. Taff was no ordinary sailor; he had been one of Scott's mainstays for many years, and he had been top man on the messdeck. Scott had a special bond with him, or so Taff thought. His death added a sickening twist to an expedition that was rapidly coming apart at the seams. Scott's judgement, having already been seriously compromised by his mistaken rejection of dogs, was now under serious pressure in terms of the choices he had made for the Final Party and the survivability of his organisation – the organisation had considered perfect in those far-off days back at Cape Evans, and which he was at pains to defend in his final writings.

References

1 Louisa Young. *A Great Task of Happiness*, pp. 156–7

2 Edward Wilson. *Diary of the 'Terra Nova' Expedition*, p. 178

3 *op. cit*, p. 179

4 Apsley Cherry-Garrard. *The Worst Journey in the World*, p. 347, n. 28

5 Roland Huntford. *Scott and Amundsen*, p. 519

6 Admiral Edward Evans. *South With Scott*, p. 178

7 Apsley Cherry-Garrard. *op. cit*, p. 395

8 Karen May and Sarah Airriess. 'Could Captain Scott have been saved? Cecil Meares and the "second journey" that failed.' p. 264

9 *ibid.*

10 Captain R.F. Scott. *Scott's Last Expedition:* Vol. II *Being the Reports of the Journeys & the Scientific Work Undertaken by Dr. E. A. Wilson and the Surviving Members of the Expedition*, p. 300

11 Admiral Edward Evans. *op. cit*, p. 188

12 Apsley Cherry-Garrard. *op. cit*, p. 368

13   David Crane. *Scott of the Antarctic*, p. 528

14   Robert Falcon Scott. *Journals.* Editor's Appendix III, p. 469

15   Colin Bull and Pat F. Wright (eds.). *Silas*, p. 221

16   Kenneth J. Carpenter. *The History of Scurvy and Vitamin C*, p. 241

17   Apsley Cherry-Garrard. *op. cit.*, p. 407

18   Robert Falcon Scott. *op. cit.*, p. 358

19   Admiral Edward Evans. *op. cit.*, p. 228

20   Edward Wilson. *op. cit.*, p. 230

21   Robert Falcon Scott. *op. cit.*, p. 368

22   *op. cit.*, p. 387

23   Sue Limb and Patrick Cordingley. *Captain Oates*, pp. 193–4

24   Commander Evans. *The Strand Magazine*

25   *ibid.*

26   M.E. Markham and F.A. Markham. *The Life of Sir Albert Hastings Markham*, p. 97

27   Robert Falcon Scott. *op. cit.*, p. 371

28   *op. cit.*, p. 375

29   Edward Wilson. *op. cit.*, pp. 231–2

30   Louisa Young. *op. cit.*, p. 141

31   George Seaver. *Edward Wilson of the Antarctic*, p. 274

32   Robert Falcon Scott. *op. cit.*, Editor's Appendix III, p. 470

33   Gordon G. Giesbrecht and James A. Wilkerson. *Hypothermia, Frostbite and Other Cold Injuries*, p. 15

34   Edward Wilson. *op. cit.*, p. 237

35   From this point on in this chapter, references to Robert Falcon Scott, *Journals*, are given with his dates only

36   Edward Wilson. *op. cit.*, p. 238

37   *op. cit.*, p. 240

38   Roger Mear and Robert Swan. *In the Footsteps of Scott*, p. 103

39   Edward Wilson, *ibid.*

40   Sue Limb and Patrick Cordingley. *op. cit.*, p. 198

41   Gordon G. Giesbrecht and James A. Wilkerson. *op. cit.*, p. 40

42   Edward Wilson. *op. cit.*, p. 240

43   *op. cit.*, p. 242

44   *op. cit.*, p. 243

45   Gordon G. Giesbrecht and James A. Wilkerson. *ibid.*

46   Edward Wilson. *op. cit.*, p. 243

26

THE LAST MARCH

The death of Taff Evans marked a profound shift in the conduct and progression of the team's homeward journey. Wilson's journal goes overnight
from fairly lengthy entries to a terse couple of sentences. Even this threadbare
reportage ceases after just ten more days. So far as Scott was concerned, it is likely
that Taff's death initiated a period of profound introspection and a review of his
options. If Taff's death had been accidental, a fall into a crevasse for example,
neither the leadership nor the organisation would have been to blame. As it was,
in spite of the fact that he would later lament the 'astonishing failure' of a man who
was thought to be the 'strongest man of the party' (in 'Message to [the] Public'),
his own records – which were now impossible to erase – clearly show the danger
of injury in such a hostile environment, especially when combined with brutally
heavy work.

With hindsight, Scott must have realised that it had been a mistake to take a
man with a nasty cut on the knuckle. He had had the choice of two fit and uninjured
men, Lashly and Crean, of whom Crean was the fresher. Some might say that it
took hindsight to know what Crean was capable of; but equally, Scott should have
known his men and rated Crean accordingly. Scott biographers have invariably
covered for him by suggesting he didn't know about Taff's injury, but that seems
highly unlikely. What is almost certain, on the other hand, is that he was in denial
of the implications.

It probably took a few days for the full shock of Taff's death to sink in, and for
its meaning in terms of his judgement to become clear. Having taken some consolation perhaps from Wilson's collection of geological samples, Scott's mood must
have now have been adversely affected again. Without having discovered anything
new in terms of the route or the Pole, the very least that might have been expected
of him would have been to bring his men back in one piece, as HR Mill later
remarked. In fact, many would say it should have been his duty. And now that

prospect had also gone, again as a result of his own poor judgement, as he probably feared many would claim. The journey that had started with such high hopes was disintegrating before his very eyes. For a man already prone to depression, Evans' death must have been utterly devastating. It probably took a superhuman effort for him to keep going at all.

Taking account of their overworked bodies and minds, cold injuries, weight loss, worn clothing and equipment, demoralisation and shock, they needed all the help they could get to get back to base. It was just about possible. They were approximately on schedule and, providing there were no problems finding their depots, they had a fighting chance of getting through. Scott is certain to have realised that it would be touch-and-go, and that they could not afford any brakes on their progress. In light of this, we have to ask why he chose to drag, rather than depot, the 35 lbs of geological samples Wilson had collected coming down the Beardmore. Anyone doubting the significance of 35 lbs extra weight is invited to do their own experiment and lift the equivalent. The failure to depot the specimens and other redundant equipment at this point suggests that Scott may already have been considering endgame options.

He had anticipated staying another year, as the order for more ponies, dogs, and supplies shows, and as his planned date of return from the Pole dictated. This means that there was going to be every opportunity, if they so wished, to collect any depoted materials during the next season. Right now, they needed to be selective in what they put on the sledge. Scott did the opposite. In addition to all those rocks, they had a camera and tripod they were not going to use again, and a heavy theodolite which was now surplus to requirements. It arguably always had been. Neither of the returning teams had a theodolite, while Amundsen did not take one at all on his Pole journey.

In addition, as Gran reports, they had a load of old clothing and empty bags on the sledge. Gran: [1]

> It was incredible how much they had crowded on the sledge. Apart from the geological specimens ... there were masses of empty sacks and tattered clothing. I think they could have saved themselves the weight.

He kept the camera and the theodolite on the sledge nearly all the way, leaving them behind only two days before the last camp. Teddy later claimed that they had '150 lbs of trash' on their sledge. Exaggeration or not, it suggests that whatever their physical state or the supplies available on the Barrier, the team's biggest problem was the excess baggage, and what that meant in terms of what was going on in Scott's mind.

As already noted, one of Scott's most unfortunate reflexes was that of evading responsibility for his mistakes and failures. It had its roots in childhood and adolescence and was a defensive response, understandable in the context of the blame-cultures to which he was subject. The Royal Navy had its fair share of time-servers and the well-connected occupying positions for which they were poorly qualified. It was fertile breeding ground for the self-exculpatory reflexes to which middle-ranking officers especially, in a fiercely competitive environment, were prone. In that sense, he couldn't be blamed, and it could be seen as an appropriately defensive response to circumstances, rather than a personal shortcoming. However, although counterintuitive for him, it would have been better for his mental health, as well as his career, if he had been able to own up and take responsibility for his mistakes.

His inner conflicts – guilt, self-loathing, contrition, anger, self-pity and impatience – were all related to this issue. He knew he did it – on a deeper, probably inarticulate, level, he must have known that he made excuses and evaded responsibility, but he couldn't help himself. It explains why he was so tormented and haunted by feelings of low self-worth. It was that suppressed awareness that caused his depression, his anxiety, and his stress. After the excruciating *mea culpa* at the Pole, old reflexes had started to creep back in, and had once again become part of the interwoven fabric of self-blame and self-exculpation, even at the cost of his own ultimate integrity and the truth of the historical record.

He was undoubtedly in denial of it, but Scott was personally responsible for the death of the Pole Party. Historians have, by and large, accepted his version of events – blaming the weather, starvation, the failure of Taff and Oates, and everything in between, all while ignoring the extraordinary fact that Scott weighed down his sledge with what was, to all intents and purposes, a load of redundant equipment and a pile of rocks.

They should have cached the geological specimens and any other items they could do without at the start of the Barrier phase. Without a shadow of doubt, anyone serious about getting home would have done so. There were plenty of landmarks at the bottom of the Beardmore he could have used as markers for a depot. They were in a race against time, but rather than doing what he could to speed their progress, he did the opposite and slowed them down with a sledge that was much heavier than it need, or should, have been. In these circumstances it was incomprehensible, unless he had an ulterior motive.

It is impossible to know when Scott's plan for the Party to die en route changed from an option to an intention; but by the time they started the Barrier stage, the evidence suggests the balance had started to shift towards it. Notably, he also starts to prepare his audience by amplifying his lamentations and ominous predictions. Nobody would claim that what they were doing was easy, but that this genuine tragedy ended up being parodied on Monty Python is a measure of the flights of melodrama and theatricality with which Scott infused his narrative. The tone, the content, the commissions and the omissions were dictated by his need to impress his audience with the hardships and suffering, in order to deflect the suspicion that it was his leadership, rather than the horrors of the Barrier that were responsible for their demise.

They started off with a few decent meals, supplemented by pony meat and Taff's share of pemmican and biscuits. Thin optimism alternates with anxiety about the surfaces and complaints about the absence of wind to help them with the sail. Scott predicts a continuation of these difficulties for the next three or four days, although he had no way of knowing. The surfaces were like 'pulling over desert sand without the least glide in the world'. All the more reason, one would have thought, for dumping any unnecessary weight. The idea of redeeming the journey, at least partially, with a haul of geological samples was clearly seductive, but it should never have been more important than their lives. The fact that Polar man-haulers have been known cut off the handles of their toothbrushes to save weight puts the decision to haul 35 lbs of rocks – not to mention a load of further redundant stuff – into perspective.

It wasn't as though Scott was unaware of the significance of even small amounts of unnecessary weight. Some ten years before, Skelton's comments on the imminent departure of Scott on a preliminary journey on the *Discovery* Expedition, are evidence that Scott was well aware of the importance of weight. Skelton: [2]

> ... the Captain's party are going on Saturday to the Bluff. Shall be jolly glad to get rid of them. While they are preparing, the Ward Room becomes a simple nursery, Shackleton 'gassing' & 'eye serving' the whole time, ponderous jokes flying through the air, articles being weighed to a hundredth of a pound, instructions being given not to beeswax the thread or to go easy with brass eyelets on account of the extra weight. Really the whole thing makes one 'feel tired'. Of course the Skipper's ideas are on the whole perfectly right, that is one must be careful about weights, & a pound saved here & there soon mounts up, but he is 'fussy' about it ...

Little rays of cheer over having had an opportunity to dry their sleeping bags penetrate the gloom, but not for long.

19 February, Scott: [3]

> I wonder what is in store for us, with some little alarm at the lateness of the season.

As a matter of fact, they were approximately on his 144-day schedule, according to which they were not expected home until 22 March.

Temperatures were mild for the time of year on 20 February (between -13 and -15 F), but they had 'the same terrible surface'. He writes that they were leaving deeply ploughed tracks, and they were not so fit as they were, and again:

... the season is advancing apace.

The next day, the 21st, was unseasonably mild (-9.5 to -11 F), but the marching was almost as bad as the day before:

Heavy toiling all day, inspiring gloomiest thoughts at times.

It is impossible to imagine a victorious Scott dragging along like this, in spite of advancing scurvy, which was almost certainly affecting their energy levels.

21 February again:

We never won a march of 8.5 miles with greater difficulty, but we can't go on like this.

Would he have continued dragging all that surplus baggage if he had been first at the Pole? Of course not. He would have been making for home with all possible speed. But Scott says nothing about his options for making the marching easier.

There is a record [4] of what Teddy Evans made of Scott's decision to keep a load of dead weight on the sledge: a letter auctioned at Christie's in September 2000, from Teddy to 'Lal' Gifford, written on board the *Terra Nova* on 6 February 1913, shortly after he had received the news about the death of the Polar Party, and commenting on Scott's decision to carry his geological specimens with him to the last. Christie's:

Evans reports his shock at hearing of the loss of the Southern Party ('Capt. Oates, the Inniskilling Dragoon came out of it best of all ... By Jove he was a fine MAN'), commenting on the poor distances Scott's party was making – 'I had a narrow squeak, thank God I was not included in the advance party' –and condemning Scott's decision to keep his geological records: 'It seems to me extraordinary that ... they stuck to all their records & specimens, we dumped ours at the first big check. I must say I considered the safety of my party before the value of the records & extra stores – not eatable. Apparently Scott did not. His sledge contained 150 lbs of trash, he ought to have left it, pushed on & recovered the specimens & records this year'. Evans attempts to mitigate his harshness with the claim that he is 'not criticizing but deploring this fact', but points out that his own records had been recovered, as Scott's would have been. He observes that the Polar Party were probably too weak to have completed their journey in any case, and speculates as to the influence of scurvy on their condition.

Apart from an incidental mention of the specimens at the end of the journey, there is no word in Scott's journal about the decision to drag '150 lbs of trash'. This silence has successfully obscured the issue for a century – with the collusion of biographers and historians, who have either ignored it altogether or attached little importance to it. 150 lbs is the equivalent of dragging a 10.7-stone person – it almost suggests they could have put Oates on the sledge without extra hardship, especially when he became less able to pull as his feet got worse. But even if we allow for exaggeration and say it was half, 75 lbs is, especially in those circumstances, a tremendous extra weight. Perhaps people have shrunk from facing up to the enormity of what it implied, and not been prepared to be vilified by Scott's army of impassioned defenders.

On 22 February it continued mild (-2 F). Scott laments, however, that

> There is little doubt we are in for a rotten critical time going home, and the lateness of the season may make it really serious.

Again, he had always expected to be out at that time. He complained when there was no wind, but also when there was wind, because then it would be in the wrong direction. Similarly, the surfaces were almost always bad, because it was either too warm or too cold. Now, the wind had picked up, but it was still no good because instead of filling their sail it covered the homeward track and they steered too far to the east. It was a gloomy position as he foresaw the difficulty returning. Wilson and Bowers allegedly tried to keep up morale, which only adds to the pathos.

The weather continued mild by Barrier standards, and two days later they reached the Southern Barrier Depot. The last diary entry we have for Oates is for this day, 24 February. It contains the laconic: [5]

> Dug up Christopher's head for food but it was rotten.

His mother later destroyed Oates' journal, so all we have are the fragments his sister Violet managed to transcribe before it was lost, and it isn't now known whether he made any entries after the 24th. They picked up ten full days' provision with less than 70 miles to go to the next depot.

There is no further mention of the extra food and supplies made available by the absence of Taff Evans. Scott noted a shortage of oil, however, which Lashly had not mentioned when he passed through with the last Supporting Party. It was all too easy to imply that the blame for the shortage of oil rested with previous parties. It was a theme which later newspaper reports would pick up on, only just stopping short of blaming them, and by implication Teddy Evans, for the disaster. Nowhere does Scott take responsibility for not addressing the known problem of the leaky oil tins. By the evening he was despondent again because of a really terrible surface, and laments again:

24 February:

> I don't know what to think, but the rapid closing of the season is ominous.

The rapidly closing season has now been mentioned four times within six days. It sounds increasingly like he is setting his readers up for disaster.

The situation, however, was not as dire as he made out. They had about 28 days left of the 144-day plan to do roughly 350 miles – an average of about 12.5 miles per day. According to Cherry, the Second Return Party, numbering just two fit men and a seriously ill Teddy Evans, had averaged 11.2 geographical miles per day. [6] This means that with a determined and motivated leader the odds would have been in their favour. Temperatures were bearable, and they had enough food to get them to the next depot. They were short of oil, but not disastrously so.

On 25 February, although the pulling was still very hard, Scott does admit that the tracks were easy to see, and that they were getting into better ski drawing again. However, after an 'excellent' lunch, incongruously, he hopes for better things in the afternoon. They didn't do too badly that afternoon, and clocked up a total of 11.4 miles for the day.

It was beginning to look like they were in with a chance of getting home, and that may have been why, on the 26th, there was another notable shift. Suddenly, we start to hear about very cold nights, cold feet at the start of the march, not enough food, and a woeful shortage of oil. Nevertheless, the temperature at the end of the day is given as -21 F – cold enough, but average for the time of year, and again they had made 11.5 miles in 'wonderfully fine' weather. In the night, however, the temperature allegedly drops to a minimum of -37 F – very unusual for the time of year in that location.

It's the start of the infamous 'cold snap', concerning which there is bitter and profound criticism of Professor Susan Solomon's *The Coldest March* from Professor Krzysztof Sienicki, who accuses her of data dragging, fabrication of meteorological data, and fallacious analysis. [7]

It is indeed curious that Scott historians in general have accepted his temperature data without question, to the extent of constructing an elaborate theory about an unusual – if not unique – weather event around them. All things considered, it is much more likely that Scott stretched the severity of the temperatures as part of a set of apparently plausible explanations for the failure, and eventual demise, of what remained of the Polar Party. He must have thought he could safely assume that no one would ever be in a position to question his data.

According to Scott, after having been down to -37 F on 26 February, there was a run of -40, -37.5, -41.5, and -40 F on the four following nights. These are seriously anomalous temperatures for that time of year in that locality. Modern automated weather stations record daily averages for the end of February of between -20 and -22 F. [8] Five nights in a row of these unseasonable temperatures stretch plausibility to breaking point. Scott goes even further in his letter to Sir Francis Bridgeman, where he claims that it has been -40 'for well-nigh a month', and in the 'Message to [the] Public', in which he states that

> On the Barrier in lat. 82^0 ... we had -30^0 in the day, -47^0 at night pretty regularly ...

In his letter to Kathleen he also mentions a temperature of -40.

In both these letters and in the 'Message to [the] Public', Scott mentions temperatures using phrases such as 'well-nigh a month' and 'pretty regularly', which do not fulfil criteria for evidence.

From 27 February there are no more diary entries, however cursory, from Wilson. In one of his death-tent letters to Oriana he says that life had become too much of a struggle to keep up his journal. Notably, however, it coincides with the start of the unseasonably cold weather, and it means that from this date forward we have only Scott's day-to-day temperature data. Birdie had stopped keeping his diary some time before this. Dates given for Birdie's cessation of notes vary; but both Bowers biographers George Seaver and Anne Strathie agree that Birdie made his last diary entry on 3 February, while Strathie tells us he stopped making records in his navigation book on 27 February, and his logbook on 12 March. [9, 10] Unless there is clear evidence that he was taking readings himself, and not simply noting what Scott told him, any extant temperature data from Birdie after 27 February should be treated with caution. The same goes for Wilson, who records a temperature of -37 F for the nights of 26 and 27 February, and stops making entries altogether after that.

Whether or not it is the case, as Professor Sienicki claims, that the team made a collective pact to commit altruistic suicide on the basis of Utilitarian Doctrine, it could have been one of Scott's reasons. (Utilitarianism is the doctrine that the good is whatever brings the greatest happiness to the greatest number of people.) We know what Kathleen had told him. As we can safely assume he was depressed, he may well have agreed with her that she and 'the boy' would be better off without him. Sienicki's collective altruistic suicide theory does provide an explanation for the fact that Wilson, Bowers, and Oates went along with the decision to haul non-essentials and trash. They outnumbered him, and would have been capable and justified in relieving Scott of command, on the basis that he was endangering their lives. There is also apparent corroboration of Scott's reasons for the disaster in Wilson's and Bowers' last letters home – without the least mention of the specimens or trash from either – which obviously added credibility to his claims.

In his last letters, Wilson writes just a couple of sentences regarding short fuel, food, and intense cold, but nearly everything else is about his faith and trust that all is according to God's will. He seems to have chosen his words very carefully, writing that they are 'all done up', and that they have struggled to the end. Birdie tells his mother that it was all about the low temperatures, lack of food and fuel, and that they were held up by their sick companions. But ultimately, he also attributes their deaths to God's will. There remains the fact, however, that they appear to have participated – for whatever reasons – in the way the Last Journey turned out.

Does the Utilitarianism theory provide sufficient explanation for the apparently deliberate manipulation of events on the Last Journey? Wilson, for example, in one of his last letters to Oriana, writes that they had done what they thought was best, which could be interpreted as a hint that there was a pact to commit Utilitarian suicide. But what about Oates? There cannot have been any part of his wretched progress that he would have volunteered for.

The problem that won't go away is that big extra weight on the sledge. Without it, there is the distinct possibility that they would have made it home. There seems little reason why Wilson and Bowers would not have wanted to get back – national honour and loyalty to Scott notwithstanding. Even an extra mile per day from the start of the Barrier would have seen them to One Ton Depot and beyond, almost within sight of home. However, if they had made a Utilitarian pact, it means that Wilson and Bowers not only agreed to commit suicide, but also the manner in which – meaning painfully and drawn-out, dragging a load of redundant weight until a location had been reached where they were likely to be found, there to lie down and wait for death.

Doubts must have surrounded the plan, however good it may have sounded in theory. Wilson and Bowers might have argued that people would see through it by recognising how obviously wrong it had been to drag unnecessary weight. Scott might have assured them he knew how to handle it. We have seen how adept he was at employing a judicious silence. Wilson's presence on the first (*Discovery*) journey is an obvious example. Instead, he paints a picture of unrelenting hardship, and blames science and Wilson for the stones. He might have guessed that their deaths at the end of it would shame any remaining doubters into silence.

It still seems a lot for Wilson and Bowers to commit to and, as far as Oates is concerned, a non-starter. We know that Scott was habitually reluctant to share his plans, and he may also have been reluctant to rely on the team's ongoing assent to a plan of which he would be the main beneficiary. Because another problem with the Utilitarian suicide pact theory is that Wilson and Bowers may not have thought that their families (or the world in general) would be better off without them. Bowers had a doting mother and sisters, and Oriana was devoted to Wilson, and he to her and his family. Would they have been willing to pay the price in terms of their nearest and dearest, who would be likely to feel that the greater good would be better served by their survival?

There is a memorial plaque to Scott in St Paul's Cathedral with the inscription 'Death is swallowed up in victory.' It is from the Bible, 1 Corinthians 15:54. The English Standard Version reads:

> When the perishable puts on the imperishable, and the mortal puts on immortality, then shall come to pass the saying that it is written: Death is swallowed up in victory.

Whoever decided the wording on the plaque must have felt that Scott had attained a kind of immortality by the manner and circumstances of his death. Scott would not have presumed to think such a thought, but the seed of the idea may have been present in the back of his mind.

Nevertheless, as committed Christians, Wilson and Bowers would not have been open to the idea of premeditated suicide. It is more likely, in our view, that they took things one day at a time; never sure that what they were doing was right, inwardly conflicted by their loyalty to Scott, and whether they had the right or the power to intervene.

Wilson and Bowers did not carry the weight of responsibility for the Pole defeat and the death of Taff Evans. Their future did not depend on the outcome of the expedition. Scott had by far the greater vested interest in portraying the outcome as heroic in some sense. Unfortunately for the rest of the team, Scott's version of heroic tended towards martyrdom, whereas someone like Shackleton would have taken pride in bringing everyone safely home, regardless of the attainment or otherwise of the stated objective. Spinning their defeat as a martyrdom in the service of a moral ideal bears the hallmarks of the Scott way. It played to his strengths, especially his literary talent.

But that meant that they had to be found. If they weren't, his journal would be lost, and with it his chance to shape the way their deaths would be perceived by history. Not only that, if his records and the photos were never found, no one would ever even be sure that they had stood at the South Pole at all, albeit in heart-breaking circumstances. Reaching a place where they and their records would be likely to be found was, therefore, essential. It provides a very satisfying explanation as to why they expired just 11 miles away from a major depot – something over which people have scratched their heads for generations.

What further explanations might one explore as to why the others went along with Scott's decisions and explanations? In view of the whole team's deafening silence about having dragged a pile of rocks, and bearing in mind that God's will may only have been invoked as the post-hoc way Wilson and Bowers reconciled themselves to the outcome, it might be useful to look to logical inference and psychological dispositions for plausible explanations. It might also be interesting to attempt an overview of what their options were.

The first, most obvious, point is the fact that they *were* all so quiet about those rocks, but then Scott had made sure of that by taking over journal duties. Nevertheless, under normal circumstances one might have expected the odd note from Wilson or Bowers, surely. It is hard to believe that a few lines were beyond them. With Scott's beady eye on them, however, it would not have been so easy – it seems to have been impossible.

We can probably dismiss the notion that the team simply carried on dragging in a benumbed kind of way, like a bunch of zombies. Teddy Evans, in his letter to 'Lal' Gifford, makes no comment other than to deplore the fact that Scott didn't dump the non-essentials – but it is simply not credible that they never considered their options. Nevertheless, the weight of the sledge might have been the 'elephant in the room'; its continued existence assured by a collective reluctance to broach the subject. Wilson was so much more than just a member of the team, but even he might have baulked at a confrontation. He too was accustomed to tiptoeing around Scott's anger and depression. They were probably all reluctant to risk one of Scott's pained and rejecting tirades. Instead, taking it one day at a time, they may have hoped that the next day might be better than the last, and that Scott might decide to cache the stones after all.

They didn't have a hope. Those specimens were crucial to Scott's plan, and the key to understanding how he worked it all out – with scant consideration, it seems, for the lives of the rest of the team. Perhaps it is because Professor Sienicki cannot accept the idea that Scott deliberately took the team with him into oblivion that he surmises they must have agreed to it. It is by no means unique, however, for sufficiently depressed people to take others with them. While it is true that their daily mileage decreased coming down the Beardmore – which, according to Professor Sienicki, is the point at which they made their collective decision to die – the decrease in mileage was also due to the difficult terrain on the Beardmore.

It is likely that Wilson was key to what happened on that Barrier Journey. It all comes down to the dynamics underlying the structure of that team, and the psychological make-up of its members. Wilson was loyal and devoted to Scott, whatever his mistakes or misjudgements. In thrall to Scott's depressive martyrdom, and afraid that taking away those specimens might break him by removing the last remaining thread of meaning and purpose of the journey, the compassionate concern that certainly Wilson and, to a large extent also Bowers, had for him might have rendered Scott immune to intervention in case it should add to his pain. They seem not to have gone near the subject.

As important, however, must have been that Wilson did not have it in him to depose Scott and take over as leader. He was identified with his role as Scott's right-hand man, enabler, apologist, partner and support, never his rival or challenger for the leadership. Scott was identified with and entrenched in his role as leader. He literally owned the expedition, and that made it impossible for anyone to question, never mind challenge, his leadership. They could criticise him, scoff behind his back, abandon him even, as some did back at Cape Evans, but they could never take his expedition away from him.

For Wilson it was also an emotional commitment. To override Scott's authority would have meant a betrayal of everything Wilson stood for in terms of the obligations of loyalty, integrity and personal trust. Nevertheless, there might still have been the potential for persuading Scott to take a different course. The question is then why Wilson, Bowers and Oates do not appear to have made a case for reducing the weight of the sledge. The answer may simply be that they did, but that they failed. Besides, Wilson may not have been passionate enough about it.

If you valued your life, in a life-or-death situation Wilson wasn't the sort of man you would want to be with. His letters, and the notations in his Book of Common Prayer, which he took with him on the journey (as well as a copy of the New Testament), make it clear that far from avoiding it, he looked forward to death as a way of becoming united with God. 'It is finished', he writes – being the words of Christ on the cross, telling mankind that their sins have been atoned for, and that the Kingdom of Heaven awaits them. [11] Presumably he believed that 'God's mercy' extended over everyone, including non-believers or agnostics like Scott.

The impression one gets from Wilson's notes on the paste-down of his prayer book is that he identified with the suffering of Christ. The very severity of the ordeal he was undergoing might have strengthened his belief that God was testing his faith, and his compassionate concern for Scott might have played into this fatalistic and masochistically submissive conceptualisation of events. He is likely to have felt that it was nobody's fault that they had been second at the Pole. Reiterating his faith in the rightness of all things under God, he might simply have accepted whatever reality he found himself in and looked forward to his reward in heaven.

For Scott, the reality might have been altogether more prosaic. It is possible that he never acknowledged the option to lighten the sledge. The bottom line was always that he was the boss, and he could have simply ignored the issue, silently defying anyone to bring it up. It is possible that Scott, for whom the prospect of facing the world had, plausibly, grown intolerable, may have countered any dissension or incipient mutiny by a simple refusal to depot the stones. If we suppose that Oates at least might still have been motivated, during the early part of the Barrier stage, to mount some sort of challenge, Scott could have threatened to stay behind. He could have given the team an ultimatum by saying he would not go on without the specimens. That would have been it. There is no way they could leave Scott behind. It meant that to go on would be to go on, on Scott's terms. For Scott, it would have been the simplest, if most ruthless option.

Even if it hadn't come to an actual confrontation, Scott may have hinted that keeping those rocks was the *sine qua non* for the rest of the journey. It would have put Wilson in an impossible position, while at the same time absolving him of responsibility, as had happened when he relinquished diary duties. Scott took advantage of that, even to the extent of claiming that the rocks were carried at Wilson's special request – an entry that Wilson probably never saw, and which was misleading. It would ultimately always have been up to Scott.

Wilson might also have found it hard to believe that Scott was deliberately leading them to their deaths. At the same time as his concern for Scott's mental suffering might have held him back from a confrontation, Wilson might have held on to the thought that things would turn out right somehow, perhaps with the dogs, or perhaps through a sign or an intervention from God. He may have thought there was still the potential for salvaging some – any – kind of value from what had been a largely symbolic quest from the beginning, and surviving against the odds. It is worth remembering that he expected the dogs at around half-way along the Barrier. He may have reasoned that in that case they could just about afford to hang on to the specimens and the other gear. When the dogs failed to arrive it would have been in character for him to have interpreted that as God's will, and that it was his duty to submit to it.

Bowers, for his part, would never have presumed to take over, having been conditioned all his life to do as he was ordered, even to the point of sacrificing his life. He would have deferred to the combined authority of Scott and Wilson, and is likely to have aligned himself with them. Oates, on the other hand, had always been the odd man out. On his own, he effectively had no choice but to go along with the rest of the team – which he must have increasingly realised meant almost certain death, not just for him, but for all of them. This unvarnished truth is unlikely ever to have been voiced, either by him or anyone else, as they all carried on pretending they were doing their best to get home. Or so we're told by Scott.

The decision to carry on dragging Scott's baggage is made all the more poignant by a consideration of the team's tiredness which, as well as inevitable in the circumstances, must have been exacerbated by scurvy. In the days leading up to the end of his journal, Wilson writes that they had a few 'fat pony hooshes', but they would have done nothing to ward off any emerging symptoms, as might have been the hope. They knew that fresh meat was anti-scorbutic, and probably assumed that fresh horse meat would be. It would explain why Scott did not order any fresh seal meat to be put in One Ton or Corner Depots, nor to leave instructions to that effect for the dog-sledge which was supposed to meet them. He should have, but he probably didn't think of it, and neither did Wilson.

There is some individual variation in the onset of scurvy, but now, after four months on a scorbutic diet, they must all have been affected. Unfortunately for them, horse meat does not contain vitamin C. It does contain certain other important nutrients which can help make the most of whatever traces of vitamin C are in the diet; but as the sledging rations contained none, the pony meat will have made no difference in that respect, and little to their weight loss, which must have been drastic, and which made them more vulnerable to the cold. The agony was real, there is no doubt about that. Wilson's medical notes throughout the journey had been rather succinct, which means he probably always took account of Scott's reluctance to admit to the true human cost of his method of travel. There were no specifics about their weight loss, and of course he never breathed a word about scurvy, the presence of which he would still have regarded as a shameful reflection on the organisation.

On 27 February, in addition to recording an anomalous temperature, Scott writes that they were already in a critical position, in spite of having six days' food (plus Taff's allowance of food and fuel) to last just 31 miles to the next depot – the Middle Barrier Depot – and having made a good mileage for the day of 12.2 miles. But:

> Pray God we have no further setbacks ... We may find ourselves in
> safety at the next depot, but there is a horrid element of doubt.

It seems contradictory, and they would have considered this situation far from desperate if they had bagged the Pole. If that had been the case, they would already have been a lot further on; it is well known what a positive mental attitude can accomplish. And they would not have been encumbered by rocks and rubbish. That much is certain.

Scott had ordered the dogs to come out to about half-way between Hut Point and the start of the Beardmore; but only after having restocked One Ton Depot, and depending on their condition. Realistically, Scott must have known that the men themselves had no chance of catching the ship, with or without dogs. The thinking must therefore have been that in the event of his triumph, the news could be rushed back at breakneck speed by Meares and a crack team of dogs, with just the glimmer of a chance of catching the ship and letting the world know.

There was zero enthusiasm for that journey back at Cape Evans, where everybody chose to believe that by taking the three XS rations to One Ton, they had fulfilled Scott's orders, albeit to the minimum. The feeling might have been that although Scott's chances of the Pole were slim in the face of Amundsen and his dogs, there was little likelihood of an emergency. Day after day, therefore, Scott and the team scoured the horizon in vain.

On this day, 27 February, Cherry was one day into his journey to One Ton with Dmitrii and the dogs. [12] Without Dmitrii that journey could never have happened, and he should be given credit for it. At the same time, at approximately the latitude where Meares had orders to meet them if possible, Scott and the team were 'always discussing the possibility of meeting the dogs', according to Scott. Certainly, Oates' hopes must have been pinned on the dogs, whom he correctly assumed were his last remaining chance of survival. The dogs were 200 miles away.

Bowers and Oates put on new finnesko on the 29th. A good thing, one might have thought, but it probably made things worse for Oates. If his feet were actually frozen to some extent, which is likely, it would have been better for them to have remained so until permanent rewarming could take place. This is because re-freezing of partially thawed tissue causes greater damage to that tissue, while walking on partially thawed feet causes the worst damage of all. They marched 11.5 miles that day. If Oates had been just about managing on numb and frozen feet, warmer footwear would have been potentially disastrous – as it turned out.

On 1 March, they reached the Middle Barrier Depot, but found a shortage of oil. That there was indeed a shortage of oil there is corroborated by Lashly, who writes on 30 January that his party too found a shortage, and that they took what they thought would take them to the next depot (Mount Hooper). Lashly: [13]

> There seems to have been some leakage in the one can, but how we could not account for that we have left a note telling Capt. Scott how we found it, but they will have sufficient to carry them on to the next depot, but we all know the amount of oil allowed on the Journey is enough, but if any waste takes place it means extra pre-cautions in the handling of it.

There was only just enough oil, evidently, and Lashly will have assumed that Scott would be travelling at a reasonable speed – which he was, to all intents and purposes. It should just about have sufficed.

On this day Oates disclosed badly frostbitten feet, but the next day he was on them again, marching almost ten miles. Oates' big toe had turned blue-black a month ago. One way or another, he had been suffering with his feet for months. His only relief now came from the refreezing, and therefore numbing, of what was left of living tissue.

On 3 March the outlook was 'blacker than ever', when the surface grew 'awful beyond words'. Scott:

> ... every circumstance was against us. After 4.25 hours things so bad that we camped, having covered 4.5 miles ... One cannot consider this a fault of our own – certainly we were pulling hard this morning ... The surface, lately a very good hard one, is coated with a thin

layer of woolly crystals ... and cause impossible friction on the runners. God help us, we can't keep up this pulling, that is certain.

He is setting up his public for the impending disaster.

It is extraordinary the way Scott continues to write about the difficulties of pulling the sledge without the slightest hint that he had the option to radically reduce its weight. The only way this makes sense is that he was keeping it quiet deliberately – which puts it beyond doubt that he had a hidden agenda. For a man whose object was heroic martyrdom, the scheme had a lot going for it. The extra weight held them back, while at the same time the specimens suggested a noble sacrifice in the service of science.

It is likely to have been his status as a representative of the Royal Navy – the pride of the nation – which he would have felt he had let down. As a private individual, a scientist, or an explorer-adventurer like Amundsen, he might have been able to live with the failure. As it was, he carried the prestige of the nation on his shoulders, and a way had to be found to turn the defeat – if not into a victory – then at least into a heroic defeat against impossible conditions. There would be no shame in failure, having bravely struggled against overwhelming odds. There would be redemption for the Pole defeat by dying in the attempt. Someone like Clements Markham would even feel that it added to the drama and romance of exploration. Who could honestly claim that it hasn't?

The specimens helped to spin the goal of the trip in the direction of science. It gave Markham, who might have started to feel defensive about his *beau idéal* fantasies, a lifeline insofar as he could claim the pre-eminence of science. No more sneering remarks about 'mudlarkers' now, it seems. Now that it suited him, he had the audacity to claim that the purpose of the expedition had been primarily in the interests of science.

It wasn't true. According to Diana Preston, [14] on 13 September 1909,

> Scott told an eager public: 'The main object of the expedition is to reach the South Pole and to secure for The British Empire the honour of this achievement.'

Unfortunately the quote isn't referenced, nor can it be found in *The Times* of that day. [15] It hardly matters, as an abundance of sources provide irrefutable evidence that the primary goal of the expedition was the Southern Journey, and for Scott to stand at the South Pole as the first man in history to do so.

The team's increasingly slow progress meant that they were generating less body heat, which must have compounded their susceptibility to the cold. It made it easier to blame the conditions.

4 March, Scott:

> Things looking *very* black indeed.

The surface was a bad as ever, but the temperature had actually risen (-20 F):

> ... but a colder snap is bound to come again soon. I fear that Oates at
> least will weather such an event very poorly. Providence to our aid!

Again things were not quite as bad as he made them sound. They made nine miles that day and were about 42 miles from the next depot with a week's food in hand (plus Taff's portion, again not mentioned), and '3 or 4 days' fuel'. A motivated leader would have considered that enough, and it would seem survivable to go to bed with a cup of cocoa and pemmican solid with the chill off. But according to Scott, this was the reason one of Oates' feet swelled up tremendously during the night. It seems an unlikely explanation. A more professional diagnosis was not forthcoming, however.

We are told that Wilson did what he could. Normally that would include making notes on the progression of any injury as a standard occupational procedure, even in these circumstances. The fact that he made no such notes constitutes further evidence that science was not the core mission of this expedition. Wilson was head of science. One would have expected him to record his observations of all the physical and mental processes the team underwent, as a service to science. It might have salvaged some value from the endeavour. It casts further doubt on the scientific justification for keeping those specimens on the sledge.

If there had still been a chance for Oates, it was now slipping away by the day. It must have been clear that his life hung in the balance, and that it was essential for him to get proper medical aid as soon as possible. In the event, Oates forced himself onwards, helping to drag many pounds of 'trash' for another 12 days before he crawled out into the snow to die. He may not have made it anyway, but with all the speed they could muster he might still have had a chance, and above all, it would have been the right thing to do – especially as they always had the option of depoting the specimens, many of which were duplicates of material already brought back by Shackleton, and Scott's first support team. Considering the dubiousness already apparent in the scientific credentials of this journey, Caroline Oates might have reasoned that her son died for the sake of hauling a pile of rocks pointlessly from A to B. Teddy had started to falter around the Middle Barrier Depot, which Scott had passed some days ago, but had still been brought to safety by Lashly and Crean.

Perhaps Oates' code of honour forbade him to protest on his own behalf. He identified with his Army rank and he was the type of officer who would carry out orders whether he agreed with them or not, purely as a matter of principle. But he must have known that if nothing changed, he was not going to survive. Somehow he struggled on for the next couple of days, but it was clear he was beginning to falter. On the evening of 6 March, Scott wrote:

... [Oates] is wonderfully plucky, as his feet must be giving him great pain. He makes no complaint, but his spirits only come up in spurts now, and he grows more silent in the tent ... If we were all fit I should have hopes of getting through, but the poor Soldier has become a terrible hindrance, though he does his utmost and suffers much I fear.

It was adding insult to injury to refer to Oates as a hindrance, and it was un-forgivable to make him carry the can for their failure to get through. Oates' mother knew it. You don't call someone a murderer for no reason. We can imagine how Caroline Oates must have felt seeing her suffering son described as a 'terrible hindrance'. The callousness of Scott's remarks about Oates seem to have been quietly ignored by the public, and of course the rest of the team probably never saw them. One wonders, however, how Wilson and Bowers dealt with Oates' obvious agony, while doing nothing to speed their progress. Wilson may have assuaged his conscience by doctoring Oates' feet while inwardly reaffirming his Panglossian faith. He might even have still harboured the faint hope that the dogs would arrive after all. Bowers, in spite of probably being the strongest physically, was psychologically powerless against the combined authority of Scott and Wilson.

As we know, Scott himself habitually resorted to denial in order to cope. This means that he had developed mental techniques for dealing with knowledge that threatened his ability to survive psychologically. He held himself together right to the end, which means he must have guarded himself against acknowledging that he was in any direct way responsible for Oates' predicament. Nevertheless, whatever his secret, or not-so-secret, plans for their collective demise, it must have taken an implacable death-wish to watch Oates deteriorate and not do what he could to get them home. Possibly, Wilson's doctoring allowed Scott to think every-thing possible was being done. He told himself and the world it was all because of the cold. It didn't wash with Caroline.

Oates' status as an outsider might have made it easier for Scott. Their relation-ship had never been the warmest. For his part, Oates might have stood up more for himself, but he must have felt it would be useless. He seems to have retreated into his own private hell. Scott might have reassured himself by reflecting that as far as he knew, no one was ever going to be in a position to question his temperature data and anyway, who was ever going to doubt the word, or the integrity of a man who would himself one day be found frozen to death?

7 March, Scott:

A little worse I fear. One of Oates' feet *very* bad this morning; he is wonderfully brave. We still talk of what we will do together at home.

A forlorn hope, as Scott knew perfectly well, and indeed as the tone of the statement suggests.

And now comes the following extraordinary error, magnified by Leonard Huxley, and thoughtlessly repeated even by Max Jones.

7 March:

> We are 16 from our depot. If we only find the correct proportion of
> food there and this surface continues, we may get to the next depot
> [Mt. Hooper, 72 miles farther] but not to One Ton Camp.

Their depot, 16 miles away, *was* Mount Hooper. A phantom extra depot has crept in. In the circumstances, the lack of clarity is understandable from Scott. The extra 72 miles in square brackets, added by Huxley, didn't exist. It is another example of the way Huxley assisted Scott by his 'creative' editing – not least in making it appear colder by massaging the temperatures down, as is shown by a comparative analysis of the data, and by removing entries in which Scott showed his unpleasant side. Now, he is too ready to make the next depot further away – inventing further difficulties for Scott, and justifying the failure.

Scott ends his entry for 7 March with:

> Sun bright and cairns showing up well. I should like to keep the
> track to the end.

In spite of apparently favourable conditions there is a death-knell in these words. It suggests he was planning to end it all whatever the conditions. Continuing to prepare his audience, therefore, the litany of woe resumes the next day, this time with complaints about how long he has to wait before everyone else has their foot-gear on. It creates the impression that he was ready to go on, and that he would have made better progress but for the others. He couldn't bear to blame Wilson, however, and gives him a free pass on account of his care for others.

They did 4.5 miles that morning. It was 8.5 miles now to Mount Hooper. If the dogs had not been there to replenish it, and there was another shortage of fuel, then, on 8 March:

> ... God help us indeed. We are in a very bad way, I fear, in any case.

There is no entry for the 9th, but they reached Mount Hooper that day. Lashly had written that his party had left nearly all their share of pemmican there, [16]

> ... on account of none of us caring for it, therefore we are leaving it
> behind for the others. They may require it.

He says nothing about fuel. According to Scott on 10 March, however, it was:

> Cold comfort. Shortage on our allowance all round.

This can't have been true, certainly not as far as the pemmican was concerned, as Lashly's comments confirm. And as always, they also had Taff's allowance of pemmican, biscuits and fuel. Plus his allowance of sundries like sugar, tea etc.

10 March, Scott:

> Things steadily downhill. Oates' foot worse. He has rare pluck and must know that he can never get through. He asked Wilson if he had a chance this morning, and of course Bill had to say he didn't know. In point of fact he has none ... poor Titus is the greatest handicap. He keeps us waiting in the morning until we have partly lost the warming effect of our good breakfast ... again at lunch. Poor chap! It is too pathetic to watch him; one cannot but try to cheer him up.

Again Scott blames Oates for their slow progress, and no amount of pity can make up for the callousness of the statement that Oates has no chance of getting through. It is worth noting that if it was true that Oates asked Wilson if he had a chance, it contradicts the Utilitarian theory. At the very least it suggests that if there was a pact to commit suicide, Oates was not included in it.

They marched only for half an hour on the 10th as the wind-chill was too much, according to Scott, forcing them to spend the rest of the day in the tent. This further serious delay had ominous implications for Oates. The state he was in on the morning of the 11th prompted Scott to write:

> Titus Oates is very near the end, one feels.

His condition must have become all but intolerable, and it can have been no coincidence that Scott ordered Wilson to hand over his supplies of morphine.

For the next few days they continued their agonised dragging. On the 14th, it was undoubtedly the wind-chill that was making it seem colder than it was. Scott claims a temperature of -43 F, and it must have felt like it in their thin, overworked, scorbutic condition and their worn and greasy clothing. Wilson could hardly get off his skis when they stopped to make camp, suggesting stiffness from hypothermia or scurvy, or both.

It must have been true that Oates had been slow in his last days. Apart from the awful state of his feet, it is a sign of hypothermia. Scott writes that even before they got to the Pole, Oates was feeling the cold and fatigue more than most. His feet had been deteriorating daily, layer by layer. It must have been during the night that he suffered the worst pain. During the day the feet would refreeze, numbing them, but as each night wore on the agony must have crept up on him again and again as they slowly thawed. In hospital situations, pain management is an important part of the care of someone being treated for frostbite, never mind whatever complications Oates was enduring. That he had steadily been getting more hypothermic is indicated by the fact that his hands had also begun to freeze, while his face had been freezing and thawing for months. He had been on a variable, but ultimately downward, trajectory from before they even got to the Pole.

There is a certain amount of variation in how individuals respond to hypothermia. Taff got the 'umbles', but Oates became silent and slow in his movements and the performance of tasks. Ataxia is a known sign of hypothermia – some of the signs being a general slowing-down, lack of co-ordination, and physical stiffness. Oates exhibited all of those.

Those last few days must have been purgatory for him. The memory of his famous exchange with Scott on the Depot Journey must have hung silently between them. One Ton Depot would have been reached by now if Oates' advice regarding the ponies had been followed. Scott never mentioned the issue again, and it had all but been forgotten about. But not by Oates, we can be fairly sure. It would not have made a difference to the outcome, however. If One Ton Depot had been further south, it might have made things easier for Oates by forcing an earlier end to the journey – which would have meant that he would have died in the tent together with the rest of the team, instead of on his own, forsaken by every living thing on earth.

At lunch on the 15th, Oates asked to be left behind in his sleeping-bag. Surely the kindest thing would have been for him to have taken his morphine and for the others to have stayed with him to the end. After all, none of them were going anywhere, as they must by now have known. According to Scott, Oates had been able and willing to discuss outside subjects to the very last and did not give up hope to the very end. The only hope he could have had was that the dogs would appear after all.

It must have been an uncomfortable reflection for Meares in the aftermath, as he never seriously considered going back out on to the Barrier, getting on the ship instead at the earliest opportunity. He may have been unwilling to help Scott, but Oates was a special friend to him. He may have told himself that he had no reason to suspect that Oates would be in dire straits; but if he thought Scott was a rotten expedition leader, he might have expected a rotten outcome, which should have spurred him into action on his friend's behalf. Atkinson, Oates' other ally, would have heard from Teddy – who had been one of the last to see him – that Oates was not in the best shape to go on to the Pole. Atkinson, as a medic, should have been able to predict that Oates would do badly as time went on. It makes his decision to stay at Hut Point and nurse Teddy hard to accept – his later abortive foray on to the Barrier with Keohane notwithstanding.

On the night of the 15–16 March, Oates was worse and, in Scott's words,

... we knew the end had come.

According to Scott, his mother and his regiment were in Oates' mind as he prepared himself for his final departure. There is artistic licence in the famous painting by Dolman picturing him staggering away from the tent. There was no light inside it, and the door was not left open. The tent was dark and closed behind him as he stumbled and crawled into the void. As the remaining warmth leached out of the still-warm parts of his body, he probably went in and out of altered states of consciousness, while his heart-rate will have started to slow down and become erratic. The others tried to find his body afterwards but couldn't. It suggests that his final act may have been to dig himself into the snow in a phenomenon called terminal burrowing. It is possible that Oates literally dug his own grave before losing consciousness forever.

Scott: [17]

> Poor Titus Oates has gone – he was in a bad state. the rest of us keep going and imagine we have a chance to get through but the cold weather doesn't let up at all.

If Bowers and Wilson had still imagined there was hope for them at least, both Scott's journal and his letter to Sir Edgar Speyer, dated 16 March, proves that Scott expected them all to die: [18]

> ... we have been to the Pole and we shall die like gentlemen – I regret only for the women we leave behind ...

That suggests that Wilson and Bowers had agreed to die alongside Scott at least as early as 16 March. This is not supported by their last letters in which they talk of going to One Ton to get supplies. Whom should we believe?

At this late stage, some of the weight was taken off the sledge by leaving behind the theodolite, the camera and Oates' sleeping-bag, but not the specimens. In fact, it is only now, on 17 March, that they are mentioned at all.

Scott:

> Diaries, &c., and geological specimens carried at Wilson's special request, will be found with us or on our sledge.

The almost casual mention of the specimens at this late stage is not congruent with their importance – not only in terms of their weight, but also in terms of their putative scientific importance. At the same time, disowning responsibility for keeping them on the sledge is an attempt to allay suspicion that it had anything to do with his own agenda. It is simply not credible that he would have acceded to a request of that nature if he had been serious about getting home.

The statement that diaries etc 'will be found with us or on our sledge' shows a deliberate intention to die – again inclusive of Wilson and Bowers. Unless they were in the terminal stages of scurvy, starvation, hypothermia or dehydration, there could not have been any certainty that their deaths were imminent. While they were obviously not in good shape, there is no evidence that they were in an acutely terminal state, as Scott's survival for at least another 12 days confirms. It shows that he was intending to die whatever their state and even, in fact, whatever the weather.

Wilson had not put pencil to paper again until his last letters in the death-tent to Oriana, his parents, and the Reginald Smiths. Bowers, having long since handed over diary duties to Scott, wrote nothing further until his last letters. Scott's motive for having taken over diary duties was obvious: it put him in control of the way the progress and outcome of the Last Journey would be perceived by history. If he could have known the extent to which he succeeded it would probably have surprised even him.

Whatever the truth of what went on within the team, Scott, who was skilled at the judicious omission, the subtle stretch and the calculated spin, focuses on the horrors of the journey, their diminishing progress, and the ongoing talk, allegedly, of what they would do when they got home.

In effect, he created the drama of their ultimate sacrifice while somehow evading responsibility. He made it appear to be colder than it was. He claimed that their supplies were more meagre than they were, that the surfaces were almost universally awful, that the wind was either absent, in the wrong direction or too chilling, and that their sick comrades, the shortage of fuel, and an 11-day storm were responsible for their failure. There was no mention at all of the real brakes on their progress: all that surplus baggage, and the scurvy that must have been increasingly affecting them. The extra weight would have been impossible to justify, and the scurvy would have reflected badly on the organisation.

Wilson and Bowers joined Scott in lying by omission, emphasising the weather etc in collusion with his version of events. Perhaps they did not want to appear complicit in deliberately engineering their end. Even having gone along with Scott without putting up a fight might have seemed incomprehensible to the outside world, and would have caused added pain to their families. Naturally, they had to guard against that. They were hardly likely now to express opinions that might reflect negatively on Scott – what would be the point? Besides, if they had had negative feelings towards him or his way of conducting the journey, it would seem even more incomprehensible that they had gone along with it.

Scott's version of events was partially true, which must have made it easier. After all, whatever the accuracy or otherwise of his temperature records, it was horrifically cold. It is possible that the way Scott himself ignored the weight of the sledge made Wilson and Bowers doubt their own judgement. A form of gaslighting might have been going on. Conformity studies have shown that people sometimes doubt or deny their own perceptions in order to conform to what appears to be a group consensus. In this case, it is possible that they were all making assumptions about each other concerning the specimens etc. The most independent-minded member of the team, Oates, might simply have kept his mouth shut because he had given up on the whole thing, and because he understood what Scott was doing, and why. As maybe the others did too, on some level. In short, there were any number of reasons why Wilson and Bowers might have corroborated Scott's story, including, but not limited to, those explored here. One thing is certain: any or all of those reasons were conducive to Scott's agenda.

He had to keep up the pretence that they had done everything they could to get home, which must have been why they kept going after Oates crawled out of the tent. One could ask what the point was of going any further when he (or they) had already decided to die, as his letter and journal shows. He had obviously been clear about their eventual fate, but he had to make it look like they had succumbed to the weather. Any suggestion of suicide had to be avoided at all costs. It would imply that he hadn't had the moral courage to face the world after the Pole had gone to a foreigner because he had got it all wrong. He certainly could not allow it to look like he had deliberately led the team to their deaths. It had to be a heroic martyrdom in the face of impossibly severe conditions. That was the only way the thing could be turned around, which is precisely what he did. If he had had almost anyone other than Wilson and Bowers with him, he might not have found it so easy.

All that remained was to get to a place where they and their records would be reasonably sure to be found, although not of course as far as One Ton Depot, where supplies awaited them. On one hand, for the scheme to work, the 'Message to [the] Public' had to be found, as had the journals, letters and the specimens. On the other, actually reaching the depot would make it harder to explain why they had not made a final effort to get home, stocked up with fresh supplies as they would have been.

The way Scott dealt with this problem was by allowing his foot to freeze. All these weeks he had been able to stop this from happening – but now, when they had reached a suitable place to expire, without actually receiving a boost to their chances in the form of supplies of fuel and food, he acquires a frozen foot. It was presumably true because Wilson confirms it in two of his last letters. The story about the curry powder does nothing to reduce the oddness of the coincidence that it all worked out so perfectly. Notably, neither Wilson nor Bowers became incapacitated in that way.

Nothing would have been easier. It had required constant vigilance to prevent frostbitten feet. It couldn't have been the first time he felt 'done' on the march, but until now it hadn't stopped him looking after his feet. Besides, Oates had been expected to carry on despite a frozen foot, and had managed it, so why not Scott? Scott says nothing in his 'Message to [the] Public' about a frozen foot, or the effect it had on their prospect of getting home. In fact, he claims that they had been ready to start for One Ton every day but that the weather had prevented them. Another contradiction.

While it was true that even if they had got to One Ton, Hut Point was still over 100 miles away, Bowers asserts that he was 'still strong' when they got to their final camp. Wilson considered the possibility of going to One Ton, and Scott had always been physically robust. They had got this far even with all that extra weight. With a light sledge and the will to survive, even at this late stage, it does seem to have been worth a shot at least. There must have been windows of opportunity with the weather. If they had been serious about getting home one cannot imagine them lying there, passively waiting to die for well over a week.

They had arrived at what was to be their final camp on the evening of 19 March 1912. The temperatures on the preceding days are given as -40, -35, and -40 F. On the 20th a blizzard started which continued through the 22nd and 23rd, although Scott later contradicts this by saying that they have had a continuous gale from the 21st. Gale or blizzard, outside it allegedly remained a scene of whirling drift without respite. Whatever the weather, there is a ghastly morbidity about the way they must have lain there day after day, waiting for death.

Scott stopped them with that frozen foot. It effectively halted Wilson and Bowers, who allegedly discussed a last-ditch plan to go and fetch supplies from One Ton. Even if it was only 11 miles away, it would have meant a round trip of 22 miles – without a tent, presumably, as they could not leave Scott in the open. There and back would have been too much for one day, and there could have been no guarantee that there was a spare tent at One Ton. They could have constructed an igloo for Scott as a last resort, but it would still have taken time to get there and back. And what then? It would have been beyond the two of them to drag Scott home on the sledge. This means that Scott's frozen foot effectively forced them all to stay where they were, and meant death for all three.

Scott must have gambled that the vision of a brave martyrdom would, if handled correctly, obscure any charges of incompetence or poor judgement, deliberate suicide, or even manslaughter. He probably didn't dare to hope that it would trump even Amundsen's victory, as it did, by achieving a miracle of spin in transforming a failed expedition into a moral victory – recasting the deaths of his entire team into an example for Englishmen, and transmuting his 'miserable jumble' into a thing that the country could be proud of. *Dulce et decorum est pro patria mori.*

All those letters and his skilled final apologia show that Scott was *compos mentis* for many days after they halted for the last time. The 'Message to [the] Public' shows that what was uppermost in his mind was to disown any blame for his organisation. He never took responsibility for the deaths of any of the team, except in a letter to Wilson's mother, to the effect that Wilson had never blamed him for having led him into 'this mess'. He turned the death of Taff Evans and Oates to his own advantage by implying that sacrifices had been made to look after the sick, while also blaming them for the failure to get home.

Scott:

> We could have come through had we neglected the sick.

The Pole photos show a man utterly devastated and unable to look the world in the eye. If Taff Evans and Oates were responsible, it was in the sense that their deaths robbed Scott of the final vestiges of his will to live.

The subtext of the 'Message to [the] Public' is justification and apology, suggesting underlying feelings of guilt. A core sense of shame and contrition seeps through the ostensible text of the Message, and the hearts of the public went out to him. Even those who were sceptical could sense the pathos underneath, and the agony unmistakeably etched on his face at the Pole. Despite his own best efforts at self-justification, ducking responsibility, and ignominiously suggesting the fault lay with others, behind the apparently competent exterior he was a depressed, anxious, self-deluding, self-pitying psychological mess.

If they had arrived at the last camp with a fair supply of food and fuel, as Professor Sienicki convincingly claims, it must have run down in the time they were there. In the end it must have been true that they were starving, although that is unlikely to have been the actual cause of death. We can only make an educated guess as to how long it took for Wilson and Bowers to die. Presumably because of a reluctance to go looking for unwelcome knowledge, Atkinson chose not to make a thorough examination of the bodies when they were found, and declared that there were no signs of scurvy. In the absence of anything resembling post-mortems, Atkinson's assertions as to the cause of death of any or all three cannot be regarded as proven. It is likely that he wanted to save the reputation and the dignity of those who died by not looking too carefully for evidence of scurvy.

Scott's eloquent and evocative prose, combined with the pathos of their lonely deaths in the cold, set the scene for the subdued awe which gripped the nation soon after the news was made public. It effectively nipped any critical appraisals in the bud and made such sentiments seem sacrilegious. The man has all but gained immortality: *death has been swallowed up in victory*.

Lashly afterwards always bravely maintained that Scott's team had been stopped by scurvy. It's not clear that he based this on anything other than a hunch, but obviously his experience of Teddy's plight must have played a part. He and Crean, on the other hand, did not appear to have been affected to any great extent. Crean famously walked 30 miles from Corner Camp to Hut Point, and Lashly successfully nursed Teddy while they waited for the dogs. But Lashly was no fool, and it is possible that hints of scurvy were present in most of the returning parties. Teddy writes that Atkinson's First Return Party [19]

... had some sickness in the shape of enteritis and slight scurvy

... when they got back to Cape Evans.

They had been out the least time of all, while the fact that Teddy was close to death suggests that to some degree it stalked all those who spent months away from the base.

While scurvy was likely to have sapped what was left of their energy, the short-term causes of death of the Pole Party are likely to have been dehydration and hypothermia. They must eventually have run out of fuel for melting snow, and they are likely to have been dehydrated and hypothermic to some extent when they made their last camp. Starvation would have taken longer, as would scurvy. By the time they set up camp for the last time they had extra food in the form of Taff's and Oates' allowances, and the fuel that went with it. But exhaustion, lassitude brought on by scurvy, and an ongoing loss of body heat would have made it comparatively easy to lie there day after day, waiting for death. The last letters were probably written in the first few days, when they were still *compos mentis* and physically co-ordinated enough to write.

Only Scott still had some idea of the date when he ended his last diary entry, apparently on 29 March, with the *cri de coeur:*

For Gods sake look after our people

It was ten days after they set up their last camp. He would have been the warm-est in the middle, which would explain why he lasted longest, as he seems to have. Hypothermia is suggested, by the agreement of all those who viewed the ghastly scene inside the tent, that Scott had pushed the flaps of his sleeping-bag to one side, which would indicate paradoxical undressing.

They all froze to death in the end. Bowers' prediction that it would be just sleep in the cold must have come true, although it may not have been as painless as he suggests. He and Wilson, who were in their bags when they were found, must have stopped generating heat through movement and shivering and, as a result, their body temperature will have dropped until their heart-rate slowed down and they lost consciousness. Slipping into a coma, their heart-rate would have become irregular until in the end it stopped.

While there must have been the possibility that they could have made it back to Hut Point, the idea that they might catch the ship with the news (such as it was) was, in the event, a vain hope. The ship had left on 4 March (1912), taking with her not only Meares and Simpson, for reasons to which we will return, but also Taylor, Ponting, Day, Forde, Clissold, Anton, and Teddy Evans – all of whom were either expected to go home after one season, or had other good reasons to. Those spending a second winter in the Cape Evans hut were Thomas Williamson and Walter Archer (new arrivals), Gran, Wright, Debenham, Nelson, Lashly, Crean, Keohane, Atkinson, Dmitrii, Cherry-Garrard, and Hooper.

Gran claims it was Hooper who first spotted the death-tent. Dmitrii says it was him, so does Wright. Not that it matters. Inside was a frozen horror which none of those who witnessed it would ever forget. Scott was almost unrecognisable, as someone thought it was Taff Evans at first. Gran's diary describes the scene as horrible, ugly and ghastly: [20]

> I will never forget it so long I live – a horrible nightmare could not have shown more horror than this ... [The tent] ... is snowcovered til up above the door, [with Scott] in the middle, half out of his bagg ... The frost had made the skin yellow & transparent & I've never seen anything worse in my life ...

They must have opened the sleeping-bags to identify Bowers and Wilson. They must also have removed the tent in order to take out the tent-poles and the inner lining. The bodies were then covered over again with the outer canvas, and a large cairn was built over them, after which a funeral service was held. The frozen bodies of Scott, Wilson and Bowers are currently on their way towards the edge of the Barrier. Professor Sienicki has worked out their trajectory, and their approximate current location from data about the ice-flows on the Ross Ice Shelf. There are techniques available today which could locate the grave, which is by now of course some way beneath the surface. Nevertheless, it should be possible to reach it, to disinter the bodies, and establish once and for all what state Scott, Wilson and Bowers were in when they died. Many would probably feel it would be a desecration – but the three Franklin graves on Beechey Island were exhumed, and there is no reason why this should be any different. It would serve the historical record. It would also, of course, be an absolute sensation.

References

1   Geoffrey Hattersley-Smith (ed.). *The Norwegian with Scott*, p. 217

2   Admiral Sir Reginald Skelton. *The Antarctic Journals of Reginald Skelton*, pp. 109–10

3   From this point on in this chapter, references to Robert Falcon Scott, *Journals*, are given with his dates only

4   Christie's. British Antarctic Expedition, Sale 6409, Lot 109, www.christies.com

5   Sue Limb and Patrick Cordingley. *Captain Oates*, p. 200

6   Apsley Cherry-Garrard. *The Worst Journey in the World*, p. 430

7   Krzysztof Sienicki, *Captain Scott*, p. 174

8   *op. cit.*, p. 279, Figure 7.2, data from Schwerdtfeger Station

9   George Seaver. *'Birdie' Bowers of the Antarctic*, p. 254

10   Anne Strathie. *Birdie Bowers*, pp. 213–14

11   Ross D.E. MacPhee. *Race to the End*, p. 181

12   Apsley Cherry-Garrard, *op. cit.*, p. 431

13   *op. cit.*, p. 410

14   Diana Preston. *A First Rate Tragedy*, p. 101

15   David Crane. *Scott of the Antarctic*, p. 606, n. 397

16   Apsley Cherry-Garrard. *op. cit.*, pp. 411–12

17   Heather Lane, Naomi Boneham and Robert D. Smith (eds.). *The Last Letters*, p. 17

18   *op. cit.*, p. 37

19   Admiral Edward Evans. *South With Scott*, pp. 225–6

20   Alison Flood, 'Antarctic diary records horror at finding Captain Scott's body'

27

REFLECTIONS

While Scott was on his Pole Journey, things back at Cape Evans were falling apart. Simpson, who had been left in charge, decided instead to pack up and go. Meares too had been expected to stay another winter. He too abandoned the expedition and got on the ship. Why?

We are told that Simpson responded to the call of a sick colleague back in India, deciding it was more important to relieve him than to continue to do pioneering work in Antarctica. It doesn't seem entirely convincing. An analysis of Scott's relationship with Simpson and his meteorological department may hold some answers.

As far as the expedition science went, George Simpson's meteorological lab took up the most space in the hut, and he was a highly qualified serious scientist. As has been noted, Scott involved himself quite markedly with meteorology through the winter.

Simpson, 'Sunny Jim', as he was patronisingly called, was not one of the lads, and had no need to prove himself, or the value of what he was doing. He does not appear to have ingratiated himself – quite the opposite, it seems. He tended to be critical. On one occasion after Debenham gave a lecture on volcanoes, Simpson was the chief critic 'as usual', totally disagreeing with him.

Debenham: [1]

> He [Simpson] has a very emphatic way of stating things and his vigorous 'You are completely wrong in all you say' always amuses us.

He also had an air of superiority, which Debenham felt was purely a mannerism, but which may not have endeared him in certain quarters.

It may been that Simpson's independence and autonomy irritated Scott. Simpson had raised £500 by his own effort for equipment, and [2]

... diligently followed the recommendations of the Royal Geographical Society's *Hints to Travellers* ...

It is possible that Simpson's attention to the *Hints to Travellers* suggested a
rejection of Scott's personal input.

As we know, at the end of September, Scott undertook what he calls a 'remarkably pleasant and instructive little spring journey'. On the face of it, it was unclear
what he had in mind. The geologists were already scheduled to go to that area, and
supplies had already been depoted for them by the ship. Scott seemed to be remarkably off-hand about it, going so far as to say he hadn't decided how long to
stay away, nor how far he would go.

There may have been more to this little trip than stretching his legs and brushing up on his sledging techniques, however. The clue is in the make-up of the team,
which was composed of Scott himself, Bowers, Taff Evans and Simpson. Why Simpson? All except Simpson were strong sledgers; and Scott, as usual, set a hard pace
on the trip.

Simpson had never shown an interest in sledging, and there is no indication
that he volunteered for it now. There is one satisfying explanation, however, which
makes perfect sense – not only as to why Simpson was taken on this journey, but
also why it was undertaken at all. My hypothesis is that it was all to do with
showing Simpson who was boss. Scott's hidden agenda was that by taking Simpson
away from his lab he would level the playing field, giving him an opportunity to
assert his dominance. This trip had no other purpose than that it gave Scott the
chance to show Simpson his strength on the traces and, in so doing, rub Simpson's
nose into his place in the simian hierarchy.

In in-group/out-group terms, Simpson would have been on his own, as both
Bowers and Taff were Scott's men, and some of the hardest sledgers on the expedition. In both psychological and physical terms, therefore, Simpson seems to have
been deliberately put at a disadvantage.

If the above was indeed the case, Simpson would have been left seething,
having been taken on a forced march that had nothing to do with meteorology,
which froze his face, and took him away from his lab for what he must have
suspected were Scott's personal issues. It would have further diminished Simpson's respect for Scott, as he might have felt that instead of playing ego games, he
would have been better employed putting more supplies on the trail. As would
Bowers and Taff, come to that.

Simpson's resentment and scorn would also explain the element of passive-
aggressive revenge in his decision to deny Scott the services of Wright for the last
journey to One Ton Depot with the dogs. Wright, a strong sledger and trained navigator, was instead kept at the hut to look after the lab. There was a last effort to

make it look like a reasonable decision in that Simpson sent both Wright and Cherry to Hut Point, ostensibly for Atkinson to make the final decision about who should go out; but it must have been clear what Simpson wanted, and Atkinson complied with it.

Cherry could have been shown how to keep things ticking over until Wright got back, but he was sent on that last mission to One Ton, a task they all knew he was poorly qualified to undertake. It wasn't fair on Cherry, but that was probably just tough luck as far as Simpson was concerned.

Meredith Hooper [3] tells us that the pages of Wright's diary, in which he generally expressed his thoughts, are missing for that period (February). Hooper writes that his feelings are therefore not known, but I think we can infer something from their absence.

One might argue that if the above hypothesis is true, Simpson should have declined the job of running the station in Scott's absence. If he had been resentful but undecided up to that point, however, the final push might have come when he read his instructions. These included general house management, supervising improvements to the hut, and making sure the bedding was aired. In what might have felt like a further ploy to cut him down to size, he was cast in the role of housekeeper. Perhaps that call from India gave him the perfect excuse to metaphorically tell Scott what he could do with his expedition.

Meares too abandoned the expedition. He too had been expected to stay another year. Both Simpson and Meares had important jobs to do, and carried a lot of responsibility. For them to have left in this manner indicates a lack of shared psychological ownership and investment in the outcome of the expedition. It hints at Teddy's remark about the legitimacy of expeditions which are too much to the glory of one man. Simpson and Meares might have had enough of supporting Scott's bid for immortality.

Meares allegedly claimed he had to leave because of the death of his father. It turned out later that his father had not died at that time, which suggests he invented an excuse to leave. There is nothing to suggest that Meares was anything other than a man of ordinary sensibilities, but he broke his agreement to stay and he threw over his responsibilities to the people, the dogs and the expedition. This tells us all we need to know about what his feelings were about Scott.

In a further breakdown of support for Scott, Atkinson had elected to stay at Hut Point and nurse Teddy, instead of taking the dogs out to One Ton. There wasn't much Atkinson could do for Teddy that someone else couldn't have been adequately instructed to do. While it is true that he had never been a notably strong sledger, he preferred to believe that the Pole Party were capable of reaching One Ton Depot without assistance.

Hence, rather than dwell on Scott's orders for the dogs to come out to 82 degrees, Atkinson reiterated Scott's alleged injunction not to risk the dogs and not to assume that any kind of relief operation would be necessary.

Atkinson: [4]

> Again, it cannot be too firmly emphasized that the dog teams were meant merely to hasten the return of the Southern Party and by no means as a relief expedition.

Atkinson also claimed that Cherry had left One Ton supplied with sufficient man provisions for a party of five for over a month, including several smaller delicacies. [5]

The emphasis on these instructions suggests a need to justify his decisions. Furthermore, his claim that he somehow knew that the Pole Party had perished when he decided to turn back from his attempt, together with Keohane, to 'do something', was made with hindsight.

'Doing something' does seem the right expression for whatever it was Atkinson had in mind when he set off together with Keohane – more, probably, in an attempt to assuage his own conscience than with any useful goal in mind. They set out onto the Barrier on 26 March and turned back on the 30th, with Atkinson 'morally certain' that the Pole Party was lost. According to Scott's 144-day plan, however, they weren't due in until the 22nd – which makes Atkinson's assumption somewhat premature.

If Scott had genuinely wanted to get in, it is certainly possible that he would have got to One Ton, and may even have been in time to meet Cherry and the dogs there. Scott's party was at the Southern Barrier Depot on 24 February. This was approximately 165 geographical miles from One Ton, where Cherry waited until 10 March. As 1912 was a leap year, that means that there were 14 days (not counting the day on which Cherry started on his return trip), in which to do that 165 miles. That works out at an average of 11.8 geographical miles per day (13.6 statute). While this does not allow for delays, and it would have been a lot to ask of men at the end of a long and exhausting journey, Shackleton's performance provides evidence that that kind of speed is attainable. Shackleton managed an average of 12.8 statute miles for the last 32 days of his return journey from within 100 miles of the Pole, without skis, including two days with no mileage.

Scott's team wasn't short of food, and Oates was still able to march at the Southern Barrier Depot. The slow progress must have been worse for his feet than fast, determined marching would have been. A short, sharp effort from the Southern Barrier Depot to One Ton, led by a determined and inspirational leader, could have saved the team. Oates could plausibly have made it to One Ton, and his life could have been saved by being pulled home by the dogs.

The whole team (minus Taff, who was doomed in any case) could have got home with the replenished supplies and the support of the dogs and Cherry and Dmitrii (or even better, Wright and Dmitrii; or best of all, Meares and Dmitrii). The only caveat is the extent to which they were affected by scurvy, which would itself have got worse the longer the trip was dragged out.

Clearly alive to the problem of the unnecessary weight on the sledge, Cherry, in *The Worst Journey in the World*, sought to justify Scott's decision by claiming that the dead weight made no difference: [6]

> The practical man of the world ... is scandalized because 30 lbs. [*sic*] of geological specimens were deliberately added to the weight of the sledge that was dragging the life out of the men who had to haul it; but he does not realize that it is the friction surfaces of the snow on the runners which mattered and not the dead weight, which in this case was almost negligible.

Leaving aside the odd claim that the dead weight on the sledge was 'almost negligible', this statement makes no sense on two counts. First, while it is obvious that the glide of the sledge does make a huge difference, and that much does depend on the surface, it is absurd to suggest that a heavy sledge is as easy to drag as a light one under any circumstances. Second, most of the time the surfaces were not ideal, which meant that the weight *did* make a difference, even by his own logic. They were in a race against time and scurvy. It was imperative to do absolutely everything they could to maximise their speed, and that must have included taking as much weight off the sledge as possible. It is difficult to see how anyone can possibly argue with that.

As far as Markham is concerned, his greatest achievement is an unintended one. He set in motion a train of events that culminated in one of the most popular accounts of drawn-out agony and martyrdom in the history of exploration. That this was spun into a heroic achievement is due to nothing but both Scott's and Markham's genius for presentation, the need to uphold the prestige of the nation, and an army of subsequent biographers eager to amplify and exploit the legend.

Markham must have known about the fate of the Pole Party when he sat for his portrait by George Henry, dated 1913. The news of Scott's fate had come through on 10 February 1913. Markham was in Estoril at the time. The likelihood must therefore be that the portrait was painted after he knew what had happened. In the portrait, the man-hauling statuette is still prominent. It was given to him by the officers of the *Discovery* after their return from Scott's first Antarctic foray.

Self-doubt, or admitting one's errors, were never Markham's strongest suits. He knew exactly how to project himself in such a way as to draw admiration and awe – regardless, or perhaps because of, his self-satisfaction and overbearing sense of entitlement, and regardless of the failure of his protégé. Markham's complacent expression reflects the way the Scott disaster had been turned into an object of national pride, and one for which he took a good deal of credit.

But Minna was having none of it. In July 1914, on the occasion of the unveiling of Kathleen's unremarkable statue of Wilson, Markham had done the honours and taken centre stage, even though he had hardly known Wilson. He had been deferred to, as usual. In the group photo taken in the garden at Westal (the Wilson family home in Cheltenham) afterwards, he is sitting in the middle, on a bench he shares with Minna. Minna, however, can be seen very clearly to be taking distance from him which, judging by his face, he wasn't happy about. It is a public display of rejection by Minna, confirmed by the expression on her face, and suggestive of a very different state of affairs to the unalloyed happiness Albert Markham claimed characterised their relationship. [7]

Oriana sits modestly to one side in the photo, undoubtedly because she preferred it that way. She lost her Christian faith when her brother Noel was killed on the first day of the Battle of the Somme, although she retained her faith in an 'immanent spirit of goodness', despite everything. She died two weeks before the end of WW2, at the age of 70. [8]

Next to Oriana sits Kathleen, and behind them stand Reginald Smith and his wife. Smith was the publisher of *Scott's Last Expedition: The Journals*, [9] and Wilson's dear good friend. Wilson wrote to him from the death-tent: [10]

> I and my beloved wife have loved you both from first to last God be thanked for such as you.

Reginald committed suicide by jumping out of an upstairs window on the 26 December 1916. He had been suffering from depression and psychosis. Kathleen saw Oriana at Reginald Smith's funeral and described her as an 'absurd prig'. [11]

In spite of recent attempts to reinstate her earlier reputation as a 'great' artist, Kathleen suffers from comparison with her contemporaries. Her portraiture is, by common consensus, good. Her Asquith is in the Tate. One of her best pieces is her bust of James Maxton, in the Glasgow City Art Gallery. Maxton's linear features forced a break from Rodin's enduring influence. Brancusi studied under Rodin but left after two months saying 'Nothing can grow under big trees'. Kathleen's work is to a certain extent evidence of that.

As to Kathleen's signature, or statement work, this takes the form mainly of male nudes, many of them boys or adolescents with up- or outstretched arms, in homage perhaps to Isadora and the bodily expression of emotion. The combination of youth, nudity, and surrender amounts to a melodramatic and slightly perverse overload, unrelieved by originality of execution or interpretation. The poses of her boys, as she herself called them, seem to accentuate the nudity, which is itself modelled with a 'caressing tool', as Gwynn [12] termed it, bringing it too unavoidably into focus, and casting the viewer as voyeur. Her large male blindfolded nude ('The Kingdom is Within') is unmistakably sadomasochistic and homo-erotic.

Lees-Milne tells us that although she gloried in men's bodily attractions, she was extraordinarily naive and innocent. [13] This rings true because her flirtations and romantic escapades weren't really about sex – they were all about narcissistic supply. If she hadn't been naive about sex, she might not have made those sculptures, nor photographed Peter in a similar pose, nude.

There is something a bit queasy about that nude photo of Peter, however, especially as she was also extremely possessive of him. He was teased at school about his mother's 'boys', being asked if he had modelled for them. From being put into little quasi-Greek togas as a child, which left his legs uncomfortably bare, he was always rather at the mercy of Kathleen's notions.

In adult life, he founded the organisation now know as the Wildfowl and Wetlands Trust, and co-founded the World Wide Fund for Nature. He was knighted in 1973 and died of a heart attack in 1989, aged 79. He grew from an arrogant young man into an excessively self-effacing older man, who preferred birds to people and who loved nothing better than to paint and look out of the window.

Kathleen was scathingly critical of Epstein, dismissing him as an amazing egoist, and [14]

> ... totally unable to carve the bold images which his virility and vitality conjured up.

But Kathleen's boys do not stand comparison with his hieratic colossi, and failed to go beyond representational or cultural conventions. While this does not necessarily make someone a lesser artist, her criticisms of Epstein seem rooted in a banal set of criteria. Woe betide anyone who had the temerity to warn her against 'narrow' interests, however, as Scott found to his cost when he made that mistake.

She is noted for her flippant response to hearing her husband was dead: [15]

> Oh well, never mind! I expected that. Thanks very much. I will go and think about it ...

She writes that she didn't mean it, but her subsequent behaviour is ambivalent. She writes theatrically about her 'god' being 'godly', and that he had always been her god and her conscience. She appears to have felt the strain, but there seems to have been little modification of her routines and habits. She intellectualises her feelings, such as they are, and carries on more or less as usual – at the same time drawing on notions of heroic fortitude, and rejecting discretion for the sake of what she terms 'the greatest visions of the heart': [16]

Let me maintain a high, adoring exaltation, and not let the contamination of sorrow touch me. ... Had he died before I had known his gloriousness, or before he had been the father of my son, I might have felt a loss. Now I have felt none for myself. Won't anybody understand that? – probably nobody. So I must go on and on with the tedious business of discretion. Must even the greatest visions of the heart be blurred by discretions?

There is an uncomfortable feeling that those irksome discretions included going ashore at Rarotonga the day after she learnt of Scott's death with a young South American, with whom she [17]

... sat on coral rocks in the rain and watched the breakers curl in over the reef. We returned by moonlight, wet to the skin. He did not know.

Whether or not he knew is immaterial. What matters is that she chose to do her grieving, such as it was, with a young man at her feet. What matters even more is that she writes about it in her diary. An emotionally mature woman, and certainly a newly bereaved widow, would have kept such behaviour to herself – even if, in the circumstances, she would have wanted it and allowed herself such indulgence. But Kathleen not only indulges herself, she records it.

She goes on in the same vein about the journey taking her further to New Zealand, where she was kept company by probably the same young man – although it isn't clear. During what she describes as her 'long nights of anxiety', she wrote: [18]

... the young Third Officer is the only human whom I have to turn to. He understands very little, but he is healthy and sane, and always ready to be with me when I can't sleep. He is the only person I can talk to at all, and he understands very little; but like a big dog he sits by me and is sorry.

Self-Portrait of an Artist contains both the parts that Kathleen wrote as the start of an autobiography and the diary extracts her second husband Edward Hilton Young deemed fit for publication. In spite of the fact he includes many of those entries that appear to have been written for Scott and for her eyes only, they are written in a manner which suggests the basis of an autobiography, rather than a record of her private thoughts. If that be the case, entries about young men sitting at her feet, even in those circumstances, show that the thing that gave her most comfort was a kind of silent worship, and that she was willing to risk censure in the service of her narcissistic impulse to show off by writing about it. She writes as though this is normal behaviour, and subsequent readers have not questioned it. It is not normal behaviour, and the reason people have failed to question it is evidence of a kind of gaslighting: a trick by which observers are gulled into questioning their own judgement by subtle suggestion and psychological manipulation.

When she got back to England she helped edit Scott's Last Expedition journals. Statistical analysis reveals that temperatures were deliberately altered to make it seem colder. These were not mistakes, as is suggested by Max Jones. The temperatures were massaged down by Kathleen and Huxley in the first published edition. They were too clever to alter them all in a downward direction, so they threw in a few anomalies to make it look like they were genuine mistakes. They were not. [19] The Scott Polar Research Institute still features Huxley's censored version of the journals on their website (October 2019). A facsimile of the actual diaries can be seen on the British Museum website.

The SPRI created a literally institutionalised bias in Scott's favour – bolstering and protecting his legacy, stature and reputation. The first of many uncritical biographies was given Kathleen's sanction – setting the tone, already conditioned by the mass mourning his death had occasioned. Scott's reputation remains sacrosanct. Some biographers are critical – Huntford especially – but the consensus to this day is that on the whole Scott *was* right for the job, but that he was unlucky.

In a rare departure from the official line, and referring to the letter sent by Teddy Evans to 'Lal' Gifford quoted in Chapter 26, Christie's Auction House website has this to say: [20]

> The attitude of Scott's farewell letters and 'Message to the Public', blaming his failure on 'misfortune in all risks which had to be taken' and on the 'sickness of different numbers of the party' and insisting that 'Every detail [of the preparation] worked out to perfection', was gratefully accepted by an administration (and public) eager for excuses. Scott and Wilson's decision not to leave their specimens behind has more often been advanced as evidence of the high scientific spirit of the expedition; in fact as Scott's route stayed very close to that of Shackleton's 1909 Polar attempt his specimens added very little to earlier findings. The question of whether the Polar Party might have been suffering from scurvy was little discussed in the expedition's aftermath, perhaps as threatening to shift attention from Scott's bad luck to his organisation of the expedition. It is extraordinary to find any member of the expedition, and particularly such a senior one [Teddy], making any adverse comment on Scott's decisions after his death.

After the expedition, while still in New Zealand, convalescing from scurvy, Teddy Evans wrote: [21]

> I have come to the conclusion ... that *private* Antarctic expeditions
> are public frauds for the glorification and selfish ends of the leader
> alone ... [his italics]

His opinion of Oates couldn't have been more different. Writing in *The Strand Magazine* in 1913 he says: [22]

> ... He lived always, as he died, without fear and without reproach. ...
> his memory will ever live in the pride and the affection of his fellow-
> countrymen and in the hearts of his companions as a most glorious
> example to us all.

But whatever fame, credit, respect and applause Shackleton, Amundsen, or even the illustrious Nansen achieved, none will ever equal the impact and lasting fascination with the phenomenon that was Robert Falcon Scott and his failed expeditions. Even when, or perhaps especially when, he chides himself, Scott was aware of his public. His pathetic demise conditions our perception of him, but it is the way he comes across as a person that is so seductive.

The secret of his emotional appeal is in his apparent disingenuousness. He gives the impression of being an honest man up against unfavourable odds. We are already disarmed when he berates himself, because we already know about his inner torments and insecurities. We know he is flawed, and we feel the pathos of his martyrdom.

Unlike Amundsen's narratives, Scott's diaries are full of drama, mostly of his own making. Amundsen's journals record the progress of a skilled professional and lack the fascination of the blundering amateur story we get from Scott. Our hearts break for the man who struggled all his life, only to fail in the end. If he thought his death would boost the value of his story, he was right.

But sentiment has stood in the way of sober evaluation, to the point where it is rather frowned upon to criticise Scott, as though it is not honourable nor legitimate. In Crane's view, for example, Scott and Markham were great men who must be allowed their little idiosyncrasies, and whom it would be ungenerous, hypocritical and mistaken to blame for their failures.

But ultimately the goal of Scott's expeditions was the Pole, and in that he was comprehensively beaten – not once, but twice, if we count Shackleton's near miss. And Shackleton did it with fewer men and resources and succeeded even without dogs and skis.

Scott lost more men than the rest of the heroic-age expeditions put together. Not forgetting the *Discovery* shambles, which he was very lucky to get away with, six men, including Vince and Scott himself, lost their lives as a direct result of Markham's fatuous irresponsibility and Scott's inability to admit to his own short-comings.

The ponies were always a mistake, brought for the wrong reasons. The seven Indian mules shipped down for the second season didn't thrive either – even though they were fitter and younger, able to wear show-shoes, and better behaved. It suggests that the ponies wouldn't have been up to the conditions even if they had been young and fit. And as for Fiennes' touching faith in British kindness to animals, the Indian mules that survived the journey to find the dead were shot rather than embarked for a return to civilisation.

The hut at least was a success. Having withstood a century of blighting weather, it is now the subject of ongoing restoration and stabilisation, despite the remoteness and difficulties of the job. One recent visitor described walking into it as almost like a religious experience. A sense of awe grips the visitor when they enter the space that is now so redolent with memories and images.

Scott's party were not the last to inhabit it. The aforementioned (in Chapter 23) Ross Sea Party of Shackleton's Imperial Trans-Antarctic Expedition spent a winter at Cape Evans and set out from there in October 1915 on their hellish journey to lay a chain of depots for Shackleton, who never came.

They had been the first people to set foot in the hut after the departure of what was left of the Scott Expedition, which had been only two years earlier, on 19 January 1913. It looked like they expected to return momentarily. The smell of tobacco and coal fires hung in the air. Bunks were [23]

> ... neatly stacked with clothing, some monogrammed. The names of the fallen marked the bunks. Secluded in one corner was Scott's own cubicle, lined with books. Beakers and test tubes crowded a laboratory bench. Shelves behind a cast-iron range were crammed with provisions and neat rows of crockery. Open crates spilled flour, sugar, and biscuits, as well as exotic delicacies such as canned goose-berries, liver pâté, chocolates, and smoked haddock. According to a detailed inventory left on the table by Scott's men, hundreds of pounds of food-stuffs were stowed there.

While not wanting to claim infallibility for myself, the voluminous Scott literature is full of errors. One of the most egregious is that made by Sue Blackhall, in whose book *Scott of the Antarctic*, Wilfrid Bruce, Kathleen's brother, is stated to be the same person as William Speirs Bruce, the Scottish Antarctic explorer. Another common error is when photos of the *Discovery* Expedition are frequently confused with those of the *Terra Nova*.

Even the Natural History Museum is not immune. In January 2012 they put on a very interesting exhibition in which the structure of the hut was recreated. It gave a great insight into the actual feel of the place, and an interesting book was published to accompany the exhibition. [24] Unfortunately, however, they forgot about Ponting. Ponting's photos are a very important part of what made the Last

Expedition so famous. In spite of using a photo of Ponting standing on his head to publicise the exhibition, his bed, which was in the darkroom, is not shown in their diagram of the interior of the hut, [25] and his place at the table, shown for the others in the form of a light show, was omitted. Being interested to know where Ponting sat, I emailed them about it afterwards. They never responded. There was a 'weather cupboard' projecting out of the wall of the meteorological lab, and Nelson had 'a small extension on the east side', but neither are shown in the usual published diagrams. They weren't important of course, but they were there. Needless to say, few historians have paid much attention to the spectacularly icy latrines.

Scott's main concerns on his death-bed were to deny any faults in his organisation, and to plead for the financial welfare of Kathleen and Peter. The vast majority of his last letters contain appeals for money on behalf of his wife and 'the boy'. Those letters were written mainly to canvas support for them, and to justify his failure to survive. Indeed, the family member who, by her own stated preference, stood to gain most from Scott's death was Kathleen, who was, as Scott was anxious to ensure, compensated handsomely.

Kathleen remarried, in 1922, to Edward Hilton Young. She had a second son, Wayland, who became a Labour politician, later joining the Social Democrats. Kathleen died in 1947, having lived in Barrie's old house on Leinster Corner, where she had her studio, and where Wayland's family lived until quite recently.

Teddy ended up as Admiral Lord Mountevans, 'Evans of the Broke' – famous, celebrated and loved by many, having earned the esteem in which he was held by rich and poor, in and outside the Navy. After he was raised to the Peerage in 1945, he sat in the House of Lords as a Labour member. He was a lifelong fitness fanatic and maintained an interest in wrestling. In 1947 he chaired a committee to formalise the rules of professional wrestling in the UK, which became known as the Admiral Lord Mountevans Rules.

The sad end of Edward Nelson suggests the kind of depression and despair suffered by what I assume to have been a gay man, as a result of the repressive and disapproving social climate of his day. While I can cite no evidence for it, it is a familiar trajectory. After his marriage failed, he went to live in lodgings in Aberdeen, and worked as the scientific superintendent of the Marine Laboratory at the Bay of Nigg. A year and a half later, in January 1923, he committed suicide by injecting poison into his leg. He was about 40 years old.

A wealth of notable characters and events accompany the epic of the Scott tragedy, from the prelude of Markham's adventures in Peru to the grand finale of the last pathetic journey. But for all the literature on the subject, many aspects have remained veiled. In spite of the hundreds of photos and the dozens of diaries, there is nothing in depth about the dynamics of Scott's relationship with Markham, and nothing about how being Markham's protégé affected Scott's already-fragile sense of legitimacy. Neither is there enough about how Scott's episodes of depression affected his performance, and the way acute anxiety curtailed his ability to lead effectively.

There has never been a proper analysis of where the core responsibility for the Scott drama lies. It was Markham's experiences on the Royal Navy Pacific Station, and his later participation in the Austin Expedition to the Arctic, which fed his nostalgia for the comfort and partying that were customary in the Royal Navy of his day. Those experiences formed the deep background to the ideas and ideals which informed the way the *Discovery* Expedition was set up, what its priorities were, how it should look, and what kind of man should command it.

Markham wrote extensively and kept diaries all his life, recording his impressions of people and events from an early age. His biographer was his cousin, Admiral Sir Albert Hastings Markham, 11 years his junior. Albert died in 1918, shortly after he wrote Clements' biography, which itself was written only a year after Clements' own death in 1916.

Albert naturally used Clements' diaries as his main source material. They abound in references to young men and how much he loved to be around them; how he was always organising entertainments, outings, 'larks', parties, theatrical productions, fancy dress balls etc. Even after he had left the Navy, Clements was well known for his habitual and lifelong involvement with boys.

To have omitted that part of Clements' life would have been to leave out one of his defining characteristics, a thing that was integral to his life, and without which his biography would not have made sense. It would have been tantamount to implying that there was something wrong in it. Censoring that kind of material would have meant that Albert suspected that all was not quite so innocent.

The result is that, to twenty-first-century eyes, Albert's biography seems almost comically naive. While Albert does seem to have been a sincere Christian, unsophisticated, obedient, and reticent in personal matters, he also found himself in a double bind. Censorship would have not only implied wrong-doing on Clements' part, but would also have cast doubt on Albert himself for having allowed such immoral ideas to enter his mind.

It is a pity that Scott wasn't as good an explorer as he was a creative writer – in more ways than one. Long experience of nudging, cherry-picking and narrative manipulation are evident in, for example, the way he diverts attention away from the danger inherent in dragging those rocks on his Last Journey.

The sheer plethora of reasons marshalled by Scott to justify the death of his party ought to arouse suspicions. As though martyrdom to science wasn't enough, he was also a martyr to uniquely low temperatures, sick comrades slowing him down, bad surfaces, shortages of food and fuel, the lateness of the season, a never-ending gale and a frozen foot – not to mention Amundsen's alleged duplicity. He protests too much. But it has impressed his audience who, for reasons that evidently have more to do with emotion than reason, have put their critical faculties to one side, and to this day defend the myth of the hero.

Scott's expeditions took place more than 100 years ago. There has been a huge improvement since then in tools and equipment, obviously; but less obviously perhaps, greater experience has given us greater levels of expertise, and our expectations have risen commensurately. Now, even those who make a living from amateur adventuring do so under the close supervision and support of experts. It is fair to say that in Scott's day, experts in snow travel were few and far between; and those who were expert, like Amundsen for example, used their knowledge for their own benefit, rather than to facilitate someone else's achievements. A certain allowance should be made, therefore, for Scott's lack of expertise, even though he was his own worst enemy when it came to benefitting from what knowledge was available at the time.

The claim that they died for science is entirely spurious. Even if Wilson hadn't known that many of his specimens were duplicates of materials already found and brought back previously, there was no justification for keeping them on the sledge. If those specimens had been worth risking their lives for, they would certainly have warranted extending their stay for another season. Cape Evans was fully equipped and supplied to do so, which means that any depoted equipment or materials could have been retrieved, irrespective of what may or may not have been their options with regard to the ship. The point is that, even if Scott's team had had the chance of catching the ship with a lighter sledge, he would have had the choice to stay and collect those stones in the next season – potentially saving their lives in the process.

While the Pole Party's survival was never guaranteed, Scott made sure of their failure by his clear decision to make the journey more difficult than it need have been. The final irony is that in having arrived second at the Pole, it was the photos taken by Bowers that provided irrefutable evidence that Amundsen and his team had got there first.

References

1   June Debenham Back (ed.). *The Quiet Land*, p. 109

2   Chris Turney. *1912: The Year the World Discovered Antarctica*, p. 76

3   Meredith Hooper. *The Longest Winter*, p. 203

4   Captain R.F. Scott. *Scott's Last Expedition*. Vol. II *Being the Reports of the Journeys & the Scientific Work Undertaken by Dr. E. A. Wilson and the Surviving Members of the Expedition*, Atkinson's chapter, 'The Last Year at Cape Evans', pp. 300–1

5   *op. cit.*, p. 304

6   Apsley Cherry-Garrard. *The Worst Journey in the World*, p. 565

7   D.M. Wilson and D.B. Elder. *Cheltenham in Antarctica*, p. 116, lower photo

8   Katherine MacInnes. 'Marriage by post', *The Lady*, www.lady.co.uk

9   Robert Falcon Scott. *Scott's Last Expedition: The Journals*

10   Heather Lane, Naomi Boneham and Robert D. Smith (eds.). *The Last Letters*, p. 61

11   Sara Wheeler. *A Life of Apsley Cherry-Garrard*, p. 194

12   Mark Stocker. 'Young Male Objects', p. 123

13   James Lees-Milne. *Fourteen Friends*, p. 8

14   *op. cit.*, p. 16

15   Lady Kennet. *Self-Portrait of an Artist*, p. 120

16   *op. cit.*, p. 121

17   *ibid.*

18   *op. cit.*, p. 122

19   Krzysztof Sienicki. *Captain Scott*, pp. 72–3

20   Christie's. British Antarctic Expedition, Sale 6409, Lot 109, www.christies.com

21   David Crane. *Scott of the Antarctic*, p. 528

22   Commander Evans. *The Strand Magazine*

23   Kelly Tyler-Lewis. *The Lost Men*, p. 64

24   Steve Parker. *Scott's Last Expedition*

25   *op. cit.*, p. 21, floor plan of the hut

Appendix

Message to [the] Public [1]

The causes of the disaster are not due to faulty organisation, but to misfortune in all risks which had to be undertaken.

1. The loss of pony transport in March 1911 obliged me to start later than I had intended, and obliged the limits of stuff transported to be narrowed.

2. The weather throughout the outward journey, and especially the long gale in 83° S., stopped us.

3. The soft snow in lower reaches of glacier again reduced pace.

We fought these untoward events with a will and conquered, but it cut into our provision reserve.

Every detail of our food supplies, clothing and depots made on the interior ice-sheet and over that long stretch of 700 miles to the Pole and back, worked out to perfection. The advance party would have returned to the glacier in fine form and with surplus of food, but for the astonishing failure of the man whom we had least expected to fail. Edgar Evans was thought the strongest man of the party.

The Beardmore Glacier is not difficult in fine weather, but on our return we did not get a single completely fine day; this with a sick companion enormously increased our anxieties.

As I have said elsewhere we got into frightfully rough ice and Edgar Evans received a concussion of the brain – he died a natural death, but left us a shaken party with the season unduly advanced.

But all the facts above enumerated were as nothing to the surprise which awaited us on the Barrier. I maintain that our arrangements for returning were quite adequate, and that no one in the world would have expected the temperatures and surfaces which we encountered at this time of the year. On the summit in lat. 85° 86° we had -20°, -30°. On the Barrier in lat. 82°, 10,000 feet lower, we had -30° in the day, -47° at night pretty regularly, with continuous head wind during our day marches. It is clear that these circumstances come on very suddenly, and our wreck is certainly due to this sudden advent of severe weather, which does not seem to have any satisfactory cause. I do not think human beings ever came through such a month as we have come through, and we should have got through in spite of the weather but for the sickening of a second companion, Captain Oates, and a shortage of fuel in our depots for which I cannot account, and finally, but for the storm which has fallen on us within 11 miles of the depot at which we hoped to secure our final supplies. Surely misfortune could scarcely have exceeded this last blow. We arrived within 11 miles of our old One Ton Camp with fuel for one last meal and food for two days. For four days we have been unable to leave the tent – the gale howling about us. We are weak, writing is difficult, but for my own sake I do not regret this journey, which has shown that Englishmen can endure hardships, help one another, and meet death with as great a fortitude as ever in the past. We took risks, we knew we took them; things have come out against us, and therefore we have no cause for complaint, but bow to the will of Providence, determined still to do our best to the last. But if we have been willing to give our lives to this enterprise, which is for the honour of our country, I appeal to our countrymen to see that those who depend on us are properly cared for.

Had we lived, I should have had a tale to tell of the hardihood, endurance, and courage of my companions which would have stirred the heart of every Englishman. These rough notes and our dead bodies must tell the tale, but surely, surely, a great rich country like ours will see that those who are dependent on us are properly provided for.

R. Scott.

Last diary entry [2]

<u>March 29th</u>

Since the 21st we have had a continuous gale from W.S.W. and S.W. – We had fuel to make 2 cups of tea apiece and bare food for two days on the 20th. – Every day we have been ready to start for our depot 11 miles away, but outside the door of the tent it remains a scene of whirling drift. I do not think we can hope for any better things now. We shall stick it out to the end, but we are getting weaker of course and the end cannot be far.

It seems a pity but I do not think I can write more –

R. Scott

Last Entry

For Gods sake look after our people

The last letters

Most of the last letters from Scott and his team are in facsimile in *The Last Letters*.[3] It seems superfluous to transcribe them again here.

There are some, however, that do not appear in that publication, or in which sections are missing. These are as follows.

A favourite letter from Kathleen was found on RFS's body inside a red leather wallet engraved with his initials, inside which were photos of Kathleen and Peter. The letter in full: [4]

My dear one ...

How can I guess how things will be with you when you get this ... but oh dearie I am full of hope. My brave man will win – with his own right hand and with his mighty arm hath he gathered himself the victory.

Now don't forget to brush your hair – and don't smoke so much and altogether you're a ducky darling and hurray for you!

I don't know if you'll ever get these silly little letters, and it's truly to tell you that I love your more than is at all comfy and moreover I think you are splendid.

I am glad and happy and I am getting to be very healthy and fit – when you come home we'll feel closer and closer together and the long time we've been apart will seem only a little hour.

May all the good gods conspire to bring my Con through his great difficulties with a glad heart and a constant hope.

Bless you dearest of men. K.

Appendix

Two letters from Scott to his mother: [5]

> My own darling Mother,
>
> The Great God has called me, and I feel that the news of it will add a fearful blow to the heavy ones that have fallen on you in life. But take comfort in that I die at peace with the world, and I myself not afraid – not perhaps believing in all that you hold to so splendidly, but still believing that there is a God – a merciful God. I wish I could remember that I had been a better son to you, but I think you will know that you were always very much in my heart and that I strove to put you into more comfortable circumstances.
>
> I join dear old Arch, both of us having given the life you gave us, to our country. The country owes you the debt – Willy will look after you, but you will have the small sum of money I was able to save, and Willy will buy an annuity.
>
> I hope so that you remain in your – [unfinished]

Scott and Kathleen had agreed that his savings should go to his mother.

> My dear dear Mother,
>
> I wish you could have been spared this blow and indeed it has been most supremely unfortunate, for the risks I have taken never seemed excessive.
>
> For myself I am not unhappy, but for Kathleen, you and the rest of the family my heart is very sore.
>
> Still I hope for all that I leave a memory to be proud of – we have done a very big journey and failed only by a very narrow margin.
>
> God bless you, dear – I die feeling that your material comfort will be looked after to the end. I wish I had been a greater comfort to you.
>
> Your loving son Con.

The following letter does appear in *The Last Letters*. However, the editors edited out the sentence 'Finally, I want you ... neglect them'. *Cf.* 'Last letter of Captain Scott finally revealed ...' [6]

To Sir Francis Charles Bridgeman, undated:

> My Dear Sir Francis
>
> I fear we have shipped up – a close shave. I am writing a few letters which I hope will be delivered some day. I want to thank you for the

friendship you gave me of late years, and to tell you how extra-ordinarily pleasant I found it to serve under you. I want to tell you that I was not too old for this job. It was the younger men that went under first. [Finally, I want you to secure a competence for my widow and boy. I leave them very ill provided for, but feel that the country ought not to neglect them.] After all we are setting a good example to our countrymen, if not by getting into a tight place, by facing it like men when we were there. We could have come through had we neglected the sick.

Good-bye and good-bye to dear Lady Bridgeman

Yours ever

R. Scott

Excuse writing – it is -40, and has been for nigh a month

All letters in *The Last Letters*

These are:

Scott to:

Kathleen
Wilson's mother
Mrs Bowers
Reginald and Mrs Smith
Sir George Egerton
Sir Edgar Speyer
JM Barrie
Joseph Kinsey

Wilson to:

his parents
Oriana
Mrs Oates
Reginald Smith

Bowers to:

his mother

Oates to:

> his mother (3 January 1912, on the Plateau)

Further letters not in *The Last Letters*

Scott to:

> Sir William Ellison Macartney (his brother-in-law)
> Sir Lewis Beaumont

References

1   Robert Falcon Scott. *Journals: Captain Scott's Last Expedition*, pp. 421–2

2   *op. cit.*

3   Heather Lane, Naomi Boneham and Robert D. Smith (eds.) *The Last Letters*

4   'Final letter to Captain Falcon Scott from wife made public for the first time'. *The Telegraph*, 18 March 2012, www.telegraph.co.uk

5   Stephen Gwynn. *Captain Scott*, pp. 230–1

6   'Last letter of Captain Scott finally revealed in full – 101 years on'. University of Cambridge, www.cam.ac.uk

BIBLIOGRAPHY

Works cited

Aldridge, Don. *The Rescue of Captain Scott.* Tuckwell Press, East Linton, 1999

Anderson, Verily. *The Last of the Eccentrics: A Life of Rosslyn Bruce.* Hodder and Stoughton, London, 1972

Armitage, Albert Borlase, Lieut., R.N.R. *Two Years in the Antarctic: Being a Narrative of the British National Antarctic Expedition* (1905). Edward Arnold, London, 1905. Kessinger Publishing, LLC, Legacy Reprints, www.kessinger.net

Aubert, Serge; Skelton, Judy; Frenot, Yves; and Bignon, Alain. *Scott and Charcot at the col du Lautaret: 1908 Trials of the first motor driven sledges designed for transport in the Antarctic.* Published by collaboration between the Joseph Fourier Alpine Station (University of Grenoble I and CNRS), the Paul Emile Victor French Polar Institute (IPEV) and the Scott Polar Research Institute of Cambridge University (SPRI). Les cahiers illustrés du Lautaret, 2014 – n°. 5

Back, June Debenham (ed.). *The Quiet Land: The Diaries of Frank Debenham, Member of the British Antarctic Expedition 1910–1913.* Bluntisham Books, Huntingdon and the Erskine Press, Harleston, 1992

Baughman, T.H. *Before the Heroes Came: Antarctica in the 1890s.* University of Nebraska Press, Lincoln and London, 1994; Bison Books, 1999

Baughman, T.H. *Pilgrims on the Ice: Robert Falcon Scott's First Antarctic Expedition.* University of Nebraska Press, Lincoln and London, 2008

Beattie, Owen and Geiger, John. *Frozen in Time: The Fate of the Franklin Expedition.* Bloomsbury, 1987

Bernacchi, L.C., O.B.E. *Saga of the "Discovery".* Blackie & Son Limited, London and Glasgow, 1938

Berne, Eric, M.D. *Games People Play: The Psychology of Human Relationships.* Penguin Books, 1968

Berton, Pierre. *The Arctic Grail: The Quest for the North West Passage and the North Pole, 1818–1909.* McClelland and Stewart, Toronto, 1988

Birkin, Andrew. *J M Barrie and the Lost Boys: the real story behind Peter Pan.* Yale University Press, 2003

Blackhall, Sue. *Scott of the Antarctic: We Shall Die Like Gentlemen.* Pen & Sword [Discovery] Books Ltd, Barnsley, 2012

Borchgrevink, C.E., F.R.G.S. *First on the Antarctic Continent: Being an Account of the British Antarctic Expedition, 1898–1900*. George Newnes, Limited, London, 1901. Digital reprint by Cambridge University Press, Cambridge Library Collection, 2014

Buczacki, Stephan. *My darling Mr Asquith: The extraordinary life and times of Venetia Stanley*. Cato & Clarke, Stratford-Upon-Avon, 2016

Bull, Colin and Wright, Pat F. (eds.). *Silas: The Antarctic Diaries and Memoir of Charles S. Wright*. Ohio State University Press, 1993

Carpenter, Kenneth J. *The History of Scurvy and Vitamin C*. Cambridge University Press, 1986; paperback edition, 1988

Cherry-Garrard, Apsley. *The Worst Journey in the World*. First published by Constable And Co., 1922; Pimlico (Random House), London, 2003, with an introduction by Sara Wheeler

Coleman, E.C. *The Royal Navy and Polar Exploration. Vol. 2: From Franklin to Scott*. Tempus Publishing Limited, Stroud, 2007

Crane, David. *Scott of the Antarctic*. Harper Perennial (HarperCollins), London, 2005, 2006

Christie's. British Antarctic Expedition, 1910–1913, Sale 6409, Lot 100, 21 September 2000, www.christies.com

Christie's. British Antarctic Expedition, 1910–1913, Sale 6409, Lot 109, 21 September 2000, www.christies.com

Day, David. *Antarctica: a Biography*. Oxford University Press, 2013

Day, David. *Flaws in the ice: in search of Douglas Mawson*. Scribe Publications Pty Ltd, Brunswick, Australia, 2013

Doorly, Captain Gerald S. *In the Wake*. Robertson & Mullens Ltd, Melbourne, undated; Foreword by Admiral Sir Edward R.G.R. Evans, K.C.B., D.S.O., 1936

Doorly, Captain Gerald S., R.N.R. *The Voyages of the 'Morning'*. Smith, Elder & Co., London, 1916. Facsimile edition by Nabu Public Domain Reprints, www.openlibrary.org/publishers/Nabu Public Domain Reprints

Dundee Heritage Trust. 'Letter from Sir Clements Markham instructing Colbeck'. www.dhtcollections.com

Ellmann, Richard. *Oscar Wilde*. Penguin Books, London, 1988

Evans, Admiral Edward R.G.R. *South With Scott*. Collins Clear-Type Press, Library of Classics, London and Glasgow, 1924

Evans, Commander R.N., C.B. 'Captain Oates: My Recollections of a Gallant Comrade'. *The Strand Magazine: An Illustrated Monthly*. Vol. XLVI, July to December. George Newnes Ltd, London, 1913

Ferrar, Sue. 'Paths are Made by Walking: The Beginnings of a Plan for a Biography of Hartley Travers Ferrar'. PCAS14 Supervised Project, ANTA604, unpublished, www.ir.canterbury.ac.nz

Fiennes, Sir Ranulph. *Captain Scott*. Hodder and Stoughton, 2003

Flood, Alison. 'Antarctic diary records horror at finding Captain Scott's body', *The Guardian*, 12 December 2018, www.theguardian.com

Foldy, Michael S. *The Trials of Oscar Wilde: Deviance, Morality, and Late-Victorian Society*. Yale University Press, New Haven, 1997

Gay, Peter (ed.). *The Freud Reader*. First published by W.W. Norton & Company, Inc., 1989; Vintage (Random House), London, 1995

Geleng, Otto. 'Gay Travel in Sicily', www.strangersguide.wordpress.com

Giesbrecht, Gordon G. and Wilkerson, James A. *Hypothermia, Frostbite and Other Cold Injuries: Prevention, Survival, Rescue, and Treatment*. Second edition, The Mountaineers Books, Seattle, 2006, 2010

Gombrich, E.H. *The Story of Art*. First published by E.P. Dutton, New York, 1950; 13th edition by Phaidon Press Limited, Oxford 1978, 1979

Gordon, Andrew. *The Rules of the Game: Jutland and British Naval Command*. Naval Institute Press, Annapolis, Maryland, 2012

Gwynn, Stephen. *Captain Scott*. Penguin Books, Harmondsworth, 1929, 1939

Hattersley-Smith, Geoffrey (ed.). *The Norwegian with Scott: Tryggve Gran's Antarctic Diary 1910–1913*. Translated by Ellen Johanne McGhie (*née* Gran). Hermann Gran/National Maritime Museum, Her Majesty's Stationery Office, 1984

Hayes, J. Gordon. *Antarctica: A Treatise on the Southern Continent*. The Richards Press, London, 1928

Heffer, Simon. *High Minds: The Victorians and the Birth of Modern Britain*. Random House, London, 2013

Hooper, Meredith. *The Longest Winter: Scott's Other Heroes*. John Murray, London, 2011

Howard, Elizabeth Jane. *Slipstream: a Memoir*. Pan Books (Pan Macmillan Ltd), London, 2003

Huntford, Roland. *Nansen*. Abacus (Little, Brown and Company), London, 2001, 2005

Huntford, Roland. *Race for the South Pole: The Expedition Diaries of Scott and Amundsen*. Continuum, London, 2010; paperback, 2011

Huntford, Roland. *Scott and Amundsen: Their Race to the South Pole*. Revised and updated version, Abacus ((Random House (USA) Inc. and Time Warner Books UK (London)), 1999, 2003. Originally published as *Scott and*

Amundsen, Abacus, 1979; then as *The Last Place on Earth*, Abacus, 2000, 2002

Huntford, Roland (ed.). *The Amundsen Photographs*. Hodder and Stoughton, London, 1987

Huxley, Elspeth. *Peter Scott: Painter and Naturalist*. Faber and Faber, London, 1993

Huxley, Elspeth. *Scott of the Antarctic*. Weidenfeld and Nicolson, London, 1977

Huysmans, Joris-Karl. *Against Nature (A Rebours)*. Translated by Robert Baldick, 1956. Penguin Books (Classics), London, 2003

Jimack, P.D. 'Introduction'; *see* Rousseau, Jean-Jacques, *Émile*

Jones, Aubrey A. *Scott's Forgotten Surgeon: Dr Reginald Koettlitz, Polar Explorer*. Whittles Publishing, Dunbeath, 2011

Jones, A.G.E. *Polar Portraits: Collected Papers*. Caedmon of Whitby, North Yorkshire, 1992

Kay, H. Alison (ed.). *H.M.S. Collingwood 1844–1848 (Pacific Station): From the Journals of Philip Horatio Townsend Somerville, R.N.* The Pentland Press, Edinburgh, 1986

Keltie, John Scott and Mill, Hugh Robert. *Report of the Sixth International Geographical Conference: Held in London, 1895*. John Murray, 1896. New York Public Library, Americana Collection, www.archive.org

Kennett, Lady (Kathleen, Lady Scott). *Self-Portrait of an Artist: From the Diaries and Memoirs of Lady Kennett*. John Murray, London, 1949

Lane, Heather; Boneham, Naomi; and Smith, Robert D. (eds.). *The Last Letters: The British Antarctic Expedition 1910–13*. The Polar Museum, The Scott Polar Research Institute, Cambridge, 2012

Lees-Milne, James. *Fourteen Friends*. John Murray, London, 1996

Limb, Sue and Cordingley, Patrick. *Captain Oates: Soldier and Explorer*. Pen & Sword [Military] Books Ltd, Barnsley, 2009

MacInnes, Katherine. 'Marriage by post', *The Lady*, www.lady.co.uk

MacPhee, Ross D.E. *Race to the End: Scott, Amundsen and the South Pole*. American Museum of Natural History and Sterling Publishing Co., Inc., 2010; The Natural History Museum, London, 2011

Markham, Admiral Sir Albert H., K.C.B. *The Life of Sir Clements R. Markham K.C.B., F.R.S.* John Murray, London, 1917. Facsimile edition by Forgotten Books, 2012, www.forgottenbooks.org

Markham, Sir Clements. *Antarctic Obsession: A personal narrative of the origins of the British Antarctic Expedition 1901–1904*. From the manuscript held in the Scott Polar Research Institute, Cambridge, entitled 'The Starting of the

Antarctic Expedition: A Personal Narrative', edited and introduced by Clive Holland. Bluntisham Books and the Erskine Press, Harleston, 1986

Markham, Clement [*sic*] Robert. *Franklin's Footsteps: A Sketch of Greenland Along the Shores of which His Expedition Passed, and of The Parry Isles, Where the Last Traces of it Were Found*. Chapman and Hall, London, 1853. Facsimile edition by Nabu Public Domain Reprints, www.penlibrary.org/publishers/Nabu Public Domain Reprints

Markham, Clements R., C.B., F.R.S. *The Arctic Navy List; or, A Century of Arctic & Antarctic Officers, 1773–1873, Together with a List of Officers of the 1875 Expedition, and their Services*. The Vintage Naval Library, MCMXCII. Griffin & Co., London, 1875. Facsimile edition by The Naval & Military Press, Dallington, East Sussex, 1992

Markham, Sir Clements R., K.C.B., F.R.S. *The Lands of Silence: A History of Arctic and Antarctic Exploration*. Cambridge University Press, 1921. Facsimile edition by Hardpress Publishing, Classic Series, Miami, www.hardpress.net

Markham, Clements Robert, C.B., F.R.S. *The Royal Geographical Society and the Arctic Expedition of 1875–6: A Report*. Cambridge University Press, 1877; digital reprint, 2012

Markham, the Rev. David Frederick. *A History of the Markham Family*. Printed by John Bowyer Nichols and Sons, London, 1854. Facsimile edition by Forgotten Books, Classic Reprint Series, 2012, www.forgottenbooks.org

Markham, M.E. and Markham, F.A. *The Life of Sir Albert Hastings Markham*. Cambridge University Press, 1927; Cambridge Library Collections, digital reprint, 2014

May, Karen and Airriess, Sarah. 'Could Captain Scott have been saved? Cecil Meares and the "second journey" that failed.' *Polar Record* 51 (258), pp. 260–273 (2015). Cambridge University Press, 2014

McGoogan, Ken. *Race to the Polar Sea: The Heroic Adventures of Elisha Kent Kane*. Counterpoint, Berkeley, 2008

Mear, Roger and Swan, Robert. *In the Footsteps of Scott*. Jonathan Cape, London, 1987

Miell, Dorothy; Phoenix, Ann; and Thomas, Kerry (eds.). *DSE212 Mapping Psychology*, Book 1. Open University, Milton Keynes, 2007

Mill, Hugh Robert. *Hugh Robert Mill: An Autobiography*. Longmans, Green and Co Ltd, London, 1951

Mill, Hugh Robert. *The Siege of the South Pole: The Story of Antarctic Exploration – Primary Source Edition*. Alston Rivers, Limited, London, 1905. Facsimile edition by Nabu Public Domain Reprints, www.openlibrary.org/publishers/Nabu Public Domain Reprints

Mills, Leif. *Men of Ice*. Caedmon of Whitby, North Yorkshire, 2008

Mountevans, Admiral Lord, K.C.B., D.S.O., LL.D. *Adventurous Life*. Hutchinson & Co. (Publishers) Ltd, London, 1946

Mountevans, Admiral Lord, K.C.B., D.S.O. *From Husky to Sno-Cat: A Short Survey of Polar Exploration Yesterday and Today*. Staples Press Limited, London, 1957

Murray, George, F.R.S. (ed.). *The Antarctic Manual for the Use of the Expedition of 1901*. Royal Geographical Society, London, 1901. Facsimile edition by Scholar Select, www.wordery.com/scholar-select-publisher

Nansen, Fridtjof. *Farthest North: Being the Record of a Voyage of Exploration of the Ship "Fram" 1893–96 and of a Fifteen Months' Sleigh Journey by Dr. Nansen and Lieut. Johansen*. Vols. I and II. Harper and Brothers, New York and London, 1897. Facsimile (illustrated) editions in two volumes by The Echo Library, Fairford, 2012, www.echo-library.com

Osborn, Lieut. Sherard. *Stray Leaves from an Arctic Journal; or, Eighteen Months in the Polar Regions, In Search of Sir John Franklin's Expedition, in the Years 1850–51*. George P. Putnam, New York, M. DCCC. LII. Facsimile edition by The Echo Library, Fairford, 2010, www.echo-library.com

Paglia, Camille. *Sexual Personae: Art and Decadence from Nefertiti to Emily Dickinson*. Yale University, 1990; Penguin Books Ltd, London, 1992

Painter, George D. *Marcel Proust*. Penguin Books Ltd, Harmondsworth, 1983

Parker, Steve. S*cott's Last Expedition*. Natural History Museum, London, 2011, 2012 (with updates). The exhibition of this title is published by collaboration between the Natural History Museum in London, Canterbury Museum in Christchurch, New Zealand and Antarctic Heritage Trust New Zealand

Parry, Sir W.E., R.N., F.R.S. *Journal of the Third Voyage for the Discovery of a North-West Passage*. [Unattributed publisher], 1889. Facsimile reprint by Dodo Press, www.dodopress.co.uk

Ponting, Herbert G., F.R.G.S., F.R.P.S., F.Z.S. *The Great White South, or, With Scott in the Antarctic, Being an Account of Experiences with Captain Scott's South Pole Expedition and of the Nature of Life in the Antarctic*. Duckworth, London, 1921

Pound, Reginald. *Evans of the Broke: a Biography of Admiral Lord Mountevans K.C.B., D.S.O., LL.D*. Oxford University Press, 1963

Pound, Reginald. *Scott of the Antarctic*. World Books (by arrangement with Cassell & Company Limited), London, 1966, 1968

Preston, Diana. *A First Rate Tragedy: Captain Scott's Antarctic Expeditions*. Constable, London, 1997

Quartermain, L.B. *South to the Pole: The Early History of the Ross Sea Sector, Antarctica.* Oxford University Press, London, 1967

Regis, Amber (ed.). *The Memoirs of John Addington Symonds: a Critical Edition.* Palgrave Macmillan, 2016, www.palgrave.com

Rousseau, Jean-Jacques. *Émile.* Translated by Barbara Foxley, Introduction by P.D. Jimack. Everyman (J.M. Dent), London, 1993, reprinted 1995

Schama, Simon. *Citizens: A Chronicle of the French Revolution.* Penguin Books, London, 1989

Scott, Robert Falcon. *Journals: Captain Scott's Last Expedition.* Edited with an Introduction and Notes by Max Jones. Oxford World's Classics, Oxford University Press, 2005

Scott, Robert Falcon. *Scott's Last Expedition: The Journals.* First published by Smith, Elder & Co., London, 1913; Second edition John Murray, London, 1927; Methuen, London, 1983

Scott, Captain R.F., R.N., C.V.O. *Scott's Last Expedition.* In two volumes arranged by Leonard Huxley, with prefaces by Sir Clements Markham, K.C.B., F.R.S. Vol. I *Being the Journals of Captain R.F. Scott, R.N., C.V.O.*; Vol. II *Being the Reports of the Journeys & the Scientific Work Undertaken by Dr. E. A. Wilson and the Surviving Members of the Expedition.* Smith, Elder & Co., London, 1913

Scott, Captain Robert F. *The Voyage of the Discovery.* Classics of World Literature, Wordsworth Editions Limited, Ware, 1905, 2009

Seaver, George. *'Birdie' Bowers of the Antarctic.* John Murray, London, 1938, 1944

Seaver, George. *Edward Wilson of the Antarctic: Naturalist and Friend.* John Murray, London, 1933

Seaver, George. *Scott of the Antarctic: A Study in Character.* John Murray, London 1940

Seaver, George. *The Faith of Edward Wilson.* John Murray, London 1948, 1949

Shackleton, Emily and Mill, Dr. Hugh Robert. *Rejoice My Heart: The Making of H.R. Mill's "The Life of Sir Ernest Shackleton": The Private Correspondence of Dr. Hugh Robert Mill and Lady Shackleton, 1922–33.* Preface by the Honourable Alexandra Shackleton, Introduction by T.H. Baughman. Adélie Books, Santa Monica, 2007; produced in cooperation with the Scott Polar Research Institute, Cambridge

Shackleton, Sir Ernest, CVO. *The Heart of the Antarctic: The Farthest South Expedition 1907–1909.* First published in two volumes by William Heinemann, 1909; subsequent popular edition in one volume, Heinemann, 1910; Penguin Books, London, 2000

Showalter, Elaine. *Sexual Anarchy: Gender and Culture at the Fin de Siècle.* Virago Press Limited, London 1992

Sienicki, Professor Krzysztof. *Captain Scott: Icy Deceits and Untold Realities.* Open Academic Press and Villa Europa Ltd, Berlin and Warsaw, 2016

Skelton, J.V. and Wilson, D.M. *Discovery Illustrated: Pictures from Captain Scott's First Antarctic Expedition.* Reardon Publishing, Cheltenham, 2001

Skelton, Admiral Sir Reginald, KCB, CBE, DSO. *The Antarctic Journals of Reginald Skelton; 'Another Little Job for the Tinker'.* Researched and edited by Judy Skelton. Reardon Publishing, Cheltenham, 2004

Solomon, Professor Susan. *The Coldest March: Scott's Fatal Antarctic Expedition.* Yale University Press, 2001

Speak, Peter. *DEB: Geographer, Scientist, Antarctic Explorer: A Biography of Frank Debenham, OBE, MA, DSc.* Polar Publishing Limited, Guildford, in association with The Scott Polar Research Institute, Cambridge, 2008

Speak, Peter. *William Speirs Bruce: Polar Explorer and Scottish Nationalist.* National Museums of Scotland Publishing, Edinburgh, 2003

Steger, Will and Bowermaster, Jon. *Crossing Antarctica.* Alfred A.Knopf, Inc., New York, 1992

Stocker, Mark. ' "Young Male Objects": the ideal sculpture of Kathleen Scott'. *Sculpture Journal*, 22.2 (2013), pp. 119–27

Strathie, Anne. *Birdie Bowers: Captain Scott's Marvel.* The History Press, Stroud, 2012

Taylor, Griffith. *With Scott: The Silver Lining.* Smith, Elder & Co., London, 1916. Facsimile edition by Forgotten Books, Classic Reprint Series, 2015, www.forgottenbooks.org

Thomson, David. *Scott's Men.* Allen Lane (Penguin Books Ltd), London, 1977

Tyler-Lewis, Kelly. *The Lost Men: The Harrowing Story of Shackleton's Ross Sea Party.* Bloomsbury, London, 2007

[Unattributed writer]. 'Dictionary of Canadian Biography: Osborn, Sherard'. Volume X (1871–1880), www.biographi.ca

[Unattributed writer]. 'HMS *Resolute*', Wikipedia, www.e.em.wikipedia.org

[Unattributed writer]. 'Last letter of Captain Scott finally revealed in full – 101 years on'. University of Cambridge, www.cam.ac.uk

[Unattributed writer]. 'Life on Board the Discovery: the Great Sledge Journey'. *Otago Witness*, 15 April 1903. Papers Past, www.paperspast.natlib.govt.nz

[Unattributed writer]. 'Mid-Victorian RN vessel HMS Collingwood'. www.pdavis.nl

[Unattributed writer]. 'Prince Luigi Amedeo, Duke of the Abruzzi'. Wikipedia, www.en.m.wikipedia.org

[Unattributed writer]. 'Whaling – South Georgia Heritage Trust', www.sght.org

Vaknin, Sam. *Malignant Self-love: Narcissism Revisited.* Narcissus Publications, Skopje, 2015

Walton, D.W.H. 'Profile: Albert Borlase Armitage'. British Antarctic Survey, Cambridge. *Polar Record*, 22(140): 511–18 (1985)

Weinberg, Gerald M. 'Beyond Blaming', AYE Conference, 5 March 2006. Blame. Wikipedia, www.en.m.wikipedia.org

Wheeler, Sara. *Cherry: A Life of Apsley Cherry-Garrard.* Vintage (Random House), London, 2002

Wheeler, Sara. *Terra Incognita: Travels in Antarctica.* Vintage (Random House), London, 1997

Williams, Isobel. *Captain Scott's Invaluable Assistant: Edgar Evans.* The History Press, Stroud, 2012

Wilson, A.N. *The Victorians.* Hutchinson, London, 2002

Wilson, D.M. and Elder, D.B. *Cheltenham in Antarctica: The Life of Edward Wilson.* Reardon Publishing, Cheltenham, 2000

Wilson, Edward. *Diary of the Discovery Expedition: To the Antarctic Regions 1901–1904.* Edited from the original mss. in the Scott Polar Research Institute, Cambridge, by Ann Savours. Blandford Press, London, 1966

Wilson, Edward. *Diary of the 'Terra Nova' Expedition to the Antarctic 1910–1912.* An account of Scott's last expedition edited from the original mss. in the Scott Polar Research Institute and the British Museum by H.R.G. King. Blandford Press Ltd, London, 1972

Worden, J. William. *Children and Grief: When a Parent Dies.* The Guildford Press, New York, 1996

Yelverton, David E. *Antarctica Unveiled: Scott's First Expedition and the Quest for the Unknown Continent.* University Press of Colorado, Boulder, 2000

Young, Louisa. *A Great Task of Happiness: The Life of Kathleen Scott.* Papermac (Macmillan Publishers Ltd), 1996

Further reading

Alberge, Dalya. 'How Scott's No 2 was left out in the cold'. *The Times*, Monday 29 March 2004, p. 7

Alberge, Dalya. 'Letters shed light on Constance Wilde's mysterious death'. *The Guardian*, Friday 2 January 2015, p. 13

Amundsen, Roald. *The South Pole: an Account of the Norwegian Antarctic Expedition in the 'Fram', 1910–1912*. Translated from the Norwegian by A.G. Chater, first published by John Murray, 1912. First paperback edition by Hurst & Company, London, 1976; second impression C. Hurst & Co. (Publishers) Ltd and Mrs Anne Christine Jacobsen, Oslo, 2001

Aronson, Theo. *Prince Eddy and the Homosexual Underworld*. Thistle Publishing, London, 2013

Aston, Felicity. *Alone in Antarctica*. Summersdale Publishers Ltd, Chichester, 2013

Bacon, Admiral Sir R.H., K.C.B., K.C.V.O., D.S.O. *The Life of Lord Fisher of Kilverstone, O.M., G.C.B., G.C.V.O., LL.D, Admiral of the Fleet*. In two volumes, Vol. 1. Doubleday, Doran & Company, Inc., New York, 1929. Kessinger Legacy Reprints, www.kessinger.net

Barczewski, Stephanie. *Antarctic Destinies: Scott, Shackleton and the Changing Face of Heroism*. Hambledon Continuum, London 2007

Bernacchi, L.C., O.B.E. *A Very Gallant Gentleman*. Eyre and Spottiswoode, London, 1933; Keystone Library, 1942

Bernacchi, Louis, F.R.G.S. *To the South Polar Regions: Expedition of 1898–1900*. Sir George Newnes, Bart., 1901. Facsimile edition by Pierides Press, 2011

Bickel, Lennard. *Shackleton's Forgotten Men: The Untold Tale of an Antarctic Tragedy [...: The Untold Tragedy of the Endurance Epic]*. Pimlico (Random House), London, 2001

Bown, Stephen. *The Last Viking: The Life of Roald Amundsen, Conqueror of the South Pole*. Aurum Press Ltd, London, 2012

Brent, Peter. *Captain Scott and the Antarctic Tragedy*. Weidenfeld and Nicolson, London, 1974

Brown, Jonathan. 'Art of the Antarctic: The works of a painter who joined Captain Scott's fateful voyage to the South Pole are to go on sale'. *The Independent*, 21 May 2010, pp.16–17

Burg, B.R. *Boys at Sea: Sodomy, Indecency, and Courts Martial in Nelson's Navy*. Palgrave Macmillan, Basingstoke, 2007

Chaney, Lisa. *Hide-and-Seek with Angels: A Life of J.M. Barrie*. Hutchinson, London, 2005

Cook, Frederick Albert, M.D. *Through the First Antarctic Night 1898–1899: A Narrative of the Voyage of the "Belgica" among Newly Discovered Lands and over an Unknown Sea about the South Pole*. Doubleday & McClure Co., New

York, 1900. Facsimile edition by Hardpress Publishing, Classics Series, Miami, www.hardpress.net

Costigan, Paul; Gray, Michael; Murphy, Shane; Newton, Gael; and Wright, Joanna (contributors and consultants). *South with Endurance: Shackleton's Antarctic Expedition 1914–1917. The Photographs of Frank Hurley*. From the Archives of The Royal Geographical Society, London, The State Library of New South Wales, Sydney, & The Scott Polar Research Institute, Cambridge. Bloomsbury, London, 2004

Day, David. 'Fire and ice: Douglas Mawson and Robert Scott's widow'. *The Australian*, October 26, 2013

Debenham, Frank, O.B.E. *In the Antarctic: Stories of Scott's Last Expedition*. John Murray, London, 1952

Dixon, Norman. *On the Psychology of Military Incompetence*. Pimlico (Random House), London 1976

Duerden, Nick. 'An awfully big adventure'. Section 2, *The Independent*, Tuesday 25 February 2014, pp. 31–2

Duncan, Isadora. *My Life*. First published Victor Gollancz Limited, London, 1928. First Sphere Books edition, 1968

Edholm, O.G. and Gunderson, E.K.E. (eds.). *Polar Human Biology: the Proceedings of the SCAR/IUPS/IUBS Symposium on Human Biology and Medicine in the Antarctic*. William Heinemann Medical Books Ltd, 1973

Edmonds, Antony. *Oscar Wilde's Scandalous Summer: The 1894 Worthing Holiday and the Aftermath*. Amberley Publishing, Stroud, 2014

Ellis, Commander A.R., R.N. (ed.). *Under Scott's Command: Lashly's Antarctic Diaries*. Taplinger Publishing Company, New York, 1969

Festinger, Leon. *A Theory of Cognitive Dissonance*. Stanford University Press, California, 1957, 1985

Foucault, Michel. *The Will to Knowledge: The History of Sexuality; Volume 1*. Éditions Gallimard, 1976. Translated from the French by Robert Hurley, Random House, Inc., 1978. Penguin Books, London, 1978, 1998

Fuchs, Sir Vivian and Hillary, Sir Edmund. *The Crossing of Antarctica: The Commonwealth Trans-Antarctic Expedition 1955–58*. Cassell & Company Limited, London, 1958

Girouard, Mark. *The Return to Camelot: Chivalry and the English Gentleman*. Yale University Press, New Haven, 1981

Gray, Louise. 'Ice age: Unseen portraits of polar explorers'. *The Daily Telegraph*, Monday 21 September 2009

Gregor, G.C. *Swansea's Antarctic Explorer: Edgar Evans, 1876–1912.* City Archives Publications: Studies in Swansea's History, no. 4. Swansea City Council, 1995

Hayes, J. Gordon. *The Conquest of the South Pole.* Thornton Butterworth Ltd, London; Keystone Library, 1936

Herbert, Kari. *Heart of the Hero: The Remarkable Women who Inspired the Great Polar Explorers.* Saraband, Glasgow, 2013

Herbert, Kari and Lewis-Jones, Huw. *In Search of the South Pole.* Conway (Anova Books Ltd), London, 2011

H. Montgomery Hyde. *The Other Love: An Historical and Contemporary Survey of Homosexuality in Britain.* Heinemann, London, 1970

Hough, Richard. *Admirals in Collision.* Hamish Hamilton, London, 1959

Hunter, Carol. *Vitamins: What They Are and Why We Need Them.* Thorsons Publishers Limited, Wellingborough, 1983

Huntford, Roland. *Shackleton.* Abacus (Little, Brown and Company), London, 1996; fifth reprint, 2001

Irvine, Chris. 'Daily suffering of explorers on worst journey in world'. *The Daily Telegraph*, Thursday 17 September 2009, p. 15

Jones, Max. *The Last Great Quest: Captain Scott's Antarctic Sacrifice.* Oxford University Press, 2003

Kamler, Kenneth, M.D. *Doctor on Everest: Emergency Medicine at the Top of the World – A Personal Account Including the 1996 Disaster.* The Lyons Press, New York, 2000

Kosiński, Sylweriusz; Darocha, Tomasz; Sadowski, Jerzy; and Drwiła, Rafał (eds.). *Hypothermia: Clinical Aspects of Body Cooling: Analysis of Dangers: Directions of Modern Treatment.* Jagiellonian University Press, Crakow, 2016

Lewis-Jones, Huw. *Face to Face: Polar Portraits.* Conway (Anova Books Company Ltd), London; in association with Polarworld, on behalf of the Scott Polar Research Institute, 2009

Lewis, Michael. *The Navy in Transition 1814–1864: A Social History.* Hodder and Stoughton, London, 1965

Ludlam, Harry. *Captain Scott: The Full Story.* W. Foulsham & Co. Ltd., London, 1965

Marshall, Howard (Re-told By). *With Scott to the Pole.* Country Life, London, 1936

Mawson, Douglas. *The Home of the Blizzard: A True Story of Antarctic Survival.* St. Martin's Griffin, New York, 2000

Maxtone-Graham, John. *Safe Return Doubtful: the Heroic Age of Polar Exploration*. First published by Barnes & Noble Books, USA, 1999; first UK edition by Constable and Company Limited, London, 2000

McGrath, James and Bates, Bob. *The Little Book of Big Management Theories … and How to Use Them*. Pearson Education Limited, Harlow, 2013

McKee, Christopher. *Sober Men and True: Sailor Lives in the Royal Navy 1900–1945*. Harvard University Press, Massachusetts, 2002

McSmith, Andy. ' "Excuse the writing – it's been minus 40": The full text of the Antarctic explorer's final note to his naval commander is released 101 years after his death'. *The Independent*, Friday 29 March 2013, p. 3

O'Connell, Fergus. *Leadership Lessons from the Race to the South Pole: Why Amundsen Lived and Scott Died*. Praeger (ABC-CLIO, LLC), Santa Barbara, Denver and Oxford, 2015

O'Hare, Mick. 'Other Side of a Polar Tragedy'. *The New European*, #125, 20 December 2018, pp. 23–7, www.theneweuropean.co.uk

Palin, Sir Michael. *Erebus: The Story of a Ship*. Hutchinson, London, 2018

Priestley, Raymond Edward. *Antarctic Adventure: Scott's Northern Party*. E.P. Dutton & Company, New York, 1915. Facsimile edition by Forgotten Books, Classic Reprint Series, 2015, www.forgottenbooks.org

Rees, Jasper. *Blizzard: Race to The Pole*. BBC Books, London, 2006

Riffenburgh, Beau. *Terra Nova: Scott's Last Expedition*. The Polar Museum, Scott Polar Research Institute, Cambridge, 2011

Riffenburgh, Beau. *The Myth of the Explorer: The Press, Sensationalism, and Geographical Discovery*. Oxford University Press, 1994

Savours, Ann (ed.). *Scott's Last Voyage: Through the Antarctic Camera of Herbert Ponting*. Sidgwick & Jackson, London, 1974

Scott, Peter. *The Eye of the Wind: An Autobiography*. Hodder and Stoughton, London, 1961

Shackleton, Sir Ernest. *South: The Story of Shackleton's Last Expedition 1914–17*. Edited by Peter King. Pimlico (Random House), London, 1999

Smith, Michael. *I Am Just Going Outside: Captain Oates – Antarctic Tragedy*. Spellmount Limited, Stroud, 2006

Smith, Michael. *Shackleton: By Endurance We Conquer*. Oneworld Publications, London, 2014

Spufford, Francis. *I May Be Some Time: Ice and the English Imagination*. Faber and Faber Limited, London, 1996

Steegmuller, Francis. "*Your Isadora*": *The Love Story of Isadora Duncan & Gordon Craig.* Macmillan & The New York Public Library, New York, 1974; Macmillan, London, 1974

Steele, Commander Gordon, V.C., R.N. *The Story of the Worcester.* George G. Harrap & Co. Ltd, London, 1962

Strange, Carolyn and Bashford, Alison. *Griffin Taylor: visionary, environmentalist, explorer.* University of Toronto Press, Toronto and Buffalo, 2009

Tarver, Michael C. *The Man Who Found Captain Scott: Antarctic Explorer and War Hero, Surgeon Captain Edward Leicester Atkinson DSO, AM, MRCS, LRCP, Royal Navy (1881–1929).* Pendragon Maritime Publications, Brixham, 2015

Turley, Charles. *The Voyages of Captain Scott: Retold from 'The Voyage of the "Discovery"' and 'Scott's Last Expedition'.* With an Introduction by Sir J.M. Barrie, BART. Smith, Elder & Co., London, 1914

Turney, Chris. *1912: The Year the World Discovered Antarctica.* Pimlico (Random House), London, 2013

[Unattributed writer]. 'Encounters at the end of the world'. Review of Turney, Chris. *1912: The Year the World Discovered Antarctica* (Bodley Head edition). Also review of Francis, Gavin. *Empire Antarctica: Ice, Silence and Emperor Penguins.* Chatto & Windus, 2012. *The Guardian*, Saturday 24 November 2012, p. 10

[Unattributed writer]. 'Scott starved to death on return from Pole'. *The Daily Telegraph*, Friday 29 June 2012, p. 15

Voltaire (François-Marie Arouet). *Candide, or, Optimism.* Translated by John Butt, 1947. Penguin Books (Classics), London, 1947

Williams, Isobel. *With Scott in the Antarctic: Edward Wilson, Explorer, Naturalist, Artist.* The History Press, Stroud, 2008

Wilson, David M. *The Lost Photographs of Captain Scott.* Little, Brown, London, 2011

Winton, John. *Hurrah for the Life of a Sailor!: Life on the lower-deck of the Victorian Navy.* Michael Joseph, London, 1977

Worsley, Frank Arthur, Commander. *Endurance: an Epic of Polar Adventure.* Jonathan Cape and Harrison Smith, Inc., New York, 1931

Wrangell, Ferdinand, Admiral. *Narrative of an Expedition to the Polar Sea, in the Years 1820–23.* Harper and Brothers, New York and London, 1842. Kessinger Legacy Reprints, www.kessinger.net

Wright, Sir Almroth E., M.D., F.R.S. *The Unexpurgated Case Against Woman Suffrage.* [Unattributed], 1913. Facsimile edition, unattributed

INDEX

Index

Index

Printed in Great Britain
by Amazon